Civil litigation

Laurence Olivo and Mary Ann Kelly

2003
EMOND MONTGOMERY PUBLICATIONS LIMITED
TORONTO, CANADA

Copyright © 2003 Emond Montgomery Publications Limited. All rights reserved. No part of this publication may be reproduced, stored in a retrieval system, or transmitted, in any form or by any means, photocopying, electronic, mechanical, recording, or otherwise, without the prior written permission of the copyright holder.

Printed in Canada.

Edited, designed, and typeset by WordsWorth Communications, Toronto.
Cover design by Susan Darrach, Darrach Design.

We acknowledge the financial support of the Government of Canada through the Book Publishing Industry Development Program (BPIDP) for our publishing activities.

Olivo, Laurence M., 1946–
    Civil litigation/Laurence Olivo and Mary Ann Kelly.

(Working with the law)
Includes index.
ISBN 1-55239-077-2

    1. Civil procedure — Ontario   2. Actions and defenses — Ontario.
I. Kelly, Mary Ann, 1948–   II. Title.   III. Series.

KEO1119.O45 2003   347.713'05   C2003-901277-8
KF8840.ZB3O45 2003

To Joyce, as always, and to Stan Gershman, professor emeritus, colleague, friend, and tireless advocate for quality education of legal paraprofessionals.

— L.M.O.

To the memory of my father, Henry Kelly.

— M.A.K.

Contents

List of figures

Preface

In the past, when we taught civil litigation subjects to students in law clerk programs, we both noticed that students were able to master individual rules of procedure but were often unable to see how these rules fit into the process of getting a case to trial. In short, students were unable to see the forest for the trees. To solve this problem, members of faculty contributed to a collection of materials that supplemented the commercially published annual edition of the *Rules of Civil Procedure*. When the supplemental materials grew to the size and weight of the Toronto telephone book, but with much less coherence, we realized that we had better do something.

This book is our solution. Using a case study, which involves the misadventures of the fictional Abigail Boar, you will follow the process of a typical civil action, looking at both the forest and the trees, and using exercises at the back of each chapter to practise analytic and drafting skills. We hope that you will gain an understanding of the process as a whole, as well as a grasp of specific procedures.

This book would probably not have appeared without our students' helpful comments on what was lacking in our teaching materials and the encouragement of our colleagues in the School of Legal and Public Administration and the School of Office Administration at Seneca College. The suggestions of students and colleagues, both solicited and otherwise, were welcome even if the proffered advice was not always followed. Any errors or omissions are, of course, the responsibility of the authors, and we welcome your assistance in correcting them. An e-mail to laurence.olivo@senecac.on.ca or maryann.kelly@senecac.on.ca will bring any problems to our attention.

The text reflects the law generally and the *Rules of Civil Procedure* in particular as of February 2003. The Rules Committee of the Superior Court is not inactive. Changes to the rules are to be expected from time to time, and care must be taken to see that your knowledge remains current. This text is designed to be used in conjunction with one of the commercially published annual versions of the *Rules of Civil Procedure*, and you should always refer to the text of the rules when examining a particular procedure or step in the process.

Laurence Olivo
Mary Ann Kelly
Toronto, February 2003

An overview of the civil litigation process

CHAPTER 1

Overview of a civil law suit

This chapter presents the "big picture" of how a civil proceeding unfolds. The balance of the book fills in the details. In order to help you see both the big picture and later the details, we start by setting out a fact situation involving Abigail Boar and her various difficulties. Using Abigail's story, we demonstrate how a civil case progresses from the initial stage of hiring a lawyer to the final stage of appealing a trial judgment.

FACT SITUATION: THE SAD TALE OF ABIGAIL BOAR

Introduction

It is now time to introduce you to the unfortunate Abigail Boar, who set out to buy a sports car and ended up with serious injuries resulting from the apparent negligence of others involved in what lawyers usually refer to as a "slip and fall case." We will follow Abigail's case from the time Abigail consults a lawyer, through the various pretrial stages, to trial in the Ontario Superior Court.[1] As we proceed, we will discuss the steps that are taken, including the preparation of many of the documents that are required in a civil action. The facts set out here present a broad outline of what occurred. As we proceed we will add more detail where it is required.

Facts

Abigail Boar is a 28-year-old securities analyst employed by Megadoon Investments Ltd. She is earning more money than she thought she would and decides the time has come to do some conspicuous consuming, so she buys her first car. After talking to friends, she decides the right kind of car for her is a two-seater sports coupe. On September 14, year 0, she decides to go after dinner to look at the hot new line of sports coupes manufactured by the Skank Motorcar Company Ltd., which are being sold at Rattle Motors Ltd. After work, she stops at Barbeerians, a trendy bar frequented by financial types, where she has a quick dinner and two glasses of wine. She then walks over to Rattle Motors Ltd. at 1240 Bay Street, Toronto.

At about 6:00 p.m., Fred Flogem, a salesperson employed by Rattle Motors, notices that there is some oil on the floor next to the Super Coupe model. He peers underneath the car and discovers oil leaking from underneath the engine. Because this is hardly good advertising for a new car, Fred does not want to draw customers' attention to the problem by cleaning up the mess immediately. Instead, he shuts off two of the four spotlights that illuminate the Super Coupe, hoping that no one looking at the car will notice the mess on the floor. Fred intends to clean up the mess when there are no customers in the showroom, or when the showroom closes for the day.

Abigail walks in the front door of the showroom at about 7:30 p.m. There are several sports cars on display. On seeing her come in, two salespersons get up from their desks and make a beeline for Abigail. Linda Lucre gets there first, so the second salesperson, Fred Flogem, sits down again and busies himself with some paperwork. Abigail tells Linda what she is looking for, and Linda shows her the floor models. Abigail looks at one car and then walks over, with Linda behind her, to look at another. The second car is in an area of the showroom where two of the four spotlights on the car are off so that the side of the car near to the wall is in relative darkness. As Abigail walks around to the darker side of the car, she steps into some oil, slips, loses her balance, and falls, striking the left side of her head against the side of the car. Abigail is knocked unconscious. Her body twists as she falls heavily to the floor with the result that she fractures her right wrist and several bones in her right arm.

Linda goes to her office and phones for an ambulance. Abigail is taken to Toronto Hospital, where she is treated. She remains there four days. The broken bones in her wrist and right arm are set in a cast. Because of the head injury, Abigail remains for neurological observation and is then sent home, where she remains for a further 6 weeks until the cast is taken off her arm. After that, she goes to physiotherapy once a week for 10 weeks.

After she is released from hospital, Abigail has no memory of slipping and falling. She continues to have chronic lower back pain and headaches. She is unable to walk long distances or sit at her desk at work for prolonged periods. Abigail, who is right-handed, has limited mobility in her right arm and is unable to work at her computer for more than 10 minutes at a time without experiencing pain.

She returns to work on March 1, year 1 for a month. However, because of chronic pain and her difficulty using a computer, which is essential for her job, Abigail then goes on long-term disability.

Before her accident, Abigail was an avid tennis player and a good amateur violinist. After her accident, she is unable to enjoy these activities and is far less active, both physically and socially, than she had been. She used to be a lively individual: cheerful, with a good sense of humour. She has, since the fall, become quieter and more withdrawn and has difficulty sleeping. Her family physician has begun treating her for depression, prescribing an antidepressant and painkillers.

At the time of the accident, Abigail was earning $80,000 gross per year. Her employer does not have a short-term sick leave plan but does have a long-term disability plan that pays Abigail 60 percent of basic monthly earnings after four months' absence from work resulting from illness or injury.

Abigail has consulted I.M. Just, a lawyer, and intends to sue Rattle Motors Ltd. and Fred Flogem because she believes they are responsible for the injuries she sustained.

AN OVERVIEW OF THE CIVIL LITIGATION PROCESS

Now that you have met Abigail, we can turn to a general description of what happens after she decides to sue.

Generally, a civil proceeding can be divided into the following stages:

1. hiring of a lawyer,

2. preliminary investigations and research,

3. commencement of proceedings,

4. exchange of pleadings (statement of claim and statement of defence),

5. examinations for discovery of the parties and discovery of documents,

6. motions,

7. pretrial conference and trial preparation,

8. trial, and

9. appeals.

Figure 1.1 lists the principal rules of procedure that relate to these steps.

Hiring of a lawyer

Unless she is suing in Small Claims Court, where people often represent themselves, as a practical matter Abigail needs to hire a lawyer either to negotiate a settlement or to take her case to trial. Rattle Motors and Fred Flogem, the likely defendants in a personal injury case, are probably covered by insurance taken out by Rattle to cover its own torts and those of its employees. If so, Rattle's obligation is to notify the insurer immediately of a potential claim. The insurance company will then hire and direct lawyers to act for Rattle and Fred because it is the insurance company that will have to pay Abigail if the case settles or if she wins at trial. For that reason, the insurance company controls the conduct of the case and instructs the lawyers even though Rattle and Fred are the defendants. If Rattle is not insured, it must hire and instruct its own lawyer to represent it and Fred. If there is a conflict between Fred and Rattle concerning any issue in dispute, Fred must be separately represented. If not, one lawyer can act for both.

How does Abigail go about choosing a lawyer? She could seek a recommendation from friends or relatives, call the lawyer referral service at the Law Society of Upper Canada, or look in the Yellow Pages. Any lawyer can take her case, but she would be wise to choose one who practises personal injury law. Because many people are injured in circumstances that give rise to legal remedies, personal injury law is a high-volume area with many lawyers to choose from.

Once Abigail has made a choice, she should formally engage the lawyer's services by signing a retainer. A retainer is a contract between a lawyer and a client that sets out a description of the work to be done by the lawyer and the terms and conditions for the payment of **fees** and **disbursements** by the client. The lawyer may also ask Abigail to pay a deposit to be applied to future fees and disbursements. This deposit is also called a retainer.[2] Abigail and her lawyer may make other arrangements for the paying of legal fees. It is not uncommon for personal injury lawyers to take no fees or disbursements at the beginning of a case; instead, they are often paid what they are owed out of the trial judgment or settlement. A lawyer who loses a case is still entitled to be paid for services rendered. However, collecting fees from clients in these circumstances is not easy, particularly if clients do not have the resources to pay and feel that the lawyer's services have produced nothing of value.

fees
payment to lawyers for services rendered

disbursements
amounts lawyers pay on behalf of clients to third parties that lawyers can recover from clients

FIGURE 1.1   STEPS IN AN ACTION

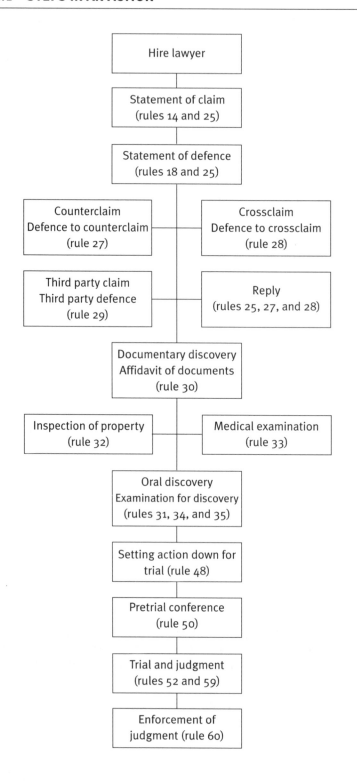

Note that a **contingency fee**, where a lawyer is paid a percentage of the judgment *only* if he or she wins the case, is not permitted in Ontario except in limited circumstances.[3] The rationale for this is that a lawyer's personal financial interest in a client's case might interfere with the lawyer's objective and disinterested advice to the client. It is hard, so the theory goes, to be "disinterested" and "objective" about the outcome when the lawyer's fees depend on whether the case is won or lost. Contingency fees are permitted in the United States and in most other Canadian provinces. As of 2003 they are permitted in Ontario. In the meantime, the courts have greatly lowered the barriers to using contingency fees.

In deciding what to charge Abigail, the lawyer may consider several factors:

- the amount of money at stake in the action,

- Abigail's ability to pay,

- the amount of time the lawyer will spend on the pretrial stage and the trial,

- the degree of complexity of the legal and/or factual issues, and

- the degree of success the lawyer is able to achieve.

Once Abigail has retained a lawyer, she will be interviewed at some length by the lawyer or the law clerk to determine the facts of the case, who the witnesses are, and who the other parties are. From this information, the lawyer has to decide whether Abigail has a good **cause of action** or not.

Preliminary investigations and research
DETERMINING THE CAUSE OF ACTION

In order for the lawyer to decide if there is a good cause of action, the lawyer has to ask whether or not the facts, as related by the client, identify a legal right or issue that gives rise to a legal remedy for the client. If there is a cause of action, the lawyer must then consider whether there is sufficient evidence to prove the facts. In the end, the evidence must lead the **trier of fact** to conclude that it is more probable than not that the facts set out by the client are correct. To put it another way, facts are conclusions that can be drawn by assessing the evidence.

If there is not enough evidence to prove the facts, the lawyer may have to advise the client not to continue with the case. The facts as Abigail relates them disclose that there is probably negligence on the part of Fred Flogem, for which Fred's employer, Rattle Motors, is vicariously liable and perhaps directly liable. Negligence is Abigail's cause of action.

RELATIONSHIP BETWEEN PROOF AND EVIDENCE

In a civil case, the burden of proof is on the plaintiff, who is obliged to prove her case on the balance of probabilities — that is, the plaintiff must show the court that it is more likely than not that her version of the case is true. The plaintiff establishes her version of the facts through the evidence of witnesses and other types of evidence. The facts and the evidence which proves those facts focus on two issues: who is liable or at fault and how much is to be paid to compensate the plaintiff for the damage done.

There are four main types of evidence:

contingency fee
fee payable to a lawyer only if he or she wins the case for a client

cause of action
legal right to sue to obtain a legal remedy

trier of fact
judge or jury whose job is to determine the facts of the case from the evidence

1. *Testimonial evidence.* The lawyer will determine from Abigail who the likely witnesses are and will interview any witness who is willing to talk to him or her. It is unlikely that the defendants, Fred and Rattle Motors, would be willing to talk to Abigail's lawyer, and they certainly would be advised by their lawyer not to. If the lawyer can discover the identity of any bystanders who saw the accident, the lawyer will want to interview them. Abigail's doctors will be interviewed about the injuries she sustained. Any witness interviewed should be asked to sign a statement setting out what they said in the interview. This can be used as a reference for the lawyer and as notes to refresh the memory of the witness at trial. If a witness says he or she saw nothing, a signed statement to that effect will prevent the witness from surfacing later with damaging information.

2. *Documentary and demonstrative evidence.* Any document, diagram, photograph, video tape, or audio tape may contain relevant evidence. In Abigail's case, there may be accident reports written by Fred or Linda, medical emergency admission reports, reports from Abigail's physician, from the rehabilitation staff, and from Abigail's employer concerning her return to work. Demonstrative evidence is also included, such as a diagram of the car showroom, photographs of the showroom taken with the floodlights around the car turned on and off, and photographs of Abigail in her cast and showing her injuries. These documents are all admissible in evidence once the person who made the record proves their authenticity. In some cases, such as a doctor's report, a document is admissible without having its maker give evidence.

3. *Physical evidence.* This evidence consists of physical objects, such as the car's leaking engine or oil pan.

4. *Expert evidence.* This evidence usually consists of reports by experts asked to comment on some aspect of the case. The reports of Abigail's doctors constitute expert evidence.

CLOSE OF PRELIMINARY INVESTIGATION: CONSIDERATION OF WHETHER AND HOW TO PROCEED

At this point, Abigail has retained a lawyer, I.M. Just, who has found out the basic facts and made some preliminary investigations from which he can give Abigail advice on how to proceed. Abigail finds out that if she is successful in her action, she will obtain a judgment in her favour in which she will receive monetary compensation called **damages**. As a successful litigant, Abigail will also recover some of her legal fees and disbursements from the defendants because an award of costs is usually given to the party who is successful at trial. However, if Abigail loses, she will not recover any money for her injuries, and she will have to pay some of the legal costs incurred by the successful defendant. She will also have to pay her own legal fees and disbursements in full.

damages
compensation awarded by a court for harm done

It is important that Abigail consider her options carefully. The outcome of her case may be uncertain for a variety of reasons. The legal issues involved may not be clearly resolved. There may be conflicting decisions on the point in issue. More usually, the problem lies with the facts: Is there convincing evidence that will prove the facts of Abigail's case? If, on the lawyer's advice, Abigail thinks she has a good case, she may elect to start a legal proceeding to recover the remedy she seeks.

Commencement of proceedings

COURT JURISDICTION

As a plaintiff in a civil proceeding, Abigail must choose between two possible courts: the Small Claims Court and the Ontario Superior Court of Justice. In order to decide which court Abigail should sue in, it is necessary to understand the basis for a court's jurisdiction — its power to hear a case and grant remedies.

There are three types of jurisdiction:

1. *Jurisdiction over the subject matter of the lawsuit.* Does the court have the power to hear this type of case and provide the remedies Abigail seeks? For example, if the court has jurisdiction only over criminal law matters, it does not have jurisdiction to hear Abigail's lawsuit. Similarly, if Abigail were seeking an injunction as a remedy, she could not do so in Small Claims Court because this court has no authority to grant this remedy. In Ontario, the Superior Court of Justice can hear civil cases dealing with any subject other than a subject over which the Federal Court of Canada has exclusive jurisdiction or a subject that has been allocated by statute to a particular court. It can also grant any civil remedy known to law: injunctions, declarations of rights, orders for the return of property, and monetary damages. The Small Claims Court, by contrast, is restricted to making orders for the return of personal property and the payment of money.

2. *Jurisdiction over the monetary amount claimed in the lawsuit.* The issue here is whether a court has the power to order payment of the amount of money being claimed. As of April 2001, the Small Claims Court's monetary jurisdiction was raised to $10,000. This means that the court may grant a judgment for the payment of money for any amount up to and including $10,000 exclusive of interest and costs. However, it has no authority to give judgment for more than that amount. The Superior Court, on the other hand, has an unlimited monetary jurisdiction. It can grant judgment for any amount of money, including an amount within the jurisdiction of the Small Claims Court.[4] Because Abigail's injuries are serious, she will choose the Superior Court because her damages exceed $10,000. The lawsuit will be more expensive to conduct than it would be in Small Claims Court, where proceedings are simpler and less formal.

3. *Territorial jurisdiction.* Does the court have the power to hear a case where the events the case is based on or the parties' residence is outside its geographical jurisdiction? In general, courts in Ontario have territorial jurisdiction over cases where the event giving rise to the lawsuit or the parties are in Ontario. But questions will arise if some of the events took place in another jurisdiction or if one or more of the parties resides outside Ontario. For example, if Abigail had gone to Buffalo, New York to buy her car and had been injured there, if events leading up to the injury occurred in Buffalo, or if the defendants resided there, could Abigail or should Abigail sue in Ontario or New York? The answer to this kind of question is

often complicated. As an issue of private international law, it is often determined on a case-by-case basis on a test of the balance of convenience to the parties.[5]

Even within Ontario, there can be issues of territorial jurisdiction that affect the court Abigail must choose. While she is suing in the Ontario Superior Court of Justice, the *Rules of Civil Procedure* require her as plaintiff to name the place of trial within Ontario, although the Superior Court can change the place of trial if it decides that the place is inconvenient to all parties on the balance of probabilities. Abigail is free, however, to commence proceedings in any *office* of the court in Ontario — for example, in Thunder Bay, Toronto, or Brampton. Whatever court office in whatever judicial region she chooses, she will have to file all documents in that office, even if she has named another location for trial. If, for example, she commences proceedings in Brampton but names Toronto as the place of trial, she and the defendants will file all documents in Brampton, and her lawyer will be responsible for transferring the court file to Toronto when the pretrial part of the proceedings has been completed.

RULES OF CIVIL PROCEDURE

In commencing proceedings, Abigail must use the appropriate court forms and follow the procedural rules for conducting a civil case. These rules are set out in the Ontario *Rules of Civil Procedure*. (We will refer to these henceforth as "the rules," as lawyers do.) The rules are actually regulations made pursuant to the *Courts of Justice Act*. The power to make the rules is vested in the Civil Rules Committee, consisting of staff from the Ministry of the Attorney General, members of the judiciary, and lawyers. Rule 1.07 provides a procedure for creating practice directions. The purpose of a practice direction is to allow the senior judge in a judicial region to customize the rules and create additional procedures to deal with problems that are specific to that region and are not covered by existing rules. For example, because of difficulties in scheduling trials in the Toronto region, there is a practice direction under rule 5.2 that requires counsel to complete certain forms to facilitate the trial-scheduling process there. The additional procedures in this practice direction are presumably not necessary for the administration of justice in other judicial regions, where they do not apply. It is now clear that a practice direction carries the force of law and must be followed. Previously the status and validity of practice directions were questioned because there was no clear authority for creating them. Rule 1.07 now sets out a procedure for creating practice directions. To bring some consistency and uniformity to practice directions, the power to authorize a practice direction is vested in the chief justice of the Superior Court.

You should become familiar with the practice directions that operate in the judicial region where cases you work on are heard. When these are created, they appear in the *Ontario Gazette* and are posted in the regional courthouses. They are also announced in the *Ontario Reports*, the law society's publication of Ontario cases, which all lawyers receive. The *Ontario Annual Practice* reproduces practice directions next to the rules to which they apply. It also contains an index of published practice directions, so you can easily locate the one you are looking for. Other commercially published versions of Superior Court practice materials also contain this information.

MOTIONS

At first glance, it seems that all you need to do is read a rule and follow it. The rules appear to be clear, but like all legal rules they require interpretation. Because the parties are in an adversarial position, both Abigail's lawyer and the defendants' lawyers are likely to use the rules to attempt to gain the upper hand or assert a position that will be helpful to them. Where one party seeks to use a rule against another party that is allegedly violating the rule, there is a procedural dispute that the court must sort out at the pretrial stage. This is done when one party brings a motion. A motion is a proceeding brought within the main action to settle a procedural issue that has arisen at the pretrial stage. A judge, or in some cases a junior judicial official called a master, will hear submissions from counsel on a motion, read submitted material, and decide the issue by making an order. An order on a motion usually does not dispose of a case on its merits, although this can happen. For example, if Abigail had made a claim not recognized by the law, the defendants could bring a motion to strike out her statement of claim and dismiss her action. If the court was persuaded by the defendants that Abigail did not have a legal reason for suing, the court could strike out her statement of claim, and that would be the end of her case. But this is most unusual. Motions are discussed in more detail later in this chapter.

ACTIONS AND APPLICATIONS

Abigail's lawyer is now ready to start the case or, in the language of the rules, to "commence proceedings." In Ontario, there are two ways for a plaintiff to commence proceedings. Abigail can start an **action** by issuing a statement of claim, or she can start an **application** by issuing a notice of application. Usually a party commences an action. Applications are used when a statute or the rules require them, or when there are no serious factual disputes and the matter turns on an interpretation of law. Otherwise, a plaintiff must proceed by way of an action. An action has a much longer and more complex pretrial procedure than an application. It is largely devoted to giving the parties the opportunity to review evidence and determine facts before trial. In an application, where there is usually little in the way of factual disputes, we have a much simpler and less time-consuming pretrial procedure. There is no need to conduct discovery or otherwise investigate the facts exhaustively. The trial is more like a hearing with no oral evidence. Each party's lawyer spends most of the hearing time on legal arguments, with the evidence introduced by the use of sworn written statements called affidavits.

The facts and issues in Abigail's case are complex and crucial to her proving negligence against the defendants. It is appropriate that her case proceed as an action rather than as an application.

action
one of the two procedures by which a civil matter is commenced in the Superior Court; the other such procedure is an application

application
one of the two procedures by which a civil matter is commenced in the Superior Court; the other such procedure is an action

Exchange of pleadings: Statement of claim and statement of defence

STATEMENT OF CLAIM

I.M. Just is now ready to commence proceedings by starting an action with a statement of claim. He prepares this document, which sets out

- the remedies Abigail is asking for, referred to as the "claim for relief";

- the identification of the parties in terms of their legal status — for example, Abigail and Fred are individuals, and Rattle Motors Ltd. is a corporation; and

- the facts on which Abigail relies, as well as statements of the laws that entitle her to a remedy.

With the statement of claim, he also files a form called "Information for Court Use," which provides the court with information about the causes of action and whether the case is using any special procedure. Once it is prepared, the document is taken by a law clerk or office courier to the local office of the Superior Court to be issued. After the law office courier pays the prescribed fee for issuing a claim, the registrar opens a court file, assigns the case a court file number which is placed on the document, and issues the statement of claim by sealing and signing the document on behalf of the registrar of the court. As the registrar is doing this to the original, the lawyer's clerk makes a **true copy** of the statement of claim. The lawyer's clerk does this by copying on a copy of the statement of claim the information the court clerk has put on the original. The true copy goes into the court file, and the lawyer's clerk brings the original back to the law office. The lawyer pays the prescribed fee of \$157[6] to the court on Abigail's behalf. If Abigail's case were urgent and I.M. Just did not have time to draft a statement of claim, I.M. Just could issue a **notice of action**, and file the statement of claim later. This might happen if Abigail had not sued until the limitation period for her cause of action had almost run out. To preserve a client's rights before the limitation period expires, a lawyer can use a notice of action to start the lawsuit and "stop the clock" on the soon-to-expire limitation period.

Once the statement of claim is issued, all further filed documents must bear the appropriate **general heading** identifying the court, the court file number, the names of the parties, and the name of the document. The names of the parties and the status in which they are suing or being sued that appears within the general heading is referred to as the **title of proceedings**. If there are many defendants or plaintiffs, the case is generally referred to by the short title of proceedings, used on the **backsheet** of the court forms. In Abigail's case, the short form is *Boar v. Rattle Motors Ltd. et al.* Figure 1.2 shows the general heading of the statement of claim, including the title of proceedings, where Abigail sues Rattle Motors and Fred Flogem in the Superior Court.

Figure 1.3 shows the backsheet for this statement.

Now that I.M. Just has issued the statement of claim, he must serve a copy of it on the defendants within six months from the date on which the claim was issued. Because defendants do not know they have been sued until they are served with the first document in the lawsuit against them, the rules are strict about ensuring that they are properly served with the first or originating document.

SERVING THE STATEMENT OF CLAIM

The statement of claim, the originating document in this case, must be served personally on the defendants or must be served by a permitted alternative to personal service. Personal service means that the statement of claim must be handed directly to the defendant if the defendant is an individual. Service is effective even if the defendant refuses to take the document, tears it up, or throws it away. Therefore a process server can simply hand a copy of the document to Fred. But what about serving Rattle Motors? There are special rules for serving individuals on behalf of a

---

true copy
copy of an original document that is like the original in every particular, including copies of alterations, signatures, and court file numbers

notice of action
document informing defendants that they have been sued

general heading
heading on all court documents identifying the court, the parties, the status of the parties, and the name of the document

title of proceedings
part of the general heading that identifies the parties and their status in a lawsuit

backsheet
part of every court document, containing the name and address of the lawyer who prepared the document, the short title of proceedings, the court and court file number, and a large space reserved for court officials to make entries on

FIGURE 1.2   GENERAL HEADING OF STATEMENT OF CLAIM (FORM 4A)

Court file no. `01-CV-1234`

ONTARIO
SUPERIOR COURT OF JUSTICE

BETWEEN:

Abigail Boar

Plaintiff

and

Rattle Motors Ltd. and Fred Flogem

Defendants

corporation. Here, a process server can serve the corporate defendant by handing a copy of Abigail's statement of claim to the manager of Rattle Motors Ltd.

It is also possible to use one of the three alternatives to personal service to serve an originating document.

1. If I.M. Just knows that Rattle Motors and Fred have lawyers acting for them in this lawsuit, he can serve the lawyers' office. This is valid service, provided that the lawyers sign a document stating that they accept service on behalf of the defendants. To do that, the lawyers should have instructions from the clients to accept service on their behalf.

2. I.M. Just can send a copy of the claim to the defendants' last-known addresses by ordinary mail with an acknowledgment of receipt form (these are pink postcards, available from the post office, addressed to the sender and attached to the recipient's envelope). Service is valid and effective if the recipient signs the pink acknowledgment card and mails it back to the sender.

3. I.M. Just can deliver the statement of claim in an envelope to the defendant's residence and leave it with an apparently adult person who appears to be a member of the household. He can then mail a copy of the claim to the defendant the next day. This mode of service applies only to Fred Flogem.

SUBSTITUTED SERVICE

All of the methods of service that we have discussed so far assume that I.M. Just knows or can find out the defendants' last-known addresses and that the defendants are actually there. But what if Fred has moved and no longer works at Rattle Motors? Or what if he is evading service? I.M. Just may have tried personal service and the alternatives to personal service and failed to serve him. If I.M. Just does not know exactly where Fred is, the other modes of service will be ineffective. In these situations, plaintiffs can ask the court to permit them to use substituted service. I.M. Just must suggest a method of service that satisfies the court that there is a reasonable probability that Abigail's statement of claim will come to Fred's attention. Depending on what seems likely to be most effective, the court may order service by

FIGURE 1.3   BACKSHEET (FORM 4C)

Abigail Boar
PLAINTIFF(S)

(Short title of proceeding)

and

Rattle Motors Ltd.
DEFENDANT(S)

Court file no. 01-CV-1234

ONTARIO SUPERIOR COURT OF JUSTICE

Proceeding commenced at Toronto

STATEMENT OF CLAIM

Name, address and telephone number of plaintiff's solicitor or plaintiff:

I.M. Just
Law Society No. 17888 Q

Just & Coping
Barristers and Solicitors
365 Bay Street - 8701
Toronto, Ontario, M3J 4A9

tel. 416-762-1342
fax 416-762-2300

Solicitors for the Plaintiff

PART I   An overview of the civil litigation process

registered mail, or service on a close relative or friend with whom the defendant appears to be in touch, or service by an announcement in the newspaper. Whatever method is ordered by the court, once I.M. Just does what the order says, Fred is presumed to be served, even if he did not actually receive a copy of the statement of claim. Abigail can continue with her lawsuit.

OTHER FORMS OF SERVICE

There are special rules for personally serving corporations and other legal entities, such as estate executors, trustees, mentally incompetent persons, and children. There is another set of rules for serving a party who does not reside or carry on business in Ontario. There are often special procedural rules that must be followed when serving someone who lives in a foreign country. Those who reside outside Ontario are given more time to respond to the lawsuit.

Once the originating document is served, the rules for service are relaxed, as those parties with an interest in the lawsuit are now presumed to know about it and about their obligations to respond. Subsequent documents may be served in a variety of ways:

- by mailing a copy to the opposite party's lawyer's office (this document is deemed to be served on the fifth day after it is mailed);

- by physically delivering a copy to the lawyer's office and leaving it with an employee, usually a receptionist;

- by depositing a copy at a document exchange of which the lawyer is a member if the copy is date-stamped as received by the document exchange (this document is deemed to be served on the day after the document exchange receives it);

- by faxing a copy to the lawyer's office, including a cover sheet setting out information that the document is being served by fax and showing who served it (some documents may not be served this way);

- by sending a copy to the lawyer's office by courier (this document is deemed to be served two days later); and

- by e-mailing a document to the lawyer's office, provided that the sender indicates in the e-mail message who he or she is and provided that the lawyer served in this way e-mails back an acceptance of the document served (this document is deemed to be served on the day following the day the message is sent).

PROOF OF SERVICE

Someone who is served with a document, whether originating or not and whatever the mode of service, may deny that he or she was served. If so, that person claims to have no notice of the lawsuit. This can be problematic. A defendant who does not respond to a claim will find that the plaintiff may still proceed in that defendant's absence.

A defendant who claims he or she was not served, and finds that he or she has been sued or that a judgment has been obtained, may move to set aside the proceedings or set aside the judgment. If the defendant is successful, the plaintiff may have to start all over from the beginning with added expense and delay. It is therefore important that I.M. Just is careful to ensure that he serves the defendants and can prove it. This is particularly important for originating documents, such as a statement of claim, which give notice to the defendant that he or she has been sued. It is less crucial with subsequent documents because a misadventure of service does not mean the action has to be restarted.

Proof usually consists of an affidavit of service, in which the person who served the document swears that he or she did so and describes the method of service, the date, and other details. The rules permit the affidavit of service to be written right on the backsheet of the originating or subsequent document. Where a lawyer accepts service, his or her endorsement is proof of service. Where service is through a document exchange, the document exchange's date stamp is sufficient evidence to prove service. No additional affidavit is required.

STATEMENT OF DEFENCE

Now that I.M. Just has served Fred and Rattle Motors Ltd. with Abigail's statement of claim by personally serving the defendants or by using an alternative to personal service, the defendants must respond to the statement of claim by serving and filing a statement of defence. If they are served in Ontario, they have 20 days to file a statement of defence. If they are served elsewhere in Canada or in the continental United States, they have 40 days. If they are served anywhere else on the planet, they have 60 days to file a defence. If time is running out before they have finished preparing a defence, they may file a notice of intent to defend. As with a notice of action, this extends the time for filing the statement of defence for a further 10 days.

Generally, plaintiffs in the same proceeding do not have conflicts of interest and are represented by the same lawyers. A plaintiff cannot be forced to have others join him or her as plaintiff. One lawyer may also represent multiple defendants, provided that their defences do not conflict. For example, if one defendant says the plaintiff's injuries were caused by the acts of the other defendant, there is a clear conflict if the other defendant denies liability. Fred and the manager of Rattle Motors will have to decide if one lawyer can represent both. In this case, Rattle Motors will be vicariously liable for the acts of its employee even if it did not itself commit separate acts of negligence. In cases like this, where both the employer and employee are sued, they are usually represented by one lawyer because it is likely that the employer or its insurer will end up paying any damages. If a conflict develops between the defendants, however, a lawyer is obliged to tell both defendants that he or she can no longer act for either of them and to help arrange for separate representation.

Let us assume that one lawyer represents both defendants. This lawyer reviews Abigail's claim, which sets out a concise statement of the facts but not the evidence by which these facts are to be proven. The claim should also identify the cause of action and set out the legal principles that Abigail relies on. Finally, the claim should set out the remedies sought. After reviewing this document the lawyer may advise one of three possible responses to the claim:

1. *Do nothing.* In this case, Abigail will obtain a default judgment.

2. *Bring a motion to dismiss on the ground that the claim discloses no known cause of action.* This type of motion is rare and unlikely in our case because Abigail's claim is not unusual.

3. *File a statement of defence.* In this statement, a lawyer sets out defences which, if proved, will result in Abigail's claim being dismissed. The defendants must admit those paragraphs in Abigail's claim with which they agree. They must then deny those paragraphs which contain statements with which they disagree. They must then identify those paragraphs in the claim about which they have no knowledge. They must also set out their own version of the facts and the law they rely on. This last requirement is sometimes referred to as an affirmative defence because it consists of more than denials of the plaintiff's claim. Those paragraphs of Abigail's claim that the defendants admit are deemed to be proved and need not be proved at trial. This is one of the ways in which the pleadings serve to narrow the issues before trial.

After the statement of defence has been served on Abigail's lawyer and filed in court, I.M. Just reviews it. If he finds that the statement of defence has raised an issue or facts related to that issue that were not dealt with in the statement of claim, Abigail may serve and file a reply to the statement of defence. For example, if the defence states that Abigail showed up at the showroom in an intoxicated state, the defendants may argue that there was contributory negligence on Abigail's part. Abigail may need to serve and file a reply denying that she was intoxicated if those facts and issues were not covered in the statement of claim. If the plaintiff simply wishes to deny the defendant's defence generally, there is no need to file a formal reply.

OTHER PLEADINGS

In some cases, there are other types of legal issues that may result in other pleadings. Suppose Abigail sues Fred and Rattle Motors but not Skank Motorcar Company Ltd., the manufacturer of the Super Coupe. If the two defendants think that it was not their negligence but the negligent manufacturing of the Super Coupe that caused Abigail's damages, they may issue a third party notice to add Skank to the proceedings. This is a notice to the manufacturer which says that the defendants hold Skank wholly or partly responsible for Abigail's damages, so that if they are found liable, they will argue to have that liability transferred to the manufacturer, whom they are adding as a third party. They must send Skank all the pleadings to date, and Skank may file a defence against the claim made by the defendants against it. Skank is also entitled to raise any defence against the plaintiff's claim in the main action that the other defendants did not raise but could have raised. Thereafter, Skank is treated as a defendant in the main proceeding, and the third party issues are part of the trial of the main action, although in some cases they may be tried separately. It is also possible for a third party to deny liability and claim that the fault, if any, is that of a fourth party. This would result in the issuing of a fourth party notice with the fourth party having the same rights as the third party.

If one defendant has a claim against the other defendant that is related to events or transactions in the main action, the defendant with the claim should file a crossclaim against the other defendant. In a case like Abigail's, this is most likely to occur with respect to a claim for contribution by one defendant under the *Negligence Act*. That Act permits one defendant to have the degree of liability between the defendants assessed to determine how much each should pay, and it allows a defendant that settles the action to claim financial contributions from other defendants. In our case, Fred may wish to argue that if the defendants are liable to Abigail, Rattle Motors is 90 percent responsible for Abigail's injuries. If Fred seeks to pin most of the responsibility on Rattle, he needs to do it by crossclaim against Rattle. The recipient of a crossclaim may counterclaim against the crossclaimant or file a defence to the crossclaim. A crossclaim is not dependent on the main action but is usually tried with it.

If either defendant can argue that Abigail acted in some way to cause them a legally recognized injury, the defendant can file a counterclaim with the statement of defence. Abigail would then have to respond with her own statement of defence to counterclaim.

Once a reply has been made to every defence filed, or the time for replying has expired, pleading stage is complete. Facts that are admitted do not have to be proved at trial. Facts that are not admitted must be proved. For example, if Rattle Motors and Fred admit that Abigail sustained the injuries and suffered the damages she claims but deny that the damages resulted from their negligence, damages are admitted and need not be proven at trial. However, Abigail will still have to prove negligence because liability is not admitted. Both parties will have to advance evidence to prove facts on the issue of negligence.

Because a party can only introduce evidence relevant to the facts as pleaded, evidence relating to facts that were not pleaded but should have been pleaded cannot be admitted. This happens rarely, but when it does happen it can be fatal to the party who forgot to plead a necessary fact to support his or her case. Sometimes the party can ask the judge to let the party amend the pleadings, but the other party will object, and the judge may decide that it is too late to permit amendments and reopen the pretrial stage for discovery on these "new" facts if the case is already at trial. This is one of the reasons it is necessary to read statements of claim and defence carefully to ensure that the pleadings fit the theory of your case.

Examinations for discovery of parties and discovery of documents

The pleadings should set out the case from each party's point of view. You should now know the basic facts in dispute, the legal issues, the case your law firm has to prove, and the case it has to meet. The pleadings are a concise statement of material facts — a lot of the details are missing. For this reason each party is entitled to have discovery of the other party's case to obtain more information about the supporting evidence and details. There are a number of different types of discovery available, including medical examinations and inspections of places or property. For example, Fred and Rattle Motors may request Abigail to submit to a medical or psychological examination about her neurological problems by a medical professional of its choice. The evidence from that examination can be received in the form of the doctor's ***viva voce* evidence** or the doctor's report. Abigail, on the other hand, may wish to have a lighting expert and an expert on flooring examine Rattle Motor's showroom. Discovery in the form of inspection of property is available to her because she does not have possession of the property or a right to enter it for the purposes of inspecting it. These types of discovery are used only in those actions where they are helpful. The main types of discovery used in almost every civil case are discovery of documents and oral examination for discovery.

***viva voce* evidence**
oral evidence

DISCOVERY OF DOCUMENTS

The rules require all parties to prepare an affidavit of documents in which they disclose under oath the identity and nature of every document that might be relevant to the action they now have or had previously. Abigail, for example, must disclose all of the subsequent medical records that underlie her claim that she suffered specific serious injuries. Rattle Motors must disclose any reports it has concerning leaking oil pans on the Super Coupe. Documents are given a broad interpretation and may include computer disks, audio and video tapes, photographs, and other media of communication. All documents that a party has or had must be listed. If the document is still in existence and obtainable, it must be produced for inspection by the other side. Usually, each side provides the other with copies of its own documents.

An exception to the disclosure rule exists with respect to documents for which a party claims legal privilege. For example, solicitor–client correspondence is routinely claimed as privileged based on the solicitor–client privilege. Similarly, documents or reports prepared specifically because of the litigation are also privileged and need not be produced. If privilege is claimed for a document, it must be listed but does not have to be produced at trial. If a party decides to waive the privilege and rely on the document for the party's own case at trial, then the privilege is lost, and the document must be disclosed. However, where a document is not privileged it must be listed in the affidavit of documents and produced.

EXAMINATION FOR DISCOVERY

Once documentary discovery has taken place, the parties usually arrange for an examination for discovery. Here, each party's lawyer is entitled to question the other party under oath about the case, the statement of claim or defence, and the documents disclosed in the discovery of documents process. Questions can be wide ranging. If a party does not know the answer to a question, he or she may be asked to undertake to provide an answer or produce a document later. On a lawyer's advice, the party either accepts or rejects the undertaking. If the undertaking is rejected, the party asking the question may bring a motion to compel the other party to re-attend at his or her own expense to answer the question, provided that the judge on the motion agrees that the question is a proper question.

These examinations are held outside court, usually in an office rented for the purpose. Abigail would be present with her lawyer to answer questions put to her by the lawyer for Rattle Motors and Fred. Fred and a representative of Rattle Motors may attend to observe and to advise their lawyer. Abigail may also be present when her lawyer questions the defendants in their lawyer's presence. Also present is a court reporter or stenographer to take down a record of the proceedings. This record can be used in preparing both for cross-examination of a party and for preparing a client for examination-in-chief at trial. Where a party gives different answers or tells a different story from the one given at discovery, the discovery transcript can be used to challenge the credibility of the evidence given by the party at trial. The transcript can also be used to "read in" admissions by the opposite party on issues and facts in the case, although this is more likely to be done on a "request to admit" before trial. We discuss "requests to admit" later in this chapter.

Motions

Thus far, we have been describing how a civil action proceeds. It appears to be orderly and without any procedural disputes. On occasion, we have made reference to one or the other of the parties applying to the court for an order concerning the conduct of the action. For example, if a lawyer omits an essential fact or legal issue from a statement of claim, he or she can ask the court for permission to amend the claim to add the missing information. But how do you ask the court? The answer is that you bring a motion to obtain the relief or remedy you request. Motions are generally proceedings within an action and may be brought at any time during the proceedings, including at trial. Their purpose is to settle a dispute about some procedural point that the parties are unable to resolve themselves. On a motion, the court hears argument by the parties and then issues an order that resolves the problem. Such orders rarely decide the case on the merits and bring it to an end. Instead, the parties usually do as the order directs and get on with the case. Appeals from orders made on motions are rare. The right to appeal this kind of order is restricted, and it is usually too expensive and time-consuming since the issues are often procedural and not crucial to ultimate success. Examples of procedural motions include motions to extend the time for filing pleadings, motions for particulars (details) of allegations in a statement of claim or defence, and motions to compel a party to produce documents or attend discovery. Occasionally, a motion may decide the case without a trial: A motion for default judgment will do this where a defendant has failed to file a defence. A motion to strike out a statement of claim as disclosing no cause of action may do this as well.

Motions are usually made on notice to the other party. The party who brings the motion, called "the moving party" whether plaintiff or defendant, serves the "the responding party" with a notice of motion. The notice of motion tells the responding party what the moving party wants the court to do and provides a brief statement of the reasons why the moving party is entitled to the order. The notice of motion also sets out the documents or sources of information relied on. Evidence on the motion is usually given by affidavit rather than orally. The affidavit sets out the facts that entitle the moving party to the relief claimed in the notice of motion. The responding party may also file an affidavit or other documents to support its case and may bring a crossmotion for relief. Counsel then appears before a judge or master of the Superior Court and presents the case orally. The judge or master decides the issues raised in the motion and issues an **order**. If a motion is made at trial, it is not necessary to use formal notices of motions because the parties are already before the court. While motions are generally made on notice, some motions may be made without notice to the other side. An example is a motion for substituted service of a claim when the other party cannot be located for service.

One motion that might occur when pleadings have been exchanged is a motion for summary judgment. While a default judgment may be obtained if the defendant files no statement of defence, a summary judgment is obtained when a party argues that the other party's pleadings disclose no triable issue. If the motion is successful, a judgment should issue — to dismiss the action if a defendant brings the motion, or to grant judgment if a plaintiff brings the motion. If the issue is one of law alone, the judge may decide it. If it involves questions of credibility or facts which are disputed, the judge is more likely to use the motion to narrow the issues, establish facts, and order a speedy trial. If, for example, the defendants bring a motion for summary

order
generic term used in the *Rules of Civil Procedure* to describe commands issued by courts on motions and at trials

judgment to dismiss Abigail's action on the basis that the limitation period for tort actions has expired, they must file affidavits as to when the accident occurred and when the action was commenced, with reference to the pleadings and perhaps discovery transcripts. On a motion for summary judgment, the facts of a case must be simple and unambiguous. There are heavy cost penalties for a party that brings a futile and unnecessary motion.

Pretrial conference and trial preparation

The parties have now exchanged pleadings, discoveries have been completed, and usually any motions necessary to ensure compliance with the rules have been brought, heard, and determined. The parties need no more information before trial. At this point, lawyers and their clients often assess their chances for success at trial, weighing the pros and cons of their case. Most cases get this far because there is a dispute about the facts. No lawyer will tell a client with certainty that he or she will win or lose; when facts are disputed, much will depend on the credibility of witnesses, which is hard to assess.

In this atmosphere and at this stage, either side or both sides may attempt to settle the case. If the parties reach a settlement, they file a consent to dismiss the action on the basis of the terms of the settlement. If the settlement involves payments by one side to the other, the action is not dismissed until the payment is made to prevent the payer from reneging on the promise. The parties may pursue informal discussions, or they may make formal written offers — the latter have some important consequences if they are rejected. Briefly, if a formal offer to settle is made, it is made in writing to the other side, and a sealed copy is filed with the court. If the other side accepts the offer on its terms and within the time during which the offer is open for acceptance, the case is over. But if the offer is rejected and the party who rejected the offer does not do as well at trial as he or she would have done had he or she accepted the offer, there are negative cost consequences.

For example, if Abigail is offered $300,000 to settle but thinks she can get $500,000 at trial, she may reject the offer. However, if she recovers only $200,000, she will receive costs only to the date the offer was made, and she will be deprived of costs thereafter. Further, the defendant is entitled to the usual costs from the date the offer was made to the date of judgment. If Abigail made an offer to Fred and Rattle Motors and they rejected it, and if Abigail received a judgment that was equal to or better than the offer she made, Abigail will receive costs to the date the offer was made and a higher cost award from the day the offer was made to the date of judgment. In a long and complex lawsuit, legal costs can reach a significant amount. This may make litigants think twice about forging ahead when they find that a large part of the judgment is eaten up by their obligations to pay their own and part of their opponent's legal costs.

SETTING THE CASE DOWN FOR TRIAL

If the case does not settle on the close of discoveries, either party may signal that he or she has completed all necessary information-gathering steps, all motions, and is ready to go to trial. This is done by filing a trial record after serving it on the other party. Sixty days after that is done, the court registrar will put the action on the trial list by setting the case down for trial. If no party sets the matter down for trial, there are provisions for the registrar to force the action on for trial, or to dismiss the action for want of prosecution after giving notice to the parties. Cases are tried in the order in which they are placed on the trial list. There are three separate lists: one for jury trials, one for non-jury trials, and one for speedy trial.

TRIAL RECORD

The trial record is a booklet with grey cardboard covers. It is prepared for the use of the trial judge by the party who sets the action down for trial. It contains a table of contents, a copy of each of the pleadings filed, and a copy of any orders made at the pretrial stage as a result of motions. The back cover of the record is set up as a backsheet, with a large blank space for the judge to write his or her **endorsement**. The endorsements are handwritten notes recording the judge's decision, though not usually the judge's reasons for his or her decision.

endorsement
judge's handwritten order or judgment from which a successful party is expected to prepare a formal draft of the order or judgment

PRETRIAL CONFERENCE

After the matter has been set down, either party may request a pretrial conference. Though not mandatory under the rules, the parties are encouraged to avail themselves of the opportunity to use a pretrial conference. Each party serves on the other and files with the court a pretrial conference memorandum that sets out the issues between the parties. The lawyers, with the parties, appear before a pretrial conference judge. The role of the judge is to listen to the lawyers, review the issues with them, and give a frank assessment of the case. The idea here is that an impartial judge may inject a dose of reality that may facilitate settlement, particularly where the parties are being obstinate. The judge's goal is to promote settlement and, failing that, to narrow the issues in order to speed up and simplify the trial. Unless the parties consent, the judge who conducts a pretrial conference does not preside at the trial of the matter.

REQUESTS TO ADMIT

As a means to speeding up the proof of facts at the trial, either party at any time may serve on the other a **request to admit**. The party served with a request to admit is being asked to admit the truth of a fact or the authenticity of a document. The party receiving the request must admit, deny, or refuse to admit, and explain any refusal to admit. Failure to respond leads to a finding that the fact is deemed to be admitted, or the document is deemed to be authentic. An admission, as noted earlier, eliminates the need to prove that fact at trial and can reduce the time it takes to try the case.

request to admit
document in which one party requires the other to admit the truth of a fact or the authenticity of a document

ASSIGNMENT COURT

After the pretrial conference or after both parties have consented to dispense with the pretrial conference, the action is placed on a controlled list for trial. As the case gets closer to the top of the list, it goes to a weekly assignment court, where the lawyers appear and, with the judge, set a specific date for trial. However, if cases ahead of it on the list settle on the eve of trial, the list may collapse, and the parties may suddenly find that their trial date has moved up. Similarly, another trial may take longer than estimated, and the parties' case may be delayed.

PRETRIAL PREPARATION

Once you know your client is going to trial, there is much to do. I.M. Just needs to decide what witnesses he will call to provide the evidence that will prove the facts alleged. Abigail will obviously give evidence of what happened to her. In addition, I.M. Just will have to use a **summons to a witness** to ensure that other witnesses attend trial and give evidence. If a witness has relevant documents that he or she can speak about, the summons should direct the witness to bring those documents to court. Because Abigail's medical reports are important evidence on the issue of damages, I.M. Just must give notice of his intent to produce these records at trial. The records will be admitted in evidence unless the opposite party wishes to cross-examine the doctor or maker of the report. There are other notices that might have to be served, though perhaps not in this case — for example, one party may serve a notice to introduce business records, such as invoices or an account record. As with medical reports, business records may be admissible without the maker of the record having to prove their validity and authenticity. I.M. Just and the defendants' lawyer may wish to prepare a trial brief. This brief includes a list of witnesses, what they will say, what opposing witnesses are likely to say, and contains points about cross-examining witnesses. It may also include matters for opening and closing argument and a guide for proving each fact necessary to the case.

Time must then be spent preparing witnesses for their examinations-in-chief and cross-examinations and preparing demonstrative and other physical and documentary evidence for trial.

summons to a witness
order of a court telling the person named on the summons to attend a trial and give evidence

A VARIATION: CASE MANAGEMENT SYSTEM

You should be aware that in Toronto and Ottawa there is a mandatory case management system for most civil actions. This does not change the basic steps in an action, but it does two things that the rules do not require. First, it imposes mandatory time limits on completion of steps in a proceeding by establishing a timetable immediately after the action commences. The timing and scheduling of the case is now in the hands of the courts rather than in the hands of the parties or their lawyers. The result is that cases move through the system much more quickly than they did when lawyers controlled the timing. Second, it simplifies and in some cases eliminates some of the procedural aspects that most contribute to wasting time and increasing cost. For example, the process for motions is greatly simplified. It also introduces some steps not otherwise required by the rules: Both case mediation and pretrial conferences are mandatory under case management. The ultimate goal of case management is to move a case rapidly through the system, structuring opportunities for settlement and getting the matter tried quickly if settlement is unsuccessful.

Trial

Because Abigail is the plaintiff, her lawyer opens her case, perhaps with an opening statement to explain what the case is about. The statement may be brief because it is presumed that the trial judge has read the trial record and knows that this is a "slip and fall" negligence case with issues concerning both liability and damages. But it will be necessary to have an opening statement if this is a jury trial, because jurors know nothing of the case until the lawyers tell them in the opening statements. I.M. Just then calls his witnesses, probably starting with Abigail. He examines

Abigail in chief, and the defendant's counsel cross-examines her. The same sequence is followed with the plaintiff's other witnesses. When I.M. Just has finished presenting Abigail's case through the testimony of witnesses, he closes the case. At this time, the defendants open their case. If their lawyers think that the evidence adduced from the plaintiff's witnesses does not prove the facts alleged by the plaintiff, they may move that the action be dismissed and elect not to call evidence. But it is more likely that they will not run this risk, and that they will call the first witness. The case then proceeds with examination and cross-examination of the defence witnesses. When the defendants close their case, each side sums up, the plaintiff going first.

Having heard the evidence, read the documents, and heard counsel, the trial judge may then decide the case on the spot. But if the judge needs to think about the issues, he or she reserves judgment and gives judgment on a later date. If the judge reserves judgment, he or she may also issue written or oral reasons for judgment. These reasons may be reported in the law reports or be available through an online service such as Quicklaw.

JURY TRIALS

If Abigail had wanted a jury trial, she is required to have issued a jury notice before the close of pleadings and discovery. The defendants could then have moved to have the jury notice struck out on the ground that the case was not appropriate for a jury. This usually happens when the evidence is technical or complex, although it is harder to strike out a jury notice on these grounds than it once was.

If the matter proceeds before a jury, the trial takes longer than it does before a judge sitting alone. This is because juries are not experienced in trying cases or knowledgeable about the law. Lawyers may have to move more slowly in questioning witnesses and be more thorough in their summing up and in their opening remarks. At the end of the trial, the judge charges the jury, giving a neutral summing up of the evidence and explaining how the law is to be applied to whatever facts the jury finds. The judge carefully drafts the charge, bearing in mind suggestions by the lawyers. It is up to the jury to assess the evidence to determine what facts have been proven from the evidence it has heard. The judge tells the jury what the law is in his or her charge. Unlike the situation in the United States, civil juries are relatively rare in Canada.

JUDGMENT

At the end of the trial, the judge gives judgment. If there is a jury, it gives a verdict on which the judgment is based.[7] If Abigail is successful, she will be given a judgment requiring Fred and Rattle Motors to pay her damages for her injuries. Each defendant may be ordered to pay a specific share if the judge assesses liability for each of them, or they may be jointly and severally liable to pay. Abigail is likely to receive general damages for her pain and suffering, and special damages for her out-of-pocket expenses, which cover her actual out-of-pocket expenses and other **pecuniary** losses caused by the defendants' negligence. She will receive prejudgment interest from the date that she was injured to the date of judgment, and she will also be awarded postjudgment interest on the amount of the judgment from the day of judgment to the day of payment of that judgment. If Abigail wins her case, she is likely to be awarded partial indemnity costs, which amount to one-third to two-thirds of

pecuniary
of monetary value

her actual legal costs, based on a cost grid or table. If Abigail is not successful, her claim will be dismissed. She will not receive anything. The successful defendants will receive their partial indemnity costs, which Abigail will have to pay.

A judgment in Abigail's favour does not mean that she will simply receive a cheque. A judgment is a command to pay, but if the defendants choose not to pay up voluntarily, Abigail will have to take steps to enforce her judgment. Abigail can file **writs of seizure and sale** against Fred and Rattle Motors. She can then direct the sheriff of Toronto or the sheriff of any county in which she has filed a writ and the defendants have property to seize and sell the property under the authority of the writ. Abigail then satisfies her judgment from the proceeds of the sale. For example, the sheriff could seize Fred's bank account or sell his car or house. The sheriff could also seize the property on which Rattle Motors has its building, as well as its inventory of cars. Alternatively, Abigail could **garnishee** Fred's wages or any amounts due to either defendant from third parties. A garnishee order is sent to third parties who owe money to either defendant, telling them to pay the funds due to the defendant to the sheriff to be held to satisfy the judgment.

writ of seizure and sale
order from a court to a sheriff to enforce the court's order by seizing and selling the defendant's property and holding the proceeds to satisfy the judgment debt to the plaintiff; also known as a writ of execution

garnishee
order directed to a third party who owes money to a defendant as a means of enforcing a judgment

EFFECT OF THE JUDGMENT

Once a judgment is given, it is final and may not be challenged unless it is appealed. The matter is then said to be *res judicata*, which means that any issue tried and decided in a court proceeding cannot be relitigated in a subsequent proceeding.

res judicata
Latin phrase meaning that a matter decided by a court is final and incapable of being relitigated in a subsequent proceeding

Appeals

The rules and the *Courts of Justice Act* provide for an appeal from almost any trial court's decision. In some circumstances, appeals are heard by the Divisional Court, a branch of the Superior Court. In Abigail's case, which originated in the Superior Court, the appeal (if the damages are substantiated) is heard in the Ontario Court of Appeal, the highest court in the province. If, for example, the defendants felt that the damage award for Abigail's pain and suffering was excessive and not supported by legal principle or the evidence, they could appeal by filing a notice of appeal in which they set out the grounds on which the appeal is based. Here the defendants are called the "appellants" in the title of proceedings because they are appealing the trial decision. Abigail will be called the "respondent" on the appeal.

The appellants are required to file with the court a statement of fact and law, which sets out the facts of the case, the legal issues raised on appeal, and a brief resume of the law on which they rely. I.M. Just will file a statement of fact and law in reply. The appellants will also order those parts of the trial transcript that are required to support their factual and legal arguments. The transcripts and documents that were exhibits at trial are the only evidence. No witnesses are heard on an appeal.

The Court of Appeal has very broad powers, but it exercises them sparingly and with discretion. The court may affirm the trial decision, reverse it, or vary it. It may substitute its own decision for that of the trial judge, though this is unusual. More often, a new trial is ordered. In most cases, the appeal is dismissed and the trial decision affirmed. The major reason why most appeals fail is because the appeal court will not interfere with the findings of fact made by the trial court, even if the appellate judges would have come to a different conclusion if they had been adjudicating at trial. The appellate judges will not substitute their findings of fact for those of the trial judge if there was any reasonable basis for the trial judge's drawing the con-clusions that he or she did from the evidence at trial. The reasoning is that the trial judge saw and heard the witnesses and, from personal observation, was able to draw conclusions about credibility which the Court of Appeal, having only the tran-scripts of evidence, is not in the position to do. Therefore, errors of fact rarely give rise to a successful appeal, leaving major errors of law as the main basis of a suc-cessful appeal. If the trial judge misapplied the law, the appellate court can identify the error and vary the judgment without a new trial. If a jury was improperly charged on the law and reaches an erroneous verdict, a new trial is ordered because a jury's reasoning process is unknown.

If appealing to the Ontario Court of Appeal is difficult, appealing from that court to the Supreme Court of Canada is even more so. Anyone who can pay for it can appeal from a Superior Court trial judgment. You do not need the appellate court's permission. While your chances may be poor, they worsen at the Supreme Court of Canada. In order to appeal from the provincial appellate court to this court, you need the Supreme Court's permission, which is called "leave to appeal." To get leave to appeal, you need to show that there are conflicting lines of case authority in different provinces or that the matter you are raising is a public policy issue of great importance.

You have had a broad overview of how a civil action proceeds through to trial and appeal. We can now begin to examine the process in more detail in subse-quent chapters.

CHAPTER SUMMARY

In this chapter, using Abigail Boar's claim for negligence against the defendants Rattle Motors Ltd. and Fred Flogem, we have followed the conduct of a civil action through the Ontario Superior Court of Justice to the Court of Appeal. The proce-dure began when Abigail hired I.M. Just to sue on her behalf. I.M. Just conducted preliminary investigations to determine if there was a good cause of action against the defendants. Once the decision to sue was made, proceedings were com-menced with the issuing of a statement of claim. The defendants answered with a statement of defence. When both sides exchanged pleadings, the pleading stage closed, and the parties proceeded to oral examinations for discovery and discov-ery of each other's documents. Until the end of discovery, the parties could bring motions to resolve disputes concerning the application of procedural rules in this case. Once discovery ended, the matter was set down for trial by filing a trial record, and a pretrial conference was held. The parties then proceeded to prepare for trial. At the end of the case, the judge gave judgment, and the parties considered their options on appeal.

KEY TERMS

fees

disbursements

contingency fee

cause of action

trier of fact

damages

action

application

true copy

notice of action

general heading

title of proceedings

backsheet

viva voce evidence

order

endorsement

request to admit

summons to a witness

pecuniary

writ of seizure and sale

garnishee

res judicata

NOTES

1 Civil cases where the remedy sought is less than $10,000 may be tried in Small Claims Court. This court has its own rules of procedure, which are less formal and complex than those used in the Superior Court. This text is about the civil process in the Superior Court. For a discussion of the rules of procedure in Small Claims Court, see Laurence Olivo, *Debtor–Creditor Law and Procedure* (Toronto: Emond Montgomery, 1999).

2 The use of the word "retainer" to describe both the contract for services and the deposit paid by a client for services to be rendered is confusing. The reason for this usage is that the payment of a deposit served to retain the services of a lawyer, even if there was no written contract of retainer. Hence, the deposit was often described as "the retainer" even where a separate "contract of retainer" was signed. To further the confusion, however, some retainers are not deposits to be set off against future accounts rendered by the lawyer but are payments made directly to a lawyer for agreeing to be available to provide unspecified services for a given period of time. This practice is common in commercial law, where a company may have a law firm on an annual retainer.

3 A contingency fee is permitted in a class action under the *Class Proceedings Act, 1992*, SO 1992, c. 6, for example.

4 A claim for under $10,000 usually goes to Small Claims Court, and there can be cost penalties for suing in the Superior Court for a small amount of money. However, there are reasons for suing for small sums in Superior Court that the court will recognize as appropriate: a test case on which many other similar cases depend, or a novel cause of action should be brought in a higher court.

5 "Balance of convenience" is a practical, fact-based test in which the court examines how difficult, expensive, or time consuming it is for the parties to try the case in one location rather than another. If the plaintiff has chosen a location,

a defendant who wishes to change location needs to show that he or she is at a great disadvantage because of the residence of witnesses, travel costs, and similar matters.

6 As of the time of writing; the fees increase from time to time.

7 Unless the verdict is completely against the weight of the evidence, in which case the judge will set the jury's verdict aside and substitute the verdict that should have been given. This is unusual, however.

REFERENCES

Carthy, James J., W.A. Derry Millar, and Jeffrey G. Cowan, *Ontario Annual Practice* (Aurora, ON: Canada Law Book, published annually).

Class Proceedings Act, 1992, SO 1992, c. 6.

Courts of Justice Act, RSO 1990, c. C.43.

Negligence Act, RSO 1990, c. N.1.

Olivo, Laurence, *Debtor–Creditor Law and Procedure* (Toronto: Emond Montgomery, 1999).

Ontario Gazette

Ontario Reports

Rules of Civil Procedure, RRO 1990, reg. 194.

REVIEW QUESTIONS

1. What are the principal steps in a civil lawsuit?

2. How does Abigail Boar go about retaining a lawyer?

3. What is a retainer?

4. What are the usual terms of a retainer?

5. What is a contingency fee and can a lawyer accept one?

6. How are legal fees determined?

7. What does it mean to have a good cause of action?

8. What is the standard of proof in a civil matter, and what kinds of evidence meet this standard?

9. Give examples of the kinds of evidence in question 8 that may arise in Abigail's case.

10. What matters are considered in determining a court's jurisdiction? Which court should Abigail sue in?

11. What is the relationship between a practice direction and the *Rules of Civil Procedure*?

12. What are the two types of civil procedure, and how do they differ?

13. How does an action commence, and what is the function of the first document?

14. How is a statement of claim issued?

15. What are originating documents and how are they served?

16. What happens if you cannot find a defendant for service because he or she has moved or gone on vacation?

17. What might happen if the defendant never saw the statement of claim and the plaintiff signed default judgment when no defence was filed?

18. What choices do Fred and Rattle Motors have when served with a statement of claim?

19. What other pleadings might one find in a civil case, and what is their function?

20. What is discovery?

21. What is a motion, and what is its purpose?

22. When the parties have completed pleadings and discovery, how do they get on the list for trial?

23. What is case management?

24. If Abigail obtains a judgment in her favour, does she sit back and wait for the defendants to send her a cheque?

25. What does it mean when we say the issue of liability in Abigail's case is *res judicata*?

26. Why is an appeal from a decision in Abigail's case based on an error of fact unlikely to succeed?

DISCUSSION QUESTIONS

1. The primary purpose of the *Rules of Civil Procedure* is to reduce cost and delay. Discuss.

2. Suppose Abigail arrived drunk at the showroom and was staggering when she slipped on the oil. Suppose that she took a fancy to Fred and made unwelcome physical advances. Suppose Fred felt he had not been negligent in any way. And suppose that Rattle Motors discovered that there had been numerous incidents of leaking oil pans on the Super Coupe. How might these situations change the type of pleadings used?

PART II

From commencement of proceedings to close of pleadings

CHAPTER 2

Procedure before commencement of proceedings

INTRODUCTION

When a client brings a civil litigation matter to the law office, there are a number of steps that both the lawyer and the legal staff must complete before going to the court office to issue the statement of claim. Before the claim issues, the apparent facts must be assessed to figure out what the cause of action is. Is the lawyer commencing the action in time or has the limitation period passed? You will have to perform a number of checks: Is the defendant solvent and worth suing? Have you named the defendant correctly for the purposes of the suit? Is any of the claim covered by insurance? You must prepare a retainer for the client to sign if he or she is to retain your firm's services. Then you will have to set up a client account or have the firm's accounts office or bookkeeper do it. Finally, you will open and set up an office file.

DETERMINING THE CAUSE OF ACTION AND OTHER PRELIMINARY STEPS

Is there a good cause of action?

After Abigail tells I.M. Just the story of her misfortune, I.M. Just must decide if the facts as related by Abigail amount to the breach of a legal right that gives rise to a remedy. In Abigail's case that is not difficult. The facts as disclosed indicate that some acts of Fred Flogem, Rattle Motors Ltd., and Skank Motorcar Company Ltd. caused her injuries and may amount to negligence. Therefore, in Abigail's case, the breach of the duty of care that caused her injuries amounts to a breach of a legal right and gives rise to the remedy of monetary damages. This breach is her legal reason for suing, or her cause of action.

Although this is a straightforward situation where the cause of action is easy to identify, it is not always so simple to determine the cause of action from the facts. For example, in what is now a landmark case,[1] a woman (known by the name Jane Doe to preserve her privacy) sued the Metropolitan Toronto Police and various individual officers in tort for failing to warn her of the danger of sexual assault she faced from a serial rapist. This man sexually assaulted Doe. Her argument was that the police had a duty to warn her, given their knowledge of the case, particularly because she alleged that the police used her as bait to catch the perpetrator. When she commenced her proceeding, the defendants brought a motion to dismiss her statement of claim on the grounds that it disclosed no reasonable cause of action. Their argument was that the police had by statute and at common law a general duty to the public, but that they had no specific duty to an individual in Doe's situation. To hold otherwise, they argued, would put them in the position of being an insurer of everyone's safety and liable to everyone who was a victim of crime. On the face of things they had a good argument, and the decision on the motion went through several stages of appeal.

Many lawyers would have told Doe that while she may have been treated badly, she had no reasonable cause of action because the duty owed by the police had never been extended as far as Doe was claiming it should be extended. However, she persevered and eventually won her case. While Doe faced an uphill fight on this issue, the common law does evolve; old principles and established causes of action are refined and extended. The courts are aware of this and scrutinize a novel cause of action carefully. Just because courts have not previously granted remedies, there is no reason why they cannot extend the law. In *Doe*, the court held that if the claim discloses a cause of action — a tort — the fact that it is novel is of no concern. For the purpose of assessing a case of this type, the facts in the pleadings are presumed to be true. If they disclose a cause of action with some chance of success, though novel, the action should proceed to trial.

Not every claimed cause of action will succeed, even if the facts are proved. For example, if I invite you to dinner, and you promise to come but do not show up, I may be mortified, humiliated, and have my feelings hurt, but the law of contract does not enforce this type of promise. Neither will the tort of deceit be applicable in this situation. The courts are not ready to extend legal rights and remedies to take into account what the law currently regards as a trifling matter — although that could change.

You need to be aware that even if there is a good cause of action, the client might be advised not to sue. Suppose Abigail were fired by her employer without just cause. She could then sue for salary in lieu of having been given reasonable notice.[2] If, however, the day after she was fired, she landed another job that paid more than the job she had been dismissed from, Abigail did not suffer any damages. Instead, she improved her position. Although she has a good cause of action in that her contract of employment was breached, she suffered no damages and would receive no remedy. There is therefore no rational basis for her to continue with the suit.

Correctly naming individual defendants

Suing in the wrong name can result in an unenforceable judgment. For example, if you are suing Fred Flogem and obtain a judgment in that name, the judgment is useless if it turns out that Fred's real first name is Frederico, but that he informally changed it to Fred. Legally, Frederico Flogem exists, but Fred Flogem does not, at least for the purposes of enforcing a judgment. Therefore, getting the proposed defendant's name right is important.

Verifying a name

If the proposed defendant was born in Ontario, married in Ontario, or died in Ontario,[3] you may fill out and file with the Office of the Registrar General an application for a certificate or a search. Figure 2.1 reproduces such an application. It will be several weeks before you get the information you want, but you can expedite the process by paying a higher fee. You can also conduct the search yourself at the registrar's office at the Macdonald Block, 900 Bay Street, Toronto. Note that you have to explain why you want the information you are requesting. Privacy legislation limits the right of the government simply to hand out this information. However, law firms are not likely to be questioned, and if you have a legitimate reason for requesting the information, you will not be refused. For information about fees and other requirements, phone 416-325-8305 or 1-800-461-2156.

If the proposed defendant was *not* born in Ontario but resides there now, you may be able to verify his or her name by a driver's licence search, a search of the name of owners and lessors of motor vehicles registered in Ontario, or a driver record search. For the first two searches, use a Ministry of Transportation address request application, which is reproduced in figure 2.2. For the third search, request a statement of driving record form, which is reproduced in figure 2.3 and available from the Safety and Regulation Division of the Ministry of Transportation. For information about forms, fees, and other requirements, call the Ministry of Transportation at 416-235-2999. You may get further information about possible Internet searches by contacting the ministry by e-mail at lao@mto.gov.on.ca.

Correctly naming businesses

To get the name of a business right you must know the form of business entity used by the proposed defendant. If the business is a sole proprietorship — that is, a business carried on by an individual using the individual's name — then searching the individual's name may be sufficient.

However, suppose that the proposed defendant carries on business using a business name:

- If the business is incorporated, you must sue the corporation in its legal corporate name.

- If the business is a sole proprietorship, it is best to sue the individual who is the sole proprietor in his or her own legal name, but you can also sue in the business name.

- If the business is a partnership, you may sue in the partnership name or sue the partners individually in their own names.

Naming the proper parties to a lawsuit will be discussed in chapter 5. For now, we will concentrate on verifying the names of proposed defendants that are businesses.

All businesses being carried on in Ontario must register their business name with the Companies and Personal Property Security Branch of the Ministry of Consumer and Business Services. If you submit a business name on a search, it will result in the identification of the individual person if the business is a sole proprietorship. If the business is a partnership, submission of the business name will result in identification of the partners registered at the time of the search. Similarly, if the business is a corporation, submission of the business name will get you the correct legal corporate name. Remember that when you sue a corporation, you have no choice concerning how to name the company: Its proper legal name must be used. Do not be surprised if the corporate name that turns up has no relation to the business name

FIGURE 2.1   REQUEST FOR BIRTH, MARRIAGE, OR DEATH CERTIFICATES

Ministry of Consumer and Commercial Relations
Office of the Registrar General

Request for Birth, Marriage or Death Certificates

You can only use this form to get certificates for births, marriages or deaths that happened in Ontario. We keep records of births for 95 years, marriages for 80 years and deaths for 70 years. If you need older records, contact the Archives of Ontario. You can find more information on the opposite page. **Please PRINT clearly in blue or black ink and sign Section 4.**

If you have any questions, please contact the **Office of the Registrar General** at **1-800-461-2156** or **416-325-8305**

1. Your name and address

Your name (First, middle, last)	Street number and name	Apartment
City, town or village	Province	Postal code

2. What documents do you want?

Please read the opposite page to find out if you're qualified to receive the certificate you're asking for.

Birth certificate

Name on birth certificate (Last, first, middle – if married, use last name at birth)	Date of birth day / month / year
Place of birth (City, town or village)	Sex	Father's name (Last, first, middle)
Mother's name at birth (Last, first, middle)	Any other last name used by mother

How many copies of each type of certificate do you want? Print number in the appropriate box. (There is a charge for **each** certificate.)

☐ Certificate (includes basic information, such as name, date and place of birth)   ☐ Long form (contains all registered information, including parents' information and signatures)   ☐ Confirmation letter (a letter saying the birth is on file)

Marriage certificate

Name of groom (Last, first, middle)	
Name of bride (Last name before marriage, first, middle)	Any other last name used
Date of marriage day month year	Place of marriage (City, town or village)

How many copies of each type of certificate do you want? Print number in the appropriate box. (There is a charge for **each** certificate.)

☐ Certificate (includes basic information, such as names, date and place of marriage)   ☐ Long form (contains all registered information, including signatures)   ☐ Marriage letter (usually needed to get married in some other countries)

Death certificate

Name of deceased (Last, first, middle)	Date of death day month year	Sex	Age
Place of death (City, town or village)	If the person was married, name of husband or wife (Last, first, middle)		
Father's name (Last, first, middle)	Mother's name (Last name before marriage, first, middle)		

How many copies of each type of certificate do you want? Print number in the appropriate box. (There is a charge for **each** certificate.)

☐ Certificate (includes basic information, such as name, date and place of death)   ☐ Long form (contains all registered information, including signatures)

3. Fees and payment   Please read the *Fees and payment* section on the opposite page to find out how much you have to pay.

How are you paying?

☐ Cheque or money order. Please make payable to: Minister of Finance **OR** ☐ VISA or ☐ MasterCard   Total amount enclosed $

Name of cardholder:	Signature of cardholder	Card number	Expiry date (m/y)

4. Important information and signature

By signing below, you are stating that you are qualified to receive this information. (See the opposite page for more details.) **If you're sending someone else to pick up the certificate for you, you must send a signed note giving them permission to pick it up for you.**

Why are you requesting the certificate?	What is your relationship to the person named on the certificate? (eg: self, mother, father)		
Your signature X	Date signed day month year	Home telephone number ( )	Work telephone number ( )

Personal information contained on this form is collected under the authority of the Vital Statistics Act, R.S.O. 1990, c.V.4 and will be used to provide certified copies, extracts, certificates, or search notices. Questions about this collection should be directed to: The Deputy Registrar General, Office of the Registrar General, P.O. Box 4600, Thunder Bay ON P7B 6L8. Telephone 1-800-461-2156 or 416-325-8305.

11076 (6/98)

Français au verso

FIGURE 2.2 ADDRESS/RESTRICTED RECORD SEARCH APPLICATION

Ministry of Transportation Ontario | Ministère des Transports | Licensing and Control Branch | Direction des permis et de l'immatriculation

Address / Restricted Record Search Application
Demande d'adresse / recherche restreinte dans le dossier

1. Requester Information
Renseignements sur le requérant

To be picked up / *Le requérant passera prendre la réponse* ☐

To be mailed / *À expédier par la poste* ☐

Application Date / *Date de la demande* — Y/A M D/J

Your File No. / *N° de votre dossier*

Telephone No. / *N° de téléphone*

Driver's Licence No. / Authorized MTO User Identification
N° du permis de conduire / Identification du client autorisé du MTO

Date of Birth (if not licensed) / *Date de naissance (si sans permis)* — Y/A M D/J

Name and Address of Individual / Company / *Nom et adresse de la personne / compagnie*

Ministry Use Only
Réservé au ministère

Off. No. | Report No.

Y/A M D/J | Fee Paid $

Personal Identification Viewed (State name of document)

☐ Completed / Processed
Was Authorized Request Package given?

Yes ☐ No ☐

Identification viewed when picked up

State the specific reason and purpose why this information is required. / *Donnez la raison précise pour laquelle vous désirez ces renseignements.*   Self / *Pour soi* ☐   Business / *Pour une entreprise* ☐

Signature of Authorized MTO User / *Signature du client autorisé du MTO* _____ Date Y/A M D/J

2. Instructions / *Directives*   Please see other side for descriptions of the products listed below. Check off a box(es) and provide all information about vehicle / driver being searched. Fees are as noted by each box. Make cheque or money order payable to the Minister of Finance. / *Vous trouverez au verso la description des produits énumérés ci-dessous. Veuillez cocher une ou plusieurs cases et fournir tous les renseignements sur le véhicule / conducteur faisant l'objet de la recherche. Le montant des droits est indiqué à chaque case. Libeller les chèques ou mandats à l'ordre du ministre des Finances.*

A ☐ $12.00 / *12 $*   Current Vehicle, Owner and Plate Information / *Renseignements actuels concernant le véhicule, son propriétaire ou son immatriculation*

☐ $12.00 / *12 $*   History of Vehicle, Owners and Plates for the past 3 years / *Historique du véhicule, de son ou ses propriétaires ou immatriculation au cours des 3 dernières années*

Date of Birth (if individual) / *Date de naissance (dans le cas d'un particulier)* Y/A M D/J

Vehicle Identification No. (VIN) / *N° d'identification du véhicule (NIV)*

Ontario Licence Plate No. / *N° d'immatriculation de l'Ontario*

Owner's Name and Address or RIN / *Nom et adresse du propriétaire ou NIC*   Postal Code / *Code postal*

B ☐ $12.00 / *12 $*   Vehicle Owner and Plate Information on: / *Renseignements sur le propriétaire du véhicule ou son immatriculation le :*   Y/A M D/J

Vehicle Identification No. (VIN) / *N° d'identification du véhicule (NIV)*

Ontario Licence Plate No. / *N° d'immatriculation de l'Ontario*

C ☐ $12.00 / *12 $*   Registrant Identification Number (R.I.N.) Summary / *Résumé - Numéro d'identification du conducteur (N.I.C.)*

Registrant Identification No. (R.I.N.) or Driver's Licence No. / *Numéro d'identification du conducteur (N.I.C.) ou n° du permis de conduire*

Owner's Name and Address / *Nom et adresse du propriétaire*   Postal Code / *Code postal*

D ☐ $12.00 / *12 $*   3 Year Driver Record Search with Address / *Recherche dans le dossier sur 3 ans avec adresse*

☐ $12.00 / *12 $*   Extended Driver Record Search (includes address) / *Recherche complète dans le dossier sur 5 ans (comprend l'adresse)*

☐ $12.00 / *12 $*   5 Year Driver Record Search / *Recherche dans le dossier sur 5 ans*
☐ with Address / *avec adresse*   ☐ without Address / *sans adresse*

☐ $5.00 / *5 $*   Commercial Vehicle Record / Driver Abstract / *Dossier de véhicule utilitaire / Résumé du dossier de conducteur*

See the back of the form for descriptions and information on persons authorized to make a request. / *Voir à l'endos de cette formule la description des recherches et l'information sur les personnes autorisées à faire une demande*

Date of Birth / *Date de naissance* Y/A M D/J   Sex / *Sexe*   Driver's Licence No. / *N° du permis de conduire*

Driver's Name and Address / *Nom et adresse du conducteur*   Postal Code / *Code postal*

E ☐ $6.00 / *6 $*   Document copy required (such as Insurance Information) / *Copie d'un document requise (p. ex. renseignements sur l'assurance)*

☐ $6.00 / *6 $*   Additional - Certified copy of each search or document for legal purposes / *Copie certifiée supplémentaire de chaque recherche ou document à des fins juridiques*

☐ $5.00 / *5 $*   Additional - Certified copy of Commercial Vehicle Record / *Copie certifiée supplémentaire du dossier du véhicule utilitaire*

What type of document do you require? / *De quel type de document avez-vous besoin?* _____

3. Affirmation Statement / *Attestation*   If you are not an authorized MTO User, please sign the affirmation statement below. / *Si vous n'êtes pas un client autorisé du MTO, signez l'attestation ci-dessous.*

I understand that I must state the reason I am requesting the information. I affirm that the information I provided is true. If any of the information I provided is knowingly false, I understand that I may be held liable and charged with offences set out in the Highway Traffic Act. / *Je sais que je dois indiquer la raison pour laquelle je demande les renseignements. J'atteste que les renseignements que j'ai fournis sont exacts. Je sais que si j'ai sciemment fourni des renseignements erronés, je peux en être tenu responsable et accusé d'avoir commis une infraction aux termes du Code de la route.*   Y/A M D/J

Signature of Affiant / Applicant
Signature du déclarant / requérant _____ Date

SR-LC-112 98-07

Original - DMS

FIGURE 2.3 APPLICATION FOR DRIVER RECORD SEARCH

Ministry of Transportation — Ontario

Ministère des Transports

Licensing and Control Branch

Direction des permis et de l'immatriculation

Application for Driver Record Search
Demande de recherches au dossier d'un conducteur

Application Date / Date de la demande
Y/A M D/J

☐ To be picked up / L'auteur de la demande passera prendre la réponse

☐ To be mailed / À expédier par la poste

Your File No. / N° de votre dossier

Telephone No. / N° de téléphone

Name and Address of Individual / Company
Nom et adresse de la personne / compagnie

State the reason why this information is required.
Donnez la raison pour laquelle vous désirez ces renseignements.

Head Office Use Only
Réservé au bureau principal
Name of Driver

Ministry Use Only / Réservé au ministère
Personal Identification Viewed (State name of document)

Report No.

Office No.

Fee Paid
$

Account No.

Please provide all known information.
Veuillez fournir tous les renseignements connus .

Driver's Licence No. / N° du permis de conduire

Date of Birth / Date de naissance
Y/A M D/J

Sex / Sexe

Age, if birthdate unknown
Âge, si la date de naissance est inconnue

Driver's Name / Nom du conducteur
Last Name, First Name and Middle Initial / Nom de famille, prénom et initiale

Street Number and Name or Lot, Concession and Twp. / N° et rue ou lot, concession, canton

Apt. No. / App. n°

City, Town or Village / Ville ou village

Postal Code / Code postal

Previous Address / Adresse précédente

Reason for Return of Application
Raison du renvoi de la demande

Request for Search / Demande de recherches   Check appropriate box(es) / Cochez la ou les cases appropriées

☐ Driver (complete driving record covering a three year period)
Conducteur (Veuillez fournir un dossier du conducteur complet pour une période de trois ans)

☐ Driver (while driving Commercial Motor Vehicles only - C.V.O.R.)
Conducteur de véhicules utilitaires seulement (I.U.V.U.)

☐ Certified copy of each search for legal purposes
Copie certifiée conforme de chaque recherche à des fins juridiques

Fees / Droits

$ 12.00 for each search request.
$ 6.00 for copy of each document.
$ 6.00 additional for each certified copy.

12 $ pour chaque demande de recherches.
6 $ pour chaque copie d'un document.
6 $ de plus pour chaque copie certifiée.

Please make cheque or money order payable to the Minister of Finance. / Libellez les chèques ou mandats à l'ordre du ministre des Finances.

Remarks / Remarques

The Ministry may decline to supply information unless satisfied that it is required in connection with a matter involving a driver.
Le ministère peut refuser de fournir les renseignements demandés s'il estime que la demande ne se rapporte pas à une question relative au conducteur.

Applicant's Signature
Signature de l'auteur(e) de la demande

Send application with fees to:
Envoyez les demandes et les droits au :

Ministry of Transportation
Data Management, East Bldg.
2680 Keele Street
Downsview, Ontario M3M 3E6

Ministère des Transports
Gestion des données
2680, rue Keele, édifice est
Downsview (Ontario) M3M 3E6

SR-LC-34 96-11

Performance Management / Évaluation de la performance

used. Rattle Motors Ltd. could turn out to be Soho Investment Ltd. Or it could be a "numbered company," 1234 Ontario Ltd. There is nothing sinister about this. If the company intends to use the business name that it used before its incorporation, it does not matter what the limited company is called, and the number initially assigned to a new corporation by the Companies and Personal Property Security Branch of the Ministry of Consumer and Business Services will do as well as anything else.

To conduct a search, use the service requisition in respect of unincorporated businesses, which is reproduced in figure 2.4, for partnerships and sole proprietorships. Using this form, you may request a copy of a business names report identifying individual persons using a business name, a copy of actual business registration documents showing names and addresses of individuals, or a certificate of non-registration showing that a business name that may be in use has not been registered. Note that if your client has not registered a name but wishes to sue in that name, his or her action will not be allowed to proceed until the name has been registered.

To search the name of a corporation, use the request for corporation information, which is reproduced in figure 2.5, or the expedited version of the form if you need a faster response, which is reproduced in figure 2.6. The corporation profile report will provide you with the address of the corporation and its proper name. Other documents are also available, including copies of the articles of incorporation, filed when the corporation was incorporated, and annual returns, which identify the individuals who currently are officers of the corporation. Business and corporate searches are conducted at the public search office, Company Information, Ministry of Consumer and Business Services, 2nd floor, 375 University Avenue, Toronto. Searches are done in person, though Internet searches are coming. For information on Internet searches, check http://www.oncorp.com. This site has information on Companies Branch searches. In the meantime, there are companies that will conduct the search for you personally for a fee. Information about conducting searches can be obtained by telephoning 416-314-8880.

CITY DIRECTORIES AND TELEPHONE BOOKS

City directories, such as *Might's Directories* and *Bower's Directories*, often allow you to use one piece of information to obtain other relevant information. Directories are indexed by name, address, and telephone number. For example, telephone numbers are set out in ascending order and will lead you to a name and address with which the telephone number is associated. If you have only an address, an entry will tell you the name of the person living there, and it will tell you much about that person: how long he or she has lived there, whether he or she owns or rents, the average income for the area, and other demographic information.

An ordinary telephone book can be used if you know a name. Even if the spelling of the name is not right, a telephone directory can lead you to alternative spellings, one of which might be correct. These types of reference resources can be found in the reference sections of larger public libraries.

Impecunious clients and opponents

Cost is a factor in determining whether to sue or not. The probable costs should be discussed candidly with the client in relation to the probable relief to be obtained.

FIGURE 2.4   SERVICES REQUISITION IN RESPECT OF UNINCORPORATED BUSINESSES

 **Ontario**

Ministry of
Consumer and
Commercial Relations

Ministère de
la Consommation
et du Commerce

Companies Branch
Direction des compagnies

Services Requisition In Respect of Unincorporated Businesses
Demande de recherche sur des entreprises non constituées en personne morale

See Instructions and Description of Products on Reverse
Les instructions et les descriptions des documents se trouvent au verso.

Identify Search/Product Required By marking 'X' in Appropriate Box
Indiquez le service requis en cochant la case appropriée.

Searches for business names ending in "Corporation", "Limited" or "Incorporated", or
any abbreviation thereof, cannot be processed on this form.

Les recherches ne peuvent pas être effectuées sur des entreprises constituées en personne morale,
notamment celles dont le nom comporte, en entier ou en abrégé, le mot "Limitée" ou "incorporée".

Column headers (A–F):
- Business Names Report / Rapport sur les noms commerciaux — A
- Document Replica / Copie de document — B
- BNLP Document List / Liste des documents - NC/SC — C
- Partnership Business Names List / Liste des noms commerciaux (SNC/SC) — D
- Certificate of Non-Registration / Certificat de non-enregistrement — E
- Expired Search / Période de recherche expirée — F

Unincorporated Business Name Raison sociale de l'entreprise non constituée en personne morale	Business Identification Number, if known. N° d'identification de l'entreprise, si connu.	A	B	C	D	E	F
1.						UNCERTIFIED / NON CERTIFIÉ CERTIFIED / CERTIFIÉ	
2.						UNCERTIFIED / NON CERTIFIÉ CERTIFIED / CERTIFIÉ	
3.						UNCERTIFIED / NON CERTIFIÉ CERTIFIED / CERTIFIÉ	
4.						UNCERTIFIED / NON CERTIFIÉ CERTIFIED / CERTIFIÉ	
5.						UNCERTIFIED / NON CERTIFIÉ CERTIFIED / CERTIFIÉ	

Client Name / Nom du/de la client(e) — Attention / Personne à contacter :

Address / Adresse :

Telephone No. / N° de téléphone

Signature / Signature — Date / Date

☐ Mail Out
Envoyer par courrier

☐ Pick up
Prendre livraison

Pick-up box # N° de la boîte	Account # / N° de compte	Sub-Account / Compte auxiliaire	Access I.D. / Mot de passe

Ministry Use Only / Réservé au ministère							
Request # / N° de la demande	Pull / Retrait	Copies / Copies	Pages / Pages	Time in / Arrivé	Time Out / Départ	Fee / Droits	Clerk / Commis

07094(12/97) CD394

FIGURE 2.5 REQUEST FOR CORPORATE INFORMATION

Ontario

Ministry of Consumer and Commercial Relations

Ministère de la Consommation et du Commerce

Companies Branch Direction des compagnies

Request for Corporation Information
Demande de renseignements sur une personne morale

Please use separate forms for electronic and non-electronic products.
Veuillez utiliser des formules distinctes si vous désirez obtenir des documents électroniques et non électroniques.

See instructions and Description of Products on Reverse
Les instructions et les descriptions des documents se trouvent au verso.

Please check appropriate box for product requested and whether uncertified or certified.
Veuillez cocher les cases appropriées pour indiquer les documents désirés et s'ils doivent être certifiés ou non.

For faster service, please provide the Ontario Corporation Number below.
Afin d'accélérer le service, veuillez indiquer ci-dessous le numéro de la personne morale en Ontario.

Electronic Search Products / Documents électroniques

Column headers (diagonal): Profile Report / Rapport de profil (A), Document List / Liste de documents (B), Business Names List / Liste de raisons sociales, Certificate of Status / Certificat de statut (C), Cert. of No Record / Cert. d'absence de dossier (D), Cert. of Non-Filing / Cert. de non-dépôt (E), (F)

	Corporation Name / Dénomination sociale	Ontario Corp. No. / Numéro de la personne morale en Ontario	A	B	C	D	E	F
1.			UNCERTIFIED NON CERTIFIÉ / CERTIFIED CERTIFIÉ					
2.			UNCERTIFIED NON CERTIFIÉ / CERTIFIED CERTIFIÉ					
3.			UNCERTIFIED NON CERTIFIÉ / CERTIFIED CERTIFIÉ					
4.			UNCERTIFIED NON CERTIFIÉ / CERTIFIED CERTIFIÉ					
5.			UNCERTIFIED NON CERTIFIÉ / CERTIFIED CERTIFIÉ					

Non-Electronic Search Products / Documents non électroniques

Column headers (diagonal): Cert. Copies of Document / Copies certifiées conformes (G), Copy of Notice where profile not avail. / Copie de l'avis s'il n'y a pas de profil disp. (H), TC Files (copies) / Dossier - transf. (copies) (I), Microfiche (J)

	Corporation Name / Dénomination sociale	Ontario Corp. No. / Numéro de la personne morale en Ontario	G	H	I	J
1.			UNCERTIFIED NON CERTIFIÉ / CERTIFIED CERTIFIÉ			
	Name of Document(s) and Date(s) required / Nom du ou des document(s) and date(s)					
2.			UNCERTIFIED NON CERTIFIÉ / CERTIFIED CERTIFIÉ			
	Name of Document(s) and Date(s) required / Nom du ou des document(s) and date(s)					
3.			UNCERTIFIED NON CERTIFIÉ / CERTIFIED CERTIFIÉ			
	Name of Document(s) and Date(s) required / Nom du ou des document(s) and date(s)					

Client Name / Nom du/de la client(e)	Attention / Personne à contacter :
Address / Adresse :	

Signature / Signature	Date / Date	Telephone No. / N° de téléphone

☐ Mail Out / Envoyer par courrier
☐ Pick up / Prendre livraison

Pick-up box # / N° de la boîte	Account # / N° de compte	Sub-Account / Compte auxiliaire	Access I.D. / Mot de passe

07249(12/97)

FIGURE 2.6   REQUEST FOR CORPORATE INFORMATION — EXPEDITED SERVICE

Ministry of Consumer and Commercial Relations	Ministère de la Consommation et du Commerce	Companies Branch Direction des compagnies

Request for Corporation Information
Demande de renseignements sur
une personne morale

EXPEDITED SERVICE / SERVICE ACCÉLÉRÉ

This form is to be used for immediate counter service ONLY / Formule à utiliser SEULEMENT pour un service au comptoir immédiat

See Instructions and Description of Products on Reverse
Les instructions et les descriptions des documents se trouvent au verso.

Please check appropriate box for product requested and whether uncertified or certified.
Veuillez cocher les cases appropriées pour indiquer les documents désirés et s'ils doivent être certifiés ou non.

For faster service, please provide the Ontario Corporation Number below.
Afin d'accélérer le service, veuillez indiquer ci-dessous le numéro de la personne morale en Ontario.

Electronic Search Products Only / Documents électroniques seulement

Column headers (diagonal):
- A — Corp. Profile Report / Profile de la société
- B — Document List / Liste de documents
- C — Business Names List / Liste de raisons sociales
- Certificate of Status / Certificat de statut
- Cert. of No Record / Certificat d'absence de dossier
- Cert. of Non-Filing / Cert. de non dépôt

	Corporation Name / Dénomination sociale	Ontario Corp. No. / Numéro de la personne morale en Ontario	A	B	C	D	E	F
1.			UNCERTIFIED / NON CERTIFIE					
			CERTIFIED / CERTIFIE					
2.			UNCERTIFIED / NON CERTIFIE					
			CERTIFIED / CERTIFIE					
3.			UNCERTIFIED / NON CERTIFIE					
			CERTIFIED / CERTIFIE					
4.			UNCERTIFIED / NON CERTIFIE					
			CERTIFIED / CERTIFIE					
5.			UNCERTIFIED / NON CERTIFIE					
			CERTIFIED / CERTIFIE					

Client Name / Nom du/de la client(e)	Attention / Personne à contacter :
Address / Adresse :	
	Telephone No. / N° de téléphone
Signature / Signature	Date / Date

☐ Mail Out / Envoyer par courrier
☐ Pick up / Prendre livraison

Pick-up box # / N° de la boîte	Account # / N° de compte	Sub-Account / Compte auxiliaire	Access I.D. / Mot de passe

Ministry Use Only / Réservé au ministère

Request # / N° de la demande	Pull / Retrait	File / Dossier	Fiche / Fiche	Copies / Copies	Time in / Arrivé	Time Out / Départ	Pages / Pages	Fee / Droits	Clerk / Commis

07250(12/97)

If Abigail's chances of establishing liability are good, she is likely to be awarded substantial damages. Because the corporate defendant is likely to carry insurance, the chances of being paid those damages are very good. Consequently, even if Abigail does not have a lot of spare cash, I.M. Just may be prepared to take his payment at the end of the case, as is common in many personal injury actions. Her lawyer may also take the case on a contingency-fee basis, which is becoming permissible in Ontario. In this case, Abigail would pay nothing, but if she won, I.M. Just would be paid by taking 20–30 percent of the damage award as his fee.

If the case is more speculative or uncertain, the client can be billed on a periodic basis. Payment by instalments the client can handle is common in litigation cases. A client who cannot pay may have to go without a remedy unless the lawyer is prepared to act on a ***pro bono*** basis. Legal aid is virtually unobtainable in civil cases. "Justice," as an English appeals judge once observed, "is like the Ritz Hotel. Anyone who has the price of a room may stay there."

If your opponent is **impecunious**, there is another set of problems to consider. If you get a judgment against the defendant, will he or she be able to pay it? If Rattle Motors has no assets and is teetering on bankruptcy, it may be better not to sue and to make a claim in the ensuing bankruptcy instead. Otherwise, you may spend both money and effort to win a case and then be left with a paper judgment — that is, a judgment that is of no more value than the paper it is written on because the client has no money or assets to pay it.

Determining solvency

If the solvency of the potential defendant is an issue, there are some searches that can be done to determine whether or not the defendant is worth suing.

If the defendant has been successfully sued before, but the judgment has never been paid, there is likely to be a writ of seizure and sale (also called a writ of execution) on file in the sheriff's office in the county or judicial region where the defendant resides or carries on business. If the writ has been unsatisfied for some time, you know that a previous judgment creditor has sued and been unsuccessful in recovering anything on the judgment debt. In addition, the writ of execution can confirm the proper name or spelling of the name of the defendant so that he, she, or it will be correctly named in the statement of claim if you do proceed.

A number of outstanding writs of execution indicate that the proposed defendant has generally been defaulting on claims. They may also indicate that the proposed defendant is adept at hiding assets.

If the writs are all recently filed, it may mean that judgment creditors are closing in and that bankruptcy may be imminent. Suing is a waste of time if the proposed defendant is **judgment-proof**. If the proposed debtor goes bankrupt, the plaintiff may obtain more by making a claim as an unsecured creditor in the bankruptcy proceedings.

Finding no writs of execution on file may indicate that the proposed defendant is solvent, but it may also indicate that you may not have searched the regions where the writs are lodged. The problem with searching writs of execution is that there is no province-wide system that can be searched. You need to search the files in each county or judicial region where the proposed defendant has or is likely to have had assets.

pro bono
abbreviation of a Latin term *pro bono publico*, meaning "for the public good," used where a lawyer takes on a case without charging a fee as part of a duty to see that justice is done

impecunious
insolvent

judgment-proof
unable to pay any amount of a judgment

Even if there are writs on file, if the proposed defendant has not gone bankrupt, it may be useful to sue anyway and obtain judgment. The reason for taking this approach is that the *Creditors' Relief Act* requires that execution creditors (all those who have filed writs of execution) share on a pro rata basis if any execution creditor succeeds in seizing and selling assets. When assets are seized and sold, the sheriff is obliged to distribute a share of the money to each of the execution creditors in proportion to what they are owed. This means that execution creditors with large judgments receive a larger share of the money than those who have judgments for smaller amounts. There are some exceptions: family support creditors and tax authorities take precedence over other creditors.

HOW TO CONDUCT A SEARCH OF EXECUTIONS

You need to complete a sheriff's request for a certificate, which is reproduced in figure 2.7. This form is obtainable from the sheriff's office, which is usually located in the local Superior Court office. Addresses for the local court office and the sheriff's office can be found in the blue pages of your local telephone directory. Give the full name of the debtor, and if the person is an individual, include a middle initial. If the debtor is not an individual — for example, if the debtor is a company — be sure to give the debtor's proper legal name. File the certificate in the sheriff's office where the debtor is likely to have lived, had assets, or carried on business. In Toronto, you can use an online computer to do your search of the Toronto files. You will get the information immediately and can then ask for copies of the writs. However you conduct the search, if the certificate turns up writs, you can ask for further particulars of who the execution creditors are, how much the judgments are for, and whether they have been paid in part. Often talking to other execution creditors or their lawyers will give you some insight into whether the defendant is worth suing.

BANKRUPTCY SEARCH

If insolvency is an issue or is probable, in addition to an execution search, you may wish to conduct a bankruptcy search. This search is useful to see if the proposed defendant has gone or is about to go bankrupt. If the defendant is bankrupt, there is no point in suing; instead, the plaintiff will file proof of the claim. If the claim is in order, the creditor may recover some of the money owing but is unlikely to see all of it. Secured creditors are entitled to seize their secured property to satisfy the debt owing to them and to do so ahead of the claims and rights of unsecured creditors claiming through the trustee.

Because of the bankruptcy rules, there is often little of value left for unsecured creditors, such as the plaintiff. For this reason, the plaintiff may recover no more than 10 or 20 cents on each dollar owed because the secured creditors have already taken major assets.

There are two ways to go bankrupt:

1. an unpaid creditor can put a debtor into bankruptcy using a petition for bankruptcy, or

2. the debtor can make an assignment in bankruptcy or a proposal.

If a creditor has petitioned the proposed defendant into bankruptcy, you must do a name search at the Office of the Superintendent of Bankruptcy in Ottawa. This

FIGURE 2.7   REQUEST FOR CERTIFICATE

Ontario

Ministry of the Attorney General	Office of the Sheriff	Court House 361 University Avenue Toronto, Ontario M5G 1T5
Ministère du Procureur général	Bureau du shérif	Palais de justice 361, avenue University Toronto, (Ontario) M5G 1T5

Request for Certificate/*Demande de certificat*

(Please print Names clearly/Veuillez écrire lisiblement en caractères d'imprimerie)

Do you require Abstract?:/*Avez-vous besoin d'un relevé?:* YES/OUI ☐   NO/NON ☐   FEE/FRAIS

SHERIFF TORONTO/LAND TITLES TORONTO 66 SEARCH AS TO WRITS OF EXECUTION, ABSTRACT OR CERTIFICATE OF LIEN AGAINST THE REAL AND PERSONAL PROPERTY:	*SHÉRIF DE TORONTO/BUREAU D'ENREGISTREMENT DES DROITS IMMOBILIERS, N° 66 RECHERCHE CONCERNANT LES BREFS D'EXÉCUTION, RELEVÉS OU CERTIFICATS DE PRIVILÈGE VISANT LES BIENS MEUBLES OU IMMEUBLES DE:*

SURNAME/*NOM DE FAMILLE*	GIVEN NAMES/PRÉNOMS
....	....
....	....
....	....
....	....
....	....
....	....
....	....
....	....
....	....
....	....

FIRM NAME/*NOM DU CABINET:* ....

....

REFERENCE/*RÉFÉRENCE:* ....

....

CAUTION: PLEASE CHECK YOUR CERTIFICATE PRIOR LEAVING THE OFFICE   *REMARQUE: VEUILLEZ VÉRIFIER VOTRE CERTIFICAT AVANT DE QUITTER LE BUREAU.*

can be done by telephone at 613-941-2863 or by fax at 613-941-9490. If the proposed defendant made an assignment or proposal, a search must be conducted at the offices of the official receiver. There are four offices in Ontario:

- 69 John Street South, 2nd floor, Hamilton, L8N 2B9, tel. 905-572-2874;

- 451 Talbot Street, Room 302, London, N6A 5C9, tel. 519-645-4034;

- 255 Argyle Avenue, Ottawa, K1A 0C8, tel. 613-995-2994; and

- 25 St. Clair Avenue East, Toronto, M4T 1M2, tel. 416-973-6486.

A search of the official receiver's records will also show if a business is in receivership.[4] You do not need to conduct these searches for every proposed defendant, but it is reasonable to do so when you know or suspect that the proposed defendant is or is about to become insolvent. Your client will not thank you for wasting time and money on getting a judgment that cannot be successfully enforced.

Insurance

Always review a client's insurance policies. Rattle Motors Ltd. is likely to have occupier's insurance covering precisely the kind of situation that arises in Abigail's case. Subject to a deductible, damage awards must be paid by the insurance company. If so, you should advise the insurer immediately that there is a claim. Insurance companies usually have their own lawyers and prefer to have them defend the case. Your firm should not be taking steps to defend unless the insurer instructs you to do so or unless it is necessary in order to preserve a defendant's rights.

The insurer may resist providing coverage on the ground that the client has failed to comply with the terms of the policy or on the ground that the claim falls outside the terms of the policy. The lawyer for Rattle Motors Ltd. should try to persuade the insurer to defend on a non-waiver basis. This means that the insurer defends, but it reserves the right to make a claim against the insured for any amount the insurer has to pay out on the insured's behalf. If this happens, Rattle's lawyer may still act for its client, not against Abigail, but against Rattle's insurers on the issue of whether the insurance company is obliged to cover the claim. If the insurance company refuses to honour a claim, Rattle's lawyer should proceed to defend and serve a third party notice on the insurer.

I.M. Just should check to see if Abigail's homeowner's insurance, workplace health insurance, or any other policy of insurance provides any coverage. Sometimes homeowner's policies are very broad and may provide full or partial coverage for her losses. If so, this may eliminate some issues and remedies in the case, or it may make it unnecessary to sue if the loss is completely covered by the insurer. Abigail must be assisted in making a claim as quickly as possible, and I.M. Just's office should take steps to see that she fully complies with the terms of the policy. If the insurance company seeks to recover what it paid from the defendants, you may need to take initial steps to safeguard Abigail's right to sue, until the insurance company takes control of the litigation.

Conflicts of interest

Your law firm will need to ensure that in representing a client it does not have a conflict of interest. The rules about conflicts of interest have become more complicated as large law firms merge, join international networks, and acquire partners from professions other than law. The new rule 2 of the law society's rules of professional conduct make several things clear:

- A lawyer cannot act against a former client on the same or a similar matter on which he or she acted for that client previously.

- When one lawyer in a firm acted for a former client, his or her partners cannot later act against that client unless the former client consents or the interests of justice demand it.

- A lawyer can act for two clients on the same matter on a joint retainer; however, if a conflict develops, the lawyer must cease acting for both clients. Further, there is no confidentiality between the two clients so that information to one client cannot be withheld from the other. If a lawyer is acting for both Fred and Rattle Motors and the lawyer has a continuous and ongoing professional relationship with Rattle, Fred must be advised of that fact.

- When a lawyer transfers from firm A to firm B and discovers that firm B is acting against firm A's client *and* the lawyer has actual knowledge of confidential matters about firm A's client, firm B must transfer the case to another firm, unless firm A's client consents to firm B's staying on the case. The former client may consent if the transferring lawyer agrees not to communicate with the lawyers handling the case against firm A's client.

Fortunately, our case is simpler. I.M. Just is practising with a salaried lawyer as an associate and can easily tell if he has any conflict of interest. If he did have such a conflict, he would be obliged to tell Abigail at once and help her find another lawyer.

When a case comes into the office, the names of the defendants and the client should be cross-checked against names on closed files, using either client cards or computerized client lists. There is software available that is designed to run conflict checks of this sort. However, this may not catch all conflicts.

For example, in one case lawyer A, an associate in a firm, sued a charitable organization on behalf of an employee. The organization was headed by B, and the lawsuit turned on B's conduct toward the employee. There was no apparent conflict between the parties because lawyer A and the firm had never acted for either party before. However, a chance remark by a partner led to the discovery by lawyer A that the partner had acted for B in another matter and knew a great deal about B. At that point, there was a conflict of interest, although the case was well underway. The parties agreed that the partner with knowledge of B's affairs would not discuss any aspect of the case with A.

LIMITATION PERIODS

Care should be taken to determine when the cause of action is complete. In Abigail's case, this occurs at the moment she comes to rest in a pool of oil on the showroom floor. All the acts that caused her damages have occurred, so an action may now be commenced against the defendants, although the extent of those damages may not be known for some time. Lawyers sometimes say at this point that "the cause of action has accrued." From this moment, the clock begins to tick and the limitation period begins to run.

Negligence is a tort. At common law, the limitation period was six years, but under the new Ontario *Limitations Act, 2002* the basic limitation period for almost all causes of action, including Abigail's, will be two years from the time the events occurred (s. 4) or could reasonably be discovered (s. 5).

Sometimes it is difficult to tell when the cause of action is complete. For example, if you are negligently exposed to excessive radiation that might cause cancer, you may not be able to sue because the cause of action does not accrue until you are actually diagnosed with cancer. If you never get cancer, you cannot sue because the cause of action did not accrue.

There are other issues concerning the discovery of the cause of action. Usually, time begins to run when the act or omission occurs. But, as noted above, the *Limitations Act, 2002*, in s. 5, sets out situations where time does not begin to run when the act or omission occurs. Rather, it begins to run when the plaintiff can show that a reasonable person knew or ought reasonably to have known that the act occurred and they could move to obtain a legal remedy.

When a client has given you the basic facts, you then have to determine the specific cause of action and the applicable limitation period. Under the *Limitations Act, 2002*, the period is almost always two years from the time the cause of action arose, or from when it could reasonably be discovered.

However, there are exceptions. Some of the more notable exceptions are:

- Minors and persons under disability: limitation periods are generally suspended until a litigation guardian is appointed; at that point the limitation period begins to run (ss. 6 to 9).

- Where the cause of action involves assault or sexual assault, limitation periods are suspended while the plaintiff is physically, mentally, or psychologically unable to act. The plaintiff in such a case is presumed to be unable to act. If the defendant thinks the limitation period should be running, he or she must present evidence to rebut the presumption (s. 10).

- In some circumstances, where a limitation period is suspended, the limitation period runs for a maximum of 15 years, with some exceptions. Where a person is mentally, physically, or psychologically incapable of starting proceedings, or where a person is a minor and not represented by a litigation guardian, the limitation-period suspension might exceed 15 years (s. 15).

- For some causes of action there is no limitation period: proceedings for a declaration of a right where there is no damage claim, proceedings to enforce or obtain a family law domestic agreement for support, and proceedings by the Crown to collect taxes, reclaim welfare benefits, or recover on defaulted student loans (s. 1).

- If a limitation period is set out in another act, it does not apply unless it is set out as an exception in the schedule at the back of the act (s. 19).

There is also a transition rule to cover transitions between the old limitation rules and those under the new Act.

Note that the new *Limitations Act* only affects causes of action arising under Ontario law. If a lawsuit involves a federal statute, you need to look at the limitation periods set by federal statutes.

RETAINERS

Once Abigail has decided to retain I.M. Just to represent her, and I.M. Just has agreed to act, their agreement should be incorporated into a contract of **retainer**. The retainer should be more than just a brief notation of a contractual relationship. It should set out all of the major terms governing the relationship. Because the lawyer is an expert in these matters, and the client is dependent on the lawyer for sound and honest advice, there is said to be a **fiduciary relationship**: the lawyer is obliged to ensure that the client is treated fairly and scrupulously. One of the ways to ensure this is to explain the terms of the retainer and spell out the corresponding duties and obligations of both lawyer and client.

The retainer must:

- identify the names of the parties (law firm and client);

- identify the work to be done ("to commence proceedings against Rattle Motors for personal injuries arising out of an incident"); and

- be signed by the client to indicate that she has agreed to retain the firm.

The retainer should:

- make clear that other members of the law firm, such as other lawyers, clerks, and staff, may work on the file;

- set out the hourly rate for these individuals;

- indicate that the rate changes periodically, and the client is obliged to pay at the new rate for work done after the date on which the rate changes;

- indicate that if the client is dissatisfied with an account, he or she has the right to have the account assessed by the court;

- indicate the amount of the deposit required before work under the retainer begins;

- indicate that the client will be billed at stated intervals, that the client will be required to pay further deposits, and that interest will be charged on overdue accounts;

- make clear that deposits are credited to future accounts rendered;

- make clear that any settlement funds are paid to the law firm, from which accounts will be paid before the balance is paid to the client; and

- indicate that the lawyer will advise the client and that it is the client's obligation, on being given advice, to give the lawyer instructions when asked to do so.

retainer
contract between a lawyer and client describing the services to be provided by the lawyer and the terms of payment by the client; also refers to a cash deposit to be used by a lawyer to pay future fees and disbursements as they are incurred

fiduciary relationship
one-sided relationship where one party relies on the other party's honesty and advice given in the reliant party's best interests

FIGURE 2.8   RETAINER

DATE: Sept. 16, year 0

CONTRACT OF RETAINER

BETWEEN:

Just & Coping, Barristers and Solicitors

and

Abigail Boar

1. I, Abigail Boar, retain you as my solicitors to commence proceedings against Fred Flogem and Rattle Motors Ltd. in respect of injuries sustained by me in an accident on September 14, year 0.

2. I understand that I have retained the firm, and not just an individual lawyer, and that other lawyers and staff may work on my case.

3. I understand that the hourly rates of those who may work on my file are as follows:

    I.M. Just, lawyer: $250/hour
    N.O.T. Coping, lawyer: $200/hour
    Edward Egregious, law clerk: $75/hour

4. I understand that the hourly rates of office staff may increase by no more than 5 percent on the first day of March, Year 1, and on the first day of March in subsequent years. I agree to pay the increased amount for work done after the date on which the rates change.

5. I understand that if I am dissatisfied with the amount of the account, I have the right to have that account assessed by the court.[*]

6. I understand that before work begins under this retainer, I am required to pay a deposit of $3,000 to be credited against accounts when rendered. I understand that I may be required to furnish future deposits from time to time to cover future fees and disbursements.

7. I understand that I must pay accounts promptly when they are rendered and that interest is chargeable on overdue accounts at the rate of 18 percent per year.

8. In the event settlement funds are received, I direct that they be paid to I.M. Just in trust, and that you may deduct any fees or disbursements owing at the time settlement funds are received, on rendering an account to me, and that the balance of the settlement funds will then be paid to me.

9. I understand that it is my obligation, on receiving advice and being asked for instructions, to provide you with instructions as requested.

Signed: *Abigail Boar*   *September 16, year 0*

---

[*]   We have yet to see this in a retainer or hear of a lawyer who conveys this information as a matter of course to clients; but in our view, given the fiduciary nature of the relationship, this information should be in the retainer.

CLIENT ACCOUNTS

Once the client has retained the firm, a client account must be opened. A bookkeeper or the bookkeeping department may do this, or you or other office staff may do it. The law society has strict rules about keeping the lawyer's own money separate from money the lawyer holds on behalf of clients. Clients' money is to be kept in a separate trust account or accounts. A lawyer's own money is kept in a general account. If a large sum is being held for a client for more than a few days, the lawyer may open a separate trust account; otherwise trust funds are deposited into one trust account for all clients.

Funds held in trust include settlement payments and retainer deposits made by clients. Abigail's $3,000 deposit, for example, does not go into I.M. Just's general account but into the firm's trust account. Part of it can be transferred from the trust to the general account when I.M. Just renders his account. If there is any of the deposit left, it remains in trust as a credit on any amount the client may owe in future.

In order to accurately record client money transactions, the firm sets up a client ledger card or a computer version of one. On this card, all monies received on behalf of the client and all debits for expenses chargeable to the client are recorded. Each firm has a method of tracking client expenses so they eventually can be billed to the client ledger card, using petty cash vouchers for cash transactions on behalf of the client, and cheque requisitions for cheques for the client's case (for example, to pay the court fee to issue the claim). These forms authorize a withdrawal from the firm's general account and allow the expense to be tracked so it can be debited to the client on the ledger statement. In addition, there is a disbursement journal in which all in-office expenses are recorded so they can be charged to the client's account. Included, for example, are photocopying charges, long distance telephone calls, and delivery of documents by office staff.

Chapter 19 examines how this information is used to prepare a client's account, as well as a **bill of costs**, when a client has been awarded costs as a successful litigant, and these amounts have to be determined and assessed.

bill of costs
list of allowable fees and disbursements that is used by an assessment officer to assess a litigant's costs after the litigant is successful in obtaining judgment; differs from an account because it does not include all fees charged to a client

Docketing

While actual disbursements incurred on the client's behalf can be tracked and recorded from cheque requisitions, petty cash vouchers, and disbursement journal entries, all of which are recorded on the ledger card, we still need to record the fees to be charged. As you may recall, the lawyers and law clerks charge an hourly rate. In order to determine how many hours they put in on Abigail's file, they need to keep track of their time. They do this by using either a computerized or manual docketing system. Units of time are broken down into tenths of an hour, each tenth being a six-minute block of time. On a docket sheet, the time and the nature of the work are recorded. When a client account is billed, the docket slips are assembled, and the time is totalled.

If the law clerk, Edward Egregious, spent about 45 minutes doing a first draft of the statement of claim on September 28, his docket slip would look something like the one in figure 2.9. Whoever has charge of the file collects the docket slips. It is also important not to discard the docket slips when the account is rendered. Should the client move to assess the account, the burden is on the lawyer to justify the amount of time spent on the case. That is a lot easier to do, and the lawyer will be much more believable, if he or she has docket slips that were made at the time the work was done and show what work was done. It is also easy to forget to docket. Interestingly, when dockets are not kept carefully, many lawyers tend to underestimate and undercharge clients for the time spent on the matter.

It is important for law clerks to document their time. For one thing, it can be charged to clients on an account. For another, a clerk who has docketed his or her time is making a case for a raise by showing the chargeable value of the work done by that clerk.

FILE ORGANIZATION

A file must be opened for Abigail's case. In a small firm, this may be an informal process, done by the lawyer, law clerk, or office assistant. In a larger firm, a central file office may do it. However it is done, there are certain practices that, with variations, are usually followed.

The case must be assigned a file number and case name. This may be as simple as the name of the client, "A. Boar," or the name followed by further information. In this case, it might be "Boar v. Rattle et al.," using a short form of the title of proceedings. This will be useful if Abigail has several files dealing with different legal matters with this law firm. If Abigail were the defendant, the name on her file might read "Boar ats Rattle." The letters "ats" mean "at the suit of" and indicate that the client is being sued by Rattle. After the name, a file number is assigned. It may be as simple as a sequential number, followed by the year the file was opened. For example, "231/02" indicates the 231st file opened in 2002. In larger firms, the system may also record the category or subject matter, identity of the lawyer opening the file, and provide other such information. For example, "231/02-FL-IMJ" indicates the 231st file opened in 2002, that this file is a family law file, and that it was opened by I.M. Just.

Because it is difficult to work on the case if the file or part of it goes missing, a law firm may have rules about how files are stored. In a small firm, the lawyer who has carriage of the file may simply store it in his or her filing cabinet, where anyone who is working on it can find it. In larger firms, where there are more people working on a case and centralized filing is used, the centralized filing office may control the file. This means files must be checked in and out like library books. It may also mean that files cannot remain out overnight or leave the office unless special procedures are followed. This prevents inadvertent loss or the misplacing of files and is also a security measure. Files contain original documents, some of which may be valuable, and are full of confidential and privileged information. Access to them needs to be controlled.

Once opened, the file must be set up and organized. The main file is a large file folder with the case name and file number on the outside. Inside the main folder are subfiles with differently coloured subfolders to identify them at a glance. The office should have a system for maintaining a consistent colour code for subfiles. Otherwise confusion reigns.

The main file should include a file management checklist, such as the one shown in figure 2.10, for noting when necessary steps have been taken or are to be taken. Anyone in the office who picks up the file will know at a glance what the status

FIGURE 2.9   DOCKET SLIP

Boar, A.			Rattle Motors Ltd. et al.			28/09/yr0		.7
Client			Matter			Date		Time
X								Edw E.
Drafting	Meeting	Court	Research		Telephone	Misc.		Initial
First draft of statement of claim								

is and what has to be done next. You will also find the file management checklist useful as a study guide for your course because it provides a practical step-by-step overview of the litigation process.

Subfiles

The following list describes the subfiles usually used in a litigation case and their contents. The contents of subfiles vary from law firm to law firm:

- correspondence: includes all correspondence sent and received in sequential order, with the oldest correspondence on the bottom of the pile;

- pleadings: includes copies of all pleadings, including motions;

- evidence: includes witness statements, factual memos, expert reports, photographs, and other demonstrative evidence;

- discovery: includes all discovery transcripts, documents produced with the affidavit of documents, and discovery exhibits in sequential order;

- law: includes research memoranda, copies of relevant cases, and research notes;

- client documents: includes all original client documents;

- opponents documents: includes all originals and copies not in other subfiles; and

- accounts: includes all statements of account, dockets, and disbursement records.

Tickler systems

A file management checklist is not a substitute for an automatic reminder of crucial deadlines. The law society and the Lawyer's Professional Indemnity Corporation (the law society's malpractice insurance body) require all lawyers to maintain a reminder system as a form of protection against professional negligence claims by clients arising from missed deadlines, especially missed limitation periods.

FIGURE 2.10 FILE MANAGEMENT CHECKLIST

Court file no.: _____   Lawyer: _____

Reference: _____   File no.: _____

Document	Date served	Date filed	Document	Date served	Date filed
Notice of action			Request for other side's answers to undertakings		
Statement of claim			Answers to undertakings received		
Notice of intent to defend			Security for costs		
Statement of defence			Motions		
Reply					
Defence and counterclaim					
Defence and crossclaim			Trial record and setting down for trial		
Third party claim			Waiver of privilege (10 days) (rules 30.09, 31.07)		
Third party defence			Notice of expert witness (10 days) (rule 53.03)		
Offer to settle			Notice for business records (7 days) (rule 35)		
Affidavit of documents (plaintiff)			Notice for medical reports (7 days) (rule 52)		
Affidavit of documents (defendant)			Trial brief		
Notice to admit			Authorities brief		
Notice of examination			Summons		
Examination for discovery					
List of undertakings					
Client's answers to undertakings					

The reminder system may take the form of a desk calendar or day book, or it may be a computerized reminder system. It should give several reminders before the crucial date comes for doing something: 30 days, 1 week, 3 days before the date, and then the date itself. Lawyers, clerks, and office assistants must take responsibility for checking the tickler system daily. At the time a file opens, the law clerk should note the expiry date of the limitation period, as well as the dates for serving and receiving pleadings and taking other steps in the proceeding. If the file falls under the case management system, it will also be necessary to enter the dates of the mandatory timetable for steps in the proceeding. Failure to set up, maintain, and check a tickler system may amount to professional misconduct and can lead to malpractice claims and higher insurance premiums for the lawyer.

CHAPTER SUMMARY

In this chapter, we discussed some of the steps taken by a law firm when it accepts a client's case. We began by assessing the facts as related by the client to determine if there was a good cause of action based on whether rights of the client had been breached and whether damages arose from the breach. We then conducted various searches to identify and name the right individuals or businesses as parties so that the correct person is sued on behalf of the client. We then determined whether the potential party was solvent and able to pay a judgment or was "judgment-proof" and not worth suing. Various searches were identified to determine whether the proposed defendant was insolvent. We also determined if the client could afford to pay for a lawsuit, noting that civil litigation is rarely funded by legal aid. The issue of insurance coverage was explored with the client because insurance may cover the claim and make a lawsuit unnecessary for a plaintiff. If acting for an insured defendant, proper notice of a claim must be given to the insurer. We explored whether a conflict of interest arose for the lawyer with the new or a former client. If so, the lawyer might need to turn the case over to someone else. Next, limitation periods were checked to see if the lawsuit was timely. We observed that once a firm decides to act for a client, the client needs to sign a formal retainer setting out the contractual relationship between the lawyer and the client. Office systems were activated for the client. An account ledger card was opened to record receipts and disbursements on this client's behalf, and methods of tracking the client's costs and expenses were identified. We noted that of particular importance is the need to docket all work done so that fees can be charged accurately. Suggestions were made about how a litigation file should be organized and maintained, and how time limits in the file can be kept track of.

KEY TERMS

pro bono	retainer
impecunious	fiduciary relationship
judgment-proof	bill of costs

NOTES

1 *Doe v. Metropolitan Toronto (Municipality) Commissioners of Police* (1990), 74 OR (2d) 225 (Gen Div.).

2 An employer can terminate an employee if the employee's services are no longer necessary or desired but must pay an amount equal to the salary for the period that would have been required had notice been properly given. If an employer has just cause to dismiss an employee, however, no notice need be given.

3 Estates can be liable for acts of proposed defendants during their lifetimes.

4 This can happen when a business defaults on a secured loan, the terms of which give the creditor the right to run the defaulter's business or to liquidate assets.

REFERENCES

Bower's Directories [by city] (Toronto: Metropolitan Cross Reference Directory, annual).

Creditors' Relief Act, RSO 1990, c. C.45.

Doe v. Metropolitan Toronto (Municipality) Commissioners of Police (1990), 74 OR (2d) 225 (Gen. Div.).

Law Society of Upper Canada, *Rules of Professional Conduct* (Toronto: LSUC, 2001) (also available at http://www.lsuc.on.ca/).

Limitations Act, RSO 1990, c. L.15.

Limitations Act, 2002, SO 2002, c. 24, sched. B (not yet in force as of February 1, 2003).

Might's Directories [by city] (Toronto: Might Directories Limited, annual).

Williams, J.S., *Limitation of Actions in Canada*, 2d ed. (Toronto: Butterworths, 1980).

REVIEW QUESTIONS

1. Roger Redoubt was hit by a car while walking along the left side of a road. Roger has always been tone deaf. As a result of the accident, he suffered some painful injuries to his legs, which have now healed, and a concussion. However, since the accident, he is no longer tone deaf and is able to play the violin like a maestro. Does Roger have a good cause of action?

2. If a client is advancing a cause of action that has not been previously recognized, should a lawyer tell him or her to sue anyway?

3. Why is it important to be accurate about the names of the parties you are suing or on whose behalf you are suing?

4. Why does a plaintiff need to know if a defendant has judgment creditors or is bankrupt?

5. What searches should a law clerk make in the ordinary course of preparing to commence proceedings?

6. Does it matter whether the defendant went into bankruptcy voluntarily or was petitioned?

7. What insurance issues should be covered with the client?

8. Describe two situations that might give rise to conflicts of interest in a law office.

9. What steps do you need to take to safeguard a client from the expiry of limitation periods?

10. What should be included in a retainer?

11. What needs to be done to set up and maintain a client's account?

12. Describe how a client file is organized.

DISCUSSION QUESTIONS

1. Read the following memorandum:

   To: Edward Egregious, law clerk
   From: I.M. Just, lawyer
   Re: Boar v. Rattle Motors et al.

   We have been retained by Abigail Boar. I wish you to conduct the usual searches to verify the name of the individual defendant, known to us as Fred Flogem, and to make sure we have the correct business name for Rattle Motors. I suspect Rattle is a limited company. Please prepare the necessary search forms in draft.

   I have heard rumours that Rattle is in financial difficulty and want to ensure it is solvent before suing it. Please prepare the documentation to search executions, and tell me what I need to do for a bankruptcy search.

2. Using your own name or that of a friend, business, or parent, find out as much information as you can from *Might's Directories* or *Bower's Directories*.

CHAPTER 3

Client management and interviewing

INTRODUCTION

In many law offices, it is the law clerk who has the most ongoing contact with the client as the case proceeds. It is often the law clerk who is involved in preliminary interviewing of the client and who speaks to him or her on the telephone. Therefore, it is important that the law clerk have some basic interviewing and some effective client management skills. It is important to remember that client contact is not just about getting information. It is also about conveying information to the client.

OBTAINING INFORMATION FROM THE CLIENT

Much of the initial and ongoing contact with the client involves information gathering. A lawyer needs to know as much about the facts of the case as possible in order to plan the case.

When clients come to the office for a meeting, make certain they are seen in private. They should also have an appointment time that is uninterrupted by telephone calls. A law office may be very busy but clients need to know that the office will not be so busy that staff cannot spend time on their case. The best way to convey this is to give clients undivided attention during their arranged appointments. Be alert, make eye contact, and listen to what they are telling you.

Interviewing is a skill, and there are many books written on the subject. Here is a short overview of some techniques that may be helpful.

Ask the client **open-ended questions**. Questions such as "What would you like to tell me about the case?" or "Is there something more I should know about the facts?" are open-ended questions. They do not box clients in. Open-ended questions encourage clients to tell the story in their own way and to convey information that is important to them. Sometimes clients may talk too much about matters that are of no consequence to the case. It is a good idea to try to redirect clients back to the issues by asking short clarifying questions to help them focus. A question that starts with, "So, what you're saying is" may be enough to turn their minds back to their narrative.

Once clients have finished relaying their story, you can then ask questions that tend to narrow the issues and focus on matters that require more elaboration. While the client has been talking, you have been deciding what parts of the story are more important or what further information you may need about certain points.

open-ended questions
questions that allow the persons interviewed to choose what they want to talk about to the interviewer

narrow questions
questions in which the interviewer tries to elicit specific information

Narrow questions tend to direct the conversation. By asking narrow questions, the questioner can get at specific points. For instance, Abigail Boar may have related her story to you about the slip and fall in the Rattle Motors showroom. You may want to ask some details about the lighting or how many drinks she had before ambling over to look at cars.

Listen carefully to what the client is saying. Taking notes is a good idea, but try to do so unobtrusively. You can encourage a client to continue by nodding or making small verbal responses such as "uh-huh." If clients are upset or expressing their feelings, you can show empathy by saying things like, "So, you are frustrated and angry." Litigation is often a very emotional experience for clients, and it is perfectly acceptable to acknowledge your clients' feelings if they are raising them.

There are some common mistakes made by many people who are "listening." Some of these are:

- jumping in to add comments when clients are telling their stories;

- fidgeting with paper or tapping a pencil or pen;

- answering a question with a question;

- pretending to understand a situation when they do not understand it; and

- using clichés, such as "I hear you."

COMMUNICATING WITH THE CLIENT

Taking a case through the litigation process can take a long time. You know what has happened on the file, but the client does not. One of the major complaints that clients have about litigation is that their lawyer's office does not keep them informed of the progress of the case or that no one returns their telephone calls. Therefore, it important to establish, right at the beginning, when and how their lawyer or you will be communicating with them.

There are several issues in establishing proper communications with clients. It is wise at the outset to advise clients how often during the litigation process you will be providing them with updates. Tell clients how the office will keep them informed. The method of communication must fit a client's understanding and ability to understand. It is useless to tell a client that you will fax or e-mail information if the client has no equipment for receiving fax or e-mail messages. It is not safe to assume that all clients have access to a computer.

Ask clients how they wish to receive communications. Do they prefer telephone contact or written communications? If they prefer to speak to someone on the telephone, it is a good idea to send a confirming letter to ensure that there is no misunderstanding about what was said.

Ensure that all the client contact information is correct. Do you have the correct mailing address and postal code, the correct e-mail address, the correct telephone or fax number? If your clients have both a home and a business telephone number, find out which number is the most convenient for them. Do not call clients at their place of business unless they indicate that that is the best manner of communicating with them. If you telephone, ensure that you do not leave too much information with whoever answers the telephone. Clients may not have advised people that they are involved in litigation and may not be happy to have it revealed to a co-worker in a message from the lawyer's office. It should be sufficient to say no more than, "This is Joe Clerk calling from Susie Seneca's office. Would you please ask Ms Client to call me?" There is no need to say that Susie Seneca is a lawyer or that you are her law clerk.

Once the method of communication has been settled, it is a good idea to determine how often clients can expect to hear from the law office. Will you update them once a month? Will you contact them only at certain milestones in the process? If so, determine what the milestones are and approximately when they will occur. Let clients know whether to expect a formal written report or an informal telephone chat.

One effective method for communicating with clients is sending them copies of relevant documents as they come into or leave the office. In this way, clients are kept abreast of developments as they occur. Some documents that may be sent to clients are:

- copies of all correspondence the office sends or receives on the matter,

- pleadings and court documents, and

- memorandums to file confirming communications or meetings.

Find out if your law office has a standard maximum length of time that it takes to return a client's telephone call. If such a standard exists, make sure you adhere to it. Often the standard is one business day. Whether there is an office standard or not, it may be a good personal policy to try to return client calls within 24 hours. If a lawyer is tied up in court and unable to return the call, make certain that this information is conveyed to the client.

It is also important to establish how clients will keep the office informed of developments in the case or new information pertaining to the litigation. They should be advised if there are certain things they should be watching for in terms of facts or situations.

When a practical and effective method and time frame of communication with the client is set up, the client has more confidence in the process and is less likely to inundate the office with telephone calls that interrupt work and create stress for all involved.

CHAPTER SUMMARY

This chapter introduced some general techniques and practices used in dealing with clients in a law office. It set out practical suggestions to guide you in interviewing clients and witnesses, including the appropriate use of open-ended and narrow questions to elicit information relevant to a case. The chapter also discussed appropriate techniques for maintaining communication with clients to ensure that the client receives necessary information in a timely fashion.

KEY TERMS

open-ended questions

narrow questions

REVIEW QUESTIONS

1. Give three examples of open-ended questions:

2. Considering the Boar case, give three examples of narrow questions you might ask Abigail.

3. What should you not do while interviewing a client or a witness?

4. Why is it important to maintain communication with the client as the case progresses?

5. What sort of information should clients receive from a law firm?

DISCUSSION QUESTION

1. Work in pairs for the following listening exercise. Look at the list of comment starters below. One student chooses any of the statements listed and uses it to begin speaking for a few minutes.

   When the first student is finished, the second student paraphrases the first student's comments. Take turns speaking and listening.

   - I would like to take a trip to ... because ...
   - One thing that I feel strongly about is ...
   - I am taking this course in college because ...
   - My favourite television show is ... because ...
   - When I go to a party ...
   - This college is ...
   - When I graduate, I would like to ...
   - My ideal job is ...

CHAPTER 4

Introduction to the Rules of Civil Procedure and the Courts of Justice Act

INTRODUCTION

The Courts of Justice Act and the law of equity

The *Courts of Justice Act* sets out the jurisdiction of the Ontario courts, the way those courts function, and other matters related to the makeup and operation of the courts. For instance, the Act tells you the route from court to court that must be followed on an appeal, it provides for the use of French and English as the official languages of the court, it spells out the names of the courts and their jurisdiction, and it requires that court hearings be open to the public except in special circumstances. It even tells you how to address judges in the courtroom.

Until the late 19th century, there were two types of courts: the common law courts and the courts of equity. The common law courts applied **common law** principles, and the courts of equity dealt with the **law of equity**. These two separate sets of legal rules created a complicated and sometimes rigid system that made it difficult for litigants and lawyers. A major court reform about a hundred years ago merged the two courts. This was a statute that joined the courts and was a predecessor to the *Courts of Justice Act*. Now any Superior Court in Ontario can apply both the common law and the law of equity. Superior Court judges have the power to give an equitable remedy to a party in a proceeding. They can grant injunctions and specific performance of contracts.

common law
law that is made by judges following precedents set by higher courts; often called "case law"

law of equity
type of law developed several hundred years ago in England wherein judges, rather than following precedents, look at the issues in a case and apply certain principles to ensure a fair outcome

The Rules of Civil Procedure

The *Courts of Justice Act* requires that a Civil Rules Committee be set up. This committee has the responsibility for making the rules of practice for the Superior Court of Justice and the Court of Appeal. The *Rules of Civil Procedure* are actually regulations to the *Courts of Justice Act*.

Under s. 66(2) of this Act, the rules committee may make rules for the Superior Court of Justice and the Court of Appeal in relation to the practice and procedure of those courts in all civil proceedings. Other committees set the rules for family law matters and criminal matters. The Small Claims Court also has its own rules; therefore the rules made by the Civil Rules Committee do not apply in that court.

It is the Civil Rules Committee that makes and amends the *Rules of Civil Procedure*. Because the committee is made up of judges, lawyers, representatives of the provincial attorney general and court administrators, its members are familiar with the manner in which courts operate from a number of different perspectives.

WORKING WITH THE RULES

The rules tell you everything you need to know about preparing a civil case for court. Your first task is therefore to learn how to use them.

Finding rules

The index at the back of the rules can lead to a long roundabout search if you do not know what you want to find. A preferable way to find a rule is to use the following three-step technique:

1. Look at the "summary of contents" at the beginning of the rules, and choose a rule that looks relevant.

2. Go to the "table of contents," which follows the summary of contents; look at the outline of what is covered in that rule, and choose a section.

3. Turn to the rule, and look through the section to find the information that is required.

The summary of contents provides a general overview of the rules. The table of contents breaks the summary into smaller components according to the various subsections of the rule. Because the summary allows an overview of the rules, it also assists you in seeing where the particular component you are searching for fits into the entire scheme.

Some rules are much easier to find and read than others and do not require all three steps, but until you are familiar with the rules, it is best to follow this technique.

Definitions and application of the rules: Rules 1 and 2

A court case runs in a fairly predictable manner from start to finish. The rules, for the most part, are set out in the same chronological order that a court case follows. The first steps you must take are set out in the first rules. In fact, the very first rules tell you the basic things that you need to know.

Rules 1.01 and 1.02 tell you where and how the rules are to be applied.

Rule 1.03 is one of the most important rules because it is the definition rule. There are many words and terms used continually throughout the rules, and this rule defines those terms. You must be careful when reading the rules that you do not apply everyday interpretations to the words in them. An ordinary word may have a different meaning in the context of the *Rules of Civil Procedure*. For instance, the word "holiday" means not only statutory holidays, as you might expect, but rule 1.03 also defines a "holiday" to mean a Saturday and a Sunday.

Over time, you will become familiar with the list of words that are defined in rule 1.03, but until you do, every time that you read a new rule, you should go back to rule 1.03 to check that there are no words in the rule you are reading that have a special definition.

Rule 2 spells out the consequences of not following the rules properly. The rules do not set up a system of proceeding that is so rigid that parties lose the right to continue with their case if they do not comply with the them. On the contrary, the court usually allows parties to correct their mistakes or to bring their documents or steps into compliance. However, such mistakes or failures in compliance cost your client money and time, and it is therefore essential that you always try to comply with the requirements of the rules.

Practice directions

The rules are applied in the same manner throughout the Ontario Superior Court of Justice. However, there are courts all over Ontario, and the administrative needs of one court may be quite different from those of another. For instance, jurisdictions with a high volume of cases, such as Toronto and Ottawa, may require special procedures to facilitate the management and organization of courts in those regions. These special procedures would make no sense in a court that has many fewer cases. Therefore, rule 1.07 provides that the chief justice of the court may give a **practice direction** to the other judges and lawyers who are active in that region. A practice direction is like a memorandum that outlines how a particular court operates in specified areas. The practice direction is operable only in the courts named in the practice direction and not in all Ontario courts. Nevertheless, the practice direction must be followed in the courts where it applies.

practice direction
instructions set out by a chief justice to inform lawyers about special procedures that must be followed in particular courts as a result of administrative needs

In the *Ontario Annual Practice*, the practice directions precede the rule to which they relate. As an example, there are a number of different practice directions that apply to the procedure for bringing motions in various judicial regions in the province. These precede rule 37, which is the rule dealing with motions.

You must always check to find out if there is a practice direction relating to the litigation step you wish to take in the court where you are proceeding with your client's case. The court may refuse to file your documents if they do not comply with what is required under a practice direction.

COMPUTATION OF TIME: RULE 3

The rules require that many steps in a court proceeding be taken within certain time limits. For instance, there are time limits for the service and the filing of documents. Rule 3 tells you how to compute the time. You might ask why there needs to be a special rule to tell you how to count time when it is something everyone knows how to do. Counting time, according to the rules, is different from counting time in ordinary life. For instance, if someone told you on Thursday that you had three days to do something, you would probably think that meant you had until Sunday. However, if you were counting in the time prescribed by the rules, your answer would be different.

Under rule 3.01(1)(a), when you count days, do not count the first day, but count the last day. For example, rule 34.05 requires you to give a party who lives in Ontario not less than two days' notice of the time and place for examinations for discovery. If you give notice on Monday, you do not count Monday as the first day.

Tuesday is the first day, and Wednesday is the second. Since you count the last day as a full day, the earliest you can require the party to attend for examination is Wednesday.

Where the rules have a time limit of *less* than seven days, holidays are not counted as days (rule 3.01(1)(b)). If the time limit required by the rule is more than seven days, you do count the holidays. Under rule 1.03, "holiday" includes Saturdays and Sundays. This means that if a rule requires three days to do something, you do not count Saturdays, Sundays, or other holidays listed under the definition of "holiday" in rule 1.03.

When the last day for taking a step in the court proceeding falls on a holiday, the step may be taken on the first day afterward that is not a holiday (rule 3.01(1)(c)). Therefore, if the third day falls on a Saturday, the deadline is extended until Monday, assuming that Monday is not a holiday. If Monday is a holiday, then the next day that is not a holiday after Saturday is the following Tuesday.

If you serve a document other than an originating process after 4:00 p.m. or on a holiday, the document is regarded as served on the next day that is not a holiday (rule 3.1(1)(d)). This means that if you served a document on Friday afternoon at 4:15 p.m. and the following Monday is Labour Day, the rules regard the document as being served on the Tuesday after Labour Day.

Although rule 3.01(2) permits the court to extend or shorten the time, you must bring a motion to ask for the court to do this, and it will cost the client more money. Therefore, it is important to try to keep the time limits as required by the rules.

FORMAT FOR COURT DOCUMENTS

The rules tell you what a court document should look like. Rule 4 prescribes in specific detail the format and content of court documents, provides for the use of electronic documents, tells you how to issue and bind documents, and gives all the other information you need to make your documents easy to read. Although instructions on how to prepare documents might seem far removed from conducting a court hearing, the documents are an integral part of the proceeding. The first impression that a judge has of your client's case arises when he or she reads your documents in preparation for a hearing or a trial.

In addition, during the court proceeding, it is necessary for the lawyers to refer the judge to parts of the documents that have been filed. It can be very irritating to a judge to try to find his or her way around a set of court documents that are not properly formatted or are badly written. Court documents may reflect on the lawyer and the law firm. Therefore, you want to make them as professional and as reflective of the seriousness of the client's case as you can.

Format of documents: Rule 4.01

Rule 4.01 gives specific requirements for the set up of documents to be filed in any court proceeding. Documents are to be typewritten and double spaced with a margin of 40 mm on the left side of the text. The font must be at least 12 point or 10 pitch size. Remember that fonts that are too small are extremely difficult to read. White paper must be used and the pages must be 216 mm by 279 mm. This is standard 8.5 × 11 inch stationery. Do not be tempted to use legal sized paper. It is not acceptable in part because it is difficult to fit into the court files. You may use single-sided or double-sided pages.

If you use electronic documents, you must be certain that the documents are produced on software that is approved by the Ministry of the Attorney General of Ontario.

Contents of Documents: Rule 4.02

Every document in a court proceeding must have both a general heading and a backsheet. In addition, there are requirements for the contents of the body of the particular document.

GENERAL HEADING: RULE 4.02(1)

This is a standard beginning for every document. There is a precedent for the general heading in the forms that are attached to the rules. The general heading for an action is in Form 4A and for an application is in Form 4B. Note that the form number is the same as the rule number related to it. Each general heading must contain:

- the name of the court;

- the court file number, if one has been issued by the court (if you are preparing the first document in the case and it has not yet been served or filed, there will be no court file number, but if you are preparing documents in an ongoing case, you must make sure that the file number is properly put on the document so that it will make its way to the proper court file); and

- the title of the proceeding (this is a fancy way of saying "the name of the case"). The title of the proceeding is sometimes called the "style of cause." This is an old-fashioned term that some lawyers still use. What is the title of the proceeding? If Abigail Boar is suing Rattle Motors Ltd., the title of the proceeding is *Boar v. Rattle Motors Ltd.*

If there are more than two parties, you can use the name of one plaintiff and one defendant. For example, *Boar v. Rattle Motors Ltd.* ***et al.*** is the short title of proceedings where Abigail Boar sues Fred Flogem and Rattle Motors.

et al.
Latin phrase meaning "and others"

BODY OF THE DOCUMENT: RULE 4.02(2)

The body of each document must contain:

- the title of the document (is it a notice of motion, an affidavit?);

- the date the document was prepared;

- the name, address, and telephone number of the person filing the document; and

- the address of the court.

If the person filing the document is a lawyer, the lawyer's name, address, and telephone number appears on the document. If a party has no lawyer and is representing himself or herself, the party's name, address, and telephone number goes on the document. It is a good idea to put a fax number on the document as well since some documents can be served by fax.

BACKSHEET: RULES 4.02(3) AND 4.07

Every court document must have a backsheet. The prescribed form for a backsheet is form 4C. Judges usually write their endorsements on the backsheet, so it is an important part of the document. Figure 1.3 in chapter 1 shows an example of a backsheet. An endorsement is a short summary of the order that the court has made.

The backsheet must contain:

- the short title of the proceeding;

- the name of the court and the court file number;

- the location of the court office where the proceeding is commenced;

- the title of the document (is it a notice of motion, an affidavit?);

- the name, address, telephone, and fax number of the lawyer serving or filing the document;

- if the person filing is a lawyer, the Lawyer's Law Society ID number; and

- the fax number, if possible, of the person being served.

In addition, if the document is an affidavit, the backsheet must also contain the name of the deponent and the date when he or she swore that the document was true.

There are usually many types of documents filed in a court proceeding. In a long case with many parties, the documents are often brought into the court on trolleys. The rules prescribe a method for telling the documents apart. They are given different coloured backsheets. Being able to tell the documents apart is very useful in a proceeding because it makes for easier access. The judge and lawyers do not need to search through a stack of documents that all look the same.

Records for motions, applications, trials, and appeals must have a light blue backsheet. Transcripts of evidence must have a light grey backsheet, except for transcripts that are to be used on an appeal. Those must have a red backsheet. Although not all court documents require a special colour for the backsheet, you should check rule 4.07 to make certain that the document that you are preparing does not require a special colour. If it does not, you can use ordinary white bond for the backsheet.

CHAPTER SUMMARY

In this chapter, we looked at the *Courts of Justice Act*, and you were introduced to the *Rules of Civil Procedure*. These rules provide a detailed set of directions as to how a court proceeding is conducted in the Ontario Superior Court of Justice and the Ontario Court of Appeal. For the most part, the rules are laid out in the same order as the chronological progress of a court case. It is essential to learn how to use the rules. Until you are familiar with them, we suggest that you use the "three-step" approach described in this chapter.

Rule 1 tells you where and how the rules are to be applied. It also contains a list of definitions that are crucial to your understanding of the rest of the rules. Rule 1 also provides that the chief justice may give practice directions about certain court procedures to the judges and lawyers in a particular court region. These directions must be followed.

Rule 2 spells out the consequences of not complying with the *Rules of Civil Procedure*. Although every effort must be made to follow the rules properly, the court has the ability to dispense with compliance if the interests of justice make it appropriate to do so. However, seeking the court's permission to dispense with compliance after a mistake has been made is costly to a client and should be avoided.

Many steps in the litigation process involve time limits. Rule 3 tells you how to count time when the rules prescribe a time limit. You must be able to use this rule in reference to the definition section in rule 1.03 to ensure that you are applying the correct usage of the terms and mechanisms contained in rule 3.

Rule 4 prescribes the format and general content of all court documents. It also tells you the size, colour, and paper that are required for each type of court document. Your documents provide the material for a judge's first impression of your client's case, and it is therefore essential that the documents be presented in a professional manner.

KEY TERMS

common law

law of equity

practice direction

et al.

REFERENCES

Carthy, James J., W.A. Derry Millar, and Jeffrey G. Cowan, *Ontario Annual Practice* (Aurora, ON: Canada Law Book, published annually).

Courts of Justice Act, RSO 1990, c. C.43.

Rules of Civil Procedure, RRO 1990, reg. 194.

REVIEW QUESTIONS

1. Using the three-step process outlined in this chapter, find the rule (or rules) that:

   a. provides for service of a document on a corporation,

   b. permits the amendment of pleadings,

   c. prescribes how to commence a proceeding in the Ontario Superior Court of Justice,

   d. requires a title of proceeding on all court documents,

   e. requires that service of originating process must be personal,

   f. permits service of court documents on a party's lawyer,

   g. tells when an appointment for an examination for discovery can first be served,

h. determines the contents of a motion record, and

i. determine the contents of a trial record.

2. To what courts do the *Rules of Civil Procedure* apply? Name the rule that tells you that.

3. What rules apply in Small Claims Court? How do you know?

4. What is the definition of "judgment"?

5. Are there special forms that you must use under the rules? If so, where do you find them?

6. What form gives you a precedent for a backsheet?

7. Must you include a fax number in your documents?

8. What rule applies to the contents of an affidavit?

9. What colour backsheet belongs on an application? What rule applies?

10. What rule tells you who should make an affidavit for a corporate party?

11. How and where do you issue and file a document?

12. Who must sign a practice direction for the Superior Court of Justice?

DISCUSSION QUESTIONS

1. A motion record is served on Brad Pout on Friday May 10 at 4:25 p.m. It is returnable — that is, it is to come to court — on May 20. However, Brad is entitled to six days' notice of the return date. Was he served in time?

2. Your firm wants to have a motion in court on Tuesday July 3 and must give three days' notice. What is the last possible day you can serve the opposite party with the motion record?

CHAPTER 5

Identification of parties, joinder of claims and parties

INTRODUCTION

We know that the parties to an action are called "plaintiff" and "defendant." But it is not always clear who the plaintiff or defendant is, or who should be included as a party. Can Abigail's boyfriend be a plaintiff because he has lost the pleasure of the company of the pre-accident Abigail? Can Skank Motorcar Company Ltd. as a party defendant? Can you join Barbeerian's, where Abigail had two glasses of wine before going to the car showroom? How about Abigail's employer: Haven't Abigail's injuries cost Megadoon Investments something? Would it make a difference procedurally if Abigail were under 18 or mentally disabled? If any of the defendants were partnerships, are there things you would need to do?

In this chapter, we examine the relevant rules of procedure to determine the answers to some of these questions. Set out below are the rules we examine and the issues they address:

- rule 5: who should be included as a party to a lawsuit;

- rule 5: which claims can be included together in one lawsuit;

- rule 6: how separate proceedings may be joined together into one proceeding;

- rule 7: how parties who are under a disability are represented in proceedings;

- rule 8: how partnerships and sole proprietorships are named as parties;

- rule 9: how estates and trusts sue and defend civil suits;

- rule 10: how unidentified persons with an interest in the issues are joined to civil suits;

- rule 11: how an interest in a lawsuit may be given by a party to a non-party, who then joins the proceeding;

- rule 12: how many persons who have the same interest in a lawsuit may be joined together to be represented by one plaintiff or defendant; and

- rule 15: whether a party to a lawsuit must be represented by a lawyer.

Our primary focus is on joinder of claims and parties (rule 5), consolidation of claims (rule 6), parties under disability (rule 7), and proceedings on behalf of and against sole proprietorships and partnerships (rule 8). You will encounter these basic rules for procedural matters often. The other rules and procedures are encountered less often unless you work in specialized areas of practice, such as estate litigation. We nevertheless include a general discussion so that if you find yourself working in these areas, you will have some familiarity with the procedural requirements.

JOINDER OF CLAIMS AND PARTIES: RULE 5

Abigail is suing Rattle Motors Ltd. and Fred Flogem for negligence concerning the failure to clean up the oil spill. But she may also have a claim against Skank Motorcar Company Ltd. arising from the defective design or manufacture of the oil pan on the Super Coupe. Should Skank and Abigail's claim against it be joined to a lawsuit that is, in some respects, about something else? Must all defendants be involved with all issues in the main lawsuit, whether their personal interest in them is minor or major? Rule 5 provides guidance in answering these questions.

Remember the basic principle in rule 1.04(1): the aim of the rules is to reduce cost and delay in the process of resolving disputes. Rule 5 is a more specific version of that general principle tied to the issues of what claims can be joined together in a lawsuit and what parties can be included as either plaintiffs or defendants. The thrust of rule 5 is that all parties with an interest in an issue in the litigation should be before the court in one hearing, so that all persons with an interest have a chance to be heard and are bound by one judgment. Generally, the rules frown on multiple proceedings involving an event, transaction, or factual issue. However, where one proceeding would be prejudicial to a party, the parties or the issues may be separated.

Joining claims

There are three procedural guidelines for joining claims set out in rule 5.01:

1. If a plaintiff has several claims against one party, he or she may join those claims together in one proceeding.

2. If a plaintiff has different claims against different defendants, he or she may include all of the claims against the defendants in one proceeding, even if some defendants have no interest in some claims made against other defendants.

3. A plaintiff may sue in more than one capacity. For example, a party may have been injured and sue for his or her own injuries, but that party may also be the litigation guardian for a child injured in the same accident. In that case, in the capacity of litigation guardian, the party makes claims for the child's injuries, and in a personal capacity, the party makes claims on his or her own behalf.

For example, if Abigail sued Fred and Rattle Motors for negligence, she might also sue Barbeerian's for continuing to serve her alcohol when she was intoxicated. These are separate incidents of negligence involving different parties. The only link the defendants have to each other is Abigail. But indirectly the issues involving the separate defendants are linked because they are part of the same transaction, event, or series of events. If Abigail were partly intoxicated, some of the liability for her injuries may lie with Barbeerian's, so she would include all claims she may have against any defendant. This is particularly important since the court might have to apportion liability among all defendants who were causally linked to Abigail's injuries.

However, the rule is flexible, and the court may refuse to join all of the plaintiff's claims together if some of the claims are disconnected from the others. For example, after the accident, Abigail's change in personality may have had a negative impact on her relationship with her boyfriend, to whom she had just become engaged. Suppose he breaks off the engagement? If she has a claim against him for engagement gifts she gave him, demanding their return, should she join that claim to her negligence action against the other defendants? There is some link between the claims. But for the accident, the relationship would likely have continued. The fact that the claim against the boyfriend might be in contract rather than in tort is not important. But a causal link such as this may be so remote that a court would hold it to be prejudicial to the other defendants to require them to spend time and money on a contractual issue in which they have no interest, direct or indirect, and that does not affect their cases. In this situation, the court might order that the contractual issue be severed from the negligence issues, and that the action against the boyfriend be tried separately. This means that if Abigail pursues both claims, she must do so in two separate lawsuits, which may raise costs and result in more stress for her. In considering whether to join claims or sever them, a court must balance the prejudice and relative inconvenience to all parties.

Joinder of parties

At least initially, the plaintiff can decide what claims to include in a lawsuit, with the understanding that where it is both fair and possible, all claims that are logically related should be disposed of in one proceeding. We now turn to rule 5.02 and the issue of when parties can join or be joined in a lawsuit.

PLAINTIFFS

To be joined as plaintiffs in the same proceeding, the plaintiffs or applicants must have the same solicitor of record and must assert claims arising out of the same event, series of transactions, or occurrence where a common question of law or fact may arise or where joining the parties may "promote the convenient administration of justice." There are two essential requirements. First, the same lawyer must represent all plaintiffs in the proceeding. This means that while the plaintiffs may advance different claims, there are no conflicts of interest among them with respect to those claims. Second, the claims must be related because they arise out of the same events where either it is convenient in terms of cost and delay to join the plaintiffs or there is a common question of fact and law that links the plaintiffs, even if some of the claims are different.

For example, suppose Abigail were a key employee so that her injuries caused loss of profits to her employer because she was unable to work. Abigail might sue for her injuries, and the employer might sue for its profit loss. The claims are different, but there is no conflict of interest between the plaintiffs. There is a common question of fact or law (whether the defendants were negligent), and the claims arise out of the same occurrence (the accident). This case might well proceed with the two plaintiffs, represented by one lawyer, making claims in one proceeding. Otherwise, each plaintiff would need to sue separately. They would also have to sue separately if any conflict between them made them adverse in interest to each other. Lawyers must be alert to this and warn multiple plaintiffs that if a conflict develops, other lawyers must represent them both separately, and their cases must be divided and tried separately.

DEFENDANTS

While plaintiffs must be united and not in conflict to proceed together, this is not the case for defendants. Defendants may have little interest in each other, be at each other's throats, and be separately represented. If defendants are in agreement on their defence, are united against the plaintiff's claim, and have no conflict of interest with each other, they may be joined in the same proceeding as defendants and be represented by the same lawyer, subject to the development of a conflict of interest. But it is the plaintiff who decides who the defendants are, simply because it is the plaintiff who decides whom to sue. Most lawyers follow the "sue everybody in sight" approach, particularly in the early stages of a case. Everyone who might be liable or who should be bound by the judgment is included initially. Later, often after discovery when the plaintiff has assessed his or her case, the plaintiff may discontinue proceedings against some of the defendants, though he or she may have to pay some costs to do so.

Guidelines as to who may be added as defendants are set out in rule 5.02(2)(a) to (e).

1. *Persons against whom the plaintiff makes claims arising out of "the same transaction or occurrence, or series of transactions or occurrences" may be joined as defendants.* These claims may be made against defendants who acted together or who acted separately from each other. If a claim against one defendant fails, it can be made alternatively against another defendant. The uniting factor is not the relationship between the defendants or between the defendants and the plaintiff; it is the relationship of all to an occurrence or transaction. For example, Abigail may sue Barbeerian's, Fred, Rattle Motors, and Skank Motorcar. Her reason for suing each is different, but they are each connected to an occurrence: the accident that gave rise to damages for which they are allegedly liable in various ways.

2. *Persons who are linked together by a common fact or issue of law may be joined as defendants.* For example, if a plaintiff seeks to determine who among several people share an interest in property, all of those people may be made defendants because of their link to and interest in an issue of law (the ownership of property). In this case, the plaintiff may seek a declaration as to who is entitled to the property rather than damages.

3. *All potential defendants may be joined in the proceeding when the plaintiff is not sure who is liable and from whom a remedy can be obtained.* This is the basis for the "sue everybody in sight" rule. In medical malpractice, there may be several medical practitioners who are responsible for the plaintiff's injury, but because of the nature of treatment or the patient's state

or both, the patient may not know who among all the doctors, nurses, and other medical professionals caused the damage. The plaintiff therefore sues them all.

4. *All potential defendants may be joined when the plaintiff has sustained a loss caused by more than one defendant, even where there is no factual connection between the potential defendants* and *there is doubt as to which defendant caused what damage.* This rule applies to a situation where, for example, a plaintiff was physically injured in an accident and then taken to a hospital where negligent medical staff did physical damage. The nature of the physical damage may prevent the plaintiff from knowing which potential defendant caused what part of the damage. In this case, this rule permits the plaintiff to sue everyone involved. This situation differs from that contemplated by the previous subrule. Here we think various defendants each did some damage. In the previous situation, we think that one or more defendants did all the damage, but we do not know which one was responsible. While the rules seems to contemplate distinct situations giving rise to joinder of defendants, you will find that often several of the subrules can apply to a case.

5. *Notwithstanding the failure of a case to come within the first four rules, defendants may be joined if joinder promotes the convenient administration of justice.* The term "convenient" incorporates the concept of "balance of convenience." The court, in examining balance of convenience, looks to see if joinder will cause the proceeding to be less expensive and less time-consuming for the parties, on the whole, without prejudicing a party's right to a fair trial.

Joinder of necessary parties: Rule 5.03

As a general rule, the court has the power to join in a proceeding any person whose presence is necessary to decide the issues in the case. This means, for example, that if a person who is not a party to the proceeding will be affected by a decision, that person should have standing as a party in the proceeding.

If a plaintiff claims a remedy to which another person is also entitled, the plaintiff is obliged to join the other person to the proceeding. If there is no conflict of interest and if the add-on agrees by filing a consent under rule 5.04(3), the add-on is joined as a plaintiff. If the add-on does not consent or objects, he or she is added as a defendant so as to be bound by the decision. While the add-on cannot be compelled to be a plaintiff, he or she cannot easily prevent being made a defendant. In general, if a person who is not a party to the proceeding could be affected by the decision, he or she should be added as a defendant. As a general rule, if a plaintiff is in doubt, the plaintiff should add the person as a defendant, even if there is no claim made against that defendant, so that the defendant is bound by the judgment. This is important because a **judgment *in personam*** is more common than a **judgment *in rem***. A judgment *in personam* arising, for example, from a negligence action is binding only on the parties; a judgment *in rem* arising, for example, from a declaration of land ownership, binds the parties, but it also binds non-parties. If you are declared the owner of Pink Acre, then you have an interest superior to the whole world, even though the whole world was not a party to the proceeding.

judgment *in personam*
judgment that is binding only on the parties to the proceeding

judgment *in rem*
judgment that is binding on everyone, whether a party to the proceeding in which the judgment is pronounced or not

In the event that a plaintiff fails to include a necessary party, any person can apply to the court to be made a party, or the court can add a party on its own motion. The ground for such addition brings us back to the main principle: a party is added where his or her presence is necessary for the court to completely determine the issues in the proceeding. Similarly, under rule 5.03(6) the court may also permit someone who ought to be joined to be relieved of that obligation. Remember that being joined to a lawsuit is expensive and time-consuming. Rule 5.04(1) confronts this issue as well.

Rule 5.04 generally recognizes that the naming of parties to a lawsuit is primarily left to the plaintiff, not to the court. Plaintiffs can make errors in including people who should have been left out and in omitting people who should have been included. Rule 5.04 gives the court broad powers to correct the errors of litigants. It does not require the dismissal of a case where persons have been wrongfully included or omitted. It allows the court to determine the dispute without the presence of a person who should have been added, but without prejudice to that person's rights, which may be litigated in a subsequent proceeding. The court may also add, substitute, or drop parties, or correct the name of a party who was incorrectly named in the lawsuit, without the lawsuit having to be dismissed and restarted against the correct parties. This power is consistent with rule 2.01, which treats procedural errors as irregularities rather than nullities. However, if the failure to include a party is so prejudicial that it cannot be compensated for by costs and an adjournment, then the failure may result in a nullity notwithstanding rule 2.01. For example, if a party was omitted and the limitation period has expired, it is prejudicial to add the party at that time.

Claim by an assignee of a chose in action

Rule 5.03(3) contains specific provisions about assignments of the right to sue. An **assignee** is a person to whom a right, usually a contractual right, has been transferred. A **chose in action** is a type of property that is intangible — that is, its value does not lie in its physical properties but in what it represents. For example, a cheque is a chose in action; its value lies not in the printed piece of paper that it physically is, but in what it represents: the promise to pay the sum written on it.

Where an **assignor** has assigned his or her right to a debt or other chose in action, the assignee acquires all the rights the assignor had, including the right to sue to collect the debt or the value of a chose in action. However, rule 5.03 requires that the assignor be added as a party. But the assignor need not be added if the assignment was absolute, so that the assignor retains no further rights in the asset *and* notice in writing of the assignment has been given to the person obliged to pay the debt or deliver up the chose in action. If, for example, the assignor assigned a chose in action as security for a loan, the assignor may redeem the security on payment of the loan. In that case, the assignor must be included as a party. Also, if the debtor or defendant was not given notice of the assignment, the assignor is still a necessary party.

assignee
person to whom rights, usually contract benefits, are granted by an assignor

chose in action
intangible personal property whose value lies in what it represents

assignor
person who grants contract rights to an assignee

Relief against joinder

We have already noted, under rule 5.04, how a court has the power to correct joinder errors without making the lawsuit a nullity. But sometimes, the correct joinder of parties results in a cumbersome proceeding that causes judges and lawyers to flee in horror. Relief from this situation is available under rule 5.05. Where a case is unduly complicated or will be delayed or prejudice a party because of joinder of multiple claims or parties, the court may take a number of procedural steps. It can order separate hearings. For example, if Abigail sued Fred, Rattle Motors, and Skank Motorcar for negligence, and her employer for wrongful dismissal all in one proceeding, the court could break the matter into two separate proceedings. It could also order claims in one proceeding to be transferred to another proceeding or allow costs to a party compelled to attend part of a proceeding in which it has no interest. It can also **stay proceedings** against one defendant while a proceeding against another defendant is completed and bind the party against whom proceedings are stayed by the findings of fact and law made in the previous proceeding. This rule may be invoked when the same issues affect both defendants, so that trying both is repetitious, and the decision in the first case is justly binding on the defendant in the stayed proceeding.

stay proceedings
stop proceedings for a given or indefinite period, pending the fulfillment of a condition, without dismissing the proceedings

CONSOLIDATION OR HEARING TOGETHER: RULE 6

Just as the court may order parties or issues to be severed from a proceeding and tried separately when convenient, so may the court order the consolidation of separate proceedings. As a means of reducing cost and delay, the court will combine separate proceedings, where possible, rather than have several related proceedings continue separately. An additional reason for consolidation is that the courts wish to avoid two or more decisions on an issue or fact that is common to both proceedings. Inconsistent decisions are to be avoided because they lead to further proceedings by way of appeal, instability, and uncertainty — all things that the common law tries to eliminate.

Under rule 6.01(1)(a) to (c), proceedings may be consolidated when:

- there is a common question of law or fact (not just common issues or questions raised by litigants);

- the relief claimed arises out of the same fact situation; or

- there is some other good reason for consolidation, leaving the court broad discretion to deal with each case on its facts within the confines of the principles stated above.

Rule 6.01 also goes on to give the court broad powers to direct how a consolidated proceeding is to be conducted justly in relation to the parties with minimal cost and delay. The two proceedings can be consolidated to be heard together as one proceeding, with the plaintiff presenting all its issues and evidence and the defendants following. However, if it is logical to have one issue or set of issues heard first because this is necessary to render a decision on a second set of issues, the court may order the cases to be consolidated but tried one after the other.

For example, if Abigail sues Fred in one proceeding and Rattle Motors in another, it may make sense to consolidate the two into one proceeding but to try the case against Fred first. If Fred turns out not to be liable for failing to mop up the oil, there may be no case against Rattle Motors to answer. If Rattle is allegedly liable for failing to direct Fred and Fred is not liable, neither logically is Rattle Motors. If the plaintiff's first case fails, her second case can be dismissed without further evidence being heard, saving time and money for all of the parties.

The court also has the power to stay one proceeding until the other is heard or asserted as a counterclaim by the defendant in the plaintiff's action. In practical terms, the court is free under rule 6.01(1)(d) and (e) to control its own process and customize consolidation orders to save time and money and to yield a just result. In rule 6.01(2), the court is given the power to make an order for directions that may dispense with service of a notice of listing for trial and abridge the waiting time for placing a case on the trial list. In fact, the court can order the matter to proceed immediately and fix a date for trial. Note the use of the motion for directions to break procedural log-jams and clean up procedural messes. Lawyers generally have carriage of how an action proceeds, who gets sued, and what issues are included. Each lawyer is focused on his or her client's needs, and if there are multiple issues and parties, there needs to be some objective supervision. If a case is going from a straightforward matter to chaos with multiple parties, proceedings, and issues, a party may use a motion for directions to sort out the mess. However, as case management becomes more common, this should become less of a problem. Case management judges and masters, assigned to a case from the beginning, have more control over how the case progresses than in non-case-managed proceedings. They have charge of the timetable, and they can see problems developing and head them off at an early stage, probably on their own initiative.

PARTIES UNDER A DISABILITY: RULE 7

The common law has long barred parties who are not of "full age and capacity" from initiating and defending lawsuits on their own. The reasoning here is that children and mentally ill adults do not have the judgment, experience, or resources to engage in litigation on their own, just as they may not contract on their own in some cases. They are not barred from suing and being sued, however, since access to the courts is a fundamental right. Instead, they may exercise rights as litigants but must have a mentally competent adult or a public body assist them in the enterprise. The rules governing the duties and procedures to be followed by a **litigation guardian** are set out in rule 7.

Minors and mentally incapacitated persons are generally referred to in rule 7 as "persons under disability"; this term replaces the now-derogatory terms "infant," "imbecile," or "lunatic" previously used at common law and under older statutes. Persons under disability must have a litigation guardian. Such people include:

- a minor;
- a person who is mentally incapable of understanding proceedings and instructing counsel on an issue in those proceedings, whether the person has a guardian or not;[1] and
- an **absentee** under the *Absentees Act*.

The court can dispense with litigation guardians in an appropriate case. A sophisticated minor, almost 18 years of age, may be allowed to proceed without a litigation

litigation guardian
competent adult who directs and takes responsibility for the litigation of a legally disabled party, such as a minor, an absentee, or a mentally disabled person

absentee
person whose rights or interests are being determined in a proceeding and whose whereabouts are unknown

guardian if the court thinks this is appropriate. The other instance where a litigation guardian is not needed involves an application for a declaration that a person is incompetent. Where a litigant seeks to declare someone mentally incompetent so as to appoint a guardian to make decisions about the alleged incompetent's property and person under the *Substitute Decisions Act, 1992* the alleged incompetent need not have a litigation guardian appointed under rule 7 unless the court requires it.

To make some sense of the law in this area, you need to understand that, under legislation, if a person is unable to manage his or her own assets because of mental illness or another infirmity, the law provides for a procedure to have the person declared mentally incompetent. Such a declaration means that the person could not manage day-to-day life decisions, especially concerning his or her money and assets. Note that not all mental illness is equivalent to legal mental incapacity. A person may be a schizophrenic and suffer specific delusions but be able to manage his or her own business affairs. If so, the court does not often intervene to appoint a guardian. But if the person cannot manage his or her business affairs, to prevent waste to the person's estate or harm to him or her physically, the court can order one or more people to act as the committee of the incompetent person, after making a finding of mental incompetence. This is the route that is followed if someone suffers from Alzheimer's disease or some other form of dementia.

In addition, a person who recognizes that he or she can no longer handle his or her own affairs or who wishes to provide for that situation when it occurs, may voluntarily, without a finding of mental incompetence, make his or her own arrangements for someone to manage his or her estate. This is done by appointing a person to take on this task under a power of attorney. No court order is or was required for this. The person granted power of attorney has the power to enter into contracts and generally deal with the assets of the person who made the appointment. In addition, the law also provides for a power of attorney for personal care, in which an individual may appoint a person to make decisions about personal care, including medical decisions, when and if the person making the appointment is no longer able to do so. Again, no court order is required. It is not uncommon for an elderly person to grant a younger, trustworthy relative both a power of attorney regarding property and a power of attorney for personal care to make decisions about health care.

Rule 7.01(3) is a transition section that takes into account new legislation in the mental health area introduced between 1990 and 1995. A person who was named as the committee of a mental incompetent in the older legislation, to represent the incompetent in proceedings, continues as a litigation guardian. Where there was no individual to do this and the public trustee was appointed to act for the mental incompetent under the *Mental Health Act*, the public guardian and trustee continues to act as litigation guardian. You should note that the rules generally are littered with such transition provisions when older legislation is amended or repealed and replaced. Often only the terminology is changed, but read the relevant rule and the legislation referred to carefully because there may be substantive changes as well.

Litigation guardians for plaintiffs

Rules 7.02(1) and (2) lay out a complete code governing litigation guardians for a plaintiff or applicant. Any person who is not under a disability may act as the litigation guardian of a person under a disability. No court order is required. The assumption is that a person under a disability who has a cause of action also has friends or relatives who will step in. This is almost always the case for minors. Where a person is mentally incapable, it may be more complicated, especially if the mental incapacity is connected to homelessness or substance abuse and the individual has become disconnected from friends and family. If Abigail were a minor, or were mentally incapacitated, she would be identified in the title of proceedings as "Abigail Boar, by her litigation guardian, Henrietta Boar, Plaintiff."

If Henrietta were suing for her own damages as well as acting as litigation guardian for Abigail, the title of proceedings would read "Abigail Boar, by her litigation guardian, Henrietta Boar, and Henrietta Boar personally." The same formats would be used if Abigail and Henrietta were defendants instead of plaintiffs.

Mentally incapable persons may have existing representatives act as litigation guardians without a court order unless the court orders otherwise. If a mentally incapable person has a guardian, or had a committee under older legislation, or voluntarily appointed an attorney[2] to manage his or her affairs under a power of attorney, that person may act as litigation guardian. However, in the case of a power of attorney, the power to act as a litigation guardian must have been included as one of the powers under the power of attorney appointing him or her. If the public guardian and trustee acted for an incompetent, as would be the case where there was no relative to appoint as committee or attorney under a power of attorney, and the person was sued, the public guardian and trustee would act as litigation guardian.

While no court order is required to appoint a plaintiff's litigation guardian, an individual who seeks such an appointment must file a certificate or a sworn affidavit setting out the nature of the disability. The affiant must also generally show that he or she is a proper person to act as litigation guardian and that there is no conflict of interest. The affiant must also agree to pay any costs awarded against him or her or against the plaintiff. If neither the affiant nor the plaintiff resides in Ontario, they may be asked to provide security for costs as well (rule 7.02(2)).[3]

The body of a sample affidavit to be filed with the court pursuant to rule 7.02(2) is set out in figure 5.1.

This affidavit uses the provisions of rule 7.02(2) as an outline to set out the information required. The affidavit also uses the language and vocabulary of the rule with simple modifications. Why make the job of drafting harder than it is?

Litigation guardians for defendants

Rule 7.03(1) provides a detailed code governing the appointment of litigation guardians for defendants or respondents. Generally, a defendant's litigation guardian must be appointed by the court unless

- the defendant is a minor with an interest in an estate or trust (in which case he or she is represented by the **children's lawyer**);

- the defendant is mentally incapable or an absentee and either has a guardian, attorney under a power of attorney, or a committee, all with authority to act as litigation guardian; or

- the defendant is mentally disabled, in which case he or she is represented by the public guardian and trustee.

children's lawyer
official of the Ontario Ministry of the Attorney General whose office oversees the rights of some minors involved in civil litigation and custody disputes

FIGURE 5.1 AFFIDAVIT FILED PURSUANT TO RULE 7.02(2) (FORM 4D)

Court file no. 01-CV-5678

ONTARIO
SUPERIOR COURT OF JUSTICE

BETWEEN:

Abigail Boar, a mentally incapable person,
by her litigation guardian,
Henrietta Boar

Plaintiff

and

Rattle Motors Ltd. and Fred Flogem

Defendants

AFFIDAVIT OF HENRIETTA BOAR

I, Henrietta Boar, of the City of Toronto, in the Province of Ontario, MAKE OATH AND SAY:

1. I consent to act as litigation guardian for Abigail Boar, the plaintiff in this action.
2. I have given written authority by way of a retainer signed on September 16, year 0 to I.M. Just to act as solicitor in this proceeding.
3. The plaintiff, as a result of her injuries, is unable to concentrate, understand complex concepts, or take any interest in her surroundings. She is depressed and passive. Dr. Alice Wunderkind, a psychologist who has examined the plaintiff, advises me that the plaintiff is unable to instruct her solicitor in this proceeding. Now marked exhibit A to my affidavit is a copy of the medical report of Dr. Wunderkind dated September 29, year 0, when this assessment was made.
4. Both the plaintiff and I are ordinarily resident in Ontario.
5. I am the mother of the plaintiff.
6. I have no interest in the proceeding adverse to that of the plaintiff.
7. I acknowledge that I have been informed by my solicitor that I may be liable to personally pay any costs awarded against me or against the plaintiff.

Sworn before me at the	)
City of Toronto,	) *Henrietta Boar*
Province of Ontario,	) Henrietta Boar
on October 16, year 0.	)
Commissioner for Taking Affidavits	)

A person who is to act as a litigation guardian for a mentally incapable defendant, must file a certificate or affidavit under rule 7.03(10) signifying ability and willingness to act. If the litigation guardian is the public guardian and trustee or the children's lawyer, the affidavit is abbreviated and omits material dealing with potential conflict of interest between the guardian and the disabled party.

A person who seeks to act as a litigation guardian must file a notice of motion asking to be appointed before acting for the disabled defendant, and must support the motion with the affidavit or certificate referred to in rule 7.03(10). If a litigation guardian is already acting for a plaintiff, he or she may defend a counterclaim without bringing a motion (rule 7.03(3)).

A sample affidavit to be filed pursuant to rule 7.03(10) is set out in figure 5.2.

If no one moves to become litigation guardian for a defendant, the plaintiff may move for the appointment of a litigation guardian for the defendant. The moving party must also serve a request to appoint a litigation guardian on the defendant, personally or by an alternative to personal service. This notice may be served with the originating documents, but must be served at least 10 days before the **return date** of the motion. The motion may be made without notice to a defendant, but it is necessary to move to dispense with notice in the notice of motion. This may be done as part of the motion to appoint by asking for leave to proceed without serving the disabled defendant and, if leave is granted, for an order appointing a litigation guardian. This eliminates the need for bringing a motion to dispense with service separately. If the goal is to appoint the children's lawyer or the public guardian and trustee as the defendant's litigation guardian, those bodies must be served with the motion (rule 7.03(4) to (9)).

Figure 5.3 sets out form 7A, the notice to appoint a litigation guardian for a defendant. With modifications, it can be used to appoint a litigation guardian for the plaintiff.

return date
the date on which the
motion will be heard by
the court

Representation of a disabled person when no one volunteers to be litigation guardian

Being a litigation guardian is not considered one of life's joys. The litigation guardian undertakes to be responsible for costs awarded against him or her or against the party with a disability. There are disabled plaintiffs and defendants with no relatives, no friends, and no one to step in and help. Where no one comes forward for the plaintiff or defendant, and where a plaintiff moves to have someone appointed as a litigation guardian for a defendant where there is no likely person available, the court may appoint:

- the children's lawyer to represent a minor, or

- the public guardian and trustee to represent a person who is mentally incapable and has no guardian or attorney under a power of attorney.

If the disabled party is both a minor and mentally incapable, the court may appoint either the public guardian and trustee or the children's lawyer (rule 7.04(1)). Where a disabled person is not a party and the court deems that he or she should be, then the party must be added. The children's lawyer or the public guardian and trustee, as the case may be, is appointed as litigation guardian.

FIGURE 5.2   AFFIDAVIT FILED PURSUANT TO RULE 7.03(10) (FORM 4D)

Court file no. 01-CV-7890

ONTARIO
SUPERIOR COURT OF JUSTICE

BETWEEN:

Henry Smoke

Plaintiff

and

Abigail Boar

Defendant

AFFIDAVIT OF HENRIETTA BOAR

I, Henrietta Boar, **of the** City of Toronto, **in the** Province of Ontario, **MAKE OATH AND SAY:**

1. This is an action for breach of contract brought against the defendant.
2. The cause of action arose on or about April 10, year 0, and the action was commenced on July 19, year 0.
3. The defendant was served with a statement of claim and a notice requesting appointment of a litigation guardian on July 24, year 0.
4. The defendant suffers from Alzheimer's disease. As a result, she often behaves impulsively, suffers from delusions, and is unable to understand the issues in this lawsuit or give instructions to counsel.
5. The defendant ordinarily resides in Ontario.
6. I, the proposed litigation guardian, am the daughter of the defendant.
7. I am ordinarily resident in Ontario.
8. I consent to act as litigation guardian in this proceeding. I am a proper person to be appointed as litigation guardian. I have no interest in the proceeding that is adverse to that of the defendant. I understand that I may incur costs that may not be recovered from the other party.

Sworn before me at the)	
City of Toronto,)	*Henrietta Boar*
Province of Ontario,)	Henrietta Boar
on November 24, year 0.)	
Commissioner for Taking Affidavits)	

FIGURE 5.3   REQUEST FOR APPOINTMENT OF LITIGATION GUARDIAN (FORM 7A)

Court file no. 01-CV-1011

ONTARIO
SUPERIOR COURT OF JUSTICE

BETWEEN:

Abigail Boar

Plaintiff

and

Maxim Furtwangler

Defendant

THE PLAINTIFF BELIEVES THAT YOU ARE UNDER A LEGAL DISABILITY. As a party under disability, you must have a litigation guardian appointed by the court to act on your behalf in defending this proceeding.

YOU ARE REQUIRED to have some proper person make a motion to this court forthwith to be appointed as your litigation guardian.

IF YOU FAIL TO DO SO WITHIN TEN DAYS after service of this request, the plaintiff may move without further notice to have the court appoint a litigation guardian to act on your behalf.

Date: July 14, year 0
TO: Maxim Furtwangler
123 DeCory Street
Toronto, Ontario, M4R 1Z6

Just & Coping
Barristers and Solicitors
365 Bay Street - 8701
Toronto, Ontario, M3J 4A9

I.M. Just
tel. 416-762-1342
fax 416-762-2300

Solicitors for the Plaintiff

The children's lawyer and the public guardian and trustee are government officials. Their departments operate with high case loads and with limited resources. This is particularly true for the public guardian and trustee, where staff have large workloads. In dealing with people's property, they also often have contentious and adverse relationships with the relatives of mentally disabled persons.

Powers of the litigation guardian

Once appointed, a litigation guardian may make any decision and take any step a litigant of full capacity can make. This includes retaining and dismissing counsel and being advised by and instructing counsel. This includes taking further proceedings, such as counterclaims, crossclaims, and third party claims. A litigation guardian, other than the children's lawyer and the public guardian and trustee cannot act on his or her own. He or she must retain a lawyer to represent the disabled party in court (rule 7.05).

Removing a litigation guardian

Being a family member or friend of a person with a disability does not necessarily make a person capable as a litigation guardian. There are provisions to remove a litigation guardian where the court thinks it is appropriate or it is otherwise required. If a minor reaches the age of majority, the litigation guardian may file an affidavit setting out that fact, and the registrar will grant an order authorizing the action to continue without the litigation guardian. The order will be served on all other parties.

An order in form 7B to continue a proceeding where a party has reached the age of majority is set out in figure 5.4. It can be modified for a party whose incapacity has ended.

Note that this is one of the few instances where the title of proceedings changes after litigation commences. Similarly, if a person is under disability for other reasons — mental incapacity, for example — and the incapacity ends, the litigation guardian or the party may move to continue the proceeding without the litigation guardian. This order is served on all other parties

If the court is of the opinion that the litigation guardian is not acting in the best interest of the party under disability, the court may remove the litigation guardian and substitute the children's lawyer, the public guardian and trustee, or any other person (rule 7.06).

Protection against default judgment

When a defendant fails to defend an action, the plaintiff can note the plaintiff in default and move without notice for default judgment. If the claim is for a liquidated amount that is easily calculated by objective standards — such as a debt and interest on it — the clerk may sign immediate judgment. Because a litigation guardian may inadequately represent a disabled party or there may be difficulty in finding a litigation guardian or getting him or her to respond, it is easy for a plaintiff to move quickly for a default judgment. However, if a plaintiff moves for default judgment and the responding party is under disability, the defendant may not be noted in default without leave of a judge of the court. If the plaintiff knows of the disability, he or she is obliged to serve a motion to note (the defendant) in default, on the litigation

FIGURE 5.4   ORDER TO CONTINUE (FORM 7B)

Court file no. 01-CV-1415

ONTARIO
SUPERIOR COURT OF JUSTICE

BETWEEN:

Emily Boar, a minor, by her
litigation guardian, Abigail Boar

Plaintiff

and

J.S. Bach Ltd.

Defendant

ORDER TO CONTINUE

On the requisition of the plaintiff, Abigail Boar, and on reading the affidavit of Abigail Boar, filed, which states that the minor, Emily Boar, has reached the age of majority on August 14, year 0,

IT IS ORDERED that this proceeding continue by Emily Boar, without a litigation guardian and that the title of the proceeding be amended accordingly in all documents issued, served, or filed after the date of this order.

Date: August 17, year 0

Signed by: _____   Address of
court office: Court House
393 University Avenue
Toronto, Ontario, M5G 1Y8

---

guardian of a person under disability, and on the children's lawyer if the defendant is a minor, unless the public guardian and trustee is the litigation guardian (rule 7.07).

Approval of settlements for parties under disability

Neither a party under a disability nor a litigation guardian has the power to settle a proceeding on behalf of a disabled party or make a settlement before proceedings are commenced without the approval of the court. This reflects a long-standing common law rule that the courts need to oversee and supervise settlements made by parties under disability to ensure that they are not taken advantage of. An unapproved settlement is not binding on the disabled party, who may have up to six years after the disability ends to sue again. For example, a minor who is injured at age 4 by the defendant's negligence can, after turning 18, sue the defendant and may have as long as six years from the time he or she turns 18 to do so before the limitation period expires.

Rule 7.08 sets out a procedural code for obtaining approval of a settlement for a disabled party. If a claim is settled before proceedings are commenced, the parties must, by application to a judge, ask for approval of the settlement by the court. If proceedings have been commenced, approval of the court must be obtained on a motion within the proceedings. The application or motion for approval must be accompanied by an affidavit of the litigation guardian, setting out the facts, the reasons for settling, and the opinion of the litigation guardian as to the proposed settlement. The lawyer acting for the litigation guardian must, by affidavit, set out his or her position on the proposed settlement. This requirement is intended as a safeguard against an improvident agreement by a litigation guardian who ignores a lawyer's advice. It puts the court on notice to examine the matter further. If the litigation guardian is acting on a lawyer's advice, the lawyer's affidavit will usually mirror the litigation guardian's.

If the person under disability is a minor over the age of 16, the consent of the minor should be filed unless the court orders otherwise.

If a judge has any qualms or questions about the propriety of the settlement, he or she may direct the material to be served by the moving party on the public guardian and trustee or on the children's lawyer, depending on the circumstances. The official served must report back to the court orally on the return date of the motion or in writing with recommendations. Reasons for recommendations in connection with the proposed settlement must also be provided.[4]

PARTNERSHIPS AND SOLE PROPRIETORSHIPS: RULE 8

There special rules for suing sole proprietorships and partnerships. These two forms of business organizations share an important legal characteristic. The individuals who own the businesses are personally liable for the business debts, and the business, regardless of its name, is not a separate entity from the individuals who own it. By contrast, the liability of shareholders as the owners of a corporation for the corporation's acts is limited; the corporation is a legal person separate from its owners, so that only the corporation is liable for its actions.[5]

Suing partnerships

If your law firm is going to sue a partnership, the suit is usually brought in the partnership's name, which you verify by a business name search. If so, the judgment may be enforced only against the partnership's assets. If Rattle Motors were a partnership, you could seize its real property — for example, its land and showroom, office furniture and equipment, bank account, income from sales, automobiles, and other inventory. But you could not seize the personal assets of partner A, B, or C. If partner A had a house, bank account, and car, none of which was used in the partnership business, this property could not be seized to enforce the judgment against the partnership (rule 8.06(1)).

However, a plaintiff may be interested in seizing partnership assets *and* personal assets of the partners to enforce and satisfy a judgment. After all, partners are liable at common law for the debts and liabilities of the partnership, and the rules of procedure do not change the substantive law. Rule 8 makes provision for a plaintiff to claim against partnership assets and a partner's personal assets. If your law firm wishes to enforce a judgment against an individual partner, when it serves originating process against a partnership, it must also serve a notice to an alleged partner, in form 8A, stating that the individual partner was a partner at the time stated in the notice (usually when the cause of action arose). The person is then deemed to be a partner unless he or she files a statement of defence in his or her own name, denying that he or she was a partner at the relevant time. An example of a notice to an alleged partner is set out in figure 5.5.

The names of the parties in the title of proceedings are set out as follows if you are naming only the partnership: "BOAR v. RATTLE MOTORS." If you also include individual partners, the title of proceedings looks like this: "Boar v. Rattle Motors, and Sam Slipp and Bob Chaterjee, Partners."

If you seek to fix personal liability on partners by giving them notice under form 8A, you need to know who they are. Think about a large law firm. Of the 200 lawyers, perhaps 150 may be partners. Further, as lawyers pursue career opportunities, several lawyers may become partners and several may leave the partnership in a given year. The firm name may not be any help. Most large firms use the names of just one or two partners, and other types of businesses may use commercial names that do not include the names of any partners. If you wish to know who the partners were five or six years ago, the business records of the Companies and Personal Property Security Branch of the Ministry of Consumer and Business Services will not be helpful because they contain mostly current records. Rule 8.05 provides the answer to a plaintiff's problem. Where there is a proceeding brought by or against a partnership, rule 8.05 entitles any party to serve a notice on the partnership requiring the partnership to set out the names and addresses of partners for the time period or date specified in the notice. In this way, a party can find out who the partners are, and then serve partners individually with the notice in form A, provided that this is done within 15 days of receiving the information. If the partnership wants to stall and prevent liability from resting on the individual partners by not providing the information, the rule provides a solution: The action will be stayed if the partnership is a plaintiff, and the defence will be struck out if it is a defendant.

Suppose a claim against a partnership gives rise to crossclaims between partners, where one partner, for example, claims that the other promised to indemnify him or her from suits by the plaintiff, or claims that he or she was not a partner when the plaintiff's cause of action arose. If one partner's defence is different from or adverse to the positions of other partners or the partnership, that partner may apply to the court on motion for leave under rule 8.02 to file a separate defence. If the partner denies being a partner at the relevant time, he or she may file a separate defence pursuant to rule 8.03(2) and rule 8.04(a).

Once the plaintiff has a judgment in a proceeding against a partnership, he or she may enforce it against partnership assets. If a partner was named individually, the plaintiff may also enforce against that person's personal property, provided that the procedure for giving the individual partner notice under rule 8.03 was followed. Rule 8.06(3) provides further relief for a plaintiff who failed to name an individual

FIGURE 5.5 NOTICE TO ALLEGED PARTNER (FORM 8A)

Court file no. 01-CV-1516

ONTARIO
SUPERIOR COURT OF JUSTICE

BETWEEN:

Abigail Boar

Plaintiff

and

Rattle Motors Ltd.

Defendant

NOTICE TO ALLEGED PARTNER

YOU ARE ALLEGED TO HAVE BEEN A PARTNER on Sept. 14, year 0 in the partnership of Rattle Motors, named as a party to this proceeding.

IF YOU WISH TO DENY THAT YOU WERE A PARTNER at any material time, you must defend this proceeding separately from the partnership, denying that you were a partner at the material time. If you fail to do so, you will be deemed to have been a partner on the date set out above.

AN ORDER AGAINST THE PARTNERSHIP MAY BE ENFORCED AGAINST YOU PERSONALLY if you are deemed to have been a partner, if you admit that you were a partner or if the court finds that you were a partner, at the material time.

Date: October 4, year 0

I.M. Just
Just & Coping
Barristers and Solicitors
365 Bay Street - 8701
Toronto, Ontario, M3J 4A9
tel. 416-762-1342
fax 416-762-2300

Solicitors for the Plaintiff

TO: Adolphus Ambrose
123 Elm Street
Scarborough, Ontario, M8Y 2Z8

under rule 8.03. Here, if the plaintiff obtains judgment against the partnership and then seeks to enforce it against a defendant not previously named, the plaintiff must apply to a judge on a motion for leave to enforce against a named individual. The order is granted if the individual admits or is found to be a partner at the relevant time.

Sole proprietorships

Sole proprietors are treated as if the individual were a partner and the sole proprietorship were a partnership. A plaintiff may sue the sole proprietor in his or her own name or the business name and compel the business to reveal who the sole proprietor was at the relevant time. A plaintiff who sues the business in the business name can enforce against business assets only. It is therefore wise to sue both the business and the individual, especially because assets are more likely to be informally intermingled than is the case with partnerships.

Assume that Priscilla Plant is a sole proprietor carrying on business under the name "Prissy's Plants." If you were suing the sole proprietor as an individual, the title of proceedings would describe the defendant as "PRISCILLA PLANT." If you sued the defendant in her own name and the business name, the title of proceedings would be "PRISCILLA PLANT CARRYING ON BUSINESS AS PRISSY'S PLANTS."

Suing corporations

A corporation is required by law to include in its name some indication that it is a corporation with limited liability. It does this by having the words "Limited," "Incorporated," "Ltd." or "Inc."[6] following its name or as part of its name. However, your client may have dealt with what he or she thought was a business called "Prissy's Plants." You will need to search that name, which will tell you whether you are dealing with a sole proprietorship, partnership, or corporation, and who its principals are. If the defendant turns out to be a corporation, the plaintiff *cannot* sue in the business name. He or she must sue in the proper corporate name as revealed in your search.

ESTATES AND TRUSTS AS PARTIES: RULE 9

We now turn to some rules governing the naming, joining, and severing of parties and issues in litigation involving trusts and estates. A trust is a means of holding property where the legal owner is acting for the benefit, not of himself or herself, but for the benefit of beneficiaries of the trust, who are also the beneficial owners of the trust assets. If a grandmother wants to give a minor grandchild the benefit of a large capital fund, she may, as the grantor, set up a trust, where the person she names as trustee is the legal owner and controls the assets for the benefit of the minor, who cannot directly get at the capital and waste the assets. An estate is similarly structured, though the grantor who creates the trust through a will is deceased. The **executor** or **estate administrator** acts in the interest of the estate beneficiaries. The same is true for trusts.

Rule 9 sets out procedural rules for naming parties. The general rule is that an estate or trust may sue or be sued by naming the administrator, executor, or trustee as the estate representative, without naming the beneficiaries specifically because

executor
person appointed by a will maker to administer an estate under the provisions of the will; a female executor is sometimes called an executrix

estate administrator
person appointed by a court to administer an estate where there is no will or where the appointment of an executor is ineffective

they are deemed to be included. There are some exceptions where beneficiaries must be named:

- a suit to contest the validity of a will;

- a suit brought to interpret a will;

- a suit to remove an executor, administrator, or trustee;

- a suit alleging fraud against an executor, administrator, or trustee; and

- a suit to force the administration of an estate or the carrying out of the terms of a trust where the trustee, executor, or administrator has failed to or refused to act (rule 9.01(1), (2)).

Where there is more than one executor, administrator, or trustee, what happens if one does not agree to join the others as plaintiff? Because they may have some liabilities and an interest in the outcome, they are joined as respondents or defendants even though no claim is made against them. This is done so that they will be in the lawsuit and bound by the judgment. In addition, the court may order any creditor or beneficiary to be added as a separate party (rule 9.01(3), (4)).

If an estate has no administrator or executor, your law firm will sue the estate in its own name and apply to the court for the appointment of a litigation administrator (rule 9.02). The proceeding can then continue, and any order will be binding on the estate and its beneficiaries. A litigation administrator can be an estate creditor with an interest in defending the plaintiff's lawsuit, a relative or business partner of the deceased, or a trust company that will accept the appointment. Estate departments of trust companies routinely administer estates under wills and charge a fee for doing so. The appointment of a litigation administrator will depend on the facts and circumstances of the case and whether there are estate assets that make the effort worthwhile.

Rule 9.03 is a child of rule 2.01 in that it prevents accidental slips, omissions, and errors from derailing a lawsuit by making it a nullity. An error is treated as an irregularity that can be cured by the court, subject to costs or an adjournment to compensate the other side from being unduly disadvantaged.

If an administrator or executor commences proceedings on behalf of an estate before the grant of probate has confirmed the appointment, the proceeding is deemed to be properly constituted, provided that the administrative grant is approved. The title of proceedings for an action commenced by or against an estate by naming the estate as a party — for example, the Estate of Abigail Boar — results in an irregularity, and the court may simply order that the action continue against the personal representative of the estate, with the title of proceedings being amended accordingly. If your law firm sues a deceased person in his or her own name, or if a party it has sued dies before it starts the suit, the court can order that the title of proceedings be amended so that the personal representative of the estate is the named party. If the court appoints a litigation administrator and then finds there was an executor or administrator already appointed under a will or otherwise, the action continues against the previously appointed executor or administrator.

In the event that an action is not properly constituted, as noted in the situations above, the court may order that the case be properly constituted and continue, but the proceeding is stayed until the errors are corrected. If the corrections are not made — for example, by applying for a litigation administrator — the proceeding can be dismissed. The court may also order that an executor or administrator be relieved of personal liability if he or she paid money out of an estate to beneficiaries before becoming aware of a proceeding against the estate, provided that he or she acted in good faith (rule 9.03).

UNIDENTIFIED AND UNASCERTAINED PARTIES AND REPRESENTATION ORDERS: RULE 10

In cases like Abigail's, there is no difficulty telling who the parties are or might be. Abigail's claim against Barbeerian's or Skank Motorcar may be more speculative and uncertain than the one against Fred Flogem and Rattle Motors. However, you can identify these entities as parties, and define and describe the claim against them, including the damages for which they may be responsible.

But consider, for example, an estate where the beneficiaries include grandchildren and great grandchildren of specific persons named in a will. If someone challenges the validity of the will, rule 9(2)(a) requires that the beneficiaries be made parties to the proceeding. The persons named in the will can easily be added, but what about the class of grandchildren? It is possible that we may not know at the time who all of the individuals in the class are. Some of these persons are not yet born or may never be born but may have an interest. Rule 10 provides a procedure for representing those who have an interest in the outcome of a proceeding where either the interest or the person cannot be ascertained or the person cannot otherwise be represented.

The provisions of the rule apply to certain types of proceedings:

- the interpretation of documents, such as contracts and wills, that create rights and interests, and proceedings that interpret the provisions of a statute, regulation, or other Act of a government body that affect rights and interests;

- the interpretation of a question or issue that has arisen in the administration of an estate or trust;

- the approval of a sale, purchase, settlement, or other transaction involving interests that cannot be ascertained or where the members of a class of persons are not known;

- the variation of the terms of a trust because the provisions did not take into account some state of affairs that prevents the trust's objects from being carried out (for example, if the trust authorizes payments to a class of beneficiaries to "advance their station in life," does this authorize flying lessons for one of the beneficiaries?);

- the administration of an estate where a question about its administration arises; and

- any other matter where it appears necessary to make a representation order.

Rule 10.01(1) gives the court considerable leeway in deciding when to make such an order. Generally, when there appears to be a present, future, or even a contingent interest (an interest contingent on the fulfillment of a condition precedent) of persons who are unborn or not yet ascertained, a representation order can be made. An order may also be made if a person is a member of a class whose interests may be affected even if the identity of the individual is not yet known. Where a large number of people are affected by the interpretation of a government regulation or a provision of a pension fund, for example, you may not know whether the class member is still alive or whether he or she still qualifies as having an interest. You may know who the persons in the class are but may not be able to find them or serve them all. In these cases, the procedural shortcut is to have one person represent the interests of all. Rule 10 governs situations similar to class proceedings, which are covered by rule 12, but rule 10 is a broader provision.

Once a representation order is made, the person named in it becomes a party, representing the class of persons identified in the order — the unborn grandchildren of Fred Flogem, for example. The person or class of persons named in the order as being represented is bound by any judgment or order made in the proceeding. This means that one of Fred's grandchildren cannot come forward and say that he or she was not consulted, had no notice, and is therefore not bound. If a settlement offer is made to, and accepted by, the representative of the class, the members of the class are bound by the settlement. An individual class member may escape from the settlement in some circumstances, although the test for doing so is a difficult one to meet (see rule 10.01(3)).

If an estate of a deceased person has an interest in an issue in a case and there is no executor or administrator, the judge may order the proceeding to continue in the absence of an estate representative. The judge may also name a representative for the purpose of the proceeding, in which case the estate of the deceased person is bound by the outcome (rule 10.02).

Although a judge may make a representation order in an appropriate case, the judge in the case or in a subsequent case can order the person or estate not to be bound provided that

- the order was obtained by fraud,

- the interests of the person appointed and the estate or person represented were in conflict, or

- there is a good reason to set the representation order aside (rule 10.03).

Because a court's discretion under rule 10 is broad, we need to look at case law. The purpose of rule 10 is to encourage a quick means of resolving contentious proceedings without having to resort to the more cumbersome class proceeding procedure covered by rule 12. The test that should be applied by the court in considering whether or not to make a representation order is not whether the members of the group can be found or ascertained, but whether it is more convenient to issue a representation order than to insist that each member of the class be served and allowed to participate. The court must also check to see that there is no conflict between the members of the class and the representative (rule 10.03).[7] In fact, the representative of the class should have all of the crucial characteristics of the class members. In a pension case, for example, the representative of the class of retirees must have the same characteristics as the retirees in the class who are affected by the issue in question: The representative must be a retiree, from the same occupation, with a right to the same types of benefits.

TRANSFER OR TRANSMISSION OF INTEREST: RULE 11

Rule 11 gives you directions about what to do if the legal status of a party changes in the course of an ongoing proceeding. For example, if Abigail Boar starts an action as a plaintiff in her own name and then dies, her legal status changes. The lawsuit must be continued in the name of her estate's executor or administrator. Another example occurs where the rights being litigated are transferred by assignment from one person to another. For example, a person becoming bankrupt transfers his or her property to a trustee in bankruptcy for the general benefit of creditors. Whatever the reason, rule 11.01 requires a proceeding to be stayed until the court makes an order to continue the proceeding by or against the "new" litigant — for example, the estate executor or the trustee in bankruptcy. The new litigant is not usually personally liable: The estate is the focus of the judgment, not the estate executor who is the "new" party.

The order is obtained on requisition from the registrar, on the filing of an affidavit by any party setting out the fact that the interest or liability of a party has been transferred. A formal motion is not necessary because the matter is usually a procedural formality. If, however, the transmission is contested, the requisition may be challenged by bringing a motion to set aside the order to continue. An example of the registrar's order to continue, form 11A, is set out in figure 5.6.

CLASS PROCEEDINGS: RULE 12

While rule 11 gives the court general powers to make one person the representative of a class in ordinary litigation, it is also available for the less complex representative or class proceeding. Rule 12 contains specific procedures that apply to actions certified as class proceedings under the *Class Proceedings Act, 1992*. The Act and rule 12 are designed to deal with proceedings more complex than those to which rule 11 applies. It is necessary to know something about the Act before we examine rule 12. What follows is an overview of the highlights that make a class proceeding or class action different from other types of civil proceedings. If you are involved in a class proceeding, there are other resources you should use that provide detailed procedural guides.[8]

Overview of the Class Proceedings Act

Suppose Abigail Boar bought a Super Coupe in its first model year, along with several thousand others. Within the first year the car was on the market, there were frequent reports of sudden engine failure. In about 30 percent of the cases, the engine failure also led to car fires, which caused serious injuries. Approximately 10 percent of the engine failures involved serious accidents, with injuries, but no car fires. In Abigail's case, let us suppose that the engine failed, but Abigail was able to steer her car off the road, so that she was uninjured. When she consulted I.M. Just, she discovered that there have been a number of incidents involving the Super Coupe.

The purpose of the *Class Proceedings Act, 1992* is to allow numerous potential plaintiffs or defendants to have their claims considered as members of a class represented by one plaintiff or defendant. This allows justice to be done by allowing many small claims to be considered. Otherwise, no claim might ever have been

FIGURE 5.6   ORDER TO CONTINUE (FORM 11A)

Court file no. 01-CV-5864

ONTARIO
SUPERIOR COURT OF JUSTICE

BETWEEN:

Abigail Boar

Plaintiff

and

Rattle Motors Ltd. and Fred Flogem

Defendants

ORDER TO CONTINUE

On the requisition of Henrietta Boar and on reading the affidavit of Henrietta Boar, filed, which indicates that on July 24, year 1 Abigail Boar, the plaintiff in this action, died, and her right of action was transferred to her estate, of which Henrietta Boar is the representative, as the executrix of the estate of Abigail Boar,

IT IS ORDERED that this proceeding continue and that the title of the proceeding in all documents issued, served, or filed after the date of this order be as follows:

Date: February 6, year 3

Signed by: _____

Address of
court office: Court House
393 University Avenue
Toronto, Ontario, M5G 1Y8

A party who wishes to set aside or vary this order must make a motion to do so forthwith after the order comes to the party's attention.

Where a transmission of interest occurs by reason of bankruptcy, leave of the bankruptcy court may be required under section 69 of the *Bankruptcy Act* (Canada) before the proceeding may continue.

made because of the expense. The Act also eliminates the possibility of the courts having to deal with a torrent of separate lawsuits.

I.M. Just, or the lawyer of any claimant, can apply to certify a proceeding as a class proceeding, in which case Abigail and all others with claims against the defendant, Skank Motorcar Company Ltd., may be separated into classes and subclasses. Here all would be included in the class claiming for product failure, but there would also be subclasses for those who were injured in car fires and for those who were otherwise injured. Because Abigail suffered only from product failure, she is a member of the main class but not the subclasses. The purpose of this arrangement is to require class members to incur expense only on issues that affect them. Each class or subclass would have a representative plaintiff. The representative must have all the relevant attributes or qualities of the class on the issues that concern the class. Often the court will have to sort out competing class action claims by a variety of plaintiffs.

The lawyers for the plaintiff whose action is certified by the court face problems and opportunities. The firm will require staff and resources to administer the proceeding, identify the members of the class, and process their claims. At the same time, if the suit is successful, the fees, which are payable on a contingency basis, will be lucrative for the firm.[9]

Under the *Class Proceedings Act, 1992*, a potential plaintiff cannot be involuntarily joined to another plaintiff's proceeding and can opt out of a class proceeding (s. 9). If Abigail wants to go it alone, she may apply to the court to do so.

Once a proceeding is certified, potential plaintiffs need to know about it so that they can contact the lawyer for the class representative and have their claims included. To facilitate the process, the court requires that a public notice be prepared, approved by the courts, and published as a legal notice, or sent by mail or by any other means (ss. 17 to 22). In Abigail's case, the court may require the defendant to furnish a list of all purchasers, in which case Abigail may receive a registered letter or a couriered letter giving her notice of the proceeding.

Individual legal or factual issues involving a class or subclass may be tried separately. Thus, one class proceeding may give rise to several subproceedings (see s. 27). Abigail, for example, may be included in the class that suffered property damage but not in the classes that sustained personal injuries.

If the representative party agrees to settlement, the court must approve the settlement because it affects other class members (s. 29). Abigail will receive notice of the settlement and be entitled to voice objections as a class member.

Because running a representative proceeding is speculative and expensive, s. 33 of the Act permits lawyers for a class to be paid their costs on a contingency-fee basis. This has not been permitted in ordinary civil actions in Ontario, but soon will be.

class proceeding fund
public fund of the Law Foundation of Ontario, administered by the Law Society of Upper Canada, to provide funding for the costs of class actions which otherwise might be beyond the financial reach of the parties

Because the costs incurred before trial by a law firm are high, the Act permits the law firm for a class representative to apply for funding for disbursements at various points in the class proceeding from the **class proceeding fund**. This fund, which is administered by the Law Society of Upper Canada, was set up to provide funding for class proceedings, especially where there are many individual class members with small claims.

If the plaintiff receives assistance from the class proceedings fund, a successful defendant in the proceeding is entitled to claim payment of costs awarded by the court from the fund.

Application of rule 12 to class proceedings

Rule 12 deals with certain procedural requirements of class proceedings. After the names of the parties and as part of the title of proceedings, there must appear the words "Proceeding under the *Class Proceedings Act, 1992.*" These words must be included in all court documents, commencing with the notice of motion to certify the proceeding as a class proceeding (rule 12.02). An example is set out in figure 5.7.

A class member as well as the class representative may be examined for discovery. Only parties are usually subject to examination for discovery. Admissions in the class member's discovery transcript can be read into the record at trial (rule 12.03(1)). Parts of rule 31, setting out the basis for examining non-parties, do not apply because that matter is covered in rule 12. Similarly, the sanctions under rule 34 for a class member who does not cooperate in the discovery process do not apply because they include dismissal of the proceeding. If Abigail were summoned as a class member and refused to cooperate in the discovery process, the proceeding should not be dismissed against the class representative, who is the actual party, because of Abigail's misconduct.

If the plaintiff has received financial support from the class proceedings fund, the Law Foundation of Ontario is entitled to notice of any motion or request for an order for costs or an assessment of costs after costs have been awarded. The fund's representative is entitled to make submissions, cross-examine witnesses, and present evidence on the issue of costs, including appeals on the issue of costs (rule 12.04). This makes sense because the fund may well be paying the costs that are being disputed.

Judgments and orders made in a class proceeding, including an order approving a settlement, must contain provisions

- detailing how the award will be distributed to class members and how the costs of making the distribution will be paid,

- outlining the payments owing on a contingency agreement between the lawyer and a representative party,

- detailing the payment of costs of the proceeding, and

- detailing payments of any levy to the fund (rule 12.05).

Defendants with the same interest may defend a proceeding on behalf of or for the benefit of all defendants and may be authorized as a class in a class proceeding for that purpose (rule 12.07).

Where there are many members of an **unincorporated association** or a trade union and it would be unduly expensive and complicated to apply to certify a class proceeding, one or more of the members may be authorized to commence a proceeding on behalf of and for the benefit of all (rule 12.08). Note that this rule is restricted to unincorporated associations and trade unions, so that a mass of individuals with a common interest is not able to use this rule. Rule 12.08 is also only available to plaintiffs. A plaintiff suing a voluntary association or trade union would have to name all the members of the association as defendants or commence a class proceeding.

unincorporated association
association of persons formed to carry out a specific purpose and not formally incorporated

FIGURE 5.7   NOTICE OF PROCEEDING UNDER THE CLASS PROCEEDINGS ACT, 1992

Court file no. 00-00-0000

ONTARIO
SUPERIOR COURT OF JUSTICE
Proceeding under the Class Proceedings Act, 1992

BETWEEN:

Abigail Boar

Plaintiff

and

Skank Motorcar Ltd.

Defendants

REPRESENTATION BY A LAWYER: RULE 15

As a general rule, an individual is entitled to represent himself or herself in every court in Canada, including the Supreme Court of Canada. This does not mean it is a good idea. There is a saying among lawyers that "a lawyer who represents himself has a fool for a client." As you already can see, knowledge of and experience with both substantive law and procedure is necessary to conduct a case, as is detachment and objectivity. Advocacy skills are also necessary. Most non-lawyers lack these skills and experiences. If you are dealing with a party who is acting in person, be prepared for the proceeding to go more slowly and for there to be numerous irregularities as parties stumble through the pretrial stages. Abigail could represent herself, and might do so if she cannot afford to hire a lawyer. Legal aid is very difficult to obtain in civil proceedings.

There are some parties that *must* be represented by a lawyer in proceedings in the Superior Court[10]: they include parties who are acting in a representative capacity, parties under a disability, and parties that are corporations unless the court grants leave for someone else to represent the corporation. Where, for example, an individual is sued along with a corporation that he or she controls, the individual has a right to represent himself or herself and may be granted the right to represent the corporation as well.

Once Abigail has retained I.M. Just and instructed him to commence proceedings, I.M. Just and his firm have the authority to proceed. I.M. Just's name, address, telephone, and fax number appear on the backsheet of every court document, starting with the originating process. Since I.M. Just is a member of a firm, both his name and the firm's name must be disclosed, along with his individual phone number or extension. Once the proceeding is commenced, the court will note and record I.M. Just's name and the firm name from the backsheet, making I.M. Just the **solicitor of record**. I.M. Just or a member of his firm is then obliged to appear

solicitor of record
lawyer recognized by the court as the legal representative of a party in a proceeding

for Abigail unless she fires him or he obtains the court's permission to be removed from the record.

Requiring a solicitor to prove authority to act

Anyone may require a solicitor of record to state in writing whether he, she, or the client authorized the commencement of proceedings. If there is no authority to proceed, the court may stay or dismiss the proceeding (rule 15.02). This rule is not often used, but it may be resorted to, for example, where there are warring factions in a privately held company or association and one such faction questions the company's proceedings.

Changing lawyers

What happens if Abigail is unhappy with I.M. Just and wishes to fire him and hire Brenda Smart to carry on the case? What usually happens is that once Brenda Smart agrees to take the case, she prepares a notice of change of solicitors (form 15A), indicating that Abigail has changed lawyers, and serves it on I.M. Just and every other party or the lawyer for every other party, if the other party is represented by counsel (rule 15.03(1)). Then, with an affidavit of service or other proof of service, the notice is filed in the court office. The court amends its records to show who the new solicitor of record is. A notice of change of solicitors in Abigail's case is set out in figure 5.8.

Similarly, a party who has been representing himself or herself must also give notice, and serve on all other parties and file with the court, a notice of appointment of a solicitor in form 15B, with proof of service (rule 15.03(2)). An example of the notice is set out in figure 5.9.

A party who has a lawyer but who wishes to dispense with the lawyer's services and represent himself or herself may do so by serving his or her lawyer and all other parties with a notice of intention to act in person in form 15C (rule 15.03(3)). The notice should be filed in court with proof of service. An example of the notice is set out in figure 5.10.

Solicitor's lien

When a client changes lawyers, the former lawyer is entitled to a lien on the client's documents in the former lawyer's possession until the client has paid his or her account with the law firm. A party may bring a motion for an order to determine what, if any, right the former lawyer has to maintain and enforce the lien (rule 15.04).

Lawyer's request to be removed as solicitor of record

A client is free to change or remove a lawyer at will, but how does a lawyer get rid of a client? Once the lawyer is "on the record" as solicitor of record, he or she is expected to represent and protect the client's interest until the matter is concluded, the client serves a notice under rule 15.03, or the court makes an order relieving the lawyer of the responsibilities as solicitor of record. The lawyer cannot "fire" a client just because the client is difficult or obnoxious.

There are two primary reasons for a court's granting an order relieving a lawyer of the obligation to act for a party: the client has refused to pay the lawyer's account or the client refuses to give the lawyer instructions when asked for them. Refusal to

FIGURE 5.8   NOTICE OF CHANGE OF SOLICITORS (FORM 15A)

Court file no. 01-CV-5864

ONTARIO
SUPERIOR COURT OF JUSTICE

BETWEEN:

Abigail Boar

Plaintiff

and

Rattle Motors Ltd. and Fred Flogem

Defendants

NOTICE OF CHANGE OF SOLICITORS

The plaintiff, formerly represented by I.M. Just of Just & Coping, Barristers and Solicitors, has appointed Brenda Smart as solicitor of record.

Date: July 25, year 1

Brenda Smart
Barrister and Solicitor
1201 Bay Street - 458
Toronto, Ontario, M1P 2B9

TO:
I.M. Just
Just & Coping
Barristers and Solicitors
365 Bay Street – 8701
Toronto, Ontario, M3J 4A9
tel. 416-762-1342
fax 416-762-2300

AND TO:
Huey Sue
Barrister and Solicitor
65 False Trail
Toronto, Ontario, M6Y 1Z6

tel. 416-485-6891
fax 416-485-6892

Solicitor for the Defendants

FIGURE 5.9   NOTICE OF APPOINTMENT OF SOLICITOR (FORM 15B)

Court file no. 01-CV-8864

ONTARIO
SUPERIOR COURT OF JUSTICE

BETWEEN:

Abigail Boar

Plaintiff

and

Rattle Motors Ltd. and Fred Flogem

Defendants

NOTICE OF APPOINTMENT OF SOLICITOR

The plaintiff, Abigail Boar, **formerly acting in person, has appointed**
I.M. Just of Just & Coping, Barristers and Solicitors, **as**
solicitor of record.

July 25, year 1.

TO:
Huey Sue
Barrister and Solicitor
65 False Trail
Toronto, Ontario, M6Y 1Z6

tel. 416-485-6891
fax 416-485-6892

Solicitor for the Defendants
Just & Coping
Barristers and Solicitors
365 Bay Street - 8701
Toronto, Ontario, M3J 4A9

I.M. Just
tel. 416-762-1342
fax 416-762-2300

Solicitors for the Plaintiff

FIGURE 5.10   NOTICE OF INTENTION TO ACT IN PERSON (FORM 15C)

Court file no. 01-CV-8864

ONTARIO
SUPERIOR COURT OF JUSTICE

BETWEEN:

Abigail Boar

Plaintiff

and

Rattle Motors Ltd. and Fred Flogem

Defendants

NOTICE OF INTENTION TO ACT IN PERSON

The plaintiff, Abigail Boar, formerly represented by I.M.
Just as solicitor of record, intends to act in person.

Date: July 26, year 1

Abigail Boar
72 Sumach Street
Toronto, Ontario, M4R 1Z5
tel. 416-928-0001
fax. 416-928-0002

TO:
Just & Coping
Barristers and Solicitors
365 Bay Street - 8701
Toronto, Ontario, M3J 4A9

I.M. Just
tel. 416-762-1342
fax 416-762-2300

Solicitors for the Plaintiff

AND TO:
Huey Sue
Barrister and Solicitor
65 False Trail
Toronto, Ontario, M6Y 1Z6

tel. 416-485-6891
fax 416-485-6892

Solicitor for the Defendants

give instructions also includes giving instructions that are unlawful and that would require the lawyer to breach the rules of professional conduct or his or her duties as an officer of the court. In this case, because of rules requiring the lawyer to keep the client's confidence, the lawyer cannot usually reveal what the client has requested. Instead, the lawyer states that he or she is unable to obtain instructions.

To do this, a lawyer must serve the client with a notice of motion for an order to be removed as solicitor of record. The client must be served personally, by an alternative to personal service, or by mailing the motion to the client's last-known address. There are special rules for serving parties under a disability: The litigation guardian must be served along with the children's lawyer if the party is a minor, and the public guardian and trustee must be served in every other case. Corporations are also given notice in the motion to remove the solicitor from the record that they must retain new counsel or other suitable representation within 30 days after being served. The notice must inform the corporation that failure to obtain new representation may result in the case being dismissed, or the corporation's defence being struck out.

The affidavit to support the motion must give the court some reason to take the lawyer off the record because leaving the client unrepresented can have serious consequences for the client. The affidavit need not give details and should not violate solicitor–client privilege by revealing the contents of any disagreement on strategy or tactics between the lawyer and the client. A sample affidavit is set out in figure 5.11.

CHAPTER SUMMARY

This chapter was primarily concerned with joinder and severance of parties and issues from one proceeding into other proceedings. We began by examining the rules for determining who can be a party to a lawsuit and which claims can be included in a lawsuit. We noted that, where possible, unless it is prejudicial or inconvenient, all proper parties and claims should be included in one proceeding rather than several because this usually reduces cost and delay. We then turned to special rules governing lawsuits for and against parties under disability. We noted that minors and those with a mental incapacity must be represented by litigation guardians. If none can be found, the parties must be represented by the children's lawyer and public guardian and trustee, respectively.

Partnerships and sole proprietorships can sue or be sued in their business name or in the name of the owners. There are special provisions to assist you in finding out who the owners are or were at the relevant time. There are also provisions to include them as parties, particularly if you want their individual as well as their business assets available to satisfy a judgment.

Estates and trusts, unascertained persons, and the transmission by assignment of an interest in a lawsuit from a party to a non-party were also examined with respect to who is, or who represents, a party in proceedings. For more complex representative actions, we set out the highlights of the *Class Proceedings Act, 1992* and examined the specific procedural rules governing some aspects of class proceedings. Finally, we examined the circumstances in which a party can represent himself or herself as well as the circumstances in which a party must have a lawyer. We also examined the procedure for both lawyers and clients where someone wished to change lawyers once proceedings had started.

FIGURE 5.11 AFFIDAVIT IN SUPPORT OF MOTION FOR REMOVAL AS SOLICITOR OF RECORD (FORM 4D)

Court file no. 01-CV-8864

ONTARIO
SUPERIOR COURT OF JUSTICE

BETWEEN:

Abigail Boar

Plaintiff

and

Rattle Motors Ltd. and Fred Flogem

Defendants

AFFIDAVIT

I, I.M. Just, **lawyer in the law firm of** Just & Coping, **of the** City of Toronto, **in the Province of Ontario, MAKE OATH AND SAY:**

1. I am the solicitor of record for Abigail Boar, the plaintiff in this proceeding and, as such, have knowledge of the matters deposed to in this affidavit.
2. I commenced proceedings on behalf of the plaintiff with a statement of claim and have received the statement of defence filed by the defendants. The defendants have served a notice for examination for discovery to be held on February 10, year 1. I have repeatedly called and left messages for the plaintiff, and have written to advise her of the date for discovery and the need to prepare for it. She has not answered my letters, nor has she returned my calls or otherwise contacted me or given me instructions.
3. I am unable to act on behalf of the plaintiff without instructions from her.
4. The plaintiff's last-known address is 72 Sumach Street, Toronto, Ontario, M4R 1Z5.
5. I make this affidavit for an order to be removed as solicitor of record for the plaintiff.

Sworn before me at the)	
City of Toronto,)	*I.M. Just*
Province of Ontario,)	I.M. Just
on February 1, year 1.)	
)	
Commissioner for Taking Affidavits)	

KEY TERMS

judgment *in personam*

judgment *in rem*

assignee

chose in action

assignor

stay proceedings

litigation guardian

absentee

children's lawyer

return date

executor

estate administrator

class proceeding fund

unincorporated association

solicitor of record

NOTES

1 See ss. 6 and 45 of the *Substitute Decisions Act, 1992*, SO 1992, c. 30, as amended.

2 "Attorney" as used here does not mean lawyer; it means a person who is authorized to act as an agent for another person.

3 If a person does not reside in Ontario, he or she probably has no assets in Ontario against which to enforce an order to pay costs. For that reason, a non-resident may be asked to post security for costs by depositing an asset or title to an asset with the court.

4 The children's lawyer has issued a memorandum setting out the information it requires and how it should be contacted. This document is reproduced in most commercially published versions of the rules.

5 There are some narrow exceptions. A shareholder may be liable for a corporate act in some circumstances for an amount equal to the value of his or her shares. Where the owner of all shares is also the directing mind of the corporation and uses it to shield himself or herself from liability, the court may "lift the corporate veil" and allow a plaintiff to sue the owner directly. But this is very unusual.

6 Or the French equivalent of these words.

7 See *Police Retirees of Ontario Inc. v. Ontario Municipal Employees' Retirement Board* (1997), 35 OR (3d) 177 (Gen. Div.); *Bruce (Township) v. Thornburn* (1986), 57 OR (2d) 77 (HC).

8 M. Cochrane, *Class Actions: A Guide to the Class Proceedings Act, 1992* (Aurora, ON: Canada Law Book, 1992); *Ontario's New Class Proceedings Act: Are You Prepared?* (Toronto: Law Society of Upper Canada, 1992). These sources became available right after the Act was proclaimed. Since they are a decade old, they should be used with caution, and cases cited should be rigorously updated.

9 See s. 5 of the *Class Proceedings Act, 1992*.

10 A party is free to represent himself or herself or use an agent in Small Claims Court.

REFERENCES

Absentees Act, RSO 1990, c. A.3.

Bankruptcy and Insolvency Act, RSC 1985, c. B-3, as amended.

Bruce (Township) v. Thornburn (1986), 57 OR (2d) 77 (HC).

Class Proceedings Act, 1992, SO 1992, c. 6.

Cochrane, M., *Class Actions: A Guide to the Class Proceedings Act, 1992* (Aurora, ON: Canada Law Book, 1992).

Mental Health Act, RSO 1990, c. M.7.

Ontario's New Class Proceedings Act: Are You Prepared? (Toronto: Law Society of Upper Canada, 1992).

Police Retirees of Ontario Inc. v. Ontario Municipal Employees' Retirement Board (1997), 35 OR (3d) 177 (Gen. Div.).

Rules of Civil Procedure, RRO 1990, reg. 194.

Substitute Decisions Act, 1992, SO 1992, c. 30.

REVIEW QUESTIONS

1. Abigail Boar would like to sue Fred Flogem for negligence in one proceeding, Rattle Motors Ltd. for negligence in another, and Skank Motorcar Company Ltd. in a third. Can she do this?

2. Can Abigail force defendants into the same lawsuit when the defendants have claims against each other?

3. In deciding to join or sever parties or issues, the court uses the balance of convenience test. Explain what this test is.

4. What are judgments *in personam* and *in rem*?

5. Can a party avoid joinder?

6. Can the court order two or more proceedings to be consolidated?

7. Suppose Abigail is 6 instead of 26 and wants to sue. Can she?

8. Why might a litigation guardian have to post security for costs?

9. How is a litigation guardian for a defendant appointed?

10. Who acts as litigation guardian if no one comes forward on behalf of the party under disability?

11. What obligations does a litigation guardian have toward a party under disability and toward the opposite party?

12. What happens if no one comes forward to act as litigation guardian for a defendant?

13. What happens if the court is not satisfied that there is an appropriate person to appoint as litigation guardian?

14. Can a litigation guardian be removed?

15. Suppose Fred Flogem is a party under disability and fails to file a statement of defence. Can Abigail sign default judgment?

16. Can a litigation guardian settle a case on behalf of the party under disability?

17. If Rattle Motors is a sole proprietorship owned by Fred Flogem, who should Abigail sue?

18. Would it make a difference if Regina Rattle and Fred Flogem owned Rattle Motors as partners?

19. When does a partner file a separate statement of defence from that of the partnership?

20. Suppose you do a name search of Rattle Motors and discover that Rattle is a trade name. The business is owned by 1234 Ontario Ltd. What party do you sue?

21. Whom does I.M. Just sue if he discovers that Abigail's estate has no estate representative?

22. If your law firm sues Abigail and she dies after the action is commenced, can you continue to sue her?

23. How does a class proceeding differ from other types of representative proceedings?

24. What must be done to turn a lawsuit into a class proceeding?

25. May any litigant represent himself or herself in a proceeding?

26. What does the phrase "on the record" mean?

27. What does Abigail need to do if she wishes to change lawyers or remove her lawyer and represent herself?

DISCUSSION QUESTIONS

1. Herkimer Spittoon, aged 26, is an electrical engineer and brother of Sam Spittoon. On August 4, year 2, Herkimer suffered brain injuries when he was involved in an automobile collision. As a result of the injuries, he suffers from mood swings and impulsive behaviour, when he goes on wild spending sprees. He has little sense of financial reality, and does not understand that he is living on a small disability allowance and does not have the income he once had. He also does not understand or accept advice on the management of his financial affairs. A creditor has sued him for purchases he made on April 4, year 0. The claim was issued on June 4, Year 0 and served on June 6, year 0. Both Sam and Herkimer live in Toronto. Sam has just become aware that Herkimer has been sued. Sam has come to the law office you work in for some advice because Herkimer is ignoring the whole business.

   a. Explain to Sam why Herkimer cannot defend this action by himself, and explain what must be done.
   b. Explain to Sam what his duties are as litigation guardian.
   c. Draft the body of Sam's affidavit, assuming he is moving to be appointed litigation guardian.

2. Johnson Eversharp retained Huey Sue to act for him in a complicated piece of commercial litigation. The pleading stage has closed, and the opposition has served Huey with a notice of examination for discovery of Johnson to be held on August 14, year 0. On August 3, year 0, Huey's law clerk phoned Johnson but got the answering machine. This happened on four subsequent days. Phone calls and e-mails to Johnson's home got no better results. The date of discovery is rapidly approaching. Huey decides that this client is not cooperating and wants to get off the record before there are further difficulties. The client still has $1,000 to his credit in the law office trust account, which will cover services to date. Draft the body of Huey's affidavit.

CHAPTER 6

Commencing proceedings

INTRODUCTION

In Ontario, you start a court proceeding in one of two ways: You bring either an action or an action. Rule 14.02 requires that a proceeding be commenced by way of an action unless either a specific rule or a statute requires otherwise. Rules 65 to 68, for example, require a proceeding to be commenced other than by way of action, but the vast majority of court proceedings are commenced by way of action.

PROCEEDINGS COMMENCED BY WAY OF ACTION

Rule 14.01(1) requires that all proceedings, either by way of action or by way of application be commenced with an originating process. Generally, the originating process that starts an action is a statement of claim, the precedent of which can be found in form 14A (general actions) or form 14B (mortgage actions). Some exceptions to this can be found in rule 14.03(1)(a) to (e).

Abigail Boar's action does not fit into exceptions, so her case will proceed by way of action and the originating process will likely be a statement of claim. But perhaps Abigail has been uncertain whether she wants to sue the defendants. She spends so much time thinking about what she is going to do that the limitation period for starting an action against Rattle Motors and Fred Flogem may be running out.

It takes time to properly draft a statement of claim and perhaps Abigail only goes to see a lawyer three days before the limitation period on her case is about to expire. This is a relatively common situation because most people without any legal training do not realize that limitation periods exist.

A **limitation period** is the time in which a plaintiff may sue another person whom he or she believes may be legally responsible for causing him or her damage. The limitation period in most cases is two years, but once the limitation period has passed, a plaintiff loses forever his or her right to sue. It is therefore very important that the court proceeding be started before the limitation period expires.

If I.M. Just, Abigail's lawyer, does not have enough time to draft a lengthy and detailed statement of claim before the limitation period expires, he can instead issue a notice of action under rule 14.03(2). Figure 6.1 sets out a notice of action for Abigail's case.

limitation period
specified time within which court proceedings must be commenced

The issuing of a notice of action stops the limitation period and gives Abigail 30 more days from the date the notice of action is issued to serve and file the statement of claim. If a notice of action is used, the form for the statement of claim changes a bit. Instead of using the general form 14A, the plaintiff who files a notice of action first must file a statement of claim using the prescribed form 14D. The claim made by the plaintiff in the notice of action is usually the same as the claim that is later made in the statement of claim. But sometimes more information about the plaintiff's claim comes to light after the notice of action has been filed. In that case, rule 14.03(5) allows the plaintiff to alter or extend the claim stated in the notice of action.

Issuing and filing originating process

The statement of claim is prepared in the lawyer's office. During this part of the procedure, the court is not involved. The lawyers and law clerks meet the client, take down the necessary information, and start the evidence-gathering process. Chapter 7 deals with how to draft a statement of claim. This chapter deals with initiating the court proceeding.

The court has no knowledge of a case until it receives the first court document. This is the originating process in an action that is a statement of claim or a notice of action. The step that notifies the court that a proceeding has been commenced is called "**issuing**." A statement of claim and all other originating processes must be issued in order to commence a proceeding.

issuing
official commencement of court proceedings whereby documents that are originating processes are signed by the registrar, dated, sealed with a court seal, and given a file number

The process of issuing is dealt with in rule 4.07. In order to issue Abigail's statement of claim, her lawyers must have the law clerk, or someone else from their office, take the document to the court office to have the registrar sign it, date it, and put a seal on it. It is the court seal that lets the other side know that the court proceeding is genuine. During the issuing, the registrar also assigns a court file number to the action. At this point, the court opens a file, which will later hold other court documents relating to the case. Until the registrar assigns a court file number, the space on the statement of claim for the number remains blank. Once a number is assigned, this number must appear on every other pleading when it is prepared in the law office.

Only in very small court offices does the registrar personally sign each originating process. In big court offices, as in Toronto, numerous court staff who work in the issuing office are designated by the registrar to sign the documents on his or her behalf.

Issuing the document also requires the payment of a fee. If you were the law clerk sent to the court by Abigail's lawyer, in order to issue the claim, you would have to take a cheque from the law firm, made out to the minister of finance in the required amount. The current fee for various court functions can be obtained by calling the court office or by checking on the Ontario government's Web site under the Ministry of the Attorney General. You can find the site at http://www.gov.on.ca. You should take two copies of your document with you. Only one copy will be signed and sealed. The original signed and sealed document will be returned to you, and the court will keep a copy in its file.

While the court clerk is signing and preparing the original, you need to create a true copy for the court to keep in its file. This is done by copying by hand, everything that the clerk is writing on the original. You put the signature of the registrar in quotation marks to indicate that it is a copy of the signature and not the original. On your copy, you put a circle on the document in the same place that the clerk affixes

FIGURE 6.1   NOTICE OF ACTION (FORM 14C)

Court file no. 01-CV-1234

ONTARIO
SUPERIOR COURT OF JUSTICE

BETWEEN:

Abigail Boar

Plaintiff

and

Rattle Motors Ltd. and Fred Flogem

Defendants

NOTICE OF ACTION

TO THE DEFENDANT

A LEGAL PROCEEDING HAS BEEN COMMENCED AGAINST YOU by the plaintiff. The claim made against you is set out in the statement of claim served with this notice of action.

IF YOU WISH TO DEFEND THIS PROCEEDING, you or an Ontario lawyer acting for you must prepare a statement of defence in Form 18A prescribed by the Rules of Civil Procedure, serve it on the plaintiff's lawyer or, where the plaintiff does not have a lawyer, serve it on the plaintiff, and file it, with proof of service, in this court office, WITHIN TWENTY DAYS after this notice of action is served on you, if you are served in Ontario.

If you are served in another province or territory of Canada or in the United States of America, the period for serving and filing your statement of defence is forty days. If you are served outside Canada and the United States of America, the period is sixty days.

Instead of serving and filing a statement of defence, you may serve and file a notice of intent to defend in Form 18B prescribed by the Rules of Civil Procedure. This will entitle you to ten more days within which to serve and file your statement of defence.

IF YOU FAIL TO DEFEND THIS PROCEEDING, JUDGMENT MAY BE GIVEN AGAINST YOU IN YOUR ABSENCE AND WITHOUT FURTHER NOTICE TO YOU. IF YOU WISH TO DEFEND THIS PROCEEDING BUT ARE UNABLE TO PAY LEGAL FEES, LEGAL AID MAY BE AVAILABLE TO YOU BY CONTACTING A LOCAL LEGAL AID OFFICE.

IF YOU PAY THE PLAINTIFF'S CLAIM, and $500.00 for costs, within the time for serving and filing your statement of defence, you may move to have this proceeding dismissed by the court. If you believe the amount claimed for costs is excessive, you may pay the plaintiff's claim and $400.00 for costs and have the costs assessed by the court.

FIGURE 6.1 CONTINUED

Date: January 4, year 1

Issued by: _____

Address of

court office: Court House
                393 University Avenue
                Toronto, Ontario, M5G 1Y8

TO:

Rattle Motors Ltd.
1240 Bay Street
Toronto, Ontario, M8H 0K8

AND TO:

Fred Flogem
21 Cypress Boulevard
Scarborough, Ontario, M8Q 1P3

tel. 416-886-1123

---

truing up
making a handmade copy of a document at the court counter

the court seal. Inside the circle, write the word "seal." This process of making a true copy at the court counter, while your document is being issued, is called "**truing up**" the document. Once the original has been issued, the clerk will give it back to you and take your true copy for the court file. The original sealed document is kept in the client's file in the law office. You can then make copies of it on a photocopier for serving on the other side.

If you start your action with a notice of action instead of a statement of claim, it is only the notice of action that is issued. The statement of claim is filed with the court when it is ready. This means that the court seal is on the notice of action and not on the statement of claim.

Whether the action is started by a statement of claim or a notice of objection, you must also file form 14F, Information for Court Use (see figure 6.2).

Issuing and filing in Toronto and Ottawa courts

Toronto and Ottawa courts have a special procedure called "case management," which is set out in rule 77 and described in detail in chapter 21. You should remember, however, that if you are doing anything in the Toronto or Ottawa courts, you should check the regular procedure in the rules for that step, and then check the case management rule to see what exceptions or additions might be involved.

Time limits for serving the statement of claim

Once the statement of claim is issued, you can serve it on the other side. Chapter 8 deals with the specific steps required to serve a court document. Very simply, service of a document means giving a copy of the document to the other side. Abigail's lawyer will have to ensure that both Rattle Motors and Fred Flogem are given copies of the claim according to the methods prescribed in the rules.

FIGURE 6.2   INFORMATION FOR COURT USE (FORM 14F)

Form 14F

Courts of Justice Act

INFORMATION FOR COURT USE

Court file no. 01-CV-1234

SUPERIOR COURT OF JUSTICE

B E T W E E N:

Abigail Boar

Plaintiff

and

Rattle Motors Ltd. and Fred Flogem

Defendants

INFORMATION FOR COURT USE

This action is for:

collection	☐	construction lien	☐
motor vehicle	☐	negligence	☒
real property	☐	landlord/tenant	☐
contract/commercial	☐	trust/fiduciary duty	☐
wrongful dismissal	☐	medical malpractice	☐
estates	☐	other professional malpractice	☐
bankruptcy	☐	other	☐

Rule 76 (Simplified Procedure) applies to this action   ☐ yes
    ☒ no

Rule 77 (Civil Case Management) applies to this action   ☒ yes
    ☐ no

If Rule 77 applies, choice of track is:

Fast ☐   Standard ☒

Date of Issue: January 4, year 1

Just & Coping, Barristers and Solicitors
365 Bay Street – 8701
Toronto, ON M3J 4A9

I.M. Just
tel 416-762-1342
fax 416-762-2300
Solicitors for the Plaintiff

Rule 14.08(1) requires that the statement of claim be served within six months after it is issued. This means that you want to be certain of the defendant's location before you issue the statement of claim. Otherwise, you may spend more than six months looking for him or her. If your statement of claim cannot be served within six months, you will have to bring a motion before the court to extend the six-month time period. Usually, if there is a good reason why the statement of claim could not be served within the time period, an extension of time will be granted. In Abigail's case, we know the location of Rattle Motors and Fred Flogem.

If Abigail's lawyer must start the proceeding with a notice of action because a limitation period is about to expire, you do not serve the notice of action separately on the defendant. Both the notice of action and the statement of claim in form 14D are served on the defendant together. You have six months to serve the documents together, but the six months starts running as soon as the notice of action is issued, not when the statement of claim is filed later with the court.

In Toronto and Ottawa, there are special case management rules in place that add some different steps to the process of issuing and filing. These steps are provided in rule 77 and are dealt with in chapter 21.

Electronic issuing and filing of documents

The Ministry of the Attorney General has started a special project in Toronto to test electronic issuing and filing of documents. For now, the project is limited to the Toronto court, but eventually it is expected to be put into all court offices across the province. It is expected to cut down and perhaps to eliminate most of the paper that is filed in court proceedings. To be part of the project, a lawyer or law firm must sign up and have special e-mail accounts with the court office. The fee for issuing the statement of claim is charged to these accounts automatically when the lawyer or law firm uses the electronic system instead of having staff appear personally in the court office. If your law office is a participant, you will issue your statement of claim electronically by sending it to the court office by way of the special e-mail system. This is much faster than standing in line at the court office and waiting for your turn to have a court clerk issue your document. The rules say that if the electronic system is used, the document is considered issued when the court's computer accepts it and a court file number is attached to it. It is at that point that the six-month period for service begins to run.

PROCEEDINGS COMMENCED BY WAY OF APPLICATION

A court proceeding in the Ontario Superior Court of Justice may also be brought by way of application instead of action. Although proceeding by way of application is much faster and more expeditious than proceeding by way of action, the use of applications is limited. A proceeding must proceed by way of action unless a statute or the rules say it is to be commenced in some other manner (rule 14.01(1)).

There are a number of rules that require a proceeding by way of application instead of by way of an action.[1] In addition, rule 14.05(3) provides a list of types of situations where plaintiffs can proceed by way of application. Therefore, the first step is deciding whether or not the case you are commencing is one that can be commenced by way of application. If it does not fit in one of the categories provided by the rules and no statute authorizes you to proceed by way of application, then you must proceed by way of action and follow the steps outlined above in relation to actions.

There has been a recent change to the rules. Rule 14.05(3)(h) now permits an application to be brought on any matter where there are no material facts in dispute. Material facts are those central to the case.

If you can commence the action by way of application, you use a different originating process than you do with an action. In an application, you start the proceedings with a notice of application. The general form for a notice of application is form 14E, but there is a special notice of application if your application is for judicial review under rule 68 or is a proceeding to register an order from the United Kingdom for enforcement by the Ontario court under rule 73. For judicial review, you commence the application with a notice of application for judicial review using form 68A. For the registration of an order from the United Kingdom, you must use form 73A.

In addition to rule 14, rules 38 and 39 spell out the procedure and the evidence that are to be used on applications.

In an application, the parties are not called the plaintiff and the defendant. Instead, they are the applicant and the respondent. The application must state the rule or statute under which it is made and set out the precise relief sought and the grounds for the relief. It should list the documentary evidence that will be used in the hearing of the application. All applications are brought before a judge. A master has no jurisdiction to hear an application (rule 38.02).

Because a notice of application is an originating process, the court must issue it before it is served on the other side. It must then be served on all parties at least 10 days before the date of the hearing unless it is served outside Ontario. Then it must be served at least 20 days in advance.

One of the reasons that an application is a much faster procedure than an action is that it relies mostly on **affidavit** evidence. The affidavit is usually served on the respondent along with the notice of application. An affidavit is a sworn document that lays out the facts that a party is relying on. It is evidence in the proceeding. It must be clear, precise, and based on the knowledge or belief of the person who is swearing that the facts in the affidavit are true. See chapter 9 for more information on drafting affidavits.

affidavit
written statement setting out the evidence of the person who swears or affirms its contents are true

A respondent who has been served with a notice of application serves and files a notice of appearance in form 38A. An example of a notice of appearance is set out in figure 6.3. A respondent who does not serve and file the notice of appearance cannot file material, examine a witness, or take other steps in the proceeding, and is not entitled to any further notice of other steps in the application.

Applications heard in Toronto and Ottawa

Since proceedings in the Toronto and Ottawa courts are case managed, if you commence an application in this court, you must refer to rule 77 for additional requirements.

Material for use on the application

The applicant is required to serve and file an application record and a **factum**, along with proof of service, at least two days before the hearing of the application. A factum

factum
document that sets out the facts, statutes, and cases that a party relies on to obtain a favourable decision

FIGURE 6.3   NOTICE OF APPEARANCE (FORM 38A)

Court file no. 03-CL-8926

ONTARIO
SUPERIOR COURT OF JUSTICE

BETWEEN:

Dinglehoofer Office Supplies Ltd.

Applicant

and

Donaldson Printing Corporation

Respondent

APPLICATION UNDER the *Business Corporations Act*, RSO 1990, c.
B.16, ss. 207-18 and s. 248, as amended.

NOTICE OF APPEARANCE

The respondent intends to respond to this application

Date: March 10, year 2
Tilley Townsend
Barrister and Solicitor
10 Winding Road
Newmarket, Ontario
Tel 905-666-1010
Fax 905-666-1011

Solicitor for the Respondent

TO:
Fair and Duguid
Barristers and Solicitors
50 Justice Way
Suite 1000
Toronto, Ontario
M9V 6J2
Bonnie Fair
Tel 416-555-1225
Fax 416-555-1226

Solicitors for the Applicant

is a document that sets out the facts and the law on which the party relies. Rule 38.09 provides that an application record must contain the following information:

- a table of contents;

- a copy of the notice of application;

- a copy of all affidavits and other material served by any party for use on the application;

- a list of all relevant transcripts of evidence in chronological order, but not necessarily the transcripts themselves; and

- a copy of any other material in the court file that is necessary for the hearing of the application.

All of the above must be bound together in consecutively numbered pages and be in the order given.

The respondent must serve and file his or her factum, stating the facts and the law on which the respondent relies, at least four days before the hearing. The factum must be bound both front and back with white cover stock paper. For more information about factums, refer to chapter 20 on appeals.

If the respondent believes that the applicant's record is incomplete, he or she may serve and file his or her own application record. The respondent's application record must contain a table of contents, the exhibits relied on, and copies of any other material that the respondent intends to rely on at the hearing.

If for any reason either or both parties believe that an application record or a factum is not necessary for the hearing of the case, they may bring a motion before a judge, asking for an order dispensing with the application record and factum.

A party who wishes to rely on an transcript of evidence must file a copy of the transcript in accordance with rule 34.18. It must be filed at least two days before the hearing of the application.

Disposition of an application

After the judge has heard the application, he or she may grant the relief the applicant is seeking, dismiss the application, adjourn the application, or direct that the matter go to trial. If the application is ordered to trial, it is turned into an action.

Evidence on an application

Evidence on an application is presented in an affidavit, which is a sworn document laying out the facts in the case. It must be based on the personal knowledge or belief of the person who makes it and swears it to be true. The person who makes the affidavit is called the **deponent**. Although the evidence is written down and not given in court through witnesses, the opposite party has a right to cross-examine the deponent on the facts he or she claims to be true. On cross-examination, a lawyer for the opposite party asks questions to test the credibility of the deponent. The cross-examination takes place in the office of an official examiner or a reporting service (rule 34.02(1)). The evidence is recorded word-for-word, and a transcript is prepared. If a party wishes to present the cross-examination at the hearing, it does so by filing a copy of the transcript.

deponent
person who makes an affidavit

A lawyer who wants to cross-examine a witness on an affidavit must serve and file all the affidavits he or she intends to rely on in the hearing of the application. It is only then that he or she may cross-examine a deponent for the other side. Once a lawyer has conducted a cross-examination, he or she cannot file any more affidavits for his or her client without permission from the court.

For more information on affidavits and cross-examinations, you may refer to chapter 9 on motions and chapter 14 on discovery.

Place and date of hearing of the application

The applicant names the place of hearing, which is usually the court nearest the place where the applicant resides. However, an application under the *Tenant Protection Act, 1997* is held in the county where the property is located (rule 38.03(1.1)).

You may pick any date for the hearing of the application when a judge is scheduled to hear applications as long as the hearing is estimated, by the lawyer, to take less than two hours. You need not obtain the date from the court before you complete and serve the notice of application (rule 38.03(2)). However, if the hearing is to take longer than two hours, a date must be obtained from the court office first unless it is an urgent case (rule 38.03(3)). An urgent matter may be scheduled for any day that applications are being heard in the court, even if it is going to take more than two hours to argue. In some courts, practice directions apply to the scheduling of applications, and you must therefore check if a practice direction exists for the court in which you wish to bring an application.

Figure 6.4 sets out a notice of application in form 14E.

CHAPTER SUMMARY

In Ontario, we have seen that all civil proceedings are commenced by way of application or by way of action. The rules require a proceeding to be commenced by way of action unless a statute or the rules require that it should be commenced by way of application.

The document that starts a court proceeding is called an originating process. There are different types of originating processes, depending on the type of court proceeding that is being started. All of the originating processes are listed under the definition in rule 1.03. Generally, the originating process that starts an action is a statement of claim. All originating processes, including a statement of claim, must be issued by the registrar of the court. A statement of claim must be served on the defendant within six months after it is issued. If the action is commenced by a notice of action, it is served along with the statement of claim. There are additional requirements for issuing a statement of claim in Toronto and Ottawa courts because these courts are case managed.

If the case is one that is proceeding by way of application, the originating process is a notice of application. We noted that it must also be issued before it is served, and it must be served at least 10 days before the hearing of the application. Once the application has been commenced, rule 38 dictates how the application proceeds through the court process. Rule 39 specifies what evidence can be brought. An application record and a factum must be filed in all applications.

FIGURE 6.4   NOTICE OF APPLICATION (FORM 14E)

Court file no. 03-CL-8926

ONTARIO
SUPERIOR COURT OF JUSTICE

BETWEEN:

Dinglehoofer Office Supplies Ltd.

Applicant

and

Donaldson Printing Corporation

Respondent

APPLICATION UNDER the *Business Corporations Act*, RSO 1990,
c. B.16, ss. 207-18 and s. 248, as amended.

NOTICE OF APPLICATION

TO THE RESPONDENT

A LEGAL PROCEEDING HAS BEEN COMMENCED by the applicant.
The claim made by the applicant appears on the following page.

THIS APPLICATION will come on for a hearing on March 10, year 2,
at 10:00 a.m., at Osgoode Hall, 130 Queen Street West, Toronto,
Ontario, M5H 2N5.

IF YOU WISH TO OPPOSE THIS APPLICATION, to receive notice of
any step in the application or to be served with any documents in the
application you or an Ontario lawyer acting for you must forthwith prepare
a notice of appearance in Form 38A prescribed by the Rules of Civil
Procedure, serve it on the applicant's lawyer or, where the applicant does
not have a lawyer, serve it on the applicant, and file it, with proof of service,
in this court office, and you or your lawyer must appear at the hearing.

IF YOU WISH TO PRESENT AFFIDAVIT OR OTHER DOCUMENTARY
EVIDENCE TO THE COURT OR TO EXAMINE OR CROSS-EXAMINE
WITNESSES ON THE APPLICATION, you or your lawyer must, in
addition to serving your notice of appearance, serve a copy of the
evidence on the applicant's lawyer or, where the applicant does not have
a lawyer, serve it on the applicant, and file it, with proof of service, in the
court office where the application is to be heard as soon as possible, but
at least two days before the hearing.

IF YOU FAIL TO APPEAR AT THE HEARING, JUDGMENT MAY BE
GIVEN IN YOUR ABSENCE AND WITHOUT FURTHER NOTICE TO
YOU. IF YOU WISH TO OPPOSE THIS APPLICATION BUT ARE
UNABLE TO PAY LEGAL FEES, LEGAL AID MAY BE AVAILABLE TO
YOU BY CONTACTING A LOCAL LEGAL AID OFFICE.

FIGURE 6.4 CONTINUED

Date: February 26, year 2

Issued by: _____

Address of
court office: Court House
                393 University Ave.
                Toronto, Ontario, M5G 1Y8

TO:

Donaldson Printing Corporation
3276 College Street North,
Toronto, Ontario, M7Y 4F7

APPLICATION

1. **The applicant makes application** pursuant to the Ontario *Business Corporations Act*, RSO 1990, c. B.16, s. 207, for
   a. an order that the voluntary winding up of the respondent corporation be continued under supervision of the court;
   b. the costs of the application; and
   c. such other order as seems just to this court.

2. **The grounds for the application are:**
   a. the applicant is a creditor of the respondent corporation, which is currently in the process of being voluntarily wound up;
   b. the respondent corporation owes the applicant a debt for supplies in the amount of $5,000.
   c. it is not in the interests of the contributories and creditors that the proceedings should be continued under the supervision of the court for the following reasons:
      i. (*here set out reasons*)
   d. the applicant relies on the provisions of the *Business Corporations Act,* RSO 1990, c. B.16, ss. 207–218 and s. 248.

3. **The following documentary evidence will be used at the hearing of the application:**

   affidavit of Bradley Pittbottom, president of the applicant corporation, dated February 20, year 2 and the exhibit referred to therein.

Date of issue: February 26, year 2
Fair and Duguid
Barristers and Solicitors
50 Justice Way
Suite 1000
Toronto, Ontario, M9V 6J2

Bonnie Fair
Tel. 416-555-1225
Fax 416-555-1226

Solicitors for the Applicant

After the parties have presented their cases at the hearing of the application, the judge may dismiss the application, grant the relief the applicant is seeking, or adjourn the matter. These resolutions are similar in any other type of hearing. However, the judge has an additional option on an application: he or she may order that the application be turned into an action. If this occurs, any further steps in the case must follow the procedural requirements for an action.

KEY TERMS

limitation period

issuing

truing up

affidavit

factum

deponent

NOTE

1   See rules 5.01, 66.01, 67.01, and 69.01.

REFERENCES

Limitations Act, 2002, SO 2002, c. 24, sched. B.

Rules of Civil Procedure, RRO 1990, reg. 194.

Tenant Protection Act, 1997, SO 1997, c. 24.

REVIEW QUESTIONS

1. What are the two ways that a court case may be commenced in Ontario?

2. What is the originating process that usually commences an action? Can another originating process be used to start an action?

3. What is an issued document?

4. What do you have to do to "true up" an issued document, and when do you do it?

5. Why is it important to get as much information about the location of the defendant as possible before you issue the statement of claim?

6. Your client was one week away from the expiry of the limitation period under the *Limitations Act, 2002* when she contacted your office. You did not have time to prepare a statement of claim so you filed a notice of action to stop the limitation period from running out. Twenty-nine days after you issued the notice of action, you filed your statement of claim. How much time do you have left to serve the statement of claim?

7. Must you serve the notice of action on the other side?

8. Will Abigail Boar commence her court case by way of application or by way of action?

9. What is the procedure for obtaining a hearing date for an application?

10. What are the contents of an application record?

11. Under what circumstances would a respondent file an application record?

DISCUSSION QUESTION

1. Brad Pout, an avid horse enthusiast, met an experienced horse trader, Tom Craze. They discussed their mutual interests over lunch on several occasions and decided to go into partnership to carry on the business of buying horses. Brad contributed $100,000 to the partnership and Tom was to buy the horses, but he contributed no money. They did buy and sell many horses and made a big profit but they eventually had a falling out. Tom now wants to dissolve the partnership. There is $300,000 in the partnership bank account. Tom wants his half of the $300,000 because he says that he contributed all the work. Brad says Tom is only entitled to $100,000, which amounts to 50 percent of the profit after Brad deducts the money he put into the partnership in the beginning. Tom is relying on s. 5 of the *Partnership Act*, which allows a partner to make an application to the court for a dissolution of the partnership when circumstances have arisen that make it fair for the partnership to be dissolved. He wants the court to order that he receive $150,000 from the partnership's remaining assets. Draft a notice of application for Tom.

CHAPTER 7

Drafting pleadings

INTRODUCTION

In this chapter, we turn to some of the matters you must consider in drafting statements of claim and defence as well as replies to statements of defence. Drafting issues involving notices of application are dealt with in chapter 9 because procedurally and in terms of format notices of application have more in common with motions than they have with statements of claim. The procedural aspects of commencing an action are discussed in chapter 6.

GENERAL DRAFTING CONSIDERATIONS

Getting organized

Before you start to draft a statement of claim or other pleading, you need to think about what you wish to say and organize your material. As a law clerk, you will usually be working under the supervision of a lawyer. Speak to him or her to be sure you understand your instructions and the theory of the case. The theory of the case is the focus or basis of liability on which you organize the facts and decide which facts are relevant. For example, if I.M. Just's theory is that Abigail Boar was injured solely because of the negligence of Fred Flogem, you include only allegations about what Fred did or did not do properly. You do not include statements to show that Rattle Motors Ltd. or Skank Motorcar Company Ltd. is liable. If, on the other hand, I.M. Just's theory is that Fred was negligent, Rattle Motors is responsible for Fred's acts, and Skank Motorcar negligently manufactured the car that caused the oil leak, you include allegations about Skank Motorcar and statements of law that Rattle Motors is responsible for the negligent acts of its employees. What you plead depends on the theory of the case.

Assemble and review the interview notes from meetings with the client and with any witnesses. Also review client documents, expert reports, or any other evidentiary material you have. Summarize the evidence on the facts that you will plead. If there is no hope of proving a fact because there is no evidence to support it, the fact should not be pleaded, and the supervising lawyer may need to revise his or her theory of the case.

Peruse precedents for other statements of claim in the firm's files. Most firms keep precedent binders, and you should too, starting with the forms and documents you create in this course and other courses as assignments and projects. A precedent can show you the proper format, act as a guide for drafting an outline, and sometimes give you the standard language to express a certain claim or principle of law. But precedents should be used with caution. You are unlikely to find a statement of claim into which you can simply plug in Abigail's name. You need to look at precedents critically, being prepared to use your own language to express your meaning and purpose. Be aware that many precedents, particularly older ones, use what is called the common law drafting style — an archaic legal style that is repetitious and full of jargon. Mercifully, it is fast disappearing as young lawyers in Ontario are trained to use plain language drafting techniques. Plain language has been part of the bar admission curriculum since 1990 and has had some impact on drafting. This style, also referred to as the Citibank style, originated with loan agreements used by the First National City Bank of New York, a major American commercial bank. The simpler and clearer documents used by the bank have been credited with reducing the volume of the bank's litigation by reducing the ambiguity of the documents. Plain language drafting has since spread throughout the common law world. This plain language style is also used in modern Ontario statute drafting, and the contrast with older statutes is startling. Do not be afraid to use simple language to express your meaning. Cut to the chase. Avoid legal jargon such as "the plaintiff states and the fact is" or "the defendant alleges." Instead, say "the plaintiff states" or "the defendant states."

Prepare an outline. The format of the statement of claim and defence as outlined in forms 14A and 18A sets this out in part, but you still need to outline the facts and law you rely on.

Type out or dictate a first draft. With minimal polishing, this can be forwarded to a client for comment and feedback. A client will often have important corrections to make to basic facts as pleaded. As you revise and go to later drafts, be sure to label the draft with the date so you do not mistakenly rely on an earlier imperfect draft.

Revise and polish the draft after getting client and lawyer feedback. A law clerk should forward what he or she thinks is the final draft to the lawyer before serving and filing the pleading in question.

Check for internal consistency. If you make a cross-reference to another paragraph in the claim or to a fact alleged elsewhere in the claim, be sure your reference is in the right place.

Give the document a fast read to see that it flows logically and that the facts and law as pleaded support the theory of the case.

Language and tone

You already know that you should avoid jargon and legalese. Most commentators think that it is best to use simple language in pleadings. Facts should be simply stated as facts. You need not search the thesaurus for a string of colourful adjectives to describe Abigail's pain. It is sufficient to describe it as "chronic and severe pain in the neck and back," for example. Use relatively short, blunt sentences that are devoid of flowery language. If a fact is material, it should be stated positively, and if possible, in a separate sentence. Tell the story in a logical way so that the reader can follow it. Usually, telling a story chronologically works well. Use an outline to be sure that you have included everything that is material and that the story flows logically.

DRAFTING STATEMENTS OF CLAIM
Format

The format of a claim is in part prescribed by rule 14 and form 14A.[1] It consists of the following, discussed in sequential order:

GENERAL HEADING AND TITLE OF PROCEEDINGS

The format for this is prescribed by form 4A. It must head every court document, including a statement of claim.

PRESCRIBED TEXT

Generally referred to as **boilerplate**, this is the part of the statement of claim that follows the general heading and title of proceedings. It begins with the words "TO THE DEFENDANT." The language here is prescribed by the rules, and the wording must appear in every claim. Fortunately, there is litigation software available that reproduces this and eliminates the need for copy typing and pre-printed forms. The boilerplate for the generic statement of claim, form 14A, is reproduced in figure 7.1 at the end of the chapter.

boilerplate
standard wording that is part of every copy of a particular type of document

The only information you need to plug into the boilerplate is the address of the court office, the date that the claim is issued, and an amount for costs. This should not be an astronomical sum and should reflect the cost of an uncontested action where the claim is paid right after it issues. An amount approximating $500 or $600 should be sufficient.

You will also need to prepare form 14F: information for court use. This form indicates what the main claim in the action is for and whether rule 76 (simplified procedure) and rule 77 (case management) apply. If rule 77 applies, you also need to indicate whether the proceeding will be on the fast or standard track. Form 14F must be served and filed with every statement of claim. Figure 6.2 in chapter 6 sets out a completed form 14F.

Format of pleadings: Rule 25.02

The body of the pleadings following the boilerplate is set out in consecutively numbered paragraphs. As far as possible, each allegation should be set out in a separate paragraph. This may make for some two- or three-sentence paragraphs, which may seem short to you, but they are appropriate for pleadings.

Claim for relief: Rule 25.09

The claim for relief, which is paragraph 1, begins with the words "The plaintiff claims." In it, you set out each head of damage together with an amount, where that amount is known, in separate subparagraphs. Other relief claimed, such as an injunction or a declaratory judgment, must be specified as well. If there is more than one plaintiff, the claims for each must be set out separately. If there is more than one defendant, you are obliged to set out how much you claim from each defendant for each claim you make unless the claim is made against all defendants jointly. Remember that each defendant is entitled to know the details of the claim made against him or her by each plaintiff.

general damages
monetary damages for pain and suffering that cannot be determined on the basis of a formula

special damages
monetary damages that are specific, ascertainable, and measured on an objective basis; sometimes referred to as out-of-pocket expenses

Abigail is likely to claim **general damages** and **special damages**. It is not always possible at the beginning of a lawsuit to determine what special damages will be at trial. For example, Abigail has become depressed and may be prescribed antidepressants. At the time the claim issues, she may have spent $300 for these, but she does not know how much she will have spent by the time of trial. Rule 25.06(9) provides a solution. The plaintiff is permitted to claim special damages calculated to the date of pleading and undertake to deliver particulars of further claims when known and, in any event, within 10 days of the start of the trial.

You should always claim prejudgment and postjudgment interest, which are available under ss. 127 to 30 of the *Courts of Justice Act* but will not be awarded unless they are specifically claimed. Prejudgment interest runs from the date the cause of action arises until judgment or payment so you need to insert that date. In this case, the cause of action arose on September 14, year 0, when Abigail was injured. Postjudgment interest runs from the date of judgment until payment. Because you do not know these dates, the bare claim is sufficient.

You must also claim costs: Failure to claim them means they may not be awarded. The practice has developed among some lawyers of claiming costs on a substantial indemnity basis. This is a punitive costs award, and judges award it when one party has behaved badly or improperly in the course of the litigation. In our view, you should simply claim costs without elaborating unless you believe this is a case for a punitive costs award — for example, where one side has tried to hide evidence or has behaved maliciously. In that case, a claim for substantial indemnity costs is appropriate. Otherwise, you should refrain from overstating your claim. When you do that, you raise your client's expectations, which cannot be fulfilled, and you fool neither your opponent nor the judge.

Most lawyers include a final claim for "such further relief as seems just to this court." This is probably unnecessary, but nearly all lawyers do it. It amounts to a security blanket to cover claims you should have made but did not. In fact, if you seek specific relief, you must state it in your claim, or the court cannot grant the relief at trial. This is because your opponent will say, with justification, that he or she is prejudiced in his or her defence because if the defendants had been aware of the claim at the beginning of the case, they would have prepared to defend it and presented their case differently. In a situation like this, the security blanket in the claim for relief will not help you. If there is a variation on a claim that is made within the scope of the pleadings, the security blanket is probably unnecessary. But most lawyers continue to put it in as if it were some kind of legal rabbit's foot or lucky charm. So, with misgivings, we include it too.

Abigail Boar's claim for relief against Fred Flogem and Rattle Motors Ltd. is set out in paragraph 1 of her statement of claim, which appears in figure 7.2 at the end of the chapter.

Cast of characters

After the claim for relief, which is set out in paragraph one, you identify in subsequent numbered paragraphs each plaintiff and each defendant. If a party is an individual, you say so. If it is relevant, you may wish to add a party's occupation, and you should add a general address, consisting of a town or city and province or state. Street addresses are not used as a matter of custom. The purpose of setting out the residence of an individual or, in the case of a party that is not an individual, the place where it carries on business, is to identify whether a party is a non-resident for purposes of service, determine whether the party should post security for costs, and identify other territorial jurisdiction issues. If the party is not an individual, its status should be set out: corporation, non-profit corporation, Crown corporation, or government agency, for example. This paragraph may also briefly describe the party's involvement in the case. An example of a cast of characters appears in paragraphs 2 to 4 of Abigail Boar's statement of claim, which is set out in figure 7.2.

Facts and law underlying the claim

In the subsequent paragraphs, you tell Abigail's story. Before doing this, however, we need to discuss a number of basic rules of pleading that apply to the drafting of claims and defences. There are also some rules that apply only to the drafting of defences, which we will discuss later in this chapter.

Plead material facts but not evidence: Rule 25.06(1)

You must plead a concise statement of material facts on which the party relies, but not the evidence that will be used to prove the facts of your case. There are three elements to this rule:

- Be concise.

- Plead material facts.

- Do not plead evidence.

"Concise" tells you not to use 15 words when 5 will do. Avoid flowery language and excessive use of adjectives. Keep sentences and paragraphs reasonably short, confining a material fact to a single sentence where possible. Don't be surprised to find yourself writing paragraphs of two to three sentences. This is probably not what you learned in English class, but then you weren't being asked to do this kind of specialized writing.

"Material facts" are the facts that are necessary to prove or defend the claim based on your theory of the case. Before you can know what the material facts are, you must be familiar with both the events involved in the case and the law that applies to the situation. For example, in Abigail's case, the material facts concern her slipping and falling on the oil on the floor. Because the law involved is the law of negligence, material facts will be those that show negligence by the defendants. Here your facts include the lawful entry of Abigail into the area where the oil spill was, the lack of lighting, the fact that Fred knew about the spill, the fact that he did nothing to clean it up, the fact that Abigail was not warned or protected, the fact that she fell, and the fact that she was injured. What may not be relevant in this instance, though it may be interesting, are the facts that Fred is married with five children, that Abigail is very fond of the colour red, and that she had a happy childhood. Similarly, it is of no relevance to Abigail's claim that Rattle Motors has sold far fewer cars this year than last and is teetering on bankruptcy. This last fact may be relevant in enforcing a judgment against Rattle Motors, but it is irrelevant to making a claim for negligence against it. Some of these facts may be relevant in some situations but not others. For example, if Abigail were going to participate in a psychological study relating colour preference to personality, then her preference for the colour red would be relevant indeed.

"Not pleading evidence" is the last element of this rule. Evidence of a material fact is information from which a material fact may be proven or deduced. For example, to state "the plaintiff fell because there was oil on the floor" is to state a material fact. But to go on to say "Abigail knew Fred was negligent because Fred admitted to Abigail that he knew about the spill and had not cleaned it up" is to set out the evidence (the admission) used to prove the material fact.

Pleading points of law: Rule 25.06(2)

Rule 25.06(2) permits you to plead any point of law in a claim or defence that is relevant to your case. If you are drawing a legal conclusion, the rule requires you to set out the facts on which that conclusion is based. For example, suppose Abigail wishes to claim against Rattle Motors by raising the issue that it is vicariously liable for the acts of its employees. To plead this principle of law, she needs to set out the material facts that underlie it: that Fred is an employee of Rattle Motors and that the acts of negligence complained of were done by Fred in the course of his employment. If you are pleading a statute or regulation as part of a point of law, be sure to give the full citation.

Pleading conditions precedent: Rule 25.06(3)

A condition precedent is something that must be done before one is legally entitled to do something else. For example, if one party refuses to close a real estate transaction, the other party may tender on the party refusing to close. In order to successfully tender, the tendering party must have met the conditions precedent for tendering by showing that he or she was ready, willing, and able to close the transaction before tendering. In an action, if one party alleges that he or she tendered on the other, this rule says that the allegation alone is sufficient, and that it is not necessary to also plead that the party was ready, willing, and able to close the transaction. In other words, you need not plead the performance of the conditions precedent to tendering. The performance of the conditions precedent are presumed without your having to state them. If the opposing party believes that the tendering process was defective because you had not fulfilled the conditions precedent, that party must say so in his or her response to your pleading, specifying the nature of the defect.

Inconsistent pleadings: Rule 25.06(4)

It is considered appropriate to plead inconsistent or apparently contradictory allegations in a claim or defence, provided that it is clear that the statements are made in the alternative. For example, in a negligence action involving a car accident, it is not always clear to the plaintiff, especially in the early stages of an action, exactly what acts of the defendant constitute negligence. The other driver may have failed to apply the brakes in time, or he or she may have been talking on a car phone and not paying proper attention, or his or her car may have been poorly maintained. In this situation, it is permissible to plead as follows: "the defendant failed to keep a proper lookout; or in the alternative, he failed to apply his brakes; or in the further alternative, his brakes malfunctioned because he had not properly maintained and serviced his vehicle." In this case, evidence on discovery or at trial may show that one or the other of these facts is correct.

The important thing is that the evidence at trial has to correspond to the case as pleaded. If the evidence shows that the negligence of the defendant was different from what the plaintiff said it was in his or her claim, the plaintiff may have his or her case dismissed for failing to prove the claim as pleaded. You are therefore encouraged to plead broadly and in the alternative where there is factual uncertainty of the type described here so that the range of possibilities pleaded will cover what is revealed at trial to have occurred.

The rule about pleading alternative versions presumes that of five versions pleaded in the alternative, one will be factually correct. But go back to our example of a motor vehicle collision: What if it turns out that the car had malfunctioning brakes *and* the driver was talking on the car phone and was not paying attention to the road. In this case, your pleading will catch the problem because you have covered both causes of the collision. However, if you suspect there is more than one cause but you are not sure which it is at the time of pleading, it is permissible to plead "the defendant failed to keep a proper lookout. *Further or in the alternative*, he failed to properly maintain his brakes so that they functioned properly."

No contradicting an allegation in a previous pleading: Rule 25.06(5)

Rule 25.06(5) identifies a situation where inconsistent or alternative pleading is not permitted. You may not in your reply to the statement of defence plead facts that contradict the facts in your earlier pleading or raise a new cause of action. If you wish to do so, you must move to amend your earlier pleading to include the new cause of action or to amend the facts in your previous pleading so that the facts in the claim are consistent with those in the reply. If you were allowed to plead different versions of the facts in the claim and the reply, you can see what the problem would be for the defence. The defendants have no procedural vehicle to counter the contradictory allegation (there is no statement of defence to a reply) nor do they know the case they have to meet, which is the prime purpose of pleadings. The purpose of a reply is not to permit the plaintiff to split her case, but to allow her to reply to issues raised in the statement of defence that were not covered in the claim.

At the same time, you do sometimes have to deal with a fact that is relevant but occurred after the statement of claim was issued. For example, if Abigail Boar recited her injuries as the basis for her damages in her claim, and then later more symptoms developed that indicated more serious injuries, she can get the new facts before the court. Rule 14.01(4) allows a party to rely on a fact that occurs after a proceeding commences, even though it is not specifically pleaded. However, the party relying on a new fact not connected to a fact previously pleaded should move to amend pleadings to include it. The purpose of this rule is to allow a party who has sustained damage to include damage discovered after pleadings where there is some relationship between the facts as pleaded and the facts as discovered later.

Pleading notice: Rule 25.06(6)

You can usually plead that notice was given by simply saying so: "The plaintiff gave the defendant notice to quit the premises." However, if the form of notice is material, you need to go into more detail. For example, if notice to a tenant to quit commercial premises must be given by registered mail, it is appropriate to plead it: "The plaintiff gave the defendant notice to quit the leased premises by giving notice in writing sent by registered mail to the defendant."

Pleading documents or conversations: Rule 25.06(7)

This rule echoes the requirement in rule 25.06(1) that pleadings be concise. If you are pleading the contents of a conversation, you need merely state the effect or purpose of a conversation or a document without repeating the precise conversation or document in its entirety. The exception to this rule occurs where the exact language is material, in which case the precise wording should be set out and surrounded by quotation marks.

Pleading the nature of an act or a state of mind: Rule 25.06(8)

This rule states that where the intentional torts of fraud, misrepresentation, or breach of trust are pleaded, the full facts underlying these allegations must be pleaded with more particularity or detail than pleading usually requires. The second branch of the rule says that if you are pleading a mental element such as malice, intent, or acting knowingly, it is permissible to state that the party acted with malice, or acted knowingly, or with intent without explicitly connecting the relevant allegations to specific factual events. The reason for this is that there is rarely a smoking gun when an allegation of malice is made — that is, the allegedly malicious party is unlikely to say, "I am motivated by my malice to act in this way." Instead, malice must be inferred from surrounding circumstances, which may be pleaded as facts. It is then up to counsel, in his or her submissions at trial, to use the facts as pleaded to make the appropriate inferences and draw the appropriate conclusions.

Place of trial

At the end of the claim, following the format of form 14A, you must state the place where you propose that the action be tried. Note that this may not be in the same city or region that the action was commenced. If so, remember that it is the plaintiff's responsibility to requisition the transmission of the court file from the court where the action was commenced to the court where the action is to be tried. This should be done once all pretrial matters have concluded and nothing further is to go into the file before trial.

Body of a statement of claim

The narrative part of Abigail Boar's claim begins at paragraph 5 and continues to the end of figure 7.2. Paragraphs 5 to 9 take you chronologically and sequentially through the events immediately leading up to the accident. They omit a lot from the original summary of Abigail's story as immaterial and irrelevant to the cause of action. It does not matter, for example, what Abigail's motivations were in deciding to buy the Super Coupe, nor whom she worked for, nor what her age was. These matters are not material to the issue of negligence.

At paragraph 10, we switch to describing Abigail's injuries and their effects. We provide the particulars of the damages, both general and special, that are described briefly in the claim for relief in paragraph 1. Paragraphs 10 to 11 describe the injuries themselves in a crisp matter-of-fact way, and paragraphs 12 to 15 describe the consequences for Abigail. The consequences are described chronologically in the sense that the earliest known consequences are described first, but information is also grouped by its effect on Abigail's lifestyle — an important factor in determining the extent of general damages. We do not connect specific injuries to special or general damages. That will be done in submissions later in the proceedings, although some lawyers do plead by identifying special and general damages. There is nothing wrong with that approach; it is simply a style preference. There is lots of room for good pleading in a variety of styles.

DRAFTING STATEMENTS OF DEFENCE

A statement of defence must follow the format prescribed by form 18A. It begins with the same general heading and title of proceedings (including the court file number) as used in the statement of claim. It then sets out the title, "STATEMENT OF DEFENCE." Paragraph 1 sets out admissions of allegations in the statement of claim, paragraph 2 sets out denials of allegations in the statement of claim, and paragraph 3 sets out allegations in the claim of which the defendants have no knowledge. After that, defendants set out in consecutively numbered paragraphs each allegation on which they rely for their defence, containing their version of the facts. All of the general rules of pleading in rule 25.06 apply to drafting statements of defence. Also applicable are some specific rules in rule 25.07.

Pleading admissions: Rule 25.07(1)

The defendant must admit every allegation of fact in the statement of claim that he or she deems to be correct by admitting that the paragraph containing it is accurate. For example, Fred and Rattle Motors will probably admit the allegations in paragraphs 2, 3, and 4 because these paragraphs accurately describe the legal status of the parties. But they probably will not admit much else. Many of the allegations that they may admit are in paragraphs that have allegations that they will not admit because their admission would hamper the defence. For example, look at paragraph 8: "The Super Coupe model was in an open area of the showroom, where two of the four spotlights on the car were off, so that one side of the car was well illuminated, and the other was not well illuminated."

The defendants may wish to admit that the car was in an open area and that some of the lights were off. But they may hotly deny that the area was not well illuminated. They may allege, for example, that there was other perfectly adequate lighting. If so, their best bet is to deny the allegation in the paragraph altogether and plead their own version later in the statement of defence. This gives them more control as to how they present their defence in terms of both substance and content, and it prevents them from inadvertently admitting something while trying to admit part of a paragraph. Rule 25.02 asks that you confine each allegation to one paragraph so that a paragraph can be admitted if the allegation is true. But often, as in our case, a paragraph will contain an allegation that cannot be admitted in its entirety. In that case, deny it and proceed.

Figure 7.3 (at the end of the chapter) presents the joint statement of defence of Rattle Motors Ltd. and Fred Flogem. In it, Fred and Rattle Motors admit Abigail's allegations in paragraph 1. We are assuming there is no conflict between the defendants on any issue.

Pleading denials: Rule 25.07(2)

If there are allegations that the defendant denies are true, he or she must deny the allegations by identifying the paragraph in the claim that contains them. Again, if some of the contents of the paragraph are to be admitted and some denied, then it is best to deny the whole paragraph and plead your version later in the defence. If you are silent on the allegations in a paragraph, they are deemed to be admitted. Each paragraph of the claim must be scrutinized carefully and critically. When in doubt, deny. Most lawyers follow this practice with the result that after (usually) admitting the paragraphs identifying the parties, they deny most, and often all, of the other paragraphs in the claim. You will note below that the defendants have neither admitted nor denied paragraph 1, the claim for relief, and paragraphs 5 and 6, which are non-controversial facts that may be omitted from the list of denials and can be admitted. It follows logically, and also according to the rule, that an allegation which is not denied or admitted is deemed to be admitted. But what happens when a defendant comes across an allegation that he or she cannot deny or admit because he knows nothing of it? In that case, it is permissible for the defendant to state that he or she has no knowledge of the allegation, in which case the plaintiff must prove it. It is not necessary for the defendant to deny the claim for relief if damages are claimed because damages are deemed to be in issue unless the defendant admits them (rule 27.07(6)).

Paragraph 2 of Fred and Rattle's statement of defence, set out in figure 7.3, contains their denial of Abigail's allegations.

Different version of the facts must be pleaded: Rule 25.07(3)

It is not sufficient for the defendant merely to deny the plaintiff's version of the facts. If the defendant has a different view of the facts, he or she is obliged to set it out in consecutively numbered paragraphs after having dealt with admissions and denials in paragraphs 1 and 2 of the statement of defence.

This is an appropriate place to deal with paragraphs in the statement of claim where the defendant wishes to deny some and admit other allegations: "The defendants admit that some of the spotlights on the Super Coupe were not lit but deny that the area around the car was not well illuminated." The rule explicitly prohibits a bare denial without an explanation. Before the creation of this rule, you might have seen statements of defence which simply denied the plaintiff's allegations: "The defendants deny every allegation in the statement of claim and put the plaintiff to the strict proof of them." This rule eliminates that approach.

Plead affirmative defences: Rule 25.07(4)

If a defence is more than a denial of the legal basis for the plaintiff's claim — for instance, a denial by the defendants that they were negligent — it is necessary to set out further defences and the facts on which they rest. For example, Abigail did not mention that she had two glasses of wine before coming to the defendants' premises. But if the defendants know of it, they may want to plead contributory negligence specifically. In the alternative, they may want to claim that Abigail became the sole author of her own misfortunes when she voluntarily put herself into an intoxicated state and, for that reason, fell and injured herself. If the defendants take this route, they are introducing a new issue, with new facts to support their position on that issue. As we will see, the plaintiff is entitled to deal with it in her reply to the statement of defence.

Effect of denying the existence of an agreement: Rule 25.07(5)

Where an agreement is alleged in a pleading, a denial of it in the statement of defence is deemed to be no more than a denial of the making of the agreement or a denial of facts from which an agreement can be implied by law. It is not to be construed as a denial that the alleged agreement was legal or sufficient in law to have an effect. If the defendant wishes to deny the legality or legal sufficiency of an agreement, he or she must set out the particulars on which he or she relies. For example, if a defendant denies entering into a lease with a plaintiff, it is sufficient to deny that there is a lease between the parties. If, however, the defendant also wishes to allege that the lease is invalid, he or she must state that the lease is invalid and give particulars — for example, it was not signed by the parties or a copy was not delivered to the defendant as required under its terms.

DRAFTING REPLIES

A reply to a statement of defence is necessary only when the defendant has pleaded a version of the facts or raised issues in the statement of defence that are different from the facts pleaded in the claim. A reply should be used in the following two situations:

1. Where a plaintiff contests the version of the facts as pleaded in the statement of defence, he or she should deliver a reply to the statement of defence, setting out his or her version of the facts unless this has been covered in the claim (rule 25.08(1)).

2. Where the defendant has raised a defence with which the statement of claim does not deal, the plaintiff should respond to this defence in the reply.

Other than in these two situations, no reply should be issued. If no reply is issued, the plaintiff is deemed to have denied the allegations in the statement of defence. In dealing with the version of facts set out in the defence, the plaintiff should admit any allegation of fact in the defence that is correct. If the defence alleges an agreement, the reply may deny it, in which case the denial is a denial of the making of an agreement or of the facts from which an agreement may be implied by law. It is not to be construed as a denial of the legality or legal sufficiency of the agreement (rule 25.09(2)). This must be pleaded specifically, as is the case under rule 25.07(5).

Figure 7.4 (at the end of the chapter) sets out Abigail Boar's reply to the statement of defence. You will notice in this example that the plaintiff does not bother to deny allegations she has already dealt with in the claim, but she denies those new allegations that allege intoxication, contributory negligence, exaggeration of damages, malingering, and failure to mitigate. None of these issues were raised in the claim, but having been raised in the defence, they must be answered if there is a version that the plaintiff wishes to advance — as is the case here, where Abigail states that her drinking did not contribute to her injuries. She also deals with the defendant's allegations about malingering, exaggerating her injuries, and failing to take steps to mitigate her damages. Remember that allegations in the reply cannot be inconsistent with or contradict statements in the claim. The defendant has to know which version of the facts the plaintiff is relying on. Where a reply is inconsistent with the claim, it is likely that the claim needs to be amended.

DEMAND FOR PARTICULARS

While a pleading must be a concise statement of material facts, it must not be so concise that it is impossible to respond to. While the modern version of the rules emphasizes the need to give full disclosure before trial to promote settlements, lawyers, for strategic reasons, often try to hold back as much information as possible. One of the ways of doing this is to plead enough to cover an issue without revealing important details. Those adopting this strategy hope that the lack of specificity will not be noticed and that the opponent can then be taken by surprise. This is a risky approach because a court may conclude that this kind of strategy amounts to trial by ambush. Penalties may await those who pursue this strategy. One should not assume that the other side is stupid. Other lawyers also know these strategies, and your opponent has a remedy when facing a pleading that is too general. Rule 25.10 permits a party to request particulars. If you receive such a request, you must supply the details requested. The initial request and the response to it may be by letter between law offices. But if the request is not answered within 10 days or if a party refuses to comply because he or she believes the request is unwarranted, the party making the request may ask the court on a notice of motion to order particulars. In considering the motion, the court asks itself whether the pleading is clear enough so that the opposite party can frame an answer to the issues raised and will not be surprised at trial. The information provided constitutes further detail of material facts; it is not so detailed as to amount to evidence.

Suppose Abigail had pleaded that as a result of her fall, she suffered "severe and catastrophic injuries that prevented her from working." This does not indicate what the injuries were or how they prevented Abigail from working, so the defendants cannot determine whether the damages claimed have any basis in fact. The defendants might then write to I.M. Just and ask him to provide details. They will likely be interested in knowing what specific injuries she sustained, the treatment for those injuries, the specific activities that the injuries prevent her from engaging in, the prognosis, her attempt to mitigate her damages, and whether she attempted to return to work.

STRIKING OUT PLEADINGS

Occasionally a pleading is so defective in failing to follow rule 25 that, on a motion by the other side, the court may strike out all or part of the pleading (rule 25.11). Usually the court gives leave to amend the pleading, but on occasion it strikes out a wholly unmeritorious pleading without leave to amend, in which case plaintiffs may have their claim dismissed or defendants may have judgment signed against them.

There are three general grounds for the court to strike all or part of a pleading or other document under rule 25.11:

- the contents of the pleading "may prejudice or delay the fair trial of an action";

- the contents are "scandalous, frivolous or vexatious"; and

- the contents constitute an "abuse of the process of the court."

A pleading may be defective because it violates all or one of these grounds. Generally, allegations that cannot be proven are deemed to be prejudicial because the opponent is being asked to respond to allegations or issues on which no proof can or will be offered. For example, if Abigail pleads the contents of documents that are not admissible in court, she cannot prove the allegations because she cannot present admissible evidence on them.[2] Therefore, the defendants should not have to respond to those allegations: it would not be fair, and that is what "prejudicial" really means. Similarly, allegations that stray well beyond the issue involved in the lawsuit may simply lengthen the pretrial and trial without being relevant to the matter being decided. A barrage of allegations only tenuously connected may be deemed to be improperly delaying proceedings if the issue being litigated involves only one dispute in the barrage.

A pleading is scandalous, frivolous, or vexatious when a fact is set out that could be proved but that would not be allowed to be proved. For example, if Fred and Rattle Motors wanted to undermine Abigail's credibility by showing her to be a person of low character, they might make various allegations about her general dishonesty. If these allegations are not relevant to the issues raised in the proceeding, then while they may be true and could be proved, they would likely not be allowed to be proved. This is not because they are scandalous[3] or shocking in the ordinary sense, but because they are irrelevant and immaterial to the issues being tried and are introduced solely to add "atmosphere." Some courts have asked whether the allegation can have any effect on the outcome. If not, it is probably scandalous, frivolous, or vexatious. If the issue in the lawsuit concerned Abigail's allegedly fraudulent behaviour, allegations about her general honesty, no matter how embarrassing or scandalous in the ordinary sense, are relevant and ought not to be struck out.

Any of the "bad" pleading behaviour described in the preceding paragraphs may also constitute an abuse of process, particularly when it is done knowingly or intentionally.

Where a pleading is attacked on an issue that goes to the court's jurisdiction or otherwise might lead to a final order disposing of the case in its entirety — either through dismissal of the action, or granting of judgment on the motion to strike a pleading — the motion should be brought before a judge, not a master. Masters have the jurisdiction to deal with procedural matters, but they do not usually have the power to make orders that finally dispose of the rights of the parties.

CHAPTER SUMMARY

In this chapter, you were introduced to the rules and conventions governing the drafting of claims, defences, and replies. We examined some of the steps that must be taken to organize material and information, develop a theory of the case, prepare outlines, and use sample precedents before drafting the document. When drafting you should try to use simple language that is clear and direct.

We then examined specific rules in rule 25, which governs all pleadings, as well as specific rules governing defences and replies. We illustrated how these rules work by setting out a claim, defence, and reply in Abigail Boar's case. Finally, we looked at what may be done if pleadings are inadequate, examining demands for particulars as well as motions to strike out pleadings that are manifestly defective.

KEY TERMS

boilerplate

general damages

special damages

NOTES

1 Form 14A is the generic version of a statement of claim. The subsequent versions of form 14 deal with various specialized types of claims.

2 *F. (M.) v. Sutherland*, July 5, 2000, doc. CA C32601 (Ont. CA).

3 Some cases use the word "embarrassing" in the same way that the word "scandalous" is used. The words have roughly the same meaning: immaterial, irrelevant, and introduced to create an atmosphere so as to make the other side look bad. Similarly, the terms "scandalous," "frivolous," and "vexatious" tend to be used synonymously in cases.

REFERENCES

Courts of Justice Act, RSO 1990, c. C.43.

F. (M.) v. Sutherland, July 5, 2000, doc. CA C32601 (Ont. CA).

Occupiers' Liability Act, RSO 1990, c. O.2.

Rules of Civil Procedure, RRO 1990, reg. 194.

REVIEW QUESTIONS

1. Edward Egregious, I.M. Just's law clerk, has just interviewed a client and intends to transcribe his notes into a statement of claim and issue it. Have you any advice for him?

2. Can Edward claim $15,000 for costs in the space provided on the boilerplate for costs?

3. Edward thinks that paragraphs in a pleading should be lengthy and detailed. Is he correct?

4. Edward wants to know the order in which you present information in the claim. Tell him what that order is.

5. In the following paragraphs, indicate which parts are material facts and which parts are evidence.

   a. The plaintiff states that the area was not properly lit. A lighting expert who examined the site confirmed this.

   b. The plaintiff states that the area was not properly illuminated. The defendant admitted this to the plaintiff at the time of the accident.

c. The standard of care exercised by the defendant was well below the standard followed by other engineers. One engineer referred to the standard as "antique," claiming no one she knew used it.

d. The defendant drove her car down Mill Lane at an excessive rate of speed for the road conditions. The speed was in excess of the stated speed limit.

e. In borrowing from the plaintiff, the defendant failed to disclose that he was about to be petitioned into bankruptcy. The defendant knew this because he had had a letter from another creditor advising him that he would be petitioned into bankruptcy if he did not pay what was owing.

6. In drafting Abigail's claim, suppose Edward set out the facts leading to Abigail's fall, the damages sustained, and then followed with a statement that the defendant Fred was negligent and caused harm to the plaintiff, for which the corporate defendant is legally responsible. How would you advise him in improving his efforts?

7. Suppose Elizabeth Egret placed an order to buy some Framitses. The contract requires a 10 percent deposit before Egmont Pigeon will ship the goods. In her claim for delivery of the goods, Elizabeth states that she demanded delivery in accordance with the terms of the contract but that the defendant neglected or refused to deliver the goods. Is that a sufficient statement of her right to delivery?

8. Edward wants to plead that Fred was negligent in turning off the spotlights or in the alternative that he did it knowingly or with reckless intent. Can he do this?

9. Is it permissible for Edward to plead negligence in the claim and to state in the reply to the statement of defence that the defendants conspired to injure Abigail intentionally?

10. If Abigail has a claim that rests on the contents of a 10-page contract, does she need to quote the whole contract in the statement of claim?

11. If Abigail wants to claim that Fred attempted to defraud her, is it sufficient for her to state that Fred acted fraudulently?

12. If Abigail commences the proceeding in Brampton but wishes to have it tried in Toronto, what does she do?

13. Fiona Flapdoodle must prepare the defendant's statement of defence. She wants to know what she needs to include and in what order.

14. If a defendant wishes to deny that he or she entered into an agreement, how does the defendant do it?

15. When should a reply be issued?

16. In what situations should you demand particulars?

17. When might a lawyer move to strike all or part of a pleading?

DISCUSSION QUESTIONS

1. Sarah Jacobs, her husband Jack Jacobs, and her 15-year-old daughter Mary kept their boat at Tom's Marina near their cottage. Since summer was approaching, they wanted to arrange to get their boat ready for the season. The Jacobs went to Tom Shanks's marina on May 24, 1999. When the Jacobs arrived at the marina, Tom Shanks, the owner and sole proprietor, was not there, but his long-time employee Kevin Coaster was in the main office. Kevin said that he would take them down the dock to their boat. He knew a shortcut along a dock at the side of the marina office. The Jacobs followed Kevin. As they were walking along the dock, several planks gave way because they were rotten. Sarah fell against a support beam, hitting the lower part of her face and then her arm as she fell backwards into the water. Mary injured her ribs when she also fell against the support beam. The Jacobs have come to your law firm. They want to sue for their injuries. Draft a statement of claim.

2. Your law firm is acting for Tom Shanks. He is very annoyed with Kevin Coaster since he had told Kevin repeatedly that Kevin was not to take the shortcut because the dock is a mess and there are a lot of rotten boards. He also says Kevin was not supposed to be at work that day and that the marina was to be shut and locked until he arrived later. Tom wants you to draft his defence.

FIGURE 7.1 STATEMENT OF CLAIM (GENERAL) (FORM 14A)

STATEMENT OF CLAIM

TO THE DEFENDANT

A LEGAL PROCEEDING HAS BEEN COMMENCED AGAINST YOU by the plaintiff. The claim made against you is set out in the following pages.

IF YOU WISH TO DEFEND THIS PROCEEDING, you or an Ontario lawyer acting for you must prepare a statement of defence in Form 18A prescribed by the Rules of Civil Procedure, serve it on the plaintiff's lawyer or, where the plaintiff does not have a lawyer, serve it on the plaintiff, and file it, with proof of service in this court office, WITHIN TWENTY DAYS after this statement of claim is served on you, if you are served in Ontario.

If you are served in another province or territory of Canada or in the United States of America, the period for serving and filing your statement of defence is forty days. If you are served outside Canada and the United States of America, the period is sixty days.

Instead of serving and filing a statement of defence, you may serve and file a notice of intent to defend in Form 18B prescribed by the Rules of Civil Procedure. This will entitle you to ten more days within which to serve and file your statement of defence.

IF YOU FAIL TO DEFEND THIS PROCEEDING, JUDGMENT MAY BE GIVEN AGAINST YOU IN YOUR ABSENCE AND WITHOUT FURTHER NOTICE TO YOU. IF YOU WISH TO DEFEND THIS PROCEEDING BUT ARE UNABLE TO PAY LEGAL FEES, LEGAL AID MAY BE AVAILABLE TO YOU BY CONTACTING A LOCAL LEGAL AID OFFICE.

(Where the claim made is for money only, include the following:)

IF YOU PAY THE PLAINTIFF'S CLAIM, and $_____ for costs, within the time for serving and filing your statement of defence, you may move to have this proceeding dismissed by the court. If you believe the amount claimed for costs is excessive, you may pay the plaintiff's claim and $500.00 for costs and have the costs assessed by the court.

Date: _____   Issued by: _____

Address of
court office: _____

_____

TO: *(Name and address of each defendant)*

FIGURE 7.2 STATEMENT OF CLAIM OF ABIGAIL BOAR (FORM 14A)

Court file no. 01-CV-1234

ONTARIO
SUPERIOR COURT OF JUSTICE

BETWEEN:

Abigail Boar

Plaintiff

and

Rattle Motors Ltd. and Fred Flogem

Defendants

STATEMENT OF CLAIM

TO THE DEFENDANTS

A LEGAL PROCEEDING HAS BEEN COMMENCED AGAINST YOU by the plaintiff. The claim made against you is set out in the following pages.

IF YOU WISH TO DEFEND THIS PROCEEDING, you or an Ontario lawyer acting for you must prepare a statement of defence in Form 18A prescribed by the Rules of Civil Procedure, serve it on the plaintiff's lawyer or, where the plaintiff does not have a lawyer, serve it on the plaintiff, and file it, with proof of service, in this court office, WITHIN TWENTY DAYS after this statement of claim is served on you, if you are served in Ontario.

If you are served in another province or territory of Canada or in the United States of America, the period for serving and filing your statement of defence is forty days. If you are served outside Canada and the United States of America, the period is sixty days.

Instead of serving and filing a statement of defence, you may serve and file a notice of intent to defend in Form 18B prescribed by the Rules of Civil Procedure. This will entitle you to ten more days within which to serve and file your statement of defence.

IF YOU FAIL TO DEFEND THIS PROCEEDING, JUDGMENT MAY BE GIVEN AGAINST YOU IN YOUR ABSENCE AND WITHOUT FURTHER NOTICE TO YOU. IF YOU WISH TO DEFEND THIS PROCEEDING BUT ARE UNABLE TO PAY LEGAL FEES, LEGAL AID MAY BE AVAILABLE TO YOU BY CONTACTING A LOCAL LEGAL AID OFFICE.

IF YOU PAY THE PLAINTIFF'S CLAIM, and $500.00 for costs, within the time for serving and filing your statement of defence, you may move to have this proceeding dismissed by the court. If you believe the amount claimed for costs is excessive, you may pay the plaintiff's claim and $500.00 for costs and have the costs assessed by the court.

FIGURE 7.2   CONTINUED

Date: January 4, year 1

Issued by: _____

Address of
court office: Court House
393 University Avenue
Toronto, Ontario, M5G 1Y8

TO:

Rattle Motors Ltd.
1240 Bay Street
Toronto, Ontario, M8H 0K8

AND TO:

Fred Flogem
21 Cypress Boulevard
Scarborough, Ontario, M8Q 1P3

tel. 416-886-1123

CLAIM

1. The plaintiff claims, against both defendants:
   a. general damages in the amount of $200,000;
   b. special damages in the amount of $3,649 to the date of this pleading. The full extent of special damages is not yet known, but full particulars will be furnished before the date of trial.
   c. prejudgment interest from September 14, year 0 to the date of payment or judgment pursuant to the *Courts of Justice Act*, RSO 1990, c. C.43;
   d. postjudgment interest from the date of judgment to the date of payment pursuant to the *Courts of Justice Act*, RSO 1990, c. C.43;
   e. costs of this action; and
   f. such further relief as seems just to this court.
2. The plaintiff is an individual who resides in the City of Toronto, in the Province of Ontario, and at the relevant time was a customer lawfully on the premises of the corporate defendant.
3. The defendant Fred Flogem is an individual who resides in the City of Toronto, in the Province of Ontario, and at the relevant time was an employee of the corporate defendant.
4. The defendant Rattle Motors Ltd. is a business corporation, incorporated under the laws of Ontario with business premises in the City of Toronto, in the Province of Ontario.
5. On September 14, year 0, at about 7:30 p.m., the plaintiff entered the retail automobile premises owned and operated by the defendant Rattle Motors Ltd. at 1240 Bay Street, in the City of Toronto, in the Province of Ontario, in order to view a Super Coupe, which she was thinking of purchasing, in the showroom.

FIGURE 7.2 CONTINUED

6. She was met at the door by Linda Lucre, a salesperson employed by the corporate defendant, who showed her some of the automobiles displayed on the showroom floor.

7. The plaintiff saw a Super Coupe model on the showroom floor and walked over to have a better look at it.

8. The Super Coupe model was in an open area of the showroom, where two of the four spotlights trained on the car were off, so that one side of the car was well illuminated while the other was not well illuminated.

9. The plaintiff walked around to the side of the car near the wall, which was in relative darkness. She walked onto a part of the floor that was covered with oil. Because of the restricted lighting, she did not see the oil, slipped on it, lost her footing, and fell.

10. As a result of the fall, she struck her head, suffered a concussion, and lost consciousness. She also fractured her right wrist and several bones in her right arm.

11. Following the fall, the plaintiff was hospitalized for 4 days and the plaintiff's arm was in a cast for 6 weeks; she suffered much pain and discomfort. In addition, she was required to attend for physiotherapy for 10 weeks after her cast was removed.

12. As a result of these injuries, the plaintiff suffers from pain in her arm and head as well as chronic lower back pain, and is unable to walk long distances or sit at a desk for long periods. She has limited mobility in her right arm and is unable to work at a computer keyboard for more than 10 minutes without experiencing pain. The plaintiff is right-handed and severely disadvantaged by these injuries.

13. Since she sustained these injuries, and as a result of them, the plaintiff has become far less active physically than she had been before the accident, and she is far less cheerful and gregarious than she had been. She is now quieter, more withdrawn, and has difficulty sleeping. She also suffers from depression. Before being injured, the plaintiff was an avid tennis player and a competent amateur violinist. Since sustaining the injuries, and as a result of them, she is unable to engage in either activity. She also has suffered some memory loss. In particular, she has no memory of sustaining the injuries complained of.

14. Since the plaintiff sustained these injuries, she has been unable to return to her work as a securities analyst. She returned to work for the month of March, year 1, but because of chronic pain, and difficulty using a computer which is essential to her work, she was unable to continue. She has been off work since April 1, year 1, and on long-term disability, where she remains at the time of pleading.

15. The plaintiff has suffered catastrophic and permanent injuries, and it is unlikely that she will ever be able to return to work as a securities analyst. At the time of injury, she earned $80,000 per year in this

FIGURE 7.2 CONTINUED

occupation. She would likely have had a lengthy career with a high level of income, had she not been injured.

16. The defendant Fred Flogem, a salesperson employed by the corporate defendant, caused the plaintiff's injuries through his negligence, for which the corporate defendant is at law responsible. The particulars of negligence are as follows:

a. He was aware that there was oil on the floor and knew or ought to have known that the oil constituted a danger to the safety of persons such as the plaintiff.

b. He knew or ought to have known that he had a duty to see that persons such as the plaintiff did not come to harm while on the premises.

c. He failed to clean up or remove the spill expeditiously, although he had the opportunity and the means to do so.

d. He turned off lighting that illuminated the area where the plaintiff fell, with the intention of making the oil spill less visible or noticeable to persons such as the plaintiff. By so doing, he negligently, or in the alternative knowingly, created a situation of danger for the plaintiff.

e. He knowingly created a situation of danger for the plaintiff by deliberately not taking steps to clean up the spill so as to hide a defect in the automobile from the plaintiff and other customers.

17. The corporate defendant is responsible for the injuries sustained by the plaintiff as a result of its negligence, the particulars of which are as follows:

a. It failed to take such care as was reasonable to see that the plaintiff entering the corporate defendant's showroom would be reasonably safe while on the property. The plaintiff pleads and relies on the *Occupier's Liability Act,* RSO 1990, c. O.2.

b. It failed to instruct its employees, including the individual defendant, in maintaining safe premises.

c. It knew or ought to have known that the floor area where the plaintiff fell was unsafe for the plaintiff.

d. It failed to maintain a system of inspection to ensure that the showroom was safe for persons on the premises, including the plaintiff.

e. In the alternative, it knowingly permitted the area where the plaintiff fell to remain in an unsafe condition so as not to attract customer attention to a defect in the car it was selling.

The Plaintiff proposes that this action be tried at Toronto.

FIGURE 7.2   CONTINUED

Date of issue: January 4, year 1

```
Just & Coping
Barristers and Solicitors
365 Bay Street - 8701
Toronto, Ontario, M3J 4A9

I.M. Just
tel. 416-762-1342
fax 416-762-2300

Solicitors for the Plaintiff
```

FIGURE 7.3   STATEMENT OF DEFENCE (FORM 18A)

Court file no. 01-CV-1234

ONTARIO
SUPERIOR COURT OF JUSTICE

BETWEEN:

Abigail Boar

Plaintiff

and

Rattle Motors Ltd. and Fred Flogem

Defendants

STATEMENT OF DEFENCE

1. The defendants admit the allegations contained in paragraphs 2, 3, and 4 of the statement of claim.
2. The defendants deny the allegations contained in paragraphs 7, 8, 9, 10, 11, 12, 13, 14, 15, 16, and 17 of the statement of claim.
3. The plaintiff entered the corporate defendant's premises at about 7:30 p.m. on September 14, year 0. She indicated to Linda Lucre, a salesperson on the showroom floor at that time, that she was interested in purchasing a Super Coupe.
4. Lucre showed the plaintiff several automobile models. Then the plaintiff walked over, on her own, to look at another model. She walked around the car and fell.
5. The defendants admit that there was a small pool of oil on one side of the car but claim that it was easily visible to any reasonably prudent person who could have avoided it without difficulty.
6. The defendants admit that two of the four spotlights were off but deny that the area was not well illuminated. The defendants state that the area was well and clearly illuminated. Any hazard, if there was one, which is specifically denied, could easily be seen and avoided.
7. The defendants admit that the plaintiff fell and appeared to lose consciousness momentarily. She also appeared to injure her lower right arm in the fall.
8. The defendants state that the plaintiff, before coming to the corporate defendant's place of business, had consumed two glasses of wine and that she was intoxicated when she entered the defendant's premises.
9. The plaintiff fell solely as a result of her intoxication. Any injuries she sustained were solely the result of her own intoxicated state and not any acts of the defendants.
10. With respect to paragraphs 10, 11, 12, 13, 14, and 15 of the statement of claim, the defendants deny that the plaintiff suffered such injuries as described. Further

FIGURE 7.3 CONTINUED

or in the alternative, the defendants state that the plaintiff has exaggerated both the extent of her injuries and the consequences of them.

11. With respect to the plaintiff's allegation that she cannot return to work, the defendants state that the plaintiff is exaggerating her injuries and that she is a malingerer. In the alternative, the defendants state that the plaintiff has failed to mitigate her damages.

12. With respect to the allegations of negligence in paragraph 16, the defendant Flogem states that he knew there was oil on the floor but that it was contained and did not constitute a danger to any reasonably prudent person. The defendant Flogem admits that he turned off two of the four spotlights, but he specifically denies that he created a situation of danger for the plaintiff because the area in question remained well illuminated and safe for a reasonably prudent person.

13. The defendants therefore request that this action be dismissed with costs.

Date: January 12, year 1

Huey Sue
Barrister and Solicitor
65 False Trail
Toronto, Ontario, M6Y 1Z6

tel. 416-485-6891
fax 416-485-6892

Solicitor for the Defendants

TO:

Just & Coping
Barristers and Solicitors
365 Bay Street – 8701
Toronto, Ontario, M3J 4A9

I.M. Just
tel. 416-762-1342
fax 416-762-2300

Solicitors for the Plaintiff

FIGURE 7.4 REPLY TO STATEMENT OF DEFENCE

Court file no. 01-CV-1234

ONTARIO
SUPERIOR COURT OF JUSTICE

BETWEEN:

Abigail Boar

Plaintiff

and

Rattle Motors Ltd. and Fred Flogem

Defendants

REPLY

1. The plaintiff denies the allegations in paragraphs 6, 7, 8, and 9 of the statement of defence.

2. The plaintiff admits that she had two glasses of wine at dinner, well before she entered the corporate defendant's premises, and she denies that she was intoxicated. She neither contributed to nor solely caused her fall and subsequent injuries.

3. The plaintiff states that she has made every effort to fully regain the good health she enjoyed before being injured, following medical advice and undertaking therapy and treatment as advised. Further, she was eager to return to work and did so for a period of one month but was unable to carry out her duties, which required extensive use of a computer, solely because of her injuries. The plaintiff specifically denies that she has exaggerated the extent and consequences of her injuries and denies that she has been malingering or has failed to mitigate her damages.

Date: February 2, year 1

Just & Coping
Barristers and Solicitors
365 Bay Street – 8701
Toronto, Ontario, M3J 4A9

I.M. Just
tel. 416-762-1342
fax 416-762-2300

Solicitors for the Plaintiff

TO:
Huey Sue
Barrister and Solicitor
65 False Trail
Toronto, Ontario, M6Y 1Z6

tel. 416-485-6891
fax 416-485-6892

Solicitor for the Defendants

CHAPTER 8

Service of court documents

INTRODUCTION

Once the initiating documents have been prepared, Abigail, as plaintiff, must let the court know that she wants to begin a court case, and she must let the defendants know about the details of the case that she is bringing against them. The process in which the plaintiff lets the court know about the case is called "issuing." We looked at issuing documents in chapter 6. The process in which she gives a copy of her pleadings or documents to the defendants is called "**service**."

As soon as the defendants know about Abigail's case against them, they will have a chance to prepare their defence to the allegations that Abigail is making. The defendants must give Abigail a copy of any documents they prepare in the case. (All the documents that are prepared in a court proceeding must be given to the other side.) It is through service of the documents that the parties exchange formal information about the court case. When service of the documents has been completed according to the rules, we say that service has been "effected."

Not only must the defendants know the details of the case that is brought against them, the court must also be satisfied that each side has provided the other side with their pleadings. Therefore, when pleadings are served, an additional document, proving service according to the rules, must be filed in the court along with the documents. This process is called providing "proof of service." Service is proven by way of affidavit. The person who served the document must, in writing, provide the details of how the document was served and swear that the details are true. The affidavit is called an affidavit of service, which appears as form 16B or 16C.

Rule 16 tells you how documents are to be served within Ontario. Rule 17 tells you how they are to be served if the other party is not in the Province of Ontario. Rule 4.05 tells you how documents are to be issued and filed in the court.

Although all documents in the court proceeding must be served on the other side, the rules require different methods of serving the document depending on the type of document. If a document is an originating process, it must be served in a different manner than other pleadings.

service
process by which documents are brought to the attention of a party in accordance with the rules or a court order

SERVICE OF AN ORIGINATING PROCESS

A document that is an **originating process** must be served either personally or by an alternative to personal service (rule 16.01(1)). If you are not certain whether the document with which you are working is an originating process, you must look

originating process
first document in a lawsuit that tells parties that they are being sued

at the definition of originating process in rule 1.03. If a pleadings is an originating process, it will be listed there. Any document not listed there is not an originating process and therefore does not need to be served using personal service or an alternative to personal service.

Personal service

There are not many originating processes that the rules specify can only be served personally, although there are some, such as a petition for divorce. Documents that specifically require personal service must be served in one of the ways outlined in rule 16.02. Where the rules require that a particular document in a proceeding be served personally, there is no alternative available. The document must be served according to rule 16.02.

According to rule 16.02(1)(a), personal service on an individual can be made by leaving a copy of the document with the person that you wish to serve. But if the individual is a person under a disability, there are special provisions as to how they are to be served personally (rule 16.02(1)(j) and (k)). For instance, if a party is a minor, the document is served on the minor's litigation guardian or, if there is no litigation guardian, on the minor *and* a parent who has custody of the child. Leaving the document with either the parent or the litigation guardian of the minor qualifies as personal service on the minor.

There are also specific provisions in rule 16.02 governing personal service on a corporation, a municipality, a partnership, a sole proprietorship, and other entities. When you are serving a document that requires personal service under the rules and the party is not a competent adult individual, refer to rule 16.02 to determine the manner in which you are required to serve your document.

Service by way of alternative service

If an originating process is not specifically required by the rules to be served personally, it can be served by means of an alternative to personal service. When a rule says a particular document can be served either personally or by an alternative to personal service and you decide to serve it by an alternative to personal service, you must look at rule 16.03, which lists the only alternatives to personal service permitted by the rules. There are three general alternatives to personal service and a fourth special provision for alternative service that relates only to corporations in Rule 16.03.

1. *Acceptance of service by a lawyer: Rule 16.03(2).* If the party to the proceeding has a lawyer, you may serve the lawyer with the document. However, this type of alternative to personal service is valid only if the lawyer agrees to accept the service on behalf of his or her client and signs a copy of the document acknowledging that he or she has accepted service. Most lawyers are not willing to do this unless they have specific permission from their client because by accepting service for their client, they are representing to the court that they have the authority to do so.

2. *Service by mail to the last-known address: Rule 16.03(4).* Service by mail is an effective alternative to personal service only if the person who is being served signs and returns the acknowledgment of receipt card, form 16A, which is sent along with the document that is being served. Form 16A appears

in the exhibit attached to figure 8.5. If the party fails to return the card, service is not valid.[1] Do not use this method unless you know beforehand that the party you are serving is cooperative and will return the card.

3. *Service at place of residence: Rule 16.03(5).* You may use this alternative method of service only if you have attempted, at least once, to serve the document personally. Then you may leave the document, in a sealed envelope, at the residence with a person who appears to be an adult. However, the same day or the day after you leave the document with someone at the residence, you must also send another copy of the document by mail to the person to be served.

4. *Service on a corporation: Rule 16.03(6).* This rule applies only when you wish to serve a corporation by an alternative to personal service. You may use this alternative method only after you have tried to effect personal service on the corporation and you find that the corporation is not at its last address registered with the Ministry of Consumer and Business Services. In that case, you may mail the document to the last registered address. It is quite possible that the corporation will not receive the document. However, because a corporation is required by statute to keep its records with the ministry up to date, the corporation's own failure to comply with legal requirements is the cause of this situation.

For example, if Abigail Boar tried to serve Rattle Motors Ltd. and found that it was no longer at its last-known address, her lawyer's clerk would do a search for the corporation's records with the Ministry of Consumer and Business Services. If the corporation had registered a new address with the ministry, Abigail would need to effect service at the new address. However, if Rattle Motors had failed to notify the ministry of its new address, Abigail's lawyer could simply have mailed the documents to that address and service would have been effected in accordance with the rules.

DOCUMENTS THAT CAN BE SERVED ON A PARTY'S SOLICITOR OF RECORD

Although a document that is an originating process can only be served personally or by an alternative to personal service, there is an additional service option available for a document that is not an originating process. A document that is not an originating process can usually be served on a solicitor of record for the party. This means that there are three options for the service of a document that is not an originating process:

1. it can be served personally,

2. it can be served by an alternative to personal service listed in the rules, or

3. it can be served on a party's solicitor of record.

Service can only be on a solicitor of record, not on a lawyer that the party may have consulted or retained in the past for a case. A lawyer becomes a solicitor of record only if he or she has either filed documents in a particular proceeding on behalf of the party or if he or she has appeared in court in this proceeding for the party.

Rule 16.05(1)(a) to (f) sets out how a solicitor of record may be served with documents that would otherwise require personal service or an alternative to personal service. These methods are:

- mailing a copy of the document to the lawyer's office,

- leaving a copy of the document with the lawyer or an employee in the lawyer's office,

- faxing a copy to the lawyer's office,

- e-mailing a copy of the document to the lawyer's office,

- sending a copy to the lawyer's office by courier, or

- depositing a copy of the document at a document exchange of which the lawyer is a member.

Service by fax on a solicitor of record

If you serve a solicitor of record by fax, there are special conditions under rule 16.05 to make this method of service effective.

- You must attach a cover page that includes all of the information required in rule 16.05(3).

- If a document is longer than 16 pages, you may serve it by fax only between 4:00 p.m. and 8:00 a.m. unless the party gives prior consent for you to serve it during another time period (rule 16.05(3.1)).

- If you serve by fax between 4:00 p.m. and midnight, service is not effective until the next day (rule 16.05(1)(d)).

- You may not serve a motion record, application record, trial record, appeal book, or book of authorities by fax unless the party being served gives prior permission for you to do so (rule 16.05(3.2)).

Service by e-mail on a solicitor of record

To effect valid service on a solicitor of record by e-mail under rule 16.05(1)(f), the following conditions must be met:

- The message to which the court document is attached must contain all the information required by rule 16.05(4), including the name of the person transmitting the message and his or her address, telephone number, fax number, and e-mail address; the date and time of the message; and the name and telephone number of a contact should there be transmission problems.

- The solicitor of record who is being served provides an e-mail response saying that he or she is accepting service and giving the date of the acceptance.

- If the e-mail acceptance of service by the solicitor of record is received between 4:00 p.m. and midnight, service is deemed to have occurred the next day.

Service on a solicitor of record by courier

Since someone must sign for a courier delivery, there is an independent record of receipt of the document in the solicitor of record's office, but it is important to note that service is effective on the second day following the day the courier was given the document to serve unless the second day is a holiday. In this case, service is deemed to have occurred in the next day that is not a holiday (rule 16.05(2.1)).

Service on a solicitor of record through a document exchange

A document exchange is a centralized service that has been formally set up by lawyers to send and receive court documents. At one time it was a common method of serving documents, but with service by fax and e-mail now permitted, these exchanges are not as widely used as they once were. Many law firms still use them, however. For service on a solicitor of record through a document exchange to be valid, the solicitor of record must be a member of that document exchange, and a copy of the document being served must be date stamped by the document exchange in front of the person who is depositing the copy for service (rule 16.05(c)). Service then becomes effective on the first day that is not a holiday after the document has been deposited and date stamped.

SUBSTITUTED SERVICE AND DISPENSING WITH SERVICE

Sometimes it is extremely difficult to effect service according to the rules. It may be that parties cannot be located despite the best of efforts, or it may be that parties are doing everything they can to avoid service. The fact that you have not been able to serve the opposite side does not mean that you cannot proceed with a lawsuit. If every effort has been made to serve a party and service has not been possible, the lawyer for the party trying to serve the documents may bring a motion for an order for substituted service or for an order dispensing with service.

A party that obtains an order dispensing with service has the court's permission to proceed with its case without serving the other side. It is only in the most exceptional circumstances that a party is granted an order dispensing with service. The reason is that the other side would have no notice of the party's court proceeding and therefore no opportunity to answer the allegations made against it.

However, an order for substituted service is relatively common in litigation. Such an order permits a party to use a method of service not prescribed by the rules. When the court makes an order for substituted service, it will also make an order specifying exactly what method of service may be substituted for the method required by the rules. Often this means that the party requesting substituted service may place a notice in a newspaper or serve by ordinary mail. An order for substituted service specifies when the service becomes effective (rule 16.04(2)). For example, the order might say service is effective on the 10th day following the publishing of the notice in the newspaper.

PROOF OF SERVICE

Once you have served the document according to the rules, you must prepare another document that proves to the court that you have served your document on the other parties. The court requires this proof because if parties fail to file documents or to appear in court, if it can be proven that they had proper service of all relevant documents, the court will be prepared to make a decision about the case in their absence. The court does not accept any document for filing unless you file proof of service at the same time.

There are three methods of proving service:

1. affidavit of service,

2. certificate of service by the Sheriff, or

3. proof of acceptance or admitting of service by the other side.

Affidavit of service

Documents are usually served by a person hired specifically to effect service or by a member of the law firm, usually the law clerk dealing with the file. The server must provide evidence to the court that the party whom they served was served according to the rules. The server does this by way of an affidavit of service. An affidavit is a document sworn under oath or affirmed that can constitute evidence in a court proceeding. The person who serves the document must give details of the steps he or she took to effect service.

An affidavit of service is set out in form 16B. Figures 8.1 to 8.5 provide precedents for affidavits of service in various circumstances. The affidavit of service need not be a separate document. Many law offices use a stamp that is put on the backsheet of the copy of the document that is to be filed with the court. When documents must be served in a hurry, these stamps are often used. The stamp is completed when the document is served, and it can be signed and commissioned at the court office.

Certificate of service by sheriff

sheriff
official appointed by the provincial government to assist in various court-related functions, such as the enforcement of orders and judgments

Each judicial area in the province has a **sheriff**. He or she is a judicial official who is appointed under the *Public Service Act* and who has certain duties involving the courts and the judicial system. Each sheriff has numerous people who work under his or her supervision.

At one time, one of the duties of the sheriff was to serve court documents. The party serving the document would be charged a fee to have a sheriff's officer go out and serve the documents. Now the sheriff's duties have been changed, and sheriffs only serve documents involving the enforcement of judgments and orders. This means that if you have documents that involve enforcement — for example, a writ of seizure and sale or a garnishment — you may either have them served by a private process server or have them served by the sheriff.

When the document is served through the sheriff's office, the sheriff's officer prepares a certificate of service by sheriff. This precedent is form 16C, which appears as figure 8.6. It contains much of the same information that an affidavit of service contains. All the details concerning the steps taken to effect service are included in

FIGURE 8.1 AFFIDAVIT OF SERVICE BY LEAVING COPY WITH ADULT AT RESIDENCE (FORM 16B)

Court file no. 01-CV-1234

ONTARIO
SUPERIOR COURT OF JUSTICE

BETWEEN:

Abigail Boar

Plaintiff

and

Rattle Motors Ltd. and Fred Flogem

Defendants

AFFIDAVIT OF SERVICE

I, Joe Splitz, **of the** City of Toronto, **in the** Province of Ontario, **MAKE OATH AND SAY:**

1. I am the process server for the law firm of Just & Coping, Barristers and Solicitors, and as such have knowledge of the matters to which I herein depose.

2. I served Fred Flogem with the statement of claim by leaving a copy on January 6, year 1, at 2:30 p.m., with Belinda Flogem, who appeared to be an adult member of the same household in which Fred Flogem is residing, at 21 Cypress Blvd., Scarborough, Ontario, M8W 1P3 and by sending a copy by regular lettermail on January 6, year 1 to Fred Flogem at the same address.

3. I ascertained that the person was an adult member of the household by means of the fact that she identified herself as Fred Flogem's wife and confirmed that she was over 18 years of age.

4. Before serving the documents in this way, I made an unsuccessful attempt to serve Fred Flogem personally at the same address on January 5, year 1.

Sworn before me at the	)
City of Toronto,	)
in the Province of Ontario,	)
on January 6, year 1.	)
	)
Commissioner for Taking Affidavits	)

Joe Splitz

Joe Splitz

FIGURE 8.2 AFFIDAVIT OF SERVICE ON SOLICITOR OF RECORD (FORM 16B)

Court file no. 01-CV-1234

ONTARIO
SUPERIOR COURT OF JUSTICE

BETWEEN:

Abigail Boar

Plaintiff

and

Rattle Motors Ltd. and Fred Flogem

Defendants

AFFIDAVIT OF SERVICE

I, Cynthia Patel, **of the** City of Toronto, **in the** Province of Ontario, law clerk for Huey Sue, Solicitor for the Defendant, **MAKE OATH AND SAY:***

1. I served Abigail Boar, the plaintiff, with the statement of defence, dated January 14, year 1, by sending a copy by fax to 416-762-2300 on January 14, year 1 to I.M. Just, Just & Coping, Barristers and Solicitors, the solicitors for the plaintiff.

Sworn before me at the)	
City of Toronto,)	*Cynthia Patel*
in the Province of Ontario,)	Cynthia Patel
on January 15, year 1.)	
)	
Commissioner for Taking Affidavits)	

* *When serving a lawyer by mail, substitute the following:*

1. I served Abigail Boar, the plaintiff, with the statement of defence, dated January 12, year 1, by sending a copy by regular lettermail on January 14, year 1 to I.M. Just, Just & Coping, Barristers and Solicitors, the solicitors for the plaintiff, at 365 Bay Street—8701, Toronto, Ontario, M3J 4A9.

When serving a lawyer by courier, substitute the following:

1. I served Abigail Boar, the plaintiff, with the statement of defence, dated January 12, year 1, by sending a copy by UPS to I.M. Just, Just & Coping, Barristers and Solicitors, the solicitors for the plaintiff, at 365 Bay Street—8701, Toronto, Ontario, M3J 4A9.
2. The copy was given to the courier on January 12, year 1.

FIGURE 8.3   AFFIDAVIT OF PERSONAL SERVICE ON CORPORATION (FORM 16B)

Court file no. 01-CV-1234

ONTARIO
SUPERIOR COURT OF JUSTICE

BETWEEN:

Abigail Boar

Plaintiff

and

Rattle Motors Ltd. and Fred Flogem

Defendants

AFFIDAVIT OF SERVICE

I, Joe Splitz, **of the** City of Toronto, **in the** Province of Ontario,
MAKE OATH AND SAY:

1. I am the process server for the law firm of Just & Coping, Barristers and Solicitors, and as such have knowledge of the matters to which I herein depose.
2. On January 5, year 1 at 2:35 p.m., I served Rattle Motors Ltd. with the statement of claim by leaving a copy with Sunil Tharper, president and general manager, at the corporation's place of business at 1240 Bay Street, Toronto, Ontario, M8H 0K8.

Sworn before me at the)	
City of Toronto,)	*Joe Splitz*
in the Province of Ontario,)	Joe Splitz
on January 6, year 1.)	
)	
Commissioner for Taking Affidavits)	

FIGURE 8.4   AFFIDAVIT OF PERSONAL SERVICE ON INDIVIDUAL (FORM 16B)

Court file no. 01-CV-1234

ONTARIO
SUPERIOR COURT OF JUSTICE

BETWEEN:

Abigail Boar

Plaintiff

and

Rattle Motors Ltd. and Fred Flogem

Defendants

AFFIDAVIT OF SERVICE

I, Joe Splitz, **of the** City of Toronto, **in the** Province of Ontario,
MAKE OATH AND SAY:

1. I am the process server for the law firm of Just & Coping, Barristers and Solicitors, and as such have knowledge of the matters to which I herein depose.
2. On January 5, year 1, at 2:35 p.m., I served Fred Flogem with the statement of claim by leaving a copy with him at 21 Cypress Boulevard, Scarborough, Ontario, M8Q 1P3.
3. I was able to identify the person by means of his confirmation that he was Fred Flogem.

Sworn before me at the)	
City of Toronto,)	*Joe Splitz*
in the Province of Ontario,)	Joe Splitz
on January 6, year 1.)	
)	
Commissioner for Taking Affidavits)	

FIGURE 8.5   AFFIDAVIT OF SERVICE ON DEFENDANT BY MAIL (FORM 16B) WITH ACKNOWLEDGMENT OF RECEIPT CARD (FORM 16A) ATTACHED AS EXHIBIT

Court file no. 01-CV-1234

ONTARIO
SUPERIOR COURT OF JUSTICE

BETWEEN:

Abigail Boar

Plaintiff

and

Rattle Motors Ltd. and Fred Flogem

Defendants

AFFIDAVIT OF SERVICE

I, Edward Egregious, **of the** City of Toronto, **in the** Province of Ontario, **MAKE OATH AND SAY:**

1. I am a law clerk for the firm of Just & Coping, Barristers and Solicitors, solicitors for the plaintiff, and as such have knowledge of the matters to which I herein depose.
2. On January 5, year 1, I sent to the defendant Fred Flogem by regular lettermail a copy of the statement of claim.
3. On January 12, year 1, I received the acknowledgment of receipt card, attached here as exhibit A, bearing a signature that purports to be the signature of Fred Flogem.

Sworn before me at the	)	
City of Toronto,	)	*Edward Egregious*
in the Province of Ontario,	)	Edward Egregious
on January 12, year 1.	)	
	)	
Commissioner for Taking Affidavits	)	

FIGURE 8.5 CONTINUED

Court file no. 01-CV-1234

ONTARIO
SUPERIOR COURT OF JUSTICE

BETWEEN:

Abigail Boar

Plaintiff

and

Rattle Motors Ltd. and Fred Flogem

Defendants

TO: Fred Flogem

You are served by mail with the documents enclosed with this card in accordance with the Rules of Civil Procedure.

You are requested to sign the acknowledgment below and mail this card immediately after you receive it. If you fail to do so, the documents may be served on you in another manner and you may have to pay the costs of service.

ACKNOWLEDGMENT OF RECEIPT

I ACKNOWLEDGE that I have received a copy of the following documents:

Statement of claim of Abigail Boar, issued January 4, year 1

Fred Flogem

Fred Flogem

(The reverse side of this card must bear the name and address of the sender and the required postage.)

THIS IS EXHIBIT A REFERRED TO
IN THE AFFIDAVIT OF
EDWARD EGREGIOUS,
SWORN BEFORE ME ON

Commissioner for Taking Affidavits

FIGURE 8.6   CERTIFICATE OF SERVICE BY SHERIFF (FORM 16C)

CERTIFICATE OF SERVICE BY SHERIFF

I, Joe Shmoe, sheriff's officer of the Township of Vaughn, certify that on March 1, year 2, at 10 a.m., I served Donald Donaldson with a writ of seizure and sale by leaving a copy with him at 400 Starry Lane, Woodbridge, Ontario L47 9V6. I was able to identify the person by means of his confirmation that he was Donald Donaldson.

Date: March 1, year 2

Joe Shmoe

Joe Shmoe

---

the document. The certificate is often put right on the copy of the served document that is filed with the court.

If you use the sheriff to serve the enforcement documents, the sheriff's office will provide you with a completed certificate. Although you will not need to prepare the document itself, you should know what it looks like.

Proof of acceptance or admitting of service by the other side

When you are serving a document, very often the lawyer for the other side will admit service. It is a good idea to put the following wording on the backsheet of the document to be filed with the court:

Service of a copy of this
document admitted on
_____(date)_____
_____(signature)_____
Solicitors for

The lawyer for the party being served, or one of the staff in his or her office, may be willing to fill in the date and sign for the document. This signature tells the court that the other side agrees that it has been properly served according to the rules. There is no need to prepare an affidavit of service. The copy of the document on which service has been admitted can be filed with the court without any further proof of service being required.

It is not always possible to use this method of proof because the lawyer for the opposite side may not be in the office when the document is served and may not have left instructions with a staff member to admit service. _It is very important that you never admit service of any document unless you have been given specific instructions by the lawyer you work for to do so._ If there is a problem with the service — for example, if it is not in keeping with the rules — and service has been admitted, the service cannot usually be challenged later.

Acceptance of service works the same way as admitting service, but the wording that is put on the backsheet of the document being served is slightly different.

> Service of a copy of this
> document accepted on
> (*date*)
> _____
> (*signature*)
> _____
> Solicitors for

The acceptance wording is used when you are serving a lawyer with an originating process under rule 16.03(2) as an alternative to personal service. If you are serving a solicitor of record with a document that is not an originating process under rule 16.05, you use the admittance of service wording.

SERVICE OUTSIDE THE PROVINCE

Sometimes one of the parties to the proceeding lives or is located outside Ontario. When serving a party outside the province, in addition to following rule 16, you must also follow any additional procedures prescribed by rule 17. This means that an originating process served outside the province must still be served personally or by an alternative to personal service under rule 16. However, you must also look at rule 17 to see if there are additional steps that must be taken or additional procedures that must be followed.

Rule 17.01 changes the definition of originating process by adding an additional document to the list contained in rule 1.03. Counterclaims against parties to the main action and crossclaims are also included as originating processes for the purpose of serving someone outside the province.

Not all documents served outside the province can be served without a court order, although many can. To determine whether your case is one in which you can serve outside the province without a court order, you must first look at rule 17.02. If your case is one of the types of cases listed under this rule, you may serve outside the province without leave, or permission, from the court. If your case is not one of the types listed under rule 17.02, you must first bring a motion to get leave from the court to serve the party who is out of the province (rule 17.03). The motion is usually a motion without notice. The court grants leave for a type of case not listed in rule 17.02 only if it can be satisfied that the courts in Ontario are the appropriate courts to hear the case.

Where an originating process is being served outside the province without leave under rule 17.02, you must state which part of the rule you are relying on to serve without leave (rule 17.04(1)). For instance, if you are serving someone in Manitoba with a statement of claim in a case that involves the breach of a contract made in Ontario, your statement of claim must contain a paragraph that states that fact and mentions rule 17.02(f)(i). Rule 17.02(f)(i) says that you do not need leave from the court to serve a document on a party when the case involves a claim relating to a contract made in Ontario.

If you are dealing with a claim that requires leave to serve outside the province, the order that grants leave must also be served along with the originating process (rule 17.04(2)).

Rule 17.05 deals with the method of service you must use when serving documents outside Ontario. Basically, when you want to serve an originating process outside the province, you may do so by having the document personally served or served by an alternative to personal service as described in rule 16. In addition, you may also serve by whatever method of service is permissible in the other jurisdiction as long as that method of service is likely to bring the document to the attention of the person being served.

However, if you want to serve an originating process in a foreign country, you must first find out if that country is a **contracting state** to the *Hague Convention on the Service Abroad of Judicial and Extrajudicial Documents in Civil or Commercial Matters*. This is the international treaty, or agreement, that Canada has entered into with many other countries. All the countries that have signed the treaty are called "contracting states." They have agreed that they will help litigants from the other countries serve documents. If you are dealing with a country that is part of the treaty, you must send your documents to the central authority in Ontario. That central authority then sends the documents to the central authority in the other country. The central authorities are government offices in each country that have signed the treaty. The central authority in the other country takes care of serving the documents and preparing the proof of service, which it will send back to you. A country that is a convention state will provide whatever proof of service is legal in that country, and it will be acceptable as good proof in an Ontario court (rule 17.05(4)).

To find out whether a country is a contracting state to the convention, you may look at the Web site for the Hague Conference on Private International Law at http://www.hcch.net/e/status/stat14e.html. You may also telephone the Department of Foreign Affairs in Ottawa at 613-995-1050 or fax the department at 613-992-2467.

If you have documents you wish to serve, you may call the document authentication officer at 613-992-6602 or send a fax to 613-944-7078.

The central authority for Ontario can be contacted as follows:

Ministry of the Attorney General
Courts Administration
Ontario Court of Justice
Court House
393 Main Street
Haileybury, ON P0J 1K0
Canada

tel.: 705-672-3395

A party that has been served outside Ontario can bring a motion, in an Ontario court, to set aside service of an originating process or to stay or stop the proceeding as long as the party commences the motion before filing any documents. When dealing with such a motion, the judge looks at whether the documents have been properly served under the rules and whether the Ontario court is the proper court in which to hear the proceeding. When you wish to serve a document in a contracting state, you must complete forms 17A, 17B, and 17C. You are usually required to provide a translation of the document as well.

contracting state
country that is a signatory to a contract or convention

CHAPTER SUMMARY

This chapter introduced the various methods that must be used to serve a document under the rules. Generally, there are specific methods set out for the service of a document that is an originating process and other methods set out for documents that are not.

You must first look to see if there is a specific rule relating to the document you want to serve that requires a specific method of service. If not, an originating process may be served either by personal service through one of the methods listed in rule 16.02 or by an alternative to personal service listed in rule 16.03. Only the alternatives to personal service listed in that rule may be substituted for personal service.

If a document is not an originating process and the party is represented by a solicitor of record, it is possible to serve the document on the lawyer by one of the methods provided in rule 16.05. If the party is representing him- or herself in the proceeding, a document that is not an originating process may be served by mail to the address provided by the party on the originating process or by personal or alternative service.

If it is impossible to serve a person because the person is avoiding service or cannot be found, the party wishing to serve the document may bring a motion to ask for an order of substituted service or an order dispensing with service. It is only in the most extraordinary circumstances that a court will make an order dispensing with service.

Once service has been effected according to the rules or a court order, the person who served the document must make an affidavit that provides evidence of the steps he or she took to serve the document. However, it is not necessary to prepare an affidavit of service if the solicitor for the opposite party admits or accepts service and certifies that he or she has done so on the backsheet of the served document. Likewise, no affidavit is necessary where the document has been left in a document exchange. The stamp of the document exchange on the document is sufficient service.

A document may be served outside Ontario without leave of the court if the case is listed in rule 17.02. If the case is any other type of case, the party wishing to serve the document must obtain a court order first. If you wish to serve a document on a person who is in a contracting state to the *Hague Convention on Service Abroad of Judicial and Extrajudicial Documents in Civil or Commercial Matters*, the person must be served, in accordance with rule 17.05(3), by a central authority in the country where the party is located.

KEY TERMS

service

originating process

sheriff

contracting state

NOTE

1   This is not the same as registered mail. Form 16A must be used.

REFERENCES

Hague Convention on Service Abroad of Judicial and Extrajudicial Documents in Civil or Commercial Matters, November 15, 1965. See *Hague Conference on Private International Law* at http://www.hcch.net/e/status/stat14e.html.

Public Service Act, RSO 1990, c. P.47.

Rules of Civil Procedure, RRO 1990, reg. 194.

REVIEW QUESTIONS

1.   How do you effect service on a partnership?

2.   When can you serve a motion record on a lawyer by fax?

3.   Julie Giudice served the defendant's solicitor of record by mail with a document that was not an originating process. The document was mailed on Friday September 23. What date will service be effective?

4. A process server wants to serve Frasier Croon with a statement of claim. He goes to Frasier's house and finds the cleaning woman there alone. The process server leaves a copy of the statement of claim with the cleaning woman and mails a copy to Frasier at the same address on the same day. Is this good service? Explain your answer.

5. Jaspal wants to serve a 15-page statement of defence on the solicitor of record for the plaintiff. He is running out of time and decides to serve the document by fax at 9:30 a.m. Is this good service?

6. You are a law clerk for Seneca and Associates, Barristers and Solicitors, 1750 Finch Avenue East, Toronto, Ontario, M2J 2X5. Your client is John Ahab, who is suing Moby's Whale of a Time Inc., a chain of restaurants, for negligently leaving a bone in his sushi. You have just served Moby's Whale of a Time Inc. with a statement of claim. You went to the restaurant closest to the law office, at 5910 Yonge Street, North York, Ontario, M7U 4T8 and left a copy with the manager of the restaurant, Ishmael Bosun. Draft an affidavit of service. If there is any necessary information that you think is missing, make it up.

7. You sent the process server out to serve a sole proprietorship personally. When the process server comes back, he produces an affidavit saying he left a copy of the statement of claim with Ginny, the assistant cashier at the place of business. Is this service adequate?

8. In the following situations, will it be necessary to seek leave of the court to serve a party with an originating process outside Ontario.

   a. Joe died in Ontario. His heirs want to sue his nurse, Betty, whom they believe removed some of Joe's property from his home after he died, and they want the property to be returned.

   b. Stacey lives in Toronto. She was in a car accident in New York State. She wants to sue the owner of the car that hit hers. He also lives in Ontario.

   c. The parties made a contract in Manitoba, but since they knew that one of the parties was moving his business to Toronto the next month, they agreed to a term in the contract that the law of Ontario should govern.

   d. George wants to seek custody of his son Benny, who is living with him in Barrie, but the child's mother lives in Montreal.

9. You are a law clerk with the firm of MacDonald, Reed, and Buss. Your supervising lawyer is Jacqueline Reed. The address of the firm is:

MacDonald, Reed, and Buss
Barristers and Solicitors
200 Bay Street, Suite 1100
Toronto, Ontario, M5V 3T3
Tel.:   416-595-5000
Fax: 416-595-5050
E-mail: MDRB@sympatico.ca

Your law firm acts for the plaintiffs, Yorkful Developers Inc. The defendant is Louis LaFrance. The process server is Jacky Dillhopper. Jacky phones and tells you he has effected service on Louis LaFrance by attending at his residence at 100 Bloor Street North, Toronto, Ontario, M6Y 4R7. He left a copy with Louis's wife, Celine, after she identified herself as Louis's wife. Draft an affidavit of service for Jacky to sign when he gets back to the office.

CHAPTER 9

Motions

INTRODUCTION

This chapter is about motions procedure and the preparation of **motion** documents. You will notice that both the procedure and the documents are very similar to those used in applications. This is not accidental. Documents and procedures in motions and applications are designed to be dispatched in a summary fashion, with a short timeline between raising a legal issue and obtaining an answer from the court.

Purpose of motions

The purpose of a motion is to settle issues that arise in the course of civil litigation, usually before trial.[1] We have already identified some circumstances where motions are required to resolve a problem of pretrial procedure: a motion to join parties to a lawsuit, a motion to strike out pleadings, and a motion to demand particulars. It used to be, and sometimes still is the case, that a party with money to spend would try to delay proceedings by bringing one motion after another and drive up the legal costs at the pretrial stage. The opposing party, if more financially limited, would soon be forced to drop the lawsuit or settle on disadvantageous terms. This practice was sometimes referred to as "motioning the other side to death." The rules discourage this kind of litigation strategy, and the courts have the power to award punitive costs against the parties who resort to them. In some cases, the courts award costs against lawyers who engage in these dark arts (rule 57.07). The court may also bar a party from bringing further motions unless the court's permission is first obtained (rule 37.16).

But there are often good reasons to bring motions. Suppose that I.M. Just, Abigail Boar's lawyer, has read the statement of defence stating that the area around the Super Coupe was properly illuminated and therefore safe. That matter is now an issue between the parties. To help settle it, I.M. Just asks Huey Sue, the defendants' lawyer, to permit a lighting engineer to come to the showroom and examine the lighting. Huey refuses to permit this. So I.M. Just decides to bring a motion to ask the court to order an examination of the premises by the lighting engineer.

Motions with notice: Overview of procedure

While we will look at various aspects of motion procedure in detail, here we set out a general overview of the process of bringing a motion with notice.

The moving party prepares a notice of motion and a supporting affidavit and serves it on the responding party at least four days before the motion is to be heard.

motion
proceeding within the main proceeding to settle an issue, usually one that has arisen at the pretrial stage

return of a motion
day on which a motion is "returned" to court for a hearing; the hearing date is also referred to as "the return date"

The day picked for the **return of the motion** depends on the practices in the court where the motion is returnable. In Toronto, an appointment for motions before both judges and masters must be obtained before serving the responding party. This is discussed in more detail in the appendix to this chapter.

The place for the return of a motion on notice is where the responding party's lawyer has his or her office or where the responding party lives, if the responding party is representing himself or herself. The parties may also consent to a venue other than those prescribed by the rules. If the solicitor of record has more than one office, it is the office listed in the court file that is relevant. Remember that the responding party may be the plaintiff or defendant.

The responding party may serve an affidavit or other evidentiary material or a crossmotion and supporting documents on the moving party until three days before the hearing.

A motion record must be prepared, usually by the moving party, consisting of the notice of motion, affidavits, and any other documents in use by the parties. It is then filed in the court where the motion is to be heard three days before the hearing. This requires the parties to observe time limits for serving each other and requires cooperation. Otherwise, each side files its own motion record: the moving party no later than three days before the hearing, the responding party two days before the hearing.

official examiner
individual who is licensed to operate a business to conduct out-of-court examinations, such as cross-examinations on affidavits and discoveries

Either party may ask to cross-examine the maker of an affidavit that is filed on the motion. This is done out of court before a court reporter or **official examiner**, and the transcript, or a part of it, may be used at the hearing. If the parties have not allowed enough time for cross-examination between the date the motion is served and its return date, the request to cross-examine is made on the return date of the motion; if the request is granted, the motion is adjourned pending completion of cross-examination. The rules require that a party who seeks to cross-examine should move to do so "with reasonable diligence." Because cross-examination causes delay, its misuse may lead to an imposition of cost penalties on the party that improperly resorts to it or the court may deny permission for cross-examination altogether (rule 39.02(3)). A party who cross-examines on an affidavit may not file supplementary affidavits responding to what was said in cross-examination without the court's consent. This puts an end to the old practice of serving a responding affidavit after cross-examination, followed by a response to the responding affidavit, and so on, which caused both delay and confusion.

There are some additional burdens on a party who cross-examines. The party bears the expense of ordering a transcript of the cross-examination for the court and for other parties. The party must also pay partial indemnity costs of every adverse party on the motion unless the court orders otherwise (rule 39.02(4)).

Parties may wish to file factums, which are statements of fact, law, and case references; they are not required on all motions, but the practice is recommended and encouraged by the judiciary.

summary proceedings
proceedings designed to be conducted quickly and with reduced formality

Hearings are **summary proceedings**. Oral evidence is not heard; instead, counsel make submissions, referring to affidavits and other documentary evidence, including cross-examination transcripts.

The successful party on the motion then drafts the order from the judge's or master's endorsement, obtains approval as to form from the unsuccessful party, and has the order issued and entered by the court.

MOTIONS WITHOUT NOTICE

There are certain types of motions that may be brought without notice. For example, if you have been unable to serve a defendant with a statement of claim, you may bring a motion for substituted service, as you saw in chapter 8. The motion is brought in the court where the proceeding was commenced (rule 37.03(1)),[2] but no notice to the other side is required. You file the notice of motion and the affidavit or other evidence you will use, appear before the judge or master, and make submissions. A notice of motion should be filed to set out the issues in advance for the judge or master and for the other party. Any party affected by the order must be served with a copy of the order immediately, along with a copy of the motion, and all the documents used on it. In that way, the process is reasonably transparent because the party, though not present, gets to see what was before the court. If the moving party misled the court, the other party will become aware of that fact and can take action to set the order aside. Because a motion without notice is rather one-sided, an affidavit must give full and fair disclosure and must be more neutral in tone than it would be had the motion been made on notice (rule 39.01(6)).

If the judge or master is of the opinion that the motion should not have been brought without first giving notice, he or she may dismiss the motion or adjourn it until the other party is served, and he or she may direct that any order made be served on the non-attending party (rule 37.07(5)).

JURISDICTION TO HEAR A MOTION

In the Superior Court, there are two types of judicial officials who decide legal issues and who can decide motions: a **master** and a judge. Masters have a more limited jurisdiction than judges do, and they sit in courts where the volume of cases is high, such as in Toronto and Ottawa. In other judicial regions, judges hear all motions.

Where you have a choice as to whether the motion is heard by a judge or master, you must decide before whom it should come. As a general rule, a motion that can be heard by a master must be heard by a master. If you schedule it before a judge, he or she will refuse to hear it, and you will have to appear again before a master, wasting both time and money.[3]

The master's jurisdiction is more circumscribed. Rule 37.02(2)(a) to (g) lists those matter which a master *cannot* hear:

master
minor judicial official with limited jurisdiction to hear and decide specific legal issues identified by the rules or a statute

- A master cannot hear a matter that has been given exclusively to a judge by a statute or regulation.

- A master cannot change an order that was made by a judge.

- A master cannot shorten or lengthen the time for doing something in an order made by a judge.

- A master cannot give a consent judgment where there is a party under disability — such as a minor — involved.

- A master cannot make an order that affects the liberty of a person — for example, because an order for contempt of court may result in jail time, contempt motions must be brought before judges.

- A master cannot make orders under s. 4 or s. 5 of the *Judicial Review Procedure Act* such as interim orders or orders extending the time for filing applications for judicial review.

- A master cannot make orders on an appeal.

Subject to these restrictions, masters have the power to make orders.

OBTAINING A HEARING DATE

In large regions such as Toronto, motions are heard every day. In small centres, there is often a "motion day,"[4] where a judge usually hears all motions filed since the last motion day. Generally, the moving party may choose any date on which motions are heard without needing first to obtain a date from the court office. When choosing a date, however, it is a good idea to check with the responding parties to the motion to be sure that counsel will be available. This will avoid wasting time and money on adjournments and rescheduling.

In Toronto, the practice for obtaining a hearing date for nearly all motions is governed by a motions and applications advisory notice, effective September 1, 2002. This is discussed in more detail in the appendix to this chapter.

Generally, if you are involved with a motion to be heard in a court or region where you are not familiar with local scheduling and hearing practices, it is a good idea to call the court office to find out what is required.

NOTICE OF MOTION

The primary document you need to prepare is the notice of motion. This tells the other side the issue that you wish to have decided, the remedy you seek, and the reason you believe you are entitled to the remedy. The document also lists the materials you intend to rely on. The prescribed form is form 37A, and the relevant rule is rule 37.06, which sets out the information required:

1. *To whom the motion is made.* Is the motion made to a master or to a judge? Check rule 37.02(2).

2. *Time, date, and place where the motion will be heard.* Try to arrange a convenient time with the responding party. Where applicable, get the date and time confirmed with the court.

3. *Whether the motion is to be heard orally or in writing.* The lawyer will make oral or written submissions. Evidence in either case is by affidavit. You need permission from the court to proceed with oral evidence.

4. *Legal basis or grounds that support the remedy requested.* Briefly list a rule, statute, case, or legal principle if relevant.

5. *Documentary evidence you rely on.* Affidavits and other documents should be identified by the date the document was created and the maker of the document if this is not obvious.

6. *Name, address, and fax number of the lawyer for the moving party.* Provide the same information for the lawyers who are being served on behalf of the responding party.

Figure 9.1 sets out Abigail's motion for an order for inspection of the defendants' premises. The relevant rule is rule 37. Have a look at it, and notice that its language is incorporated into the motion itself.

AFFIDAVITS AS EVIDENCE ON MOTIONS AND APPLICATIONS

One of the ways in which hearings on motions and applications are speeded up is by using affidavit evidence instead of having witnesses give evidence orally. What a witness would have said in examination-in-chief is reduced to a sworn statement. If cross-examination is desired, arrangements need to be made to cross-examine the deponent on the contents of his or her affidavit. The transcript of that cross-examination is used with the affidavit itself at the hearing. The process of adjourning a motion or application to permit cross-examination and obtain transcripts may end up costing more and taking more time than using oral evidence on the motion or affidavit.

Drafting affidavits

The basic requirements for affidavits are set out in rule 4.06. Form 4D sets out a prescribed format.

USE THE FIRST PERSON FORM

The statements in affidavits are set out in the first person singular ("I"), although joint affidavits may be used where appropriate, in which case the first person plural ("we") must be used.

IDENTIFY THE DEPONENT

Before setting out the first numbered paragraph, give the deponent's full name, followed by the municipality and province where the deponent resides. Set out the deponent's status — for example, as a party, solicitor for a party, or officer of a corporation — so that the testimony can be seen in context. Two examples of paragraphs identifying a deponent are set out below. The second example, although not in conformity with the directions in form 4D, is often used.

> I, Eldred Klump, of the City of Brampton, in the Regional Municipality of Peel,[5] consulting electrical engineer, MAKE OATH AND SAY:

> I, Eldred Klump, of the City of Brampton, in the Regional Municipality of Peel, MAKE OATH AND SAY:
> 1. I am a consulting electrical engineer, retained by the plaintiff, and as such have knowledge of the matters sworn to in this affidavit.

SET OUT STATEMENT IN CONSECUTIVE PARAGRAPHS

Much like a statement of claim or defence, the affidavit is divided into consecutively numbered paragraphs, with each paragraph confined as far as possible to a specific statement of fact. Again, this may mean that many paragraphs are just two or three sentences long. The writing should be concise. However, it is not limited to material facts, and evidentiary material may be set out.

FIGURE 9.1   MOTION FOR ORDER FOR INSPECTION OF PREMISES (FORM 37A)

Court file no. 01-CV-1234

ONTARIO
SUPERIOR COURT OF JUSTICE

BETWEEN:

Abigail Boar

Plaintiff

and

Rattle Motors Ltd. and Fred Flogem

Defendants

NOTICE OF MOTION

THE PLAINTIFF will make a motion to the court on Monday October 16, year 1 at 10:00 a.m., or as soon after that time as the motion can be heard, at 393 University Avenue, Toronto, Ontario, M5G 1Y3.

PROPOSED METHOD OF HEARING: The motion is to be heard

❑ in writing under subrule 37.12.1 (1);
❑ in writing as an opposed motion under subrule 37.12.1 (4);
☒ orally.

THE MOTION IS FOR an order permitting Eldred Klump, consulting electrical engineer, to inspect the level of lighting in the automobile showroom operated by the corporate defendant at 1240 Bay Street in the City of Toronto, Province of Ontario, on such terms and at such times as the court considers just.

THE GROUNDS FOR THE MOTION ARE that there is an issue between the parties as to the adequacy of lighting in the corporate defendant's showroom, and it is necessary to determine that issue in this proceeding to carry out an inspection of the corporate defendant's premises to examine the lighting, pursuant to rule 32 of the rules of civil procedure.

THE FOLLOWING DOCUMENTARY EVIDENCE will be used at the hearing of the motion:

1. Statement of claim filed January 4, year 1;
2. Statement of defence filed January 12, year 1; and
3. Affidavit of Eldred Klump sworn October 3, year 1.

FIGURE 9.1 CONTINUED

Date: September 16, year 1

Just & Coping
Barristers and Solicitors
365 Bay Street – 8701
Toronto, Ontario, M3J 4A9

I.M. Just
tel. 416-762-1342
fax 416-762-2300

Solicitors for the Moving
Party (Plaintiff)

TO:

Huey Sue
Barrister and Solicitor
65 False Trail
Toronto, Ontario, M6Y 1Z6

tel. 416-485-6891
fax 416-485-6892

Solicitor for the Responding
Parties (Defendants)

SIGN AND SWEAR THE AFFIDAVIT

The deponent must sign the affidavit at the end, or foot, after he or she has been affirmed or sworn by a commissioner for taking oaths and affidavits. Every lawyer is a commissioner and is authorized to swear affidavits. Law clerks employed in law offices may apply through their offices to the provincial government to become commissioners while employed in that law office and doing work for it. A lawyer signs the **jurat** as commissioner when he or she has sworn the deponent. A non-lawyer signs the jurat and also applies his or her commissioner's stamp, identifying the law office for which he or she works and the date of the expiry of the commission. A lawyer's commission does not require use of a stamp.

jurat
part of an affidavit that appears at the bottom on the left side of the page and begins with the words "Sworn (or affirmed) before me"

An affidavit is commissioned when it is being used in an Ontario proceeding. If it is being sworn for use in another province or in a foreign jurisdiction, it should be notarized instead, and the notary's seal should be affixed next to the notary's signature.

Where a lawyer commissions an affidavit without a seal and the signature is an illegible scrawl, the lawyer should print his or her name underneath the signature. The standard jurat[6] is set out in figure 9.2.

WHEN HEARSAY IS PERMISSIBLE

The content of an affidavit, like the evidence on a witness's oral examination-in-chief, is usually restricted to matters of which the deponent has personal knowledge. Hearsay is not permitted unless it falls into one of the numerous exceptions to the

FIGURE 9.2   STANDARD JURAT (FORM 4D)

Sworn before me at the) City of Brampton,) **in the** Regional Municipality) of Peel,) **on** October 3, year 1.)	*Edward Klump* ———————————— Edward Klump

I.M. Just
————————————————
I.M. Just

Commissioner for Taking Affidavits   )

---

hearsay rule. However, this requirement, set out in rule 4.06(2), is subject to the qualifications set out in rule 39.01(4) and (5).

If the affidavit is for use on a motion, it may contain statements of the deponent's information and belief, provided that the deponent identifies the source of the information and states that he or she believes the information to be true. In this instance, hearsay is admissible.

This rule also applies to affidavits used on applications, provided that the source of the information is revealed, the deponent states that he or she believes it to be true, and the *facts in question are not contentious*. Therefore hearsay is admissible, provided that it is not disputed. Where a contentious statement is included, the proper response is to move to strike out the objectionable part of the affidavit.

Using an example from Abigail Boar's case, the usual method for expressing information and belief is as follows: "I am informed by Abigail Boar, the plaintiff in this action, and I believe that she was unable to see the oil spill because of inadequate lighting at the site of her fall."

EXHIBITS TO AFFIDAVITS

Occasionally the deponent's statement refers to a document or other material. The document or other material should be clearly described and given an exhibit number (usually a letter), which is stamped on a copy of the document. If the exhibit to be attached or filed is a copy, the deponent should so state. Once it is made an exhibit, the document or other material should be made available to other parties and the court. This can be done in one of two ways: (1) it can be attached to the affidavit or (2) it can be referred to in the affidavit and filed in court. Rule 4.06(3) prescribes language for each of the two ways of dealing with exhibits, and you should take care to use the appropriate word formula. Examples from Abigail's case appear below.

- If the exhibit is attached, write "Now *shown to me*, marked exhibit A, *and attached to this affidavit* is a copy of the bar bill of Abigail Boar from Barbeerian's restaurant, dated September 14, year 0."

- If the exhibit is shown to the deponent and filed, write "*Now produced and shown to me*, and marked exhibit A is a copy of the bar bill of Abigail Boar from Barbeerian's restaurant, dated September 14, year 0."

Law firms usually use an exhibit stamp with blank spaces to be filled in with the exhibit number or letter, the name of the deponent, and the date of the affidavit.

FIGURE 9.3   EXHIBIT STAMP

```
┌─────────────────────────────────┐
│        This is exhibit           │
│               A                  │
│      to the affidavit of         │
│         Eldred Klump             │
│             dated                │
│      October 3, year 1           │
│                                  │
│          I.M. Just               │
├─────────────────────────────────┤
│   Commissioner for Taking Affidavits │
└─────────────────────────────────┘
```

The person who commissions the affidavit signs in the space provided. The stamp is reproduced in figure 9.3.

Figure 9.4 shows what Eldred Klump's affidavit in the Abigail Boar case looks like. Figure 9.5 sets out the affidavit filed by Sunil Tharper on behalf of Rattle Motors Ltd.

MOTION RECORDS

Assume for the moment that you have now obtained a date for the motion, determined who hears it, prepared a notice of motion and affidavit, and served this on the responding party. The responding party has served its documents on you. You are now ready to prepare a motion record.

Why use a motion record?

Formerly when a motion was brought, the moving party served and filed a motion and affidavit, and the responding party served and filed an affidavit. On each filing, the court clerk stamped the incoming document and put it in the appropriate court file, noting the day of the motion. On the day before the motion, the clerks brought the court file to the judge or master who was to hear the matter. The judicial official then found himself or herself with a court file full of documents in no particular order. If the matter was complex, there might be hundreds of pages. The judge or master would go through the file, looking for the notice of motion and the appropriate affidavits, and reading what he or she hoped was the correct material. To introduce some order into this chaos, the rules were amended to require a motion record to be filed containing all the material necessary for hearing and determining the motion. Only the motion record would be delivered to the judge or master unless a party separately requisitioned the whole file. It was now no longer necessary for judges and masters to fumble around in search of the appropriate documents.

Contents of a motion record

Rule 37.10(2) sets out what a motion record should have in it in consecutively numbered pages:

- an index, headed by a general heading and title of proceeding, describing each document, identified by its nature or date, including exhibits filed or

FIGURE 9.4 AFFIDAVIT OF ELDRED KLUMP (FORM 4D)

Court file no. 01-CV-1234

ONTARIO
SUPERIOR COURT OF JUSTICE

BETWEEN:

Abigail Boar

Plaintiff

and

Rattle Motors Ltd. and Fred Flogem

Defendants

AFFIDAVIT OF ELDRED KLUMP

I, Eldred Klump, **of the** City of Brampton, **in the** Regional Municipality of Peel, **MAKE OATH AND SAY:**

1. I am a consulting electrical engineer, retained by the plaintiff, and as such have knowledge of the matters sworn to in this affidavit.
2. I am advised by I.M. Just, lawyer for the plaintiff, and I believe that there is a disagreement between the parties as to whether or not there was adequate illumination in the area where the plaintiff allegedly fell in the showroom of Rattle Motors Ltd.
3. There are Building Code and other standards for safe and adequate lighting for various areas in buildings, including showrooms.
4. It is possible to measure the amount of light at the location in question and check the measurements against known standards.
5. The information obtained from these tests would be relevant in assisting the court in making findings as to the adequacy of the lighting in question.
6. In order to properly measure the light, it is necessary for me to enter the showroom of the corporate defendant, adjust the lights in the location where the plaintiff fell as they were on the day of the accident, and take measurements of the light available.

Sworn before me at the)	
City of Brampton,)	*Eldred Klump*
in the Regional Municipality)	Eldred Klump
of Peel,)	
on October 3, year 1.)	
)	
Commissioner for Taking Affidavits)	

FIGURE 9.5 AFFIDAVIT OF SUNIL THARPER (FORM 4D)

Court file no. 01-CV-1234

ONTARIO
SUPERIOR COURT OF JUSTICE

BETWEEN:

Abigail Boar

Plaintiff

and

Rattle Motors Ltd. and Fred Flogem

Defendants

AFFIDAVIT OF SUNIL THARPER

I, Sunil Tharper, president and general manager of Rattle Motors Ltd., **of the** City of Toronto, **in the** Province on Ontario, **AFFIRM:**

1. I have read the affidavit of Eldred Klump, sworn October 3, year 1 and filed on behalf of the plaintiff in this proceeding.
2. On or about February 1, year 1, the corporate defendant's directors decided to renovate its automobile showroom to better display the automobiles that the company sells.
3. The renovations were extensive, involving a complete gutting of the interior and replacement of flooring, ceilings, showroom windows, and offices.
4. In the course of carrying out this renovation, all of the prerenovation lighting, including spotlights or pot lights, was removed, and new lighting was installed.
5. The new lighting is of a different type from the old lighting and is placed differently. In particular, the spotlighting now used is of the halogen type, rather than the conventional incandescent floodlight type.
6. Since the lighting fixtures and the illumination they cast are completely different from the lighting that was used at the time the plaintiff fell, the inspection proposed by the plaintiff would serve no purpose.
7. The defendants have consulted a lighting expert, Elihu Dunck, who has prepared a report in which he advises that it would now be impossible to carry out the tests and inspections proposed by the plaintiff, and that the inspection would be of no assistance to the court. Now shown to me and attached hereto and marked exhibit A to this affidavit is a report dated October 5, year 1 from Elihu Dunck to the defendant's lawyer, which sets out Mr. Dunck's opinion.

Affirmed before me at the	)
City of Toronto,	) *Sunil Tharper*
in the Province of Ontario,	) Sunil Tharper
on October 6, year 1.	)
	)
Commissioner for Taking Affidavits	)

attached to affidavits and identified by exhibit numbers (figure 9.6 sets out a motion record index for the case of Abigail Boar);

- a copy of the notice of motion;

- a copy of all affidavits and other material served by any party;

- a list of all relevant transcripts in chronological order (if the transcript or the part relied on is short, it may be included in the motion record; if it is too long for that, be sure it is in the court file, and requisition the court file for the motion); and

- a copy of any other material in the court file that might be relevant to the issues on the motion (often lawyers file copies of the pleadings to provide a context) or that may be required by the court.

Although it is not required, it is a good idea to use tabs to separate documents so the judge or master can easily find what the lawyer is referring to in argument. Rule 4.07 requires that a motion record be bound with a light blue backsheet.

Figure 9.6 sets out the motion record index in the case of Abigail Boar.

Responding party's motion record

If enough time is allowed for both parties serving each other with their motion material and there is cooperation, one motion record can usually be prepared for use by the parties and the court on the motion. This is the approach preferred by judges and masters, who dislike having to shuffle through several sets of documents. However, where the responding party is not satisfied that the record is complete, he or she may prepare a responding party's motion record to include those documents which he or she thinks should be included. The motion record should have a table of contents describing the documents included that were omitted from the moving party's motion record (rule 37.10(3)). It must be served on other parties and filed two days before the hearing. A responding party's motion record is required where the moving party refuses or neglects to include a court document that the responding party wishes included or where the responding party decides that a document is required after the moving party's motion record has been filed.

Factums for use on motions

Although not yet mandatory, the rules encourage parties to serve and file a factum for use on a motion. This is particularly useful with long or complex motions involving issues of law. A factum is required if a motion is opposed and in writing. It is also required on certain types of motions in some regions — for example, on a motion for summary judgment in Toronto. A factum can set out in neutral terms the facts of the case, concise arguments on these facts, and statements of the principles of law relied on, including case references. A motion factum is simply a version of the type of factums that have long been filed on appeals (rule 37.10(6)).

SERVICE OF MOTIONS AND MOTION RECORDS

The requirements for service of motion material are scattered through rules 37 and 39. Generally, you should pick a return date that is far enough in advance so that

FIGURE 9.6   MOTION RECORD INDEX

Court file no. 01-CV-1234

ONTARIO
SUPERIOR COURT OF JUSTICE

BETWEEN:

Abigail Boar

Plaintiff

and

Rattle Motors Ltd. and Fred Flogem

Defendants

MOTION RECORD INDEX

Tab	Document	Page
1	Notice of motion brought by the plaintiff, returnable on October 16, year 1	2
2	Affidavit of Eldred Klump, sworn October 3, year 1	3
3	Affidavit of Sunil Tharper, sworn October 6, year 1	4
3a	Exhibit A to the affidavit of Sunil Tharper, sworn October 6, year 1: report from Elihu Dunck, dated October 5, year 1	5
4	Statement of claim, issued January 4, year 1	7
5	Statement of defence, dated January 12, year 1	10

you will have time to serve your documents, receive the responding party's documents, and file a complete motion record on time. But where time is of the essence, here are the steps you must follow:

1. *Determine the location.* Unless there is consent or the matter is urgent, the place of hearing should be where the lawyer for the responding party has his or her office (rule 37.03(2)).

2. *Serve the motion.* The notice of motion, supporting affidavit, and other documents must be served at least four days before the hearing (rules 37.07(6) and 39.01(2)).

3. *File the notice of motion.* The notice of motion with proof of service must be filed at least three days before the day of the hearing (rule 37.08(1)).

4. *File the affidavit.* The moving and the responding parties may file affidavits and other supporting documents at least two days before the hearing, which gives a responding party more time to file (rule 39.02).

5. *File the motion record.* A motion record should be filed at least three days before the date of hearing. If it contains all the documents necessary for the

motion, there is no need to follow the separate rules for filing motions and affidavits that are noted above.

6. *File the responding party's motion record.* If required, this should be served and filed at least two days before the hearing (rule 37.10(3)). This rule is also consistent with the rule requiring filing of affidavits two days before the hearing. Everything that is going to be filed must be with the court two days before the hearing so that the judge or master can read the documents before the hearing.

Remember that these are filing and service deadlines. You could find yourself:

- serving the opposing party on day 1;

- filing your motion record on day 2 (in which case the record is likely to be missing the responding party's material);

- being served with the responding party's material on day 3;

- having the responding party filing his or her own motion record, including the affidavit served on you, on day 3; and

- attending the hearing on day 5.

If the matter is an emergency, both the notice and the service and filing rules may be suspended (rules 2.03 and 37.07(2) to (4)). When proceeding this way, it is wise to ask in the notice of motion for "leave to dispense with service of this notice of motion" and "leave to abridge the time for serving and filing the notice of motion and supporting affidavits" on the grounds that the matter is urgent. If leave is granted, you can proceed with the substantive part of the motion.

ABANDONED MOTIONS

A party who has made a motion, has served but not filed it, and who does not appear in court is deemed to have abandoned the motion. However, a party who makes a motion may abandon it by delivering a notice of abandonment. In either case, the responding party is likely to have done some work and spent some legal fees getting ready to respond. Provided that the moving party served the motion, the responding party is entitled to immediate costs of the motion unless the court specifically orders otherwise. This means that the responding party may move to assess costs without waiting for the trial judgment. If the responding party appears on a motion that has been abandoned, he or she can ask the court to fix costs immediately, saving the need for a separate assessment of costs, and yet another court attendance. A notice of abandonment is set out in figure 9.7.

However, for emergency motions in Toronto, you still need to obtain a date beforehand from the Motions Scheduling Unit. For details, see the appendix to this chapter.

MOTIONS MADE WITHOUT ORAL ARGUMENT

The usual way to argue a motion is for counsel to appear at the hearing on the return date and to make submissions orally with references to the motion, affidavits,

FIGURE 9.7 NOTICE OF ABANDONMENT

Court file no. 01-CV-1234

ONTARIO
SUPERIOR COURT OF JUSTICE

BETWEEN:

Abigail Boar

Plaintiff

and

Rattle Motors Ltd. and Fred Flogem

Defendants

NOTICE OF ABANDONMENT

TAKE NOTICE that the moving party, Abigail Boar, wholly abandons
the motion returnable on October 16, year 1.

Date: October 10, year 1

Just & Coping
Barristers and Solicitors
365 Bay Street - 8701
Toronto, Ontario, M3J 4A9

I.M. Just
tel. 416-762-1342
fax 416-762-2300

Solicitors for the Moving
Party (Plaintiff)

TO:
Huey Sue
Barrister and Solicitor
65 False Trail
Toronto, Ontario, M6Y 1Z6

tel. 416-485-6891
fax 416-485-6892

Solicitor for the Responding
Parties (Defendants)

transcripts, or other documents. However, there are some circumstances where a motion does not require anyone to appear at a hearing.

Motion on consent

If a motion has been made and the responding party consents to the order sought, the moving party needs to file a consent and a draft order along with the notice of motion. A judge simply signs the order after reviewing the consent (rule 37.12.1(2)). You may wish to contact the court office to find out the procedure for filing a consent motion. Some regions ask moving parties to indicate on the motion that it is returnable during "the week of" followed by a date, for example, rather than on a specific day.

Unopposed motion

If the motion has been served and the responding party signals that he or she does not oppose it, the moving party should file a notice from the responding party that the motion is unopposed, together with a draft order (rule 37.12.1(3)). The notice should indicate that there is no opposition to the order sought. An example of the wording of such a notice is set out in figure 9.8.

Motions without notice

Motions without notice may be made in writing. For example, a motion for substituted service may not require oral argument. The notice of motion should make it clear what the moving party requires, and the affidavit should provide all of the evidence and facts a master would need to grant the order.

Opposed motions in writing

Where a motion is opposed and the issues are not overly complicated, the moving party may propose in the notice of motion that there be no oral argument and that the documents on the motion be submitted to the court. This is attractive because it saves the cost of a hearing, but most lawyers are loath to give up the opportunity for oral argument because it gives them the chance to gauge the court's reaction to the arguments. However, the elimination of oral argument is the way of the future for some procedures since it saves time and money. If the moving party wishes to take this route, the motion must be served 14 days before the return date. The moving party must serve a motion record *with* the notice of motion, a draft order, and a factum for a motion in writing, and at the same time file all of this with the court.

Within 10 days of being served, the responding party must serve and file a consent to the order, a notice that the order is not opposed, or a motion record with a notice that the responding party agrees to have the contested motion dealt with in writing without oral argument. In this case, the responding party must also file a factum.

If the responding party requires oral argument, he or she serves the moving party with notice that the responding party intends to make oral argument as well as file material. The moving party must then decide whether to appear and argue the motion or rely on his or her motion record and factum (rule 37.12.1(4)).

FIGURE 9.8   NOTICE THAT MOTION IS UNOPPOSED

Court file no. 01-CV-1234

ONTARIO
SUPERIOR COURT OF JUSTICE

BETWEEN:

Abigail Boar

Plaintiff

and

Rattle Motors Ltd. and Fred Flogem

Defendants

NOTICE THAT MOTION IS UNOPPOSED

TAKE NOTICE that the defendant, Rattle Motors Ltd.
(responding party), does not object to the order sought by
the plaintiff (moving party) to permit an inspection by a
lighting engineer of the defendant's premises at 1240 Bay
Street, Toronto, Ontario, M4H 0K8.

Huey Sue
Barrister and Solicitor
65 False Trail
Toronto, Ontario, M6Y 1Z6

tel. 416-485-6891
fax 416-485-6892

Solicitor for the Responding
Parties (Defendants)

TO:
Just & Coping
Barristers and Solicitors
365 Bay Street - 8701
Toronto, Ontario, M3J 4A9

I.M. Just
tel. 416-762-1342
fax 416-762-2300

Solicitors for the Moving
Party (Plaintiff)

CHAPTER SUMMARY

In this chapter, we examined the procedures for making motions, beginning with an overview of the procedure for a motion on notice. We then saw how motions without notice are dealt with, how to determine whether a motion should come before a master or a judge, and how to obtain a hearing date, noting the way in which practice directions in Toronto have complicated motion procedure there. We then examined the requirements for notices of motion and affidavits, focusing on criteria and rules for drafting and preparing these documents. Following this discussion, we turned to the preparation of motion records and to the rules governing time limits for serving motion materials. Finally, we examined the consequences of abandoning a motion and looked at the requirements and procedure for bring a motion in writing without oral argument.

APPENDIX: OBTAINING A MOTION HEARING DATE IN TORONTO

Until recently, there was a confusing collection of practice directions for procedures on various types of motions in Toronto. All of these were designed to spread out the motion workload so that the Toronto judges and masters could handle it efficiently, but case-managed and non-case-managed motions were handled differently, as were motions before judges and masters. There were also other specialized procedures for other areas such as estate, commercial list, and construction lien matters.

As of September 2002, there is one procedural guide for scheduling and bringing motions in Toronto, the *Superior Court of Justice Motions and Applications Procedure — Toronto Region*. If you are involved with Toronto motions, you should obtain a copy of this document, and any amendments, from the Toronto Court Office and read it carefully. Highlights are set out here:

1. There is a specific procedure for scheduling masters' and judges' motions in almost all cases, case-managed or non-case-managed. Estate list, commercial list, and some other motions are not covered by this practice direction.

2. To schedule a motion:

    a. You must check with counsel for the responding party to decide on a suitable date, and estimate how long the motion will take, provided that it will not take more than two hours.

    b. Call 416-327-5292 or e-mail the Motions Scheduling Unit at jus.g.mag.csd.civilmotionscheduling@jus.gov.on.ca to determine whether the date selected is available, and to book it if it is.

3. If the motion will take more than two hours, obtain a special appointment from the Motions Scheduling Unit:

    a. Your notice of motion will not have a fixed date. Instead, it will indicate that it will be heard on a date to be fixed by the court.

    b. With the responding party, you will have to work out a timetable of all steps to be taken prior to the argument of the motion, including the dates on which those steps will be completed. You must also include in the timetable the dates for exchange of motion documents with the responding party.

c. Serve the timetable with your notice of motion so that the responding party can review it.

d. As the moving party, you will have to file this timetable with your motion record. There is no special form for the timetable.

e. If the responding party does not agree to the timetable, either party can ask for a case conference to fix the timetable.

f. Once the timetable is complete and either fixed by the court or agreed to, the Motions Scheduling Unit will provide the parties with a court date.

4. If a motion is before a judge and will take more than one full day, you will need to have a case conference before the judge in charge of long motions to deal with timetables and other procedural matters. The judge will assign it to a trial list "for the week of" rather than for a specific date. This means that counsel will have to be sure to be available for that week, without having much advance notice of when the motion will actually be heard.

5. All motions, long or regular, must be confirmed by 2:00 p.m. two business days before the motion is to be heard. Confirmation may be made by fax to 416-327-5484 or by e-mail to jus.g.mag.csd.civilmotionsconfirmation @jus.gov.on.ca. Figure 9.9 shows the confirmation form for all judges/ masters civil motions/applications.

6. Urgent or emergency motions can be scheduled by calling the manager of the Motions Scheduling Unit at 416-326-1843.

7. If the motion is about discovery undertakings or objections involving more than five questions, there are special procedures. You are required to use a chart in prescribed form (schedule B to the practice direction) to list disputed discovery questions and the issues surrounding them.

KEY TERMS

motion	summary proceedings
return of a motion	master
official examiner	jurat

NOTES

1 In a proper case, rule 37.17 permits a motion to be brought before a proceeding has been commenced, provided that the moving party undertakes to commence proceedings promptly.

2 A motion without notice may also be brought in the court nearest to the residence of any party or nearest to the office of the solicitor of record of any party.

FIGURE 9.9 CONFIRMATION FORM FOR ALL JUDGES/MASTERS CIVIL MOTIONS/APPLICATIONS

ONTARIO
SUPERIOR COURT OF JUSTICE
CASE MANAGEMENT SCHEDULING UNIT

383 University Avenue, 10th Floor
Toronto ON M5G 1E6
Telephone: (416) 327-5292; Fax: (416) 327-5484
E-mail: jus.g.mag.csd.civilmotionsconfirmation@jus.gov.on.ca

CONFIRMATION FORM FOR ALL JUDGES/MASTERS
CIVIL MOTIONS/APPLICATIONS

COURT FILE NUMBER:

SHORT TITLE: _Boar v. Rattle Motors Ltd. et al._

Jurisdiction of Motion:
☐ Judge   ☒ Traditional Master   ☐ Case Management Master   _Smith_
(Name of Managing Master)

I, _I. M. Just_ , COUNSEL FOR THE MOVING
PARTY/~~APPLICANT~~, CONFIRM:

☒   I HAVE DISCUSSED WITH _Huey Sue_ , OPPOSING
COUNSEL/PARTY, THE MATTER REFERRED TO ABOVE AND CONFIRM,

OR

☐   I HAVE BEEN UNABLE TO CONFIRM WITH OPPOSING COUNSEL/PARTY BECAUSE
_____,

THAT THE MOTION/APPLICATION LISTED TO BE HEARD ON _Monday_ THE _16th_ DAY OF _October_, ~~2002~~ _YR 1_ IS:

(TICK ONE BOX ONLY):

☐ WITHDRAWN ON CONSENT   ☐ CONSENTED TO

☐ UNOPPOSED, ALL OTHER ISSUES   ☐ OPPOSED, COST ISSUE ONLY

☐ ADJOURNED ON CONSENT TO: _____(DATE BOOKED WITH SCHEDULING UNIT)

☐ OPPOSED ADJOURNMENT TO BE REQUESTED BY: _____

☒ OPPOSED ON ISSUES AS SET OUT IN THE NOTICE OF MOTION/MOTION FORM

☐ OPPOSED ONLY ON THE FOLLOWING ISSUES: _____

TIME ESTIMATE REQUIRED: _1_ HOURS _25_ MINUTES   ☐ MORE THAN ORIGINALLY ESTIMATED

THE FOLLOWING MATERIALS (MOVING AND RESPONDING) HAVE BEEN FILED FOR USE ON THIS MATTER.

1. _Statement of claim, Jan. 4, YR 1_   4. _Affidavit of Sunil Tharper, sworn Oct. 6, YR 1_
2. _Statement of defence, Jan. 12, YR 1_   5.
3. _Affidavit of Eldred Klump, sworn Oct. 1, YR 1_ 6.

October 12, YR 1
Date & Time

I. M. Just
Solicitor for moving party (please type or print clearly)

416 - 762 - 1342   imjust@isp.on.ca
Telephone Number and Email Address

TO: SCHEDULING UNIT
FAX: 416-327-5484   CONFIRMATIONS ONLY – NO FILINGS WILL BE ACCEPTED
EMAIL: jus.g.mag.csd.civilmotionsconfirmation@jus.gov.on.ca

NOTE:
❑   CONFIRMATION OF MOTION MUST BE FAXED OR E-MAILED BY 2:00 P.M. TWO DAYS PRIOR TO THE
      SCHEDULED DATE OF HEARING
❑   IF CONFIRMATION IS NOT RECEIVED BY THE SCHEDULING UNIT, THE SCHEDULED MOTION/APPLICATION
      WILL BE NOTED AS ABANDONED
❑   NO LATE MATERIALS WILL BE ACCEPTED BY THE COURT
❑   THIS FORM SHOULD BE COPIED TO OPPOSING COUNSEL/PARTY

3 A master's motion, as a matter of convention, may be brought before a judge in an emergency if no master is available.

4 Often this is a "motion morning" or a "motion afternoon." Once you know the court where the matter must be heard, call the court office to find out when the motion time is.

5 While the form calls for the municipality and the county or region as a residential description, the City of Toronto, since the abolition of the former Municipality of Metropolitan Toronto, is no longer part of a county or region. The practice has grown up of describing a deponent residing in Toronto as residing in the City of Toronto, Province of Ontario.

6 The wording of the jurat changes slightly when it is sworn by two or more deponents, when it is sworn by a blind or illiterate person, or when it is sworn by a person who does not understand the language in which it is written. If the deponent is blind or illiterate, the jurat must indicate that the deponent had it read to him or her, that he or she understood it, and that he or she signed it or made his or her mark (usually an "X"). If the deponent does not understand the language, the jurat must indicate that a named person interpreted the affidavit and swore to translate it correctly.

REFERENCES

Judicial Review Procedure Act, RSO 1990, c. J.1.

Rules of Civil Procedure, RRO 1990, reg. 194.

REVIEW QUESTIONS

1. What is the purpose of motions?

2. What does the phrase "motioning the other side to death" mean, and how may the practice be prevented?

3. Explain to your client what happens when a motion is brought.

4. Indicate whether a master can hear the following motions:

    a. a motion to strike out parts of a statement of claim

    b. a motion to commit a witness to jail for failure to appear at trial when summonsed

    c. a motion to vary an order made by Judge Jeffreys

    d. a motion to join parties to the lawsuit

    e. a motion for a judgment on consent where 16-year-old Rory is a party

5. Suppose your firm wishes to bring a "long motion" in Toronto. Is there anything special you should do?

6. When can hearsay be used in an affidavit?

7. What is included in a motion record?

8. What is the purpose of a motion record?

9. a. Today is March 2. Your instructing lawyer wants to bring a motion on notice returnable March 5. Can she do it? Why?

   b. When is the last day the lawyer could have filed a motion record?

   c. When is the last day the responding party could have filed a responding party motion record?

10. Can a law firm bring a motion, change its mind, and abandon the motion without consequences?

11. Suppose your law firm wishes to make a motion in writing, rather than have an oral hearing. Can it?

DISCUSSION QUESTIONS

1. Read and respond to the following memorandum:

   To: E. Egregious, law clerk
   From: I.M. Just, lawyer
   Re: *Boar v. Rattle Motors Ltd. et al.*

   When we brought a motion for inspection of Rattle Motor's showroom, under rule 32, we were surprised to hear that the defendant had gutted the interior of the showroom and destroyed important evidence. I don't believe that this renovation had anything to do with marketing cars. I want to bring a motion to have the defendant found in contempt for the intentional destruction of evidence. But before I do that, I want to examine Sunil Tharper, the manager, on this issue. Write me a brief memo setting out what authority there is for doing this.

2. Read and respond to the following memorandum:

   To: E. Egregious, law clerk
   From: I.M. Just, lawyer
   Re: *Boar v. Rattle Motors Ltd. et al.*

   I have just received a report from Diedre Kuflesnout. She is an automobile engineer and a member of the Society of Automotive Engineers. She is a consultant and expert on assessing mechanical and design defects in cars. Her report indicates that leaking oil pans on new models, affecting about 12 cars in 1,000, have plagued the year 0 Super Coupe. The expected rate of leaking pans would be about 1 car in 2,000 had there been no problem. There is also information that the manufacturer was aware that there might be a problem and did nothing. Although we are about to start discoveries, I want to add Skank Motorcar Company Ltd., the manufacturer of the Super Coupe, as a party defendant in this lawsuit. Find out what rule gives me the right to do this, and then draft the notice of motion and an affidavit in my name setting out the reasons why the proposed defendant should be added. Also advise me as to whether we would likely have to pay costs and what rights the other defendants might have.

CHAPTER 10

Default judgment

INTRODUCTION

Once you have served the plaintiff's statement of claim, the defendant must serve you with a statement of defence within the time provided for in the rules. If you receive no statement of defence, the defendant is deemed to have admitted the truth of the facts in the statement of claim and admitted liability. The plaintiff may then obtain a judgment against the defendant in default of a defence. The plaintiff may also obtain a default judgment if a defence was delivered but was struck out without leave to file another (rule 19.01(2)). Where there are several defendants and one has not delivered a defence, and the plaintiff has not noted that defendant in default, a defendant who has delivered a defence can require the registrar to order the plaintiff to note the non-filing defendant in default (rule 19.01(3)).

While obtaining a default judgment is a paper process, it can now be done electronically where the hardware is available. E-filing, which is likely to become a more common feature in civil procedure, will reduce the number of tedious attendances at the court office.

If a claim is a liquidated amount, there is a quick and straightforward administrative process for obtaining a judgment for the amount due. Most debt collection cases are liquidated claims — for example, claims for payment for goods sold or services rendered or for repayment of loans.

Abigail's claim against Fred and Rattle Motors, however, is not liquidated. Her claim for general damages cannot be calculated by using a simple, objective formula. Even her special damages, which can be calculated that way, are still accruing, so we do not know what they will total. In this kind of case, even though the defendant is deemed to have admitted the truth of the facts in the statement of claim and to have admitted liability, the plaintiff is obliged to prove the monetary value of damages on a motion to a judge. Evidence may be given by affidavit or orally in a hearing if the court requires it. An affidavit, usually the plaintiff's, details her injuries, pain, treatment, and post-injury disabilities by way of general damages; it also provides details of her special damages. Affidavits of other witnesses provide other evidence that supports the claim for damages.

In this chapter, we examine both the summary method of signing default judgment for liquidated damages before the registrar and the method whereby a judge assesses general damages.

DEFAULT JUDGMENT FOR A LIQUIDATED DEMAND

To obtain or sign default judgment on behalf of a plaintiff, you must prepare certain documents and file them with the registrar of the Superior Court (actually with a clerk at the public counter in the court office of the region where the action is commenced). If the documents are properly prepared and in order, the clerk acts on the registrar's behalf to sign judgment for the full amount of the claim, prejudgment interest, and costs. Be sure that your claim is accurately stated and that your calculations are accurate because it is embarrassing and time-consuming to amend a judgment later to correct an error.

Consider another of Abigail's claims. Hieronymus Bloggs owes Abigail Boar $38,182.79 for the financial analysis services provided by Abigail. Payment should have been made on July 28, year 0, and interest runs on overdue amounts at the rate of 12 percent per annum. On September 26, year 0, I.M. Just issued a claim on Abigail's behalf and served it on Hieronymus. No statement of defence was received, and I.M. Just intends to sign default judgment on October 17, year 0. The cost of issuing a claim is $157. You paid a process server $41 to serve the claim and provide you with an affidavit of service. You have receipts to attach to the bill of costs for all disbursements. GST is chargeable on all fees and on disbursements that are services, such as photocopies, fax, postage, and service of pleadings at 7 percent. GST is not chargeable on government fees, such as the $157 paid to issue the statement of claim.

Forms required to sign default judgment

The following are the forms required to sign default judgment:

- an affidavit of service, proving service of the statement of claim, and the original statement of claim;

- a requisition of default judgment, noting the defendant in default;

- a bill of costs (the original and two copies) to provide a basis for fixing the amount of costs;

- a draft judgment (the original and two copies);

- a requisition for a writ of seizure and sale;

- a writ of seizure and sale (the original and two copies); and

- a cheque, payable to the Ontario Superior Court of Justice to issue the writ of seizure and sale (rules 19.01 and 19.04).

The defendant may be noted in default separately by filing a requisition to note the defendant in default. But it saves some time and paper to note the defendant in default as part of the requisition for default judgment. The effect of noting the defendant in default is to note pleadings closed, which bars the late filing of a statement of defence.

The requisition for default judgment requires you to state that the claim is liquidated and that it comes within the class of claims for which you may sign default judgment. You also show on this form how much is owing, less payments made by the debtor, if any.

Procedure for signing judgment

Set out below is a step-by-step guide to signing default judgment.

PREPARE A REQUISITION FOR DEFAULT JUDGMENT

You will need the original statement of claim attached to the process server's affidavit of service so that the clerk can see when the claim was served, where it was served, and satisfy himself or herself that the time for filing the defence has elapsed. Remember that the time runs from the time of service, not from the time the claim was issued. Figure 10.1 at the end of the chapter shows a completed requisition for a default judgment.

1. On the requisition itself, after the words "TO THE LOCAL REGISTRAR AT," type in the word "Toronto." After this, type "I REQUIRE you to note the defendant (*name*) in default in this action and that pleadings be noted closed against the defendant on the ground that the defendant has failed to file a statement of defence within the time provided for in the *Rules of Civil Procedure*."

2. Check off the basis for signing default judgment.

3. Indicate whether any payments have been made on account with respect to the claim. If some payments have been made, complete part A; if none have been made, complete part B.

4. If some payments have been made, indicate the principal amount claimed, without interest. Then show the payment on account, and show how much of that payment is allocated to interest and how much to principal. At common law, amounts received are applied first to outstanding interest. If there is any amount remaining, it is applied to outstanding principal. After allocating the payment received, indicate the principal amount outstanding. This is "total A" on the form.

5. With respect to the calculation of prejudgment interest, indicate the date on which the claim was issued and the date on which the cause of action arose. This allows the clerk (and you) to determine how many days of interest your client is entitled to, and what the appropriate rate is if interest is calculated under the prejudgment interest provisions of the *Courts of Justice Act*. If you have not previously learned how to apply the prejudgment and postjudgment interest rules, see chapter 17.

6. Show how the prejudgment interest is calculated. Calculate simple interest unless you have a contractual right to compound interest. Calculate interest on the principal amount outstanding from the date of the last payment previously identified in the form. To do this, count the number of days from the date of the last payment to the date on which judgment is to be signed (the last "end date" in the form). Then multiply that number by the annual rate of interest, multiply that result by the principal amount owing, and divide by 365. This is "total B" on the form.

7. From the calculations in 6 above, enter total B, and from the calculations in 4 above, enter total A in order to fill in the total amount for which to sign judgment.

8. If no payment was received, then complete part B, indicating amount A, the total amount of the claim less interest. Provide the interest data,

including the date on which the claim arose and was issued. Then show your interest calculations, using simple interest unless you have a contractual right to compound interest and have claimed this in your statement of claim. Count the number of days from the date the cause of action arose to the date of judgment, and do the calculations as described previously for part A (part payments received). Add the sum claimed (total A) to the interest claimed (total B) to determine the amount for which the judgment is to be signed.

9. Complete part C, "Postjudgment interest and costs." Insert the rate of postjudgment interest that applies (this is either a rate contractually agreed on between the parties or the rate set by statute for the quarter in which the judgment is signed), and indicate the basis for claiming interest. Then check off whether you wish the registrar to fix costs or have the costs assessed later. The usual practice is to have the registrar fix the costs based on your bill of costs, which you prepare in accordance with the rules. This is much quicker and less expensive than coming back at a later date to have the costs assessed. One might ask to have a bill of costs assessed if costs to the plaintiff had been much higher than is usually the case in a default judgment situation. In this situation, having costs assessed might be worth the time and expense because costs are fixed in accordance with flat rates based on a "normal" proceeding.

PREPARE A BILL OF COSTS

See figure 10.2 at the end of the chapter for Abigail's bill of costs. In a default judgment situation, as in most civil cases, the loser pays some of the winner's legal costs on a **partial indemnity** scale. The basis for assessing lawyers' fees on a bill of costs is the costs grid in tariff A, Solicitor's Fees and Disbursements. It includes set amounts for lawyers' fees for performing certain services. The assessment officer may increase the set amount if he or she believes it is unreasonably low for the work done. The high end of each fee level was designed for use in Toronto, where fees are generally higher than elsewhere. The fee actually charged by the lawyer to his or her client may be much higher than the grid allows. But lawyers' out-of-pocket expenses are another story. Under tariff A, part II "disbursements," payments are nearly on a dollar-for-dollar basis. For example, travel costs paid to a witness may amount to what it actually cost the witness to travel. There are limits on some part II disbursements. For example, fees paid to an expert witness may be $500 per day, but part II allows a maximum of $350 per day, subject to the discretion of the assessment officer. If costs are fixed, you are limited to a claim for what you actually paid or $350, whichever is less. Court and sheriff fees can be recovered in full. The items usually included in the bill of costs on default judgment are as follows:

1. *Pleadings.* Hours times appropriate hourly rate in the costs grid (the more experience a lawyer has, the higher the hourly rate on the grid).

2. *Court fees paid to issue statement of claim.* $157.[1]

3. *Fees paid to serve statement of claim.* Tariff A, part II, reasonable cost backed by attached receipt.

partial indemnity
usual order for costs, based on a cost grid that establishes hourly rates for tariff items listed in the grid; provides less than full recovery for the client

4. *Assessment of costs and signing order (default judgment).* Hours times appropriate hourly rate in the costs grid.

5. *Fee paid to file requisition for default judgment.* $90.

In the bill of costs, fees and disbursements are recorded in separate columns and totalled. Disbursements include tariff A, part II items, as well as court fees and sheriff fees. If for any reason you wish to recover costs on a **substantial indemnity** basis, this is a claim for a full recovery of costs and is best dealt with by being set down for hearing before an assessment officer, although it is possible to have these costs fixed.

substantial indemnity costs scale, usually used as a punitive costs award, that results in near indemnity for the winner on a dollar-for-dollar basis

DRAFT A JUDGMENT

Draft a judgment such as the one shown in figure 10.3 (at the end of the chapter), and make two copies of it. A judgment is a one-paragraph document in which you must insert the sum claimed, composed of the principal amount and interest (taken from the requisition for default judgment), and the costs (taken from the bill of costs). Remember to include a sentence saying, "This judgment bears interest at the rate of ___ percent per year from its date." If this statement is not present in the draft judgment, even though interest is claimed in the statement of claim and identified in the requisition for default judgment, the clerk may not insert the phrase for you, and you may not obtain postjudgment interest.

PREPARE A REQUISITION FOR A WRIT OF SEIZURE AND SALE

The requisition, which is set out in figure 10.4 at the end of the chapter, is directed to the sheriff of each county, region, or district where you think the debtor has assets. If the debtor has assets in more than one area, you must refer in the requisition to each sheriff's office in which you intend to file a writ of seizure and sale. Be sure to set out the name of the debtor accurately. Include the amount to be seized, the amount of costs claimed, and the applicable postjudgment interest rate, all of which can be copied from the judgment.

PREPARE A WRIT OF SEIZURE AND SALE

This writ is set out in figure 10.5 at the end of the chapter. You should prepare an original and one copy of it for each sheriff's office in which you plan to file it. When you obtain the default judgment and pay the fee to issue the writ, file the original and one copy with the sheriff's office, along with a covering letter instructing the sheriff to file the writ in the land registry and land titles system (if there is one). If the writ is not filed in the land titles system, the writ will not attach the execution debtor's land registered in the land titles system. Filing the writ with the sheriff is sufficient to attach an interest in land registered in the land registry system. Check with the sheriff's office to ascertain the fee for filing with the land registry system.

To complete each writ, fill in the blanks, using the judgment and the requisition for a writ of seizure and sale as the source of the relevant information. Keep one copy of each writ for your office file. Remember to complete the backsheet by adding in the fee paid to the province to issue the writ, and the fee paid to the lawyer for doing the work. The sheriff is entitled to add these costs to the amount on the face of the writ that may be collected from the debtor in the future.

To cover the cost of issuing each original writ of seizure and sale, check the current court's and sheriff's fees tariff.

DEFAULT JUDGMENT FOR AN UNLIQUIDATED DEMAND

Where a claim is not liquidated and the defendant has defaulted on a defence, or where the registrar is uncertain about a liquidated claim and refuses to sign default judgment, the plaintiff must bring a motion before a judge against the defendant to claim judgment on the statement of claim.

Evidence of damages

Where the claim is unliquidated, more detail is required than in the case of a liquidated claim. Initially, this detail is provided by way of affidavit evidence. If the judge is satisfied with the contents of the affidavit, he or she may grant judgment in accordance with the motion. But if there is any doubt, the judge can order that the matter proceed to trial for an assessment of damages. The judge may also decide that the claim is without merit — for example, if the claim concerns a breach of a right of the plaintiff that the law does not recognize. In that case, it does not matter whether the plaintiff can prove damages. If there is no right of action, the claim is dismissed even though the defendant has not put in a defence.

Contents of the affidavit

Where the statement of claim discloses a breach of the plaintiff's rights, the affidavit need only focus on the damages. Abigail's affidavit would describe the accident very briefly and focus on her injuries, convalescence, recovery, treatment, and the consequences of the injury on her social life, employment, and general enjoyment of life. An exhibit should be attached to the affidavit, listing the totals for special damages, such as medications, homecare assistance, and income loss. You may wish to have an affidavit from Abigail's doctor with medical reports about her prognosis attached as exhibits. You may want an affidavit from her employer or from the human resources person who has handled her work disability issues. You may also wish to have affidavits from one or two of her acquaintances who can describe the pre- and post-injury Abigail to show how the injuries have affected her daily life.

If a judge decides that oral evidence should be heard, the witnesses who made the affidavits will testify, and the topics covered will be the same as those covered in the affidavits.

Figure 10.6 (at the end of the chapter) shows what Abigail's affidavit might look like. Because it includes both evidence from which factual conclusions can be drawn and the facts themselves, it appears to be like a detailed version of the paragraphs in Abigail's statement of claim that deal with damages. Since liability is deemed to be admitted, little space is devoted to that issue.

SETTING ASIDE DEFAULT JUDGMENT

Often a plaintiff will serve a defendant, and the defendant will not respond. While the plaintiff is entitled to assume that the defendant's lack of response is simply an admission of the plaintiff's case, that is not always the case. Where, for example, the defendant has been served by an alternative to personal service, he or she may have been unaware of the case against him or her because service was ineffective. For example, the plaintiff may have attempted personal service at the defendant's residence and followed up, following rule 16.03(5), by delivering and then mailing the statement of claim to the defendant at his or her residence. Perhaps the defendant was out of town, and the letters were just left for him or her. The defendant may return to find that there is now a judgment against him or her. In other cases, the defendant is served and turns the claim over to a lawyer with instructions to defend; the lawyer then inadvertently misses the time limit. In these cases, rule 19.08 provides that a judgment signed by the registrar or a judgment made after motion to a judge may be set aside or varied by the court. The noting of the defendant in default may also be set aside, which technically reopens pleadings and allows a statement of defence to be filed. The cases make clear that the defendant must satisfy the court on three factors if the judgment is to be set aside:

1. the default must be adequately explained as the result of a mistake or error on the part of one or more of the parties,

2. the motion to set the judgment aside must be brought promptly, and,

3. the defendant must disclose a plausible defence that cannot be decided without cross-examination or further judicial inquiry.[2]

Figure 10.7 (at the end of the chapter) sets out the kind of affidavit that can be used to set aside a default judgment.

SETTING ASIDE ORDERS ON MOTIONS

What rule 19.08 does for default judgments, rule 37.14 does for orders made on motions. Any order made by a judge or master on a motion, or made by a registrar, may be set aside by bringing a motion to set aside or vary the order in question.

When motion to set aside may be brought

Anyone who is affected by an order made on a motion without notice may move to set the order aside. The person need not be a party to the proceeding. The breadth of this rule demonstrates the safeguards that are built into the rules where a motion is made without notice. Where a motion is made with notice and a responding party or other interested person fails to appear through inadvertence, mistake, or insufficient notice, that person may move to set the motion aside. Here, because of the short minimum period for serving and filing, a responding or interested party may not have enough time to prepare adequately. In a case like this, it is appropriate to tell the moving party that the time period is too short and ask for an adjournment. If the moving party refuses, rule 37.14 provides an adequate, if cumbersome, remedy. If a person is affected by an order of a registrar, he or she may move to set the judgment aside.

Motion procedure

The rule requires that a motion be brought immediately on finding out about the order. The motion is returnable on the first available day that is at least three days

TABLE 10.1 ROUTES FOR SETTING ASIDE ORDER ON MOTION

Nature of original order	*Before whom motion to set aside should be made*
Order of a registrar	Judge or master in accordance with rule 37.03.
Order of a judge	1. Judge who made the order in any place where the judge is sitting. 2. Any other judge in accordance with rule 37.03.
Order of a master	1. Master who made the order in any place where the master is sitting. 2. Any other judge or master in accordance with rule 37.03.
Order of a judge of Court of Appeal or Divisional Court	1. Judge who made the order. 2. If the order was made by a panel of judges, the panel that made it.

after the service of the motion (the minimum notice period under the rules). Rule 37.14(3) to (6) tells you before whom a motion may be brought, depending on who made the original order. This is necessary because of jurisdictional issues. A master does not have the power to set aside a judge's order. Table 10.1 summarizes the routes to follow to set aside an order made on a motion.

CHAPTER SUMMARY

In this chapter we examined the procedure for obtaining a default judgment when the defendant fails to file a statement of defence. We noted the difference between a liquidated claim, where the registrar of the court signs judgment as an administrative act, and an unliquidated claim, where the plaintiff is obliged to present evidence to show what the quantum of damages should be. We noted how to prepare the necessary documentation for a default judgment (requisition, bill of costs, draft judgment, requisition for a writ of seizure and sale, and a writ of seizure and sale). We then examined what is required to set aside a default judgment both for judgments and for orders made on other kinds of motions.

KEY TERMS

partial indemnity

substantial indemnity

NOTES

1 As of August 2001; the fees change every year or so.

2 See *Grieco v. Marquis* (1998), 38 OR (3d) 314 (Gen. Div).

REFERENCES

Courts of Justice Act, RSO 1990, c. C.43.

Grieco v. Marquis (1998), 38 OR (3d) 314 (Gen. Div.).

Rules of Civil Procedure, RRO 1990, reg. 194.

REVIEW QUESTIONS

1. Under what circumstances can a plaintiff apply to sign default judgment?

2. Explain the difference between a liquidated and an unliquidated claim.

3. What documents must you present to the court in order to sign a default judgment?

4. What is the function of the requisition for default judgment?

5. Suppose the defendant defaults on his or her defence but pays some money on account of the amount claimed. How does this affect the process of signing default judgment?

6. What determines the prejudgment and postjudgment interest rate you ask for?

7. How do you determine the amounts that go into a bill of costs?

8. In what circumstances do you need to requisition more than one writ of seizure and sale?

9. If you wish to set aside a default judgment, what must you show to the court?

10. Explain how setting aside an order under rule 37.14 differs from setting aside a judgment under rule 19.

1. Read and respond to the following memorandum:

   To: Law clerk
   From: Lawyer
   Re: *Ulock v. Foot*
   Date: April 26, year 1

   We issued a claim against Murgatroyd Ulock on March 23, year 1. Ulock had signed a promissory note to our client, Squeezem Ltd., for $20,000 on August 1, year 0. The note was due on December 1, year 0. It provided for interest at 11 percent per year from the time it was past due until payment. Interest has been claimed on this basis. The claim was thus for $20,000 plus interest on the overdue amount. On March 1, year 1, Ulock paid $2,000 on account, but he has paid nothing since. Ulock was served with the statement of claim on March 24, year 1. Because Ulock has not defended, and the time for filing a defence has passed, please prepare the necessary documents to sign default judgment on April 28, year 1. The original statement of claim and affidavit of service is in the file, together with a receipt for $53.21 for service of the claim and a receipt for $157 for the court fee paid to issue the statement of claim. It is rumoured that Foot owns property in Toronto and Oshawa.

2. Read and respond to the following memorandum:

   To: Law clerk
   From: Lawyer
   Re: *Foot ats Ulock*
   Date: April 30, year 1

   I have just learned that default judgment has been signed on April 28, year 1 against our client, Ophelia Foot, on a promissory note made to Murgatroyd Ulock. Foot brought the statement of claim in two weeks ago, and I meant to draft a defence. The defence is to be based on the fact that Ophelia does not speak or read English, she thought she was signing a lease rather than a promissory note, and Ulock misled her and intended to defraud her. Unfortunately, I spilled coffee all over the statement of defence, put it on the radiator in the copier room to dry out, and then forgot about it. I think the cleaners threw it out, so I do not have a copy, though I remember it was a simple claim on a promissory note. Draft a notice of motion and affidavit in support in my name so that we can move to set aside default judgment.

FIGURE 10.1   REQUISITION FOR DEFAULT JUDGMENT (FORM 19D)

Court file no. 01-CV-7777

ONTARIO
SUPERIOR COURT OF JUSTICE

BETWEEN:

Abigail Boar

Plaintiff

and

Hieronymus Bloggs

Defendant

REQUISITION FOR DEFAULT JUDGMENT

TO THE LOCAL REGISTRAR AT TORONTO

I REQUIRE you to note the defendant, Hieronymus Bloggs, in default in this action and that pleadings be noted closed against the defendant on the ground that the defendant has failed to file a statement of defence within the time provided for in the *Rules of Civil Procedure*.

I REQUIRE default judgment to be signed against the defendant Hieronymus Bloggs.

Default judgment may properly be signed in this action because the claim is for

ⵝ a debt or liquidated demand in money
❑ recovery of possession of land
❑ recovery of possession of personal property
❑ foreclosure, sale or redemption of a mortgage

ⵝ There has been no payment on account of the claim since the statement of claim was issued. *(Complete Parts B & C.)*
OR
❑ The following payments have been made on account of the claim since the statement of claim was issued. *(Complete Parts A & C.)*

FIGURE 10.1 CONTINUED

Part A — PAYMENT(S) RECEIVED BY PLAINTIFF

(Complete this part only where part payment of the claim has been received. Where no payment has been received on account of the claim, omit this part and complete Part B.)

1. Principal

Principal sum claimed in
statement of claim (without interest) $ . . . .

Date of Payment	Amount of Payment	Payment Amount Principal	Applied to Interest	Principal Sum Owing
TOTAL	$	$	$	A $ . . . .

2. Prejudgment interest

(Under section 128 of the Courts of Justice Act, *judgment may be obtained for prejudgment interest from the date the cause of action arose, if claimed in the statement of claim.)*

Date on which statement of claim was issued . . . .

Date from which prejudgment interest is claimed . . . .

The plaintiff is entitled to prejudgment interest on the claim, calculated as follows:

(Calculate simple interest only unless an agreement relied on in the statement of claim specifies otherwise. Calculate interest on the principal sum owing from the date of the last payment. To calculate the interest amount, count the number of days since the last payment, multiply that number by the annual rate of interest, multiply the result by the principal sum owing and divide by 365.)

Principal Sum Owing	Start Date	End Date (Date of Payment)	Number of Days	Rate	Interest Amount

(The last End Date should be the date judgment is signed.)

TOTAL B $ . . . .

Principal Sum Owing (Total A above) $ . . . .
Total Interest Amount (Total B above) $ . . . .

SIGN JUDGMENT FOR . . . . $ . . . .

FIGURE 10.1 CONTINUED

PART B — NO PAYMENT RECEIVED BY PLAINTIFF

(Complete this part only where no payment has been received on account of the claim.)

1. Principal

   Principal sum claimed in
   statement of claim (without interest) A $ 38,182.79

2. Prejudgment interest

   (Under section 128 of the Courts of Justice Act, *judgment may be obtained for prejudgment interest from the date the cause of action arose, if claimed in the statement of claim.)*

   Date on which statement of claim was issued . . September 26, year 0 . . . .

   Date from which prejudgment interest is claimed . . . . . July 29, year 0 . . .

   The plaintiff is entitled to prejudgment interest on the claim, calculated as follows:

   (Calculate simple interest only unless an agreement relied on in the statement of claim specifies otherwise. To calculate the interest amount, count the number of days and multiply that number by the annual rate of interest, multiply the result by the principal sum owing and divide by 365.)

Principal Sum Owing	Start Date	End date (Date of Judgment)	Number of Days	Rate	Interest Amount
38,182.79	July 29, year 0	Oct. 17, year 0	76	12%	904.07

TOTAL B $ 904.07

Principal Sum Owing (Total A above) $ . . 38,182.79

Total Interest Amount (Total B above) $ 904.07

SIGN JUDGMENT FOR . . . . $ . . 39,086.86

FIGURE 10.1 CONTINUED

PART C — POSTJUDGMENT INTEREST AND COSTS

1. Postjudgment interest

   The plaintiff is entitled to postjudgment interest at the rate of 12
   percent per year,

   ❏ under the *Courts of Justice Act*, as claimed in the statement of
   claim.

   or

   ☒ in accordance with the claim made in the statement of claim.

2. Costs

   The plaintiff wishes costs to be

   ☒ fixed by the local registrar.

   or

   ❏ assessed by an assessment officer.

Date October 17, year 0 .... *I.M. Just* ....

(Signature of plaintiff's solicitor or plaintiff)

*(Name, address and telephone and fax
numbers of plaintiff's solicitor or plaintiff)*

```
              Just & Coping
         Barristers and Solicitors
           365 Bay Street - 8701
         Toronto, Ontario, M3J 4A9

                   I.M. Just
            tel. 416-762-1342
            fax 416-762-2300

       Solicitors for the Plaintiff
```

FIGURE 10.2   BILL OF COSTS (FORM 57A)

Court file no. 01-CV-7777

ONTARIO
SUPERIOR COURT OF JUSTICE

BETWEEN:

Abigail Boar

Plaintiff

and

Hieronymous Blogg

Defendants

BILL OF COSTS

AMOUNTS CLAIMED FOR FEES AND DISBURSEMENTS

FEES OTHER THAN COUNSEL FEES

1. Preparing and drafting statement of claim,
   I.M. Just, October 16, year 0   1 hour
2. Signing default judgment and assessing costs   0.6 hour
   Fee for I.M. Just, Barrister and Solicitor,
                         1.6 hours x $250 = $400

                                    TOTAL FEES: $400

DISBURSEMENTS

1. Paid to issue statement of claim $157.00
2. Paid to serve claim $41.00
3. Paid to file requisition for default judgment $90.00

                                                  $288.00

GST [RO145892]   nil
TOTAL DISBURSEMENTS $288.00
TOTAL FEES AND DISBURSEMENTS $688.00

STATEMENT OF EXPERIENCE
A claim for fees is being made with respect to the following lawyers:

Name of lawyer	Years of experience
I.M. Just	12 years

FIGURE 10.2 CONTINUED

TO:
Huey Sue
Barrister and Solicitor
65 False Trail
Toronto, Ontario, M6Y 1Z6

tel. 416-485-6891
fax 416-485-6892

Solicitor for the Defendants

THIS BILL assessed and allowed at $ this   day of

Registrar,
Ontario Superior Court of Justice

FIGURE 10.3   DEFAULT JUDGMENT (DEBT OR LIQUIDATED DEMAND) (FORM 19A)

Court file no. 01-CV-7777

ONTARIO
SUPERIOR COURT OF JUSTICE

BETWEEN:

Abigail Boar

Plaintiff

and

Hieronymus Bloggs

Defendant

JUDGMENT

On reading the statement of claim in this action and the proof of service of the statement of claim on the defendant, filed, and the defendant having been noted in default,

1. IT IS ORDERED AND ADJUDGED that the defendant pay to the plaintiff the sum of $39,086.86 and the sum of $688.00 for costs of this action.

   This judgment bears interest at the rate of 12 percent per year from its date, and the costs bear interest at the rate of 12 percent per year from its date.

Date: October 17, year 0

Signed by: _____

**Address of
court office:** Court House
393 University Avenue
Toronto, Ontario, M5G 1Y8

FIGURE 10.4   REQUISITION FOR WRIT OF SEIZURE AND SALE

Court file no. 01-CV-7777

ONTARIO
SUPERIOR COURT OF JUSTICE

BETWEEN:

Abigail Boar

and

Hieronymus Bloggs

REQUISITION FOR WRIT OF SEIZURE AND SALE

TO THE LOCAL REGISTRAR at Toronto

I REQUIRE a writ of seizure and sale pursuant to an order of this court made on October 17, year 0 in favour of Abigail Boar

directed to the Sheriff of the City of Toronto
to seize and sell the real and personal property of

Surname of individual or name of corporation/firm, etc.		
1. Bloggs		
First given name *(individual only)*	Second given name *(individual only)* *(if applicable)*	Third given name *(individual only)* *(if applicable)*
Hieronymus		

and to realize from the seizure and sale the following sums:

(a) $ 39,086.86 and interest at 12 percent per year commencing on
October 17, year 0

Amount of payment   *Due date*

(a) $_____ and interest at _____ percent per year on the
payments in default commencing on the date of default;

(b) 688.00 for costs together with interest at 12 percent per year
commencing on October 17, year 0; and

(c) your fees and expenses in enforcing this writ.

Date: October 17, year 0

Just & Coping
Barristers and Solicitors
365 Bay Street - 8701
Toronto, Ontario, M3J 4A9

I.M. Just
tel. 416-762-1342
fax 416-762-2300

Solicitors for the Plaintiff

FIGURE 10.5   WRIT OF SEIZURE AND SALE (FORM 60A)

Court file no. 01-CV-7777

ONTARIO
SUPERIOR COURT OF JUSTICE

BETWEEN:

Abigail Boar

and

Hieronymus Bloggs

WRIT OF SEIZURE AND SALE

TO the sheriff of the City of Toronto

Under an order of this court made on October 17, year 0, **in favour of** Abigail Boar

YOU ARE DIRECTED to seize and sell the real and personal property **within** the City of Toronto

Surname of individual or name of corporation/firm, etc.
Bloggs

First given name (individual only)
Hieronymus

and to realize from the seizure and sale the following sums:

(a) $ 39,086.86 **and interest at** 12 **percent per year commencing on** October 17, year 0

Amount of payment   *Due date*

(a) $_____ and interest at _____ percent per year on the payments in default commencing on the date of default;

(b) $688.00 **for costs together with interest at** 12 **percent per year commencing on** October 17, year 0; **and**

(c) your fees and expenses in enforcing this writ.

YOU ARE DIRECTED to pay out the proceeds according to law and to report on the execution of this writ if required by the party or solicitor who filed it.

Date: October 17, year 0

Issued by: _____

**Address of
court office:** Court House
393 University Avenue
Toronto, Ontario, M5G 1Y8

FIGURE 10.5 WRIT OF SEIZURE AND SALE — BACKSHEET (FORM 60A)

Abigail Boar

and

Hieronymus Bloggs

(Short title of proceeding)

Court file no. 01-CV-7777

ONTARIO SUPERIOR COURT OF JUSTICE

Proceeding commenced at Toronto

**WRIT OF
SEIZURE AND SALE**

Creditor's name: Abigail Boar

Creditor's address:

c/o Just & Coping
Barristers and Solicitors

Solicitor's name:

I.M. Just
Law Society No. 178888Q

Solicitor's address:

Just & Coping
365 Bay Street – 8701
Toronto, Ontario, M3J 4A9
Tel. no.: 416-762-1342
Fax no.: 416-762-2300

Solicitor for the Plaintiff

FEES		
Fee	Item	Officer
$42.00	Paid for this writ	
$15.00	Solicitor's fee for issuing writ	
	First renewal	
	Second renewal	
	Third renewal	

RENEWAL	
Date	Officer

FIGURE 10.6   AFFIDAVIT OF ABIGAIL BOAR

Court file no. 01-CV-1234

ONTARIO
SUPERIOR COURT OF JUSTICE

BETWEEN:

Abigail Boar

Plaintiff

and

Rattle Motors Ltd. and Fred Flogem

Defendants

AFFIDAVIT OF ABIGAIL BOAR

I, Abigail Boar, **of the** City of Toronto, **in the** Province of Ontario,
MAKE OATH AND SAY:

1. I am the plaintiff in this proceeding and as such have
    knowledge of the matters set out in this affidavit.
2. I slipped on oil on the floor of the showroom of the
    corporate defendant. My fall and subsequent injuries were
    solely the result of the negligent acts of the defendants.
3. As a result of the fall, I struck my head, suffered a
    concussion and lost consciousness. I also fractured my
    right wrist and several other bones in my right arm. I
    was taken to the Toronto Hospital emergency room, where
    my fractures were set and my arm was put in a cast. I
    was hospitalized and also underwent neurological
    examination for my head injury.
4. My arm was in a cast for six weeks. I was in great pain
    for the first two weeks and was unable to sleep or rest
    without medication to mask the pain. I required homecare
    assistance. Because I am right-handed and my right arm
    was immobilized, I was unable to dress myself or look
    after myself.
5. I had to undergo 10 weeks of physiotherapy to help
    restore mobility to my right hand and arm.
6. Since the accident, I have also suffered from headaches
    and chronic lower back pain. I am unable to walk long
    distances or sit at a desk for long periods. I have not
    recovered mobility in my right arm, and I am unable to
    work at a computer keyboard for more than 10 minutes
    without great pain.
7. As a result of these injuries, I have been far less
    active and less outgoing than I had been. I have become
    withdrawn and morose. I can easily become upset by
    little things that would not have bothered me in the
    past. I am often tired and have difficulty sleeping
    because of the chronic pain from my back and head
    injuries.

FIGURE 10.6   CONTINUED

8. Before I was injured, I was outgoing and gregarious, an avid tennis player, and a competent amateur violinist. Since I was injured, I have become uninterested in maintaining my social life, and I am unable to engage in the sports and cultural activities from which I formerly derived much pleasure.

9. I have also suffered some memory loss, which has interfered with both my employment and my social life.

10. I have been unable to return to work as a result of my injuries. My work as a securities analyst requires me to sit at a desk and computer keyboard for lengthy periods of time. I also now have difficulty focusing and concentrating on my work because of memory loss and chronic pain. I tried to return to work but was able to work only for a month before my employer and I agreed that I was no longer able to perform my duties. I have been on long-term disability from April 1, year 1 and am unlikely to be able to return to my former employment.

11. At the time of the accident, I was earning $80,000 per year plus benefits worth another $20,000. My work performance was excellent. I expected to work another 25 years and retire early at age 51. I am advised by Eatom Shredlu, the vice-president of human resources at Megadoon Investment Ltd., and believe, that my salary would likely have increased on average about 6 percent per year during my career had I continued my work for this employer.

12. I am advised by Dr. Morris Furgazy, a neurologist, and I believe, that I am unlikely to be employable in any office position on a permanent basis because of my mental disabilities arising from my accident and my physical inability to perform office work.

Sworn before me at the)	
City of Toronto,)	*Abigail Boar*
in the Province of Ontario,)	Abigail Boar
on February 18, year 1.)	
)	
Commissioner for Taking Affidavits)	

FIGURE 10.7   AFFIDAVIT TO SET ASIDE DEFAULT JUDGMENT

Court file no. 01-CV-1234

ONTARIO
SUPERIOR COURT OF JUSTICE

BETWEEN:

Abigail Boar

Plaintiff

and

Rattle Motors Ltd. and Fred Flogem

Defendants

AFFIDAVIT OF HUEY SUE

I, Huey Sue, **of the** City of Toronto, **in the** Province of Ontario,
AFFIRM:

1. I am the lawyer for the defendants and as such have knowledge of the matters deposed to in this affidavit.
2. On January 4, year 1, the defendants were served with the statement of claim in this action.
3. On January 6, year 1, I met both defendants and arranged to file a statement of defence. Attached hereto and marked exhibit A to my affidavit is a copy of the proposed statement of defence in this proceeding.
4. The defendants have a good defence to the plaintiff's claim. It is the position of the defendants that the plaintiff was intoxicated at the time of the accident and that her injuries were wholly the result of her intoxicated condition, rather than the result of any alleged act of negligence by either defendant, which negligence, if any, is denied by the defendants.
5. Because of the pressures of practice, I overlooked the passage of the time for filing the statement of defence.
6. I discovered my oversight on January 28, year 1. I attempted immediately to file the statement of defence, but I learned that the defendants had been noted in default and that a default judgment had been entered.
7. On January 29, year 1, I served the plaintiff with a notice of motion to set aside the noting of pleadings closed and the default judgment in this action.

Affirmed before me at the	)	
City of Toronto,	)	*Huey Sue*
in the Province of Ontario,	)	Huey Sue
on January 28, year 1.	)	
	)	
Commissioner for Taking Affidavits	)	

CHAPTER 11

Summary judgment: Rule 20

INTRODUCTION

Once the pleadings have been delivered, one of the parties may take the position that there is no issue that needs to be tried. For example, Abigail Boar, the plaintiff, may believe that the defendants, Fred Flogem and Rattle Motors, have raised no defence known in law to her claim. On the other hand, the defendants may take the position that Abigail does not have sufficient evidence to make a case against them.

In such circumstances, either the plaintiff or the defendant may bring a motion for summary judgment. If the plaintiff brings the motion, she will ask the court to make a final judgment in her favour. If the defendants bring the motion for summary judgment, they will ask for a dismissal of all or part of the plaintiff's case. Rule 20 provides the procedure for summary judgments.

Summary judgment is a final decision about the case that is made by the court without a trial. The parties may not rely on their pleadings in trying to persuade the court that there is no issue for trial. They must provide the court with an affidavit setting out the facts on which they are relying. The affidavits may be based on the information supplied by others that the deponent believes to be true. However, basing a motion for summary judgment on affidavit evidence may be risky. The court may **draw an adverse inference** if the affidavits contain material based solely on information and belief and not on the direct, personal knowledge of the deponent. For example, the court may take the view that the reason that no direct personal knowledge evidence has been presented is that there is none.

The affidavits of the party responding to the motion must do more than deny the allegations of the moving party or say that more evidence may be available at trial. The material must set out specifics facts showing that there is a genuine issue for trial (rule 20.04(1)).

In addition to the affidavits they wish to rely on in the motion for summary judgment, each party must also serve and file a factum at least two days before the hearing of the motion (rule 20.03). A factum is a document that gives a concise summary of the facts in the case and sets out the case law and the statutes that the party is relying on to support its position. Factums are dealt with in more detail in chapter 20.

draw an adverse inference
make a factual determination that is contrary to the interests of a party

TEST FOR GRANTING SUMMARY JUDGMENT

The test for summary judgment in a simplified procedure is different from the test in a regular action; see chapter 23. The first situation in which summary judgment is available occurs when the court is satisfied that there is no genuine issue for trial. For instance, in Abigail's negligence action, if the defendants can establish that the plaintiff's case is statute barred because it was commenced outside the time set in the *Limitations Act, 2002*, they would be able to satisfy the court that there is no genuine issue for trial. In such a case, the court must grant summary judgment.

The second situation in which summary judgment is available occurs when the parties agree to have all or part of the case dealt with on a motion for summary judgment and the court agrees that it is an appropriate case for this treatment. Summary judgment based on this criterion is discretionary. The court may decide that the matter is better left to trial.

A motion for summary judgment may be brought before a master or a judge. However, if a motion based on a question of law is brought before a master, it must be adjourned for hearing before a judge (rule 20.04(4)).

If the court decides that the only genuine issue for trial is the amount of money to which the moving party is entitled, the court can order a trial limited to that issue or grant judgment in favour of the moving party and direct a **reference** to determine the exact amount (rule 20.04(3)).

reference
judicial proceeding used when it is necessary to delve into an issue in detail before a decision can be reached

Summary judgments are often sought in cases involving debt issues because a plaintiff may obtain judgment for all or part of a debt claim at an early stage in the proceedings without the cost and delay of discovery and trial.

If the court determines on the motion that a summary judgment is not appropriate in a particular case, or is only partially applicable, the court can make a number of orders regarding the trial:

1. It may make an order specifying that certain facts or issues are not in dispute in order to narrow the scope of the trial.

2. It may order that the trial be placed on a special list of cases requiring speedy trial or that the case be set down for trial within a specified time.

3. It may give directions or impose terms, including an order for security for costs, an order for payment into court of all or part of the claim, or an order prescribing the way in which discovery is to be conducted.

Summary judgment can be a very effective litigation tool in that it can, in appropriate cases, avoid costly and time-consuming procedures. However, if a party improperly uses the rule, the court may apply cost sanctions. If the moving party is unsuccessful and the court determines that the motion for summary judgment was unreasonable, it may fix the responding party's costs on a substantial indemnity basis and order the moving party to pay them forthwith (rule 20.06).

Where there are many claims in an action, summary judgment may address only some of those claims, leaving others to be determined through the trial process. A plaintiff who obtains summary judgment may proceed against the defendant for any other relief he or she is claiming. In an appropriate case, the court may order a stay of the summary judgment until the entire matter, including any crossclaim, counterclaim, or third party claim, is dealt with.

CHAPTER SUMMARY

In this chapter, we have seen that summary judgment is a final decision that is made about a case by a court without a trial. Either the plaintiff or the defendant may bring a motion for summary judgment, which must be accompanied by affidavit evidence and factums. The test for granting a summary judgment is that there is no genuine issue for trial. A summary judgment may be granted either in whole or in part.

The parties may agree to have the case determined in this manner; however, the court is not obligated to grant a summary judgment and may direct that the case proceed by way of a full trial. Debt cases are often dealt with by way of summary judgment. Summary judgment may prove to be an effective litigation tool to avoid costly and time-consuming trials, but there can be severe cost consequences for seeking summary judgment in an inappropriate situation.

KEY TERMS

draw an adverse inference

reference

REFERENCES

Limitations Act, 2002, SO 2002, c. 24.

Rules of Civil Procedure, RRO 1990, reg. 194.

REVIEW QUESTIONS

1. Set out the steps you would take and the documents you would prepare to bring a motion for summary judgment.

2. What must a party show to obtain a summary judgment?

3. What sort of evidence should be used in support of the motion?

4. If a party is unsuccessful on a motion for summary judgment, are there consequences?

CHAPTER 12

Counterclaims, crossclaims, and third party claims

INTRODUCTION

A simple proceeding involves only two parties: the plaintiff and the defendant. As you know, the plaintiff can sue more than one defendant in the proceeding, as Abigail Boar is doing. She believes both Fred Flogem and Rattle Motors Ltd. are responsible for her injuries, and she is suing them both. In Abigail's case, there are multiple defendants.

It is also possible to have multiple plaintiffs in a proceeding when several people claim that they suffered damages caused by the defendant or group of defendants. But a proceeding can become more complicated than this. The rules provide for a number of different combinations of plaintiffs and defendants and outline the pleadings and the procedures for each. These pleadings are the counterclaim, the cross-claim, and the third party claim.

When you first try to sort out the nature of these other pleadings, they may seem extremely complicated because of the additional parties and steps involved. However, when reviewing the procedures, keep in mind the basic principle: All parties should know the legal claim made against them and have the opportunity to answer the claim. Remember the basic pleadings in an action: the statement of claim, the statement of defence, and the reply. All of the other pleadings follow the same general principles.[1]

COUNTERCLAIMS: RULE 27

The defendant may wish to sue the plaintiff in the proceeding. Maybe the defendant was seeking legal advice about suing the plaintiff, but the plaintiff was the one who issued the statement of claim first. The legal system and the rules have an interest in resolving disputes between parties in the most cost-effective and efficient manner. To force the defendant who wants to sue the plaintiff to commence a proceeding separate from the one already commenced by the plaintiff would be more expensive and time-consuming than allowing the defendant to bring his or her action against the plaintiff at the same time.

counterclaim
claim made by the
defendant in the main
action against the plaintiff
or against the plaintiff
and other persons

main action
primary case brought by
the plaintiff against the
defendant

When a defendant sues a plaintiff, this is called a "**counterclaim**." The proceeding in which the plaintiff is suing the defendant is then called the "**main action**."

In a counterclaim, the defendant in the main action must be suing the plaintiff in the main action. The defendant can also sue anyone else in his or her counterclaim, as long as the original plaintiff is one of the persons being sued.

There is no restriction as to the basis for the defendant's counterclaim against the plaintiff. It may have the same subject matter as the claim in the main action, or it may have a completely different subject matter. Assume that Abigail Boar did not go to Rattle Motors to buy a car on the day that she fell. Assume instead that she had already bought the car and went into the dealership that day to make a payment on the car she had purchased. After she slipped and fell, she refused to make additional payments on the car. Rattle Motors wants to enforce its contract of sale against her. Therefore, when she starts her action against Rattle, it counterclaims against her for the debt owing. Abigail is suing Rattle for the tort of negligence, and Rattle is suing Abigail on a contract.

Assume as well that Abigail's boyfriend purchased the car with her and also entered into a sales contract with Rattle Motors. He has made no further payments on the car either, and Rattle wants to sue him too. Rattle can add him to the counterclaim, even though he is not one of the parties in the main action. As long as Rattle is suing Abigail, the plaintiff in the main action, it may also include her boyfriend in the counterclaim.

Pleadings in a counterclaim

The possible pleadings in a counterclaim are:

1. statement of claim (form 14A), delivered by the plaintiff in the main action;

2. statement of defence and counterclaim (form 27A or 27B), delivered by a defendant in the main action who is making a counterclaim against the plaintiff in the main action;

3. defence to counterclaim (form 27C), delivered by the plaintiff in the main action who wishes to defend against the counterclaim; and

4. reply and defence to counterclaim (form 27D), delivered by the plaintiff in the main action who wants to reply to the defendants' statement of defence in the main action and defend against the counterclaim.

Statement of defence and counterclaim

The defendants commence the counterclaim by including it in the same pleading as their defence to the main action. Instead of being called a "statement of defence," it is called a "statement of defence and counterclaim." There are two forms for this pleading: form 27A and form 27B. Form 27A is used when the defendant is suing only people who are parties to the main action. Form 27B is used if the defendant is adding someone to the counterclaim who is not a party to the main proceeding. If Rattle Motors were suing only Abigail, it would use form 27A. If it were also suing Abigail's boyfriend, because the boyfriend is not a party to the main action, it would use form 27B. Figure 12.1 at the end of the chapter sets out a statement of defence and counterclaim.

There is a major distinction between the two forms. Because form 27A is not an originating process, it does not need to be issued. However, because form 27B brings in a new party to the proceeding, it is an originating process. It must therefore be issued within the time prescribed in rule 18.01 for delivery of the statement of defence or any time before being noted in default — that is, within 20 days if the statement of claim was served in Ontario, 40 days if it was served elsewhere in Canada or in the United States, or 60 days if it was served anywhere else in the world.

Form 27B must also contain a second title of proceeding showing the plaintiff by counterclaim and the defendants by counterclaim. In our example, Rattle Motors is the plaintiff by counterclaim, and Abigail and her boyfriend are the defendants by counterclaim (rule 27.03).

The statement of defence and counterclaim (form 27A or 27B) raises two separate issues for the plaintiff in the main action. She has been served with a defence to her claim in the main action and with a new claim against her by the defendant. In the main action, in which Abigail is suing Rattle Motors in negligence, she may want to reply to any new issue that Rattle has raised in its defence. In addition, Abigail will want to raise her defence against Rattle Motor's claim for payment for the car. Her boyfriend will also want to raise his defence against Rattle.

Defence to counterclaim or reply and defence to counterclaim

If Abigail has no reply to Rattle Motor's defence in the main action but wants to defend herself against Rattle's counterclaim, she must file a defence to counterclaim, form 27C, within 20 days after being served with the statement of defence and counterclaim. Figure 12.2 at the end of the chapter sets out a defence to the counterclaim. If Abigail's boyfriend or any other defendant who is not a party to the main action wishes to file a defence to the counterclaim, that person has 20 days, 40 days, or 60 days to file a statement of defence and counterclaim, depending on the place of service (rule 27.05(3)).

If Abigail wants to file a reply to Rattle Motor's defence in the main action and raise a defence on the counterclaim, she must include the defence to the counterclaim in the reply. This means she first addresses all the issues she wishes to address in reply and follows those paragraphs with all the points she wishes to raise in the defence to the counterclaim.

If Rattle wants to reply to Abigail or to another defendant's defence and counterclaim, it may do so in form 27D within 10 days after being served with the defence to the counterclaim (rule 27.06).

Amending defence to add counterclaim

If the defendants in the main action deliver a statement of defence and then decide they want to bring a counterclaim, they may amend their statement of defence to add the counterclaim and deliver the amended pleading, as long as the counterclaim is against the plaintiff and someone else who is already a party to the main action. But if the counterclaim brings in a defendant who is not a party to the main action, the defendants may amend their pleading to add the counterclaim only with leave of the court (rule 27.07).

Trial and disposition of the counterclaim

A counterclaim that goes to trial is usually heard at the end of the trial of the main action. However, if it appears that the counterclaim may delay, complicate, or prejudice a party, the court may order separate trials or may order that the counterclaim proceed as an action separate from the main action (rule 27.08(1) and (2)).

Sometimes, the defendant may not dispute the plaintiff's claim in the main action but may want to assert a counterclaim. Conversely, the plaintiff may not dispute the counterclaim but may want to proceed with his or her claim in the main action. In such a situation, the court may either stay or grant a judgment in the undisputed part of the case and then hear the claims that are disputed. If the plaintiff is successful in the main action and the defendant is successful on the counterclaim — that is, if each party wins the part of the case it brought against the other — the court may dismiss the smaller claim and order that the difference between the two damage awards be paid (rule 27.09).

For example, assume that Abigail Boar wins her negligence action against Rattle Motors, and Rattle is ordered to pay her $75,000. Rattle, however, also wins its counterclaim for the money still owing on the car, which is $10,000. In this instance, the court may dismiss Rattle's case and order Rattle to pay Abigail $65,000, the difference between the two claims.

CROSSCLAIMS: RULE 28

crossclaim
claim brought by one defendant whom the plaintiff is suing against another defendant whom the plaintiff is suing

co-defendant
one defendant in multi-defendant proceeding

A **crossclaim** is a claim made by one defendant against another defendant in the main action. Rule 28 governs the procedure on a crossclaim. The rule provides that crossclaims may be brought only in certain limited circumstances. These circumstances exist if:

1. the **co-defendant** is or may be liable to the defendant for all or part of the plaintiff's claim;

2. the co-defendant is or may be liable to the defendant for an independent claim for damages or other relief, arising out of the same transaction or occurrence involved in, or related to, the main action;

3. the co-defendant should be bound by the determination of an issue arising between the plaintiff and the defendant; or

4. the defendant is claiming a contribution from a co-defendant under the *Negligence Act* (rule 28.01(1) and (2)).

In short, the crossclaim must have a direct relationship to the main action in terms of subject matter and some level of joint liability to the plaintiff in the main action. For instance, Abigail is suing both Fred Flogem and Rattle Motors Ltd. for negligence. Fred and Rattle Motors are therefore co-defendants. If Fred believes that he did nothing to cause Abigail's fall and that Rattle created an unsafe showroom and is totally responsible for Abigail's injuries, Fred can bring a crossclaim against Rattle. However, if Fred wants to start an action against Rattle for unpaid wages, that issue has no connection to the main action and is not a proper subject for a crossclaim.

crossclaiming defendant
defendant in the main action who commences a crossclaim against one or more of the other defendants in that action

defendant on the crossclaim
defendant in the main action against whom a crossclaim is brought

The defendant in the main action who brings the crossclaim is referred to in the rules as the **crossclaiming defendant**. The defendant against whom the crossclaim is brought is called the **defendant on the crossclaim**. In our example, Fred is the crossclaiming defendant, and Rattle is the defendant on the crossclaim.

Pleadings in a crossclaim

The following is a list of pleadings on a crossclaim:

1. statement of claim (form 14A), delivered by the plaintiff in the main action against more than one defendant;

2. statement of defence (form 18A), delivered by any defendant who is not crossclaiming;

3. reply (form 25A), delivered by the plaintiff in the main action to answer any new issues raised in the statement of defence;

4. statement of defence and crossclaim (form 28A), delivered by a defendant who wishes to answer the plaintiff's claim against him or her and bring a crossclaim against one of the other defendants being sued by the plaintiff in the main action;

5. defence to crossclaim (form 28B), delivered by the co-defendant against whom the crossclaim has been commenced; and

6. reply to defence to crossclaim (form 28C), delivered by the defendant who is bringing the crossclaim and who wants to reply to issues raised by the co-defendant he or she is suing on the crossclaim.

Statement of defence and crossclaim

A crossclaim is included in the same document as the statement of defence and is called a statement of defence and crossclaim (form 28A). Figure 12.3 at the end of the chapter sets out a statement of defence and crossclaim. If the defendant has already filed a statement of defence in the main action and then decides he or she wants to bring a crossclaim, the defendant may simply amend the statement of defence under rule 26 and include the crossclaim. No leave of the court is required (rule 28.03).

The statement of defence and crossclaim must be served within the time limits for filing a statement of defence under rule 18.01 or anytime before the defendant is noted in default. It may be served after a noting in default only with leave of the court (rule 28.04(1)). There is no requirement for personal service of the statement of defence and crossclaim, unless the defendant in the crossclaim has failed to deliver a statement of defence or a notice of intent to defend in the main action.

Defence to the crossclaim

The defence to the crossclaim, form 28B, must be delivered within 20 days after service of the statement of defence and crossclaim. Figure 12.4 at the end of the chapter sets out a defence to a crossclaim. However, a defence to a crossclaim is not needed in the circumstances specified in rule 28.05. When the crossclaim is only seeking contribution or indemnity under the *Negligence Act* and the defendant to the crossclaim has delivered a defence in the main action that addresses the issues raised in the crossclaim, the defendant need not deliver a specific defence to the crossclaim. He or she can rely on the statement of defence delivered in the main action and is deemed to deny every allegation in the crossclaim.

In a crossclaim, the defendants are being sued by the plaintiff, and the crossclaim must have something to do with the plaintiff's claim in the main action.

Very often the defendant on the crossclaim will be liable for damages on the crossclaim only if the plaintiff is successful in the main action. If the plaintiff loses his or her case, none of the defendants bears any liability.

Therefore, rule 28.06 provides a procedure by which the defendant on the crossclaim may raise a defence to the plaintiff's claim against the other defendant — that is, the crossclaiming defendant. If the defendant wants to raise a defence to the plaintiff's claim against the crossclaiming defendant, he or she may do so in a separate part of the defence to the crossclaim. This part of the defence against the crossclaim must be headed with the wording "DEFENCE TO A PLAINTIFF'S CLAIM AGAINST CROSSCLAIMING DEFENDANT."

A defendant who does not defend against the crossclaiming defendant in this way is bound by any order made in the main action between the plaintiff and the crossclaiming defendant.

A defendant may be noted in default on a crossclaim just as a defendant can be noted in default in the main action. If the defendant on the crossclaim is noted in default on the crossclaim, judgment can be obtained against him or her only at the trial of the main action or on a motion to a judge. In other words, a default judgment cannot be obtained from the registrar in this circumstance.

Reply to the defence to the crossclaim

The reply to the defence to a crossclaim must be delivered within 10 days of the service of the defence to the crossclaim.

Trial of the crossclaim

The crossclaim is usually heard at the trial of the main action or immediately thereafter. However, if the plaintiff believes that the crossclaim will prejudice or delay the trial of the main action, he or she may bring a motion seeking an order that the crossclaim proceed as a separate action. The court may order a separate trial on the crossclaim, or it may impose any terms necessary to ensure that the main action is not prejudiced or delayed.

THIRD PARTY CLAIMS: RULE 29
Introduction

One or more of the defendants to the main action may take the position that the plaintiff has not named all persons who are liable for his or her injuries. For instance, assume that unbeknownst to Abigail Boar, the car on display in the showroom had a manufacturer's defect in the oil pan that caused it to leak onto Rattle Motor's showroom floor. In its own investigation into Abigail's fall, Rattle discovers this defect and believes that Skank Motorcar Company Ltd. is responsible for Abigail's injuries. But Abigail has not sued the car manufacturer. The rules provide a procedure for Rattle to bring Skank into the action. This is called a **third party claim**, and it may be commenced by a defendant against any person who is not a party to the main action but who:

third party claim
claim brought by a defendant in the main action against a person who is not already a party to the main action

- is or may be liable to the defendant for all or part of the plaintiff's claim,

- is or may be liable to the defendant for an independent claim for damages or other relief arising out of the same transaction or occurrence or series of transactions or occurrences involved in the main action, or

- should be bound by the determination of an issue arising between the plaintiff and the defendant (rule 29.01).

Pleadings on a third party claim

A third party claim is a new claim made against a person who is not a party to the main action. It is unlike a counterclaim and a crossclaim because these proceedings involve someone who is already a party to the existing proceeding. For instance, in a counterclaim, the defendant must make a claim against the plaintiff. A crossclaim involves defendants who are already parties by virtue of the fact that they are being sued by the same plaintiff or plaintiffs. There are therefore two sets of pleadings in a third party proceeding: the pleadings in the main action and the pleadings in the third party proceeding.

The pleadings in the main action are the regular pleadings: the statement of claim, the statement of defence, and the reply. The second set of pleadings between the defendant who is making the claim against the third party and the third party are:

- the third party claim (form 29A), delivered by the defendant asserting the claim and resembling a statement of claim in its form and content;

- the third party defence (form 29B), delivered by the third party to raise a defence to the claim being brought against him or her; and

- the reply to the third party defence (form 29C), delivered by the defendant asserting the third party claim.

The third party claim

Because a third party claim brings someone new into the proceeding and asserts a new claim, it is an originating process. It must be issued by the court within 10 days after the defendant delivers a statement of defence or anytime before the defendant is noted in default (rule 29.02(1)). However, if the plaintiff replies to the statement of defence in the main action, the third party claim may be issued within 10 days of the plaintiff's delivering his or her reply (rule 29.02(1.1)).

There are exceptions to these time limits for commencing a third party claim. A claim may be issued at any time if the plaintiff consents or if the court grants leave, and the court grants leave unless the plaintiff will suffer prejudice (rule 29.02(1.2)).

Like other originating processes, the third party claim must be served on the third party personally or by an alternative to personal service under rule 16.03. At the same time, the third party must also be served with all the pleadings previously delivered in the main action, any counterclaim, any crossclaim, and any other third party claim. Service of the documents must take place within 30 days after the third party claim is issued (rule 29.02(2)).

The third party claim must also be served on every other party to the main action within 30 days after the issuing, but it need not be served personally on these parties (rule 29.02(3)). Figure 12.5 at the end of the chapter sets out a third party claim.

Third party defence

The third party defence must be delivered within 20, 40, or 60 days, depending on where the third party claim is served (rule 29.03).

Once the third party has delivered a third party defence, there are several consequences that affect the third party.

- The third party must be served with any subsequent pleadings filed by any party to the main action.

- The plaintiff cannot obtain a consent judgment or note the defendant in default without notice to the third party.

- The third party has a right of discovery against any defendant to a crossclaim brought by the defendant who asserted the third party claim (rule 29.06).

Where a third party is noted in default for failing to file a third party defence, judgment may be obtained against the third party only at trial of the main action or on a motion to a judge. The registrar cannot issue a default judgment against a third party. Figure 12.6 at the end of the chapter sets out a third party defence.

Reply to third party defence

The defendant who commenced the third party proceeding has a right to reply to a third party defence within 10 days after being served with the defence.

Defence of the main action by the third party

A third party may defend against the plaintiff in the main action's claim against the defendant by delivering a statement of defence, and the third party may raise any defence open to the defendant. The reason for this rule is obvious: Since the defendant's third party claim is based on the allegation that the third party is liable for the plaintiff's damages in whole or in part, if the plaintiff is unsuccessful in the main action, the defendant will have no need or interest in pursuing the third party claim.

The statement of defence must be delivered within the standard time frames of 20, 40, or 60 days from the service of the third party claim, depending on where the third party was served (rules 29.04(3) and 29.03). The plaintiff may reply to that statement of defence within 10 days after being served.

Once the third party has delivered a statement of defence in the main action, he or she has the same rights and obligations in the main action as the defendant. The third party may seek discovery, participate in the trial of the main action, and appeal any decision made at the trial. In addition, he or she is bound by any order made in the main action between the plaintiff and the defendant who made the third party claim. In the event that the third party does not deliver a statement of defence in the main action, he or she is still bound by any order made in that action between the plaintiff and the defendant who made the third party claim.

Trial of the third party claim

After the close of pleadings in the third party claim, the claim must be listed for trial without undue delay in accordance with rule 48. It is to be placed on the trial list immediately after the main action, and it must be tried at the same time or immediately after the main action.

If the plaintiff is concerned that the third party claim will delay or prejudice the main action, he or she may bring a motion. The court may order that the third party claim be tried as a separate action or set terms for a trial of the action that will prevent delay or prejudice. However, the order or terms may not cause any injustice to the defendant or the third party.

Subsequent party claims

A third party may bring a fourth party claim against a person who is not a party to the main action as long as it meets the criteria set out in rule 29.01 for the commencement of a third party action. A fourth party may then assert a fifth party claim under the same criteria, and so on (rules 29.11 and 29.12).

CHAPTER SUMMARY

In this chapter, we have explored counterclaims, crossclaims, and third party claims.

Rule 27 governs counterclaims, a procedure in which the defendant is suing the plaintiff and any number of other persons along with the plaintiff. The basis for the counterclaim does not have to have the same subject matter as the main claim. Pleadings relating only to the counterclaim are the statement of defence and counterclaim, the defence to the counterclaim, or the reply and defence to the counterclaim. A counterclaim that goes to trial is usually heard at the completion of the trial of the main action. However, if it appears that the counterclaim may delay the main action, the court may order it to be tried separately.

Rule 28 governs crossclaims, a procedure that involves one defendant suing another defendant. The crossclaim must be directly related to the main action in terms of its content and the joint liability of the defendants to the plaintiff. Pleadings relating only to the crossclaim are the statement of defence and crossclaim, the defence to the crossclaim, or the reply to the defence to the crossclaim. The trial of the crossclaim is usually held at the same time as or immediately after the trial of the main action. However, the plaintiff may bring a motion to have the crossclaim tried separately if there is a possibility that the crossclaim could delay the main action.

Rule 29 governs third party claims, a procedure in which the defendant commences an action against a person whom the plaintiff is not suing. It must be directly related to the main action respecting subject matter and liability of the parties. The pleadings related solely to a third party claim are the third party claim, the third party defence, and the reply to the third party defence. Since a third party claim brings a new party into the proceeding, it is an originating process and must be issued by the court. The third party action is usually tried at the same time as or immediately after the main action, although the plaintiff may move to have it tried as a separate matter if it will delay the main action. A third party may make a fourth party claim and bring an additional party into the proceeding. A fourth party may bring in a fifth party, and so on.

KEY TERMS

counterclaim

main action

crossclaim

co-defendant

crossclaiming defendant

defendant on the crossclaim

third party claim

NOTE

1 You may find it helpful to locate in your rules book the chart that deals with the procedure in counterclaims, crossclaims, and third party claims and follow it as you read through this chapter.

REFERENCES

Negligence Act, RSO 1990, c. N.1.

Rules of Civil Procedure, RRO 1990, reg. 194.

REVIEW QUESTIONS

1. John Smith is suing Big Bob's Building Emporium Ltd. Big Bob believes that Diddlehopper Cleaning Ltd. bears some of the liability for the claim. What can Big Bob do? What rule applies?

2. Draft the general heading for this pleading.

3. What is the document used to bring a counterclaim? What is this document's form number?

4. In a counterclaim, is the defendant limited to suing the plaintiff in the main action?

5. What are the pleadings used on a counterclaim?

6. In what circumstances is a crossclaim available and what rule applies?

7. The defendant has already filed a statement of defence. However, he now wants to commence a crossclaim against one of his co-defendants. Do the rules permit him to do this?

8. Which of the proceedings you have studied in this chapter are originating processes?

9. John Green wishes to commence a crossclaim against his co-defendant George Black. What steps must be taken to commence the crossclaim?

10. At what stage of the proceedings may a third party claim be issued?

11. If a third party claim has been commenced, is there any step the plaintiff can take to have the third party claim heard separately from the main action?

DISCUSSION QUESTIONS

1. Kule Kiddie Fashions Inc. is being sued by Mindy McGillicuddy for a breach of contract. Mindy is claiming that Kule Kiddie did not deliver her line of spring clothing to her boutique as required under her contract with it. Kule Kiddie claims that it did not deliver the spring line of clothing because Mindy still owes $40,000 on the winter line and must pay before there will be any more clothing deliveries. What can Kule Kiddie do to recover its money from Mindy? What rule applies?

2. Kule Kiddie Fashions Inc. is being sued by Mindy McGillicuddy for a breach of contract for its failure to deliver a clothing line to Mindy's boutique. Kule Kiddie has had many business dealings with Mindy. Last year, Mindy did some clothing design work for it but did not complete the job because she left to open her own boutique. Kule Kiddie was forced to retain another designer to finish the job. The second designer charged twice as much for the job. Because it was late, Kule Kiddie lost $100,000 in income. Can Kule Kiddie bring a counterclaim in this situation?

3. Kule Kiddie Fashions Inc. wants to sue Mindy's son, Boris, an electrician. When he did some work at its factory last year, he crossed the wires, causing its major knitting machine to blow up. While Kule Kiddie was awaiting a new machine, it lost $20,000 in business. Can Kule Kiddie bring a counterclaim against Boris in the main action that his mother has commenced against it?

FIGURE 12.1 **STATEMENT OF DEFENCE AND COUNTERCLAIM (FORM 27B)**

Court file no. 01-CV-1234

ONTARIO
SUPERIOR COURT OF JUSTICE

BETWEEN:

Abigail Boar

Plaintiff

and

Rattle Motors Ltd. and Fred Flogem

Defendants

AND BETWEEN:

Rattle Motors Ltd.

Plaintiff by Counterclaim

and

Abigail Boar and James Dinglehoofer

Defendants to the Counterclaim

STATEMENT OF DEFENCE AND COUNTERCLAIM

TO THE DEFENDANTS TO THE COUNTERCLAIM

A LEGAL PROCEEDING has been commenced against you by way of a counterclaim in an action in this court. The claim made against you is set out in the following pages.

IF YOU WISH TO DEFEND THIS COUNTERCLAIM, you or an Ontario lawyer acting for you must prepare a defence to counterclaim in Form 27C prescribed by the Rules of Civil Procedure, serve it on the plaintiff by counterclaim's lawyer or, where the plaintiff by counterclaim does not have a lawyer, serve it on the plaintiff by counterclaim, and file it, with proof of service, in this court, WITHIN TWENTY DAYS after this statement of defence and counterclaim is served on you.

If you are not already a party to the main action and you are served in another province or territory of Canada or in the United States of America, the period for serving and filing your defence is forty days. If you are served outside Canada and the United States of America, the period is sixty days.

If you are not already a party to the main action, instead of serving and filing a defence to counterclaim, you may serve and file a notice of intent to defend in Form 18B prescribed by the Rules of Civil Procedure. This will entitle you to ten more days within which to serve and file your defence to counterclaim.

IF YOU FAIL TO DEFEND THIS COUNTERCLAIM, JUDGMENT MAY BE GIVEN AGAINST YOU IN YOUR ABSENCE AND WITHOUT FURTHER NOTICE TO YOU. IF YOU WISH TO DEFEND THIS PROCEEDING BUT ARE UNABLE TO PAY LEGAL FEES, LEGAL AID MAY BE AVAILABLE TO YOU BY CONTACTING A LOCAL LEGAL AID OFFICE.

FIGURE 12.1   CONTINUED

IF YOU PAY THE AMOUNT OF THE COUNTERCLAIM AGAINST YOU, and $500.00 for costs, within the time for serving and filing your defence to counterclaim, you may move to have the counterclaim against you dismissed by the court. If you believe the amount claimed for costs is excessive, you may pay the amount of the counterclaim and $400.00 for costs and have the costs assessed by the court.

Date: January 12, year 1

Issued by: _____

Address of

court office: Court House
393 University Avenue
Toronto, Ontario, M5G 1Y8

TO:

James Dinglehoofer
4747 Memory Lane,
Toronto, Ontario, M7T 8U9

Defendant by counterclaim

1. The defendants admit the allegations contained in paragraphs 2, 3, and 4 of the statement of claim.
2. The defendants deny the allegations contained in paragraphs 7, 8, 9, 10, 11, 12, 13, 14, 15, 16, and 17 of the statement of claim.
3. The plaintiff entered the corporate defendant's premises at about 7:30 p.m. on September 14, year 0. She indicated to Linda Lucre, a salesperson on the showroom floor at that time, that she was interested in purchasing a Super Coupe.
4. Lucre showed the plaintiff several automobile models. Then the plaintiff walked over, on her own, to look at another model. She walked around the car and fell.
5. The defendants admit that there was a small pool of oil on one side of the car but claim that it was easily visible to any reasonably prudent person who could have avoided it without difficulty.
6. The defendants admit that two of the four spotlights were off but deny that the area was not well illuminated. The defendants state that the area was well and clearly illuminated. Any hazard, if there was one, which is specifically denied, could easily be seen and avoided.
7. The defendants admit that the plaintiff fell and appeared to lose consciousness momentarily. She also appeared to injure her lower right arm in the fall.
8. The defendants state that the plaintiff, before coming to the corporate defendant's place of business, had consumed two glasses of wine and that she was intoxicated when she entered the defendant's premises.
9. The plaintiff fell solely as a result of her intoxication. Any injuries she sustained were solely the result of her own intoxicated state and not any acts of the defendants.

FIGURE 12.1 CONTINUED

10. With respect to paragraphs 10, 11, 12, 13, 14, and 15 of the statement of claim, the defendants deny that the plaintiff suffered such injuries as described. Further or in the alternative, the defendants state that the plaintiff has exaggerated both the extent of her injuries and the consequences of them.

11. With respect to the plaintiff's allegation that she cannot return to work, the defendants state that the plaintiff is exaggerating her injuries and that she is a malingerer. In the alternative, the defendants state that the plaintiff has failed to mitigate her damages.

12. With respect to the allegations of negligence in paragraph 16, the defendant Flogem states that he knew there was oil on the floor but that it was contained and did not constitute a danger to any reasonably prudent person. The defendant Flogem admits that he turned off two of the four spotlights, but he specifically denies that he created a situation of danger for the plaintiff because the area in question remained well illuminated and safe for a reasonably prudent person.

13. The defendants therefore request that this action be dismissed with costs.

COUNTERCLAIM

14. The plaintiff by way of counterclaim claims:
    a. the sum of $11,275.98;
    b. interest in the said amount of $11,275.98 at the rate of 5 percent per year from September 1, year 1 to the date of payment on the judgment;
    c. its costs of this counterclaim; and
    d. such further relief as seems just to this court.

15. On November 15, year -1, the defendants to the counterclaim, Abigail Boar and James Dinglehoofer, entered into a contract of purchase and sale with the plaintiff by counterclaim, Rattle Motors Ltd., for the purchase on credit of a Super Coupe, year 0 model. The full purchase price of the vehicle was $22,472.89. The price was to be paid in monthly instalments of $329.47, commencing December 1, year -1.

16. Between December 1, year -1 and September 1, year 0, the defendants by counterclaim paid the requisite amount owing each month. No payment has been made pursuant to the agreement since September 1, year 0.

17. The defendants by counterclaim have made no payment since September 1, year 0 and are currently 4 months in arrears.

Date: January 12, year 1

Huey Sue
Barrister and Solicitor
65 False Trail
Toronto, Ontario, M6Y 1Z6

tel. 416-485-6891
fax 416-485-6892

Solicitor for the Plaintiff by Counterclaim

FIGURE 12.2   DEFENCE TO COUNTERCLAIM (FORM 27C)

Court file no. 01-CV-1234

ONTARIO
SUPERIOR COURT OF JUSTICE

BETWEEN:

Abigail Boar

Plaintiff

and

Rattle Motors Ltd. and Fred Flogem

Defendants

AND BETWEEN:

Rattle Motors Ltd.

Plaintiff by Counterclaim

and

Abigail Boar and James Dinglehoofer

Defendants to the Counterclaim

DEFENCE TO COUNTERCLAIM

1. The defendants to the counterclaim admit the allegations contained in paragraphs 15 and 16 of the counterclaim.
2. The defendants to the counterclaim deny the allegations contained in paragraph 17 of the counterclaim.
3. The defendants to the counterclaim have no knowledge in respect of the allegations contained in paragraph 14 of the counterclaim.
4. The automobile that was the subject of the contract of sale between the plaintiff by counterclaim and the defendants by counterclaim has required 4 major motor repairs since purchase. For the 7 months that the defendants by counterclaim have had possession of the vehicle, the vehicle has been inoperable for all or part of 5 of those months.
5. On September 14, year 0, the defendants by counterclaim attempted to return the vehicle to the plaintiff by counterclaim, but the sales manager refused to accept the return.
6. The defendants by counterclaim allege that there has been a fundamental breach of the contract of sale by the plaintiff by counterclaim and that they are no longer liable for payments on the contract.
7. The defendants by counterclaim therefore submit that the counterclaim in this action be dismissed.

FIGURE 12.2   CONTINUED

Date: February 1, year 1

Just & Coping
Barristers and Solicitors
365 Bay Street - 8701
Toronto, Ontario, M3J 4A9

I.M. Just
tel. 416-762-1342
fax 416-762-2300

Solicitors for the Defendants by Counterclaim

TO:
Huey Sue
Barrister and Solicitor
65 False Trail
Toronto, Ontario, M6Y 1Z6

tel. 416-485-6891
fax 416-485-6892

Solicitor for the Plaintiff by Counterclaim

FIGURE 12.3   STATEMENT OF DEFENCE AND CROSSCLAIM (FORM 28A)

Court file no. 01-CV-1234

ONTARIO
SUPERIOR COURT OF JUSTICE

BETWEEN:

Abigail Boar

Plaintiff

and

Rattle Motors Ltd. and Fred Flogem

Defendants

STATEMENT OF DEFENCE AND CROSSCLAIM OF THE DEFENDANT

FRED FLOGEM

1. The defendant Fred Flogem admits the allegations in paragraphs 1, 2, and 3 of the statement of claim.
2. The defendant denies the allegations contained in paragraphs 7, 8, 9, 10, 11, 12, 13, 14, 15, 16, and 17 of the statement of claim.
3. The plaintiff entered the defendant Rattle Motors Ltd.'s premises at about 7:30 p.m. on September 14, year 0. She indicated to Linda Lucre, a salesperson on the showroom floor at that time, that she was interested in purchasing a Super Coupe.
4. Lucre showed the plaintiff several automobile models. Then the plaintiff walked over, on her own, to look at another model. She walked around the car and fell.
5. The defendant Fred Flogem admits that there was a small pool of oil on one side of the car but claims that it was easily visible to any reasonably prudent person who could have avoided it without difficulty.
6. The defendant Fred Flogem admits that two of the four spotlights were off but denies that the area was not well illuminated. The defendant Fred Flogem states that the area was well and clearly illuminated. Any hazard, if there was one, which is specifically denied, could easily be seen and avoided.
7. The defendant Fred Flogem admits that the plaintiff fell and appeared to lose consciousness momentarily. She also appeared to injure her lower right arm in the fall.
8. The defendant Fred Flogem states that the plaintiff, before coming to the defendant Rattle Motors Ltd.'s place of business, had consumed two glasses of wine and that she was intoxicated when she entered the premises.
9. The plaintiff fell solely as a result of her intoxication. Any injuries she sustained were solely the result of her own intoxicated state and not any acts of the defendant Fred Flogem.
10. With respect to paragraphs 10, 11, 12, 13, 14, and 15 of the statement of claim, the defendant Fred Flogem denies that the plaintiff suffered such injuries as described. Further or in the alternative, the defendant Fred Flogem states that the plaintiff has exaggerated both the extent of her injuries and the consequences of them.

FIGURE 12.3 CONTINUED

11. With respect to the plaintiff's allegation that she cannot return to work, the defendant Fred Flogem states that the plaintiff is exaggerating her injuries and that she is a malingerer. In the alternative, the defendant Fred Flogem states that the plaintiff has failed to mitigate her damages.

12. With respect to the allegations of negligence in paragraph 16, the defendant Fred Flogem states that he knew there was oil on the floor but that it was contained and did not constitute a danger to any reasonably prudent person. The defendant Fred Flogem admits that he turned off two of the four spotlights, but he specifically denies that he created a situation of danger for the plaintiff because the area in question remained well illuminated and safe for a reasonably prudent person.

13. The defendant Fred Flogem therefore requests that this action be dismissed with costs.

CROSSCLAIM

14. The defendant Fred Flogem claims against the defendant Rattle Motors Ltd.:
    a. contribution and indemnity for any and all claims of the plaintiff,
    b. costs of this action on a substantial indemnity basis, and
    c. such further relief as seems just to this court.

15. The defendant Fred Flogem is the employee of Rattle Motors Ltd.

16. The defendant Fred Flogem states that if the plaintiff has suffered damage, which is not admitted, such damage was caused by the negligence of the defendant Rattle Motors Ltd. and did not result from any act or omission of the defendant Fred Flogem.

17. *(Any additional facts on which the crossclaiming defendant relies are set out in the following paragraphs in the same manner as in a statement of claim.)*

Date: January 12, year 1

Huey Sue
Barrister and Solicitor
65 False Trail
Toronto, Ontario, M6Y 1Z6

tel. 416-485-6891
fax 416-485-6892

Solicitor for the Crossclaiming Defendant

TO:
Fair & Duguid
Barristers and Solicitors
380 Bay Street
Toronto, Ontario, M5H 3W5

B.E. Fair
tel. 416-927-1342
fax 416-927-2300

FIGURE 12.4 DEFENCE TO CROSSCLAIM (FORM 28B)

Court file no. 01-CV-1234

ONTARIO
SUPERIOR COURT OF JUSTICE

BETWEEN:

Abigail Boar

Plaintiff

and

Rattle Motors Ltd. and Fred Flogem

Defendants

DEFENCE TO CROSSCLAIM

1. The defendant Rattle Motors Ltd. admits the allegations contained in paragraph 15 of the crossclaim.
2. The defendant Rattle Motors Ltd. denies the allegations contained in paragraphs 16 and 17 of the crossclaim.
3. The defendant Rattle Motors Ltd. has no knowledge in respect of the allegations contained in paragraph 14 of the crossclaim.
4. *(Any facts relied on as a defence to the crossclaim must be laid out in consecutively numbered paragraphs, as they would be in a statement of defence.)*

DEFENCE TO PLAINTIFF'S CLAIM AGAINST CROSSCLAIMING DEFENDANT

7. *(If the defendant to the crossclaim wishes to defend against the plaintiff's claim against the crossclaiming defendant, pursuant to rule 28.06, further consecutively numbered paragraphs are included here. If no such defence is being raised, this part of the document is not included.)*

Date: January 25, year 1

TO: Brenda Brilliant
Barrister & Solicitor
1400 Willsa Way
Toronto, Ontario, M6V 9T7

Solicitor for the Crossclaiming Defendant

FIGURE 12.5 THIRD PARTY CLAIM (FORM 29A)

Court file no. 01-CV-1234

ONTARIO
SUPERIOR COURT OF JUSTICE

BETWEEN:

Abigail Boar

Plaintiff

and

Rattle Motors Ltd. and Fred Flogem

Defendants

and

Skank Motorcar Company Ltd.

Third Party

THIRD PARTY CLAIM OF THE DEFENDANT
RATTLE MOTORS LTD.

TO THE THIRD PARTY

A LEGAL PROCEEDING HAS BEEN COMMENCED AGAINST YOU by way of a third party claim in an action in this court.

The action was commenced by the plaintiff against the defendant for the relief claimed in the statement of claim served with this third party claim. The defendant has defended the action on the grounds set out in the statement of defence served with this third party claim. The defendant's claim against you is set out in the following pages.

IF YOU WISH TO DEFEND THIS THIRD PARTY CLAIM, you or an Ontario lawyer acting for you must prepare a third party defence in Form 29B prescribed by the Rules of Civil Procedure, serve it on the lawyers for the other parties or, where a party does not have a lawyer, serve it on the party, and file it, with proof of service, WITHIN TWENTY DAYS after this third party claim is served on you, if you are served in Ontario.

If you are served in another province or territory of Canada or in the United States of America, the period for serving and filing your third party defence is forty days. If you are served outside Canada and the United States of America, the period is sixty days.

Instead of serving and filing a third party defence, you may serve and file a notice of intent to defend in Form 18B prescribed by the Rules of Civil Procedure. This will entitle you to ten more days within which to serve and file your third party defence.

YOU MAY ALSO DEFEND the action by the plaintiff against the defendant by serving and filing a statement of defence within the time for serving and filing your third party defence.

FIGURE 12.5   CONTINUED

IF YOU FAIL TO DEFEND THIS THIRD PARTY CLAIM, JUDGMENT MAY BE GIVEN AGAINST YOU IN YOUR ABSENCE AND WITHOUT FURTHER NOTICE TO YOU. IF YOU WISH TO DEFEND THIS PROCEEDING BUT ARE UNABLE TO PAY LEGAL FEES, LEGAL AID MAY BE AVAILABLE TO YOU BY CONTACTING A LOCAL LEGAL AID OFFICE.

IF YOU PAY THE AMOUNT OF THE THIRD PARTY CLAIM AGAINST YOU, and $500.00 for costs, within the time for serving and filing your third party defence, you may move to have the third party claim dismissed by the court. If you believe the amount claimed for costs is excessive, you may pay the amount of the third party claim and $400.00 for costs and have the costs assessed by the court.

Date: May 25, year 1

Issued by: _____

Address of
court office: Court House
393 University Avenue
Toronto, Ontario, M5G 1Y8

TO:
Skank Motorcar Company Ltd.
349 Losers' Lane
Windsor, Ontario, J4T 6Y7

CLAIM

1. The defendant Rattle Motors Ltd. claims against the third party:
   a. a declaration that the third party is liable to the defendant for all or part of the plaintiff's claim that the defendant may be ordered by this court to satisfy;
   b. further, or in the alternative, contribution, indemnity, and relief in respect to any damages, interest, and costs awarded to the plaintiff as against the defendant;
   c. costs of defending the main action and the third party action on a substantial indemnity basis; and
   d. such further relief as seems just to this court.
2. The plaintiff in the main action alleges that as a result of the negligence of the defendants, she slipped and fell on a patch of oil while viewing automobiles for sale in the showroom of the defendant Rattle Motors Ltd.
3. The plaintiff in the main action alleges that as a result of her fall in the showroom of the defendant Rattle Motors Ltd., she suffered damages totalling $203,649.00, together with interest and costs.
4. The defendant Rattle Motors Ltd. denies that it is negligent and further denies any liability to the plaintiff.

FIGURE 12.5   CONTINUED

5. *(Each allegation of a material fact relied on must be set out in consecutively numbered paragraphs. The form and content should resemble the form and content of a statement of claim.)*

6. If the defendant Rattle Motors Ltd. is found at trial to be liable for the plaintiff's claim, or any part of it, then the defendant Rattle Motors Ltd. is entitled to contribution, indemnification, or relief from the third party to the full extent of the damages found and the costs of the main and third party actions on a substantial indemnity basis.

Date of issue: February 6, year 1

Huey Sue
Barrister and Solicitor
65 False Trail
Toronto, Ontario, M6Y 1Z6

tel. 416-485-6891
fax 416-485-6892

Solicitor for the Defendants

FIGURE 12.6   THIRD PARTY DEFENCE (FORM 29B)

Court file no. 01-CV-1234

ONTARIO
SUPERIOR COURT OF JUSTICE

BETWEEN:

Abigail Boar

Plaintiff

and

Rattle Motors Ltd. and Fred Flogem

Defendants

and

Skank Motorcar Company Ltd.

Third Party

THIRD PARTY DEFENCE

1. The third party admits the allegations contained in paragraphs 2 and 3 of the third party claim.
2. The third party denies the allegations contained in paragraphs 5 and 6 of the third party claim.
3. The third party has no knowledge in respect of the allegations contained in paragraph 1 of the third party claim.
4. *(Each allegation of a material fact must be set out in a consecutively numbered paragraph. The form and content should resemble the form and content of a statement of defence.)*

Date: February 16, year 1

Huey Sue
Barrister and Solicitor
65 False Trail
Toronto, Ontario, M6Y 1Z6

tel. 416-485-6891
fax 416-485-6892

Solicitor for the Defendants

TO: U.R. Smart
Barrister & Solicitor
4700 Bay Street
Toronto, Ontario, M4T 8V2

Solicitor for the Third Party

CHAPTER 13

Amending pleadings

INTRODUCTION

Ideally, before issuing a pleading, you will have carefully investigated the facts, researched the law, and drafted the claim, defence, or crossclaim. All parties should expect to be able to rely on that pleading as an accurate statement of your case right through the pretrial and trial stages. However, after a pleading has issued, often as the result of discovery, new facts emerge which expand or change a claim or defence, so that the pleading is no longer accurate. For example, if on the eve of trial, further medical tests showed that Abigail had suffered more serious mental impairment than was evident from the description of her injuries when the claim issued and when she appeared for discovery, I.M. Just would need to amend the pleadings. He would do this by adding this information to a description of the consequences of her injuries. He would also have to amend paragraph one to increase the claim for general damages. If her claim was not amended and the evidence at trial showed more serious damages than had been pleaded, Abigail would be limited to judgment for the amount she had claimed in her pleadings. The reason for this is that the defendant expects to answer the case as pleaded. If a plaintiff changes her claim, the defendant is entitled to proper notice; if it is not given, she is confined to the case as pleaded. The balance of this chapter concerns how a party goes about giving that notice.

RIGHT TO AMEND

Rule 26.01 states that the court *shall* amend a pleading at any stage of the action, including trial, unless the prejudice to the other side cannot be compensated by costs or by an adjournment. There are relatively few cases where costs and an adjournment cannot compensate the opposite party when an amendment is sought, even at a late stage. While judges usually grant the request, given the language of the rule, they often remain sceptical of a defence or claim that arises late in the proceeding. If your law firm is going to amend, it should do so at the earliest opportunity. The longer it waits, the more expensive it will be. For example, if an amendment is sought and granted on the eve of trial, it will often be on terms that the case be adjourned and that the opposite party have the opportunity to have discovery, both oral and documentary, on the issues covered by your amendment. In addition, your amendment may trigger an amendment to the opposite party's pleading as he or she pleads to your amendment. The costs of all the procedures spawned by the amendment will be borne by the party seeking the amendment.

WHEN YOU AMEND MAKES A DIFFERENCE

Before pleadings are noted closed, any party may amend his or her pleading without seeking leave of the court and without having terms imposed as a condition for making the amendment, provided that the amendment does not result in new parties being added or existing parties being deleted (rule 26.02(a)). Once pleadings have closed, then you must bring a motion (rule 26.02(b)), in which case the court follows the requirements of rule 26.01, and permits the amendment on terms unless it is so prejudicial that costs and adjournment will not adequately compensate the other party. However, if all parties consent, the amendment may be made without the court's permission on filing the consent. Any new party being added as a result of the amendment must consent as well (rule 26.02(c)).

HOW TO MAKE THE AMENDMENT

Rule 26.03, which governs the making of amendments, predates the age of the word processor. It provides one of the few instances in the rules where interlineations in pen seem to be required.

If the amendment is not extensive, consisting of a phrase or a sentence or two, it can simply be written in the appropriate place on the face of the document and underlined. If the amendment is so extensive that interlineations would make the document difficult to read, the party must file a fresh copy of the original pleading as amended, bearing the date of the original pleading, with the title preceded by the word "amended" (AMENDED STATEMENT OF DEFENCE, for example). The amended parts of the fresh pleading must also be underlined.

In each case, the registrar must note on the pleading the date on which the amendment was made and the authority for it: the order of the judge or master who permitted it, rule 26.02(a) if leave was not required because pleadings were not noted closed, or the filed consent of all parties.

If the pleading is amended more than once, each subsequent amendment is underlined an additional time. The text of the second amendment made is underlined twice to distinguish it from the previous amendment, and so on. So, for example, in figure 13.1, Abigail's claim for relief in her statement of claim set out her damages at $200,000 in paragraph 1a. It was then amended to $250,000 (and underlined once), then later amended to $400,000 (and underlined twice).

AMENDED PLEADINGS MUST BE SERVED

Every party to the proceeding, including any party added by the amendment, is to be served with the amended pleading. This includes not only the opposite party but also those added by crossclaim, third party claim, and counterclaim. Proof of service of the amended pleading must be filed "forthwith."[1] If the amended pleading is an originating process, such as a statement of claim, it need not be served personally on a party that was served with and responded to the original pleading. However, if the party has defaulted or is added as a result of the amendment, he or she must be served personally. The defaulting party's opportunity to plead and rejoin the proceeding is revived by being served with the amended pleading (rule 26.04).

FIGURE 13.1 AMENDED PLEADING

1. The plaintiff claims, against the defendant:

$250,000 $400,000
↑   ↑

a. general damages in the amount of $200,000;

The reason for this is that a defaulter with no defence to the original claim might have defence to the amended claim and may now wish to defend.

A party served with an amended pleading has 10 days to respond. If the amendment is made at an early date, while the time to respond to the original pleading is still running, then the party has the balance of the time remaining, if it is greater than 10 days (rule 26.05(1)).

If a pleading is amended and the party responded to the original but not the amended version, the party is deemed to be relying on the other party's original pre-amended pleading (rule 26.05(2)). Interestingly, the rules do not specify what form this "response" should take. Refer back to rule 1.04(2), which states that where the rules do not provide for a situation, you should proceed by analogy to the rules — in other words, find a similar process in the rules and adapt it. You might use a reply and modify it to respond to the amended pleading. Alternatively, you could develop a document called a "response to the amended statement of claim," or other amended document, with the usual general heading and title of proceedings. Then set out your response in consecutive numbered paragraphs, following the usual rules for pleadings. However, if your response also requires you to amend your pleadings, you must bring a motion to do so if pleadings are closed.

If an amendment is made at trial and is recorded on the trial record by the court reporter, no formal written order need be drafted, issued, or entered. It is likewise unnecessary to formally amend the pleading (rule 26.06).

CHAPTER SUMMARY

This chapter reviewed the process of amending pleadings. It noted the general rule that amendments are to be made unless they are so prejudicial that the other side cannot be compensated in costs or by an adjournment. We then noted how amendments are made technically on the face of the pleadings by underlining and, in some cases, by issuing a fresh copy of the original pleadings as amended. Once an amendment is made, the pleading must be served on all parties, who then have the opportunity to respond to the amended pleadings and to amend their own pleadings.

NOTE

1   "Forthwith" is not defined as a specific time period, but it means "as soon as possible."

REFERENCES

Rules of Civil Procedure, RRO 1990, reg. 194.

REVIEW QUESTIONS

1. Amir claims that you can amend pleadings at any time. Is he correct?

2. What constitutes prejudice in the context of amending pleadings?

3. When do you need leave to amend and when do you not need it?

4. How do you make amendments?

5. What happens after a pleading is formally amended?

1. Read and respond to the following memorandum:

To: E. Egregious, law clerk
From: I.M. Just, lawyer
Re: *Boar v. Rattle Motors Ltd. et al.*, amending claim

Although trial is only three weeks away, I have just had a supplementary report and updated prognosis from Ms Boar's neurologist, Dr. Morris Furgazy. In his report, dated May 30, year 2, Dr. Furgazy says that as a result of recent neurological tests, he has found that there is much more brain damage than he originally thought. Specifically, there are neurological lesions present, which cause impaired cognitive function. Originally, these looked to be transient or relatively minor, but it now appears that they are permanent and will result in much reduced ability to reason and to remember information. This changes the nature of the injury sustained and increases the damages that we should be claiming. I called Huey Sue to see if he would consent to the amendments. He refused, saying we should have had this information much earlier. We will need to move to amend.

What do you think the likely outcome of a motion to amend will be? Please draft the motion and affidavit in my name.

PART III

From discovery to trial

CHAPTER 14

Discovery

INTRODUCTION

In terms of time, and therefore cost, **discovery** takes up a large part of pretrial procedure. The purposes of discovery are:

- to discover the evidence on which the opponent relies to establish the facts of his or her case,

- to obtain admissions that will help prove your case,

- to obtain admissions that will assist you in weakening the opponent's case,

- to narrow issues for trial by requiring disclosure,

- to assess the credibility of the opposing party and your client as witnesses, and

- to determine if there is a basis for settlement before trial.

discovery
process that occurs after close of pleadings in which parties obtain more information about each other's cases before trial

OVERVIEW OF THE DISCOVERY PROCESS

Rules 30 to 33 include the basic forms of discovery that can be used. Rules 34 and 35 cover discovery procedures. An overview of these rules is set out in table 14.1.

In addition to the discovery procedures covered by rules 30 to 35, there are three other discovery-like provisions in the rules.

1. The pretrial conference covered by rule 50 creates a forum that enhances settlement and allows for narrowing of the issues if the case proceeds to trial.

2. Rule 51 facilitates a process in which the parties ask each other to admit the authenticity of a document or the truth of a fact, which narrows issues by reducing matters that must be formally proved at trial.

3. Rule 53 requires the disclosure of experts' reports before trial to reduce surprise and narrow issues.

These discovery-like procedures are discussed later in the text. In this chapter, after briefly discussing the deemed undertaking rule (rule 30.1), property inspections (rule 32), and medical examinations (rule 33), we focus on discovery of documents, oral discovery, and following up on undertakings because these procedures are featured in almost every civil action.

TABLE 14.1 OVERVIEW OF DISCOVERY RULES

Regulation of the forms of discovery: Rules 30 to 33

    Rule 30: Discovery of documents

    Rule 30: Deemed undertaking

    Rule 31: Examination for discovery

    Rule 32: Inspection of property

    Rule 33: Medical examination

Regulation of the procedure for conducting discovery: Rules 34 and 35

    Rule 34: Out-of-court oral examinations

    Rule 35: Out-of-court written discovery by questions

Deemed undertaking rule: Rule 30.1

Rule 30.1 codifies a rule, which developed at common law, that parties give an implied undertaking not to use the fruits of discovery other than in the proceeding in which the information was obtained.[1] The rule protects the privacy of parties because discovery requires them to disclose information that they might not otherwise need or want to disclose. For example, confidential client or product information is usually subject to secrecy. It ought not to be revealed to the whole world just because the parties are involved in a lawsuit. Further, the rule encourages parties to give full and frank disclosure by eliminating the risk that information will be leaked everywhere. However, once the information makes it onto the court record, it is in the public domain and no longer protected by the deemed undertaking rule.

This common law rule has now been incorporated into rule 30.1. All parties and counsel are governed by this rule with respect to any information obtained from any form of discovery under the rules (oral, written, and documentary discovery, medical examinations, and property inspections). The information obtained may be used only in the proceeding in which it was obtained (rule 30.1(1) and (3)). However, if a party uses other investigative techniques to discover information in the course of a proceeding, rule 30.1 does not cover that kind of information — it covers only information obtained through the discovery process (rule 30.1(2)). There are some exceptions: If a party consents to the use of evidence, it may be filed in another proceeding (rule 30.1(4)). If evidence is filed in court or given or referred to in a hearing, or if information is obtained from evidence given at a hearing, either orally or as a document, it may be disclosed. This exception is based on the notion that court proceedings are open, and the information given in court is public and may be disseminated generally (rule 30.1(5)(a) to (c)). Evidence obtained in one proceeding through discovery may be used against a witness to impeach the witness' credibility in another proceeding (rule 30.1(6)). If, for example, Fred gave evidence on discovery in one proceeding and in a separate proceeding gave evidence that contradicted his previous discovery evidence, counsel in the second proceeding is entitled to introduce the discovery evidence in the first proceeding to challenge Fred's credibility. The undertaking rule may be waived by the court where the interest of justice demands it (rule 30.1(8)).

Inspection of property: Rule 32

Rule 32 sets out a procedure for the inspection of property as part of the discovery process. It may be used in conjunction with rule 45, which gives the court the authority to order the preservation of property for inspection and for other purposes in connection with a proceeding. Rule 32.01(1) permits the inspection of real or personal property. The rule is broad and permissive. It allows the court to authorize the entry onto property of any person and may allow the property to be taken out of the possession of its owner, whether the owner is a party to the proceeding or not. The court may permit all kinds of tests and inspections to be carried out, though notice must be given to the party who owns or has possession of the property unless there are good reasons not to give notice (rule 32.01(3) and (4)).

Medical examinations of parties: Rule 33

This form of discovery usually occurs in cases involving claims for damages for personal injury where the plaintiff's own doctors have furnished expert medical evidence. With difficult-to-diagnose injuries, such as back problems or neurological problems, the defendants may wish to have their own expert conduct an examination. Where a party raises his or her own health or medical state as an issue, an opponent can test the allegations. Where an opponent raises the other party's medical condition as an issue, the court is more reluctant to order the party to submit to an examination. However, where the parties cannot agree on an examination, s. 105 of the *Courts of Justice Act* permits a medical examination. Rule 33 governs the procedure to be followed after an order for an examination has been made under s. 105.

MEDICAL EXAMINATION PROCEDURE

Where one party wishes to subject an opponent to an examination, he or she must being a motion, serving all parties, not just the party who is the focus of the inquiry (rule 33.01). An order under s. 105 of the *Courts of Justice Act* may name the practitioner to conduct the examination and set the terms and limits on the examination. If the circumstances warrant, subsequent examinations may be ordered (rule 33.02(1) and (2)). Within seven days of the examination, the party to be examined must provide the party requesting the examination with a copy of relevant medical reports and hospital or other records. However, records that were prepared in contemplation of litigation, and for no other purpose, and that will not be used at trial may be withheld. This may include, for example, preliminary examinations conducted at the behest of the injured party's lawyers to advise the lawyers of the nature of the injury or its cause, where the report is used to guide the lawyer to other experts whose reports eventually will be used (rule 33.04). The medical examination ordered under s. 105 is not a three-ring circus. Unless the court orders otherwise, only the person to be examined, the medical practitioner, and assistants may attend the examination (rule 33.05).

Once an examination has been conducted, its results cannot be swept under the carpet. The practitioner is required to prepare a written report of observations, test results, diagnosis, and prognosis, and deliver it to the party who requested the order for an examination. That party is then obliged to serve the report on every other party to the proceeding (rule 33.06). For a party who does not cooperate with an order under s. 105, there are the usual remedies of striking out pleadings, dismissing the action, or making such further order as is just.

DISCOVERY OF DOCUMENTS
Discovery of documents: When and what

In every action, within 10 days after the close of pleadings, every party must serve on every other party an affidavit of documents (rule 30.03(1)). The scope of what must be included is broad. The affidavit must list and disclose every document relating to any matter in issue in an action. As a general rule, when in doubt as to its relevance, include it (rule 30.02(1)).

To be disclosed, the document must be in the possession, control, or power of the party. This means that the party has the document, or has the power or right to obtain it, where the other party does not (rule 30.01(b)). If the other party has the document or can get it, you need not list it and can take the position that the other party can satisfy itself by obtaining the document itself (rule 30.01(b)).

Once listed in the affidavit of documents, every document must be produced for inspection if requested unless privilege is claimed for it. If the other party wishes to challenge a claim of privilege, it may do so by bringing a motion (rule 30.02(2)). Whether privilege may be claimed depends on what kind of document you have. There are three categories you need to consider.

1. *Solicitor–client communications to get and receive advice on issues relevant to the action.* This category is covered by solicitor–client privilege and probably includes most of the lawyer's correspondence on the file with the client and with others on the client's behalf.

2. ***Without prejudice*** *documents.* Typical of this category is settlement correspondence where offers are made on a without prejudice basis. These documents are privileged and may be described as correspondence regarding settlement between the parties.

3. *Documents for which the dominant purpose is litigation.* A document may have been created for several purposes, but if the dominant purpose was litigation, then it may be privileged.[2] For example, in one case, the lawyers for the defendant obtained a police officer's summary report of his investigation of an accident for the dominant purpose of litigation. Although the document had other purposes, such as data for traffic accident statistics, its primary purpose conferred a privilege on it.[3]

There is a special rule about insurance policies. Where there is an insurance policy that may cover a claim in all or part of a lawsuit, or may cover a settlement of a claim, the insured party, whether plaintiff or defendant, must disclose and produce the insurance policy if requested. However, no evidence about the insurance policy can be admitted into evidence unless it is relevant to an issue in the action. Its purpose is to let other parties know that the judgment can be satisfied from the insurance and to permit other parties to notify the insurer if the insured party has not done so so that the insurer is not able to deny coverage because there was a

without prejudice
term used, usually in correspondence, to indicate that an offer or admission cannot be used against its maker, admitted in evidence, or disclosed to the court

failure to give timely notice of a claim (rule 30.02(3)). Insurance companies are entitled to use technical defences to deny coverage, and they are not shy about doing so.

Subsidiary corporations, affiliated corporations, and corporations controlled by a party may be forced to produce documents in a lawsuit to which they are not parties. In this situation, the court may order a party to disclose documents in the power, possession, or control of a subsidiary, affiliate, or wholly controlled corporation. The key here is that the party controls these corporations, or at least has a right of access to information from them because of the relationship (rule 30.02(4)). The nature of the corporate relationship that ties a corporation to a party is further spelled out:

1. A subsidiary corporation is one that is directly or indirectly controlled by another. This means that the controlling corporation has a majority of voting shares or at least a large enough minority to give it *de facto* control in alliance with others.

2. A corporation is affiliated if:

   a. one corporation is a subsidiary of another;

   b. both corporations are subsidiaries of another so that they are linked; or

   c. the same person, where one corporation is a party and the other is not, controls both corporations directly or indirectly (rule 30.01(2)).

A document includes the usual paper, but it also includes all kinds of information that is stored electronically, as well as maps, videos, and films.

Affidavit of documents

The affidavit of documents has a prescribed format (form 30A for individuals and form 30B for corporations). The difference is that an officer or director of a corporation or a partner on behalf of a partnership completes form 30B, whereas an individual party completes his or her own affidavit using form 30A. The deponent must not only search his or her own records but must also take steps to inquire about the kinds of documents that might be relevant and inquire of others who may have control of various types of classes of relevant documents. After a thorough inquiry and search, the deponent swears that he or she has disclosed all documents that are relevant and in his or her power, possession, or control.

The documents are then divided into three schedules:

1. Schedule A documents are those that the deponent has or can get and that he or she will produce if asked.

2. Schedule B documents are those that the deponent has or once had but that he or she objects to producing on the ground of privilege. The basis for privilege must be stated: correspondence subject to solicitor–client privilege, documents for which the dominant purpose is litigation, or correspondence related to settlement made on a without prejudice basis.

3. Schedule C documents are those that were once in the possession, power, or control of the deponent but no longer are. It is necessary to state how control was lost and to give the present location of the documents if known.

There is also a fourth schedule, schedule D, but it is used only in cases brought under rule 76, the simplified procedure rule. Here, in addition to disclosing documents, a party also discloses the names and addresses of persons who might reasonably be expected to have knowledge of transactions or occurrences in issue. Some of these persons may be called as witnesses, and some may not, but those who eventually become witnesses should be on this list. Once the names are known, lawyers for any party may approach the potential witnesses to ask them questions. It is then up to the person contacted to decide whether he or she wishes to talk to the lawyer. There is no obligation to do so. The only obligation is to attend court and give evidence if summonsed to do so. In a proceeding that is *not* conducted under rule 76, names of persons with information can be obtained on oral discovery.

The deponent's signature must appear on the affidavit of documents. A lawyer must also sign the certificate on the form, stating that he or she informed the deponent of the requirement that full disclosure of all documents be made.

Clerk's role in the discovery of documents

Now that we have examined the basic document disclosure and production rules, and the contents of the affidavit of documents, we can turn to your role in the document discovery process.

The law clerk needs to understand both the issues involved in the action and the individual lawyer's approach to the issues in the file. This means that you need to understand the theory of the case, and how that might affect the organization of documents. The theory for Abigail's allegation of negligence, for example, is that she fell because Fred left the oil on the floor so no that one would notice it and hid it by turning down the lights.

The clerk needs to find out how the lawyer prefers information to be presented in the affidavit. The main variation is in how documents are described, for example: "letter from Dr. Morris Furgazy, neurologist, to Dr. Edwina Dhrool, family physician for Abigail Boar, regarding results of PET scan taken June 13, year 1" or "letter from Dr. Morris Furgazy to Dr. Edwina Dhrool, Abigail Boar's family physician." Either version is acceptable. The briefer version will force the opponent's lawyer to review the document and determine its relevance.

The next step is to review the client's documents. If they are numerous, and are composed of ordinary business records, it may be necessary to conduct your review on the client's premises. Otherwise, the documents can be taken to the lawyer's office. Whichever approach is taken, it is important not to disturb the way in which the client arranged the material. If a client keeps account records in a particular sequence in a shoebox, then they should remain in that sequence in that shoebox. Each document should be located, copied, identified, and put back in its original location.

The management of the documents by the law firm may be done on a variety of specialized software programs, or it may be done on a standard word-processing program, using the table and sort functions. What follows is an overview of how to prepare an affidavit of documents from client files.

Go through the client's documents in the exact order that you find them, without disturbing that order, and review them for relevance and privilege, using the guidelines discussed earlier. Number each document in each file in the sequence that they appear. This includes every phone message, invoice, memorandum, letter, videotape, and so on.

Each file can be labelled as a subfile and given a sequential number. The documents in all subfiles can then be numbered in sequence as well, starting with the first document in the first subfile and ending with the last document in the last subfile. This means that the first document in subfile 4 is not F4/D1 but may be F4/D632. In this way, each document has a unique number, allowing you to easily find a document to be produced, or one that is privileged or irrelevant, and to know how many documents there are in total.

When numbering documents, do not write on originals; instead, use small coloured stickers, writing the document number and the subfile number on the sticker.

As you assign document and file numbers, you prepare a table in which a complete list of all documents in all files can be entered. This is a master list for office use, although by using the sort function of your software later, you will be able to select documents for the schedule A list, with all necessary location details. Table 14.2 provides a format for a document table.

List each document, starting with the first document in the first subfile and going to the last document in the last subfile. Then sort the list chronologically. Undated items appear at the head or foot of the list, depending on your preference and the capabilities of your software.

Using this chronological list, you can now prepare the list for schedule A in the affidavit. From the chronological list, sort for all schedule A documents and list them in a separate table in chronological order, undated items first. The schedule A documents should now be listed in sequence (1, 2, 3) on the affidavit, and the document identifier numbers (F1/D3) previously used to locate them can be deleted from the affidavit. Most lawyers do not give individualized lists of documents for which privilege is claimed in schedule B. Rather, they identify and describe a class of documents, as the following examples illustrate:

- "all notes prepared by or on behalf of Abigail Boar in anticipation of litigation or for use in instructing counsel and prosecuting this action,"

- "all correspondence passing between the plaintiff and her solicitors," and

- "narrative prepared by Abigail Boar of events following her fall, prepared for her solicitors."

Abigail Boar's affidavit of documents

In a case such as Abigail's, most of the documentation concerns her injuries and their consequences. But to keep matters simple, let us assume we have looked through Abigail's files and found the following documents:

1. a receipt for dinner at Barbeerian's, September 14, year 0 [D1];

2. a written narrative prepared by Abigail for I.M. Just describing events after the accident, January 21, year 1 [D2];

3. a daily "pain diary" prepared by Abigail and kept on a daily basis, from November 10, year 0, recording pain and other effects of the injuries sustained [D3];

TABLE 14.2   DOCUMENT TABLE

Schedule	Date	Type	Pages	Description	Location

In the schedule column, insert A, B, or C for the relevant schedule on the affidavit of documents.

In the date column, insert the date of the document; leave it blank if the document is undated.

In the type column, indicate whether the document is an original, photocopy, video, or fax copy.

In the pages column, indicate the length of the document in pages.

In the description column, bearing in mind your lawyer's approach, enter a description of the document.

In the location column, indicate the document's location by subfile number and individual document number — for example, F3/D67.

4. Toronto Hospital records from September 14 to 16, year 0 [D4];

5. a letter from Dr. Furgazy to Dr. Dhrool, January 10, year 1, advising on treatment for Abigail [D5];

6. a prescription, October 14, year 0 [D6];

7. a prescription, October 21, year 0 [D7];

8. a prescription, November 3 year 0 [D8]; and

9. a birthday card from Aunt Emma, August 31, year 0 [D9].

Because there are not many documents, you would not necessarily arrange them in subfiles, but if you did, you could create the following subfiles and place the documents in them:

- F1 receipts: D1, D6, D7, D8;

- F2 medical records: D4; and

- F3 correspondence and memorandums: D2, D3, D5, D9.

D2 is privileged because it was prepared for use by her lawyer in this litigation. You can eliminate D9 from the affidavit because Abigail's birthday is not relevant to the issues in the action. It is included in the office list but will not appear in the affidavit. The rest are clearly relevant to the issues and belong in schedule A.

Figure 14.1 shows Abigail Boar's affidavit of documents.

Inspection of documents

Once the other parties have received an affidavit of documents, they have a right to inspect any of the documents in schedule A. They may do this by serving a request to inspect documents (form 30C). An example of a request to inspect documents is set out in figure 14.2.

FIGURE 14.1   AFFIDAVIT OF DOCUMENTS (FORM 30A)

Court file no. 01-CV-1234

ONTARIO
SUPERIOR COURT OF JUSTICE

BETWEEN:

Abigail Boar

Plaintiff

and

Rattle Motors Ltd. and Fred Flogem

Defendants

AFFIDAVIT OF DOCUMENTS

I, Abigail Boar, of the City of Toronto, in the Province of Ontario, the plaintiff in this action, MAKE OATH AND SAY:

1. I have conducted a diligent search of my records and have made appropriate enquiries of others to inform myself in order to make this affidavit. This affidavit discloses, to the full extent of my knowledge, information and belief, all documents relating to any matter in issue in this action that are or have been in my possession, control or power.

2. I have listed in Schedule A those documents that are in my possession, control or power and that I do not object to producing for inspection.

3. I have listed in Schedule B those documents that are or were in my possession, control or power and that I object to producing because I claim they are privileged, and I have stated in Schedule B the grounds for each such claim.

4. I have listed in Schedule C those documents that were formerly in my possession, control or power but are no longer in my possession, control or power, and I have stated in Schedule C when and how I lost possession or control of or power over them and their present location.

5. I have never had in my possession, control or power any document relating to any matter in issue in this action other than those listed in Schedules A, B and C.

Sworn before me at the	)
City of Toronto,	) *Abigail Boar*
in the Province of Ontario,	) Abigail Boar
on February 10, year 1.	)
	)
Commissioner for Taking Affidavits	)

FIGURE 14.1   CONTINUED

CERTIFICATE OF SOLICITOR

I CERTIFY that I have explained to the deponent the necessity of making full disclosure of all relevant documents.

Date .January 14, year 1.   .... *I.M. Just* ....

                                                    I.M. Just

SCHEDULE A

Documents in my possession, control or power that I do not object to producing for inspection.

1. Receipt for dinner from Barbeerian's: September 14, year 0
2. Prescription: October 14, year 0
3. Toronto Hospital records: September 16, year 0
4. Prescription October 21, year 0
5. Prescription November 3, year 0
6. Pain diary, November 10, year 0 to date of this affidavit
7. Letter from Dr. Furgazy to Dr. Dhrool, January 10, year 1

SCHEDULE B

Documents that are or were in my possession, control or power that I object to producing on the grounds of privilege.

1. Written narrative describing post-accident events, prepared for counsel for the purpose of conducting litigation: January 21, year 1.
2. All correspondence passing between the plaintiff and her lawyer.
3. All notes, reports, and memoranda prepared by or on behalf of the plaintiff in anticipation of litigation or for use in instructing counsel and conducting this litigation.

Privilege is claimed on the basis that these documents were prepared in contemplation of or for the purpose of litigation or are the subject of solicitor–client privilege.

SCHEDULE C

Documents that were formerly in my possession, control or power but are no longer in my possession, control or power.

There are no such documents.

FIGURE 14.2 **REQUEST TO INSPECT DOCUMENTS (FORM 30C)**

Court file no. 01-CV-1234

ONTARIO
SUPERIOR COURT OF JUSTICE

BETWEEN:

Abigail Boar

Plaintiff

and

Rattle Motors Ltd. and Fred Flogem

Defendants

You are requested to produce for inspection all the documents listed in Schedule A of your affidavit of documents.

Date: January 23, year 1

Huey Sue
Barrister and Solicitor
65 False Trail
Toronto, Ontario, M6Y 1Z6

tel. 416-485-6891
fax 416-485-6892

Solicitor for the Defendants

TO:
Just & Coping
Barristers and Solicitors
365 Bay Street - 8701
Toronto, Ontario, M3J 4A9

I.M. Just
tel. 416-762-1342
fax 416-762-2300

Solicitors for the Plaintiff

Most lawyers do not bother with the request to inspect; instead, they usually co-operate by producing and providing copies to the other side of their client's documents in schedule A, often bound and tabbed in a binder. The affidavit of documents is not usually filed in court unless it is relevant to an issue on a motion or at trial. Its primary function is to serve as an index to the productions themselves.

However, where a party does not produce documents voluntarily, rule 30.04 sets out a procedure for obtaining them for inspection. If there are further difficulties, a court on a motion may order production. In considering an order for production, a court may order "divided production" (rule 34.04(8)). Such an order may be made where a document that is prejudicial to a party becomes relevant only after an issue in the action has been decided. The court may allow disclosure to be withheld until the issue is decided.

Without further notice or summons, documents in schedule A are to be produced at discovery of the party who swore the affidavit of documents and at trial (rule 34.04(4)).

Incomplete affidavits of documents

A party may find relevant documents after completing the affidavit of documents and producing documents. In this case, the party must make a supplementary affidavit of documents, indicating which further documents have been discovered and take the necessary steps to produce the documents (rule 37.07). Where the affidavit is incomplete or privilege is improperly claimed, the court may order cross-examination on the affidavit of documents, service of a revised and amended affidavit of documents, and disclosure and production of omitted documents. If a claim of privilege is in issue, the court may inspect the document to determine if the claim of privilege is improper (rule 30.06). Where a party fails to disclose a document or produce it for inspection on the issue whether or not it is privileged, the court may, if the document is favourable to the party withholding it, prohibit its use in evidence in the action. If the document is not favourable, the court may make any order as is just (rule 30.08). There are similar rules with respect to documents for which privilege is improperly claimed. Once a document is privileged, the other side does not get to see it or refer to it in evidence. It would be unfair to allow the party claiming privilege to take the other side by surprise by suddenly waiving privilege and introducing the document in evidence at trial. If a party does wish to waive privilege, it must do so by notice in writing 10 days before the commencement of trial. There is one exception to this rule: A party may, without giving advance notice, use the privileged document to challenge the credibility of a witness (rule 30.09).

Production from non-parties

The rules governing discovery of documents apply only to parties. What happens if a non-party has a relevant document that is not privileged and is legally beyond the reach of any party? Rule 30.10 provides an answer by permitting any party to bring a motion for the inspection (as to relevance and privilege, if claimed) and production of a document. The moving party must show that the document is relevant and that it would be unfair to require the party to proceed to trial without it. Because the motion involves someone who is not a party to the proceeding, the non-party must be served with the motion personally or by an alternative to personal service.

ORAL EXAMINATION FOR DISCOVERY
Introduction

Examination for discovery is probably the most important pretrial procedure in a civil action. It permits a lawyer to obtain admissions to prove his or her case and to undermine the other party's case. It narrows the issues that must be proved at trial and identifies evidence on which the other party relies. It also reveals the opponent's theory and strategy for proof of the case.

Thorough preparation is extremely important. The client must understand the theory of his or her case and be **wood-shedded** so that he or she is prepared to answer questions on cross-examination and deal with various cross-examination styles. The client must review the pleadings, witness statements, documents, and relevant memorandums. The client should also review with counsel the issues to be canvassed and the questions to be asked in examining the opposing party.

wood-shedded
prepared for later cross-examination by opposing lawyer

Opposing counsel tries to obtain answers that help his or her case and hurt yours. A witness who answers a question without thinking has lost many a case. David Stockwood, an experienced civil litigator, has the following suggestions to aid a witness on examination for discovery or any examination:

1. If the lawyer objects to a question, the client should not answer it unless he or she is told to do so. Objections are used sparingly because they may be seen as an attempt to hide evidence.

2. The client should listen to the question and be sure he or she understands it before answering.

3. If the client does not understand the question, he or she should say so.

4. If the client does not know the answer to a question or does not remember the answer, he or she should say so. This information can be supplied after discovery.

5. Unless the client has clear and accurate figures in writing, he or she should give an estimate.

6. The client should not rush to answer and should take time to think, if it is needed.

7. The client should be concise and should not ramble.

8. The client should not argue with opposing counsel.[4]

The client also needs to know how oral discovery works and what the physical layout is in the place where the examination occurs. Discovery is an out-of-court examination that is arranged and supervised by the lawyers. The lawyer conducting the examination, usually after consultation with opposing counsel, determines the date and time for the examination and reserves space with one of the private reporting services or, in smaller centres, with the official examiner. If a reporting service or an official examiner is used, the service or the official examiner supplies a meeting room with a long table, exhibit stamps, a Bible, and a court reporter who takes down the evidence on tape and later transcribes it. There is no judicial official present. The party being examined and his or her lawyer sit on one side of the table. The lawyer conducting the examination sits on the other side, together with his or her client, who is allowed to be present. The witness is then sworn and questioned by the opposing counsel. If the witness's lawyer believes a question is irrelevant, abusive, or otherwise improper, he or she may object to the question and tell the witness not to answer it. In this case, the lawyer states the basis of the objection for the record. The lawyer may then permit the party to answer, subject to the objection. In this case, the answer cannot be used in court later unless on a motion the court determines that the question was proper. Alternatively, the lawyer may tell the client not to answer, in which case a motion is necessary to compel the answer. Because there is no judge present to rule on an objection, if the examining lawyer wants the question answered, he or she must bring a motion to compel re-attendance to answer the question, provided, of course, that the court finds the objection improper. When the witness does not know an answer or does not have information, he or she may be asked to give an undertaking to provide the answer or information. The witness should wait for his or her lawyer to agree or not. A lawyer who is not sure "takes it under advisement." This means that the lawyer will consult with the client and provide an answer later, either refusing to give an undertaking or giving it and providing what is required. If a lawyer cuts off the client and answers the question, the client is deemed to have adopted the lawyer's answer as his or her own if the client does not object or correct the lawyer's answer (rule 31.08).

Questioning styles vary. Some lawyers hop around from issue to issue, often returning to an issue. This may result in a witness's being caught off guard and contradicting himself or herself. But the transcript from this kind of examination is often hard to follow. Other lawyers take a more chronological or sequential approach. Often the lawyer doing the discovery is a junior associate. One purpose here is to save the client from the senior counsel's fees. The other purpose is strategic, so that the party being examined is not exposed to and therefore ready for the style of questioning of senior counsel at trial.

Lawyers often agree to certain ground rules to save time. Often counsel adopts an **estoppel** technique in conducting the examination. For example, in Abigail Boar's case, counsel might ask Fred Flogem, "Can you show me anything in the correspondence with Skank Motorcar that indicates that the problem with the leaking oil pan had been fixed?" This may produce a lengthy wait, while Fred goes through the exhibits to inform himself. Instead, counsel can state, "Unless I hear from you to the contrary, may I take it that there is nothing in the correspondence with Skank Motorcar to suggest that the problem with the leaking oil pan had been fixed?" In the latter case, no undertaking need be given. Fred can look at the correspondence and report back if he finds something relevant. If he is silent, Fred is estopped, or barred, from taking the position at trial that there is something relevant in the correspondence.

More time is saved when both lawyers consult at the beginning of the examination and come to an agreement about the facts that are not in dispute. The witness can then be asked to adopt the position that certain facts have been agreed to. The facts in question can be set out in writing and made an exhibit to the discovery, so the witness does not have to be taken through each one. If the discussion about which facts might be agreed to takes place in the examination, the lawyer who initiates the discussion may ask to go "off the record." This means that the reporter will not record the discussion. This cuts the length of the transcript and its cost. Not every

estoppel
term indicating that a witness is bound by his or her original position and evidence and cannot later take a contrary position

discussion should be off the record, however. Discussions about the basis for an objection should be on the record, as the transcript of that discussion may be evidence or an exhibit in a motion to compel a party to answer the question objected to.

In dealing with documents on discovery, much time can be wasted making each document a separate exhibit. Each party usually has a pile of documents that are in schedule A of the affidavit of documents. If there are 40 documents in schedule A, the easiest thing to do is to produce copies in a tabbed binder and agree to enter them as exhibits 1 to 40 on discovery and later at trial. Any other documents that emerge can be entered separately as exhibits 41, 42, and so on after a witness has identified them and testified as to their authenticity.

Cross-examination is permitted at discovery, except on issues of credibility, which are explored at trial. This allows a lawyer to lead a witness with simple questions that can be answered "yes" or "no." This saves time and transcript space. It is permissible to ask about evidence that lies behind a statement of fact and to ask for the names and addresses of persons who have knowledge of matters in the action, whether these people become witnesses or not. Because insurance policies must be produced if they cover the liabilities raised by the lawsuit, they can be the subject of questions on discovery. A party may also be asked to disclose findings, opinions, and conclusions of experts who will give evidence, though the report does not have to be produced unless the party intends to rely on it at trial. Parties who subsequently learn the answer to a question they were asked on discovery are obliged to disclose it (rule 31.06).

Once the examination is completed, a lawyer does not terminate it but adjourns it, subject to the fulfillment of undertakings and the bringing of motions on disputed questions.

The lawyer for the party who has been examined may, at the conclusion of the examination, re-examine the party to clarify an answer, or the answer may be clarified by letter later.

In the event information is obtained that requires correction of an answer given on discovery, there is a duty to provide the correct information forthwith in writing. The writing can be treated as evidence, but an adverse party may insist that it be given in affidavit form to have the same weight as the sworn evidence given on discovery (rule 31.09(1) and (2)). If a party fails to disclose new information as required by rule 31.09, if it is favourable, he or she cannot use it at trial. If it is not favourable, the court has broad discretion to do what is just (rule 31.09(3)).

Arranging discoveries

A party to an action may examine every other party who is adverse in interest. The examination may be oral or written but not both. If a corporation or partnership is a party, get directions from your supervising lawyer before arranging for a particular representative to be examined. Counsel may examine any party once. If the corporation's counsel gets to choose who represents the company, the examination may be very uninformative. If counsel has a person in mind to question, that person should be summonsed to the examination (rule 31.03). If a person under disability is a party, the litigation guardian may be discovered, but if the disabled party is competent to give evidence, the disabled party may be examined.[5]

There is some debate over whether it is advantageous to be examined first or to examine first.[6] Some think that it is an advantage to examine first because the examining lawyer gets a chance to assess the credibility and demeanour of the opponent and take him or her by surprise. Others think that by going last, you will know more about your opponent's theory of his or her case and be able to shape your own examination accordingly. Where credibility is an issue, however, whoever goes first, the time between examinations of the plaintiff and defendant should be short, so that a dishonest party does not have the opportunity to tailor evidence. If the examinations are to last a half day each, scheduling back to back is one solution to this problem. Another solution is to have both examinations well underway before transcripts are available.

The governing rules for arranging discoveries are rules 31.04 and 34. A defendant who wishes to examine the plaintiff must have served a statement of defence and an affidavit of documents. A plaintiff who wishes to examine a defendant may do so after the defendant has served a statement of defence and affidavit of documents, or the defendant has been noted in default. The parties may also agree to other arrangements regarding timing. In any event, the person who first issues a notice of examination may examine first and complete his or her examination before being examined by the other party (rule 34.01).

Rule 34.04 sets out the procedure for compelling attendance. A notice of examination, form 34A, must be served on the solicitor of record, if there is one, or on the party personally or by an alternative to personal service. The alternative service procedure may not be used if the person is appearing as a representative of a company or other non-individual. An example of the notice of examination is set out in figure 14.3.

If a lawyer expects that the party being summonsed for examination will not appear, it may be wise to serve the party personally as well as by his or her lawyer. Then if the lawyer brings a motion for contempt, the party can be jailed if he or she has been served personally with the notice (and later with the motion). Usually, however, service on the solicitor of record will suffice.

If the person being examined resides in Ontario, he or she must be given at least two days' notice of the examination (rule 34.05). If the person resides outside Ontario, the terms and conditions of the examination, whether it is held in Ontario or elsewhere, are set by the court (rule 34.07). Examinations outside Ontario, which are governed by rules 34.07 and 36.01, are beyond the scope of this text.

attendance money
formerly called conduct money, composed of the *per diem* witness fee and an amount for transportation and lodging in accordance with tariff A

A notice of examination operates like a summons to a witness. Consequently, the party being summonsed must be served with **attendance money** in accordance with tariff A, part II. As of August 2001, $50 is allowed for each day of attendance, plus $3 for travel if the party is examined in the county or region where he or she resides. This is usually the case because a party is entitled to be examined for discovery where he or she resides. If the party is travelling farther, the travel allowance is based on the distance travelled. The accommodation and meal allowance is currently $75 per day.[7]

All of this rigmarole can be avoided, and sensible lawyers usually do avoid it, by agreeing to the time, place, and order of the examinations and to the furnishing of documents. Taking the sensible approach can save much time and money, and there is little to be gained by being unnecessarily adversarial in making these procedural arrangements.

FIGURE 14.3   NOTICE OF EXAMINATION (FORM 34A)

Court file no. 01-CV-1234

ONTARIO
SUPERIOR COURT OF JUSTICE

BETWEEN:

Abigail Boar

Plaintiff

and

Rattle Motors Ltd. and Fred Flogem

Defendants

NOTICE OF EXAMINATION

TO: Abigail Boar

YOU ARE REQUIRED TO ATTEND FOR AN EXAMINATION FOR DISCOVERY on Tuesday, September 14, year 1, at 10:00 a.m. **at the office of**

Victory Verbatim Reporting Services
Toronto Dominion Centre
66 Wellington Street West
Suite 3320, PO Box 182
Toronto, Ontario, M5K 1H6

YOU ARE REQUIRED TO BRING WITH YOU and produce at the examination the documents mentioned in subrule 30.04(4) of the Rules of Civil Procedure, and the following documents and things: All documents, as defined in the Rules of Civil Procedure, relating to any matter in this action within your possession, power, or control.

Date: August 23, year 1

Huey Sue
Barrister and Solicitor
65 False Trail
Toronto, Ontario, M6Y 1Z6

tel. 416-485-6891
fax 416-485-6892

Solicitor for the Defendants

TO:
Just & Coping
Barristers and Solicitors
365 Bay Street - 8701
Toronto, Ontario, M3J 4A9

I.M. Just
tel. 416-762-1342
fax 416-762-2300

Solicitors for the Plaintiff

Examination of non-parties

An analogy to rule 30.10, requiring production of documents from non-parties in certain circumstances, is found in rules 31.10 and 34.05(4), governing the examination of non-parties. The test for bringing such a motion is set out in rule 31.10(2), and it is a stringent one. Non-parties are strangers to the lawsuit, at least technically, and they ought not to be inconvenienced. If non-parties are required for examination, the moving party must show that:

- he or she could not obtain the information from a party on discovery, or from the person who has possession, power, or control of the information or document in question;

- it would be unfair to require the moving party to proceed to trial without the opportunity of examining the person; and

- the examination will not unduly delay the trial, create unreasonable expense for the person, or be unfair to the non-party.

If the moving party is successful, he or she must provide transcripts free of charge to the other parties. The costs of the examination cannot be recovered from other parties as part of a general costs award at trial unless the court expressly permits it. Evidence of a non-party, unlike the evidence of parties, cannot be read into evidence under rule 31.11(1).

Controlling disruptive and uncooperative behaviour

Although lawyers should know better, there are a number who cannot resist engaging in improper or disruptive behaviour, or who do not take steps to prevent their clients from behaving improperly and disruptively. Some members of the legal profession who think this is a growing problem look back to a "golden age," when lawyers behaved with civility toward other counsel and their clients. Whether the problem is or is not on the increase, the Law Society of Upper Canada, in August 2001, mailed a pamphlet on civility to all lawyers in the province, a sort of lawyer etiquette manual. With respect to discovery, and out-of-court examinations generally, the kinds of questionable conduct one might expect to encounter are set out in rule 34.14(3):

- an excessive number of improper questions, interruptions, or objections designed to wear down or distract the person being examined or to disrupt the examination completely;

- an examination conducted in bad faith (for a purpose other than that intended by the rules) or in an unreasonable manner so as to embarrass, intimidate, or oppress the person being examined (examples include using a loud, angry, and sarcastic voice, asking irrelevant and embarrassing questions, making personal remarks, and in one extreme case, pouring coffee on opposing counsel's notes and later on his lap);

- answers from a party that are evasive, unresponsive, or unduly lengthy (examples include answering questions with questions, giving irrelevant answers that do not respond to the question asked, and going on at great length about irrelevant matters); and

- neglect or refusal of a party to produce relevant documents on the examination.

A lawyer faced with this kind of behaviour has several choices. If it is only moderately disruptive, so that he or she is still getting information, it may be best to ignore it. Let the examination transcript speak for itself at trial if the issue of bad faith, non-responsiveness, or credibility arises, or when addressing costs at trial. An examination for discovery is not a chat among friends. Some friction, though it should be avoided, may have to be tolerated. There comes a time, however, when a lawyer is simply being stonewalled or a client is being subjected to stressful and intimidating tactics. At that point, it is appropriate to break off the examination, state that you are adjourning the examination in order to seek directions from the court for the continuation of the examination, or for an order terminating the examination or limiting its scope. If the court finds that there was improper conduct, the court may levy costs against the person who engaged in improper conduct, especially if it was wilful or in bad faith. Costs may be levied personally against a lawyer in this regard (rule 34.14(2)). The same cost penalties may be levied against a moving party who improperly adjourned an examination to bring a motion for directions.

While the motion under rule 34.14 for directions focuses on improper conduct of an examination, rule 34.15 is directed at default or misconduct by a witness on an examination including:

- failure to attend at the time and place fixed for examination,

- refusal to take an oath or make an affirmation,

- refusal to answer a proper question,

- refusal to produce a document or thing that he or she is required to produce, or

- refusal to comply with an order made under rule 34.14 to correct previously noted improper behaviour.

The remedy granted depends on the nature of the default or misconduct. If counsel considers a question to be improper, he or she can state the objection on the record and direct the client not to answer the question. If opposing counsel wishes to challenge the objection, a rule 34.15 motion is the way to do it. If the moving party is successful, the court will order the party to re-attend at his or her own expense and answer the question, and any proper questions that flow from that answer. This is not uncommon. Reasonable lawyers may honestly disagree about whether a question is proper or not. But the other kinds of misconduct identified in rule 34.15 are more likely to be unreasonable and wilful. For this misconduct, a plaintiff's action may be dismissed, or a defendant's defence may be struck out. Lesser penalties include striking out the person's evidence recorded on the transcript or in an affidavit.

The ultimate penalty, where someone refuses to attend or be sworn or continues to obstruct an examination after a rule 34.14 order has been made, is committal to jail for contempt. If a lawyer is seeking committal for contempt, the rule 34.15 motion must be served personally, and the motion must be brought before a judge because a master has no authority to make an order depriving someone of his or her liberty.

Ordering and using transcripts

Check with the lawyer responsible for the file before ordering transcripts of an examination for discovery. Depending on the issues and the complexity of the case, and whether settlement is imminent, the lawyer may not wish to go to the expense of ordering transcripts. On the other hand, it may be important to obtain transcripts quickly, in which case counsel may wish to have the transcripts expedited. This means that instead of taking several weeks, copies will be available in a few days, but the cost is high. The lawyer who conducts an examination usually orders the first copy. Included in the cost is a copy sent to the court. Parties who order subsequently do not get the second copy (rule 34.17). A party who intends to use a transcript on a motion or at trial is responsible for seeing that the transcript is filed with the appropriate court office (rule 34.18).

The transcript may be used in a variety of ways. At trial, counsel may read into the record, as part of his or her own case, all or part of the discovery transcript of an adverse party or a non-party. Counsel may later call other evidence at trial to rebut the answers given on discovery. This procedure of "reading in" is usually done by referring to the questions and answers by the question numbers. At that point, and not before, the transcript or the relevant parts should be filed with the court (rule 31.11(1)). The opposing party may ask that other parts of the transcript also be included because they qualify the answers or give them a proper context.

The transcript may be used to impeach the credibility of the deponent as a witness at trial when he or she gives an answer that contradicts the answer given on discovery. Counsel puts the discovery question and answer to the witness and asks if he or she gave that answer then. The assumption is that the discovery answer, earlier in time, is more likely to be accurate.

The transcript of any party may be read into evidence if that party has died, is unable to attend the trial, refuses to attend the trial, refuses to be sworn, or stands mute and refuses to answer questions.

If discovery is held in an action, the action is discontinued or dismissed, and a new action dealing with the same subject matter is commenced, the discovery in the first proceeding may be used in the second proceeding as if it had been the discovery transcript in the second proceeding (rule 31.11(2) to (8)).

EXAMINATION FOR DISCOVERY BY WRITTEN QUESTIONS

Written questions and answers as a form of discovery has long been in use in England, where they are called interrogatories, and in the United States, where they supplement oral discovery. Although available here under rule 35, they are rarely used. Most lawyers are not familiar with the format and find it inflexible. Most lawyers prefer the fluidity of an oral examination, where a question may be inspired by the answer to the previous question. An oral examination is especially desirable when the person being examined is uncooperative or evasive, credibility is in issue, or a lawyer needs to get a sense of what the party being examined is like. However, a written examination for discovery is much cheaper because it does not involve court reporters, rental of meeting rooms, out-of-office attendances, or the cost of transcripts. Where credibility is not an issue and the fact situation is simple, a rule 35 written discovery may be more appropriate. With the advent of case management in Toronto, case management masters may start encouraging parties to use this mode of discovery to save time and money where it is appropriate.

Serving a list of questions in form 35A on the person to be examined and on every other party commences a written examination. Once the list is served, the party waives a right to oral discovery. Answers are given by affidavit in form 35B within 15 days after being served with the list of questions. If the party objects to a question asked, he or she must state the objection in the affidavit and give reasons for refusing to answer. The examining party, after receiving the affidavit, has 10 days to serve a further list of supplementary questions, which must be answered in 15 days from the date of service of the supplementary questions. Where there is an unresolved dispute about an unanswered question, the court may order the question answered by affidavit or by oral examination. Similarly, if the answers are evasive, the court may order attendance for a complete oral examination, thereby abandoning the rule 35 process. The questions and the answers given under rule 35 may be filed and treated as transcripts at trial under rule 31.11. Figure 14.4 provides an example of questions on a written examination for discovery, and figure 14.5 provides an example of answers on such an examination.

UNDERTAKINGS AND FOLLOWUP ON DISCOVERY

When a discovery transcript has been prepared, it is often the duty of a law clerk to go through the transcript and do the following:

- prepare a summary of the transcript, noting key points; and

- prepare a list of undertakings to provide information, refusals to provide information or answer a question, and requests taken under advisement.

Many reporters list undertakings, objections, and refusals at the front of the transcript, but you would be wise to scan it yourself to be sure nothing was missed. You will also wish to note questions taken under advisement — that is, questions that the opposing lawyer wishes to think about and advise you on later.

Once you have recorded the necessary material, write to the lawyer for the other party, asking him or her to honour the undertakings, and answer the questions objected to or taken under advisement. You probably will not get a positive response on the questions objected to or taken under advisement, but there is no harm in asking. If the information is not provided and you feel it is necessary for your case, you will have to bring a motion to compel the party to re-attend and answer the questions at his or her own expense.

When you have received the answers, they should be bound together and added as an appendix to the discovery transcript.

Your law firm will be asked to provide answers to undertakings on behalf of your client. If the letter is a general request, you will have to go through your client's transcript and find the undertakings, prepare a list, and ask the client to provide answers, including answers to disputed questions if nothing much turns on them. The letter to the client should request that the answers be in writing, and you should note the question number and page of the transcript on which the question appears. The lawyer should review the client's answers and forward them in a letter to opposing counsel.

FIGURE 14.4 QUESTIONS ON WRITTEN EXAMINATION FOR DISCOVERY (FORM 35A)

ONTARIO
SUPERIOR COURT OF JUSTICE

BETWEEN:

Abigail Boar

Plaintiff

and

Rattle Motors Ltd. and Fred Flogem

Defendants

QUESTIONS ON WRITTEN EXAMINATION FOR DISCOVERY

The plaintiff has chosen to examine the defendant Fred Flogem for discovery by written questions and requires that the following questions be answered by affidavit in Form 35B prescribed by the Rules of Civil Procedure, served within fifteen days after service of these questions.

1. On what date and at what time did you notice an oil leak on the showroom floor?
2. What steps did you take upon discovering the oil leak?

• • •

Date: May 15, year 1

Just & Coping
Barristers and Solicitors
365 Bay Street – 8701
Toronto, Ontario, M3J 4A9

I.M. Just
tel. 416-762-1342
fax 416-762-2300

Solicitors for the Plaintiff

TO:
Huey Sue
Barrister and Solicitor
65 False Trail
Toronto, Ontario, M6Y 1Z6

tel. 416-485-6891
fax 416-485-6892

Solicitor for the Defendants

FIGURE 14.5 ANSWERS ON WRITTEN EXAMINATION FOR DISCOVERY (FORM 35B)

Court file no. 01-CV-1234

ONTARIO
SUPERIOR COURT OF JUSTICE

BETWEEN:

Abigail Boar

Plaintiff

and

Rattle Motors Ltd. and Fred Flogem

Defendants

ANSWERS ON WRITTEN EXAMINATION FOR DISCOVERY

I, Fred Flogem, of the City of Toronto, in the Province of Ontario, one of the defendants in this action, AFFIRM that the following answers to the questions dated May 15, year 1 submitted by the plaintiff are true, to the best of my knowledge, information and belief:

1. I first became aware of some fluid on the floor of the showroom at about 6:30 p.m. on September 14, year 0.
2. The fluid did not seem to be an urgent problem, so I left it until later to clean up and turned off the lights to discourage customers from wandering into the area.

• • •

Affirmed before me at the)	
City of Toronto,)	*Fred Flogem*
in the Province of Ontario,)	Fred Flogem
on May 20, year 1.)	
)	
Commissioner for Taking Affidavits)	

In your review of the transcript, if you note any errors in the answers or any answers that are not complete, you have an obligation to provide corrections as soon as possible. Your instructing lawyer should be notified of errors immediately.

Summaries and undertaking lists prepared from transcripts

To demonstrate how an undertaking list and summary is prepared, figure 14.6 sets out an excerpt of the transcript of Abigail Boar's evidence.

Preparation of a transcript summary

Create a two-column table. In the left-hand column, note the question number or numbers and the page number. In the right-hand column, write a brief summary of the point or issue covered. Your table should look like the one set out in table 14.3.

List of undertakings

You also need to prepare a list of undertakings to provide information later where the information was not available to answer a question on discovery. The list also includes refusals or objections to answering questions or providing documents or further information, as well as a list of questions taken under advisement. To record this information, set out a six-column table such as the one in table 14.4. The last two columns, designed for the date you receive an answer and the substance of the answer/disposition by court, are left blank for now. They will be filled in later when and if you get answers to the undertakings, or when a court deals with a refusal to answer. The table can also be used for motions to compel a party to answer an undertaking; it meets the format requirement for this type of motion in a case-managed proceeding in Toronto.

CHAPTER SUMMARY

This chapter introduced you to various discovery procedures. We began with an overview of the general purposes of discovery and discussed the deemed undertaking rule, which prevents you from using information obtained on discovery in other proceedings. We then identified and described the various forms discovery takes: discovery of documents, oral examination for discovery, inspection of property, medical examinations, and written discovery. Our primary focus in this chapter was on documentary discovery and oral discovery because these are used in practically all cases, whereas the others are narrower and more specialized in their usage. We then examined the rules for discovery of documents, noting the obligations on a party to identify and produce all non-privileged documents that are relevant. We discussed how to assist clients in collecting documentary material and how to organize it both for office use and for the preparation of an affidavit of documents. We then turned to how to set up an oral examination for discovery and described its scope and how it is conducted. Then, using sample transcripts we saw how a summary and a list of undertakings are prepared by a clerk for use by a lawyer.

FIGURE 14.6 EXAMINATION FOR DISCOVERY OF ABIGAIL BOAR

EXAMINATION FOR DISCOVERY OF ABIGAIL BOAR ON BEHALF OF FRED FLOGEM AND RATTLE MOTORS LTD., HELD SEPTEMBER 14, YEAR 1

1   Abigail Boar, sworn

2   By Mr. Sue:

3   Q1:   Madam, please state your name for the record.

4   A: Abigail Boar.

5   Q2:   Ms Boar, I understand that on September 14, year 0 you

6   entered the showroom of Rattle Motors Ltd. to look at new

7   cars.

8   A: Yes.

9   Q3:   What time did you arrive there?

10   A: About 7:30 p.m.

11   Q4:   What time did you leave work?

12   A: About 5:30.

13   Q5:   How did you spend the time between leaving work and ar-

14   riving at the car showroom?

15   A: I walked to a restaurant, Barbeerians, had dinner with a

16   friend, and then I walked on alone to Rattle Motors.

17   Q6:   Ms Boar, I am producing and showing to you a restaurant

18   receipt from Barbeerian's, dated September 14, year 0.

19   Can you identify this receipt?

20   A: Yes, it is mine for my dinner that evening. I had dinner with

21   a friend.

22   Q7:   I notice that the bill includes two glasses of wine. Did you

23   drink both glasses?

24   A: Yes, it was a fine Bordeaux. When I drank the first glass, it

25   was very fine, and not the plonk it often is, so I had another,

26   to savour it. And very nice it was, raspberry overtones with

27   a hint of oak. Yes, very fine indeed.

28   Q8:   You mentioned a friend. Please tell me the name and ad-

29   dress of that friend.

30   Mr. JUST: Just a moment. Who that person is is entirely irrelevant to

31   the issues; Ms Boar will not provide that information.

32   Mr. SUE: I am entitled to the names and addresses of witnesses.

33   Mr. JUST: We will take it under advisement.

34   Q9:   Now, Ms Boar, you claim that the lighting on the premises

35   was inadequate for you to see the oil on the floor. Aside

36   from your own inability to see the oil, do you have any ex-

37   pert evidence or reports that indicate the lighting was not

38   adequate?

39   Mr. JUST: Just a moment, counsel. You have no right at this time to

40   any experts' reports we might have on hand, and we are

41   refusing to produce any such report at this time.

FIGURE 14.6 CONTINUED

1	Q10:	Well, Ms Boar, can you summarize what the findings are
2		in any report on the adequacy of lighting that you may
3		have?
4	A:	Well, we have one, but I only glanced at it, and I don't re-
5		member what it actually said.
6	Q11:	Will you undertake to review the report and provide me
7		with a summary of its findings and conclusions?
8	Mr. JUST:	We will examine our records and provide you with the in-
9		formation you request.
10	Q12:	What kind of shoes were you wearing when you got to the
11		showroom?
12	A:	Swamp green dress shoes with a narrow 4-inch heel.
13	Q13:	Would you describe your footwear as giving you good foot
14		and ankle support when you are walking?
15	A:	Well, they are really for office wear. I wouldn't go rock
16		climbing in them.
17	Q14:	Ms Boar, do you have any accident insurance that covers
18		personal injuries you sustain?
19	A:	Yes, I think Mr. Just gave you the particulars of it.
20	Q15:	Will you please provide me with a copy of the policy?
21	Mr. JUST:	No, we will not give you that undertaking. You have all of
22		the information that you require.

TABLE 14.3 SUMMARY OF TRANSCRIPT OF EXAMINATION OF ABIGAIL BOAR

Q1-2, p. 1	introduction of Boar, setting context
Q3-8, p. 1	Boar accounts for time after work, dinner with friend with two drinks before going on to Rattle
Q9-11, pp. 1-2	Boar asked for lighting expert's report and her recollection of what it said: didn't recall what it said
Q12-13, p. 2	Boar describes her footwear at time of accident, and whether it was safe or suitable
Q14-15, p. 2	Boar acknowledges she had accident insurance, refusal to provide copy of policy

TABLE 14.4   SUMMARY OF UNDERTAKINGS, OBJECTIONS, AND ADVISEMENTS

UNDERTAKINGS CHART

Outstanding undertakings given on the examination of Abigail Boar				**dated** September 14, yr 1	
Issue & relationship to pleadings or affidavit, if any	Question No.	Page No.	Specific undertaking	Date answered or precise reason for not doing so	Answer/Disposition by Court
1. Whether to provide name and address of dinner companion (defence, par. 8 & 9; reply, par. 3)	8	1	Advisement		
2. Provision of expert lighting report	9	1	Refused		
3. Provision of summary of lighting expert report	10-11	2	Undertaking		
4. Provision of accident insurance policy	15	2	Refused		

KEY TERMS

discovery

without prejudice

wood-shedded

estoppel

attendance money

NOTES

1   *Goodman v. Rossi* (1995), 125 DLR (4th) 613 (Ont. CA).

2   *General Accident Assurance Co. v. Chrusz* (1997), 34 OR (3d) 354 (Gen. Div.), var'd. 37 OR (3d) 790 (Div. Ct.), rev'd. 45 OR (3d) 321 (CA).

3   *Ferber v. The Gore Mutual Insurance Co.* (1991), 3 CPC (3d) 41 (Gen. Div.).

4   David Stockwood, *Civil Litigation*, 4th ed. (Toronto: Carswell, 1997), form 25, at 239.

5   Rule 31.03(5); also see (6), (7), and (8) with respect to assignees, trustees in bankruptcy, and nominal parties.

6   Supra footnote 4, at 74.

7   Tariff A, part II, 21. Always consult the current tariff before issuing a cheque because the tariffs change from time to time.

REFERENCES

Courts of Justice Act, RSO 1990, c. C.43.

Ferber v. The Gore Mutual Insurance Co. (1991), 3 CPC (3d) 41 (Gen. Div.).

General Accident Assurance Co. v. Chrusz (1997), 34 OR (3d) 354 (Gen. Div.), var'd. 37 OR (3d) 790 (Div. Ct.), rev'd. 45 OR (3d) 321 (CA).

Goodman v. Rossi (1995), 125 DLR (4th) 613 (Ont. CA).

Rules of Civil Procedure, RRO 1990, reg. 194.

Stockwood, David, *Civil Litigation*, 4th ed. (Toronto: Carswell, 1997).

REVIEW QUESTIONS

1. What is the purpose of discovery?

2. What forms of discovery are available in a civil action?

3. What is the deemed undertaking rule?

4. Can you run tests on property during an inspection under rule 32?

5. Under what circumstances will a medical examination be ordered as a form of discovery?

6. What documents must be disclosed?

7. What determines whether a document is privileged?

8. The plaintiff's lawyer would like to see the defendant's insurance policies. Can she?

9. Company A is a defendant in a lawsuit. A minority of company A's and company B's shares are held by company C, but the minority is large enough to give company C total control because the rest of the shares in companies A and B are widely dispersed. Company B has some documents that are relevant to the plaintiff's claim against company A. Can the plaintiff demand this document from company A?

10. How does a law clerk organize client materials for an affidavit of documents?

11. How do lawyers obtain the schedule A documents to inspect them?

12. What should you do if you notice that a document was omitted from the affidavit of documents or that an answer given in oral discovery was in error?

13. Can a lawyer obtain production from a non-party?

14. How should you prepare a witness for an examination for discovery?

15. Describe for the client the physical environment where discovery takes place.

16. How do lawyers control the discovery process?

17. How can lawyers shorten the process of entering exhibits?

18. How do you arrange discoveries?

19. Can a lawyer examine a non-party for discovery?

20. What kinds of misconduct at discovery do the rules contemplate and how is it controlled?

21. How do you obtain transcripts of the examination?

22. When would you be likely to use a written question-and-answer discovery format?

23. What do you need to do with a transcript when it comes back from the reporter?

DISCUSSION QUESTIONS

1. Read and respond to the following memorandum:

   To: Law Clerk
   From: Lawyer
   Re: Examination of Phineas Whipsnade

   We act for Henry in a family law dispute. Wendy claims that the property she owns in which Henry claims a half interest is heavily mortgaged to her father, Phineas Whipsnade. If this is so, Henry's share is likely peanuts. If it is a load of codswallop, as I suspect it is, then Henry may well get a bundle. On discovery, Wendy claimed she had no mortgage documents in her possession, power, or control.

She said it was an unregistered equitable mortgage, based on a promissory note giving the property as security. She said she didn't have a copy of the note and claimed her father had the original. I wrote to Phineas requesting that he provide me with a copy and let me examine the original. That was two weeks ago, and I have had no answer.

Please write a short memorandum telling me what our options are.

2. Read and respond to the following memorandum:

To: E. Egregious, law clerk
From: I.M. Just
Re: *Boar v. Rattle Motors Ltd. et al.*

Attached is a copy of a transcript of the examination of Fred Flogem for discovery. Please prepare a summary and a list of undertakings, objections/refusals, and questions taken under advisement. Also prepare a draft notice of motion to compel Fred to re-attend at his own expense to answer unanswered questions and provide documents. Assume that Fred will not respond to the refusals, objections, or advisements.

EXAMINATION FOR DISCOVERY OF FRED FLOGEM ON BEHALF OF
ABIGAIL BOAR, HELD October 21, year 1

1		Fred Flogem, affirmed
2	By Mr. Just:	
3	Q1:	Sir, will you please state your name for the record.
4	A:	Fred Flogem.
5	Q2:	I understand that you are employed as a salesperson for
6		Rattle Motors Ltd. and that you were present on the pre-
7		mises on September 14, year 0.
8	A:	Yes.
9	Q3:	I understand at about 6:30 p.m. you spotted an oil leak on
10		the floor by the Super Coupe.
11	A:	Well, there was some fluid on the floor, but I didn't know
12		for sure it was oil, or that it came from a leak.
13	Q4:	Well, Freddie boy, did you think the spirits of the air sud-
14		denly dropped this stuff out of the sky?
15	Mr. SUE:	I object to that question, and Mr. Flogem will not answer it.
16		It is not necessary to use that sarcastic and flippant tone,
17		calculated as it is to intimidate and harass the witness.
18	Q5:	Well, Mr. Flogem, where did you think this stuff came
19		from?
20	Mr. SUE:	I object to the question. It is not relevant where it came
21		from. He has already acknowledged in his answers that it
22		was there, and that is sufficient.
23	Q6:	Mr. Flogem, do you have an insurance policy covering the
24		damages claimed in this action?
25	A:	Me? Not personally, but I believe Rattle Motors has a
26		policy, or at least so I have been told.

1	Q7:	Can you furnish me with the particulars of the policy?
2	A:	Well, not off hand. Sunil, the manager, has a copy, I think,
3		but I have never seen it, and I have no idea where it is.
4	Q8:	Will you undertake to find out what the particulars are?
5	A:	Well, Sunil has it with him, and he is out of town, so I don't
6		know.
7	Mr. SUE:	We will take it under advisement.
8	Q9:	After you saw the fluid on the floor, what did you do?
9	A:	Well, I thought I would clean it up later, and to discourage
10		anyone from going into the area, I turned off two of the
11		four spotlights in that part of the room.
12	Q10:	Why did you put off cleaning this up?
13	A:	Well, it wasn't much of a spill, it was mostly under the car,
14		and it didn't seem urgent.
15	Q11:	Did you have any information before September 14, year
16		0 that Skank Motorcars had issued an alert about leaking
17		oil pans on the Super Coupe model?
18	A:	Well, I think there were some letters, but I haven't read
19		them.
20	Q12:	Can you provide me with copies of those letters?
21	A:	Well —
22	Mr. SUE:	No, he cannot because he does not have them or have
23		access to them.

Pretrial procedures

INTRODUCTION

Once the parties have completed the discovery process, it is time to think about going to trial. As we have discussed, the discovery process gives both sides a good opportunity to examine the case of the opposite party and determine whether or not they have a chance of winning their case at trial. During discovery, the parties often decide to settle the case.

Rules 46, 47, 48, 50, and 51 are the major rules dealing with pretrial procedures. The various procedural steps are as follows:

1. determining the place of trial: rule 46;

2. deciding whether the case will be tried with a jury and issuing a jury notice if so: rule 47;

3. listing the case for trial: rule 48;

4. pretrial conference: rule 50; and

5. dealing with admissions: rule 51.

PLACE OF TRIAL: RULE 46

The general rule is that the plaintiff chooses the place of trial, but some statutes specify where a trial must take place. If the case is governed by a statute that prescribes where the trial is to be held, the plaintiff does not get to choose. The trial is held where the statute says it must be held. For example, in family law cases, any trial that involves an issue of child custody or access must take place in the county where the child resides unless a court orders otherwise (rule 70.05).

The plaintiff must make the choice of location for trial early in the game. Rule 46.01(1) requires that the plaintiff must propose the place for trial in the statement of claim. The last paragraph must indicate the plaintiff's choice. The proper wording for the paragraph, which is set out in form 14A, is "The plaintiff proposes that this action be tried in (*place*)." The place of trial proposed by the plaintiff does not need to be the same place where the proceeding is commenced.

Usually the trial is held in the place proposed in the statement of claim. However, the court has the power to order that the trial take place in a location other than the one the plaintiff has chosen (rule 46.02).

If one or both of the parties want to have the trial held in a different location than the one originally named, they must bring a motion under rule 46.03(2). Before deciding to grant an order for a change, the court must be satisfied that

balance of convenience

judicial determination of greatest convenience for all parties arrived at by judge after weighing all the relevant factors and merits of parties' arguments

- the **balance of convenience** favours holding the trial in another place, or

- it is likely that a fair trial cannot be had at the place named in the statement of claim (rule 46.03(2)).

When the court looks at the issue of convenience, it considers where the parties live and where most of the witnesses live. It also looks at whether any of the parties or witnesses suffer from a disability or an illness that would make it difficult for them to participate in a trial held in a particular location. The financial positions of the parties that might affect their ability to travel may be something else the court takes into consideration. None of these factors determines the issue, but once the court has considered all the factors involving convenience, it balances them and determines whether any of them makes it substantially more convenient to hold the trial in one place or another.

In some instances, the parties may agree that the trial be held in a place other than the place that the plaintiff names in the statement of claim. If that is the case, the court considers the wishes of the litigants but s. 114 of the *Courts of Justice Act* states that the court is not bound by the consent of the parties to change the location. Therefore, if the court, after applying the convenience and fairness test, decides that a change is not warranted, the consent of the parties is irrelevant.

In most cases, the court has a good deal of discretion in deciding whether or not to change the place of trial chosen by the plaintiff. However, if there is a statute that requires that the trial be held in a particular location and the plaintiff has not named the required location as the place for trial, the judge has no discretion. He or she must change the location to ensure it complies with the statute (rule 46.03(1)).

JURY NOTICE: RULE 47
Right to a jury trial

Section 108 of the *Courts of Justice Act* gives any party in a proceeding in the Superior Court of Justice the right to a jury trial. Whether or not a party wants a jury trial will depend on a number of factors, including the complexity of a case, the amount of sympathy or hostility the party believes that it may receive from a jury, and the length of the trial list for jury trials.

If a jury trial is chosen, the jury can hear the entire case and make a determination about whether or not the defendant is liable for damages, or it can be called in to hear only the damages part of the case. In the latter instance, the trial proceeds from the beginning without a jury. The judge makes all the determinations of facts in the case and decides whether or not the defendant is liable to the plaintiff. Then, once the liability issue has been decided, the jury is called in to determine the amount of damages that the plaintiff will receive.

There is no absolute right to a jury trial. Section 108(2) of the *Courts of Justice Act* lists the types of cases in which a jury trial is never permitted. The list includes most family law matters, cases involving equitable remedies, partition or sale of real property, and requests for injunctions. Even if the case is one where a jury trial is not prohibited under s. 108(2), a judge has the discretion to decide that a jury trial is not appropriate in a particular case. A jury notice in Abigail Boar's case is set out in figure 15.1 (at the end of the chapter).

Procedure for obtaining a jury trial

Either party can decide that it wants to have a jury trial. It then must prepare and serve a jury notice on all the other parties. The jury notice is in form 47A. It may be served any time before the close of pleadings. Once served, the notice is then filed with the court (rule 47.01).

Striking out a jury notice

If any of the other parties does not wish to have a jury trial, it can bring a motion asking that the jury notice be struck out. If the notice is struck out, the trial proceeds without a jury. There are two grounds under rule 47.02 for striking out a jury notice:

1. the jury notice is not in accordance with a statute or the rules, or

2. it is inappropriate to have a jury trial in a particular case.

NOT IN ACCORDANCE WITH A STATUTE OR THE RULES

If there is a statute that governs a particular type of case and the statute prohibits a trial by jury, a party's attempt to have a trial by jury is not "in accordance" with a statute. For example, if there were an application for custody of a child and one of the parties served a jury notice, this notice would not be in accordance with a statute because s. 108(2) of the *Courts of Justice Act* prohibits jury trials in all cases under the *Children's Law Reform Act*. The other party would bring a motion to strike the jury notice out and the court would have no choice but to grant that motion (rule 47.02(1)(a)).

A jury notice not would be in accordance with the rules if it were served after the close of pleadings. Rule 47.01 requires that the jury notice be served *before* the close of pleadings. If served after pleadings have closed, it is out of time, and it may be challenged on that basis. A motion to strike out a jury notice on the grounds that it is not in accordance with a statute or the rules may be brought before a master.

JURY TRIAL WOULD BE INAPPROPRIATE

If a jury notice cannot be struck out on the basis that it is not in accordance with the rules or a statute, it is still possible to bring a motion under rule 47.02(2) asking that it be struck out on the grounds that it is not appropriate to have a jury hear a particular case. This motion, unlike a motion to strike on the basis of not according with a statute or the rules, must be brought before a judge. A master has no jurisdiction to hear this type of motion.

When deciding whether or not a jury trial is appropriate, the judge will look at a number of issues, including the complexity of the case. If a case involves difficult questions of law, a judge may decide that it is best to proceed without a jury. It is the jury's role in a trial to determine which version of the facts is the most plausible. In a jury trial, it is the role of the judge to decide the legal issues. We call the jury "the finder of fact" for this reason. Sometimes the parties are not in a major dispute about the facts of a case: The source of their disagreement is how the law should be applied to those facts. In a case like this, there is no role for a jury, and a judge would likely decide that the case should proceed without one.

Even if the party wanting to have the jury notice struck is not successful on a motion, that party may try again to have the jury notice struck by the trial judge (rule 47.02(3)).

LISTING THE CASE FOR TRIAL: RULE 48
Setting the action down for trial: Rules 48.01 and 48.02

The court does not automatically schedule a trial once a lawsuit has been started. The parties must first let the court know that they are ready to proceed to trial. The process of letting the other side and the court know that your side is ready for trial is called **setting an action down for trial**.

Any party who has not been noted in default can set the case down for trial, but usually the plaintiff takes this step. The plaintiff is the party who has the most interest in having the case decided. For example, Abigail Boar wants to have the court decide that she is entitled to be compensated by the defendants for her injuries. It is likely that she would be the party to set the matter down for trial.

In order to set a matter down for trial, Abigail must serve and file a **trial record** (rule 48.02(1)). The trial record must be served and filed on all the parties to the action, including the parties to a counterclaim, a crossclaim, or a third party claim. Once this has been done, the trial record is filed with the court along with proof of service. The court is now aware that this case is ready for trial.

If there is a third party claim in your action, the third party must be served along with all the other parties, but there are additional procedural requirements. A party that wants to have the third party claim set down for trial must prepare a separate trial record. This third party trial record must be served on all the parties to the third party claim. Therefore, if an action has a third party claim, there are two trial records: one for the main action and one for the third party claim.

When an action is undefended — that is, when the defendant does not file a statement of defence — the plaintiff has the defendant noted in default, and the case does not proceed to trial. However, in rare instances, a judge can order that an **undefended action** proceed to trial. In that case, rule 48.03(2) requires that a trial record be prepared in the usual way, but there is no requirement that it be served on any other party. If you are setting an undefended action down for trial, you file the trial record with the court without serving anyone.

Once again, there are slightly different rules for third party claims. If a third party claim is undefended, a party that wants to set it down for trial must prepare a separate trial record for the third party claim. Rule 48.02(4) requires that the trial record for the undefended third party claim be served on the plaintiff in the main action, but no other party in the main action needs to be served. After service on the plaintiff in the main action, the trial record in the undefended third party claim can be filed with the court.

For example, suppose that Abigail Boar, the plaintiff in the main action, is suing Rattle Motors Ltd. and its employee Fred Flogem. Both Rattle Motors and Fred have served and filed statements of defence in the main action. The main action is therefore a defended action. Both Rattle Motors and Fred are planning to defend against Abigail's claim that they are liable to pay her damages because they caused her injuries. Rattle Motors has commenced a third party claim against Skank Motorcar

setting an action down for trial
procedure that a party must follow in order to have its case placed on the trial list

trial record
bound set of documents prepared by the party setting the action down for trial and containing the pleadings of all parties, any relevant orders, all notices, and certificates

undefended action
an action in which no statement of defence is delivered

Company Ltd., the manufacturer of the Super Coupe, claiming that the oil pan on the car was defective and that it caused the leak that resulted in Abigail's fall. Because Skank has also filed a statement of defence in the third party claim, the third party claim is also defended.

Abigail wants to set the main action involving herself, Rattle Motors, and Fred down for trial. I.M. Just prepares the trial record for the main action and it is served on Fred, Rattle Motors, and the third party Skank. Abigail really does not care whether Rattle's third party claim against the car manufacturer comes to trial or not. She intends to get all compensation for her injuries from Fred and Rattle Motors.

Rattle Motors, however, cares that the third party claim comes to trial because it thinks Skank Motorcar caused Abigail's injuries. Rattle's lawyer, Huey Sue, would prepare the trial record in the third party claim, serve it on all the other parties, and file it with the court. There would then be two trial records: one for the main action involving Abigail, Rattle, and Fred and the other for Rattle's third party claim against Skank.

Let's change the facts. Assume that Rattle Motors and Fred have not filed a statement of defence. There is now no third party claim because Rattle never brought one. In this example, there is only one action, the main action, and it is undefended. Nevertheless, a judge has ordered that this undefended action proceed to trial. I.M. Just would prepare the trial record and file it with the court immediately without serving it on Rattle and Fred.

Let's say that the main action between Abigail, Rattle Motors, and Fred is a defended action. In this situation, Rattle has brought a third party claim, but Skank has not filed a statement of defence. The third party claim is now undefended. If this undefended third party claim is to be set down for trial, Huey Sue must prepare a third party trial record. He does not need to serve the third party or Fred, but he must serve Abigail, the plaintiff in the main action.

When a party sets a matter down for trial and the trial is to be held in a place other than where the action was started, the party that set the action down for trial must requisition the court file to be sent to the other court.

Remember, even though most plaintiffs start their cases in the same court where they want the trial to be heard, the rules permit an action to be started in a different place than the place named for trial. If this is the situation, the court file will be located in the court where the action is commenced, and it will be needed in the other court for the trial. It will not be sent to the second court unless the party that set the action down for trial requisitions it.

A requisition is in form 4E and appears as figure 15.2 (at the end of the chapter). Once that form is prepared and sent to the registrar of the court where the action was commenced, the registrar's office will get the court file ready and send it to the trial court.

Consequences of setting an action down for trial: Rule 48.04

There can be a very long wait for cases to come to trial. Therefore, a party may be anxious to set the action down as soon as possible, but there are consequences of setting the action down that a party will want to consider before moving too quickly. By setting an action down for trial or consenting to an action's being

trial list
list kept by the registrar in
each courthouse of cases
that are ready for trial

placed on the **trial list**, a party is advising the court that it is ready for trial. Therefore, rule 48.04(1) prohibits parties from bringing any motions or conducting any further discoveries without leave of the court once they have set the action down. The other parties can bring motions and continue with discoveries if they wish. Only the party that sets the action down is prohibited from continuing these procedures. A party will want to make sure that it has brought all the necessary motions and conducted all the discoveries it will need before setting the action down.

The rule prohibiting discoveries for the party setting down the action does not mean that the other parties are not obligated to follow through on their undertakings or their other obligations listed in rule 48.04(2)(b).

The party that sets an action down for trial may seek permission from the court to bring further motions, but the court will be reluctant to grant permission to do so unless the proposed motion concerns a serious issue that could not have been brought before the action was set down. It is rare that the court will give leave to a party to initiate or continue with discoveries after the party has set the action down.

Placing the action on the trial list: Rules 48.05 to 48.13

Once the trial record is filed, the action must be placed on the trial list 60 days later by the registrar of the court (rules 48.05 to 48.09). The parties can agree that the action be listed for trial before the 60-day period has passed, but a party who consents to putting the case on the trial list loses the right to bring any further motions or to initiate or continue discoveries.

sittings
a time period during
which a specific court
may hear cases

In larger cities, the court sits all year long, so it does not matter when the trial record is filed. Once it is filed, the registrar adds the name of the action to the bottom of the list of cases that are ready for trial. However, outside major centres, the judges may not hear civil litigation matters all year. These cases are heard at certain designated periods called **sittings**. For instance, the Superior Court in Milton might have a sitting scheduled from October 15 to December 14. There is a trial list prepared for each sitting of the court. If you want your action added to the list for a particular sitting, you must file the trial record at least 10 days before the start of that sitting (rules 48.05(2) and 48.06(2)). After that time, any new cases are added to the trial list for the next scheduled sitting. The only way a case that is filed less than 10 days before the start of the sitting can go on the list for that sitting is if a motion is brought and the judge orders that the action be placed on that list.

A place on the trial list does not guarantee that the case will be heard right away. The trial lists are long, and a case is not heard until it reaches the top of the list. Usually the court notifies the lawyers as the case gets close to the top, but it is the responsibility of the parties' lawyers to keep track of where they are on the list. When the case reaches the top, the parties must be ready to go to trial. There are separate trial lists for jury and non-jury trials. Usually the jury trial list is shorter.

Rule 48.12 requires the lawyers for the parties to let the registrar's office know immediately if a case has been settled. Usually you call the registrar's office first, but the rule also requires that the settlement be confirmed in writing. If a case is settled, it is taken off the trial list. This is one of the reasons that the trial list must be monitored closely when your case gets near the top. Your case may be number 10 on the list, but if all the cases in front of you are settled and removed from the list, you will move to the top very quickly.

Status notice

Sometimes, an action is commenced and a court file is opened, but nothing much happens on it. A statement of claim and a statement of defence may be filed. Maybe the parties are taking their time negotiating a settlement, or maybe they have settled and have forgotten to terminate the action.

The registrar is responsible for making sure that there are not a lot of these cases cluttering up the court files. Rule 48.14 requires the registrar to send a notification to the parties if an action has not been placed on a trial list within two years after a statement of defence has been filed in the case. To notify the parties, the registrar sends them a status notice in form 48C. The notice says that the action will be dismissed for delay unless it is set down for trial or terminated within 90 days after service of the status notice. A lawyer who receives a status notice is required to give a copy of it to the client immediately.

If the action is not set down for trial or terminated or if a judge does not order an extension of time, the registrar makes an order dismissing the action with costs 90 days after the status notice is served. This order must also be given to the client immediately after it is served on the lawyer.

Sometimes there is a legitimate reason why the action has not been set down for trial. If this is the case, the lawyer for a party served with a status notice may request a status hearing before a judge (rule 48.14(5)). At this hearing, the plaintiff must satisfy the court that the action should not be dismissed for delay. However, the status hearing must be arranged within the 90-day period before the registrar dismisses the case. If the judge determines that there should be an extension of time, the action stays alive for the period specified by the judge. Otherwise, the judge dismisses it. Figure 15.3 (at the end of the chapter) sets out a status notice.

Contents of a Trial Record

Rule 48.03 specifies the contents of a trial record. The record must include a table of contents, all pleadings, any orders made on motion relating to how the trial is conducted, all notices, and a certificate from the solicitor of record who is setting the action down for trial. The certificate must state, among other things, that the record contains all the required documents and that pleadings have closed. Only one of the parties serves and files the trial record, and it therefore must contain the pleadings of all the parties. It is like a short history of the proceedings.

A trial record is put together in the same way as a motion record. It is bound with a light blue backsheet (rule 4.07(1)), and the pages should be numbered consecutively. The various documents should be separated by tabs to make it easy to read. An example of a trial record is set out in figure 15.4 (at the end of the chapter).

THE PRETRIAL CONFERENCE: RULE 50

The court has a major interest in seeing that matters settle before they come to trial. Litigation is expensive for the parties, but it is costly from the court's perspective as well. There must be courtrooms, court staff, and judges available to accommodate the trial procedure. The courts therefore want to see that as many matters as possible are resolved before they require trial time. The pretrial conference is one of the procedural mechanism to try to achieve settlement.

The pretrial conference is an informal meeting between the lawyers for each party and a judge. Parties who are not represented by lawyers are expected to attend, but those represented by counsel need not be present. However, many lawyers find it advantageous to have their clients with them for the pretrial conference so that the clients can give instructions should a reasonable settlement be proposed by the other side.

The pretrial conference can be requested by a judge or by one or all of the lawyers for the parties. In most jurisdictions, pretrial conferences are held in almost every case. The purpose of the pretrial conference is to settle the case and avoid a trial or, if a trial cannot be avoided, to narrow the issues for trial. A list of issues that may be considered at the conference appears in rule 50.01.

Settlement of the case

During the pretrial conference, the lawyers each outline to the pretrial judge the case they intend to present at trial. They tell the judge the evidence they will call and how they intend to present the party's interests. Once the judge has heard the two sides of the case, he or she usually states how he or she would decide the case on the basis of this evidence. The lawyers then discuss the pretrial judge's decision with their client. The pretrial judge is not making the final decision but is merely advising the parties what he or she thinks of their likelihood of success. However, a judge's opinion can be helpful in encouraging a party to accept a reasonable settlement offer if the party thinks there is a possibility that they may lose the case at trial.

It is important to prepare properly for a pretrial conference. In Toronto, there is a practice direction requiring each party to file a pretrial memorandum that outlines the party's theory of the case and the facts on which the party relies. It must be served and filed at least five days before the pretrial conference. A pretrial memorandum is a good idea, even in a jurisdiction that does not require one. A well prepared memorandum can be very helpful in persuading a pretrial judge of the merits of a client's case. An example of a pretrial conference memorandum is set out in figure 15.5 (at the end of the chapter).

The documents that a party intends to use at trial should also be made available to the pretrial judge (rule 50.05). Very often, the pretrial memorandum and the documents to be presented at trial can be included together in a pretrial brief. Because there is no formal requirement under the rules for this kind of brief, the contents are up to the party. However, most pretrial memorandums contain separate sections outlining the facts and the law that will be relied on at the trial. Expert reports and other documents can be attached, and a brief summary of each document's contents will be very helpful to the pretrial judge.

Sometimes despite the parties' efforts to settle, the case is not settled and must proceed to trial. The judge who presided at the pretrial conference may not hear the case at trial. He or she may have already heard too much informally about the case to render a decision on the evidence presented at the trial alone (rule 50.04).

Narrow the issues at trial

In many cases, it is not possible for the parties to settle all the issues between them, but it is possible to agree that certain facts are not in dispute. Although the case must go to trial, it can be significantly shorter and less costly when the parties spend time dealing only with the issues that are contested. For instance, in Abigail's case, none of the parties disputes the fact that Abigail fell while at Rattle Motors' showroom. What they do disagree on is the cause of the fall. Abigail alleges that she fell because the defendants negligently left oil on the floor, and Rattle claims she fell because she was intoxicated. If the defendants are prepared to admit that the plaintiff fell on their premises, the plaintiff need not call witnesses to prove that she fell.

It is important to determine exactly what the other side admits is true and what is not in dispute in a case. To do this, the parties can use rule 51, which governs admissions.

ADMISSIONS

Under rule 51, a party can formally request that any other party admit the authenticity of certain documents or the truth of certain facts. If a party makes an admission about a document or a fact, the party intending to rely on the document or the fact need not prove that the document is genuine and authentic or that the fact is true.

Every document relied on by a party at trial must usually be proven to be authentic. The person who wrote the letter or took the photograph or prepared the report must give evidence that the document is genuine or is a true copy of the original document. This can be very time consuming, particularly in a trial where a lot of documents are being relied on. Likewise, every fact that a party relies on must also be proved in court. Admissions remove the need for proving every element that is not in dispute.

Rule 51.02 provides that a party may serve a request to admit (form 51A) on the opposite party at any time during a proceeding. The request to admit may ask the other side to admit either a fact or a document. Any document for which a party is seeking an admission of authenticity must be attached to the request to admit unless the other side already has a copy. An example of a request to admit is provided in figure 15.6 (at the end of the chapter).

The party that receives the request to admit must respond within 20 days after the request is served. A party responds to the request to admit by preparing and serving a response to request to admit, which is in form 51B. An example of a response to a request to admit is set out in figure 15.7 (at the end of the chapter). Parties must answer each request to admit a fact or document by saying they admit or deny the fact or document. If they fail to respond to any part of the request to admit or fail to respond to the entire request, they are deemed to have admitted all the facts and documents contained in the request (rule 51.03(2) and (3)).

An admission, either in a pleading or in a response to a request to admit, and all deemed admissions can be withdrawn only with the consent of all the other parties or with leave of the court. The court only grants leave to withdraw if the party asking to withdraw can show that there is something about the fact or document that is an issue between the parties, that the admission was made through inadvertence, and that there will be no injustice to the opposite party that cannot be made up in costs. Therefore, it is important to ensure that no admissions are made without major consideration.

If an admission is significant enough, a party to whom the admission is made can seek an order in the case based on that admission by bringing a motion to a judge. An admission made under oath or affirmation — in an affidavit, in examinations for discovery, or orally in court — can be used by another party to obtain an order in an entirely different proceeding (rule 51.06).

CHAPTER SUMMARY

This chapter dealt with the decisions and the steps that must be taken to get ready for a trial. We noted that rules 46, 47, 48, 50, and 51 are the major rules dealing with pretrial procedures.

The first decision to be made is where the trial is to take place, and we noted the requirements of rule 46 in this regard. The second decision is whether or not the trial should be held before a jury or a judge alone. We noted the procedural requirements for serving and filing a jury notice and for bringing a motion to strike the jury notice under rule 47. Any party can decide to have a jury trial.

We then covered the procedure for setting a case down for trial and examined the consequences of failing to set a matter down for trial within two years of its commencement under rule 48.

We then considered the pretrial conference, an informal hearing before a judge which attempts to effect a settlement between the parties or at least to narrow the issues for trial under rule 50.

Finally we examined the matter of admissions and the procedures involved in the request to admit under rule 51.

KEY TERMS

balance of convenience

setting an action down for trial

trial record

undefended action

trial list

sittings

REFERENCES

Children's Law Reform Act, RSO 1990, c. C.12.

Courts of Justice Act, RSO 1990, c. C.43.

Evidence Act, RSO 1990, c. E.23.

Rules of Civil Procedure, RRO 1990, reg. 194.

REVIEW QUESTIONS

1. If Abigail wants to have her trial held in Toronto, when must she decide this and how must she let the defendants know?

2. Are there any limitations on Abigail's choice of place of trial?

3. If Fred does not want the trial to be held in Toronto, what must he do?

4. If the parties agree that the place for trial should be changed to London, is the court obligated to change the location?

5. Who is most likely to want to set this case down for trial, and how must that party do it?

6. What are the consequences of a party's setting a matter down for trial?

7. What is a status notice, and who sends it?

CHAPTER 15   Pretrial procedures

8. What are the purposes of a pretrial conference?

DISCUSSION QUESTIONS

1. Abigail does not want to have a jury trial. However, Fred believes he will do better with a jury than without one. He thinks the jury will not be sympathetic to Abigail if he can show that she was drunk. Can Fred ask for a jury trial even though he is a defendant?

2. If Rattle Motors Ltd. has brought Skank Motorcar Company Ltd. into the action, what must be done to set the matter down for trial?

3. If Rattle Motors has made an admission in its statement of claim that Abigail fell on its premises, what would Rattle have to do to withdraw it? What criteria would determine whether a withdrawal could be made?

FIGURE 15.1   JURY NOTICE (FORM 47A)

Court file no. 01-CV-1234

ONTARIO
SUPERIOR COURT OF JUSTICE

BETWEEN:

Abigail Boar

Plaintiff

and

Rattle Motors Ltd. and Fred Flogem

Defendants

JURY NOTICE

THE PLAINTIFF REQUIRES that this action be tried by a jury.

Date: May 3, year 3

Just & Coping
Barristers and Solicitors
365 Bay Street - 8701
Toronto, Ontario, M3J 4A9

I.M. Just
tel. 416-762-1342
fax 416-762-2300

Solicitors for the Plaintiff

TO:
Huey Sue
Barrister and Solicitor
65 False Trail
Toronto, Ontario, M6Y 1Z6

tel. 416-485-6891
fax 416-485-6892

Solicitor for the Defendants

FIGURE 15.2   REQUISITION (FORM 4E)

Court file no. 01-CV-1234

ONTARIO
SUPERIOR COURT OF JUSTICE

BETWEEN:

Abigail Boar

Plaintiff

and

Rattle Motors Ltd. and Fred Flogem

Defendants

REQUISITION

TO THE LOCAL REGISTRAR at Milton:

I REQUIRE that court file number 01-CV-1234, in the matter of Boar v. Rattle Motors Ltd. and Flogem, currently held at the Court House in Milton, be transferred to the Court House at 393 University Avenue, Toronto for trial.

May 5, year 3

Just & Coping
Barristers and Solicitors
365 Bay Street - 8701
Toronto, Ontario, M3J 4A9

I.M. Just
tel. 416-762-1342
fax 416-762-2300

Solicitors for the Plaintiff

FIGURE 15.3   STATUS NOTICE (FORM 48C)

Court file no. 01-CV-1234

ONTARIO
SUPERIOR COURT OF JUSTICE

BETWEEN:

Abigail Boar

Plaintiff

and

Rattle Motors Ltd. and Fred Flogem

Defendants

STATUS NOTICE

TO THE PARTIES AND THEIR SOLICITORS

MORE THAN TWO YEARS HAVE PASSED since a statement of defence in this action was filed. According to the records in the court office, this action has not been placed on the trial list or terminated.

THIS ACTION WILL BE DISMISSED FOR DELAY unless within ninety days after the service of this notice: (a) it is set down for trial; (b) it is terminated; or (c) a judge presiding at a status hearing orders otherwise.

A party may request the registrar to arrange a status hearing.

IF A STATUS HEARING is held, the plaintiff must show cause why the action should not be dismissed for delay, and the presiding judge may set time periods for the completion of the remaining steps necessary to have the action placed on a trial list and may order that it be placed on a trial list within a specified time, or may adjourn the status hearing to a specified date, or may dismiss the action for delay.

Date: February 26, year 3

Signed by: _____

Address of
court office: Court House
               393 University Avenue
               Toronto, Ontario, M5G 1Y8

FIGURE 15.3 CONTINUED

TO:

```
Just & Coping
Barristers and Solicitors
365 Bay Street - 8701
Toronto, Ontario, M3J 4A9

I.M. Just
tel. 416-762-1342
fax 416-762-2300

Solicitors for the Plaintiff
```

AND TO:

```
Huey Sue
Barrister and Solicitor
65 False Trail
Toronto, Ontario, M6Y 1Z6

tel. 416-485-6891
fax 416-485-6892

Solicitor for the Defendants
```

FIGURE 15.4 TRIAL RECORD

Court file no. 01-CV-1234

ONTARIO
SUPERIOR COURT OF JUSTICE

BETWEEN:

Abigail Boar

Plaintiff

and

Rattle Motors Ltd. and Fred Flogem

Defendants

TRIAL RECORD

Just & Coping
Barristers and Solicitors
365 Bay Street - 8701
Toronto, Ontario, M3J 4A9

I.M. Just
tel. 416-762-1342
fax 416-762-2300

Solicitors for the Plaintiff

Huey Sue
Barrister and Solicitor
65 False Trail
Toronto, Ontario, M6Y 1Z6

tel. 416-485-6891
fax 416-485-6892

Solicitor for the Defendants

TRIAL RECORD TABLE OF CONTENTS

Tab	Document	Page
1	Statement of claim, dated January 4, year 1	1
2	Statement of defence, dated January 12, year 1	5
3	Reply, dated February 2, year 1	9
4	Jury notice, dated May 3, year 3	12

FIGURE 15.5   PRETRIAL CONFERENCE MEMORANDUM

Boar v. Rattle Motors Ltd. and Flogem   Date: May 20, year 3

Counsel for the plaintiff:

Just & Coping
Barristers and Solicitors
365 Bay Street – 8701
Toronto, Ontario, M3J 4A9

I.M. Just
tel. 416-762-1342
fax 416-762-2300

Counsel for the defendant:

Huey Sue
Barrister and Solicitor
65 False Trail
Toronto, Ontario, M6Y 1Z6

tel. 416-485-6891
fax 416-485-6892

Counsel for the plaintiff at trial: I.M. Just

THEORY OF THE PLAINTIFF'S CASE INCLUDING FACTUAL CONTENTIONS

The plaintiff was a customer of the defendant corporation, Rattle Motors Ltd., an automobile dealership. The defendant Fred Flogem is an automobile salesperson for Rattle Motors Ltd. The plaintiff slipped and fell while in the corporate defendant's showroom, sustaining considerable physical and psychological damage. The plaintiff alleges that Rattle Motors Ltd. was negligent in permitting an oil spill to remain on the showroom floor and that Fred Flogem was negligent in lowering the showroom lighting so that the spill could not be detected.

LEGAL ISSUES RAISED IN THE PLEADINGS AND TO BE DETERMINED AT TRIAL

1. Was the defendant Rattle Motors Ltd. negligent?
2. Was the defendant Fred Flogem negligent?
3. Was there any contributory negligence on the part of the plaintiff?
4. What general damages were suffered by the plaintiff?

PLEADINGS AND RELEVANT MATTERS

1. Are the pleadings in order or do they require amendments?
    The pleadings are in order and do not require further amendments.
2. Are there any contemplated or outstanding motions?
    No.

FIGURE 15.5   CONTINUED

3. Are productions complete?
    Yes.
4. Are all the transcripts available?
    Yes.

MOTIONS

Will there be any motions at trial?
No.

ADMISSIONS

The defendants admit that the plaintiff slipped and fell while on the premises of the corporate defendant and momentarily lost consciousness, but they allege that the fall was the result of the plaintiff's intoxicated state and not of any negligence of the defendants.

BUSINESS RECORDS

Will any business records be entered under the *Evidence Act*, and has the appropriate notice been given?
No business records will be produced.

EXPERT EVIDENCE

1. Will any be called?
    Yes.
2. On what issues?
    The long-term physical effects of the injuries that the plaintiff suffered.
3. Identity of Experts
    The plaintiff will call her neurologist, Dr. Morris Furgazy.

TRIAL DATE

1. Are the parties ready for trial?
    Yes.
2. Are there times when the trial cannot proceed because of witness or other matters?
    No.
3. How long will the trial last?
    It is estimated that it will last three days.

SETTLEMENT

What are the prospects of settlement?
Settlement is not likely in this case.

FIGURE 15.5 CONTINUED

DAMAGES

The plaintiff claims:

1. general damages in the amount of $200,000; and
2. special damages in the amount of $20,769.

IS THIS A CASE WHERE IT MAY BE ADVISABLE TO DIRECT A REFERENCE?
No.
WHAT PRETRIAL ORDERS ARE REQUESTED?
None.

FIGURE 15.6 REQUEST TO ADMIT (FORM 51A)

Court file no. 01-CV-1234

ONTARIO
SUPERIOR COURT OF JUSTICE

BETWEEN:

Abigail Boar

Plaintiff

and

Rattle Motors Ltd. and Fred Flogem

Defendants

REQUEST TO ADMIT

YOU ARE REQUESTED TO ADMIT, for the purposes of this proceeding only, the truth of the following facts:

1. The plaintiff drank two glasses of wine at Barbeerian's before arriving at the corporate defendant's place of business on September 14, year 0.
2. The plaintiff was intoxicated at the time that she entered the corporate defendant's place of business.

YOU ARE REQUESTED TO ADMIT, for the purposes of this proceeding only, the authenticity (see rule 51.01 of the Rules of Civil Procedure) of the following documents:

1. Receipt for dinner from Barbeerian's, dated September 14, year 0.

Attached to this request is a copy of each of the documents referred to above.

The above document has not been attached because the plaintiff has copies.

YOU MUST RESPOND TO THIS REQUEST by serving a response to request to admit in Form 51B prescribed by the Rules of Civil Procedure WITHIN TWENTY DAYS after this request is served on you. If you fail to do so, you will be deemed to admit, for the purposes of this proceeding only, the truth of the facts and the authenticity of the documents set out above.

Date: March 15, year 3

Huey Sue
Barrister and Solicitor
65 False Trail
Toronto, Ontario, M6Y 1Z6

tel. 416-485-6891
fax 416-485-6892

Solicitor for the Defendants

FIGURE 15.6   CONTINUED

TO:

```
Just & Coping
Barristers and Solicitors
365 Bay Street - 8701
Toronto, Ontario, M3J 4A9

I.M. Just
tel. 416-762-1342
fax 416-762-2300

Solicitors for the Plaintiff
```

FIGURE 15.7 RESPONSE TO REQUEST TO ADMIT (FORM 51B)

Court file no. 01-CV-1234

ONTARIO
SUPERIOR COURT OF JUSTICE

BETWEEN:

Abigail Boar

Plaintiff

and

Rattle Motors Ltd. and Fred Flogem

Defendants

RESPONSE TO REQUEST TO ADMIT

In response to your request to admit, dated March 15, year 3, **the plaintiff:**

1. Admits the truth of fact number 1.
2. Admits the authenticity of document number 1.
3. Denies the truth of fact number 2.
4. Denies the authenticity of documents numbers: N/A.
5. Refuses to admit the truth of fact number 2 for the following reasons:
   There is no truth in the allegation that the plaintiff was, in fact, intoxicated when she entered the place of business of the corporate defendant.
6. Refuses to admit the authenticity of documents numbers for the following reasons: N/A.

Date: March 22, year 3

Just & Coping
Barristers and Solicitors
365 Bay Street - 8701
Toronto, Ontario, M3J 4A9

I.M. Just
tel. 416-762-1342
fax 416-762-2300

Solicitors for the Plaintiff

TO:
Huey Sue
Barrister and Solicitor
65 False Trail
Toronto, Ontario, M6Y 1Z6

tel. 416-485-6891
fax 416-485-6892

Solicitor for the Defendants

CHAPTER 16

Trial preparation and trial

INTRODUCTION

If the parties do not settle at the pretrial conference, it is important to start preparing for an eventual trial as soon as possible. If the evidence has not been prepared and the work done well in advance, parties can find themselves pressed for time when they suddenly realize that their action is near the top of the trial list.

ORGANIZING THE EVIDENCE

There are three types of evidence used at trial: documentary evidence, physical evidence, and the testimony of witnesses. We will examine each type in turn.

Documentary evidence

Documentary evidence consists of all written documents, such as letters and contracts, that a party wants to rely on to prove the facts of the case. Documents also include all the things that are mentioned in rule 30.01(1)(a), such as sound recordings, videotapes, film, and charts.

Most of the work done in relation to documentary evidence is done during discoveries and the preparation of the affidavit of documents. Not all the documents listed in the affidavit of documents will be used at trial. In fact, only a small portion of the existing documentary evidence will be so used. This is because the material often addresses a matter that is not at issue between the parties.

Sometime after the completion of discoveries, check with the lawyer handling the case to see what documents he or she expects will be needed should the case go to trial. Keep a note of these documents, and once the matter has passed the pretrial stage without settling, begin to make copies of the identified documents. You will need enough copies of the documents to provide them to the other side, to the court, and to any witness who will be asked to validate or otherwise give evidence related to that document. Many lawyers tend to make notes on copies of the documents they are using in the case. Make sure that the copies are clean copies — that is, that they do not have a lawyer's notes all over them.

Lawyers are urged by the court to submit joint document books. This cuts down on duplication and provides more manageable material for the judge to review. If you are using a joint document book, you will have to contact the law clerk or lawyer on the other side to determine which documents will go into the joint book.

The rules of evidence do not commonly permit a document to be introduced into evidence without a witness to authenticate it. For instance, if a lawyer wants to introduce a letter into evidence, the lawyer has the writer of the letter come to court to give oral evidence that the letter was indeed written by him or her and that his or her signature appears on the document. However, calling a witness for every single piece of material introduced at trial could add a significant amount of time to a trial. In an effort to keep a trial as short as possible, some documents are treated in a particular manner that does not require their identification by a witness.

BUSINESS RECORDS

If a party wants to introduce records that are kept by a business in the ordinary course of its operation and the records were made at or near the time of the incident that they record, the records may be admitted without calling the person who made them. For instance, if Abigail were taken to the emergency department after her fall at Rattle Motors, her lawyer could use the emergency room admission records at the trial as business records. Many people may have seen Abigail at emergency: the admission clerk, a series of nurses, a medical intern, a resident doctor, the emergency physician, and perhaps a specialist. All of these people would have written things in Abigail's chart. Without special provisions in the *Canada Evidence Act* and the Ontario *Evidence Act*, in order to admit these records, the lawyer would need to call all these people to verify the records.

The evidence statutes, however, provide that if at least seven days' notice is given to all other parties, the court may admit them without having a person there to verify them. The other parties are given an opportunity to object to the admission of the record, and an objection is argued before the court. If you are dealing with business records, you must ensure that notice of intention to introduce them as evidence at trial is served on all the other parties at least seven days before trial.

The other parties have a right to inspect the documents and may give notice to the party introducing the records that they wish to examine them. The introducing party must then produce the records within five days after receiving the notice.

MEDICAL REPORTS

Section 52 of the Ontario *Evidence Act* provides a procedure whereby medical evidence may be presented through a written report without the presence of the medical practitioner. To comply with the statute, you must give 10 days' notice that you intend to introduce the report at trial to all the other parties. The other parties have a right to review the report before trial, and a copy of the report should therefore be included with the notice.

Even if the intention is to call the medical practitioner to give evidence, if the lawyer wishes to introduce the report itself, the other side should be given 10 days' notice.

It is important to remember that "medical practitioner" refers not only to a medical doctor. Section 52 also relates to reports prepared by a chiropodist, a physiotherapist, a registered psychologist, a denture therapist, a dentist, a nurse practitioner, and many other types of health care providers covered by the *Regulated Health Professions Act* and the *Drugless Practitioners Act*.

USING A COPY OF AN ORIGINAL DOCUMENT

An original document is usually used at trial. If, for any reason, it is necessary to use a copy of the original at trial, the Ontario *Evidence Act* requires that notice be given to all the other parties at least 10 days before the trial. The notice should also provide an appropriate date and time when the other parties may come to inspect the document.

Sometimes a statute may allow for the admission of a certified copy of the original. A certified copy is a copy that the person certifying the document compares to the original and swears to be a true copy.

In title documents pertaining to a real estate transaction, the land registrar certifies the copy to be a true copy of the original. The party wishing to introduce the document must give at least 10 days' notice to all the other parties that he or she intends to introduce the certified copy. Any other party may challenge the document within 4 days of being served with the notice.

Under s. 29 of the Ontario *Evidence Act*, public or official documents may also be certified by the person who has custody or control of the document. They then may be admitted into evidence without further verification.

Physical evidence

Physical evidence consists of an actual object relating to an issue in the action between the parties. It may be brought into court and introduced into evidence. For instance, if a party were suing a manufacturer for damages caused by a faulty or unsafe product, the product may be brought into the court. In our case, Rattle Motors may want to claim that the oil spill in its showroom resulted from a faulty oil pan made by Skank Motorcar and may wish to bring the oil pan into the courtroom.

Sometimes, if the object is too large to be brought into the courtroom, the rules provide a method whereby the judge, jury, and other trial participants can go to a site outside the courtroom to look at the object or the property. This is called a "view," and it is governed by rule 52.05

Testimony of witnesses

The usual way to introduce evidence to be given by a person is to summon that person to court to give oral evidence called "**testimony**." The witnesses are asked questions by the lawyers for the parties. The judge and the jury, if there is a jury, listen to the answers. The testimony is recorded by a court reporter or a recording device that takes down every word said in the courtroom.

It is unusual for evidence at a trial to be given in affidavit form. Affidavits may be used at a trial under the ordinary procedure only with special leave of the court, although they are used in the simplified procedure.

When a witness comes to give evidence at trial, the lawyer for the party who has asked the witness to give evidence asks questions first. This is called **examination-in-chief**.

Any party who is adverse in interest to the party that called the witness then gets to ask questions. This is called **cross-examination**. The purpose of cross-examination is for the opposing side to try to shake the credibility of that witness.

testimony
oral evidence given by a witness

examination-in-chief
series of questions asked of a witness by the lawyer for the party who called the witness

cross-examination
series of questions asked of a witness by a lawyer for a party adverse in interest to the party that called the witness

Cross-examination can be gruelling, and sometimes witnesses are reluctant to attend voluntarily to give evidence.

SUMMONS TO A WITNESS

Witnesses can, however, be compelled to attend the trial. They can be served with a summons in form 53A if they are in Ontario or in form 53C if they are outside Ontario. An example of a summons in form 53A is provided in figure 16.1. A summons is a court order to a person to attend a court hearing at a certain date and time. It can also direct a person to bring certain documents with him or her. A person who does not appear can suffer severe legal consequences. A warrant may be issued for his or her arrest, and he or she can then physically be brought to court.

It is important to serve each witness with a summons even if the witness is your client's best friend and says he or she is more than willing to attend to give evidence. If witnesses have not been served with a summons and they do not appear, it is much more difficult to convince the judge to adjourn the matter until they do. If witnesses are important to your client's case and they come down with the flu or are in a car accident on their way to the courthouse, and you have not served them with a summons, it is possible that their evidence will never be heard and your client's case will be irreparably damaged.

The summons to a witness must be issued by the court. You may request a blank summons from the court office, and it will be signed by the registrar and sealed. You can then fill in the rest of the form later, at your office.

The summons must be served personally on the witness, and a cheque for the full amount of the attendance allowance and any travel allowance must accompany the summons. Attendance money is a small allowance that is set by tariff A, part II "Disbursements."

Witnesses are entitled to a payment of $50 for each day they are expected to attend a trial and give evidence. In addition, if they live in the same city or town as the courthouse, they are entitled to $3 per day travel allowance. If they live within 300 km of the courthouse, they are entitled to a travel allowance of $0.24 per km. If they live further away than 300 km, they are entitled to return airfare, mileage to the airport, overnight accommodation, and meal allowances of $75 per night.

If a witness requires an interpreter in a language other than French, the person calling the witness must provide the interpreter. In larger centres, the court usually keeps lists of interpreters who have been approved to interpret in various languages, including sign language. French interpreters are usually provided by the court.

EXPERT WITNESSES

An expert witness is permitted to give opinion evidence. An ordinary witness must stick strictly to what they saw, heard, or otherwise perceived. For instance, Fred Flogem can say that he saw oil under the car directly beneath the oil pan. He can describe the oil pan and the car, but he cannot say that, in his opinion, a defective oil pan in the car caused the leak onto the floor of the showroom. However, an engineer, qualified to design and examine cars can give his or her opinion about what caused the leak.

Before being classified as experts, witnesses must satisfy the court that they have the necessary qualifications and experience. They must also be experts in

FIGURE 16.1 SUMMONS TO WITNESS (AT HEARING) (FORM 53A)

Court file no. 01-CV-1234

ONTARIO
SUPERIOR COURT OF JUSTICE

BETWEEN:

Abigail Boar

Plaintiff

and

Rattle Motors Ltd. and Fred Flogem

Defendants

SUMMONS TO WITNESS

TO:
Donny Dilhouse
1700 Bloor Street East
Toronto, Ontario, M6Y 3K9

YOU ARE REQUIRED TO ATTEND TO GIVE EVIDENCE IN COURT at the hearing of this proceeding on July 10, year 3 **at** 10:00 a.m. **at the** Court House at 393 University Avenue, Toronto, **and to** remain until your attendance is no longer required.

YOU ARE REQUIRED TO BRING WITH YOU and produce at the hearing the following documents and things: N/A

ATTENDANCE MONEY for one day of attendance is served with this summons, calculated in accordance with Tariff A of the Rules of Civil Procedure, as follows:

Attendance allowance of $50.00 daily	$50.00
Travel allowance	$ 3.00
Overnight accommodation and meal allowance	$ Nil
TOTAL	$53.00

If further attendance is required, you will be entitled to additional attendance money.

IF YOU FAIL TO ATTEND OR REMAIN IN ATTENDANCE AS REQUIRED BY THIS SUMMONS, A WARRANT MAY BE ISSUED FOR YOUR ARREST.

Date: June 1, year 3

Issued by: _____

FIGURE 16.1   CONTINUED

Address of

court office: Court House
393 University Avenue
Toronto, Ontario, M5G 1Y8

This summons was issued at the request of, and inquiries may be directed to:

Huey Sue
Barrister and Solicitor
65 False Trail
Toronto, Ontario, M6Y 1Z6

tel. 416-485-6891
fax 416-485-6892

Solicitor for the Defendants

some area that the court recognizes as a valid area of study. For instance, a person may have studied UFOs for years, but the court may not find that to be a legitimate area of study.

A party who intends to call an expert must serve all the other parties with a report, signed by the expert, setting out his or her name, address, qualifications, and the substance of his or her proposed testimony. This report must be served at least 90 days before the commencement of the trial.

If any of the other parties wishes to call another expert to challenge the testimony of the first expert, the party must serve a similar report containing the same information pertaining to the expert. This report must be served on all the other parties at least 60 days before the start of the trial (rule 53.03).

These timelines must be met, or the court may refuse to hear the expert witness.

PREPARATION OF WITNESSES

The law clerk may be asked to help prepare the witnesses for trial. Most witnesses are not accustomed to being in a courtroom and will need some help and reassurance in getting ready to give evidence.

Most lawyers run their witnesses through the proposed examination-in-chief and may rehearse a possible cross-examination to give them experience in answering difficult questions asked by a lawyer who is challenging their testimony. Witnesses should be told some basic things about giving evidence, such as the fact that in examination-in-chief, the lawyer asking the questions is not able to help the witness find the answer. This technique is called "**leading a witness**," and it violates the rules of evidence if used during examination-in-chief. However, the opposing counsel may lead the witness in cross-examination, and witnesses must be aware that an opposing lawyer may attempt to lead them into giving answers that they do not wish to give.

Witnesses should be told that they may ask the lawyer to repeat the question. They do not need to rush their answers, but if they are too slow, they may appear to

leading a witness
asking a witness a question that suggests the answer

be avoiding the question. If they do not understand the question or do not recall something, they should say so.

Finally, witnesses should understand that they must, for the most part, rely on their recollections of the event or incident. If they use notes that were made at the time of the incident, they must be prepared to show their notes to the other party's counsel. They may not use notes unless the notes were made at the same time or almost immediately after the incident at issue. They cannot write down what they want to say just before they are called to give evidence and then use these notes to jog their memories while they are in the witness box.

In the event that the trial lasts more than one day, the witnesses may be released by the court and called back to give their evidence as the proceedings progress. Often, if an expert witness is to give testimony in a case, the court will permit them not to be at court but to be available by telephone to be called when they are needed.

Trial brief

Once all the material is organized, it is time to prepare a trial brief. A trial brief is not the same as a trial record. A trial record is for the use of the court. A trial brief is for a lawyer's use at trial. It helps the lawyer keep his or her material organized as he or she is presenting the case.

Lawyers have their own preferences for the organization of a trial brief, but it must be composed in such a way that lawyers are able to find things easily while they are on their feet and making their case in the courtroom.

Unlike the documents filed with the court, which are usually spiral-bound, the trial brief is usually in a three-ring binder so that the material can be moved around freely. A trial does not always follow a straight path, particularly if something unexpected arises, and a lawyer must be able to adapt the organization of the material to the flow of the trial.

Most lawyers will want the material organized by type and placed in the binder in chronological order. For instance, the opening and closing arguments will be in one binder, the pretrial motions in another, the witness statements and summaries of evidence in another, and the discoveries in yet another. If the material is not voluminous, some of these binders may be combined in a single binder.

The binders should be different colours so they can easily be distinguished from one another when they are sitting on the counsel table in a courtroom. There should be clearly marked tabs separating the material.

Once the trial brief has been prepared, it is time to go back and ensure that sufficient copies of proposed exhibits and transcripts have been made.

Brief of authorities

A brief of authorities puts together all the legal cases, statutes, and regulations that support your client's action. It should be organized with an index, listing the cases and the legislation. The cases and legislation must be properly cited. Tabs should be used to separate the material, and the index should identify the tab at which the material can be found. These briefs are usually spiral-bound. The judge is given a copy of the brief of authorities as are counsel for the other side. Remember that if a lawyer is referring a judge to an authority, the judge must be able to find it easily.

CHAPTER SUMMARY

In this chapter, we discussed the two steps involved in getting ready for a trial: (1) organizing the evidence and (2) assembling the materials that will be needed in the courtroom for the presentation of the case. We also discussed three general types of evidence: (1) documents, (2) physical evidence, and (3) testimony.

We observed that much of the documentary evidence in a trial is identified through discoveries. The rules of evidence require most documents to be verified in the course of the trial by calling the person who made the documents as a witness. However, there are special rules of evidence permitting business records and medical reports to be entered into evidence without calling the person who made them. In connection with testimony, we discussed summons and the need to summons even witnesses who agree to appear voluntarily.

Finally, we covered the drafting of a trial brief and the compilation of a brief or a book of authorities.

KEY TERMS

testimony

examination-in-chief

cross-examination

leading a witness

REFERENCES

Canada Evidence Act, RSC 1985, c. C-5.

Drugless Practitioners Act, RSO 1990, c. C.18.

Evidence Act, RSO 1990, c. E.23.

Regulated Health Professions Act, 1991, SO 1991, c. 18.

Rules of Civil Procedure, RRO 1990, reg. 194.

REVIEW QUESTIONS

1. What is a trial brief, and who uses it? How does it differ from a trial record?

2. What are the three types of evidence that may be introduced in a trial?

3. How is evidence usually admitted at a trial?

DISCUSSION QUESTIONS

1. Your instructing lawyer is calling Dr. Hardy Ames as an expert witness. Dr. Ames is an engineering professor at Trent University. He has a PhD in chemical engineering. What must the lawyer do to ensure that Hardy's evidence will be heard?

2. John Doe is suing Mary Smith. Draft a summons in the case for the plaintiff's witness Dan Doe. Dan lives at 1400 Winding Lane, Peterborough, Ontario, L4T 7Y6. The trial is to take place in Newmarket. There is a distance of about 120 km between Peterborough and Newmarket. The trial starts on March 15, year 1, and the witness will be needed for one day of testimony.

CHAPTER 17

Judgments

PROCEDURE FOR DRAFTING, ISSUING, AND ENTERING JUDGMENTS AND ORDERS

Introduction

When a court makes a decision, that decision is a command to one or more of the parties to do something: to pay money or to cease doing something in the case of an injunction, for example. These commands from the court are referred to as orders. They take three forms under the rules:

1. an order in form 59A, called an "order" and used for a decision on motions and applications;

2. an order in form 59B, called a "judgment" and used for a final decision in actions; and

3. an order in form 59C, called an "order on appeal" and used for a decision by an appellate court (the Court of Appeal and the Superior Court when it acts in an appellate capacity).

Make sure to determine the type of order you are drafting so that you use the correct form.

DRAFTING ORDERS AND JUDGMENTS

Order-drafting process

There are several steps to the creation of a final order or judgment:

1. obtaining the judge's or master's endorsement of the record,

2. drafting a formal order from the endorsement,

3. approving and signing the order, and

4. entering the order.

Obtaining the judge's or master's endorsement

In any proceeding, whether it is a motion or a trial, when a judge makes a decision, he or she writes or endorses the decision on the back of a trial or motion record, notice of motion, or other court document. If a judge or master wishes to give reasons for the decision, he or she may write them as part of the endorsement, if that is practical, or may state "reasons to follow" (rule 59.02). (In an appellate court, if reasons are given, an endorsement is not required.) In the rare cases where written reasons are given, they are usually written separately, typed by the judge's secretary, released to the parties, and filed in the court file.

Figure 17.1 shows what an endorsement in Abigail Boar's case might look like.

Drafting a formal order

The court does not create the final order for you. It is the responsibility of the parties to prepare the order. One of the parties, usually the one who has been successful and has a real interest in completing the process, prepares the order. You begin by going to the court file, finding, and photocopying or writing out the endorsement. Using the appropriate version of form 59, you then prepare a draft order. All orders contain the following:

- the name of the judge or officer who made it;

- the date on which it was made;

- the recital, which gives a context for the order and may include the date of the hearing and whether parties or counsel or both were present; and

- the operative parts of the order or the commands.

Each command is set out in a separately numbered paragraph. The paragraphs usually begin with "THIS COURT ORDERS AND ADJUDGES" or some variation of this phrase, depending on the court and the type of order (rule 59.03(1) to (4)). Damages are usually expressed as a total consisting of general and special damages together with prejudgment interest, if awarded, calculated to the date of the order. Costs are listed in a separate paragraph.

If the order requires payments to a minor directly or through a trustee, the order must show the minor's date of birth and address, and it must contain a direction that it be served on the children's lawyer. This ensures that an independent public agency has notice of the minor's interest, and that there is an indication of when the minority status ends (rule 59.03(5)). At that point, the minor, on becoming an adult, has the right to take charge of funds held on his or her behalf under the terms of the order.

An order for the payment of costs must direct that the costs be paid to the party, and not to the lawyer for the party. This prevents the lawyer's obtaining the funds for his or her own use. It is permissible for the payer to pay the costs to the lawyer in trust for the client, however. In this way the lawyer has to account for what is held in trust (rule 59.03(6)).

Where postjudgment interest is payable, you draft the order with a provision for the payment of postjudgment, setting out the rate at which it is payable and the date from which it begins to run. Sometimes the rate and date are left blank and filled out by the counter clerk when the order is signed.

Support orders must set out the last-known addresses of the support creditor and support debtor.

Figure 17.2 sets out what a draft judgment in form 59B might look like if Abigail Boar succeeded in getting judgment for $200,000 for general damages, $25,000 for special damages, and costs.

An order in form 59A has a somewhat different format. Set out in figure 17.3 is an order on a motion to compel Fred Flogem to re-attend and answer questions on his examination for discovery.

FIGURE 17.1   ENDORSEMENT

Abigail Boar

PLAINTIFF(S)

(Short title of proceeding)

and

Rattle Motors Ltd.

DEFENDANT(S)

Court file no. 01-CV-1234

ONTARIO SUPERIOR COURT OF JUSTICE

Proceeding commenced at Toronto

STATEMENT OF CLAIM

Name, address and telephone number of plaintiff's solicitor or plaintiff:

I.M. Just
Law Society No. 17888 Q

Just & Coping
Barristers and Solicitors
365 Bay Street – 8701
Toronto, Ontario, M3J 4A9

tel. 416-762-1342
fax 416-762-2300

Solicitors for the Plaintiff

July 12, year 3:

Judgment for the plaintiff in the amount of $53,000 and costs.

Snork, J

FIGURE 17.2   JUDGMENT (FORM 59B)

Court file no. 01-CV-1234

ONTARIO
SUPERIOR COURT OF JUSTICE

The Honourable   Friday, the 12th day
Madam Justice Snork   of July, year 3

BETWEEN:

Abigail Boar

Plaintiff

and

Rattle Motors Ltd. and Fred Flogem

Defendants

JUDGMENT

THIS ACTION was heard on July 10, 11, and 12, year 3,
without a jury at Toronto, in the presence of counsel for
all parties,

ON READING THE PLEADINGS AND HEARING THE EVIDENCE and the
submissions of counsel for the parties,

1. THIS COURT ORDERS AND ADJUDGES that the plaintiff
   recover from the defendants the sum of $200,000.00 for
   general damages.
2. THIS COURT ORDERS AND ADJUDGES that the plaintiff
   recover from the defendants the sum of $25,000.00 for
   special damages.
3. THIS COURT ORDERS AND ADJUDGES that the defendants pay
   to the plaintiff her partial indemnity costs of this
   action forthwith after assessment.

THIS JUDGMENT BEARS INTEREST at the rate of _____ per cent
per year commencing on _____.

_____
Registrar, Superior Court of Justice

FIGURE 17.3   ORDER (FORM 59A)

Court file no. 01-CV-1234

ONTARIO
SUPERIOR COURT OF JUSTICE

MASTER BELLWETHER   Friday, the 3rd
                                        day of June, year 2

BETWEEN:

Abigail Boar

Plaintiff

and

Rattle Motors Ltd. and Fred Flogem

Defendants

ORDER

THIS MOTION, made by the plaintiff for an order that the
defendant Fred Flogem re-attend at his own expense to answer
questions 4, 5, and 7 on his examination for discovery was
heard this day at Toronto,

   ON READING the affidavit of Dianne Swan, sworn and filed,
and on reading the transcript of the examination for
discovery of the defendant Fred Flogem and on hearing the
submissions of counsel for both parties,

1. THIS COURT ORDERS that the plaintiff's motion be
   dismissed.
2. THIS COURT ORDERS that costs be in the cause.

_____
Registrar, Superior Court of Justice

Approving and signing the order

Once you have drafted the judgment or order from an endorsement, you must obtain approval as to the form of the order from the other parties who are affected by it and who were present and participated in the proceeding. The lawyer for the other party checks the draft against the endorsement to see that your draft is fair and accurate. If it is, the lawyer writes on the face of the order "approved as to form" and signs his or her name and capacity as lawyer for a party in the proceeding. Then he or she returns the signed copy to you.

You then take the approved copy and an original to the office of the local registrar. If all parties who were present at the hearing have approved the order, the registrar examines the order and, if satisfied with the form, signs the order on behalf of the court.[1] If the registrar is not satisfied, he or she rejects the order and returns it unsigned. In this case, the party can either make the required corrections or, if he or she believes the registrar is in error, can obtain an appointment before the judge or master who made the order to settle the terms of the order (rule 59.04(5) to (9)).

Where the parties cannot agree on the form of the order and a party has withheld approval, the other party may obtain an order to settle the terms of the order before the registrar. The registrar examines the draft order and the endorsement and, if satisfied, signs the order. If the registrar is uncertain, he or she refers the order to the judge or master who made the order to determine whether or not it should be signed (rule 59.04(10)). If a party disagrees with the registrar's decision, he or she may obtain an appointment with the judge or master to settle the terms of the order (rule 59.04(12)).

If the referral is to a court consisting of more than one judge, the application to settle the terms of an order should be brought before the presiding judge in that court. Once the order has finally been settled, the registrar signs it (rule 59.04(12) to (16)). If a case is urgent, a lawyer can ask the judge who issued the order to sign it. In this case, the judge may do so without approval if he or she is persuaded that the matter is urgent. The judge will then sign a draft order, which you need to prepare beforehand, and write on the face of the order: "let this judgment issue and enter."

Entering the order

Once the order has been signed, it must be officially recorded and filed by the court. The court's seal is applied in the upper left-hand part of the order, just below the name of the judge or master who made the order. At the bottom, a note is affixed identifying the entry book in which the order is inserted. If the order is entered in the court records electronically or is microfilmed or photocopied, the note on the order will provide appropriate information to retrieve the order. This is done in the office of the court where the proceeding commenced. If an order is amended or varied by a subsequent order, the subsequent order is entered in the same court office as the original order, as well as in the office where the subsequent order was made. If the order is made in the Court of Appeal, it is entered both in the Court of Appeal office and in the office of the court where the action commenced (rule 59.05).

An order found to contain an inadvertent error resulting from an accidental slip or omission may be corrected on motion to the court that made the order (rule 59.06).

Where an outstanding judgment has been paid to the judgment creditor's satisfaction (even if not paid in full), it can no longer be enforced. A document attesting to the satisfaction of the judgment creditor, called a "satisfaction piece," may be filed and entered in the office of the court where the order was entered (rule 59.07).

PREJUDGMENT INTEREST
Introduction

When a party obtains judgment in a lawsuit for money to which he or she is entitled, the party is also entitled to interest because he or she has been deprived of the use of the money from the time it was owing. Interest is paid on the amount owing to compensate the party for what he or she might have earned as profit on that money or to compensate the party for the loss of the use of it. Another reason for awarding interest is to make it less attractive for the defendant to stall proceedings in the hope that the plaintiff will run out of money or the will to pursue the case. A defendant who knows that interest is running on the amount of the claim may be more inclined not to waste time and to settle the claim.

Sections 127 to 129 of the *Courts of Justice Act* set out the rules for calculating prejudgment interest. Section 127 sets out definitions of relevant terms and the formula for determining prejudgment and postjudgment interest. The person designated by the deputy attorney general calculates the basic interest rate for each quarter of the year. The rate for each quarter is available from court offices[2] and the commercially published civil procedure rules. There is also a computerized source of rate information that even does the calculations: http://www.judgmentcalc.com/. Whatever source you use, all you need to do is determine what the relevant quarter is and look up the interest rate for that quarter in the given year. The rates are set out in table form, using two tables. The first table covers rates for prejudgment interest for causes of action that arose before October 23, 1989 and for postjudgment interest in all cases, both before and after 1989. The second table sets out the rates for prejudgment interest for all causes of action that arose after October 23, 1989. Prejudgment interest is calculated differently before and after that date as a result of an amendment to the *Courts of Justice Act*, which is why we need the second table for post-1989 prejudgment interest.

Step-by-step calculation instructions

1. *Determine whether you should claim interest under the prejudgment interest rules or whether you have an alternative right to interest.* Contracts often provide an interest rate and method of calculation for any amount that may be payable under the contract, including when there is a default in payment. A contract for a loan will certainly contain an interest rate. A penalty clause may also provide for interest. Sections 128(3)(g) and 129(5) of the *Courts of Justice Act* state that neither prejudgment nor postjudgment interest is payable under ss. 127 to 129 if there is a right to interest that arises other than under these sections. If you have a right to interest that arises outside the Act, it is still a good idea to claim prejudgment interest under the Act in the alternative in the statement of claim. If your claim to a right to interest arising outside the Act is unsuccessful, you can then fall back on the Act's provisions. The clause in the claim for relief might read: "prejudgment and postjudgment interest at the rate of 14 percent in accordance with the provisions of s. 3 of the contract between the parties or, in the alternative, prejudgment and postjudgment interest in accordance with the provisions of the *Courts of Justice Act*."

2. *If you have a right to claim interest under the Act, you must classify the damages on which interest may be charged because this may determine what the rate of interest is and how interest is calculated.* There are three types of damages for the purpose of s. 128:

    a. *General rule: Section 128(1).* Money awarded under an order is generally subject to the appropriate quarterly rate for the quarter when the proceeding was commenced.

    b. *First exception: Section 128(2) damages for non-pecuniary loss for personal injury.* The rate of interest on damages for non-pecuniary loss for personal injuries does not use the quarterly rates, but instead uses the rate determined under rule 53.10, which is currently 5 percent. The type of damages you are looking for is a non-monetary loss in a personal injury action. This means the amount of general damages awarded by the court for pain and suffering or the emotional shock that results from a personal injury. Because no money was actually lost, the s. 128(2) rule was meant to limit interest to 5 percent, which was lower than the usual quarterly rates at the time the rule was made. If Abigail is awarded $100,000 in general damages for pain and suffering, use 5 percent as the interest rate for this head of damages.

c. *Second exception: Section 128(3) special damages accruing over time.* Special damages are liquidated damages. These include out-of-pocket expenses and other sums that can be determined with precision using a simple formula. They may occur all at once at the time the cause of action arises, or you may have continuing out-of-pocket expenses from the time the cause of action arose. If so, you must calculate interest every six months on these damages as they accrue. If Abigail had continuing out-of-pocket expenses for medications, you would add up her expenditures for each six-month period. Beginning with the date the action arose, you would calculate interest using the quarterly rate on the day the action was commenced on the total for the first six-month period and do the same for any other six-month period, and for any part period up to the date of the order. You may not calculate interest on interest from any previous six-month period. Total the interest separately from the special damages for each six-month or part period to determine interest under this head of damage. This interest is added to any other interest arising under other heads of damage and added to the amount of the total judgment.

3. *Identify amounts on which no interest may be charged.* Section 128(4) identifies amounts that are not subject to interest calculation. They are listed below.

a. *Exemplary or punitive damages.* **Exemplary damages** (also called aggravated damages) are awarded to compensate the plaintiff for emotional harm when a defendant's conduct has been particularly outrageous. **Punitive damages** are also awarded when a defendant's behaviour is particularly outrageous, but the purpose here is to punish the defendant to deter him or her from behaving in the impugned way again. Because these damages are penalties, interest on these amounts as a further penalty could be said to be overly harsh.

b. *Interest under s. 128.* Interest is not compounded. It is calculated separately and then added in with the other damages. However, when postjudgment interest is calculated, it is calculated on the entire judgment, including the component that is prejudgment interest.

c. *Award of costs.* The costs awarded at the time of judgment, whether fixed or to be assessed, are not subject to prejudgment interest, though they are subject to postjudgment interest.

d. *Pecuniary loss that is identified as occurring after the date of the judgment.* Sometimes a judge can identify a plaintiff's loss that is

exemplary damages
damages over and above the plaintiff's actual loss, paid to compensate the plaintiff for hurt feelings or mental stress caused by the defendant's particularly outrageous behaviour

punitive damages
damages in the nature of a fine paid to the plaintiff when the defendant's behaviour has been particularly outrageous

connected to the cause of action but that has not yet accrued. For example, in Abigail's personal injury action, a judge may be able to determine an amount for her future loss of income because she will continue to be unable to work. On this amount, no interest may be charged.

e. *Advance payment of the amount to settle a claim before judgment after the payment was made.* Suppose you owe $100 as of January 1, and you pay $75 as an advance payment to settle the claim on February 1. If the plaintiff continues to go after you for the balance, prejudgment interest on the $75 will run only from January 1, when the cause of action arose, to February 1, when that amount was paid. But interest will run on the balance, $25, for the whole period from the time the cause of action arose until judgment: from January 1 until the date of the judgment.

f. *Where the order is made on consent.* There is no prejudgment interest on an order made on consent unless the debtor agrees.

g. *Where interest is payable by a right other than under s. 128.* As noted earlier, if you have a right of interest arising, for example, under a contract, you must claim interest under the contract and not under the Act.

4. *Establish the prejudgment interest rate that applies to your damages claim.* Except for damages for **non-pecuniary** loss on personal injuries, where the interest rate is 5 percent, the applicable rate of interest is the rate for the quarter in which the action was commenced. Do not confuse this with the quarter in which the cause of action arose. The right to sue always arises earlier than the day on which you commence proceedings, and it may well be in a different quarter. You do not have to do the calculations in s. 127 to determine the rate. This is done for you in the table that is updated quarterly by the Ministry of the Attorney General. Remember, as noted earlier, that there are two tables. Use the first table (beginning with 1985) for prejudgment interest on cases where the cause of action arose before October 23, 1989 and for postjudgment interest in all cases. Use the second table (beginning with October 23, 1989) for prejudgment interest in cases where the cause of action arose *after* October 23, 1989.

non-pecuniary
non-monetary

5. *Having established the rate, calculate the prejudgment interest.* You will need to determine the following dates: (a) the date on which the cause of action arose (interest is calculated from this date); (b) the date on which proceedings commenced (the interest rate is the rate for the quarter in which proceedings commenced); and (c) the date on which the order or judgment was made (interest runs to this date). The prejudgment interest calculation formula for simple interest is:

$I = P \times R \times T$

where

I = interest,
P = amount for the head of damage on which the claim is made,
R = rate of interest from the rate for the quarter when the action was commenced, and

T = number of days from the day the cause of action arose to the day of judgment, which is expressed as a fraction of a year — for example, 40 days is expressed as $40/365$.

Suppose Abigail Boar sues her employer for wrongful dismissal when her employer terminates her employment without notice on August 12, 1999. She sues the employer on October 1, 1999 and recovers judgment with general damages of $80,000 on November 15, 2000.

1. *Determine if you have a right to interest under the Act.* In this case, there is no rate set out in a contract and no other right to interest. Therefore prejudgment interest can be claimed under the Act.

2. *Classify the damages to determine the rate and calculation mode.* The damages are general damages and come within neither exception to the general rule: They are not damages for personal injuries and they are not special damages accruing over time before judgment.

3. *Identify the amount on which no interest may be charged.* Interest may be charged on the general damages claimed; there are no claims that are exempt from prejudgment interest on these facts.

4. *Establish prejudgment interest rate for this claim.* The rate is the rate for the quarter in which the cause of action arose. August 12, 1999 is in the third quarter of 1999, and the rate must be taken from the second table for proceedings where the cause of action arose after 1989. The rate is 5.3 percent.

5. Calculate the prejudgment interest:

$I = P \times R \times T$

August 12, 1990 to August 11, 1991 (one year):

$80,000 \times 0.053 = $4,240$

August 12, 1991 to November 15, 1991 (96 days, including the day on which judgment is given):

$80,000 \times 0.053 \times 96/365 = $1,115$

$I = $5,355$

POSTJUDGMENT INTEREST
Introduction

Postjudgment interest is also available. If a party has a right to interest from the time the cause of action arose, a party has that right after judgment until he or she is paid. Postjudgment interest therefore compensates a party for the loss of the use of money that he or she should have had. It also encourages a judgment debtor to pay what he or she owes. The longer the delay, the greater the amount that must be paid.

The general principles are the same as for prejudgment interest but the calculation rules are slightly different. If an order awards periodic payments, such as in a divorce support order, postjudgment interest runs from the date each payment becomes due.

Step-by-step calculation instructions

1. *Determine the amount of the judgment.* This includes the amount of the damages, the interest on that amount, and the costs awarded.

2. *Determine the postjudgment interest rate.* This requires you to use the rate in the first table for the quarter in which judgment was given.

3. *Calculate the postjudgment interest.*

   a. Determine the day of judgment, when the interest begins to run.

   b. Count the days from the day after the order is made to the day on which payment is received. Since prejudgment interest was calculated to include the day the judgment was given, postjudgment interest starts on the next day.

   c. Calculate the postjudgment interest using the formula: $I = P \times R \times T$.

4. *Calculate the amount due on the date of payment.* Add the postjudgment interest just calculated to the amount of the outstanding judgment.

Let's assume Abigail Boar had her costs assessed at $2,000 and that she was paid on November 30, 2000.

1. *Determine the amount of the judgment.*

   The judgment was for $80,000 + costs of $2,000 + interest of $5,355 = $87,355.

2. *Determine the postjudgment interest rate.*

   The day of judgment is November 15 in the fourth quarter of 2000, and the rate in table 1 is 7 percent.

3. *Calculate the postjudgment interest.*

   Interest runs from the day after the judgment to the date of payment:

   November 16, 2000 to November 30, 2000 = 15 days

   $87,355 \times 0.07 \times {}^{15}\!/_{365} = $251.30

4. Calculate the amount due on November 30, 2000.

   $87,355 + $251.30 = $87,606.30

CHAPTER SUMMARY

In this chapter, we examined the procedural requirements involved in drafting, approving, signing, and entering orders, including challenging and varying orders that are not in accordance with a judge's endorsement. We distinguished between orders generally and orders on applications, motions, and from the Court of Appeal. We also distinguished orders generally from judgments after trial, noting the differences in form. We then turned to prejudgment and postjudgment interest, noting that prejudgment interest runs from the time the cause of action arises to the day of judgment, and is calculated on the amount of the judgment at an interest rate determined by a formula and set out in a table. We also made note of exclusions and types of damages using special calculations methods and special rates. We then turned to the calculation of postjudgment interest from the date of the order to payment, noting how the rate is established and the amount of the judgment on which it is calculated.

KEY TERMS

exemplary damages

punitive damages

non-pecuniary

NOTES

1 The procedure varies. In some places, a court clerk signs the order on behalf of the registrar. Judges can sign their own orders but rarely do so.

2 Rates for each quarter are also available on the Web at http://www.attorneygeneral.jus.gov.on.ca/english/courts/interestrates.asp.

REFERENCES

Courts of Justice Act, RSO 1990, c. C.43.

Rules of Civil Procedure, RRO 1990, reg. 194.

REVIEW QUESTIONS

1. What is the difference between a judgment and an order?

2. What is an endorsement?

3. What does it mean to "approve the order as to form"?

4. Describe the process of signing an order.

5. What happens if the order is not approved as to form?

6. What happens if the registrar refuses to sign an order because he or she is not satisfied that it is in proper form or that it correctly reflects the contents of the endorsement?

7. Where are orders entered?

8. What should you do if you pay the amount due on an order or an amount that satisfies the judgment creditor?

9. What happens if there is an inadvertent error in the judgment?

10. On what can you obtain prejudgment and postjudgment interest?

11. How do you determine the appropriate interest rate to calculate prejudgment interest?

12. How do you determine the interest rate for calculating postjudgment interest?

13. How do you calculate the interest for special damages where they continue to accrue after the cause of action arose?

DISCUSSION QUESTIONS

1. Suppose Abigail is not successful at trial. You are asked to draft the judgment. You get the court file and find this endorsement on the back of the trial record: "September 27, 2001. Action dismissed with costs. Palardeau J." The trial took place in Toronto on September 10, 12, 13, 14, 26, and 27. Counsel and parties were all present and evidence was given orally. Draft the judgment.

2. Assume the same trial dates as in question 1, but suppose that Abigail is successful. The endorsement reads: "Judgment for the plaintiff. General damages $225,000. Special damages $87,242.03. Partial indemnity costs for the plaintiff together with prejudgment interest in the amount of $12,098.21."

3. Assume Abigail obtained judgment for $100,000 for general damages for pain and suffering and $50,000 for out-of-pocket expenses or special damages, which accrued as follows: September 14, 2000 to March 13, 2001: $22,000; March 14, 2001 to September 13, 2001: $23,000; September 14 to 28, 2001: $5,000. The accident occurred on September 14, 2000. The action commenced on October 23, 2000, and judgment was granted on September 28, 2001.

4. Assume that Abigail obtained judgment on June 5, 2000 for $150,000, her costs were assessed at $10,000, and prejudgment interest was $3,000. Assume also that she was paid on October 15, 2000. Determine the amount of postjudgment interest and the total amount payable on October 15, 2000.

CHAPTER 18

Costs

INTRODUCTION

Although there are exceptions, a judge usually orders that the losing side pay part of the legal costs of the winning side. When speakers of legalese say "the costs follow the cause" or "the costs follow the event" this is what they mean: the winning side recovers some of its legal expenses from the losing side.

The jurisdiction of the court to award costs is provided in s. 131 of the *Courts of Justice Act*. The amount of costs or whether costs are awarded at all are matters totally in the discretion of the court. Although costs usually follow the event, the court sometimes awards costs or denies costs to express its disapproval of the way that one of the parties has conducted itself during the proceeding (rule 57.01(2)). For instance, if parties have prolonged the proceedings unnecessarily, the court may refuse to award them costs, even if they have won the case. Moreover, depending on the severity of the conduct during the litigation, the court may even order the winning party to pay costs to the losing side.

HOW COSTS ARE DETERMINED

In determining whether costs are to be awarded, the court uses the factors set out in rule 57.01(1). These factors include such things as the amount of money the winning party recovered in the proceeding; the complexity of the proceeding; the importance of the issues; and the conduct of any party, including conduct resulting from negligence, mistake, or excessive caution.[1] In addition, rule 57.04 provides costs sanctions if the case was brought improperly in the Superior Court rather than in the Small Claims Court. As you can see, in providing for the awarding of costs, the rules encourage parties to move their cases speedily and efficiently through the litigation process.

Costs in Ontario courts never cover the total expenses of the party to whom they are awarded. Rather, they cover only a portion of the actual legal costs of the party. The portion of the real legal costs covered depends on what scale is used to calculate the costs awarded. The court orders which scale is to be used. The two scales used are the partial indemnity scale and the substantial indemnity scale.[2] In most cases, the partial indemnity scale is used. The court usually orders that the substantial indemnity scale be used only if the party who must pay costs has done something blameworthy during the litigation.

Before January 1, 2002, when the rules relating to costs went through substantial change, the trial judge could determine both which party would be awarded costs and the actual monetary amount of the costs. Alternatively, the judge might make an order determining which party was to be awarded costs and leave the actual

fixing costs
making an order that a
specific party pay a
specific amount of costs

calculation of the amount of those costs to a court official called an assessment officer. When the judge determines not only who receives costs but also how much that person receives, this is called "**fixing costs.**" When the judge decides which party receives costs but leaves the assessment officer to decide the amount, this is called making an "assessment of costs."

As a result of the changes to rule 57 effective in January 2002, assessment of costs is the exception. The amended rule 57.01(3) provides that costs are to be fixed by the trial judge at the end of the trial. In addition, the judge must now also apply the amounts set out in the tariffs when determining the amount to be awarded (rule 57.01(3)). Only exceptional cases will be referred for an assessment. This has streamlined the process since, in most cases, the judge fixes costs and there is no need for a second hearing before the assessment officer.

Costs may also be awarded on a contested motion. Before the rule changes effective in January 2002, the motion judge or master would often leave the determination of the costs of the motion to the trial judge or award costs to the party who eventually won the case: the trial judge or the assessment officer would then determine the amount to be awarded. Rule 57.03 now requires the motions court to fix the costs of a motion in all but exceptional cases. Exceptional cases are sent for assessment of the costs. The rule also requires that the costs, whether fixed or assessed, must be paid within 30 days of their being fixed or assessed. Failure to pay may result in dismissal or stay of the proceeding or a striking out of the defence (rule 57.03(2)).

After a trial or a contested motion, the party that has been awarded costs must prepare a bill of costs in form 57A. The amounts in the bill of costs for fees are those provided in the costs grid in part I of tariff A. Part II of tariff A outlines permissible disbursements. The tariffs can be found in the *Ontario Annual Practice* volume. If the costs have been fixed, the party serves the bill of costs on the other party and files it, along with proof of service, with the court. The court then sets the amount according to the tariff.

If the costs are to be assessed, a party must follow the procedures for an assessment under rule 58 after serving and filing the bill of costs. These procedures are discussed later in this chapter.

PREPARATION OF A BILL OF COSTS

A bill of costs is form 57A and appears as figure 18.1. In order to complete the form, you need the time dockets for the client's files, showing specific work that has been done on the file and the amount of time it took to accomplish each task. You also need a copy of the cost grid in part I of tariff A as well as the order or judgment for costs, which indicates which scale is to be used in calculating the costs: partial indemnity or substantial indemnity. Figure 18.2 sets out the cost grid in part I of tariff A.

You must then sort the time dockets into tasks that involve procedures authorized by the rules, such as drafting of pleadings or attendance at a mandatory mediation session, and tasks that are services provided to the client but that are not covered by the rules, such as meetings with clients for the purpose of taking instruction.

A step-by-step guide for calculating costs is provided below.

1. *Determine the scale that the costs are to be calculated under.* This can be determined from the order or judgment.

FIGURE 18.1   BILL OF COSTS (FORM 57A)

Court file no. 01-CV-1234

ONTARIO
SUPERIOR COURT OF JUSTICE

BETWEEN:

Abigail Boar

Plaintiff

and

Rattle Motors Ltd. and Fred Flogem

Defendants

BILL OF COSTS

AMOUNTS CLAIMED FOR FEES AND DISBURSEMENTS

FEES OTHER THAN COUNSEL FEES

1. Drafting statement of claim	1.5 hours
I.M. Just, January 3, year 1	
2. Drafting reply to statement of defence	0.75 hours
I.M. Just, February 5, year 1	
3. Drafting affidavit of service	0.5 hours
Edward Egregious, law clerk, January 5, year 1	
4. Drafting affidavit of documents	
Edward Egregious, February 7, year 1	4.5 hours
I.M Just, February 9, year 1	0.5 hours
5. Attendance at examination for discovery	5.0 hours
I.M. Just, February 10, year 1	
6. Attendance at pretrial conference	2.0 hours
I.M. Just, May 20, year 3	

COUNSEL FEE

7. Attendance at trial of the matter	
I.M. Just, July 10, 11, 12, year 3	3 days x $2,500

TOTAL FEES	$10,312.50

DISBURSEMENTS SUBJECT TO GST	
Paid to process server to serve statement of claim	$60.00
Paid to official examiner	200.00
	$260.00
GST	18.20
Total disbursements subject to GST	$278.00

FIGURE 18.1   CONTINUED

DISBURSEMENTS NOT SUBJECT TO GST

Paid to issue statement of claim	$132.00
Paid to set matter down for trial	268.00
Total disbursements not subject to GST	$400.00
TOTAL DISBURSEMENTS	$678.20
TOTAL FEES AND DISBURSEMENTS	$10,990.70

STATEMENT OF EXPERIENCE

A claim for fees is being made with respect to the following lawyers:

Name of lawyer	Years of experience
I.M. Just	9 years

TO:

Huey Sue
Barrister and Solicitor
65 False Trail
Toronto, Ontario, M6Y 1Z6

tel. 416-485-6891
fax 416-485-6892

Solicitor for the Defendants

FIGURE 18.2   COST GRID (PART I, TARIFF A)

**Note: On January 1, 2002, Part I is revoked
and the following substituted:**

PART I — COSTS GRID

Where students-at-law or law clerks have provided services of a
nature that the Law Society of Upper Canada authorizes them to
provide, the fees for those services may be assessed and allowed
under this costs grid.

Where counsel has special expertise, his or her hourly rate
classification may be varied accordingly.

1. Fees other than Counsel Fee

Hourly rates for pleadings, mediation under Rule 24.1 or Rule 75.1,
financial statements, discovery of documents, drawing and settling
issues on special case, setting down for trial, pre-motion conference,
examination, pre-trial conference, settlement conference, notice or
offer, preparation for hearing, attendance at assignment court, order,
issuing or renewing a writ of execution or notice of garnishment, seizure
under writ of execution, seizure and sale under writ of execution, notice
of garnishment, or for any other procedure authorized by the Rules of
Civil Procedure and not provided for elsewhere in the costs grid.

**Note: On July 3, 2004, Part I is amended by striking out "mediation
under Rule 24.1 or Rule 75.1" and substituting "mediation under
Rule 24.1". See: O. Reg. 284/01, ss. 38(2), 39.**

	Partial Indemnity Scale	*Substantial Indemnity Scale*
Law Clerks	Up to $80.00 per hour	Up to $125.00 per hour
Student-at-law	Up to $60.00 per hour	Up to $90.00 per hour
Lawyer (less than 10 years)	Up to $225.00 per hour	Up to $300.00 per hour
Lawyer (10 or more but less than 20 years)	Up to $300.00 per hour	Up to $400.00 per hour
Lawyer (20 years and over)	Up to $350.00 per hour	Up to $450.00 per hour

2. Counsel Fee — Motion or Application

	Partial Indemnity Scale	*Substantial Indemnity Scale*
0.25 hour	Up to $400.00	Up to $800.00
1.00 hour	Up to $1,000.00	Up to $1,500.00
2.00 hours (half day)	Up to $1,400.00	Up to $2,400.00
1 day	Up to $2,100.00	Up to $3,500.00

FIGURE 18.2 CONTINUED

3. Counsel Fee — Trial or Reference

	Partial Indemnity Scale	Substantial Indemnity Scale
Half Day	Up to $1,500.00	Up to $2,500.00
Day	Up to $2,300.00	Up to $4,000.00
Week	Up to $9,500.00	Up to $17,500.00

4. Counsel Fee — Appeal

	Partial Indemnity Scale	Substantial Indemnity Scale
1.00 hour	Up to $1,000.00	Up to $1,500.00
2.00 hours (half day)	Up to $1,250.00	Up to $2,000.00
1 day	Up to $2,000.00	Up to $4,000.00

See: O. Reg. 284/01, ss. 38(1), 39.

2. *Divide the time dockets for the file into items that cannot be included in the bill of costs, items to be included as non-counsel fees, and items to be included as counsel fees.* Counsel fees are those fees directly related to the lawyer's appearance in court. These fees are calculated according to the type of court appearance and the length of time spent. For example, if the lawyer spent one hour in court on a contested motion, the allowable amount is up to $1,000. All allowable fees that do not involve a court appearance are included in the account as non-counsel fees.

3. *Determine the experience level of each of the lawyers who are claiming fees.* The cost grid shows how much a lawyer with a particular number of years of experience is entitled to claim. For example, a lawyer with more than 20 years' experience can claim up to $350 per hour on a partial indemnity scale and up to $450 per hour on a substantial indemnity scale. You claim the lawyer's actual hourly fee, as billed to the client, or $350 per hour, whichever is less. The allowable hourly fee must be calculated for each lawyer claiming fees.

4. *Determine whether any procedure to be included in the bill of costs was performed by a law clerk or a student-at-law.* Each of their permissible hourly rates is included in the cost grid.

5. *Calculate allowable disbursements.* Look at part II of tariff A to determine whether a particular type of disbursement is an allowable item in the bill of costs, and ascertain how much can be billed for each type.

6. *Attach time dockets.* You must attach the actual time dockets for the fees claimed to the bill of costs.

7. *Attach evidence of disbursements.* For disbursements claimed, you must attach copies of invoices, cancelled cheques for payment of issuing fees, and any other evidence that proves the disbursements were incurred.

ASSESSMENT OF COSTS

If the court does not fix costs at the completion of the motion or trial, the court awards costs to a particular party and refers the matter to an assessment officer for an **assessment of costs**. The assessment officer is a court official who has the responsibility of determining the exact monetary amount to be awarded to that party. In assessing the costs, the assessment officer looks to rule 58, which determines the assessment procedure.

A party entitled to costs may file a bill of costs and a copy of the order awarding costs (rule 58.03(1)). Once these documents are filed, the entitled party can then obtain a notice of appointment for assessment of costs, form 58A, from the office of the assessment officer. The notice of appointment for assessment and the bill of costs must be served on all parties who have an interest in the assessment at least seven days before the date of the assessment (rule 58.03(2)). A sample notice of appointment for assessment of costs appears as figure 18.3.

If the party entitled to costs does not serve the bill of costs for assessment within a reasonable time, the party who has been ordered to pay the costs may obtain a notice to deliver a bill of costs for assessment, form 58B, from the assessment officer and serve it on every party who has an interest in the costs issue at least 21 days before the date set for the assessment. A sample notice to deliver a bill of costs for assessment appears as figure 18.4.

Once the party entitled to costs is served with the notice to deliver a bill of costs for assessment, the entitled party must file and serve a bill of costs on every interested party at least seven days before the date set for the assessment. If the entitled party does not serve a bill of costs as required, then the assessment officer may proceed to fix the costs, without the bill of costs.

On the date of the assessment, the interested parties appear before the assessment officer. The items in the bill of costs are examined, and the parties make submissions on any items that they wish to challenge or defend. The assessment officer then reviews the items and determines whether they reflect a reasonable amount of time spent on a particular step. For instance, the assessment officer might not allow a party to claim 3.5 hours for drafting a simple notice of motion. That amount of time is excessive for a routine matter. In deciding whether the expenditure of time or any other item in the bill of costs is reasonable, the assessment officer may take into consideration the factors listed in rule 58.06(1).

The assessment officer must apply the tariffs in determining the hourly legal fees and the disbursements. The fee schedule is contained in the cost grid in part I of tariff A, and the allowable disbursements are contained in part II of tariff A. Only disbursements paid to the court are allowed unless a lawyer establishes at the assessment that a disbursement was made or incurred by the party. Sometimes, with an unusual disbursement, it may be necessary to prepare an affidavit to prove the disbursement. The assessment officer also has the authority under the rules to require a party to produce books and records for the purpose of the assessment.

In addition, the assessment officer is bound to follow any direction given by the court that made the order for costs. Pursuant to rule 57.02, the court that awards costs may provide specific directions to the assessment officer as to how the costs are to be assessed. If there is such a direction on any item, the assessment officer must follow it. For example, the court may order that an item that is not included in part II of tariff A be assessed as a legitimate disbursement.

assessment of costs
tally made by an assessment officer of a specific amount of costs payable after a court has determined which party is entitled to costs

FIGURE 18.3   NOTICE OF APPOINTMENT FOR ASSESSMENT OF COSTS (FORM 58A)

Court file no. 01-CV-1234

ONTARIO
SUPERIOR COURT OF JUSTICE

BETWEEN:

Abigail Boar

Plaintiff

and

Rattle Motors Ltd. and Fred Flogem

Defendants

NOTICE OF APPOINTMENT FOR ASSESSMENT OF COSTS

TO THE PARTIES

I HAVE MADE AN APPOINTMENT to assess the costs of the plaintiff, a copy of whose bill of costs is attached to this notice, on Tuesday July 30, year 3 **at** 2:00 p.m., **at the** Court House, 393 University Avenue, Toronto, Ontario, M5G 1Y8.

Date: July 20, year 3

_____
Assessment Officer

TO:
Huey Sue
Barrister and Solicitor
65 False Trail
Toronto, Ontario, M6Y 1Z6

tel. 416-485-6891
fax 416-485-6892

Solicitor for the Defendants

FIGURE 18.4   NOTICE TO DELIVER A BILL OF COSTS FOR ASSESSMENT (FORM 58B)

Court file no. 01-CV-1234

ONTARIO
SUPERIOR COURT OF JUSTICE

BETWEEN:

Abigail Boar

Plaintiff

and

Rattle Motors Ltd. and Fred Flogem

Defendants

NOTICE TO DELIVER A BILL OF COSTS FOR ASSESSMENT

TO THE PARTIES

I HAVE MADE AN APPOINTMENT, at the request of the defendant Rattle Motors Ltd., to assess the costs of the plaintiff on Tuesday July 30, year 3, at 2:00 p.m., at the Court House, 393 University Avenue, Toronto, Ontario, M5G 1Y8.

TO:
Just & Coping
Barristers and Solicitors
365 Bay Street - 8701
Toronto, Ontario, M3J 4A9

I.M. Just
tel. 416-762-1342
fax 416-762-2300

Solicitors for the Plaintiff

YOU ARE REQUIRED to file your bill of costs with me and serve your bill of costs on every party interested in the assessment at least seven days before the above date.

Date: July 21, year 3

_____
Assessment Officer

Following the assessment, the assessment officer must provide a certificate of assessment of costs, form 58C, that sets out the amount of the costs allowed. Once the certificate is completed, it has the same effect as an order of the court and may be enforced in the same way as a court order. A sample of a certificate of assessment of costs appears as figure 18.5.

If, at the completion of the assessment, any of the parties is unhappy with the assessment officer's decision, he or she may ask the assessment officer to withhold the certificate for seven days. During the period that the certificate is withheld, the objecting party must serve a written copy of his or her objections on every other interested party and file them with the assessment officer. Any party served with the objections may prepare a reply to the objections, serve them on the other parties, and file the reply with the assessment officer. The assessment officer, on receiving an objection, must reconsider the initial assessment and then complete the certificate of assessment, which may be amended as a result of the reconsideration. A party that is still not satisfied may appeal the assessment officer's decision to the court that made the original costs order.

ASSESSMENT OF COSTS ON SETTLEMENTS AND ABANDONED CASES

It is usually costs that have been awarded by the court at the completion of a trial or a motion that are referred to assessment. However, sometimes a case settles or is abandoned before it gets to trial. In such cases, the parties may agree that costs are appropriate. Especially where a case is abandoned, one party may believe it is entitled to costs.

It is often a condition of the settlement of a proceeding that one party pay costs. Parties that agree to costs being a condition of settling a case usually draft minutes of settlement that contain the specific amount of costs to be paid. However, where the payment of costs is a condition of settlement and the amount is not included in the settlement, the costs may be assessed pursuant to rule 57.04 by one of the parties filing a copy of the minutes of settlement in the office of the assessment officer.

Likewise, the costs on an abandoned motion, application, or appeal may also be assessed if one of the parties files

- the served notice of motion or application and an affidavit stating that the document was not filed within the time prescribed by the rules or that the initiator of the proceeding did not appear on the court date,

- a served notice of abandonment, or

- a copy of any order dismissing the case as abandoned.

COST IMPLICATIONS OF OFFERS TO SETTLE

The legal system has a major interest in having matters settle without trial. The rules provide many methods of encouraging parties to settle their disputes. One of these rules is rule 49, which deals with offers to settle. An offer to settle is a proposal made by a party to the litigation that attempts to resolve one or more of the issues

FIGURE 18.5   CERTIFICATE OF ASSESSMENT OF COSTS (FORM 58C)

Court file no. 01-CV-1234

ONTARIO
SUPERIOR COURT OF JUSTICE

BETWEEN:

Abigail Boar

Plaintiff

and

Rattle Motors Ltd. and Fred Flogem

Defendants

CERTIFICATE OF ASSESSMENT OF COSTS

I CERTIFY that I have assessed the costs of the plaintiff in this proceeding under the authority of the order of the Honourable Madam Justice Snork, dated July 12, year 3, and I ALLOW THE SUM OF $12,000.

THE COSTS ALLOWED IN THIS ASSESSMENT BEAR INTEREST at the rate of 6.75 per cent per year commencing on July 12, year 3.

Date: July 12, year 3

_____
Assessment Officer

between the parties. For example, the defendant may offer the plaintiff a portion of the damages being sought.

Rule 49 provides procedures for making and withdrawing offers. Rule 49.10 deals with the cost consequences when reasonable offers to settle are made by one party but not accepted by the party to whom they are made. The rule sets out three criteria regarding the offer to settle and its acceptance:

1. the offer to settle must have been made at least seven days before the commencement of the hearing;

2. the offer to settle must not be withdrawn and must not expire before the commencement of the hearing; and

3. the offer must not be accepted by the opposite party.

The consequences that flow from meeting these criteria are set out below.

Offer to settle made by plaintiff

If all three of these criteria are met and the offer to settle is made by a plaintiff who obtains an order at the end of the proceeding that is as good as, or better than, the offer made, the plaintiff is entitled to partial indemnity costs to the date the offer to settle was served and substantial indemnity costs from that date onward unless the court orders otherwise.

Stated another way, the plaintiff makes an offer to the defendant to settle the case for less money than the plaintiff is suing for. The defendant does not accept the plaintiff's offer, and the case goes to trial. At the end of the trial, the plaintiff wins the case, and the court awards the plaintiff the same amount of money or more than the amount that the plaintiff offered to settle the case for. The defendant may be ordered to pay higher costs than he or she would usually have to pay because the costs are based on the substantial indemnity scale from the date that the offer was made until the end of the trial.

Offer to settle made by defendant

If all three of the criteria are met and the offer to settle is made by a defendant and the plaintiff obtains an order at trial that is only as good as, or is worse than, the offer made, the plaintiff is entitled to partial indemnity costs to the date the offer was served, and the defendant is entitled to partial indemnity costs from that date onward, unless the court orders otherwise.

In this situation, the defendant has made an offer to settle the case for less money than the plaintiff is seeking from the court. The plaintiff does not accept the offer and ultimately wins the case. However, the court does not accept the plaintiff's claim for damages and instead orders the defendant to pay damages to the plaintiff in an amount that is equal to, or lower than, the amount contained in the defendant's offer to settle. Because the plaintiff could have saved the time and expense of the trial by accepting an offer that was as good as, or better than, he or she ultimately received in the judgment, the plaintiff is entitled to costs on a partial indemnity scale only to the time the offer was made. After that date, the plaintiff must pay partial indemnity costs to the defendant.

The obvious intention of this rule is to ensure that parties think carefully about rejecting any reasonable offer to settle. If they reject an offer that turns out to be either as good as, or better than, the order eventually made by the court, the rejecting party suffers cost consequences.

Because of this rule, it is wise to structure all offers to settle a case in such a way that they automatically expire either within a specified period or at the commencement of the trial. If the offer to settle does not contain an automatic expiry period, it is important to withdraw it before the commencement of a trial.

Offer made in a case with multiple defendants

In many cases, the plaintiff names more than one defendant and claims they are jointly and severally liable for damages. Rule 49.10 does not apply to the situation of multiple defendants unless the plaintiff makes an offer to settle that includes all the defendants. If the offer is made by the defendants to the plaintiff, rule 49.10 does not apply unless the offer includes all the defendants or the defendants making the offer also agree to pay the costs of any defendant not joining in the offer (rule 49.11).

Offer to contribute

If the plaintiff is suing more than one defendant and claiming that the defendants are jointly and severally responsible for the damages, one defendant can make an offer to another defendant under rule 49.12. The offer would be to contribute to the plaintiff's claimed damages in a specific amount.

A plaintiff who is suing more than one defendant, claiming that they are jointly and severally liable, is saying that they each are totally liable for all the damages. A plaintiff who wins such a case can go after any of the defendants for all the money. He or she need not take a specific portion from each of them unless the court orders otherwise. The plaintiff obviously wants to go after the defendant with the most money to collect the amount owing with the least trouble. For instance, if Abigail is successful against both the defendants Fred Flogem and Rattle Motors Ltd., unless the court orders otherwise, she is likely to seek all the money from Rattle. Rattle is more likely to have the money available because Rattle is a business, whereas Fred, who is an individual employed as a car salesman, may or may not have the funds available.

Rule 49.12 provides that Rattle can offer to split Abigail's claim with Fred on a 50/50 basis. If this offer is accepted, Rattle will pay half of Abigail's damages, and Fred will pay the other half. Rattle initiates this by serving Fred with a offer to contribute, form 49D.

If Fred rejects Rattle's offer and Abigail eventually wins her case against both of them, the court can take Fred's rejection of Rattle's offer to contribute into account when awarding costs. The court may require Fred to pay Rattle's costs, and it may require Fred to pay not only his own share of the costs to Abigail, but Rattle's share as well.

Discretion of the court to consider any offer to settle

Rule 49.13 gives the court discretion to consider any offer to settle when making an order as to costs. This means that the court is not restricted to addressing cost issues in the manner set out in the rules.

SECURITY FOR COSTS

If a plaintiff is unsuccessful, the defendant is usually entitled to costs. Collecting costs from a plaintiff who does not have sufficient assets in Ontario is difficult. Rule 56 therefore provides a method for a defendant to bring a motion to the court asking that a plaintiff be required to pay money into court to be held for the duration of the proceeding. If the plaintiff is the successful party, the money is returned at the conclusion of the case. However, if the plaintiff is unsuccessful and the defendant is awarded costs, the costs are paid out of the money held by the court. The money held in the court is called "security for costs."

Rule 56.01(1) lists the circumstances in which security for costs is available. Security is most commonly sought and granted when plaintiffs reside outside the jurisdiction and may not have sufficient assets in Ontario to satisfy an order for costs made against them.

A defendant who is not certain where a plaintiff normally resides can demand in writing that the plaintiff's lawyer declare in writing whether the plaintiff is a resident of Ontario (rule 56.02). Failure of the plaintiff's lawyer to answer the demand may result in the court dismissing or staying the case. Staying a case means suspending it.

When the case is brought by way of an action, the motion for security for costs can be brought only after the defendant has delivered a defence. Notice of the motion must be served on the plaintiff and on every defendant who has delivered a defence or a notice of intent to defend.

When the case is brought by way of application, the motion for security can be brought only after the respondent has delivered a notice of appearance. Notice of the motion must be served on the applicant and every other respondent who has delivered a notice of appearance.

Once security for costs has been ordered, the plaintiff cannot take any further steps in the proceeding until the security has been paid into court. If the plaintiff does not comply with the order for security, the court may dismiss or stay the case.

When the plaintiff has posted the security, he or she must immediately give notice to every other party that he or she has complied with the order.

CHAPTER SUMMARY

In this chapter, we have seen that s. 131 of the *Courts of Justice Act* gives the court jurisdiction to award costs and that rules 57 and 58 deal with the procedure for awarding costs and the assessment of costs. Generally, the losing party must pay costs to the successful party, but we have noted exceptions to this. The rules require that the court fix costs in all but exceptional cases, where the court may refer the case for an assessment of costs.

We observed that costs may be awarded on either a partial indemnity scale or a substantial indemnity scale. The ordinary scale is partial indemnity. Tariff A, part I sets out the scales for calculating the amount of costs to be paid in dollars. Part II of the tariff deals with the disbursements that may be included in an award of costs.

At the end of the proceeding, we saw that the party who is awarded costs must prepare, serve, and file a bill of costs. A guide was provided for preparing a bill of costs.

Since the court wants to encourage litigants to settle cases wherever possible, there are cost penalties for rejecting a reasonable offer to settle made by the opposite party pursuant to the rules. We reviewed rule 49 in this regard. Finally, we examined rule 56, which provides a procedure for requiring a plaintiff to post security for costs.

KEY TERMS

fixing costs

assessment of costs

NOTES

1 See rule 57.01(1) for a complete list of the factors to be considered in the awarding of costs.

2 Before the amendment to the rules effective January 1, 2002, partial indemnity costs were referred to as "party and party" costs, and substantial indemnity costs were referred to as "solicitor and client" costs.

REFERENCES

Carthy, James J., W.A. Derry Millar, and Jeffrey G. Cowan, *Ontario Annual Practice* (Aurora, ON: Canada Law Book, published annually).

Rules of Civil Procedure, RRO 1990, reg. 194.

REVIEW QUESTIONS

1. The plaintiff in the case of *Smith v. Jones* sued for $150,000 in damages and was successful. No offer to settle was made. What costs is a court likely to award?

2. The plaintiff in the case of *Mahoud v. Balucci* sued for $25,000. She won the case, but the court awarded her only $7,000 in damages. How might the court approach a cost award in this case? What rule would apply? Why do you think this rule exists?

3. Explain the difference between the fixing of costs and the assessment of costs.

4. Your law firm acted for an unsuccessful plaintiff in a proceeding. The court awarded costs to the defendant. Two months have passed since the making of the order, and the defendant has not yet served and filed a bill of costs. How should your firm proceed? What rule or rules should it look to for guidance?

5. Your client is a defendant being sued by a plaintiff who lives in New York State. What are the cost implications? What must be done to protect your client? What rule applies?

6. The plaintiff is suing the defendant for damages in the amount of $300,000. Following the examinations for discovery, the defendant makes an offer to settle for $200,000. The plaintiff rejects the offer. A trial takes place. The plaintiff is successful and is awarded $200,000 in damages by the court. What are the cost implications? What rule applies?

DISCUSSION QUESTIONS

1. You are the law clerk for B.A. Doowright and Associates, the lawyers for the plaintiff in the case of *Sam Sunshine v. Fast and Loose Delivery Services Ltd.* Sam has won his case against the defendant, and you must now draft a bill of costs. The court has ordered that the plaintiff shall have costs on a partial indemnity scale up to January 10, 2002 and substantial indemnity scale after that date. This order was made because the defendant had rejected an offer to settle made by the plaintiff. However, at the end of the case, the court awarded the plaintiff larger damages than those he proposed in the rejected offer. The various members of the firm who worked on this file are:

B.A. Doowright, lawyer: 21 years' experience

M.A. Blitz, lawyer: 2 years' experience

Sally Smart, law clerk

The file shows the following time docket items:

a. institution of action, including drafting pleadings: July 10, 2001

   i. Doowright: 0.5 hours
   ii. Blitz: 3.0 hours
   iii. Smart: 2.0 hours

b. discovery of documents, including drafting affidavit of documents: September 16, 2001

   i. Smart: 1.5 hours
   ii. Blitz: 1.0 hours

   c. examination for discovery: October 11 and 12, 2002

      i. Doowright: 1.5 days
      ii. Smart: 1.0 hours

   d. counsel fee at trial: February 1, 2, and 3, 2002

      i. Doowright: 3 days

   e. drafting judgment

      i. Smart: 0.5 hours

The disbursements on the file are as follows:

a. paid court $157 for issuing of statement of claim

b. paid $40 for service of statement of claim

c. paid $40 for service of affidavit of documents

d. paid $250 to expert witness at trial

Draft a bill of costs.

2. Your law firm represents the plaintiff. The defendant brought a motion to dismiss your client's action. Your law firm spent a great deal of time preparing the necessary documents, serving and filing them, and taking other necessary steps to deal with the defendant's motion, including appearing in court to argue it. Neither the defendant or his counsel appeared on the motion. You telephoned the office of the defendant's counsel and were told that the client no longer intends to ask for a dismissal of the case. Your client asks if there is anything you can do to force the defendant to pay some of her legal expenses. Is there something you can do? What is it? What rule applies?

CHAPTER 19

Statement of accounts

INTRODUCTION

If Abigail Boar wins at trial and there is no appeal, the work on her case is done, and I.M. Just will send out her final account. If the law practice is managed well, Just & Coping will have sent her interim accounts at the end of various stages in the proceeding. In most civil litigation cases, interim accounts are sent out at the close of pleadings, the conclusion of discoveries, and near the beginning of trial when pretrial preparation gets underway. Just & Coping may also have asked Abigail to **refresh the retainer** by making further deposits on account of fees when each interim account is rendered. Some personal injury lawyers will take on a case and agree to be paid at the end of the case, provided that it appears that the client will be successful, at least to the extent of covering his or her legal fees. Once contingency fees are finally permitted in Ontario, lawyers will be able to take between 15 and 30 percent of a judgment as the fee (and will get nothing if the client loses the case). Before reading this chapter, review the section of chapter 2 that deals with client accounts, particularly docketing and disbursements.

> **refresh the retainer**
> make a further deposit against future fees as a case progresses

GATHERING INFORMATION TO PREPARE THE CLIENT'S ACCOUNT

The following is a step-by-step guide to gathering the relevant information.

1. *Collect all docket slips or sheets.* If a file has been well managed, this information will have been entered periodically on docketing software. If this has not been done and paper dockets have been used, collect these for entry. If other lawyers or law clerks have worked on the file, you should include their dockets. Lawyers who are not partners (as well as those who are) have their salaries tied directly or indirectly to their billings. It is important for them to have their hours properly billed.

   If, in reviewing the file, you see that there has been work done for which there are no dockets, you should alert the lawyer with **carriage** of the file. Do not try to solve this problem yourself, and do not manufacture docket slips after the fact, even if you think they are likely to be accurate, because the law society considers this to be unprofessional conduct.

   > **carriage**
   > responsibility for a file or a case

2. *Check billable disbursements.* Disbursements are expenses paid by the law firm out of the firm's general account. These include charges for photocopying, long distance calls, courier services, fees paid to witnesses,

fees paid for expert reports, and filing fees. Some expenses, such as courier services, that generate receipts will probably be properly entered on the client ledger card, but others, such as photocopying, may not be, and you may need to search out this information.

3. *Check credits to the client's account recorded on the ledger card.* Credits include any retainer/deposits not yet billed or accounted for, and any receipts by the lawyer in trust for the client — for example, payment of a judgment. You should be able to use this information to summarize trust account transfers in a trust statement at the end of the account.

You should now be ready to prepare the draft account.

COMPONENTS OF A CLIENT ACCOUNT

An account is usually prepared on the firm's letterhead or on special account letterhead and addressed to the client. The format may vary. Some lawyers favour sending out a brief account, which simply says "for professional services rendered," followed by the total fees and disbursements. This is accompanied by a reporting letter from the lawyer, describing the work done, giving further advice if required, and informing the client that details of the account will be furnished on request. Other lawyers favour a more detailed account with a reporting letter. What follows is a description of what goes into a detailed account.

Description of fees

This is almost always presented in chronological order and tells a story that shows what work the lawyer did on a case. It may be in one long narrative paragraph, setting out the date of an activity, its description, and the time taken to do it, in 10ths of an hour — for example, .1 hour or .2 hour. If the account covers several months, it may list all activities for each month under a subheading for each month. Whatever variation is used, you should describe the activity, the date(s) on which it occurred, the person who did it, and the amount of time taken to do it.

Totalling of fees

When you have finished describing the work done, add up the work done by each lawyer or law clerk on the file, and multiply the hours by the appropriate rate. For example:

> I.M. Just, lawyer: 18.3 hours × \$250 per hour = \$4,575
> Edward Egregious, law clerk: 10 hours × \$75 per hour = \$750

Then, total the fees. To the total of \$5,325 in the above example, you must then add 7 percent GST (\$5,325 × 0.07 = \$372.75), for a grand total of \$5,697.75.

GST

GST is the federal goods and services tax. It applies to some, but not all, of the items that are billed by lawyers in an account. There is some room for interpretation as to how the tax applies to specific items, but you should note that GST is chargeable on:

- the fees charged by lawyers for their professional services, including the services of clerks, articling students, and associates; and

- services provided for the client by the lawyer's office and billed to the client such as photocopying, fees charged by a private process server, faxing charges, fees paid to court reporting services to provide space for pretrial examinations, and postage where the lawyer initially pays for the service and then bills the client.

Because the lawyer is paying GST for the latter services, he or she is entitled to pass the tax on to the client. If the client pays for some of these services directly, the firm does not levy GST. Generally, any service the lawyer pays for to assist in doing the client's work is subject to GST.

GST is not chargeable on:

- fees charged by the courts and the government, such as fees to issue statements of claim, and

- fees set by the government and listed in the tariffs, regulations, or statutes, such as the daily fee paid to a person summonsed as a witness, a fee paid to a special examiner to issue a notice of examination, a fee paid for transcripts, and fees paid to a court reporter.

Adjusting the fee

In preparing a draft account, multiply the hourly rate by the hours of work done; the lawyer may adjust the fee, usually by discounting it. Lawyers often adjust the fee based on the results for the client, the benefit to the client from those results, the complexity or difficulty of the work undertaken, and other subjective factors. For example, where the unadjusted fee is high in comparison to the benefit to the client, the lawyer may lower the fee. This reflects what an assessment officer might do if a client moves to assess the account because he or she thinks it too high.

Disbursements

After identifying all of the disbursements charged to the client's ledger, and any others not yet posted to the ledger, divide them into disbursements subject to GST and disbursements not subject to GST. Then you can add each subset of disbursements, and calculate and add in the GST.

Total fees and disbursements

You are now ready to total all fees and disbursements, including the GST. The total GST on fees and disbursements should be set out on a separate line below the total, along with the firm's GST number so that commercial clients can include this amount in any tax credits available to them.

Deduct credit balance in trust from total

If the client has a retainer/deposit held in trust, it should be credited against the amount due on the account, thereby reducing the amount owing from the client.

Balance now due

On this line, you can now record the net amount due after deducting credits from the client funds held in trust.

Signature line

Only a lawyer can sign an account. This job should not be delegated to a law clerk or other office staff.

E&OE

This acronym is a standard business account notation and means "errors and omissions excepted." This means that the lawyer is not bound by the account if the lawyer finds that he or she left something out. The lawyer can still bill for that amount subsequently.

Interest on overdue accounts

At one time, lawyers could not charge on overdue accounts because it was considered improper for professionals to do so. Times change. Interest can now be charged at up to 1.5 percent per month or 18 percent per year, putting lawyers in the same league as bank credit cards. There should be a statement just below the signature that interest will be charged at a specified rate on accounts that remain unpaid for more than 30 days after they are rendered.

Trust statement

A trust or ledger statement should appear at the end of the account to record transfers of money held in trust by the lawyer, including the purpose of the transfer. The trust statement underlies the lawyer's right to transfer money from the lawyer's trust account to his or her general account when an account is rendered to the client.

ABIGAIL BOAR'S FINAL ACCOUNT
Account information and data

Let's suppose that Abigail's case went to trial on some of the issues raised in the pleadings, that the trial lasted three days (July 10, 11, and 12, year 3), and that Abigail obtained judgment for $100,000. On July 14, year 3, I.M. Just rendered his final account, covering the period from July 1, year 3, after completion of some of the pretrial work, through to the end of trial. Abigail's previous account was rendered on June 30, and was paid for by an amount on deposit in her trust account. She has refreshed the retainer with a cheque for $10,000, deposited to I.M. Just's trust account on July 2. I.M. Just's hourly rate is $250. When attending court, litigation lawyers often charge a flat counsel fee for each day or half day in court. I.M. Just's counsel fee is $2,500 per day and $1,200 per half day. The rate charged by the firm for Edward Egregious, the law clerk, is $75.

Edward's dockets are as follows:

- July 6: arranging for issuing and serving summonses to witnesses: 0.5 hours

- July 8: meeting with witnesses: 1.0 hours

- July 10: organizing files and documents for trial: 1.0 hours

- July 10–12: attending court to assist I.M. Just, 6 hours per day for 3 days: 18 hours

- July 14: preparing account and telephone calls arranging for payment of judgment by defendants: 0.6 hours

I.M. Just's dockets are as follows:

- July 2: reading law and preparing trial brief: 8.0 hours

- July 3: reading law and preparing trial brief: 6.0 hours

- July 5: interviewing witnesses: 4.0 hours

- July 6: meeting client and preparing client for trial: 3.0 hours

- July 10, 11, 12: attending trial: 3 full days

- July 13: reporting to client: 1.0 hour

The client's ledger card shows the following entries:

- July 2, year 3: received from client further retainer of $10,000

- July 5, year 3: paid witness fees, 3 summons at $53 each per court-prescribed fee ($159)

- July 6, year 3: paid to serve summonses $45.00

- July 8, year 3: photocopying $73.20

Draft account

Figure 19.1 shows what the draft account in Abigail's case might look like.

CHAPTER SUMMARY

In this chapter, we continued to explore the docketing of hours and the recording of disbursements on the client's account, and we used this information to render an account to a client. From assembled docket sheets and disbursements recorded from the client's ledger card, we created a draft account. The account described the work done and the time taken to do it. It established the fee and total disbursements and recorded the GST charged on all fees and disbursements that are subject to GST. We also accounted for any monies received from the client in trust, using these funds to reduce the balance owing.

FIGURE 19.1   DRAFT ACCOUNT

JUST & COPING
Barristers and Solicitors
365 Bay Street – 8701
Toronto, Ontario, M3J 4A9

July 14, year 3

TO:
Abigail Boar
72 Sumach Street
Toronto, Ontario, M4R 1Z5

RE: BOAR v. RATTLE MOTORS LTD. AND FLOGEM

FOR ALL PROFESSIONAL SERVICES from and after July 1, year 3, including:

I.M. Just, July 2-3, reading law and preparing trial brief: 14 hours; I.M. Just, July 5, interviewing witnesses: 4 hours; I.M. Just, July 6, meeting client and preparing client for trial: 3 hours; E. Egregious, July 6, arranging for issuing and serving witness summonses: 0.5 hours; E. Egregious, July 8, meeting witnesses: 1 hour; E. Egregious, July 10, organizing files and documents for trial: 1 hour; E. Egregious, July 10, 11, 12, attending court to assist counsel: 6 hours per day for 3 days: 18 hours; I.M. Just, July 13, reporting to client: 1 hour; E. Egregious, telephone calls arranging for payment of judgment: 0.6 hours

OUR FEE:	$7,082.50
COUNSEL FEE: I.M. Just, 3 days at trial at $2,500 per day	$7,500.00
TOTAL FEE:	$14,582.50
GST:	$1,020.76

TOTAL FEES INCLUDING GST:	
	$15,603.26

DISBURSEMENTS SUBJECT TO GST:	
Photocopies	$73.20
Service of summonses	$45.00
TOTAL SUBJECT TO GST:	$118.20
GST:	$8.27

DISBURSEMENTS NOT SUBJECT TO GST:	
Court prescribed witness fee,	
3 summonses at $53.00 per summons	$159.00
TOTAL NOT SUBJECT TO GST:	$159.00

TOTAL FEES AND DISBURSEMENTS:	$15,888.73
(TOTAL GST IS $1,029.03 — GST # RO 12534)	

FIGURE 19.1   CONTINUED

LESS TRANSFERRED FROM TRUST: −$10,000
BALANCE NOW DUE AND OWING: $5,888.73
THIS IS OUR ACCOUNT HEREIN

JUST & COPING
Per: _____

Interest will be charged at the rate of 18 percent per annum on all
accounts outstanding for over 30 days.
E&OE

TRUST STATEMENT

Date	Transaction	Disbursement	Receipt
July 2, year 3	Received from client in trust		10,000.00
July 14, year 3	Paid to Just & Coping, Transfer of funds for fees and disbursements, invoice # year 3-1298	10,000.00	
	TOTAL TRUST	10,000.00	10,000.00
	TRUST BALANCE	NIL	NIL

KEY TERMS

refresh the retainer

carriage

REVIEW QUESTIONS

1. In a well-managed law practice, does the lawyer usually wait until the trial is over before billing the client?

2. Does a client usually make a single deposit payment when a lawyer is retained?

3. What must you do before drafting an account?

4. What should you do if dockets are missing for work you know has been done?

5. What is subject to GST?

6. Does a lawyer always establish a fee by adding up all of his or her billable hours?

7. What does "E&OE" mean?

8. May a lawyer charge interest on overdue accounts?

DISCUSSION QUESTION

1. Read and respond to the following memorandum:

   To: Law clerk
   From: Lawyer
   Re: *Farthbottle v. Blob*

   We opened this file on September 16, year 0, and it has just settled. Please draft an account to Fabian Farthbottle for the end of November of this year. My hourly rate is $250. Charge $50 for your time on the file.

   An examination of docket sheets reveals the following:

   Law clerk's dockets:

   - September 16: attending meeting with client: 1.0 hours

   - October 25: meeting client to review documents: 3.0 hours

   - October 26: organizing documents and drafting affidavits of documents: 3.5 hours

   Lawyer's dockets:

   - September 16: initial meeting with client: 1.0 hours

   - September 25: drafting statement of claim: 0.5 hours

   - September 26: telephone conversation with client concerning amendments to statement of claim: 1.0 hours

   - October 5: reviewing statement of claim and defence: 2.0 hours

   - October 10: drafting reply and defence to counterclaim: 0.5 hours

- November 21: preparing for examination for discovery: 3.0 hours

- November 21: preparing client for discovery by telephone: 2.0 hours

- November 22: attending examination for discovery: 5.0 hours

- November 24: negotiating on telephone with defendant's lawyer: 2.0 hours

- November 24: discussing offer with client on telephone: 0.2 hours

- November 25: discussion with defendant's lawyer accepting offer: 0.1 hours

Client's ledger card shows the following:

- September 16: received in trust $2,000.00

- September 16–November 25: photocopies $25.00

- September 26: fee to issue statement of claim $132.00

- September 26: service of statement of claim by process server $41.00

- October 1: postage $6.00

- October 26: fax charges $3.00

- October 30: examiner's fee for notice of examination $9.50

- November 24: discovery transcript $16.00

- November 24: court reporter's fees $100.00

- November 24: examination facilities $80.00

CHAPTER 20

Appeals

INTRODUCTION

An appeal is not a retrying of the case. Many clients misunderstand this. They think an appeal is a redetermination of the case by a higher court that will hear all the evidence presented to the **court of first instance**. This is not the function of an **appellate court**.

The client must be helped to understand that an appeal can be commenced only if the court of first instance made a legal error. It is not the role of the appeal court to hear new evidence, make new determinations of facts, or reassess the credibility of witnesses. In fact, the appeal court does not hear any witnesses. An appeal is conducted by way of written documentation and submissions of the lawyers for the parties. The submissions centre on the legal error that the appealing party claims the court of first instance made. The party commencing the appeal is called the **appellant** and the party responding to the appeal is called the **respondent**.

Rules 61, 62, and 63 deal with procedure on appeals. In addition, you must look to the *Courts of Justice Act* to determine which level of court has jurisdiction to hear an appeal.

court of first instance
court that made a decision that is under appeal

appellate court
any court that hears an appeal

appellant
party that commences an appeal

respondent
party that answers or defends against an appeal

NATURE OF THE ORDER APPEALED FROM

Once it has been decided that there are arguable legal grounds for an appeal, the next step in determining which procedure to follow is to establish whether the order appealed from is final or interlocutory in nature.

All orders can be classified as either final or interlocutory. A **final order** is one that determines all the outstanding issues in the proceeding. An **interlocutory order** is one that resolves only a particular issue in the proceeding on a temporary basis. It is not a complete determination of all the issues between the parties.

Many, but not all, motions lead to interlocutory orders. Similarly, most orders made at a trial of an issue are final. However, it is important to look at the content of the order, not the proceeding in which it was granted, to determine whether it is final or interlocutory in nature. For instance, a successful motion for summary judgment results in a final order. The order is final because all the issues in the proceeding are dealt with on the basis of summary judgment.

When trying to decide whether a particular order is final or interlocutory, it is a good idea to ask whether the order resolves all the outstanding issues between the parties or whether there are still issues to be litigated. The issue is not always cut and dried, and there are many cases in which the courts have been asked to determine whether a particular order is final or interlocutory in nature.

final order
order that resolves all the outstanding issues between the parties

interlocutory order
order that decides some of the matters at issue

There are different routes through the court system for appeals of final orders and interlocutory orders. Therefore, determining whether a particular order is final or interlocutory is the first step in establishing the procedure to be followed on an appeal.

RIGHT TO APPEAL

leave of the court
permission of the court to
take a procedural step

There is not always an automatic right to appeal an order of the court. In many instances, permission or **leave of the court** must be sought in order to commence an appeal. If the rules require that leave must be granted before an appeal can be commenced, the party wishing to appeal must bring a motion to the court that is to hear the appeal, asking for permission.

WHICH COURT HEARS THE APPEAL?

After establishing whether the order is interlocutory or final, the next step is deciding which court has the jurisdiction to hear the appeal. There are three courts that can hear appeals:

1. the Ontario Superior Court of Justice,

2. the Divisional Court, and

3. the Court of Appeal.

To determine which court has jurisdiction in each particular appeal, you must look at the *Courts of Justice Act*. Section 17 of the Act, provides that a judge of the Superior Court of Justice has jurisdiction to hear appeals from the following orders:

(a) an interlocutory order of a master or case management master;

(b) a certificate of assessment of costs issued in a proceeding in the Superior Court of Justice, on an issue in respect of which an objection was served under the rules of court.[1]

Section 19(1)(a) through (c) of the *Courts of Justice Act* provides that the Divisional Court may hear appeals from the following orders:

(a) a final order of a judge of the Superior Court of Justice,

   (i) for a single payment of not more than $25,000, exclusive of costs,

   (ii) for periodic payments that amount to not more than $25,000, exclusive of costs, in the twelve months commencing on the date the first payment is due under the order,

   (iii) dismissing a claim for an amount that is not more than the amount set out in subclause (i) or (ii), or

   (iv) dismissing a claim for an amount that is more than the amount set out in subclause (i) or (ii) and in respect of which the judge or jury indicates that if the claim had been allowed the amount awarded would have been not more than the amount set out in subclause (i) or (ii);

(b) an interlocutory order of a judge of the Superior Court of Justice, with leave as provided in the rules of court;

(c) a final order of a master or case management master.

The Divisional Court, pursuant to s. 31 of the *Courts of Justice Act*, also has jurisdiction to hear appeals from Small Claims Court matters in which the amount of the claim was in excess of $500, excluding costs.

Section 6(1)(a) through (c) of the *Courts of Justice Act* provides that the Court of Appeal has jurisdiction to hear an appeal of the following orders:

(a) an order of the Divisional Court, on a question that is not a question of fact alone, with leave of the Court of Appeal as provided in the rules of court;

(b) a final order of a judge of the Superior Court of Justice, except an order referred to in clause 19(1)(a) [an order that should be appealed to the Divisional Court] or an order from which an appeal lies to the Divisional Court under another Act;

(c) a certificate of assessment of costs issued in a proceeding in the Court of Appeal, on an issue in respect of which an objection was served under the rules of court.[2]

In summary, a final order of a judge of the Superior Court of Justice may be appealed to the Divisional Court if the monetary value of the order is less than $25,000. A final order for more than $25,000 from a judge of the Superior Court goes to the Court of Appeal. An interlocutory order of a master goes to the Superior Court of Justice on appeal, but a final order of a master goes to the Divisional Court. Table 20.1 sets out the various routes of appeal.

APPEAL TO THE DIVISIONAL COURT OR THE COURT OF APPEAL

Rule 61 applies to appeals to the Divisional Court or the Court of Appeal.

Section 20(1) of the *Courts of Justice Act* requires that an appeal to the Divisional Court be brought in the region where the proceeding is commenced. Since there is only one Court of Appeal in Ontario, at Osgoode Hall in Toronto, an appeal to that court is commenced through the court office there.

Motions for leave to appeal

There is not always a right to appeal a decision. Sometimes it is necessary to seek leave from the appellate court to appeal a judgment of a lower court. The procedure on motions for leave to appeal to the Divisional Court is similar to the procedure on motions for leave to appeal to the Court of Appeal. Because there are some procedural differences, however, we will deal with these appeals separately.

MOTION FOR LEAVE TO APPEAL TO THE DIVISIONAL COURT: RULE 61.03

A motion for leave to appeal to the Divisional Court must be served within 15 days of the making of the order unless the matter is governed by a statute that provides a different time limit. If the court reserves a decision, the 15 days starts to run on the day the decision is released.

The notice of motion, along with proof of service, must then be filed within 5 days of service in the office of the registrar of the Divisional Court in the region where the proceeding resulting in the appeal was commenced. A notice of motion for

TABLE 20.1 APPEAL ROUTES

Nature of the order made	*Court to which the appeal goes*
Final order of a judge of the Superior Court of Justice in an amount over $25,000 (exclusive of costs)	Court of Appeal
Final order of a judge of the Superior Court of Justice in an amount under $25,000 (exclusive of costs)	Divisional Court
Interlocutory order of a judge of the Superior Court of Justice (with leave)	Divisional Court
Final order of a master	Divisional Court
Interlocutory order of a master	Judge of the Superior Court of Justice
Certificate of assessment of costs issued in a proceeding in the Court of Appeal	Court of Appeal
Certificate of assessment of costs (where objection served) in a proceeding in the Superior Court of Justice for an amount under $25,000	Superior Court of Justice
Certificate of assessment of costs (where objection served) in a proceeding in the Superior Court of Justice for an amount over $25,000	Court of Appeal
Small Claims Court order for an amount over $500	Divisional Court

leave to appeal, which appears as figure 20.1, is generally in the same format as a regular motion. (See chapter 9 on motions.) However, in the portion of the form that requires a date, instead of including a date, you write "on a date to be fixed by the registrar" (rule 61.03(1)(a)).

In addition, the questions that the Divisional Court is being asked to answer, should leave be granted, must be included in the notice of motion.

On the motion for leave, you need a motion record. A motion record on an application for leave to appeal is similar to a regular motion record. The pages must be consecutively numbered, and the contents must be arranged in the following order:

1. a table of contents, describing each document, including each exhibit by its nature and date and, in the case of an exhibit, by its exhibit number or letter;

2. a copy of the notice of motion;

3. a copy of the order or decision from which leave to appeal is sought as signed and entered;

4. a copy of the reasons of the court or tribunal from which leave to appeal is sought with a further typed or printed copy if the reasons are handwritten;

5. a copy of any order or decision that was the subject of the hearing before the court or tribunal from which leave to appeal is sought;

FIGURE 20.1   NOTICE OF MOTION FOR LEAVE TO APPEAL

Court file no. 03-CA-5678

ONTARIO
SUPERIOR COURT OF JUSTICE

BETWEEN:

Abigail Boar

Plaintiff

and

Rattle Motors Ltd. and Fred Flogem

Defendants

NOTICE OF MOTION FOR LEAVE TO APPEAL

THE DEFENDANT Rattle Motors Ltd. will make a motion to the court on a date to be fixed by the Registrar.

PROPOSED METHOD OF HEARING: The motion is to be heard orally.

THE MOTION IS FOR: Leave to appeal the order of the Honourable Madam Justice Snork, **made** July 12, year 3.

THE GROUNDS FOR THE MOTION ARE:

1. Should leave to appeal be granted, the questions the court will be asked to address on the appeal are:
   a. Did the Honourable Trial Judge err in finding that the defendant Rattle owed a duty of care to the plaintiff?
   b. ...
2. *(List all further grounds for the motion.)*
3. ...

THE FOLLOWING DOCUMENTARY EVIDENCE will be used at the hearing of the motion:

1. The order of the Honourable Madam Justice Snork made July 12, year 3.
2. *(List all other documents on which you will be relying in the motion.)*

Date: July 30, year 3

Just & Coping
Barristers and Solicitors
365 Bay Street - 8701
Toronto, Ontario, M3J 4A9

I.M. Just
tel. 416-762-1342
fax 416-762-2300

Solicitors for the Plaintiff

FIGURE 20.1   CONTINUED

TO:
```
Huey Sue
Barrister and Solicitor
65 False Trail
Toronto, Ontario, M6Y 1Z6

tel. 416-485-6891
fax 416-485-6892

Solicitor for the Defendants
```

6. a copy of any reasons for the order or decision with a further typed or printed copy if the reasons are handwritten;

7. a copy of all affidavits and other material used before the court or tribunal from which leave to appeal is sought;

transcript
written record of
proceedings transcribed
word for word

8. a list containing each relevant **transcript** of evidence in chronological order, but not necessarily the transcripts themselves; and

9. a copy of any other material in the court file that is necessary for the hearing of the motion.

In addition to the motion record, the factum and the transcripts of the proceeding must be provided. A factum is a statement of the facts and the law on which the moving party is relying. Facts are determined by going through the transcripts of the trial and listing each fact, as found by the court at the trial.

The facts and law are to be set out in the document. They are to be presented in the form of a concise argument. For the overview of the contents of a factum on appeal, see the section in this chapter dealing with motions for leave to appeal to the Court of Appeal.

Three copies of the motion record, factum, and transcripts must be filed with the court, along with proof of service, within 30 days after filing of the notice of motion for leave. Three copies are required because the Divisional Court usually sits as a panel of three judges, but one judge alone may hear a motion for leave. In addition to the copies for the court, you will need copies for each of the other parties, as well as a copy for your own lawyer.

The responding party may file a motion record if he or she believes that the moving party's record is not complete. It must be filed with proof of service, within 15 days after the responding party is served with the moving party's record. The responding party's motion record must have a table of contents, followed by any additional material that the respondent believes should be before the court on the motion for leave. Responding parties may also file a factum, and in most cases they do.

Once all the documents are filed, the registrar fixes a date for the hearing of the motion. The Divisional Court is made up of judges from the Superior Court of Justice, but since the motion for leave cannot come before the same judge that made the order or judgment being appealed, the motion cannot be scheduled for any date that the judge will be sitting as a member of the Divisional Court.

Should the moving party be granted leave to appeal, the party must file a notice of appeal within seven days after leave to appeal has been granted.

One of the orders or judgments that cannot be appealed without leave is an order for costs. If only costs are being appealed, then a motion for leave must be brought in the usual way. But often costs are appealed along with another issue that does not require leave. An appeal that does not require leave of the court is called an **appeal as of right**. If the costs appeal is brought along with an appeal as of right, the leave to appeal costs is included in the notice of appeal as part of the relief sought. The motion for leave to appeal is then heard at the start of the appeal on the other issues and not on a separate date.

appeal as of right
appeal that a party has a legal right to bring and for which leave to appeal is not required

MOTION FOR LEAVE TO APPEAL TO THE COURT OF APPEAL: RULE 61.03.1

Rule 61.03.1 provides the procedure for bringing a motion for leave to appeal to the Court of Appeal. The procedure in many ways mirrors that of a similar motion to the Divisional Court. However, there are some differences.

A motion for leave to appeal to the Court of Appeal is usually heard in writing without any of the parties or their counsel attending before the court. However, once all the necessary documents have been filed on the motion, the court may decide to order that the motion be heard orally. If that is the case, the registrar fixes a date for the hearing and advises the parties. Since the Court of Appeal has its own filing system, do not put the court file number of the lower court on the notice of appeal. The registrar's office will assign a new file number to the case.

The notice of motion must state that the court will hear the motion in writing 36 days after service of the moving party's motion record, factum, and transcripts, or on the filing of the moving party's reply factum, whichever is earlier.

The notice of motion must be served within 15 days after the date of the order or decision that the party wants to appeal. It must then be filed, along with proof of service, with the Court of Appeal within 5 days of service. A motion record, factum, and transcripts must also be served on the respondent.

Unlike the rule regarding motions for leave to appeal to the Divisional Court, rule 61.03.1(4) spells out exactly what is to be put into a factum for use on a motion for leave to appeal. It should contain the following sections:

1. part I, identifying the moving party, the order or decision that party wants to appeal, and the content of the order or decision;

2. part II, containing a concise statement of the facts with any references to the transcripts given by page and line number;

3. part III, outlining any specific questions that will be put to the court of appeal if the motion for leave is granted;

4. part IV, containing a concise statement of each issue raised, immediately followed by a statement of the law and the citation for the authorities supporting that legal point;

5. schedule A, containing a list of all the authorities used in part IV; and

6. schedule B, containing the text of all relevant provisions of statutes, regulations, and bylaws on which the moving party is relying.

In addition, if your lawyer is relying on case law to support a legal argument, you should prepare a book of authorities containing all the cases or excerpts from the cases being relied on. There should be a list of the cases at the front of the book, and each case should be separated by a tab. Number all the pages in the book of authorities. The court must be provided with three copies, and the opposite parties are each served with one. It is also necessary to prepare a book for the lawyer arguing the motion. Books of authorities may be used on motions for leave to appeal to the Divisional Court, and they are always used on the appeal itself.

All the paragraphs in the factum should be numbered consecutively. This means that if the last paragraph in part I is number 5, the first paragraph in part II is number 6.

As with all documents that are prepared for court, the presentation of a factum is important. You should use tabs if they make the document more accessible. You should always use tabs for the schedules, even if you choose not to use them in any other part of the factum. If there are only a few authorities being used, you can put them at the back of the factum. However, if there are a lot of authorities, prepare a separate book called a "book of authorities," and put all the cases in it.

Three copies of the moving party's motion record, factum, transcripts, and book of authorities must be filed, with proof of service, within 30 days after the notice of motion has been filed.

The responding party may serve a motion record as well, if he or she is of the opinion that the moving party's motion record is incomplete. In any event, the responding party must file a factum organized as follows:

1. part I, containing a statement of the facts that identifies those facts given by the moving party that the responding party accepts and those with which the responding party disagrees (in addition, the responding party must incorporate a summary of any facts that he or she believes the moving party has not included in his or her factum, along with references to the evidence in the transcripts that supports these facts;

2. part II, containing the responding party's position with respect to each issue raised by the moving party, immediately followed by a concise statement of the law and a citation for the authorities related to the issue in question;

3. part III, containing a statement of any additional issues raised by the responding party, followed by a concise statement of the law on the issue and citations for the relevant authorities;

4. schedule A, containing a list of the citations for the authorities referred to in the factum; and

5. schedule B, containing photocopies of the portions of the relevant statutes, regulations, and bylaws on which the responding party is relying.

The factum must be laid out in the same fashion as the moving party's factum, with all the paragraphs numbered consecutively through all the parts.

Three copies of the factum, any book of authorities, and any motion record of the respondent must be filed with the court, along with proof of service, within 25 days of service of the moving party's factum and other documents. This means that you must prepare at least five copies of the documents: one for your lawyer, three for the court, and at least one for the opposite party. If there is more than one opposing party, you must prepare a separate set of documents for service on each of them.

In the event that the responding party raises a new issue, not addressed in the moving party's factum, the moving party is entitled to serve and file a reply factum within 10 days after service of the responding party's factum.

As with a motion in Divisional Court for leave to appeal a costs order that is joined to another issue that can be appealed as of right, the request for leave to appeal must be included in the notice of appeal as part of the relief sought. The panel of the Court of Appeal that hears the appeal as of right decides whether or not to grant leave on the costs appeal.

Commencement of appeals: Rule 61.04

The document that commences an appeal is a notice of appeal in form 61A, which is set out in figure 20.2. If leave to appeal is sought and granted, the moving party has 7 days to file the notice of appeal after leave is granted. On an appeal as of right, the notice of appeal must be served on all the parties within 30 days of the granting of the order or decision that is being appealed. The only exception to the 30-day rule comes into play if a statute prescribes another time limit for filing of the notice.

As with all court documents, there is no need to serve the notice of appeal on a party to an action who has been noted in default or a respondent in an application who has failed to file a notice of appearance unless that respondent was given permission by the court to participate in the hearing in which the order being appealed was made.

The notice of appeal must set out the relief sought by the appellant and the grounds for the appeal. In some cases, the notice of appeal is filed to protect the party's right to appeal. After the transcripts have been ordered, the appellant may wish to make some changes to the grounds or the relief sought. The notice of appeal may be amended without leave of the court at any time before the appeal is perfected. **Perfecting an appeal** means completing the procedural steps to ensure that the appeal is ready to be heard by the court. Perfecting an appeal is discussed in more detail later in this chapter.

perfecting an appeal
taking all the necessary procedural steps to ensure that an appeal is ready to be heard

In order to amend the notice of appeal, the appellant must serve a supplementary notice of appeal in form 61F and file it with the registrar, along with proof of service. The appellant must obtain leave of the court to rely on grounds or seek relief not specified in the original or supplementary notice of appeal.

The general heading for an appeal is different from the general heading of the case when it was in the court of first instance. The precedent for the general heading on an appeal is in form 61B. The short title of the case remains the same: in Abigail's case, the short title would be *Boar v. Rattle Motors Ltd. and Flogem*. However, in an appeal, the parties are no longer the plaintiff and the defendant. The party that commences the appeal is called "the appellant," and the party that is responding is called "the respondent." The general heading must identify which of the parties is the appellant and which is the respondent. For example, if Abigail appealed the decision of the trial judge, figure 20.3 sets out the general heading.

The court file number on the appeal is not the same as the file number in the lower court. The Divisional Court and the Court of Appeal both have their own filing

FIGURE 20.2   NOTICE OF APPEAL TO AN APPELLATE COURT (FORM 61A)

Court file no. 03-CA-1234

ONTARIO
SUPERIOR COURT OF JUSTICE

BETWEEN:

Abigail Boar

Plaintiff
(Appellant)

and

Rattle Motors Ltd. and Fred Flogem

Defendants
(Respondents)

NOTICE OF APPEAL

THE PLAINTIFF APPEALS to the Court of Appeal from the judgment of the Honourable Madam Justice Snork, dated July 12, year 3, made at Toronto.

THE APPELLANT ASKS that the judgment be set aside and judgment be granted as follows:

1. the respondent Rattle Motors Ltd. be found jointly and severally liable for the appellant's injuries along with the respondent Fred Flogem;
2. damages be awarded to the appellant in the full amount of her claim; and
3. the appellant be awarded costs of this appeal.

THE GROUNDS OF APPEAL are as follows:

1. the learned trial judge erred in finding that the defendant Rattle Motors Ltd. did not owe a duty of care to the plaintiff;
2. the learned trial judge erred in finding that the defendant did not breach the standard of care owed to the plaintiff; and
3. such further and other grounds as counsel may advise and this court permit.

FIGURE 20.2 CONTINUED

Date: July 30, year 3

Just & Coping
Barristers and Solicitors
365 Bay Street – 8701
Toronto, Ontario, M3J 4A9

I.M. Just
tel. 416-762-1342
fax 416-762-2300

Solicitors for the Appellant

TO:
Huey Sue
Barrister and Solicitor
65 False Trail
Toronto, Ontario, M6Y 1Z6

tel. 416-485-6891
fax 416-485-6892

Solicitor for the Respondents

FIGURE 20.3   GENERAL HEADING FOR APPEAL (FORM 61B)

Court file no. 03-CA-1234

COURT OF APPEAL FOR ONTARIO

BETWEEN:

Abigail Boar

Plaintiff
(Appellant)

and

Rattle Motors Ltd. and Fred Flogem

Defendants
(Respondents)

systems and issue the file a new number within that system. Therefore, initially leave the court file number blank when you prepare the notice of appeal. The file number will be given to you by the court office.

Along with the notice of appeal, the appellant must also serve a certificate in which he or she sets out the portion of the evidence that he or she believes to be required for the appeal. The precedent for this document is form 61C. Within 15 days of service of the appellant's certificate, the respondent must serve a responding certificate on the appellant in which he or she either confirms the appellant's certificate or sets out any additions or deletions that he or she wants to make. If the respondent fails to serve and file a certificate within the required time, the respondent is deemed to have accepted the appellant's certificate.

Instead of complying with the rules about the certificate of evidence, the parties may choose to consult each other and come to an agreement respecting the evidence to used on the appeal. If they choose this option, within 30 days of the service of the notice of appeal they must make the decision about which documents and portions of the transcripts will be needed for the court on the appeal. If the appellant has already placed an order for portions of the transcript that both parties agree will not be needed, the appellant may provide the court reporter with an amended order for the transcripts.

The purpose of the certificate of evidence or the agreement respecting the evidence is to cut down on the amount of documentation with which the Court of Appeal must deal. Not all the evidence given at a trial is required on the appeal because much of it covers issues that are not being appealed. These two procedures ensure that only the necessary evidence is filed with the court and that only one copy of each document is filed. Without the rule, both parties might file all the transcripts and copies of identical documents.

During the trial, a court reporter or a recording device would have taken down every word said in the courtroom. The written version of the trial is called the transcript. The appellant must order all the transcripts of the trial within 30 days of filing the notice of appeal and must file proof that he or she has ordered them. However, the appellant need only order the copies of the transcript of the evidence that the parties have agreed should be admitted on the appeal. It is important to keep the quantity of transcript to a minimum because transcripts are expensive and take a great deal of time to read. If the respondent has not agreed to the appellant's certificate of evidence and has required unnecessary additional parts of the transcript to be prepared, the court may impose costs against the respondent.

In any event, the transcript must not include:

- any challenge of the jury;

- the opening address of the judge;

- the opening and closing addresses of counsel;

- any part of the proceeding that took place in the absence of the jury, except an objection to the charge to the jury by the judge; or

- any objections to the admissibility of evidence, but the ruling of the judge on the objection is to be included.[3]

The court reporter should be aware of these automatic exclusions and not include them unless there is a court order requiring a normally excluded part of the transcript to be included. Therefore, if there is an order for inclusion, you should provide the court reporter with a copy when you order the transcript or as soon as possible after the order is made.

The transcripts are ordered through the court reporter who recorded the oral proceedings at the court of first instance. The reporter will provide you with confirmation that the transcripts have been ordered. You must order five copies for the court and a copy for yourself and each of the other parties. The transcripts of a fairly lengthy proceeding take quite a while to be prepared because the reporter must type them when he or she is not in court on other cases. Once they are complete, the court reporter will notify all the parties and the registrar in writing.

Court reporters have been instructed that once a transcript has been ordered for an appeal in the Court of Appeal, they may not suspend completion of the transcript on the request of a party. A court order is required to suspend completion except in legal aid cases.

On some appeals to the Court of Appeal, the parties do not have a different version of the facts. Instead, they are appealing the manner in which the trial judge applied the law to these facts. If there is no dispute as to the facts, the parties may file an agreed statement of facts rather than a transcript. This saves money and time in bringing the appeal before the court.

Cross-appeals: Rule 61.07

In some cases, the respondent may also want to appeal the same judgment that the appellant is setting to overturn, or the respondent may be satisfied with that judgment but wish to seek different or additional relief in the event that the appellant is successful on the appeal. The appeal of the respondent is a cross-appeal. The respondent wishing to cross-appeal must, within 15 days after service of the notice of appeal, serve a notice of cross-appeal on all parties whose interests may be affected or who are entitled to be heard.

A notice of cross-appeal is in form 61E. It must state the relief sought and the grounds for the cross-appeal and must be filed, along with proof of service, in the office of the registrar within 10 days of service. If the respondent does not deliver a cross-appeal, no cross-appeal may be heard, except with leave of the court.

Perfecting the appeal: Rule 61.09

Perfecting the appeal means completing all the necessary legal steps to ensure that the appeal is ready to be heard by the court. There are different time limits for perfecting the appeal depending on whether or not transcripts need to be ordered. If the appeal does not require transcripts, it must be perfected within 30 days after the notice of appeal was filed. If transcripts are required, the appeal must be perfected within 60 days of the court reporter's giving notice that the transcripts are available.

In addition to the oral evidence set out in the transcripts, the appellant or cross-appellant may require for the appeal any or all of the exhibits presented in the court of first instance. To obtain these exhibits for the appeal, the party must bring a motion before a judge of the appellate court seeking an order that they be sent to the registrar of the court hearing the appeal.

In order to perfect the appeal, the appellant must

(a) serve on every other party to the appeal and any other person entitled ...
to be heard on the appeal,

    (i) the appeal book referred to in rule 61.10,

    (ii) the exhibit book, if any, referred to in rule 61.10.1,

    (iii) a typed or printed copy of the transcript of evidence,

    (iv) an electronic version of the transcript of evidence, unless the court reporter did not prepare an electronic version, and

    (v) a typed or printed copy of the appellant's factum referred to in rule 61.11;

(b) file with the Registrar, with proof of service,

    (i) three copies of the appeal book, and where the appeal is to be heard by five judges, two additional copies,

    (ii) one copy of the exhibit book, if any,

    (iii) a typed or printed copy of the transcript of evidence,

    (iv) an electronic version of the transcript of evidence, unless the court reporter did not prepare an electronic version,

    (v) three typed or printed copies of the appellant's factum, and where the appeal is to be heard by five judges, two additional copies, and

    (vi) an electronic version of the appellant's factum; and

(c) file with the Registrar a certificate of perfection,

    (i) stating that the appeal book, exhibit book, if any, transcripts and appellant's factum have been filed, and

    (ii) setting out, with respect to every party to the appeal and any person entitled ... to be heard on the appeal, the name, address and telephone number of,

        (A) the party's or person's lawyer, or

        (B) if the party or person acts in person, the party's or person's name, address for service and telephone number.

Preparation of all the documentation on an appeal may cost a great deal and take a long time to prepare. Where compliance with the rules for perfecting the appeal would cause undue expense or delay, on motion a judge of the appellate court may make an order giving special instructions and direction.

When all of the above steps have been taken, the appeal is perfected. Once it has been perfected, the registrar sends both counsel a notice of listing for hearing in form 61G. This notice does not contain the date set for the appeal. Counsel are notified of the date at a later point.

Appeal book: Rule 61.10

Rule 61.10 sets out in detail the required content and organization of the appeal books. The registrar may refuse to accept any appeal book that does not comply with the rules or is not legible. The appeal book must contain, in consecutively numbered pages arranged in the following order, a copy of

1. a table of contents describing each document by its nature and date;

2. the notice of appeal and any notice of cross-appeal or supplementary notice of appeal or cross-appeal;

3. the order or decision appealed from, as signed and entered;

4. the reasons of the court or tribunal appealed from with a further typed or printed copy if the reasons are handwritten;

5. any earlier order or decision that was the subject of the hearing before the court or tribunal appealed from, as signed and entered, and a copy of any reasons for it, with a further typed or printed copy if the reasons are handwritten;

6. the pleadings or notice of application or any other document that initiated the proceeding or defines the issues in it;

7. any affidavit evidence, including exhibits, that the parties have not agreed to omit;

8. the certificates or agreement respecting evidence referred to in rule 61.05;

9. any order made in respect of the conduct of the appeal;

10. any other document relevant to the hearing of the appeal; and

11. a certificate (form 61H) signed by the appellant's lawyer, or on the lawyer's behalf by someone he or she has specifically authorized, stating that the contents of the appeal book are complete and legible.

Appellant's factum: Rule 61.11

An appellant's factum, which is set out in figure 20.4, is laid out in essentially the same form as the factum on a motion for leave to appeal, described earlier in this chapter. However, in addition to the four parts and the two schedules required on motions for leave to appeal, the factum for the appeal must contain a fifth part, stating the precise order that the appellate court will be asked to make, including any order for costs. The factum must also be signed by the appellant's lawyer or someone the lawyer has specifically authorized to sign in his or her place. In addition, the factum must contain a certificate

- stating that an order requiring the forwarding of the original record and exhibits has been obtained or is not needed, and

- stating how long the party will require for his or her oral argument on the appeal to the closest quarter hour.

Respondent's factum: Rule 61.12

The respondent must prepare, serve, and file the requisite copies of a factum as well. It must be delivered within 60 days after the service of the appeal book, transcripts, exhibit book, if any, and appellant's factum. In addition to the hard copies that must be delivered, the respondent must also file an electronic version of the factum with the court within that time period. The factum must be signed by the respondent's lawyer or someone specifically authorized by the lawyer to sign the document in his or her place. It is laid out in the same general manner as other factums,[4] but it must also contain a certificate

- stating that an order requiring the forwarding of the original record and exhibits has been obtained or is not needed, and

- stating how long the party will require for his or her oral argument on the appeal to the closest quarter hour.

FIGURE 20.4   APPELLANT'S FACTUM

COURT OF APPEAL FOR ONTARIO

BETWEEN:

Abigail Boar

**Plaintiff
(Appellant)**

and

Rattle Motors Ltd. and Fred Flogem

**Defendants
(Respondents)**

APPELLANT'S FACTUM

Part I: Nature of the appeal

1. There is an appeal by the plaintiff, Abigail Boar, from the judgment of the Honourable Madam Justice Snork, dated July 12, year 3, wherein Justice Snork dismissed the negligence action of the plaintiff and awarded costs in the amount of $72,000 to the defendants, Rattle Motors Ltd. and Fred Flogem.

Part II: Statement of facts

2. On September 14, year 0, the appellant slipped and fell on a patch of oil while a customer at the respondent Rattle Motors Ltd.'s place of business.
3. The respondent Rattle Motors Ltd. is a corporation in the business of selling automobiles to the public.
4. The respondent Fred Flogem is an employee of the respondent corporation, Rattle Motors Ltd.

(Here in consecutively numbered paragraphs set out the facts of the case in the manner of a statement of claim.)

Part III: Statement of issues and the law

7. The appellant respectfully submits that the learned trial judge erred as follows:
   a. in finding that the respondent Rattle Motors Ltd. did not owe a duty of care to the appellant, a customer in its place of business;
   b. in finding that the respondent Rattle Motors Ltd. did not breach the standard of care owed to the appellant;
   c. in finding that even if the respondent Fred Flogem had been negligent, the respondent Rattle Motors Ltd. was not vicariously liable for the actions of its employee;
   d. in finding that the actions of the respondent Fred Flogem were not the proximate cause of the appellant's injuries.

FIGURE 20.4 CONTINUED

8. It is respectfully submitted that the appellant was a customer at the place of business of the respondent Rattle Motors Ltd. and as such was owed a duty of care by that respondent.

M'Alister (or Donoghue) v. Stevenson, [1932] AC 562 (HL).
Hercules Managements Ltd. v. Ernst & Young, [1997] 2 SCR 165.

9. It is further respectfully submitted that the respondent Rattle Motors Ltd. breached the standard of care when its employee, the respondent Fred Flogem, dimmed the lights in the automobile showroom to hide the spillage of oil underneath one of the vehicles.

LeBlanc v. Marson Canada Inc. (1995), 139 NSR (2d) 309, at 312.

(Here, in consecutively numbered paragraphs, set out any further issues.)

Part IV: Order requested

30. It is therefore respectfully submitted that the appeal should be allowed, with costs, and that
   a. the respondent Rattle Motors Ltd. should be found jointly and severally liable with the respondent Fred Flogem;
   b. damages should be awarded to the appellant in the full amount of her claim; and
   c. the appellant should be awarded costs of this appeal.

ALL OF WHICH IS RESPECTFULLY SUBMITTED

I.M. Just

I.M. Just
Solicitor for the Appellant

A respondent who is cross-appealing must deliver an appellant's factum in the cross-appeal. It can be a separate factum from the respondent's factum or can be incorporated into the respondent's factum, and it must be delivered within the allowable times for delivery of the respondent's factum.

The appellant on the main appeal, who is also the respondent on the cross-appeal, may file a respondent's factum on the cross-appeal within 10 days after service of the respondent's factum.

RESTRICTIONS ON THE LENGTH OF FACTUMS

The rules require that the factum contain a "concise" summary of the facts and the applicable law. Although there is no limit on the length of a factum in the rules, a practice direction of the Court of Appeal states that factums should be no more than 10 pages and should never exceed 30 pages unless the case is exceptional. A lawyer who believes that the case is exceptional and that the factum must exceed 30 pages must get permission to file a longer factum from a judge of the Court of Appeal.

Exhibit book: Rule 61.10.1

This book is a collection of the documentary evidence, filed as exhibits, in the trial that the parties intend to rely on in the appeal. The parties can agree that certain exhibits from the trial may be omitted; however, unless both parties consent to the omission, the exhibit must be included.

The exhibit book is to be bound and laid out in consecutively numbered pages. There is to be a table of contents describing each exhibit by its nature, date, and exhibit number or letter. A copy of each exhibit must follow. The exhibits can be arranged in order of their date, or they can be arranged in groups, with similar documents sharing common characteristics grouped together. Do not arrange the exhibits by their trial exhibit numbers.

Book of authorities

Although there is no specific requirement for a book of authorities in the rules, it is helpful to both the court and the lawyers to prepare bound books containing copies of all the case law that a party will rely on in the appeal. There is a practice direction that provides guidelines for preparing these books. They should:

- include only the cases to which a lawyer intends to refer in oral argument before the court;

- indicate whether the appellant or the respondent filed them (lawyers for the parties should consult each other beforehand to ensure that they are not filing duplicate copies of cases);

- have a tab for each case with either a number or a letter on the tab;

- have an index of the cases and indicate the tab number or letter where the case can be found;

- have consecutively numbered pages unless the actual page number of each case is clear on the photocopy; and

- be filed, if possible, not later than the Monday of the week preceding the hearing of the appeal so that the judges on the panel have an opportunity to read them before the appeal.

You must prepare three or five copies of the book of authorities to be filed with the court, depending on how many judges will be sitting on the panel. Then there must be a copy for the lawyer for each of the parties.

Compendium of evidence and exhibits: Rule 61.12.1

Once the registrar has scheduled the appeal, counsel for each of the parties must file a compendium of evidence and exhibits, or the parties can agree to file one joint compendium.

The purpose of the compendium is to organize the most pertinent part of the evidence in a manner that makes it as easy as possible for the judges to focus on it. It must contain the following in consecutively numbered pages arranged in the following order:

1. A table of contents describing each excerpt from the transcript of evidence and each exhibit included in the compendium by its nature, date and exhibit number or letter.

2. The excerpts from the transcript of evidence referred to in the factum of the party filing the compendium (or in the factums of the parties, in the case of a joint compendium), and any additional excerpts from the transcript of evidence to which the party filing the compendium intends to refer during the hearing of the appeal (or to which the parties intend to refer, in the case of a joint compendium).

3. The exhibits referred to in the factum of the party filing the compendium (or in the factums of the parties, in the case of a joint compendium), and any additional exhibits to which the party filing the compendium intends to refer during the hearing of the appeal (or to which the parties intend to refer, in the case of a joint compendium). The exhibits shall be arranged in order by date (or, if there are documents with common characteristics, grouped accordingly in order by date) and not by exhibit number.

After the compendium has been filed, a party who decides that he or she wants to refer to an excerpt from the transcript or to an exhibit not contained in the compendium must serve and file the necessary number of copies of a supplementary compendium. Any supplementary compendium must be filed at least two days before the appeal.

Dismissal for delay: Rule 61.13

A notice of appeal must be filed within 30 days of the making of the order being appealed. Sometimes a lawyer for a party files the notice to protect the party's right to appeal, but the party may decide not to proceed. In other cases, a party may file a notice of appeal as a tactical matter in order to create a delay. The party does not order the transcript as required and may delay in perfecting the appeal.

In such instances, either the respondent or the registrar may take procedural steps to dismiss the appeal for delay. The respondent may make a motion to the registrar to dismiss the appeal with 10 days' notice to the appellant.

However, the registrar does not need to wait for the respondent to take action. Where the appellant has not

- filed a transcript within 60 days after the court reporter has provided written notice that it is ready,

- perfected the appeal within one year of filing the notice of appeal, or

- perfected the appeal within 30 days of filing the notice of appeal where no transcript is needed for the appeal,

the registrar may serve notice on the appellant to correct the default within 10 days, or the appeal will be dismissed.

Within the 10 days following the service of the respondent's motion or the registrar's notice, the appellant must perfect the appeal, order the transcript or obtain an order from the court providing him or her with an extension of time in which to take these steps. If the appellant does nothing, the registrar will dismiss the appeal for delay and award costs to the respondent.

It is not only the appellant who must act in a timely fashion on the appeal. If the respondent has brought a cross-appeal and has not delivered a factum on the cross-appeal within 60 days after he or she has been served with the appeal book, the appellant may make a motion to have the cross-appeal dismissed for delay. The respondent has 5 days in which to file the factum or obtain an order for an extension of time. If the respondent does neither, the registrar will dismiss the cross-appeal with costs.

Similar consequences apply to a party who does not act in a timely fashion on a motion seeking leave to appeal. If the moving party has not served and filed a motion record and other documents within 60 days of filing the notice of motion, the registrar may give notice to the moving party to file the record and documents within 10 days. If the defect has not been cured within 10 days, the registrar will dismiss the motion for leave with costs.

The responding party on the motion for leave need not wait the 60 days for the registrar to take action. If the motion record and other documentation has not been filed within 30 days of the notice of motion being filed, the responding party may bring a motion, on 10 days' notice, to dismiss the motion for leave (rules 61.03(2) and 61.03.1(4) to (6)). Once again, the appellant has 10 days to correct the defect or obtain an order for an extension of time. If he or she does neither, the registrar will dismiss the motion for leave to appeal with costs.

Abandoned appeals: Rule 61.14

After filing the notice of appeal, if the appellant decides that he or she does not wish to continue with it, the proper thing to do is to file a notice of abandonment in form 61K. A party who serves a notice of appeal but does not file it with the court within 10 days of service is deemed to have abandoned the appeal. A party who abandons an appeal or a cross-appeal may be liable for costs to the opposite party or parties.

If the main appeal has been dismissed for delay or abandoned, and a cross-appeal has been commenced, the respondent on the main appeal must deliver a notice of election to proceed with the cross-appeal in form 61L or bring motion to the court for directions. Otherwise, the cross-appeal will be deemed to be abandoned without costs.

Motions in appellate court: Rule 61.16

In the event a party finds it necessary to bring a motion relating to the appeal to the appellate court, parts of rule 37,[5] the general rule for motions, and rule 61.16 govern. The two rules must be read together.

There are a number of different types of motions that may be made in an appeal. Some of the motions are heard by only one judge of the appellate court. Others are heard by a panel of judges.[6] Motions in appellate courts are commenced in the same manner as other motions — that is, with a notice of motion. The notice of motion for an appellate court must, however, include a certificate stating how long the party estimates the motion will take. The notice must be served and filed at least three days before the motion is to be heard. A motion record must also be served and filed along with a factum.

If a motion is to be heard by more than one judge, the notice of motion should not set a date but should rather state that the motion is to be heard on a date to be fixed by the registrar. The registrar then arranges for a date when a panel of judges is sitting and notifies the parties.

APPEALS FROM INTERLOCUTORY ORDERS AND OTHER NON-APPELLATE COURT APPEALS

Rule 62 deals with the procedure on appeals of interlocutory orders. Appeals of this type of order lie either with a judge of the Superior Court of Justice or with the Divisional Court.

If the order being appealed is an interlocutory order of a master, a certificate of assessment of costs, or an appeal under any statute that does not specifically require another procedure for appeal, the appeal will proceed to a single judge of the Superior Court of Justice. Unlike an appeal of a final order, it will not proceed to an appellate court. Interlocutory orders that fall within any of these three categories may be appealed without leave.

If the order being appealed is an interlocutory order of a judge of the Superior Court of Justice, the appeal must be heard by the Divisional Court. However, there is no automatic right to appeal an interlocutory order of a judge. A party that wants to appeal this type of order must bring a motion seeking leave to the Divisional Court. Since the judges of the Divisional Court are the same as those who sit in the Superior Court of Justice, the judge hearing the motion for leave must be different from the judge who made the order being appealed.

The procedure on these appeals is different from the procedure on appeals of final orders, which we looked at earlier under rule 61. Rule 62.01 deals with the procedure on the appeal of interlocutory orders that do not require leave. Rule 62.02 sets out the procedure on seeking leave for appeal, when leave is required.

Commencement of the appeal

If the appeal does not require leave, it is commenced by serving a notice of appeal on all parties whose interests may be affected by the appeal. The prescribed form is form 62A. The notice of appeal must be served within seven days of the making of the order being appealed. The notice must then be filed with the court, along with proof of service, no later than four days before the appeal is to be heard.

The notice of appeal must set out the relief sought and the grounds of the appeal. The grounds must be specific and only those grounds stated in the notice may be relied on at the hearing unless the presiding judge orders otherwise. Therefore, the grounds must be carefully drafted and be as comprehensive as possible.

When determining which court must hear the appeal, you must look at rule 37.03, which governs the place of hearing of motions. The requirements for determining the place in which a motion on notice must be heard apply to this type of appeal. The appeal must be commenced in the same place where the original proceeding was commenced, where any party resides, or where the solicitor of record for any party has his or her office.

Material for use on the motion

The appellant must prepare, serve, and file both an appeal record and a factum. These must be filed in the court office, along with proof of service, at least four days before the hearing of the appeal.

Rule 62.01(7) sets out the required contents of an appeal record. It must contain, in consecutively numbered pages,

- a table of contents describing each document, including each exhibit, by its nature, date, and exhibit number, if there is one;

- a copy of the notice of appeal;

- a copy of the signed and entered order or certificate of costs appealed from, along with a copy of any reasons for judgment relating to the order or certificate; and

- any other material used at the hearing at which the order being appealed was made, which is necessary for the hearing of the appeal.

The contents of the appeal record must be set out exactly in the order listed above. The appeal record must also have a blue back cover, not the buff-coloured back cover required for appeals to appellate courts.

The title of proceedings does not change for this type of appeal, except that the words "plaintiff" and "defendant" are changed to "appellant" and "respondent." If there is more than one defendant and the appeal does not involve all of them, the names of those involved must be underlined in the title of proceedings.

The respondent must also prepare a factum and any other material that was before the judge who made the order being appealed, which is necessary for the hearing of the appeal and which has not been provided by the appellant in his or her appeal record. The factum and the additional material must be served and filed with the court at least two days before the hearing of the appeal.

The judge hearing the appeal may dispense with the requirements of the parties to file any or all of this material.

If the appellant commences the appeal by serving and filing the notice of appeal and then decides not to proceed with it, he or she should serve and file a notice of abandonment. If the appellant does not file the necessary documentation on the appeal at least three days before the hearing date, he or she will be deemed to have abandoned the appeal.

Motions for leave to appeal

If the order being appealed is an interlocutory order of a judge of the Superior Court of Justice, leave is required to bring the appeal and the prospective appellant must serve a motion within seven days after the order to be appealed was made. Rule 62.02 sets out the procedure on the motion for leave to appeal.

It is usually quite difficult to obtain leave to appeal. Leave will not be granted if one of the tests in rule 62.02(4) is met.

In preparing a motion record for leave to appeal, it is not necessary to reproduce an entirely new motion record. Remember, what is being appealed here is likely an order made on a motion. The original motion record may be requisitioned for the motion for leave. A supplementary motion record should then be prepared, containing the notice of appeal, a copy of the order being appealed, and any reasons given by the judge for making the order.

Both parties must serve and file factums on the motion. These must be filed in the court office at least two days before the hearing.

If the motion is successful and leave to appeal is granted, the moving party, who now becomes the appellant, must serve and file a notice of appeal as required by rule 61.04, along with the appellant's certificate of evidence required by rule 61.05(1). This must be done within seven days after the order granting leave to appeal is made.

STAYS PENDING APPEAL: RULE 63

During the appeal process, orders for the payment of money, other than orders for family support, are usually stayed or suspended. Only a judge of the appellate court can order that the judgment remain in effect while it is being appealed. Without such an order, the order appealed from is automatically stayed, and it cannot be enforced.

A respondent may bring a motion to have an automatic stay lifted while the appeal is winding its way through the system. The court may lift the stay totally or partially on terms that are just.

If the order being appealed is an order for relief other than the payment of money, the order is not automatically stayed when the appeal commences. A party may apply to the appellate court or to the court that made the order being appealed, however, to request a stay during the appeal. If a stay is ordered, it may be varied or set aside later through motion.

The stay comes into effect when the notice of appeal is filed, or the order granting it is made. Once the stay takes effect, no enforcement action can be taken. In order to ensure that the sheriff's office does not commence enforcement on a stayed order, a party may requisition a certificate of stay from the registrar of the court that granted the stay or the court to which the appeal was taken. This certificate can then be filed with the sheriff's office to notify the sheriff that he or she may not take any further enforcement action until the stay is lifted. If the stay is granted by an order, particulars of the order must be included in the certificate. A certificate of stay is in form 63A.

CHAPTER SUMMARY

This chapter has dealt with appeals and rules 61, 62, and 63, which govern the procedure for appeals. We have seen that rule 61 governs appeals of final orders, rule 62 governs appeals of interlocutory orders, and rule 63 governs stays pending an appeal. We have noted that there are three courts that may hear appeals in Ontario: the Superior Court of Justice, the Divisional Court, and the Court of Appeal. The *Courts of Justice Act* sets out the types of appeal that each court may hear, and we have provided an overview of the courts' jurisdiction.

We have addressed the matter of commencing an appeal, with or without the necessity of seeking leave. We have noted the various time limits and procedures in this regard. An appeal must be perfected before it is ready to be heard. An appeal is perfected when the appellant has taken all the procedural steps, including the service and filing of such material as an appeal book, an exhibit book, the transcript, and a factum. Finally, we have examined automatic stays of orders under appeal and the lifting of such stays by means of motion.

KEY TERMS

court of first instance

appellate court

appellant

respondent

final order

interlocutory order

leave of the court

transcript

appeal as of right

perfecting an appeal

NOTES

1 An objection to an assessment may be made pursuant to rule 58.10.

2 Ibid.

3 Practice direction of the chief justice of Ontario, May 1, 1993.

4 See rule 61.12 for specific detail of the content of the respondent's factum on an appeal.

5 Rules 37.02 to 37.05, 37.07(6), 37.08, 37.10, and 37.17 do not apply to motions to an appellate court.

6 See rule 61.16(2), (2.1), and (2.2).

REFERENCES

Courts of Justice Act, RSO 1990, c. C.43.

Rules of Civil Procedure, RRO 1990, reg. 194.

REVIEW QUESTIONS

1. What is the difference between a final and an interlocutory order?

2. What factors determine which court will hear an appeal?

3. What three courts hear appeals?

4. What types of appeals are heard in the Superior Court of Justice?

5. What types of appeals are heard in Divisional Court?

6. What types of appeals are heard in the Court of Appeal?

7. Identify the court to which the following judgment or orders should be appealed:

    a. a decision by a judge that Widgets Inc. has breached its contract with John Doe and that John should be awarded $60,000;

    b. a decision by a master to permit an amendment of a pleading after pleadings have closed;

    c. a decision by a Small Claims Court judge to award the plaintiff $1,500 in damages caused by his neighbour's negligence;

d. a decision by a judge at the end of trial that the defendant is not liable for the plaintiff's claim of $100,000;

e. a decision by a judge at the end of trial that the defendant is liable for the plaintiff's claim but awarding the plaintiff only $20,000; and

f. a decision by a judge of the Superior Court to strike out a jury notice after hearing the motion brought by the defendant.

8. Where does the Ontario Court of Appeal sit?

9. How much time do you have to serve a motion for leave to appeal to the Divisional Court? What rule applies?

10. How is a factum for leave to appeal to the Court of Appeal arranged? What rule applies?

11. What document commences an appeal?

12. How long does an appellant have to order the transcript for an appeal?

13. Your law firm is appealing a matter to the Court of Appeal and needs some of the exhibits from the trial. How do you obtain them?

14. In an appeal to the Divisional Court, must the respondent file a factum?

15. A party does not wish to continue with an appeal after filing a notice of appeal. How does the party terminate the appeal process?

DISCUSSION QUESTION

1. The defendant, Global Steel Works Inc., wishes to appeal a decision of the Superior Court of Justice. The decision ordered it to pay its former employee, Romeo Capulet, $250,000 for wrongful dismissal. Draft a general heading for the notice of appeal.

CHAPTER 21

Case management

INTRODUCTION

What is it?

Before the introduction of case management, lawyers, and to some extent their clients, determined the pace at which a case moved forward. Once originating process was issued, lawyers could waive many time limits imposed by the rules. For example, the statement of defence is due 20 days from the time the statement of claim is served in most cases. Defence counsel would often ask for, and get, an extension of time, simply as a matter of courtesy. And so the case would progress, at a stately and leisurely pace. The court was passive, waiting for lawyers and litigants to take the next step.

The result was that cases could take a long time to get to trial, particularly if one litigant or the other decided to employ delaying strategies, or one of the lawyers had many files on the go. Lawyers used to joke about files so old that they had moss growing on their north side.[1] In addition, there was the natural tendency among many lawyers to procrastinate about getting things done. As a student, you may be familiar with this tendency and will appreciate how it could prevent a case from moving forward quickly to trial.

These kinds of delays did not matter all that much in judicial regions where the volume of cases was low. But in larger centres, such as Toronto, it created problems. Because lawyers controlled the pace a case took getting to trial, individual decisions about when a case was to move forward at various stages of the proceeding resulted in uneven flows of cases through the court system. This created backlogs at points where court time was needed: at motions and at trial. In Toronto, a case could take a year or more getting to trial. In addition, because the court was not proactive in assisting the parties to explore settlement in a rational way, settlement was often left to the last minute, with a deal being struck at the courtroom door. This approach to settlement was wasteful for both the court system and the litigants. If a deal had been explored earlier in the process, much time and money might have been saved for the litigants. For the courts, a last minute settlement often meant collapse of the trial list because the next cases on the list were not necessarily ready to start immediately. This sometimes resulted in empty courtrooms and judges with nothing on their schedule for the day — hardly a good use of public funds.

Case management is an attempt to solve problems of cost and delay and to promote settlement at earlier stages by having the court intervene and oversee the case as it moves along, making procedural decisions and ensuring that the case adheres to a timetable so that it either settles or comes to trial within a reasonable time.

case conference

conference managed by the case management judge or master, who controls timetables and settles all procedural matters

mandatory mediation

process in which disputants are required to allow a neutral third party to facilitate their communication and assist them in negotiating a settlement

Under the case management system, once a proceeding is commenced, the plaintiff must select a track (fast or standard) with a timetable to which the litigants *must* adhere unless the court agrees to change it. The case is assigned to a case management master or, in some cases, a judge who may call a **case conference** to discuss changes to the timetable, make orders enforcing time limits, discuss settlement, and deal with a host of procedural issues. A party can also request a case conference. The case management masters and judges have powers to enforce strict compliance with set timetables, but they can also alter timetables if circumstances warrant.

Once the first defence[2] is filed, the parties are obliged to enter into and complete **mandatory mediation**, within strict time limits, early in the proceeding. This gives the parties an opportunity to explore settlement before spending time and money on what may turn out to be unnecessary litigation. It also diverts cases from the courts at an early stage, lessening the burden on the court system.

Motions are simplified and less formal than in the ordinary system. Often something that would be the subject of a motion may be disposed of informally at a case conference.

Settlement conferences are now automatic and mandatory, following mediation. Within 150 days of filing the first defence in a fast track action, and within 240 days in a standard track, all discoveries must be completed. Parties must be prepared to seriously discuss settlement and will be assigned a trial date if settlement discussions fail. In Toronto, the trial date is set when the settlement conference is scheduled.

There is an optional trial management conference to narrow issues and promote speedy trials.

Purpose of the rule

In stating the purpose of the rule, we can do no better than to quote rule 77.02 in its entirety:

> 77.02 The purpose of this Rule is to establish a case management system throughout Ontario that reduces unnecessary cost and delay in civil litigation, facilitates early and fair settlements and brings proceedings expeditiously to a just determination while allowing sufficient time for the conduct of the proceeding.

What's in?

Although rule 77.02 speaks of all of Ontario, at the time of writing, case management applies only in the following areas:

- all civil cases commenced in the Superior Court in Ottawa and the municipalities around it that formerly constituted the Regional Municipality of Ottawa-Carleton (now called the City of Ottawa); the province has reserved the right to name other areas at a later date by listing them in the schedule referred to in rule 77.01(1);

- all civil cases commenced in the former Municipality of Metropolitan Toronto and present City of Toronto before July 1, 2001 and randomly assigned to case management by the court registrar; and

- all civil cases commenced in the Superior Court in the City of Toronto after July 1, 2001, subject to some exceptions.

It is also open to the court under rule 77.01(1.1) and rule 77.11 to bring cases that are not case managed into case management. While the language is broad enough to bring a case anywhere in Ontario into case management, it would be hard to do this outside Toronto or Ottawa. Presumably the rule contemplates cases in Toronto and Ottawa that are not case managed. In Toronto, a system of **call-over courts** has been established with the aim of bringing all cases in Toronto into case management by 2004. The call-over courts are discussed in more detail later in this chapter.

What's out

The case management rules do not apply to cases commenced outside Toronto and Ottawa. Within Toronto and Ottawa, rule 77.01(2) also excludes certain types of cases. Simplified procedure cases under rule 76 are also excluded from case management under rule 77.[3] A summary of the types of exclusions is set out below, but when considering whether a case is within the case management rules, you should read rule 77.01(2) carefully, because it is likely that the rule will be amended frequently.

Exclusions to the case management rules include:

- some Superior Court family law cases in Toronto and Ottawa that are subject to family law case management rules or are otherwise excluded;

- commercial list actions in Toronto, which go on a separate civil trial list before judges with a commercial litigation background;

- a variety of estate, guardianship, and trust proceedings, many of which are governed by statutory procedural rules in addition to the *Rules of Civil Procedure*;

- mortgage actions;

- construction lien proceedings, which are governed by procedural rules and time limits found in the *Construction Lien Act*;

- bankruptcy proceedings, where there is a prescribed procedure dictated in part by the *Bankruptcy and Insolvency Act*;

- class proceedings, unless certification as a class proceeding has been denied; and

- simplified proceedings under rule 76.

call-over courts
temporary courts set up in Toronto to bring all cases commenced before July 2001 into the case management system or otherwise to ready them for trial or settlement

TRANSITION RULES

Most civil cases commenced after July 3, 2001 became subject to case management. However, on that date, there were approximately 46,000 cases underway in Toronto that were not case managed. What should be done with these cases? They are not suitable for standard case management treatment because the timetables that are an essential feature of case management operate from the time proceedings commence. The solution seemed to be to review each case, to close the court file on those that have settled or on those in which there has been no activity, and to use a modified case management system to move the others to trial quickly.

Call-over court

Between July 2001 and the end of 2004, courts will send out notices to the solicitor of record in all cases that are not case managed with a form that must be completed by counsel and returned to the court seven days before the call-over court date. If the solicitor of record indicates that the case has been settled, no one need appear, and the court will close the court file. If the case has not settled and has not been placed on the trial list within two years of the filing of a defence, the call-over court may act as if it were holding a status hearing under rule 48.14. In this situation, it may dismiss the proceeding for delay unless the matter is set down for trial within 90 days after service of the notice. The court may also inquire into the reasons for delay and set out a timetable for bringing the action to trial. If the action is proceeding, the court may establish a timetable or fix the date for a pretrial conference or for a trial.

The form to be completed by counsel is set out in figure 21.1 (at the end of the chapter) along with the notice for attendance. If no one completes the form, the case is placed on the speedy trial list under rule 48.09 on the date set out on the notice of attendance. This is not a process that lawyers or litigants may dodge. Every party who receives a notice must appear by counsel or in person if not represented. If the case has settled, all counsel must confirm this when the notice is returned to the court either on the notice itself or by filing a consent. But they need take no further action since the court will close its file. In all other cases, counsel must complete the call-over court notice, return it to the court within seven days of the scheduled hearing, and attend the hearing. The parties must then provide information about the status of the case by completing page 2 of the notice to attend. At the hearing, the court determines how the case is to proceed. It appears that this court aims to move the case onto a timetable to complete the pretrial stages and if it is ready for trial, get it on the trial list. Counsel should be prepared to set court dates, including dates for a pretrial conference and for trial.

If no one files a notice or attends call-over court, the matter remains listed on the transition trial list. It then comes up for scheduling at the transition trial court and is called to trial. If no one appears, the case is dismissed.

Presumably, the call-over courts will become extinct by 2004, when all cases have been transferred or otherwise made to disappear.

COMMENCEMENT OF PROCEEDINGS

The steps taken when proceedings commence are somewhat different from those in an ordinary proceeding. Originating process is the same as in an ordinary proceeding, but there are differences.

Forms prescribed by rule 77, including notices, certificates, and orders referred to in the rule, may be single spaced and do not require backsheets (rule 77.05(2)). The idea behind this is to save paper and reduce the size of court files to save storage space.

When commenced as part of a main proceeding, third party proceedings keep the same court file number as the main proceeding but have a suffix added. For example, if the main case number is CM1234, the third party proceeding is identified as CM1234-A (rule 77.05(1)).

When a notice of action or statement of claim is issued, the party files the pleadings as in an ordinary action along with form 14F, "Information for Court Use." There is a place on the form to check off that rule 77 applies and that the plaintiff is choosing either the fast or the standard track. The former requirement to file a notice of commencement of proceedings, but not the pleadings, was revoked.[4]

The plaintiff must choose a track on which the case is to proceed. The criteria for choosing is set out in rule 77.06(6). In general, fast track cases

- have simpler facts or issues of law,

- involve issues that are of importance to the parties rather than the public,

- have few parties,

- will not require much intervention by the case management master, and

- will not have lengthy discoveries.

All other cases go on the standard track.

While the initial choice is the plaintiff's, the defendant has the opportunity to move to change tracks, but he or she must do so before the close of pleadings or within 10 days of the filing of the respondent's affidavit. By that time, the defendant has the basic outline of the case before him or her and has enough information to decide which track is appropriate.

The choice of track involves different time limits.

Within 90 days on the fast track and within 240 days on the standard track from the filing of the first defence, the plaintiff must complete all productions of documents, discovery, and all motions arising from discovery and be ready for a settlement conference. Not later than 10 days before the settlement conference, the plaintiff must serve and file a settlement brief. The defendant must respond to this by filing his or her settlement brief within 5 days of the settlement conference.

Defendants serve on the plaintiff and file in court a statement of defence or notice of intention to defend just as in a regular action.

Commencement of proceedings sets the clock running

Issuing a claim or commencing an application sets timetables and deadlines running. Because the times allotted for completing pretrial procedures and getting a matter to trial are shorter and under the control of the courts, a lawyer must be careful about when to commence proceedings. In the days before case management, lawyers issued claims before they completed their investigation and research, and they did repair work on the pleadings later if required, adding parties and amending claims or defences. But with the timetable out of their hands, there may not be time to correct mistakes if, for example, the time for completing discoveries has passed, and the matter is being set down for a pretrial conference. Lawyers are now advised to complete as much of their investigative and research work on a case as possible before commencing proceedings, unless a limitation period is about to expire. Once a proceeding is commenced, it is expected to move from stage to stage within the time allowed by the case timetable.

CASE TIMETABLE
Deadlines that arise when proceeding commences

Once a claim is issued, regardless whether or not it is served, three time limits begin to run:

1. the six-month period to serve a statement of claim pursuant to rule 14.08(1);

2. the 180-day period in which either a defence must be filed or a default judgment must be obtained, failing which the registrar will dismiss the action as abandoned pursuant to rule 77.08; and

3. the 180-day period in which a timetable must be agreed to by all parties, or a case conference must be convened to impose one.

Periods of 180 days or six months may sound like a lot of time, but they are not. Consider what happens if you have difficulty in serving the claim after it is issued. If the claim is unliquidated and not defended, the plaintiff will need time to move for an assessment of damages under rule 19.05. Consider what will happen if you have several defendants to serve, some of whom are overseas and may have up to 60 days to file a defence. You could easily run up against the 180-day limit without having been able to obtain a default or undefended judgment. You then run the risk of having the registrar dismiss your action. You can see why you should do as much preparation ahead of time, before issuing your claim. And once having issued it, move to serve it as quickly as possible.

Deadlines that arise when the first defence is filed

If you serve some of the parties but not all of them, you may run into a second problem. A second set of time limits begins to run when the first defence is filed, regardless whether some defendants have not yet been served:

1. Within 30 days from the date the first defence is filed, the parties must name a mediator; if they fail to do so, the court will appoint one pursuant to rule 24.1.09(5).

2. Within 90 days from the filing of a first defence, the parties must complete mandatory mediation or, in the case of standard track cases, consent to an extension of time for mediation.

3. Within 150 days, the parties must complete all production and discovery and motions arising from discovery in fast track actions.

4. Within 240 days, the parties must complete all production and discovery and motions arising from discovery in standard track actions.

To put it succinctly, you have 240 days from the filing of the first defence to complete all pretrial proceedings in most cases. In a straightforward case with one plaintiff and one defendant where no motions are necessary, this is not a difficult timetable to meet. But if the case is factually and legally complex, there are multiple parties, difficulties with service, and disputes about procedure, 240 days may be very tight indeed.

Defendants and timetables

It is not only the plaintiff who must move quickly once proceedings have commenced. The defendant has even less room to manoeuvre. Because the registrar must dismiss an action if no defence has been filed and the case has not been disposed of within 180 days of the claim issuing, the plaintiff cannot extend extra time for filing a defence.

If a defendant does not have counsel at the time a claim is served, the defendant may put off retaining counsel until near the end of the time for filing a defence. This leaves little time for the defendant's newly retained counsel to conduct necessary research and investigate the matter before issuing a statement of defence. There may be a need to make crossclaims against other defendants, or a counterclaim against the plaintiff. Since these are part of the main action, they are all subject to the main action timetables on which time is already beginning to run. This in turn creates a situation where counsel will need to ask a **case management judge or master** to extend the time for filing a defence, and extend other running time limits. Asking for more time creates an extra procedural step, which makes for more cost and delay. But the important point is that someone other than counsel is overseeing the progress of the case and preventing it from getting bogged down, as often used to be the situation when a simple case became complex.

case management judge or master
court official assigned to each case managed case to ensure court control over the case on its way to trial

Because a third party proceeding, spawned from the main action, brings in a new party, the proceeding is subject to a separate timetable. It gets a case file number that is the same as that in the main action, but it has a letter added at the end to distinguish it, while keeping the two proceedings linked.

Because timelines start to run when the claim issues, it is important to do as much investigation and negotiation, including mediation, before it is required under rule 24.1. In this way, if negotiations fail, you will have done all the necessary preliminary work and will have possibly selected a mediator so that you are ready to move within the timelines set by rule 77, when the action commences.

Case management timetable

Once the case is underway under case management, the court expects to see the parties create a case management timetable. Initially, under rule 77.10(2), it is the responsibility of the plaintiff to do this when a mediator files a report or when an order exempting the case from mediation has issued. The purpose of the timetable is to set up a "schedule for the completion of one or more steps required to advance the proceeding" (rule 77.03). This means that dates may be set for the delivery of affidavits of documents, examinations for discovery, other types of discovery, or motions. Here, the parties can set their own timelines, provided that they fit them within the boundaries set by the rules. For example, depending on the track chosen, the timetable must provide for the completion of discoveries and related motions within 150 or 240 days after the first defence is filed and within 10 days before the settlement conference (rule 77.10(4)). Within those 150 or 240 days, the parties are free to arrange discoveries as they see fit. But remember to be realistic about allowing enough time to carry out the steps required in the case. Lawyers, as well as other folk, often underestimate the time required to complete a series of tasks, and it is important to stay within the deadlines established under rule 77 and other rules.

Timetable must comply with deadlines in the rules

If a timetable is filed that does not comply with the rules, the court has the power to call a case management conference to review and, if necessary, impose a timetable that complies with rule 77. The timetable should at least take the parties to completion of discoveries and right up to the settlement conference within the 150- or 240-day time limits. The parties cannot themselves extend the time limits in the rules.

Customizing the timetable and extending the deadlines in the rules

If the parties think they are going to need more time than the fast or standard track provides to complete pretrial procedures, rule 77.10 gives the court power on a motion by a party, or on the motion of a case management judge or master, to convene a case conference. At the conference, a timetable can be arranged. If the parties are uncooperative, they can be subject to sanctions.

In changing or customizing the case management timetable, counsel should be aware that some rules trigger automatic dismissal and that some timelines are running simultaneously. For example, if a lawyer is moving to extend time for mandatory mediation, he or she must also remember to extend other rule 77 times, such as the date for completing pretrial discovery before scheduling a case conference. Otherwise, lawyers may give themselves enough time for mediation but not leave enough time to complete discoveries. They then need to ask for a second case management conference.

Time requirements

Case management time requirements, and any time requirement in any rule, may be extended or abridged only by order of a case management judge or master. The key time requirements are set out below.[5]

Within 180 days from the commencement of proceedings:

1. The plaintiff must file a timetable agreed to by all parties or request a case conference to establish one (rule 77.10(2)).

2. If no defence is filed, the plaintiff must obtain default judgment or an order extending time for filing a defence by motion or case conference, or the registrar will dismiss the action (rule 77.08).

3. If the statement of claim is not served in six months, an order is required to extend time for service.

Within 30 days from the filing of the first defence:

1. The parties must name a mediator and provide the name to the mediation coordinator or obtain an order from the case management judge or master to extend the time for doing this; otherwise, the mediation coordinator will appoint a mediator, who will unilaterally set a date for mediation (rule 24.1.09(6) and (7)).

Within 90 days from the filing of the first defence:

1. The parties must complete a mandatory mediation session. In standard track cases, you may extend the time to do this on consent, or you may obtain an order. In fast track cases, you must obtain an order (rule 24.1.09(1) and (3)).

2. Rule 24.1 (mandatory mediation) requires the parties to file a statement of issues with the mediator, and the plaintiff must file a copy of the pleadings at least seven days before the first mediation session. Failure to comply with the requirements for mandatory mediation will result in a certificate of non-compliance, which automatically triggers an appearance before a case management judge or master.

Within 150 days for fast track actions and 240 days for standard track actions from the filing of the first defence:

1. The parties must complete all production and discovery and all motions arising from discovery and be ready for a settlement conference (rule 77.14(1) and (2)).

2. At least 10 days before the date of the settlement conference, the plaintiff must file a settlement conference brief, including a witness list with a summary of evidence to be given by each witness. All other parties must file their brief and witness list within 5 days of the settlement conference (rule 77.14(4) to (6)).

3. If the parties are not ready for a settlement conference, the court will schedule a case conference, revise the timetable, and possibly set sanctions.

At least 90 days prior to trial:

1. Each party must deliver any expert reports on which he or she intends to rely at trial (rule 53.03(1)).

At least 60 days before trial:

1. Each party must deliver responding expert reports on which he or she intends to rely at trial (rule 53.03(2)).

2. Each party must answer any undertakings if he or she wishes to rely at trial on the information that is the subject of the undertakings (rule 31.07(2)).

At least 30 days before trial:

1. Each party must deliver any supplementary experts' reports on which it intends to rely at trial (rule 53.03(3)(b)).

At least 7 days before trial:

1. The trial record must be filed (rule 77.14(8)).

2. Notice must be given under s. 35(3) of the Ontario *Evidence Act* regarding introduction of records made in the ordinary course of business.

Missing a time limit often triggers a case conference, which can occur automatically or at the instance of another party. This in turn can lead to the imposition of timetables or to sanctions, raising costs for your client. Rule 77 procedures and time limits will cause lawyers to introduce a form of case management to their office operations to control their practice. Gone are the days when lawyers take on all files that come in the door. It will be much more important to manage the flow of cases in the office, so that the lawyer is able to meet all deadlines, and does not end up, for example, with two cases being tried back to back, while he or she is trying to complete discoveries in a third and schedule mediation in a fourth. This will be particularly problematic for sole practitioners, who do not have a stable of associates or articling students to hand work to. Case Management Master MacLeod has set out 10 ideas to make case management work:

1. *Complete all research and investigation before you commence proceedings.*

2. *Once the claim issues, serve it immediately because time limits start running.*

3. *Once all parties have appointed counsel, try to get agreement on an early timetable.* If extensions of times beyond the limits in the rules are required, be ready to apply for an order.

4. *Watch your time limits.* Use ticklers with multiple time warnings — for example, at one month, two weeks, five days, two days, and one day before a deadline.

5. *Organize documentary production.* Organize production as soon as possible, and seek extensions over the 10-day time period where necessary.

6. *Consider the timing of mediation.* After the first defence is filed, you must name a mediator in 30 days and complete mediation in 90 days. This may be too short a time for mediation to work in some cases. Consider applying for an order to extend time, and be careful to extend other times that will be affected by the extension of mediation.

7. *Consider the timing of discoveries and the need for post-discovery motions.* It may not be possible to complete discoveries in 150 or 240 days of the filing of the first defence if, for example, there are a dozen defendants. Consider applying to extend the time.

8. *Consider using requests to admit facts and documents to narrow issues before trial.* Consider also whether you can proceed by stated case, with an agreed statement of facts, in whole or in part.

9. *Continue to watch time limits.* If the case timetable is becoming unrealistic, consider obtaining the consent of all parties to schedule a case conference and revise it or revise it on a consent motion.

10. *Focus on results.* Avoid useless procedural wrangling. The court is likely to be far less tolerant of delaying tactics than it was before mandatory case management was put in effect.

Case timetable forms

There is no prescribed form for setting out a case timetable. Lawyers have therefore been creating their own forms, such as the one for standard track actions, which appears as figure 21.2, and the one for fast track actions, which appears as figure 21.3 (at the end of the chapter). These forms have been completed and show realistic times between stages in an action.

MOTIONS

Rule 77.12 provides special rules governing motions in the case management system. To the extent that this rule conflicts with rule 37, which sets out motion procedures generally, the specific procedures in rule 77.12 prevail. There are certain unique features to motions under case management. Generally, the case management judge or master assigned to a case hears all motions. As part of the "hands-on" management by the court, a judge or master may initiate a motion if neither party does. More routine motions may be brought informally in a case conference without serving documents or making complicated scheduling arrangements. Some motions, such · as a motion to change tracks, must be brought within specific time periods. There is an abbreviated check-off motion form, form 77C, that is used on case-managed motions, and generally there is less documentation required. There is usually no need to draft, issue, or enter an order after a decision has been rendered.

Motions made before case management judge or master

Once a case is commenced, a case management judge or master must hear all motions. Motions that were within the master's jurisdiction under rule 37.02(2) must be brought before a case management master. Motions that are within the exclusive jurisdiction of a judge must be brought before a case management judge.

A case management master is assigned to the case to oversee its progress to trial or settlement. The assignment usually takes place when a case conference is convened, a party proposes to bring a motion, or a party asks for a review of a proposed case timetable. When the case is commenced, it is automatically assigned to a team of judges, and judges from that team hear the motions. In exceptional cases, the senior regional judge may assign a single judge to manage the action, and that judge will hear all motions. In some cases, the regional senior judge may assign a single judge and master or two masters to case manage a complex case (rules 77.04 and 77.09.1).

Motions before specific judicial officers

There are some motions, however, that must be brought before specific judicial officers. If you believe that your case falls under rule 77.09.01, requiring the appointment of a specific judge to manage the case and hear motions, you must bring your motion before the senior regional judge to request that a specific judge be appointed. Certain motions concerned primarily with procedural matters, which are either unopposed or on consent, may be brought before the registrar under rule 77.12(5). . The registrar must then make the order requested. This removes routine motions from the usual case management motion procedure designed for contested motions. The types of motions that may be brought before the registrar include motions to amend pleadings, add parties, or remove a solicitor from the record, provided that they are on consent or unopposed. The complete list of included motions is set out in rule 77.12(5) 1, i to ix. The registrar may also make orders on motions where no responding material is filed. This presumably identifies the motion as unopposed.

However, a responding party on a case-managed motion is not required to file a case management motion form, even if opposing a motion (rule 77.12(2.1) and (2.2)). This may be a drafting oversight, and it would be unsafe to assume that all motions on which no material is filed should be treated as unopposed. A call to responding counsel will soon settle the matter.

It is also clear that in some circumstances under rule 77.11(2), a case management judge or master may initiate hearings that will lead to orders of a type usually associated with motions. For example, rule 77.10(7) provides that where the parties have failed to comply with a timetable, the judge or master may strike out pleadings filed by the non-compliant party.

Where motions are brought

If a case commences under case management, the motion is brought before the case management judge or master to whom the case is assigned. This overrides rule 37, which requires that a motion be brought where the responding lawyer resides or where an unrepresented responding party resides.

Case management motion procedure

In some cases, procedural matters may be resolved without bringing a formal motion, even where the issue is contested. If no case conference had been held and no case management master has been formally assigned, you would usually need to call a case conference to have a master or judge assigned to manage the case and to hear the motion. Then you would need to schedule the motion and argue it in a separate proceeding. But you can use the case conference and rule 77.13(5) and (6) to ask the case management judge at a case conference to make procedural orders and give directions on procedural issues.

The first case conference may also be used to discuss the scheduling of a longer or more complex motion, possibly eliminating or narrowing some issues. You should raise the possibility of a long motion at the first opportunity at a case conference so that the master will have the opportunity to schedule it at an early and convenient date.

Where a long motion is in respect to refusals to answer questions or honour undertakings on discovery, you must complete and file a chart that sets out the details of each objection or unanswered undertaking. The chart must be in the form indicated in schedule B of the Toronto Motions Practice Direction Advisory (see the appendix to chapter 9, Motions). An example of the chart is provided in table 14.4 in chapter 14, Discovery.

Saving trees: Form 77C

A motion under case management uses form 77C, which appears at first glance to be a document requiring little creative drafting. In fact, it does allow for persuasive writing. In addition, you are not prohibited from providing additional information and attaching other documentation. Rule 77.12(2.1) contemplates that a motion may be made without supporting material or a motion record. However, most counsel want to attach an affidavit to set out supporting facts, and it is probably wise to attach the pleadings to sketch out the basic facts and positions of the parties. The responding party may want to file evidence in the form of an affidavit or may want to file a responding party's motion form, but there is no requirement that this be done.

Once a motion has been decided, rule 77.12(8) indicates that no formal order need be issued and entered, unless there is an appeal or the presiding judicial officer requires an order to be issued and entered. The judicial officer's endorsement on the motion form is the only necessary notation, and this form usually stands in for a written order.

An example of a case management motion form in form 77C is set out in figure 21.4 (at the end of the chapter).

Costs on a motion

Rule 77.12(4) requires counsel to address costs at the end of the motion. This is not new, but this rule contemplates that the judicial officer hearing the motion will fix costs at the end of the motion and order them payable forthwith. In a contested complex motion, it is a good idea to prepare a bill of costs and include receipts for disbursements so that counsel can make a complete and convincing argument on the costs issue.

Scheduling motions

Motions concerned with discovery and productions must all be completed at least 10 days before a settlement conference (rule 77.10(5)). As for the time for filing motions, the old requirement of three days' notice under rule 37 is gone, replaced by the requirement of rule 77.12(2) that form 77C be submitted to the court before the motion is heard. However, the scheduling of motions in case management cases in Toronto is subject to the provisions for scheduling motions in the Toronto courts, as set out in the Motions Practice Direction Advisory (see the appendix to chapter 9, Motions).

CASE CONFERENCE
What the case conference does

The case conference is the device used to steer a case-managed proceeding. It creates a forum where a case management judge or master can do whatever is necessary to keep a case moving forward effectively. In particular, it allows a judge or master to

- resolve issues arising under mandatory mediation;

- make procedural orders, even where no motion has been brought;

- arrange for a motion on a fixed hearing date;

- create or revise a case timetable, extending or abridging time for completing pretrial tasks;

- make arrangements for related actions and third party proceedings to be settled or tried together;

- engage in settlement discussions, if appropriate, at an early date before a formal settlement conference;

- narrow issues and establish agreed facts; and

- oversee the readying of a case for trial so that a fixed trial date remains realistic.

How and when to convene a case conference

There is no single prescribed method or time for convening a case conference. A case conference can be convened at the request of any party — for example, when a party wishes to bring a motion or on the initiative of a judge or master.

Rule 77 sets out some circumstances where the court can compel parties to attend a case conference on the initiative of either party or the court.

1. *Rule 77.10(1).* If a party fails to meet a time limit established by rule 77, a case management judge or master will convene a case conference.

2. *Rule 77.10(2) and (3).* This is the rule that a case timetable must be established once mediation is completed or dispensed with. If the plaintiff has not proposed one and no other party has acted, the court will initiate a case conference.

3. *Rule 77.10(6).* If the timetable turns out to be unrealistic or the parties are otherwise not meeting timetable requirements, a case management judge or master may convene a case conference to amend the timetable or sanction uncooperative parties.

4. *Rule 77.11(2).* This is the catch-all rule that covers the general oversight function of case management judges and masters. These judges and masters can call case conferences at any time in connection with any case management matter, including failure to comply with the rules.

5. *Rule 24.1.13.* If a party has refused to comply with the mandatory mediation rules, the mediation coordinator must refer the problem to a case management judge or master, who may convene a case conference to establish a mediation timetable, or make punitive orders for non-compliance, including striking out pleadings, dismissing actions, and awarding costs.

If no case management judge or master has been appointed to your case because there has been no need for a case conference or motion, you will need to call the case management appointments and scheduling clerk. The clerk will advise you which master is assigned to handle the case. You will then need to book the case management conference through the assigned master's registrar.

When a party requests a case conference, some masters require completion of a request for a case conference form. If you must use the form, the reason for the case conference should be stated concisely and without argument. The purpose of the form is to give notice of the issues to other parties and the case management master. An example of a request for a case conference form is set out in figure 21.5 (at the end of the chapter).

Once a case conference is initiated, the master's office sends a copy of a notice to attend a case conference to the plaintiff's lawyer, who is then responsible for serving copies on counsel for other parties and on unrepresented parties. An example of a notice to attend a case conference in person is provided in figure 21.6.

An example of a notice to attend a case conference by telephone conference call is set out in figure 21.7. (Both figures appear at the end of the chapter.)

Case management judge or master

When a situation arises requiring a case conference, the party seeking it needs to consider whether a judge or master is required. If, for example, a lawyer is bringing a motion that only a judge can hear, you should make that clear to the case management scheduling office. There is a team of case management judges, and one will be assigned to hold the case conference, hear the motion, and hear all subsequent motions. Usually, however, an assigned master will handle case management matters until trial. In some circumstances, where a case is complex, has many parties, involves several related proceedings, or has other peculiarities, a particular judge, two judges, or a judge and a master can be assigned to manage the case under rule 77.09. This can be done on consent of all parties or on a motion brought by any party.

Making effective use of case conferences

The case conference is designed to make the litigation process more efficient, and less expensive. To make good use of the conference, lawyers and legal staff need to prepare for it. An early meeting of counsel may avoid the need for convening case conferences. When a case conference is called, counsel with carriage of the file in your office should attend. Alternatively, another lawyer must be thoroughly briefed so that the conference time is not wasted. The lawyer should bring his or her calendar or scheduler so that conflicts can be avoided. A calendar is also necessary if you are seeking to extend time or amend the timetable or if another party is doing so. Lawyers may wish to consider holding the case conference by conference telephone call. This may be done by pre-arrangement with the case management master's registrar or by submissions in writing.

Powers of case management judges and masters

Masters' powers are not as extensive as judges' powers. Under rule 77.11(1), either can extend or abridge a timeline, transfer a proceeding from one track to another, adjourn a case conference, set aside an order made by a registrar, and generally make orders to carry out the purposes of rule 77. In addition, a master may make a procedural order, on consent of the parties refer a matter to alternative dispute resolution, and convene a settlement conference. A judge may do all of the things a master may do and in addition may convene a hearing and give directions for trial. Rule 37 does not fade into the sunset: A master's jurisdiction on motions is subject to the same limitations under case management as in motions that are not case managed.

SETTLEMENT CONFERENCE

The settlement conference is much like a pretrial conference in that it is designed to promote settlement before trial. But there are significant differences. Under rule 50, a pretrial conference is an option, but under rule 77.14 a settlement conference is mandatory, and so is the timing. Rule 77.14(1) says that the registrar is required to give 45 days' notice of the date of the settlement conference, which is to occur no later than 240 days after the first defence is filed for standard track actions (150 days for fast track actions). In Toronto, the practice is that the registrar sends out a notice for a trial-scheduling court appearance, at which both the settlement conference date and the trial date are fixed.

The settlement conference is usually held far enough ahead of the date fixed for trial that trial preparation, and the attendant preparation costs, have not yet been incurred. This means significant savings for the client if the case settles at the settlement conference.

Completion of pretrial steps before settlement conference

The reason why lawyers must keep track of the timing of the settlement conference is that they cannot continue to conduct pretrial proceedings, such as motions, after the settlement conference. Rule 77.14(2) requires that all examinations, production of documents, and motions arising out of examinations and productions are to be completed before the settlement conference. If that does not seem to be happening, a case conference is necessary to alter the timetable. There must be a good reason — something other than procrastination or sloth — because the case management judge or master can refuse the extend the time or apply cost penalties. The idea behind this rule is that the parties should have had full disclosure so that they know and can assess their own cases and their opponent's before discussing settlement at a settlement conference.

You should also be sure to have all medical and other expert witness reports completed and available since rule 77.14(6)(d) requires such reports to be exchanged before the settlement conference.[6]

Settlement conference brief

In order to give structure and focus to settlement conferences, all parties are required by rule 77.14(4) and (5) to file a settlement brief. The plaintiff's brief and certification under rule 77.14(2) that all discoveries and related motions have been completed must be delivered not later than 10 days before the settlement conference, with the defendant's due not later than 5 days before the settlement conference. If the parties need more time to file a settlement brief, particularly a defendant responding to issues in the plaintiff's brief, he or she should ask to convene a case conference to extend the time.

Contents of the brief

Rule 77.14(6) lists what should be in the brief:

- a concise summary of the facts, including agreed upon facts, which helps to distinguish between facts that are admitted and facts that must be proved at trial;

- a concise summary of the legal issues and the law to be relied on in the form of legal principles and their authorities, such as cases;

- a list of witnesses and a summary of each witness's evidence;

- relevant portions of transcripts, experts' reports, and other documentary evidence to be adduced at trial; and

- pleadings, including any particulars produced as a result of a demand for particulars.

The defendant's brief is shorter, consisting of anything the plaintiff omitted from his or her brief. Although the rule is silent, the brief should be cirlox-bound, have covers, and have a table of contents. It is also a good idea to include tabs for each section of material.

The contents of the brief allow a case management judge or master to know enough about the case to give a reasoned opinion on the parties' chances of success at trial, the likely costs, and the amount of time the trial will take.

Who attends the settlement conference?

Rule 77.14(3) is clear: In order to get anything done on settlement, counsel need instructions to make a deal. The lawyer with carriage of the file should be present and so should the client or a representative of the client with authority to settle the lawsuit. The conferences are scheduled to last about an hour. If more time is needed, it should be arranged through a case conference or should be spoken to in trial-scheduling court. A settlement conference is not like mediation, where the focus is on getting parties to talk their way to a deal regardless of their legal rights. A settlement conference is based on an assessment of the rights of the parties, with the case management judge or master giving views on the outcome. With properly prepared briefs, oral submissions should not be lengthy, and the conference should not take long.

Orders arising from the outcome of a settlement conference

Ideally, the only order that should arise is an order for dismissal of the action in accordance with the terms of a settlement or an order fixing a trial date for fast track actions in Toronto and for both fast and standard track actions in Ottawa in accordance with rule 77.14(7).[7] However, a case management judge or master may also make procedural orders to carry out the intent of rule 77, including ordering a case conference or trial management conference. Figure 21.8 (at the end of the chapter) sets out the practice direction regarding Toronto region trial scheduling.

TRIAL MANAGEMENT CONFERENCE

Rule 77.15 governs the trial management conference. Unlike the settlement conference, the trial management conference is optional. It may be convened at the request of a party or on the initiative of the trial judge or a case management judge or master once a trial date has been set.

The trial management conference is likely to be used when the settlement conference has not resulted in a clear picture of what will happen at trial. As noted earlier, the settlement conference is held when disclosure is complete and before trial preparation has been commenced. It is not until trial preparation is well underway that counsel decides which witnesses will be called, which facts will be admitted on a request to admit, and which facts can generally be agreed to without formal proof. The trial management conference is likely to be used in cases where one side is uncooperative or inefficient in making full disclosure, where several related cases have been joined together for trial, or where a case is complex.

Whoever is presiding over the trial management conference may exercise the powers that all judicial officers may exercise at a case management conference under rule 77.11. In addition, there are powers to ensure the parties organize the presentation of evidence in the most effective way. Before the conference is held, the plaintiff and defendant must file form 77D, the trial management conference form, at least 4 days before the trial management conference is held. If no trial management conference is convened, the form must be filed at least 14 days before trial. A review of the forms filed by the case management judge or master, or the trial judge, may identify issues that need to be resolved, and the filing may result in a judicial official convening a trial management conference if no party has requested one. The form is useful in requiring parties to think carefully about the evidence to be used, the issues outstanding, and the time it will take to try the matter. Each party completes its own form, and the picture is not complete until both plaintiff and defendant have filed their respective forms. It is important that the information on the form be complete and accurate. A sample of form 77D is set out in figure 21.9 (at the end of the chapter).

OTTAWA

Case management under rule 77 also operates in civil cases in Ottawa. However, there are some differences in practice. These distinctions may evolve over time, but at the time of writing the principal ones are set out below.

The rule does not mandate a case conference request form, but Ottawa has created one for all cases. It is simpler than the ones some case management masters in Toronto have developed for their own use (see figure 21.5). The Ottawa form is set out in figure 21.10 (at the end of the chapter).

Rule 77.10, requiring plaintiffs to file a timetable or request a case conference within 180 days of the commencement of proceedings, does not apply in Ottawa.

Motions are heard on Tuesday and Thursday mornings or by teleconference at other times. Motions must be confirmed with a motion confirmation form two days before the day of the motion. Factums and books of authorities are not required, but an outline of the summary of the argument is suggested. Dispositions are not faxed to parties. Copies can be obtained from the court file or from a computer in the civil filing office.

Settlement conference briefs are required by rule 77.14. Although there are no penalties specified in that rule, in Ottawa failure to file will result in a plaintiff's action being dismissed and a defendant's defence being struck out.

CHAPTER SUMMARY

This chapter introduced you to the mandatory case management procedure for most civil actions in Toronto and Ottawa. Case management was introduced to help reduce cost and delay in civil litigation and to reduce case volumes in the overcrowded Toronto and Ottawa courts. We noted that once a proceeding commences, plaintiffs must select a fast or standard track for the proceeding. The track imposes fixed deadlines before which various steps in the proceeding must be completed. Cases are assigned to case management masters or judges, who hear all motions and generally oversee the case. The case management authorities have the powers to enforce compliance with set timetables and to amend those timetables in appropriate cases.

The case management system has a simplified procedure for motions, allowing some motions to be made informally at case conferences. All motions involve minimal paperwork. Settlement conferences are now automatic and mandatory. If a case fails to settle, a specific trial date will be fixed by a trial-scheduling court, usually before the settlement conference is held. To ensure trials are conducted effectively, there is an optional trial management conference to narrow the issues, arrange for the effective presentation of evidence, determine who the witnesses will be, and decide how long the trial will take. Some difference between practices under rule 77 in Toronto and Ottawa were identified. An overview of the process is set out in figure 21.11 (at the end of the chapter) in the form of a case management checklist. It has been left blank so that you can make use of it in practice if you wish.

KEY TERMS

case conference

mandatory mediation

call-over courts

case management judge or master

NOTES

1 Delay in the courts is nothing new. Charles Dickens's novel *Bleak House* involves an estate litigation case, *Jarndyce v. Jarndyce*, that went on for more than a generation, with lawyers dying or retiring and being replaced by others, until most of the beneficiaries were dead, and the estate had been consumed by legal fees. This is a fictional and extreme example, but it shows that problems with cost and delay have been constant. A large part of the cause is attributed to delaying tactics and procrastination by the legal profession. The 19th-century reform that attacked this problem was the abolition of the Court of Chancery, combining law and equity in one superior court. The late 20th-century solution has been case management, which transfers control of how a case progresses from the lawyers to the courts.

2 The phrase "first defence" contemplates actions where there are several defendants filing separate defences as well as cases with only one defendant or one statement of defence for several defendants.

3 Simplified procedure cases were originally included under rule 77 but then excluded as of January 2, 2002. Rule 76 cases have their own form of case management.

4　O. reg. 457/01, which was proclaimed on December 22, 2001 and came into force on January 2, 2002. It was not surprising to find that when the courts opened after New Year's Day, there was a certain amount of confusion.

5　Adapted from C. MacLeod, "Commencing an Action and the Key New Concept: The Early Timetable," in *Civil Litigation — 100% Case Management Alert*, Advocates' Society conference, held in Toronto, May 31, 2001.

6　Rule 53.03 requires a report prepared by an expert witness that a party intends to call at trial to be served on the other parties 90 days before trial.

7　In Toronto, the trial-scheduling court sets the date for trial and the settlement conference in standard track actions.

REFERENCES

Bankruptcy and Insolvency Act, RSC 1985, c. B-3, as amended.

Construction Lien Act, RSO 1990, c. C.30.

Evidence Act, RSO 1990, c. E23.

MacLeod, C., "Commencing an Action and the Key New Concept: The Early Timetable," in *Civil Litigation — 100% Case Management Alert*, Advocates' Society conference, held in Toronto, May 31, 2001.

O. reg. 457/01.

Rules of Civil Procedure, RRO 1990, reg. 194.

Short, Donald, "Case Timetable (Fast Track)," in *Civil Litigation — 100% Case Management Alert*, Advocates' Society conference, held in Toronto, May 31, 2001.

Short, Donald, "Case Timetable (Standard Track)," in *Civil Litigation — 100% Case Management Alert*, Advocates' Society conference, held in Toronto, May 31, 2001.

REVIEW QUESTIONS

1.　Why was case management introduced in Toronto and Ottawa?

2.　What are the key features of case management?

3. What cases does case management cover?

4. What specific procedures must you follow when commencing a proceeding?

5. What time limits are set by the fast and standard tracks?

6. What do defendants have to do in a case-managed proceeding that is different from what they usually have to do?

7. When do the time limits in case management begin to run?

8. What is included in a case timetable?

9. Once a case timetable is set, is it rigidly fixed?

10. What needs to be done within 180 days of the commencement of proceedings?

11. What must be done after the filing of the first defence?

12. What is the procedure for bringing motions in case management?

13. For what purposes is a case conference convened and by whom?

14. How and when is a case conference convened?

15. What powers can case management judges and masters exercise in a case conference?

16. What are the principal features of a settlement conference?

17. What is the purpose of a trial management conference?

18. How does the application of rule 77 in case-managed proceedings in Ottawa differ from the application of the rule in Toronto?

DISCUSSION QUESTIONS

1. Read and respond to the following memorandum:

   To: E. Egregious, law clerk
   From: I.M. Just, lawyer
   Re: *Boar v. Rattle Motors Ltd. et al.*

   We have served our statement of claim, which was issued on January 4, year 2, and we have asked that the case be on the standard track in Toronto. Huey Sue is acting for both defendants and served us with his statement of defence on January 12, year 2. Because the date to choose a mediator is fast approaching, I would like to have a case conference convened to discuss early implementation of a case timetable. Please find out who we call to schedule a case conference and assign a case management master to this case, and then prepare a draft request for a case conference. Even though all masters don't require this, I think it is a good idea to use one. Also prepare a draft case timetable that fits sensibly within the standard track that I can use as a basis for discussion at the case conference.

2. Return to discussion question 2 in chapter 9 and reread I.M. Just's memorandum about Diedre Kuflesnout's engineering report. Respond to the memorandum, drafting the appropriate documents to bring the relevant motion under case management in Toronto. Also let I.M. Just know what is necessary to bring the matter before the case management master.

FIGURE 21.1   CALL-OVER COURT FORM

TORONTO REGIONAL SENIOR JUSTICE'S CALL-OVER COURT
And/or STATUS NOTICE PURSUANT TO RULE 48.14

ACTION NO: **NOTICE TO ATTEND**

Superior Court of Justice

NOTICE: **All counsel and unrepresented parties to this action are required to attend the Call-Over Court fixed for:**

DATE:
TIME:
PLACE:

Please answer the following questions [where applicable] and return this form to:

MARY D'EON, Transition Co-ordinator
393 University Avenue, 19th Floor
Toronto, Ontario, M5G 1E6
Fax Number: 416-327-4350

1) List all counsel or self-represented parties:

NAME:	NAME:
ADDRESS:	ADDRESS:
PHONE NO:	PHONE NO:
FAX NO:	FAX NO:
PARTY REPRESENTED:	PARTY REPRESENTED:
NAME:	NAME:
ADDRESS:	ADDRESS:
PHONE NO:	PHONE NO:
FAX NO:	FAX NO:
PARTY REPRESENTED:	PARTY REPRESENTED:
NAME:	NAME:
ADDRESS:	ADDRESS:
PHONE NO:	PHONE NO:
FAX NO:	FAX NO:
PARTY REPRESENTED:	PARTY REPRESENTED:

If more space is required, please attach a separate sheet.

FIGURE 21.1   CONTINUED

ACTION NO:

1) Is this action settled?   YES ☐   NO ☐

If the action is settled **ALL** counsel and self-represented parties must confirm this in writing and return the consent with this form.   Otherwise, personal attendance is required.   Counsel are not required to gown.

2) If not settled – what is the status of <u>this action</u> and <u>any other related proceeding</u>?

Comment: _____

<u>**ACTION NO. OF ALL RELATED PROCEEDINGS:**</u> _____

_____

   a) Pleadings completed?   YES ☐   NO ☐

   b) Affidavits of documents completed?   YES ☐   NO ☐

   c) Discovery completed?   YES ☐   NO ☐

   d) Experts reports available?   YES ☐   NO ☐

3) Any Motions intended to be brought?   YES ☐   NO ☐

   <u>If yes</u> –   What Motions?   _____

               Under which rules?   _____

4) Is this action ready for a pre-trial conference?   YES ☐   NO ☐

5) Is this action ready for a trial?   YES ☐   NO ☐

6) Have the parties attended mediation?   YES ☐   NO ☐

7) Approximately how long will the trial take?   _____ Days

8) JURY ☐   NON-JURY ☐

9) Has the action been affected by Bankruptcy or other transmission of interest?   YES ☐   NO ☐

Please Note: There will not be any adjournments of the Call-Over Court date. The Transition Unit does not have the authority to adjourn court dates, only the Call-Over Court judge may do so.

FIGURE 21.1 CONTINUED

NOTICE

All actions for which no form is returned and no person attends at Call-Over Court will be placed on the speedy list under Rule 48.09 for trial on

Date:
At 10:00am

At the Court House
361 University Avenue
Toronto, Ontario M5G 1T3

A court list indicating the number and location of the courtroom will be posted in the lobby on that date.

Failure to attend for trial on this date may result in dismissal of this action and an order for costs may be made against you.

INFORMATION LINE NUMBER: 416-327-3898

CALL-OVER COURT FORM – FEBRUARY 2001

FIGURE 21.2 **CASE TIMETABLE FOR STANDARD TRACK ACTION**

Court File No. ___03___ ___/2001_____

ONTARIO SUPERIOR COURT OF JUSTICE

D. SHORT

Plaintiff(s)

- and -

A. LINE

Defendant(s)

CASE TIMETABLE [STANDARD TRACK]

X **AGREED**

☐ **DATES TO BE RESOLVED**

A. Date Action Commenced: ___July 10, 2001_____ + 180 days = ___January 6, 2002_____
(Last Date to File Timetable)

Date First Defence Filed: ___September 4, 2001___ + 240 days = ___April 25, 2002_____
(Last Date for Settlement Conference)

B. Enter dates by which the various steps are to be completed. Ensure that sufficient time is allowed to accomplish the step. If counsel cannot agree on an element enter "To Be Resolved" and then each party should prepare and attach a separate schedule setting out their position on the items that cannot be agreed upon for submission to the court. The Court may by Order extend any time period.

1.	Mediator Selected By [within 30 days of First Defence]:	Date: October 1, 2001
2.	Affidavits of Documents Exchanged By:	Date: November 15, 2001
3.	**Mediation Completed By [within 90 days of First Defence] [60 more days available Rule 24.1.09(3)]:**	**Date: November 30, 2001**
4.	Discoveries Completed By:	Date: February 5, 2002
5.	Undertakings/Refusals Completed By:	Date: April 4, 2002
6.	Discovery Motions Completed By:	Date: April 29, 2002
7.	Other: PLAINTIFF'S EXPERT REPORT	Date January 15, 2002
8.	**Settlement Conference Completed By: (Max. 240 days from first defence unless Court varies)**	**Date: April 25, 2002**

TIMETABLE DATE: ___September 9, 2002_____

FIGURE 21.2   CONTINUED

Counsel to sign to evidence agreement to above schedule. Signed schedules to be exchanged with other counsel and copies of schedule to be filed at Court Office.

Counsel for Plaintiff(s):   Counsel Defendant 1:

(party)   D. Short _____   (party)   A. Line _____

(name)   _____   (name)   _____

(sgd)   _____   (sgd)   _____

(date)   _____   (date)   _____

(firm)   Tried and True _____   (firm)   Dewey Cheetham & Howe _____

(phone)   _____   (phone)   _____

(fax)   _____   (fax)   _____

(email)   _____   (email)   _____

Counsel for Defendant 2: _____   Counsel Defendant 3: _____

(party)   _____   (party)   _____

(name)   _____   (name)   _____

(sgd)   _____   (sgd)   _____

(date)   _____   (date)   _____

(firm)   _____   (firm)   _____

(phone)   _____   (phone)   _____

(fax)   _____   (fax)   _____

(Email)   _____   (email)   _____

IN THE MATTER OF UNRESOLVED DATES:

CASE CONFERENCE DISPOSITION *(If necessary)*

1.   The dates entered on the above Case Timetable in the areas previously noted "To Be Resolved" and initialed by me above are hereby established for this case.

2.

_____   _____

Date   Case Management Master

FIGURE 21.3   CASE TIMETABLE FOR FAST TRACK ACTION

Court File No.   04   /2001

ONTARIO SUPERIOR COURT OF JUSTICE

D. SHORT

Plaintiff(s)

- and -

S. SWEET

Defendant(s)

CASE TIMETABLE [FAST TRACK]

X   **AGREED**

☐   **DATES TO BE RESOLVED**

A.   Date Action Commenced: July 10, 2001_____ + 180 days =   January 6, 2002_____
                                                                    (Last Date to File Timetable)

Date First Defence Filed: September 4, 2001___ + 150 days =   ___February 1, 2002____
                                                                    (Last Date for Settlement Conference)

B.   Enter dates by which the various steps are to be completed. Ensure that sufficient time is allowed to accomplish the step. If counsel cannot agree on an element enter "To Be Resolved" and then each party should prepare and attach a separate schedule setting out their position on the items that cannot be agreed upon for submission to the court. The Court may by Order extend any time period.

1.   Mediator Selected By [within 30 days of First Defence]:   Date: October 1, 2001

2.   Affidavits of Documents Exchanged By: Date: October 15, 2001

3.   **Mediation Completed By [within 90 days of First Defence]**   **Date: November 30, 2001**
      [60 more days available Rule 24.1.09(3)]:

4.   Discoveries Completed By: Date: December 3, 2001

5.   Undertakings/Refusals Completed By: Date: January 15, 2001

6.   Discovery Motions Completed By: Date: January 25, 2002

7.   Other: Date: N/A

8.   **Settlement Conference Completed By: (Max. 150 days from**   Date: February 1, 2002
      first defence unless Court varies)

TIMETABLE DATE: __September 10, 2001_____

FIGURE 21.3 CONTINUED

Counsel to sign to evidence agreement to above schedule. Signed schedules to be exchanged with other counsel and copies of schedule to be filed at Court Office.

Counsel for Plaintiff(s):		Counsel Defendant 1:	
(party)	D. Short	(party)	S. Sweet
(name)	Joe Blow	(name)	Huey Dewey
(sgd)		(sgd)	
(date)		(date)	
(firm)	Tried and True	(firm)	Dewey Cheetham & Howe
(phone)		(phone)	
(fax)		(fax)	
(email)		(email)	

Counsel for Defendant 2:		Counsel Defendant 3:	
(party)		(party)	
(name)		(name)	
(sgd)		(sgd)	
(date)		(date)	
(firm)		(firm)	
(phone)		(phone)	
(fax)		(fax)	
(email)		(email)	

IN THE MATTER OF UNRESOLVED DATES:

CASE CONFERENCE DISPOSITION *(If necessary)*

1.   The dates entered on the above Case Timetable in the areas previously noted "To Be Resolved" and initialed by me above are hereby established for this case.

2.

_____   _____
Date   Case Management Master

FIGURE 21.4 CASE MANAGEMENT MOTION FORM (FORM 77C)

Court file no. 01-CV-1234

ONTARIO
SUPERIOR COURT OF JUSTICE

BETWEEN:

Abigail Boar

Plaintiff

and

Rattle Motors Ltd. and Fred Flogem

Defendants

CASE MANAGEMENT MOTION FORM

JURISDICTION ❏ Case management judge
☒ Case management master

THIS FORM FILED BY *(Check appropriate boxes to identify the party
filing this form as a moving/responding party on this motion AND to
identify this party as plaintiff, defendant, etc. in the action)*

☒ moving party
❏ Plaintiff _____
❏ responding party
❏ defendant/respondent name _____
❏ other — specify kind of party and name _____

MOTION MADE

❏ on consent of all parties   ❏ on notice to all parties and
                                        unopposed

❏ without notice   ☒ on notice to all parties and
                                        expected to be opposed

Notice of this motion was served on: October 6, year 2.
by means of: service on the solicitor for the defendants by
courier.

METHOD OF HEARING REQUESTED

☒ by attendance
❏ in writing only, no appearance
❏ by fax
❏ by telephone conference under rule 1.08
❏ by video conference under rule 1.08

Date, time and place for attendance or for telephone or video conference

September 16, year 1, at 10:00 a.m., Court House,
393 University Avenue, Toronto, Ontario, M5G 1Y8

FIGURE 21.4 CONTINUED

ORDER SOUGHT BY THIS PARTY *(Responding party is presumed to request dismissal of motion and costs)*

❑ Extension of time — until *(give specific date)*: _____
❑ serve claim/application   ❑ file or deliver defence
❑ complete discoveries
❑ other _____
❑ Assignment of proceeding (and related proceedings if applicable) to judge(s) for case management.
☒ Other relief — be specific

1. The plaintiff seeks an order permitting Eldred Klump, lighting engineer, to inspect the level of lighting in the automobile showroom operated by the corporate defendant at 1240 Bay Street, Toronto, Ontario, M8H 0K8 on such terms and times as the court considers just.

2. The costs of this motion.

MATERIAL RELIED ON BY THIS PARTY

☒ this form   ☒ pleadings   ☒ affidavits - specify
❑ transcript — specify   ❑ other — specify

Affidavit of Eldred Klump, sworn October 3, year 1

GROUNDS IN SUPPORT OF/IN OPPOSITION TO MOTION (INCLUDING RULE AND STATUTORY PROVISIONS RELIED ON)

There is an issue between the parties as to the adequacy of lighting in the corporate defendant's showroom, and it is necessary to carry out an inspection of the corporate defendant's premises to examine the lighting, pursuant to rule 32 of the *Rules of Civil Procedure*, in order to determine that issue.

CERTIFICATION BY LAWYER

I certify that the above information is correct, to the best of my knowledge.

Signature of lawyer *(If no lawyer, party must sign)*

I.M. Just   *LSUC #17888Q*

Date: September 4, year 1

FIGURE 21.4 CONTINUED

THIS PARTY'S LAWYER *(if no lawyer, give party's address for service, telephone and fax number)*	OTHER LAWYER *(if no lawyer, give other party's name, address for service, telephone and fax number)*
Name and firm I.M. Just, Just & Coping	Name and firm Huey Sue
Address 365 Bay Street – 8701 Toronto, Ontario, M3J 4A9	Address 65 False Trail Toronto, Ontario, M6Y 1Z6
Telephone 416-762-1342	Telephone 416-485-6891
Fax 416-762-2300	Fax 416-485-6892

DISPOSITION BY CASE MANAGEMENT JUDGE/MASTER

❑ order to go as asked ❑ adjourned to

❑ order refused ❑ order to go as follows:

_____

_____

_____

_____

Hearing method _____ Hearing duration _____ min.

Heard in: ❑ courtroom ❑ office

❑ Successful party MUST prepare formal order for signature

❑ No copy of disposition to be sent to parties

❑ Other directions — specify

_____

_____

	Judge's/Master's	Judge's/Master's
Date _____	Name _____	Signature _____

FIGURE 21.5   REQUEST FOR CASE CONFERENCE

		Court House
Master Albert's Chambers	Chambres des Pronotaire Albert	393 University Ave.
Superior Court of Justice	Cour suprieure de justice	Toronto, Ontario
Toronto Region	Région de Toronto	M5G 1E6

Registrar: (416) 326 3272
Facsimile: (416) 326 5416

Request for Case conference with Master Albert

Court file number: _____

Short Title of Proceeding: _____ v. _____
Date of request: _____

Party requesting case conference:
- Name of party: _____
- Plaintiff, defendant, third party, etc? _____
- Counsel (name, address, telephone and fax): _____
  _____
  _____
  _____
  _____

Purpose of case conference (if seeking to vary an order, attach a copy):

_____

_____

_____

_____

Proposed participants in case conference:

Party (plaintiff, defendant)	Name of Counsel	Counsel's Phone/Fax
_____	_____	_____
_____	_____	_____
_____	_____	_____

>>

(To be completed by registrar):   **Date and time of case conference appointment:** _____

Appearance _____ **or** **Telephone Conference Call** _____

If tel. conference call, telephone arrangements to be made by _____ .

FIGURE 21.6   NOTICE TO ATTEND CASE CONFERENCE IN PERSON

Court File Number: _____

SUPERIOR COURT OF JUSTICE

_____ v _____

NOTICE CONVENING A CASE CONFERENCE
(Appearance)

TAKE NOTICE that pursuant to Rule 77.13(1) of the Rules of Civil Procedure, you must attend a case conference before Master Albert in this proceeding and all related proceedings on _____, _____, at 393 University Avenue, 6th Floor, to discuss the issues raised in the litigation and to establish an appropriate timetable to meet the requirements of Rule 77 in this proceeding and any third and fourth party and other related proceedings.

COUNSEL AND UNREPRESENTED PARTIES in this proceeding and any third or fourth party or other related proceedings are required to participate in the case conference. In the event counsel cannot participate, it will be their responsibility to brief and arrange for fully informed alternate counsel to participate. At the case conference a timetable will be established or if one is in place it will be reviewed to ensure that the requirements of Rule 77.14 are met and any necessary consequential orders will be made.

THOSE PARTICIPATING must have with them calendars reflecting the future availability of counsel, parties and witnesses and should be fully familiar with the proceeding and its conduct to date. They must be prepared to schedule future events and discuss the issues in dispute.

COUNSEL FOR THE PLAINTIFF SHALL FORTHWITH SERVE A COPY OF THIS NOTICE on all counsel and unrepresented parties in this proceeding and all related proceedings to whom the notice has not been directed as set out below. If you have any questions please contact my registrar, Annette Bidlofsky, by telephone at (416) 326-3272 or by fax at (416) 326-5416.

DATED at Toronto _____.

_____

Master Carol Albert, Case Management Master

TO: _____, *solicitor for the plaintiff*

FAX: _____

FIGURE 21.7   NOTICE TO ATTEND CASE CONFERENCE BY TELEPHONE

Court File Number: _____

SUPERIOR COURT OF JUSTICE

_____ v _____

NOTICE CONVENING A CASE CONFERENCE
(Telephone Conference Call)

TAKE NOTICE that pursuant to Rule 77.13(1) of the Rules of Civil Procedure, you must participate in a case conference with Master Albert by conference telephone call on _____, at _____. _____ counsel for _____ shall make the conference call arrangements. Telephone conference arrangements are made by the responsible person connecting all parties on the telephone conference line and then calling in to Master Albert at (416) 326-3239. Any administrative inquiries shall be directed in advance to Master Albert's registrar at (416) 326-3272. If your office does not have conference facilities, use the Conference Operator service provided by your telephone service provider.

THE PURPOSE of the case conference is to discuss the issues raised in the litigation and to establish an appropriate timetable to meet the requirements of Rule 77 in this proceeding and any third and fourth party or other related proceedings.

COUNSEL AND UNREPRESENTED PARTIES in this proceeding and any third or fourth party or other related proceedings are required to participate in the case conference. In the event counsel cannot participate, it will be their responsibility to brief and arrange for fully informed alternate counsel to participate. At the case conference a timetable will be established or if one is in place it will be reviewed to ensure that the requirements of Rule 77.14 are met and any necessary consequential orders will be made.

THOSE PARTICIPATING must have with them calendars reflecting the future availability of counsel, parties and witnesses and should be fully familiar with the proceeding and its conduct to date. They must be prepared to schedule future events and discuss the issues in dispute.

COUNSEL FOR THE PLAINTIFF SHALL FORTHWITH SERVE A COPY OF THIS NOTICE on all counsel and unrepresented parties in this proceeding and all related proceedings to whom the notice has not been directed as set out below. If you have any questions please contact my registrar, Annette Bidlofsky, by telephone at (416) 326-3272 or by fax at (416) 326-5416.

DATED at Toronto _____.

_____

Master Carol Albert, Case Management Master

TO: _____, *solicitor for the plaintiff*

FAX: _____

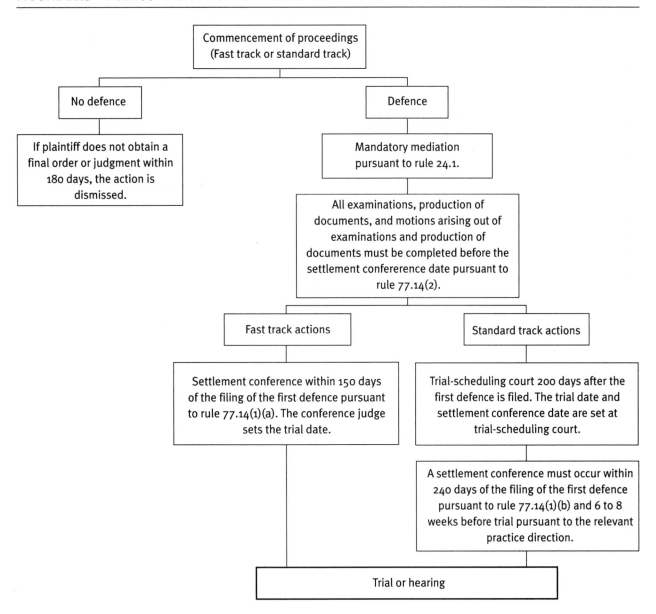

FIGURE 21.9   TRIAL MANAGEMENT CONFERENCE FORM (FORM 77D)

Court file no. 01-CV-1234

ONTARIO
SUPERIOR COURT OF JUSTICE

BETWEEN:

Abigail Boar

Plaintiff

and

Rattle Motors Ltd. and Fred Flogem

Defendants

TRIAL MANAGEMENT CONFERENCE FORM

Filed on behalf of the plaintiff, Abigail Boar

Trial Management Judge or Case Management Master: Master Slow
Date of Trial Management Conference: October 30, year 2
Trial Lawyer: Plaintiff

> I.M. Just, Just & Coping, Barristers and
> Solicitors,
> 365 Bay Street – 8701,
> Toronto, Ontario, M3J 4A9
> tel. 416-762-1342; fax 416-762-2300

Defendant

> Huey Sue, Barrister and Solicitor,
> 65 False Trail, Toronto, Ontario, M6Y 1Z6
> tel. 416-485-6891; fax 416-485-6892

Jury: yes _____   no ____x____

1. **Issues Outstanding**
   a) **liability:** admitted by the defendant
   b) **damages:** general damages are still in issue
   c) **other:** N/A

2. **Plaintiff's Witnesses**

Names	Estimated time for Examination-in-chief *(to be completed by plaintiff)*	Estimated time for Cross-examination *(to be completed at trial management conference)*
Abigail Boar	3 days	
Dr. Morris Furgazy	1 day	
Dr. Edwina Dhrool	1/2 day	

FIGURE 21.9 CONTINUED

3. **Defendant's Witnesses**

Names	Estimated time for Examination-in-chief (*to be completed by plaintiff*)	Estimated time for Cross-examination (*to be completed at trial management conference*)

4. **Document Brief**

a) Prepared: yes ____x____   no _____

b) If no, will be prepared by lawyer for the _____

and delivered by _____ (date)

c) Comment: Joint document brief including all documents of all parties.

5. **Expert's Reports**

a) Are any "reply" reports anticipated?

yes ____x____   no _____

b) If "yes," do they create any timing problems regarding readiness

for trial?   yes _____   no ____x____

6. **Admissions Made**

a) By plaintiff

b) By defendant #1

on issue of liability

c) By defendant #2

same as defendant #1

7. **Notice To Admit Facts/Documents**

a) Served by plaintiff: yes ____x____   no _____

b) If no, will be served by: _____ (date)

c) Served by defendant(s):   yes ____x____   no _____

d) If no, will be served by: _____ (date)

e) Comment: N/A

f) Would a chronology, cast of characters or chart of corporate parties with shareholders, directors, officers, etc. be useful and if so, who will prepare them?

Yes, a chronology of treatment of Abigail Boar's injuries will be prepared by the plaintiff.

FIGURE 21.9 CONTINUED

8. **Amendments to Pleadings**

a) Have all parties considered the pleadings and are any amendments likely to be sought?

No

b) If amendments are likely, will this create problems with readiness for trial?

N/A

9. **Damages**

a) Has a damages brief been delivered?

yes _____   no _____x_____

b) If "no," will one be delivered before trial?

yes _____x_____   no _____

10. **Brief of Authorities**

a) Has a brief of authorities been delivered?

yes _____x_____   no _____

b) If "no," will one be delivered before trial?

yes _____   no _____

11. **Settlement Conference**

a) Already held on September 12, year 2 by Master Slow.

b) Further settlement conference will be conducted:

yes _____   no _____x_____

c) If yes, lawyer to arrange for such conference to be held prior to (date)

12. **Readiness for Trial**

a) Estimated trial time required: 8 days

b) Are there any special circumstances which should be noted to assist in scheduling this matter for trial? (i.e. witnesses from out of town; large courtroom required due to number of lawyers or documents?)

Dr. Furgazy is on vacation during the first three weeks of November, year 2 and will not be available at that time.

FIGURE 21.10 OTTAWA CASE CONFERENCE REQUEST FORM

ONTARIO SUPERIOR COURT OF JUSTICE

SHORT TITLE OF PROCEEDING: Boar v. Rattle Motors et al.

CASE CONFERENCE FORM

REQUESTED BY:

DATE SCHEDULED:

1. Brief Statement of facts and law:

2. Purpose of the Case Conference
   a) Identification of Issues
   b) Explore methods to resolve contested issues
   c) Secure parties' agreement on a specific schedule
   d) Review and amend the timetable for the proceeding
   e) Other procedural matter (specify)

3. Disposition of the Case Management Judge/Master:

_____

_____

_____

_____

_____

_____   _____

Date   Judge/Master

Prepared by: (Law Firm)

FIGURE 21.11 CASE MANAGEMENT CHECKLIST (STANDARD TRACK ACTIONS)

* = Rule 77 Mandated action or time

EVENT	DATE	DATE EXTENDED OR AMENDED BY ORDER OF	DATE EXTENDED OR AMENDED BY ORDER OF
STATEMENT OF CLAIM ISSUED (Standard or Fast Track?)		N/A	N/A
* Defence must be filed or default obtained by 180 days or action is dismissed. (*See Note 1*)			
* Plaintiff must file consent timetable or obtain Case Conference Date by 180 days. Defendant may consider proposing one. (*See Note 2*)			
STATEMENT OF DEFENCE # of Defendants			
* When was the first Statement of Defence filed? (Obtain Case History — *See Note 1*)			
Other Defences to be filed			
MANDATORY MEDIATION (*See Note 3*)			
* Mediator must be selected and Mediation Coordinator advised failing which the Mediation Coordinator appoints a mediator from the roster (30 days after first defence).			
* Notice of Mediation must be served on all parties by lawyers 20 days before mediation.			
* Statement of Issues (Form 24.1C) to be filed 7 days before mediation.			
* Mediation to be held within 90 days of 1st defence (or in a standard track case only, may be extended a further 60 days on consent filed with Mediation Coordinator).			

FIGURE 21.11 CONTINUED

EVENT	DATE	DATE EXTENDED OR AMENDED BY ORDER OF	DATE EXTENDED OR AMENDED BY ORDER OF
Draft Timetable to be delivered. (With SOD? *See Note 2*)			
Affidavit of Documents served.			
Examinations for Discovery completed.			
Discovery Motions to be completed.			
Undertakings and Refusals answered.			
Plaintiff's Reports to be delivered.			
Defendant's Reports to be delivered.			
Third Party Reports to be delivered.			
Reply Reports to be delivered.			
SETTLEMENT CONFERENCE			
* Notice to be sent to parties (105 days after 1st defence filed)			
* Plaintiff's SC Brief must be filed 10 days before SC (ie. 230 days after 1st defence filed)			
* SC Briefs of other parties filed 5 days before SC (ie. 235 days after 1st defence)			
* SC is to be held (240 days after 1st defence filed)			
TRIAL MANAGEMENT CONFERENCE * Parties to file TMC form (Form 77D - earlier of 14 days before trial date or 4 days before TMC date)			
TRIAL DATE (set at TMC)			

NOTES:

1. **When acting for a Plaintiff**, if, within 180 days of the issuance of the claim, a) at least one defendant has not defended OR b) default judgment has not been obtained, the registrar will dismiss the action.

   When acting for a Defendant, when a Defence file comes in, obtain instructions to get the Case History from the Court which will tell you the two key dates: a) when the claim was issued, and b) when the first defence was filed.

   NO MORE WAIVERS OF DEFENCE WILL BE GIVEN BY THE PLAINTIFF

FIGURE 21.11 CONTINUED

2. **Timetable:** The obligation is on the Plaintiff to file a consent timetable within 180 days of issuing the claim, or convene a Case Conference with the Master to set one. If acting for a Plaintiff, consider suggesting one with the SOC, or on receipt of the (first?) defence. If acting for the Defendant, consider sending a suggested timetable with the SOD.

Make sure the client can abide by the timetable as well.

Case Management and Timetables mean more events in a shorter period of time. Carefully coordinate timetables on files to prevent double booking or other conflicts.

3. **Mandatory Mediation:** The rates of the Mediator are fixed by Regulation for the mandated 3 hour session (plus 1 hour mediator prep time). If the mediation extends beyond the prescribed time, the rate of the mediator must be negotiated between the mediator and the parties.

Source: "Case Management Checklist (Standard Track Actions)," in *Civil Litigation — 100% Case Management Alert*, Advocates' Society conference, held in Toronto, May 31, 2001.

CHAPTER 22

Mandatory mediation

WHAT IS MEDIATION?

Mediation is a form of **alternative dispute resolution**. It is one way for people to settle disputes or lawsuits without going to court. When a dispute is mediated, a neutral third party — the mediator — assists the parties in identifying their chief concerns and interests and helps them to negotiate a settlement that they can each live with. Mediators do not impose settlements by deciding disputes the way judges or arbitrators do. The mediator's job is to facilitate communication between the parties in a constructive way so that the parties can find their way to a satisfactory agreement. In mediation, the aim is not to identify winners or losers but to solve a problem that has led to a dispute or disagreement. The solution the parties fashion with a mediator's help may be based on factors other than the parties' legal rights.

Mandatory mediation in Ontario

In the last decade of the 20th century, the civil courts began to come to grips with problems of cost and delay in the civil court system by looking for new ways of doing things. The court system was overhauled, and the civil court rules were amended to introduce procedures, such as case management, to cut cost and delay. Another approach was to divert some cases out of the civil courts to be dealt with under various alternatives to dispute settlement in court. This approach has a history going back to the mid-20th century, when courts were divested of jurisdiction over various types of disputes. Labour relations disputes, for example, began to be dealt with by arbitrators or in some cases by labour relations boards, but not by courts. Boards and tribunals often deal with disputes without the parties being able to go to court. The court's role in these situations is restricted, ensuring that the boards or arbitrators or mediators provide a basically fair system.

The Ministry of the Attorney General introduced mandatory mediation in 1999. Eventually it will apply throughout Ontario, but currently it operates only in the Superior Court in Toronto and Ottawa,[1] and applies only to cases governed by case management under rule 77 or cases subject to rule 75.1 (estates, trusts, and **substitute decisions cases**). It was originally introduced, as was case management, as one of the pilot projects aimed at reducing cost and delay in the Superior Court.

Does mandatory mediation work?

That was the question the pilot project had to answer. The answer was that mandatory mediation was generally successful.[2] It resulted in significant reductions in the time taken to dispose of cases — a plus for clients and the courts, which can deal with the remaining cases more easily when the case load is reduced. Not surprisingly, the

mediation
process whereby a neutral third party facilitates communication between disputants and assists them in negotiating a solution

alternative dispute resolution
term used to describe various ways of settling disputes without going to court, including arbitration, mediation, and conciliation

substitute decisions cases
cases involving the *Substitute Decisions Act*, under which a person may be named to handle the property and day-to-day affairs of a person who is not mentally competent to manage his or her own affairs

costs for litigants were also reduced when mediation was wholly or partially successful.[3] A high proportion of cases, over 40 percent in both Toronto and Ottawa, were settled at or within seven days of the completion of mediation. An additional 13 percent of cases in Ottawa and 21 percent of cases in Toronto were partially settled, with some issues being taken from the table, speeding up the proceedings and reducing costs. However, there were concerns voiced by some members of the bar, particularly in Toronto. One was that mediation came too early in the proceeding under rule 24.1, before the parties were ready to consider it. Generally, the Toronto bar was more critical than the Ottawa bar of the mandatory mediation process.

MANDATORY MEDIATION IN CIVIL PROCEEDINGS: RULE 24.1

All civil case-managed proceedings that are defended in Toronto and Ottawa and that are subject to case management under rule 77 are also subject to mandatory mediation under rule 24.1. Therefore, if your case is case managed, it will also be going to mediation. The types of cases excluded from case management under rule 77.01(2) are also excluded from mandatory mediation. Note that estate, trust, and substitute decisions cases, while excluded from case management under rule 77.01(2), have their own form of mandatory mediation under rule 75.1, with different timelines and procedures from those in rule 24.1. Not every case that goes to mandatory mediation should go. For example, a case where the parties are likely to try to kill each other if they are in the same room is not a good case for mandatory mediation. Rule 24.1.05 permits a party to bring a motion for an order for exemption of a particular case from mandatory mediation, and in a case like this, the court may well grant the order.

Who conducts the mediation?

Because there is a high volume of mediation cases, it is necessary to have a great many mediators, and some administrative coordination of them. Rule 24.1.08 provides for the establishment of a mediation committee with the responsibility of developing criteria for appointing mediators, screening them, and approving them to be included on a list or roster of mediators. A mediation coordinator for each county or region where mandatory mediation has been imposed administers the list. There are a variety of certificate and diploma courses where one may train to be a mediator. There are no clear professional standards that all mediators must adhere to, and there is no single body that certifies mediators as professionals in the way that doctors and lawyers are certified. The mediation committee has broad discretion in appointing individuals to the list of mediators, and the Ministry of the Attorney General has provided some guidelines for exercising that discretion.

In any case, the litigants have some choices about who does the mediation (rule 24.1.08(2)). The mediation may be conducted by:

- a person the parties agree to, whether on the list or not, and whether the person holds himself or herself out as a mediator or not, or

- a person assigned by the mediation coordinator.

An appointment is made where the parties fail to give notice within 30 days after the filing of the first defence that they have appointed a mediator. It also occurs where no mediation session has taken place within 90 days from the time that the first defence was filed. The coordinator also appoints a mediator if he or she has not received a notice postponing mediation on consent (rule 24.1.09(1), (3), (5), and (6)). The person chosen or assigned to mediate must comply with the requirements of rule 24.1. and, in particular, must file a mediation report under rule 24.1.15(1).

Choosing a mediator

Counsel is entitled to information from any mediator, on the list or off it, and there are questions a lawyer or client should ask before a mediator is selected.

- Where did the mediator train?

- What kind of mediation experience does he or she have?

- Is the mediator familiar with rule 24.1, the court processes, and the role of mediation in a civil proceeding?

- What references can the mediator provide?

- Will the mediator agree to the fee schedule established under the rule?

- What are the mediator's fees for services above and beyond the fee schedule for the first three hours of mediation?

MEDIATION PROCEDURE STEP BY STEP
Arranging the mediation

The parties need to contact each other as soon as possible after proceedings are commenced to select a mediator because a mediation session must take place within 90 days of the filing of the first defence. However, if there are many parties or complex issues and pleadings, a lawyer can bring a motion to extend (and also to abridge or shorten) the time for mediation (rule 24.1.09(1) and (2)). The rule suggests that in addition to the number of parties and the complexity of the issues, the court will also consider extending time for mediation if a party brings a motion for determination of an issue before trial because this might change the focus of mediation if the court removes an issue from mediation by ruling on it. The court will also hold off on mediation if there is a motion for summary judgment. If the motion is successful, the lawsuit is over, and there is nothing to mediate. If a party argues that he or she cannot proceed to mediation without more facts and information, the court may extend the time to permit discovery to take place before mediation begins.

In addition, the parties may also consent to postpone a mediation session for up to 60 days without bringing a motion by filing a consent with the mediation coordinator.

While mediation can be delayed, the choice of a mediator should be made within 30 days of the filing of the first defence. It is the duty of the plaintiff to file with the mediation coordinator a notice in form 24.1A[4] setting out the mediator's name and the date of the mediation session. A sample notice appears in figure 22.1.

If the parties do not themselves choose a mediator and fix a date for the first mediation session, under rule 24.1.09(6) it is the responsibility of the mediation co-

FIGURE 22.1 NOTICE OF NAME OF MEDIATOR AND DATE OF SESSION (FORM 24.1A)

Court file no. 01-CV-1234

ONTARIO
SUPERIOR COURT OF JUSTICE

BETWEEN:

Abigail Boar

Plaintiff

and

Rattle Motors Ltd. and Fred Flogem

Defendants

NOTICE OF NAME OF MEDIATOR AND DATE OF SESSION

TO: MEDIATION CO-ORDINATOR,

1. I certify that I have consulted with the parties and that the parties have chosen the following mediator for the mediation session required by Rule 24.1: Marielle Moosetrap.
2. The mediator is named in the list of mediators for the City of Toronto.
3. The mediation session will take place on December 13, year 1.

Date: November 17, year 1

Just & Coping
Barristers and Solicitors
365 Bay Street – 8701
Toronto, Ontario, M3J 4A9

I.M. Just
tel. 416-762-1342
fax 416-762-2300

Solicitors for the Plaintiff

ordinator to assign a mediator from the list. The assigned mediator immediately fixes a date for the mediation and serves a notice in form 24.1B on all parties at least 20 days before the day for which the mediation is scheduled. This puts the mediator in a peculiar position: He or she is expected to conduct a mediation with parties who may not wish to mediate and who are not cooperating with respect to the mediation process. The mediator is also acting as the court's police force, compelling the parties to attend or risk penalties. A sample mediator's notice form is reproduced in figure 22.2.

Preparing for mediation

The lawyer needs to run the client through the requirements for mandatory mediation, including the penalties for not cooperating in the process. A lawyer must also advise the client as to the choice of mediator, whether the mediator is from the list or not. The choice may involve some negotiation with other parties. The lawyer also has to prepare the statement of issues in form 24.1C[5] and provide a copy to other parties at least seven days before the mediation session. The statement of issues is like an agenda for a meeting; it tells the parties and the mediator, who knows nothing about the case, what is going to be "on the table." A statement of issues appears in figure 22.3.

The lawyer then must prepare the client for the mediation session and provide legal and strategic advice during the mediation process. Mediation is not something to send the client to alone. The lawyer, as an officer of the court, is obliged to protect the integrity of the mediation process by participating in the process in good faith and ensuring, as far as possible, that the client participates in the process in good faith too.

Preparing the client for mediation

Unlike a pretrial conference or a settlement conference, where the client says little and the lawyer does most of the talking, a client is expected to be an active participant in mediation. This means that an intelligent and articulate client may have an advantage, which is something a lawyer with a less articulate client may have to counter by participating more actively. But a client will require careful preparation. In particular, the lawyer must

- give the client an overview of the mediation strategies and goals;

- explain to the client what the client's role is;

- remind the client that the goal is to find a mutually acceptable solution, not to beat the other side;

- discuss particular strategies with the client;

- be sure the client or the client's representative has authority to settle the lawsuit, and establish settlement ceilings;

- discuss with the client the cost, risks, and benefits of not settling during mediation;

- ensure that the client understands the theory of his or her own case, and its strengths and weaknesses;

FIGURE 22.2   NOTICE BY ASSIGNED MEDIATOR (FORM 24.1B)

Court file no. 01-CV-1234

ONTARIO
SUPERIOR COURT OF JUSTICE

BETWEEN:

Abigail Boar

Plaintiff

and

Rattle Motors Ltd. and Fred Flogem

Defendants

NOTICE BY ASSIGNED MEDIATOR

TO: Abigail Boar
AND TO: Rattle Motors Ltd. and Fred Flogem

The notice of name of mediator and date of session (Form 24.1A) required by rule 24.1.09 of the *Rules of Civil Procedure* has not been filed in this action. Accordingly, the mediation coordinator has assigned me to conduct the mediation session under Rule 24.1. I am a mediator named in the list of mediators for the City of Toronto.

The mediation session will take place on December 13, year 1 from 10:00 a.m. to 1:00 p.m., at JPR Arbitration and Mediation Services, 365 Bay Street – 400, Toronto, Ontario, M3J 4A9.

Unless the court orders otherwise, you are required to attend this mediation session. If you have a lawyer representing you in this action, he or she is also required to attend.

You are required to file a statement of issues (Form 24.1C) by December 6, year 1 **(7 days before the mediation session).** A blank copy of the form is attached.

When you attend the mediation session, you should bring with you any documents that you consider of central importance in the action. You should plan to remain throughout the scheduled time. If you need another person's approval before agreeing to a settlement, you should make arrangements before the mediation session to ensure that you have ready telephone access to that person throughout the session, even outside regular business hours.

YOU MAY BE PENALIZED UNDER RULE 24.1.13 IF YOU FAIL TO FILE A STATEMENT OF ISSUES OR FAIL TO ATTEND THE MEDIATION SESSION.

November 20, year 1

Marielle Moosetrap
1200 Yonge Street
Toronto, Ontario, M5R 1Z6
tel. 416-490-8765
fax 416-490-8766

cc. Mediation coordinator

FIGURE 22.3 STATEMENT OF ISSUES (FORM 24.1C)

Court file no. 01-CV-1234

ONTARIO
SUPERIOR COURT OF JUSTICE

BETWEEN:

Abigail Boar

Plaintiff

and

Rattle Motors Ltd. and Fred Flogem

Defendants

STATEMENT OF ISSUES

1. Factual and legal issues in dispute

The plaintiff states that the following factual and legal issues are in dispute and remain to be resolved:

1. whether oil leaking from an automobile in the corporate defendant's showroom caused the plaintiff to fall and be seriously injured;
2. whether the defendant Fred Flogem failed in his duty to the plaintiff by not cleaning up the oil spill when he became aware of it; and
3. whether the damages sustained by the plaintiff were solely the result of the defendants' negligence.

2. Party's position and interests (what the party hopes to achieve)

1. The plaintiff's position is that all of her injuries and subsequent losses and damages resulted from the negligent acts of the defendants.
2. The plaintiff hopes to receive adequate compensation for both special and general damages arising from her injuries.

3. Attached documents

Attached to this form are the following documents that the plaintiff considers of central importance in the action:

1. Statement of claim and defence
2. List of general damages sustained by the plaintiff
3. List of special damages sustained by the plaintiff

Date: December 1, year 1 _____Abigail Boar_____

FIGURE 22.3 CONTINUED

```
Just & Coping
Barristers and Solicitors
365 Bay Street - 8701
Toronto, Ontario, M3J 4A9

I.M. Just
tel. 416-762-1342
fax 416-762-2300

Solicitors for the Plaintiff
```

NOTE: When the plaintiff provides a copy of this form to the mediator, a copy of the pleadings shall also be included.

NOTE: Rule 24.1.14 provides as follows:

All communications at a mediation session and the mediator's notes and records shall be deemed to be without prejudice settlement discussions.

- ensure that the client understands the theory of the other party's case, and its strengths and weaknesses;

- advise the client how to present his or her position in the most positive and persuasive way;

- advise the client about any confidential information that should not be disclosed; and

- work with the client to develop an opening statement.

Mediation session

The parties and their lawyers must attend the mediation session. Since the session is confidential and things said in it are said without prejudice, the sessions are not public. The three-hour mediation session usually opens with the mediator's explaining to the parties the mediation process and reviewing the terms of the mediation and the issues set out in the issues statement. The mediator usually then initiates the discussion and structures it. Each party gives his or her side of the story, sets out what is important, and asks questions. Once the mediator has a sense of where the parties are, he or she helps them to develop solutions to the problem. The mediator may meet the parties while they are face-to-face or may shuttle back and forth between them while the parties stay in separate rooms. The lawyer, sitting with the client, can determine when the client needs additional advice or a break. During the break, the client can get advice from the lawyer about how to negotiate and about possible solutions.

Rule 24.1.11 makes it clear that both the client and the lawyer, if there is one, must attend the mediation session. If the claim for damages is covered by insurance, a representative with authority to bind the insurer to any agreement must also attend. Where authority to settle is required and the person with authority cannot be present, the party must arrange to have telephone access to whoever is appearing for him or her at the mediation session.

Minimal attendance requirements

Rule 24.1 mandates a three-hour mediation session, meaning that the parties must attempt mediation for at least three hours. The session may be less than that if the parties settle or if the mediator decides that there is no point in continuing. Mediation also may last more than three hours if the parties and the mediator consent. Further sessions may be scheduled if the parties agree, but no one is obliged to attempt more than three hours of mediation.

If a mediation is scheduled and a party does not appear within 30 minutes of the scheduled commencement time, the mediator cancels the session and files a certificate of non-compliance in form 24.1D[6] with the mediation coordinator. A certificate of non-compliance appears in figure 22.4.

When the mediation coordinator receives a notice of non-compliance, the coordinator refers the matter to the case management master or judge assigned to the case. If none has been assigned at this early stage in the proceedings, one will be assigned, and he or she is likely to convene a case conference. Issues of rescheduling can be dealt with and costs may be awarded to those who showed up and had costs "thrown away" because they spent time preparing for a meeting that did not happen and will need to spend time preparing again. Costs usually include payment of the mediator's fee for the cancelled session.

Completion of the mediation process

Rule 24.1.15 requires the mediator to file a report on the outcome of the mediation with the parties and the mediation coordinator within 10 days after the mediation is concluded. Because the matters discussed in mediation are confidential, the report states no more than the fact that the parties attended the mediation session and complied with the rules.

If the parties reach an agreement on some or all of the issues, you can record the terms of the agreement using a standard minutes of settlement format. If the agreement settles the matter, the minutes of settlement should be filed in court, together with an order consenting to judgment or dismissal in accordance with the terms of the minutes of settlement.

Who pays for mediation?

Mediator's maximum fees for the mandatory three-hour mediation session are set by regulation,[7] in response to charges of critics that mediation is an added, open-ended expense for clients. The fee covers one hour of preparation time for the mediator as well as the three-hour session. The client must pay lawyer's fees connected to the mediation process in addition to the cost of the mediator. The fee rises along with the number of parties involved and is shared by the parties. The current schedule, as of March 2002, is set out in table 22.1.

If the client has a legal aid certificate, or is of modest means and meets the Ministry of the Attorney General's financial eligibility requirements, mediation is provided at no cost to the client. The ministry's eligibility form is set out in figure 22.5.

TABLE 22.1   MEDIATOR FEES

Number of parties	Maximum fees for mandatory session
2	$600 plus GST
3	$675 plus GST
4	$750 plus GST
5 or more	$825 plus GST

FIGURE 22.4   CERTIFICATE OF NON-COMPLIANCE (FORM 24.1D)

Court file no. 01-CV-1234

ONTARIO
SUPERIOR COURT OF JUSTICE

BETWEEN:

Abigail Boar

Plaintiff

and

Rattle Motors Ltd. and Fred Flogem

Defendants

CERTIFICATE OF NON-COMPLIANCE

TO: MEDIATION CO-ORDINATOR

I, Marielle Moosetrap, mediator, certify that this certificate of non-compliance is filed because:

( ) (*Identify party(ies)*) failed to provide a copy of a statement of issues to the mediator and the other parties (*or* to the mediator *or* to *party(ies)*).
( ) (*Identify party(ies)*) failed to provide a copy of the pleadings to the mediator.
(x) The defendant Fred Flogem failed to attend within the first 30 minutes of a scheduled mediation session.

December 13, year 1

Marielle Moosetrap
1200 Yonge Street
Toronto, Ontario, M5R 1Z6
tel. 416-490-8765
fax 416-490-8766

FIGURE 22.5   FINANCIAL ELIGIBILITY FORM

FINANCIAL ELIGIBILITY FORM
ONTARIO MANDATORY MEDIATION PROGRAM

To be completed by litigants seeking pro bono mediation services under the MMP Access Plan.

Date: _____ Location (county): _____
        yy mm dd

Name: _____
        First   Last

1. How many people are in your family unit, including you, your spouse and any dependent children?

    1 2 3 4 5+

2. What is the total gross income of your family unit annually (or monthly)?

    ❑ No income ❑ Under $18,000 ($1,500) ❑ $18,000-26,999 ($1,500-2,249)
    ❑ $27,000-30,999 ($2,250-2,582) ❑ $31,000-36,999 ($2,582-3,082)
    ❑ $37,000-43,000 ($3,083-3,583) ❑ Over $43,000 ($3,583)

3. Does the total amount of your liquid assets exceed $1,500 including all bank accounts, bonds, stocks, RRSPs, GICs, mutual funds and similar assets? (Do not include vehicles, real property and household effects)

    ❑ yes ❑ no

4. Does your net worth exceed $6,000?

    ❑ yes ❑ no

Declaration: I, _____, of the _____ of
_____, declare that the above information is true and correct and I make this statement conscientiously believing it to be true and knowing that it is of the same force and effect as if made under oath.

Declare before me at the _____ of _____ in the province of Ontario this

_____ day of _____ 20 ___.

_____   _____
Local Mediation Coordinator Signature   Litigant Signature Counsel Signature
(if applicable)

Over and above the fees set out in table 22.1, a mediator may charge reasonable expenses, such as those incurred for renting space to conduct the mediation. However, the parties must agree to payment of these fees in advance.

MANDATORY MEDIATION IN ESTATE, TRUST, AND SUBSTITUTE DECISION PROCEEDINGS: RULE 75.1

Introduction

This section provides an overview of mandatory mediation as it applies to what is generally called estates litigation, which concerns litigation about estates, trusts, and substitute decisions under rule 75.[8] A related rule, rule 75.1, requires that a form of mandatory mediation be applied to estates cases under rule 75. Mandatory mediation under rule 75.1 closely parallels rule 24 but is adapted to suit the procedures in estates litigation. Mandatory mediation under rule 75.1 applies to cases in Toronto and Ottawa to disputed matters relating to estates, trusts, and substitute decisions (rule 75.1.01). Not every type of estate litigation requires mediation, and you should refer to rule 75.1.02(1) for the kinds of estate cases to which mandatory mediation applies.

How rule 75.1 works

There are reasons for the differences between mandatory mediation under rule 24.1 and mandatory mediation under rule 75.1. Cases under rule 75 are not under case management and follow a different timetable. Cases under rule 75 are usually brought by notice of application, which sets out a different and shorter pretrial procedure. Procedure is further complicated by rules in statutes that govern rule 75 matters. It is usual in estate cases to have a great number of parties, consisting of estate beneficiaries and classes of estate beneficiaries, not all of whom are interested in all of the issues. A mechanism is needed to avoid dragging all parties into mediation that does not concern them.

When a rule 75 proceeding has been commenced, an applicant on a notice of application is required to bring a motion for directions relating to the conduct of the mediation within 30 days of the last day on which the respondents may serve a notice of appearance. The rule does not specify a time limit for when the motion must be heard (rule 75.1.05).

On the return of the motion for directions, the order may be a formality and a foregone conclusion, or it may be lengthy and customized. Estate litigation that involves a challenge to a will or raises issues interpreting a will can be very complex. There may be scores of beneficiaries, some of whom will be affected by the order but some of who may not be. Some may be affected in different ways, or some may have one position on the outcome, and others may have another. In the complex estate case, the court may have to:

- identify the issues to be mediated and the order in which they are mediated,

- determine who has carriage of the mediation (usually the estate administrator or trustee),

- set the timetable for conducting the mediation when there are many parties with different interests, and

- decide which parties may attend the mediation and how the cost is to be shared among the parties or classes of parties.

Once an order for directions is made, the parties must select a mediator within 30 days (rule 75.1.07). The parties may choose their own mediator or select one from the roster. Care should be taken to select a mediator who has some general knowledge of substantive and procedural estate law. Once the parties have agreed to a mediator, the party with carriage of the mediation is required to give the mediator a copy of the order for directions. If the parties fail to select a mediator within 30 days, the party with carriage of the mediation is responsible for filing a request to assign a mediator with the local mediation coordinator.

When the mediator is selected (or assigned), he or she must immediately fix a date for the mediation and, at least 20 days before that, must serve on every party designated by the order for directions notice of the place, date, and time of the mediation (rule 75.1.07). At least 7 days before the mediation, designated parties must provide the mediator and the other designated parties with a statement of issues. The statement of issues, in form 75.1C, must identify the factual and legal issues in dispute and briefly set out the position and interest of the party making the statement. The party should also attach any documents that that party considers to be of relevance to its position (rule 75.1.08). Form 75.1C[9] is set out in figure 22.6. It is completed in much the same way as is the statement of issues in form 24.1C under rule 24.1.

The mediator is obliged to give a copy of his or her report on the mediation to every party and to the mediation coordinator within 10 days of the conclusion of the mediation (rule 75.1.12). An agreement is to be reported, and a breach of an agreement by any party can be enforced. If the standard three-hour mediation is not enough, and with many parties or issues it is likely not to be, the parties may consent to an order for further sessions. The fees are then to be negotiated between the parties and the mediator.

CHAPTER SUMMARY

This chapter briefly explained the purpose of mediation and its role in diverting civil cases from the court system by promoting settlement at an early date. The encouraging results of the mediation pilot project have resulted in mediation becoming mandatory for all proceedings that are case managed under rule 77. We discussed the lawyer's role in the mediation process and his or her duty in explaining to the client how mediation works.

Once a proceeding is commenced, we noted that the parties have 30 days after the first defence is filed to choose a mediator. Within 90 days of the filing of the first defence, the parties are expected to complete mediation, which is envisaged as a three-hour session. If necessary, time limits can be extended by calling a case conference under rule 77. At least 7 days before the mediation session, the parties must provide the mediator with an issues statement. On completion of the mediation, the mediator must, within 10 days, report to the mediation coordinator on the outcome of the mediation. The costs of mediation are borne by the parties, and the fees are fixed for the first three hours. The parties may, on consent, go on to further sessions, but the mediator's fees are no longer fixed. If a party does not cooperate

FIGURE 22.6   STATEMENT OF ISSUES (FORM 75.1C)

Court file no. E-1111-01

ONTARIO SUPERIOR COURT OF JUSTICE

IN THE ESTATE OF Abigail Boar,   **deceased,**
late of the City of Toronto, in the Province of Ontario,
occupation investment analyst,
who died on October 21, year 4

STATEMENT OF ISSUES

<u>1. Factual and legal issues in dispute</u>

The undersigned designated party states that the following factual and
legal issues are in dispute and remain to be resolved.

Whether or not there is a last will and testament of Abigail
Boar, subsequent to that which is dated April 4, year -4, for
which an application for probate has been made in this court.

<u>2. Party's position and interests (what the party hopes to achieve)</u>

This party is the brother of Abigail Boar, who is excluded
from the beneficiaries mentioned in the Last Will and
Testament of Abigail Boar, dated April 4, year -4. This
party believes there is a subsequent will dated April 9,
year -4, and that this will includes this party as a
beneficiary of the estate of Abigail Boar.

<u>3. Attached documents</u>

Attached to this form are the following documents that the designated
party considers of central importance in the proceeding:

1. Affidavit of Bill Boar, sworn November 5, year 1 and
   filed in this proceeding
2. Photocopy of a Last Will and Testament of Abigail Boar,
   executed by her on April 9, year -4

Date: October 23, year 4   Bill Boar
                                         2311 Baybottom Crescent
                                         Toronto, Ontario, M5R 8X3

NOTE: Rule 75.1.11 provides as follows:

All communications at a mediation session and the mediator's notes and
records shall be deemed to be without prejudice settlement discussions.

with the process, the court may impose penalties. However, in appropriate cases, the court may order that the case proceed without mediation.

We also briefly discussed mandatory mediation under rule 75.1 for contentious and disputed estate, trust, and substitute decision cases, noting differences from mandatory mediation under rule 24.1.

KEY TERMS

mediation

alternative dispute resolution

substitute decisions cases

NOTES

1 The Toronto mediation office is located at 393 University Avenue, where the Superior Court is located. The phone number is 416-314-1360 or 1-888-377-2228 (toll free). The Ottawa office is in the Ottawa Courthouse at 161 Elgin Street, second floor. The phone number is 613-239-1135.

2 The description here of the results of the evaluation of mandatory mediation is adopted from R.G. Hann and Carl Baar et al., *Evaluation of the Ontario Mandatory Mediation Program: Executive Summary and Recommendations* (Toronto: Queen's Printer, March 2001). See also "Report of the Evaluation Committee of the Ontario Civil Rules Committee for the Mandatory Mediation Rule Pilot Project," in *Civil Litigation — 100% Case Management Alert*, Advocates' Society conference, held in Toronto, May 31, 2001. The pilot project report is also available online at http://www.attorneygeneral.jus.gov.on.ca/english/courts/manmed/evalcommittee.asp.

3 But costs increase where mediation fails because the parties must pay the mediator, and there are the additional costs of lawyers preparing for mediation.

4 Form 24.1A appears to have been revoked by O. reg. 453/98, s. 2(2) as of July 1, 2001; nevertheless it still seems to be in use.

5 This form, like form 24.1A, appears to have been revoked by O. reg. 453/98, as of July 1, 2001 but seems to be still in use.

6 Form 24.1D, like forms 24.1A and 24.1C, appears to have been revoked by O. reg. 453/98, s. 2(1) as of July 1, 2001 but seems to be still in use.

7 O. reg. 451/98, as amended by O. reg. 241/01.

8 The discussion is brief for two reasons: (1) estate, trust, and substitute decisions litigation, known collectively as "estate litigation," is specialized and based on several statutes and a vast amount of case law; (2) the future of mandatory mediation in this area is uncertain. It is to continue as a pilot project until July 3, 2004, when it will either expire and disappear or be continued, probably in a much altered form.

9 This form has technically been revoked, like other mediation forms, by O. reg. 453/98, s. 2 but appears to be still in use.

REFERENCES

Hann, R.G. and Carl Baar et al., *Evaluation of the Ontario Mandatory Mediation Program: Executive Summary and Recommendations* (Toronto: Queen's Printer, March 2001).

O. reg. 241/01.

O. reg. 451/98.

O. reg. 453/98.

"Report of the Evaluation Committee of the Ontario Civil Rules Committee for the Mandatory Mediation Rule Pilot Project," in *Civil Litigation — 100% Case Management Alert*, Advocates' Society conference, held in Toronto, May 31, 2001.

Rules of Civil Procedure, RRO 1990, reg. 194.

REVIEW QUESTIONS

1. What is mediation?

2. What are the advantages and disadvantages of mediation?

3. What cases are subject to mandatory mediation?

4. Must every case-managed proceeding go through mediation?

5. How are mediators selected?

6. What must be done to prepare for mediation?

7. Who must attend the mediation?

8. How long is a mediation session?

9. What are the costs of mediation?

10. What happens if a party is not cooperative in the mediation process?

11. What happens when mediation is complete?

12. How does mandatory mediation under rule 24.1 differ from mediation under rule 75.1?

DISCUSSION QUESTION

1. Draft a statement of issues to be filed on behalf of Fred Flogem and Rattle Motors Ltd. You will want to review figures 7.2 (statement of claim), 7.3 (statement of defence), and 22.3 (Abigail Boar's statement of issues).

CHAPTER 23

Simplified procedure: Rule 76

INTRODUCTION

As we have seen in our look at the *Rules of Civil Procedure*, litigation in the Ontario Superior Court of Justice can be a complicated, expensive, and time-consuming process. A party who is suing for less than $10,000 can take the case to Small Claims Court with its straightforward and relatively fast procedure. However, if a party wants to sue for more than $10,000, there is no option but to use the Superior Court.

Not all actions in the Superior Court warrant the use of the usual lengthy procedure. Therefore, the rules provide a little halfway point between the Small Claims Court and the regular Superior Court process. This halfway point is called the simplified procedure, and it is contained in rule 76. This procedure reduces the time and expense associated with litigation.

APPLICATION OF THE SIMPLIFIED PROCEDURE

The simplified procedure *must* be used in all cases in the Superior Court in which a party is claiming $50,000 or less, exclusive of interests and costs.[1] It may also be used for claims over $50,000, provided that the parties consent. The limit does not apply only to claims for money. It also applies to claims for real and personal property valued at less than $50,000. The assessment of the value of the property is its fair market value at the time the action is commenced.

The simplified procedure is not available for actions brought under the *Class Proceedings Act, 1992*, the *Construction Lien Act*, or to divorce actions or other family law matters in the Superior Court. Actions following the simplified procedure are not subject to rule 77 and are therefore not case managed.

If there is more than one plaintiff, each plaintiff's claim must independently meet the requirements for application of the rule.

For example, if Abigail Boar sued Rattle Motors Ltd. and Fred Flogem for $25,000, and her boyfriend also decided to sue the defendants for the loss of Abigail's companionship as a result of her injuries, his claim would have to be for $50,000 or less and satisfy the other criteria as well.

COMMENCEMENT OF AN ACTION

Since it is the plaintiff who commences the action, it is also the plaintiff who must use the simplified procedure if the amount claimed is $50,000 or less. It is also the plaintiff who may elect to use the procedure for claims of more than $50,000. The statement of claim must indicate that the action is being brought under the simplified procedure. The proper wording is "This action is brought against you under the simplified procedure provided in rule 76 of the *Rules of Civil Procedure*." This wording is added at the top of the page on which the claim is commenced.

Once the action has been commenced under simplified procedure, it remains under that procedure unless the defendant in the main action, the crossclaim, or the counterclaim, or the third party objects. Objections are to be made in the statement of defence. The ground for an objection is that the amount of the claim, the crossclaim, or the counterclaim is not within the $50,000 limit. The plaintiff or the defendant who brought the claim then has the option of stating in the reply that he or she is abandoning forever the amount of the claim that exceeds the limit. If the amount in excess is abandoned, the action continues under the simplified procedure. If not, the action is continued under the ordinary procedure, and case management applies if it is otherwise an action that falls within the case management rule.

Likewise, an action that has been commenced under the ordinary procedure may continue instead under the simplified procedure if

- a party's pleading is amended to bring it within the limits for the simplified procedure;

- any crossclaims, counterclaims, or third party claims attached to the main action are within the monetary limits; and

- the parties file a consent to proceed under the simplified procedure.

If an action changes stream, from simplified to ordinary procedure or vice versa, the plaintiff must serve and file form 76A, which states what change has been made. A sample form 76A is shown in figure 23.1.

DIFFERENCES BETWEEN THE SIMPLIFIED AND THE ORDINARY PROCEDURE

The major differences between the ordinary and simplified procedures are set out below.

1. *Discovery.* No discovery is permitted on the simplified procedure, but the parties are required to have discussions within 60 days after the first statement of defence or notice of intent to defend has been filed to determine whether all the documents relating to the disputed issues have been disclosed (rule 76.08).

2. *Cross-examination.* No cross-examination on an affidavit is permitted under the simplified procedure.

3. *Examination of a witnesses.* No examination of a witness on a pending motion is permitted under the simplified procedure.

4. *Affidavit of documents.* The affidavit of documents under the simplified procedure must contain an additional schedule, schedule D, setting out the names and addresses of all potential witnesses to be called at trial. A witness who is not included in schedule D cannot be called to give evidence at the

FIGURE 23.1   NOTICE WHETHER ACTION UNDER RULE 76 (FORM 76A)

NOTICE WHETHER ACTION UNDER RULE 76

The plaintiff states that this action and any related proceedings are:

❑   continuing under Rule 76
❑   continuing under Rule 77 — fast track
❑   continuing under Rule 77 — standard track
❑   continuing as an ordinary procedure.

---

trial without an order of the court. When the affidavit of documents is served, copies of all the documents listed in schedule A must be served as well. The affidavit of documents must be served within 10 days of the close of pleadings.

5. *Motions.* Motions under the simplified procedure are significantly different from those under the ordinary procedure. These differences are discussed below.

MOTIONS

A motion is commenced with a simplified procedure motion form, form 76B, rather than with a notice of motion. Reflecting the less complicated process under the simplified procedure, this form, for the most part, involves filling in the blanks and requires little drafting. A sample of a motion in form 76B is set out in figure 23.2.

The motion is to be heard in the same court where the action was commenced unless the parties consent or the court orders that it be heard in another location. In many instances, the motion may be heard without a motion record and other supporting documents.

Many motions can be dealt with by the registrar and do not require a hearing before a judge. For example, the registrar may deal with the following types of motions if they are on consent, a consent is filed, no party is under a disability, and no responding material is filed:

- an amendment of a pleading or a notice of motion;

- an addition, deletion, or substitution of a party whose consent is filed;

- the removal of a solicitor of record;

- setting aside a noting in default;

- setting aside a default judgment;

- discharge of a certificate of pending litigation;

- security for costs in a specified amount; and

- dismissal of a proceeding without costs.

There is no need to take out a formal order unless there is an order that it be taken out or the order is being appealed. The endorsement on the motion form is all that is necessary to establish that an order was made.

FIGURE 23.2   SIMPLIFIED PROCEDURE MOTION FORM (FORM 76B)

SIMPLIFIED PROCEDURE MOTION FORM

JURISDICTION   ❑ Judge
               ❑ Master
               ❑ Registrar

THIS FORM FILED BY (*Check appropriate boxes to identify the party filing this form as a moving/responding party on this motion AND to identify this party as plaintiff, defendant, etc. in the action*)

❑ moving party
❑ plaintiff

_____

❑ responding party
❑ defendant

_____

❑ Other — specify kind of party and name

_____
_____

MOTION MADE

❑ on consent of all parties

❑ without notice

❑ on notice to all parties and unopposed

❑ on notice to all parties and expected to be opposed

Notice of this motion was served on (date):

_____

by means of:

_____
_____

METHOD OF HEARING REQUESTED

❑ by attendance
❑ in writing only, no attendance
❑ by fax
❑ by telephone conference under rule 1.08
❑ by video conference under rule 1.08

Date, time and place for conference call, telephone call or appearances

_____   _____   _____
(date)   *(time)*   *(place)*

FIGURE 23.2 CONTINUED

ORDER SOUGHT BY THIS PARTY *(Responding party is presumed to request dismissal of motion and costs)*

❑ Extension of time — until (give specific date): _____
❑ serve claim
❑ file or deliver statement of defence
❑ Other relief — be specific

_____
_____
_____

MATERIAL RELIED ON BY THIS PARTY

❑ this form
❑ pleadings
❑ affidavits — specify
❑ other — specify

_____
_____
_____

GROUNDS IN SUPPORT OF/IN OPPOSITION TO MOTION (INCLUDING RULE AND STATUTORY PROVISIONS RELIED ON)

_____
_____
_____

CERTIFICATION BY LAWYER

I certify that the above information is correct, to the best of my knowledge.
Signature of lawyer *(if no lawyer, party must sign)*

_____

Date _____

THIS PARTY'S LAWYER *(if no lawyer, give party's name, address for service, telephone and fax number)*	OTHER PARTY'S LAWYER *(if no lawyer, give party's name, address for service, telephone and fax number)*
Name and firm:	Name and firm:
Address:	Address:
Telephone:	Telephone:
Fax:	Fax:

FIGURE 23.2 **CONTINUED**

DISPOSITION

❏ order to go as asked
❏ adjourned to
❏ order refused
❏ order to go as follows:

_____

_____

Hearing Method: _____ Hearing duration: _____ minutes

Heard in: ❏ courtroom ❏ office

❏ Successful party MUST prepare formal order for signature
❏ No copy of disposition to be sent to parties
❏ Other directions — specify

_____

_____

Date _____ Name _____ Signature _____

Judge/Master/Registrar

DISMISSAL BY THE REGISTRAR

Actions proceeding under the simplified procedure rule are not case managed under rule 77. Instead, rule 76 sets up a process through which the registrar will dismiss a case that is not proceeding in a timely fashion. Rule 76.06 requires the registrar to treat an action as abandoned and dismiss it if the following conditions apply:

- no statement of defence has been filed, 180 days have passed since the originating process was filed, and nothing further has been done either to set the matter down for trial or to terminate it; or

- a statement of defence has been filed, more than 150 days have passed since the first statement of defence or notice of intent to defend has been filed, and nothing further has been done either to set the matter down for trial or to terminate it.

Before dismissing an action as abandoned, the registrar must give 45 days' notice of the pending dismissal. During the 45-day period, if the parties do nothing further, the registrar will make an order dismissing the action as abandoned.

SUMMARY JUDGMENT

Either party may move for summary judgment after the close of pleadings. The motion can be brought only before a judge in the county in which the action was commenced unless the parties agree otherwise.

As with any motion, a motion for summary judgment under the simplified procedure must be supported by evidence in the form of affidavits. A responding party is not permitted merely to deny all the allegations in the moving party's material. Responding parties must prepare their own affidavits setting out specific facts that support the refusal of summary judgment. Affidavits may be based on what the deponent was told or what he or she believes, but the court may draw an adverse inference if no direct evidence is provided from a person who has personal knowledge of the alleged facts.

A motion record must also be prepared for the motion. The record must contain the following material, arranged in the following order on consecutively numbered pages:

1. a table of contents, describing each document and exhibit by its nature, date, and in the case of an exhibit, by its exhibit number;

2. a copy of the notice of motion;

3. a copy of all the affidavits to be used; and

4. a copy of all the pleadings.

Every party must also file a factum, along with proof of service, at least two days before the hearing of the motion.

A judge must grant the summary judgment under the simplified procedure unless he or she determines that it is not possible to decide the matters at issue without cross-examination or that it would not be fair to decide the issues on the motion.

SETTING DOWN FOR TRIAL AND THE PRETRIAL CONFERENCE

Within 90 days after the first statement of defence or the notice of intention to defend has been filed, the plaintiff must serve a notice of readiness for pretrial conference, form 76C, on all the parties and file it with the court, along with proof of service. A sample form 76C is shown in figure 23.3. If the plaintiff does not take this step, any other party may do it. The filing of the notice of readiness for pretrial conference sets the case down for trial. Following the filing of the notice of readiness, the registrar schedules a pretrial conference and gives the parties at least 45 days' notice.

The parties and their lawyers are required to attend the pretrial conference unless the court orders otherwise. In addition, a party who needs approval from someone else to accept a settlement of the action must ensure that he or she has the ability throughout the conference to contact that person by telephone.

At least five days before the conference, each party must file:

- a copy of the party's affidavit of documents and copies of the documents relied on for the party's claim or defence,

- a copy of any expert's report, and

- any other material necessary for the conference.

It is not necessary to serve this material on the other parties because they will already have copies. In addition, the parties must *serve* and file:

- a two-page statement setting out the issues and the party's position with respect to them, and

- a trial management checklist (form 76D).

FIGURE 23.3 NOTICE OF READINESS FOR PRETRIAL CONFERENCE (FORM 76C)

Court file no. 01-CV-6789

ONTARIO
SUPERIOR COURT OF JUSTICE

BETWEEN:

Mabel Maddenly

Plaintiff

and

Jimmy Jingle

Defendant

NOTICE OF READINESS FOR PRE-TRIAL CONFERENCE

The plaintiff, Mabel Maddenly, is ready for a pre-trial conference and is setting this action down for trial. A pre-trial conference in the action will proceed as scheduled and the trial will proceed when the action is reached on the trial list, unless the court orders otherwise.

CERTIFICATE

I CERTIFY that there was a settlement discussion under rule 76.08.

Date: January 10, year 2

_____
Signature

Belinda Brilliant
Barrister & Solicitor
47 Tempest Road
Toronto, Ontario, M6Y 5R7

tel. 416-555-1234
fax 416-555-1235

Solicitor for the Plaintiff

TO:
George Fandoddle
Barrister & Solicitor
2001 Space Lane
Toronto, Ontario, M8U 9I4
tel. 416-666-8910
fax 416-666-8911

Solicitor for the Defendant

(Name, address and telephone and fax numbers of lawyer or moving party giving notice)

A sample trial management checklist is provided in figure 23.4.

The pretrial judge or master sets the trial date. The trial may be an ordinary trial or a summary trial under rule 76.12. If the parties cannot agree about the type of trial, the pretrial judge or master will determine which type of trial is most appropriate for the case.

Immediately after the pretrial conference, the registrar will place the action on the appropriate trial list. At least 10 days before the trial, the party that set the matter down for trial by filing the notice of readiness for the pretrial conference must serve a trial record and file it with the court with proof of service. All the parties to the main action, counterclaim, crossclaim, or third party claim must be served with the trial record.

If the trial is proceeding as an ordinary trial, the trial record is prepared in exactly the same way as the trial record for an action under the ordinary procedure (rule 48.03). If the trial is proceeding as a summary trial, the trial record must contain, in consecutively numbered pages arranged in the following order:

1. a table of contents that describes each document, including each exhibit, by its nature and date and, in the case of an exhibit, by its exhibit number or letter;

2. a copy of the pleadings, including those relating to any counterclaim, crossclaim, or third party claim;

3. a copy of any demand or order for particulars of a pleading and the particulars delivered in response;

4. a copy of any order respecting the trial;

5. a copy of all the affidavits served by all the parties for use in the summary trial; and

6. a certificate signed by the lawyer of the party filing the trial record, stating that it contains the documents listed above.

SUMMARY TRIAL

In an ordinary trial, each party calls its witnesses into the courtroom, and the witness is first questioned by the lawyer for the party who called the witness. This is called examination-in-chief. The lawyers for the other parties are then entitled to ask the witness questions on cross-examination.

In a summary trial, parties present their evidence in affidavits, eliminating examination-in-chief of witnesses at trial. Opposite parties are entitled to cross-examine witnesses in court, if necessary. Rule 76.12 sets out the order for presenting the evidence and examining witnesses at a summary trial.

A party who wants a witness presented at trial for cross-examination on affidavit must give 10 days' notice to the party who presented the affidavit. The notice is to allow the party presenting the affidavit to arrange for the deponent's attendance at trial for cross-examination.

If the parties agree to a summary trial or the pretrial judge or master orders that it proceed in that manner, a timetable for delivery of all the affidavits will be established at the pretrial conferences and the parties must abide by that schedule.

FIGURE 23.4   TRIAL MANAGEMENT CHECKLIST (FORM 76D)

TRIAL MANAGEMENT CHECKLIST

Trial Lawyer — Plaintiff (s):

Trial Lawyer — Defendant (s):

Filed by Plaintiff
Filed by Defendant
Filed by Subsequent Party

1. Issues Outstanding
    (a) liability:
    (b) damages:
    (c) other:

2. Names of Plaintiff's Witnesses

3. Names of Defendant's Witnesses

4. Admissions
    Are the parties prepared to admit any facts for
    the purposes of the trial or summary trial?   ❑ yes   ❑ no

5. Document Brief
    Will there be a document brief?   ❑ yes   ❑ no

6. Request to Admit
    Will there be a request to admit?   ❑ yes   ❑ no
    If so, have the parties agreed to a timetable?   ❑ yes   ❑ no

7. Expert's Reports
    Are any expert's reports anticipated?   ❑ yes   ❑ no

8. Amendments to Pleadings
    Are any amendments likely to be sought?   ❑ yes   ❑ no

9. Mode of Trial
    Have the parties agreed to a summary trial?   ❑ yes   ❑ no
    Have the parties agreed to an ordinary trial?   ❑ yes   ❑ no
    If the parties have not agreed about the mode of
    trial, what mode of trial is being requested by
    the party filing this checklist?

10. Factum of Law
    Will the parties be submitting factums of law?   ❑ yes   ❑ no

Unlike cross-examination in an ordinary trial, in a summary trial time limitations are placed on cross-examination of witnesses and closing arguments. All of a party's cross-examinations must be completed within 50 minutes, and each party has only 45 minutes to present a closing oral argument.

COSTS CONSEQUENCES

Since the purpose of simplified procedure is to reduce both expense and delay of litigation involving smaller amounts, there are severe cost consequences for failure to use the simplified procedure in appropriate actions. For instance, if the plaintiff proceeds to trial under the ordinary procedure seeking more than $50,000 in relief but at the end of the trial is awarded only $50,000 or less, the court can deny the plaintiff costs unless it is satisfied that it was reasonable for the plaintiff to proceed under the ordinary procedure. This ensures that plaintiffs will put appropriate thought into correctly valuing their claim before they begin the litigation.

Defendants also face potential cost consequences if they object to the actions proceeding under the simplified procedure because they say the property at issue is worth more than $50,000 and, as a result of their objection, the matter is continued under the ordinary procedure. If the court finds that the property is in fact worth $50,000 or less, the defendant will be ordered to pay the extra costs of the plaintiff that were incurred because he or she could not proceed under the simplified procedure. Any such costs will be awarded based on the substantial indemnity scale.

Any party who amends a pleading so that the action is changed from the ordinary procedure to the simplified procedure is liable for the other party's costs that were incurred because the action was originally commenced under the ordinary procedure. These costs will be awarded on a substantial indemnity basis.

CHAPTER SUMMARY

In this chapter, we have seen that the simplified procedure is a process for dealing with claims of $50,000 or less. It is not available for class action, construction lien, or family law matters. Cases involving a claim of less than $50,000 must use the simplified procedure, but cases involving a claim of more than that amount may also use this route if the parties consent. The plaintiff elects to proceed under simplified procedure but the defendants, a third party, or a party in a crossclaim or counterclaim may object by way of motion.

We have noted that the major differences between simplified procedure and ordinary procedure are that no discovery or cross-examination of witnesses on affidavits is permitted in simplified procedure, and the affidavit of documents contains an additional schedule, schedule D, which sets out the names and addresses of all the witnesses a party intends to call at trial. Motion records are not required, and the registrar has the power to deal with most simple or uncontested motions. Summary judgment is easily obtained.

We also examined the various time limits in simplified procedure. Within 60 days of the first defence being filed, the parties must hold a settlement conference to decide whether all the necessary documents have been produced and whether settlement is possible. Within 90 days, the plaintiff must set the action down for trial. The registrar will then give notice of a pretrial conference date to the parties. The parties and the lawyer must attend the pretrial conference, and if no settlement can be reached, the judge or master will set a trial date.

The trial may be a regular trial, but the matter may also proceed to a summary trial, if appropriate. In a summary trial, the parties present their evidence in affidavits and the witnesses may be cross-examined under strict time limitations.

There are severe cost consequences for failing to use the simplified procedure in an appropriate case.

NOTE

1 Rule 76 was amended, effective January 1, 2002, to raise the limit from $25,000 to $50,000. Cases in the system before January 1, 2002 still apply the $25,000 limit.

REFERENCES

Class Proceedings Act, 1992, SO 1992, c. 6.

Construction Lien Act, RSO 1990, c. C.30.

Rules of Civil Procedure, RRO 1990, reg. 194.

REVIEW QUESTIONS

1. Consider whether simplified procedure is available in the following situations:

   a. a claim for damages in the amount of $50,000;

   b. a construction lien in the amount of $25,000;

   c. a divorce action in which the total value of the net family property is $45,000;

d. a claim for damages in the amount of $75,000; and

e. a damages claim for $40,000 each by Melinda March and her daughter against George Speedy whose snowmobile ran into the March's toboggan.

2. What is the purpose of the simplified procedure?

3. What is the difference between the statement of claim in an ordinary action and the statement of claim in an action under the simplified procedure?

4. What are the major differences between the regular procedure and the simplified procedure?

5. How is an action under the simplified procedure set down for trial?

6. Your law firm's client, the CEO of a corporation, says he is too busy to attend the pretrial conference but will send his executive assistant as a representative of the corporation. Is this acceptable?

7. What is the difference between a summary trial and an ordinary trial?

8. Why is it important to use the simplified procedure in the appropriate cases?

DISCUSSION QUESTION

1. Read and respond to the following memorandum:

To: Law clerk
From: I.M. Smug, lawyer
Re: *Tome Inc. v. Joseph Apostiledes*

Our client, Joe Apostiledes, was sued by Tome Inc. for non-payment of a debt of $35,000. We have filed a statement of defence in the case, but Mr. Apostiledes has now decided he does not want legal representation and he is going to represent himself in the action. Counsel for Tome is not objecting to this motion and will not be filing any material in response.

Please prepare a motion having me removed as solicitor of record on the case.

You look in the file and see that Tome Inc. is located at 1300 Winding Lane, Toronto, Ontario, M8U 5Y7. It is represented by the firm of Tilley and Tidy, 400 Bay Street, Suite 2200, Toronto, Ontario, M7K 2Y6. Howie Tilley is the lawyer with carriage of the case. The firm's telephone number is 416-878-0000 and their fax is 416-878-0001.

Joe lives at 14 Foolhardy Way, Windsor, Ontario, N0P 4T8, and his telephone number is 613-555-1222.

Your firm is located at 1750 Cornucopia Crescent, London, Ontario, L7T U8P. The telephone number is 613-566-6666 and the fax is 613-566-6667.

Prepare the necessary form to commence the motion.

CHAPTER 24

The commercial list

INTRODUCTION

The commercial list was established in the Superior Court of Justice in Toronto for the hearing of actions, applications, and motions related to corporate and commercial matters. It is a completely voluntary method of proceeding, except for bankruptcy cases, which must be heard by placing them on the commercial list. Other cases that may be placed on the list are cases dealing with or related to

- the *Bank Act*;

- the *Ontario Business Corporations Act*;

- the *Canada Business Corporations Act*;

- the *Companies' Creditors Arrangement Act*;

- the *Limited Partnerships Act*;

- the *Pension Benefits Act*;

- the *Personal Property Security Act*;

- receivership applications and all interlocutory motions to appoint, or give directions to, receivers;

- the *Securities Act*;

- the *Winding-Up and Restructuring Act*;

- the *Credit Union and Caisses Populaires Act* relating to credit unions and caisses populaires under administration or that are being wound up or liquidated; and

- any other commercial matters that a judge presiding over the commercial list may direct be placed on the list.

Lawyers dealing with commercial law often want to have their cases on the list because the procedure for dealing with the list is speedier than the ordinary list.

The list was initially established in 1991 by a practice direction of the chief justice. As of April 2002, the original practice direction was replaced by a new practice direction that governs the procedure for the list. There is no rule dealing with any of the procedure. It is all found in the practice direction of the Honourable Justice Patrick LeSage, chief justice of the Superior Court of Justice, dated February 18, 2002.

The list is administered through the Commercial List Office, 10th floor, 393 University Avenue, in Toronto. Cases are usually heard on the 8th floor of the Court

House at that address. Only matters originating in the Toronto judicial region can be heard on the list unless the supervising judge orders otherwise.

If a case is started in the usual manner and the parties wish to transfer it to the list for hearing, the court staff in the Commercial List Office, will transfer it if all parties consent to the transfer, the proper documents are submitted, and the case involves one of the statutes or matters listed above, including bankruptcy matters.

COURT DOCUMENTS

The name of the court in the title of proceeding for cases on the list is "Superior Court of Justice — Commercial List." All notices of application or notices of motion involving the list state that the application or motion will be made to "a judge presiding over the commercial list at 393 University Avenue, Toronto."

Originating process may be issued in the Commercial List Office. In addition to the court documents needed for all actions or applications, cases to be heard on the commercial list must be accompanied by a fully completed request form and a case timetable form. These forms are not forms created by the rules and they change often. Copies of the current forms may be obtained from the Commercial List Office.

DATES FOR APPLICATIONS, MOTIONS, AND TRIALS

A realistic estimate of the time required for the hearing must be stated in the request form. Staff in the Commercial List Office schedule hearings that will take less than one day of court time. These are called "short hearings." The supervising judge schedules hearings that will take longer than one day. Each day, the supervising judge is in chambers at 9:30 a.m. to deal with urgent matters, matters without notice, consent matters, and scheduling matters. If your hearing is expected to take more than one day, the office staff will book a time for the lawyers to appear. No matter can take more than 10 minutes of the time in chambers, and all matters heard on the chambers list must be completed by 10:00 a.m. Materials to be used at the chambers appointment must be filed with the court office the day before the hearing.

If the initial hearing date is not one set by the office staff or by the supervising judge in chambers, the first court date for applications and motions is the assignment court, held on the first Monday of each month or on the first Tuesday if the Monday is a holiday. Matters in the assignment court are all scheduled for 9:30 a.m. When preparing the notice of application or the notice of motion for this type of matter, state in the notice that the application or motion is to be heard on the initial return date "and thereafter as the judge may direct."

Dates for hearing a petition in bankruptcy are also set at the assignment court on the first Monday of the month.

In order to obtain a trial date, a motion must be brought to a supervising judge in chambers, or a special appointment must be made with the court office. A trial date will not be set unless the parties have completed a case timetable. The current version of this form may be obtained from the Commercial List Office.

Counsel for the parties are expected to discuss the case timetable and, if possible, to agree on it. If they cannot agree on the schedule for the case, they must attend before the supervising judge in chambers.

If parties are not certain as to the appropriate scheduling, largely because they are negotiating scheduling issues or some other matter, the notice may simply state that the matter will be heard "on a date to be established by the Commercial List Office." The court office keeps a list of cases like this. A case remains on the list for three months, at which time it is struck off unless a judge orders otherwise.

As indicated above, a reasonable estimate of time must be made in the request form, which is to be completed for each case. The estimate should be made in conjunction with the other parties and, where possible, all counsel should sign the form. If a request form that is not signed by all counsel is submitted, the initial date will be scheduled for only a 10-minute scheduling hearing. Sometimes, although the best effort has been made to accurately estimate the time needed, it becomes obvious before the court date that more time will be required. In that case, the Commercial List Office must be advised and provided with a reason for the change.

ADJOURNMENTS AND SETTLEMENTS

Once a date has been set, the matter is expected to go ahead. Adjournments are granted in only the most exceptional circumstances. If an adjournment cannot be avoided, counsel must advise the Commercial List Office at the earliest opportunity to permit staff to reschedule the list so that time is not wasted. Counsel waiting on standby can be alerted that their matter may be scheduled, on short notice, in the vacated time slot resulting from the adjournment.

If a case has been adjourned so that settlement discussions can continue and the case is not settled within a reasonable time, a report must be made to advise the court of the status of the discussions. The report must be made within 30 days after the adjournment and may be made in court, in chambers or by letter, depending on which method is most appropriate in the circumstances.

Cases may be scheduled to be heard on a standby basis for a particular date. When a case is listed in this way, the parties should be prepared to proceed on short notice because they may get a call from the court office telling them to appear because their matter is the next on the list for that day.

CASE MANAGEMENT AND CASE SETTLEMENT

Case management under rule 77 does not apply to matters on the commercial list. However, the operation of the list is a form of informal case management. It is expected that the same judge will hear the matter through to completion. This means that if there is to be a motion on an important matter, the continuing judge must be contacted in writing by counsel in advance so that the matter may be scheduled before that judge wherever possible. The letter advising the judge of the need for a hearing on a particular issue in the case must contain a list of times when the lawyers are available to deal with the issue.

Sometimes a case-managed matter on the regular list is transferred to the commercial list, or a party may want a commercial list matter to be case managed and bring a motion requesting that direction from the judge. In such instances, the matter will be case managed, and there is a provision in the practice direction for a scheduling conference. The conference is held in order to develop a plan for the timely processing of the case through the list.

A case conference is also held no later than a month after discoveries. The purpose of the conference is to monitor the progress of the case and make efforts to settle it before trial. The plaintiff or the applicant has the responsibility of arranging the conference. The plaintiff then confers with the other parties and the court to determine a mutually agreeable date.

There is no mandatory mediation on the commercial list. However, at any time the case management judge, on the consent of the parties, may refer any issue for alternative dispute resolution. If alternative dispute resolution is ordered on a particular case, the parties must keep the case management judge apprised of the progress of the matter while it is in such resolution.

Pretrial conferences may be scheduled for entire cases or for particular issues within a case. At least five days before the conference, each party must deliver a pretrial brief to all the other parties. The brief must contain the following:

- a concise statement of facts, including the agreed facts and admissions;

- a concise summary of the issues where necessary;

- any outstanding procedural issues;

- the current settlement position of each party; and

- an estimate of the trial time.

MATERIALS FOR USE OF THE COURT AT THE HEARING

All materials that are required by the court must be filed within the times prescribed by the rules for your particular type of hearing. However, the court encourages filing of documents as early as possible. Everything must be filed by at least 2:00 p.m. two days before the hearing.

Commercial cases can be voluminous and to avoid huge files being carted around from filing to courtroom, parties are expected to notify court staff of the specific materials they want at hearings. In addition, in an effort to keep huge files in an easily accessible manner, the court suggests that counsel coordinate a common numbering scheme for the various records, transcripts, factums, authorities, and other materials intended for use by the judge. Usually, the law clerks to counsel for the parties go to the court office before the hearing to ensure that the correct materials are available to the judge.

compendium
summary of material to be referred to at a hearing, designed for easy access by judge

In addition to the documents and records used for matters on the regular list, a commercial list case may require a **compendium**. A compendium is a type of record that gives an overview of a complex case and organizes the documents to be referred to at the hearing in a way that makes it as easy as possible for the judge to locate them. A compendium usually contains a statement of the relief sought by the party and a copy of any pages from motion records, applications, or other documents that a party intends to rely on. The portions to be referred to should be highlighted. There should be a cover sheet that identifies the document from which the page has been extracted. The cover sheet should also summarize the general content of the document from which the page or pages have been extracted. If a document is only a few pages, the entire document may be included in the compendium, but if a document is lengthy and the party wishes to refer only to a portion of the document, only the portion to be referred to should be included.

The compendium should also contain the headnotes and the pages of any case authorities on which a party is relying. There is no need to include the entire case in the compendium, although it should be in the book of authorities. Only the issues being referred to should be included, and the **ratio decidendi** of the case should be highlighted.

All of these materials should be placed in a looseleaf binder. All the photocopies must be clear. The binder contents should be kept to a minimum, and wherever possible the parties should prepare a joint compendium.

If the evidence is complex or technical, the court encourages the use of diagrams, charts, lists of persons involved, point-form chronologies, and other summaries to assist in clarifying the issues and the parties. For trials, the court asks that sworn witness statements be used to replace examination-in-chief, in whole or in part, where appropriate. Statements must be exchanged with all parties well in advance of the hearing. The maker of a statement must be available at the trial for cross-examination on the statement unless the court has ordered otherwise.

In addition, draft orders should be prepared and presented by counsel for signing at the end of the hearing. Counsel for the moving party, or counsel for the plaintiff, must assist court staff in preparing the order by presenting a draft for the judge to edit. In order to facilitate the judge's editing, an electronic version of the draft order, on a disk, should be presented to the court office along with a hard copy of the draft, any handwritten endorsement of the judge, or a copy of the dictation tape. Sometimes judges' handwritten endorsements can be difficult to read. If the person drafting the order has difficulty reading the endorsement, any illegible parts should be highlighted on the copy of the endorsement so that the judge can clarify the wording of the decision.

ratio decidendi
the legal reason for the judge's decision in a case

CHAPTER SUMMARY

This chapter provided an overview of the practice direction that outlines the procedure followed for cases on the commercial list. The commercial list is a specialized list of corporate and commercial cases dealt with through an informal case management process, which allows for a speedy and efficient flow of cases through the court. Except for bankruptcy cases, which must go on the commercial list, the use of the list is voluntary.

The practice direction works with the general rules and adds to the regular procedure for cases on the commercial list. Pleadings are prepared in the same manner as regular pleadings, but the title of proceedings must appear as follows: "The Superior Court of Justice — Commercial List."

KEY TERMS

compendium

ratio decidendi

REFERENCES

Bank Act, SC 1991, c. 46, as amended.

Business Corporations Act, RSO 1990, c. B.16.

Canada Business Corporations Act, RSC 1985, c. C-44.

Companies' Creditors Arrangements Act, RSC 1985, c. C-36.

Credit Union and Caisses Populaires Act 1994, SO 1994, c. 11.

Limited Partnerships Act, RSO 1990, c. L.16.

Pension Benefits Act, RSO 1990, c. P.8.

Personal Property Security Act, RSO 1990, c. P.10.

Securities Act, RSO 1990, c. S.5.

Winding-up and Restructuring Act, RSC 1985, c. W-11.

REVIEW QUESTIONS

1. What matters may be heard on the commercial list?

2. Where are commercial list matters issued?

3. If a matter is placed on the regular list and a party wants to have it transferred to the commercial list, what is the procedure?

4. How do you obtain a hearing date for a commercial list matter?

5. When you are preparing a motion for hearing on the commercial list and no date has yet been set, what date do you put on the notice of motion?

6. What is the proper procedure for adjourning a matter on the commercial list?

7. What material is required for a pretrial hearing?

8. What is the purpose of a compendium?

CHAPTER 25

Motor vehicle insurance claims in Ontario

INTRODUCTION

Until the 1980s, cases involving personal injury and property damage resulting from the operation of a motor vehicle were handled as any other tort case. The party who was not at fault made a claim against the party who was. If the claim was not settled, the party not at fault sued the other party in tort for damages for personal injury and property loss. Because motor vehicle insurance was mandatory for all vehicles licensed in Ontario, insurance companies, through their adjusters and through lawyers retained by them, handled claims made against their insured clients. Those who were injured in motor vehicle collisions retained their own lawyers and sued the party at fault, with minimal involvement of their own insurance company.

Since there are always lots of motor vehicle accidents, there were lots of tort claims based on who was at fault. This meant that there was a large plaintiffs' personal injury bar, with many lawyers, often in small practices, able to earn a living from the high volume of motor vehicle cases. There was also a defence bar, often in larger firms, which were retained by insurance companies to handle claims made against the insurance company or its insured.

Insurance companies generally disliked this adversarial tort system of compensation for motor vehicle collisions for a number of reasons. Compensation based on fault necessitated establishing who was at fault, which usually involved lengthy and time-consuming litigation and increased the costs of doing business for the insurer, which had to litigate and then pay a claim. Because plaintiffs could opt for a jury trial, there was a perception that juries would inflate damages.

In the 1970s, across Canada and the United States a movement spearheaded by insurance companies clamoured for **tort reform**, which aimed to remove compensation for damages from motor vehicle collisions from the courts, with insurance companies simply compensating their own insured for damages sustained regardless who was at fault. The proponents of tort reform thought that this would result in far less litigation, reduce the costs of settling claims, and reduce the amounts that were paid out in some cases. The movement was largely successful, and today across Canada and much of the United States, motor vehicle claims are often handled on a **no fault** basis, where claims are paid by the claimant's own insurer. In some cases, insurance companies may try to apportion liability, as between

tort reform
campaign to change provincial legislation to limit access by motor vehicle accident claimants to civil courts in order to claim damages

no fault
term that usually refers to a system where motor vehicle insurance claims are paid out by the claimant's own insurer regardless who is at fault and without the claimant's suing for damages

themselves, on the basis of whose insured was at fault, but this does not affect their obligation to pay their own insured.

The statutory regimes set up to replace the civil tort action as a means of deciding claims vary widely. Some provinces, such as British Columbia, have set up a single public automobile insurer to insure all motor vehicles registered in the province. If both cars involved in a collision are registered in British Columbia, the government insurer simply compensates both parties for their losses without determining who is at fault. Ontario has gone through several variations of no fault insurance since 1990. At present, the system is a partial or modified no fault system. Ordinary accidents are covered by the no fault rules, where an insurer pays its own insured and passengers in the insured vehicle for their medical needs, as well as for damage to the insured's car or other property. However, if the claimant, whether insured or not, suffers a catastrophic injury, he or she may sue the person who caused the injury in tort for general damages for pain and suffering in respect of that injury, while having other personal injury and property loss damages covered under the no fault rules. A claimant involved in a dispute regarding which insurance company is responsible for making payments may need to sue or engage in private arbitration to determine the answer to that question. If there is a question about which jurisdiction's law applies to an accident, that question must be resolved in the courts.

The change in the law has changed the involvement of lawyers in motor vehicle collision cases. If a collision involves only property damage and minor injuries, there is no right to sue the party at fault for damages, and those with losses are paid by their own insurer or, if they are passengers, by the car owner's insurer. In this situation, there appeared to be no role for lawyers. The injured person sent a claim to the insurance company, which processed it and paid the claim. Many lawyers who had had a personal injury practice began to plan to take on other kinds of cases.

However, some unexpected things began to happen under the no fault regime which brought personal injury lawyers back into motor vehicle collision cases. While the insurers paid many no fault claims without any fuss, some claims were contested or refused. Insurers carefully scrutinized costly claims for injuries leading to partial disability, chronic illness, or which prevented an early return to work. Some claims were refused outright. Others, which were seen to be inflated or exaggerated, were paid in a limited fashion. It was not very long before disputes between claimants and insurance companies began to spring up. These disputes quickly began to involve lawyers, as clients looked for professional help in their struggles with insurance companies.

Today, many personal injury lawyers find that a growing part of their practice involves disputes about the payment of no fault benefits. In marshalling evidence and information, managing a case file, and completing forms, there are ample opportunities for litigation law clerks. The balance of this chapter is devoted to an overview of the dispute settlement process.

NO FAULT DISPUTE SETTLEMENT SYSTEM

These disputes are not generally settled by lawsuits.[1] Instead, the **Financial Services Commission of Ontario (FSCO)**, the body which regulates motor vehicle insurers in Ontario, handles these disputes using alternative dispute resolution techniques. Before 1998, the superintendent of insurance handled these disputes.

Financial Services Commission of Ontario (FSCO)
provincial body established in 1998 to supervise and regulate the financial services industry, including pension trusts, credit unions, cooperatives, mortgage brokers, provincial loan and trust companies, and insurance companies

Dispute Resolution Practice Code

WHERE TO FIND IT

FSCO has established a **Dispute Resolution Group** to handle disputes between insurers and claimants. It has developed a relatively straightforward **Dispute Resolution Practice Code** that describes the mechanism for settling disputes and provides procedural rules that are less formal than, but not unlike some of, the procedures described in the *Rules of Civil Procedure*. The discussion of procedures under the code in this chapter is based on the version of the code released on May 31, 2001, which was the latest version at the time of writing. Since this area is currently evolving, you are advised to update the code. There may have been changes since this book was written. If you are going to do legal work in this area, you should diarize periodic updating. Printed copies may be obtained from Publications Ontario, 880 Bay Street, Toronto, Ontario, M7A 1N8. You may also download the complete code, as updated, at no cost from the FSCO Web site at http://www.fsco.gov.on.ca/.

As arbitration and appeals increase in volume, a body of case law has begun to develop. This should be checked as part of the process of preparing a disputed claim. The complete text of case decisions is posted on a secure part of the FSCO Web site, for which a password is needed. To obtain a password, call 1-800-517-2332, extension 7202 (Toronto 416-590-7202). Summaries of decisions are reported and published by private law publishers.[2] You may obtain the forms required to access code dispute settlement procedures from an insurer, or you may download them from the FSCO Web site noted above.

WHAT'S IN IT?

The code has seven parts, divided into sections A through G. Section A contains the rules of procedure for the forms of dispute settlement employed at FSCO. There are rules governing mediation, **arbitration**, **neutral evaluation**, appeals of arbitration orders, variation of orders, and general procedures for hearings. Section B sets out guidelines issued by the superintendent of FSCO and the former superintendent of insurance for the interpretation and application of the ***Statutory Accident Benefits Schedule***. Section C contains practice notes, which are issued by the Dispute Resolution Group to explain key elements of the dispute resolution process. Section D sets out the fees and expenses payable at various stages of the procedure. An example is the fee payable on summonsing a witness to an arbitration hearing. Sections E and F contain regulations that apply to settlements and the determination of expenses. Section G contains copies of the prescribed forms used in the FSCO dispute resolution procedures.

Determining benefits

Most disputes involve the *Statutory Accident Benefits Schedule*: how much should be paid and for how long. You should refer to part B of the code and the publications referred to earlier in this chapter for detailed information and analysis of legal issues. At this point, as a law clerk or paralegal assisting with the resolution of a claim dispute, you need to know what types of insurance benefits are likely to be the subject of a dispute. This matter has two components: the type of benefit and the date on which the accident occurred.

Dispute Resolution Group
branch of FSCO that oversees the settlement and adjudication of no fault benefit disputes between claimants and insurance companies

Dispute Resolution Practice Code
user's guide to dispute settlement procedures that are available to settle no fault benefit claims

arbitration
court-like procedure where a neutral third party, chosen by the parties, hears each side of the dispute and renders a binding decision

neutral evaluation
optional procedure that may follow a failed mediation in which a neutral third party gives an assessment of the likely outcome of arbitration

Statutory Accident Benefits Schedule
schedule attached to every automobile insurance policy issued in Ontario, setting out the mandatory no fault benefits, including amounts payable or a formula for determining them

---

The following types of no fault benefits are available under current legislation for accidents that occurred on or after November 1, 1996:

1. *Income replacement benefits.* These benefits pay a claimant for lost income as a result of being unable to work because of an injury;

2. *Non-earner benefits.* These benefits are paid if a claimant suffers a complete inability to carry on a normal life if the claimant does not qualify for income replacement or caregiver benefits because he or she was not working and/or was not entitled to caregiver benefits.

3. *Caregiver benefits.* These benefits are paid if a person who is injured cannot continue as the main caregiver for someone who is under 16 or who is over 18 and requires care because of a mental or physical disability.

4. *Medical benefits.* These benefits are paid for reasonable and necessary medical expenses that are not covered by a provincial or other medical health insurance plan.

5. *Rehabilitation benefits.* These benefits are paid for things such as physiotherapy or for prosthetic devices that are not covered by the provincial health insurance plan or by any other insurance plan.

6. *Attendant care benefits.* These benefits are paid for the expenses of an aid or attendant, or for otherwise uninsured services provided in a long-term care facility, such as a nursing home or chronic-care hospital.

7. *Care manager benefits.* These benefits are paid in the case of a complex and catastrophic injury where the provision of goods and services for a person badly impaired is so complicated as to require someone to coordinate care.

8. *Death benefits.* These benefits provide a sum of money, usually a lump sum, to the survivors of a person who dies as a result of a motor vehicle collision.

9. *Funeral expenses.* These benefits pay a sum for the reasonable funeral expenses of a person who dies as a result of a collision.

10. *Other expenses.* These benefits pay sums for other losses, including the cost of home maintenance and housekeeping services or lost educational expenses while the injured person is recovering. It may also cover the cost of visiting an injured claimant. This benefit also covers the cost of repairing or replacing items that were lost or damaged as the result of the accident. It does not include damage to the automobile, which is covered under a different part of the automobile insurance policy. Also remember that in a catastrophic injury, the injured party may sue the person who caused the injury in tort for damages for pain and suffering and the loss of enjoyment of life. In a serious case, these damages could be equal to or greater than all the statutory benefits taken together.

The second matter to be considered is the date on which the accident took place because there have been three different no fault accident regimes in Ontario since 1990. If the accident occurred in 1991, the no fault benefit rules that apply are those that were in place in 1991, even though these rules are no longer the law in

Ontario. For example, the types of benefits available since 1996 are those described above. Before 1996, other benefits were available, and amounts were different, as were eligibility requirements. Table 25.1 sets out the relevant dates and references to the legislation and regulations for those dates that you must examine to determine your client's rights.

None of these rules applies to accidents that occurred before June 21, 1990.

PROCEDURAL STEPS UNDER THE CODE

How to approach code procedures

In this section, with the help of the much afflicted Abigail Boar, we will examine the basic procedure and filing rules under section A of the code. This includes mediation, arbitration, neutral evaluation, arbitration appeals, variation of an order, and general hearing procedures. There are other questions and issues beyond those covered in part A of the code, but space does not permit us to cover them here. If you are going to work in this area, or are examining the subject in depth, you should buy or download a complete copy of the code.

What does the code say?

When you learned about the civil court procedures earlier in this text, we suggested that you read the relevant *Rules of Civil Procedure* that were discussed in the text and in class. In law, the use of primary reliable sources is important. Here we suggest that you accompany your reading of this text with an examination of the primary source for our discussion: part A of the Dispute Resolution Practice Code.

Overview of procedural requirements before administrative boards and tribunals

FSCO and its Dispute Resolution Group do not constitute a court. Instead, they form a specialized body that regulates insurance. Under its enabling legislation, FSCO is given the power to set up bodies and procedures to settle disputes about a variety of things. One of those things is a dispute between claimants and insurance companies about the right to be paid no fault benefits for injuries and property losses. Instead of suing the insurance company, alternative dispute resolution procedures, such as mediation and arbitration, are used.

Administrative boards and tribunals, such as those established here by FSCO, are thought to be less expensive and faster than courts. Procedures are simplified, with the aim that a well informed person can use the system to obtain remedies without a lawyer, at least in some cases. Settlement without an adversarial hearing is a primary goal in FSCO's alternative dispute resolution system, in the belief that a compromise fashioned by the parties is more durable and legitimate than a solution imposed by a third party.

Arbitration involves simple procedures and relaxed rules of evidence — for example, admitting hearsay. The hearing atmosphere is usually much less formal than in a civil court. Arbitrators are not bound by the decisions of other arbitrators. For that reason, the case law summaries available from FSCO cannot be relied on as precedents, at least to the extent that the outcome of a previous case automatically

TABLE 25.1   NO FAULT BENEFITS

Date accident occurred	*Relevant legislation*
On or after November 1, 1996	• *Insurance Act*, including amendments under the *Automobile Insurance Rate Stability Act, 1996* • *Statutory Accidents Benefit Schedule — Accidents on or After November 1, 1996*
On or between January 1, 1994 and October 31, 1996	• *Insurance Act*, as amended by the *Insurance Statute Law Amendment Act, 1993* • *Statutory Accident Benefits Schedule — Accidents After December 31, 1993 and Before November 1, 1996*
On or between June 22, 1990 and December 31, 1993	• *Insurance Act*, also known as the *Ontario Motorist Protection Plan* • *Statutory Accident Benefits Schedule — Accidents Before January 1, 1994*

determines the outcome of the dispute you are working on. Instead, previous cases lend insights and should be treated with respect by an arbitrator as being persuasive.

While proceedings may be informal, the arbitrator is bound to meet certain minimal standards of **natural justice** or **procedural fairness**. The arbitrator must allow each side to present his or her case, and each side should know the case against it and be able to make an answer. The Superior Court has the authority to oversee the operation of administrative boards, tribunals, arbitrators, and other quasi-judicial decision makers to ensure that the parties are treated fairly. However, the court will usually not intervene on a finding of fact since it defers to the decision maker's expertise in dealing with the facts in the specialized area within his or her jurisdiction. It will also not usually interfere with a finding of law or legal interpretation unless the finding or interpretation is plainly or obviously wrong or unless it led an arbitrator to wrongly accept or decline jurisdiction over the matter in issue between the parties.

Suppose that instead of tripping on an oil spill in the Rattle Motors showroom, Abigail Boar asks to take a demonstration drive in the Super Coupe. She drives the car out of the lot and onto the road. While she is lawfully proceeding through an intersection in a northerly direction, Helmut Hapless, driving his car westerly on a cross street, fails to stop at a stop sign and hits the Super Coupe broadside. The Super Coupe is spun around, and Abigail's head strikes the door, knocking Abigail unconscious. She is hospitalized and kept under observation for three days. When she is released, she finds that she has short-term memory problems and is unable to perform the core functions of her job as an investment analyst. The Imperialist Payless Insurance Co. insures the Super Coupe. Abigail applies for and receives a variety of no fault benefits. She is paid relevant benefits, including loss of income benefits, while she is unable to work. However, six months after the injury, Imperialist Payless takes the position that Abigail is ready to return to work. Abigail still has

natural justice
basic elements of a fair hearing, including one impartial judge, the right to be told the case against one, and the right to answer it

procedural fairness
the idea that procedural rules are fair and fairly applied

short-term memory problems and now has headaches. She says that she cannot perform the core functions of her job, and she must lie in a dark, quiet room when her headaches strike. Imperialist Payless claims it will cease paying the loss of income benefit in two weeks' time. It asks Abigail to attend for an examination by its neurologist and a psychologist, and Abigail does so. Imperialist Payless takes the position that Abigail can return to work half time. Its medical experts are of the view that Abigail has exaggerated her symptoms and that she could control her headaches by taking appropriate pain medication. Abigail is averse to "messing with drugs," as she puts it, and thinks the recommended medication will create long-term health problems. Her neurologist says there is one study that links the medication in question to profound depression that can lead to suicide in a handful of cases.

If Abigail wishes to contest this decision, she must take steps under the FSCO procedure.

General rules of dispute resolution: Section A, part 1

If Abigail looks at part 1 of the code, she will find a variety of principles underlying dispute resolution procedures that are similar to some found in the *Rules of Civil Procedure*. It is clear that the lawyers involved in drafting these rules were familiar with the *Rules of Civil Procedure* and used those rules as a model. They differ in some respects: There are more procedurally prescribed opportunities to settle at all stages of the process. Because non-lawyers using these procedures may make legal errors, the commission retains the power to require parties to remedy deficiencies in their documents before being allowed to proceed.

The rules are to be given a broad interpretation to produce just and quick results. Where the rules do not provide for something that must be done, parties may develop a procedure that is similar to other procedures in the code. If parties make a technical mistake, the proceeding is not automatically terminated. However, if the error leads to the failure to prove something that must be proved or leads to a legal error, the results can be fatal to an action.

The **director of arbitrations** under s. 21 of the *Insurance Act* makes the rules, at least in theory. In reality, a committee of civil servants acting under the director's authority assembles the rules. The rules must conform to the minimum standards for Ontario boards and tribunals set out in s. 25.1 of the *Statutory Powers Procedure Act*. The director has immediate control over the process for making rules and has the power to change the rules immediately whenever he or she sees fit. This allows a good deal of flexibility to deal with procedural problems, which is important in a new rule system such as this one. It also means you should be prepared to do regular checks of the FSCO Web site to see if the rules have been updated. Remember that they were completely reworked as a new code effective on May 21, 2001. It is reasonable to expect changes as the code is fine-tuned.

Rules 2.1 and 2.2 give the director the authority to publish guidelines to tell you how the *Statutory Accident Benefits Schedule* (SABS) operates and is to be interpreted. Guidelines issued by the superintendent of insurance, the person with authority in this area before the establishment of FSCO, are also authoritative unless replaced by new rules made by the director. The guidelines are found in section B of the code. Arbitrators and mediators follow them so they function as interpretive tools, like case law.

director of arbitrations
person who oversees the arbitration, appeals, and adjudication system and who is given power under the rules to control the process

Practice notes are another interpretive tool found in section C of the code. These are procedural and administrative guidelines for users of the mediation and arbitration processes. They do not bind adjudicators, however (rules 3.1 and 3.2).

Use of a language other than English

Because FSCO is a government agency, the *French Language Services Act* applies. A person has a right to communicate with FSCO in French and to avail himself or herself of services in French, where those services are available. However, if you wish to use a language other than English or French in mediation, you must supply and pay for your own interpreter. However, in an arbitration proceeding (including appeals, variations, and revocations), the Dispute Resolution Group will arrange for and pay for an interpreter for any language other than English.

Service of documents

When Abigail decides to dispute Imperialist Payless's position, she must start with mediation and then move to arbitration if she is not satisfied with the mediator's suggestions. To commence the mediation process, she must file form A, the application for mediation. In doing so, she will have to pay attention to the requirements of rules 6 and 7. Where a document must be filed, it must be delivered to the Dispute Resolution Group using one of the methods set out in rule 7 within the time limits set out there. There are seven methods of delivery or service of a document:

1. *Personal service.* Personal service involves handing a document to an employee at the Dispute Resolution Group Office or to a party; delivery is deemed to occur when the document is actually delivered. The office address of the group, which appears on the front of all forms, is 5160 Yonge Street, 15th floor, North York, Ontario, M2N 6L9.

2. *Service by regular, registered, or certified mail.* Delivery is deemed to occur on the fifth day after mailing.

3. *Service by courier.* This service includes priority courier; delivery is deemed to be made on the day of receipt or the second day after the document is given to the courier, whichever is earlier.

4. *Service by fax.* This mode of service requires a cover page identifying the sender and noting the date and time sent, the name of the person to be served, and the number of pages sent. Delivery is deemed to occur on the day the document is sent.

5. *Service through a document exchange.* Where the person served is a member of an exchange with the right to receive documents, service is deemed to occur on the day after the document is deposited with the exchange.

6. *Service by e-mail.* Provided that the sender includes his or her e-mail address and telephone number, delivery is deemed to occur on the day the e-mail is sent.

7. *Service by other method.* Service may also be made by any other method and within any time period specified by the director. While there is no

specific procedure for substitute service, this part of rule 7 may allow you to apply to the director for permission to serve in a specific way.

While rule 6 speaks about delivery to the Dispute Resolution Group, presumably rules 6 and 7 also apply to delivery or service on an opposing party or the party's representative.

Calculation of time

Rule 8 sets out the basic means for calculating time periods in the rules, which are based on rule 3 of the *Rules of Civil Procedure*. Where there is a number of days between two events in a rule, count by excluding the date of the first event but include the date of the second. Where a time period ends on a Saturday, Sunday, or holiday, the time period ends on the next day that is not a Saturday, Sunday, or holiday. Any document filed or served after 4:45 p.m. is deemed to be served on the next business day. The 4:45 rule stops you from sending an e-mail at 11:59 p.m. on Tuesday and having it deemed to be delivered on that Tuesday instead of the next day.

Right to representation

Abigail has the right, under rule 9, to represent herself or be represented by someone else (not necessarily a lawyer). She must provide the group with contact information for herself and her representative. She and her representative must report address and telephone number changes, if any, to the group and to other parties. This is also the case if she changes her representative or decides to dispense with representation. A representative who wishes to withdraw, however, prejudices the position of the party for whom he or she acts. The representative is required to have the consent of the party, failing which the **registrar** or the adjudicator can set terms governing the withdrawal and may require the representative to continue to act, at least until someone else can step in. These controls are similar to those governing a lawyer who is retained for an action and wishes to withdraw from the case after proceedings have commenced: Either the client consents or the court must give permission, taking some care to safeguard the client's rights.

registrar
official who oversees the administration of some of the alternative dispute resolution processes offered by or through the Dispute Resolution Group

If Abigail appoints a representative, she must give written authority to the representative to discuss all issues in dispute, to negotiate, and to settle. The group may require Abigail to provide a copy of the document authorizing the representative to act. If a lawyer is acting, a detailed retainer form can be used to meet this requirement. If an agent (a law clerk or paralegal) acts, he or she can use a form like a retainer that grants authority. A power of attorney, if one exists, may be sufficient for this purpose. There is a problem, however, with authority to settle. Abigail is unlikely to want to give a representative complete freedom to settle without confirming and obtaining Abigail's express approval of the specific terms. She may want to set limits below which the representative may not go. Because this information is usually privileged, Abigail and her representative would be wise to object to revealing this information without assurances that it will be completely confidential and not made available to other parties or to the adjudicator. The other and better way to handle the problem is for Abigail to attend the mediation session — the mediator will probably require her to be there anyway.

If it appears a representative lacks authority, the adjudicator may adjourn the proceeding until authority has been obtained or verified.

Persons under disability

Rule 10 covers persons under disability. Abigail will be presumed capable unless she has been found mentally incapable under ss. 6 to 22 of the *Substitute Decisions Act* or unless she is a minor.

If she is mentally incapable, she must be represented by a court-appointed guardian of property, the public guardian and trustee, or a person appointed under a continuing power of attorney with authority to deal with property.

If the person is a minor, a parent who lives with the minor may represent the child, as may a custodial parent. Otherwise, a court-appointed guardian may act, or the children's lawyer may act if no one else is available.

If, in the course of a mediation, arbitration, or other proceeding, it appears that a party may be mentally incapable, though not so found by a court, there is a procedure for dealing with mental capability as a preliminary issue. A party or an adjudicator can raise the issue. The adjudicator has the power to appoint a spouse, same-sex partner, or near relative, if that person is both willing and able to act. Failing that, the adjudicator may notify the public guardian and trustee to take steps under the *Substitute Decisions Act* to appoint someone to act. The person appointed must submit any settlement to the courts for approval and review, as is usual in the case of a mentally incapable person.

Limitation periods

If Abigail wants to dispute Imperialist Payless's decision, how long does she have? Rule 11 provides the answer. She has two years from the date on which she received written notice from the insurer of its refusal to pay the amount claimed, to file an application for mediation, neutral evaluation, or arbitration. A party may file an application for arbitration within 90 days of receiving a mediator's report or within 30 days of receiving a report of a neutral evaluator. If the party wishes to proceed from mediation to arbitration, it appears that both processes must be commenced, though not necessarily completed, within the two-year time frame.

The relevant timelines are set out below.

1. Apply for mediation within 2 years of denial of benefits.

2. A mediator should be assigned within 3 weeks of your application.

3. Complete mediation within 60 days of the filing of the application.

4. The report of the mediator is issued within 7 business days of the conclusion of mediation.

5. Apply for arbitration within 2 years of denial of benefits or within 90 days of the report of the mediator.

6. An arbitrator is assigned within 5 business days of the receipt of the application.

7. Dates for a prehearing are available within 6 to 8 weeks from the receipt of the application.

8. Dates for holding an arbitration hearing are available within 4 to 6 months from the conclusion of the prehearing discussion.

9. An arbitration hearing usually takes about 3 days, depending on the complexity of the issues.

10. An arbitration order is issued 60 to 85 days after the conclusion of the hearing.

11. A written arbitration hearing is usually completed within 60 days of filing for arbitration.

12. An order on a written arbitration is issued on the later of 60 days after the last day on which you could file a reply to the application or 30 days after the last day on which the parties are required to file written submissions.

13. File an appeal from an arbitrator's order within 30 days of the date of the order.

14. A decision in the appeal should be issued 60 to 85 days after the conclusion of an oral or written appeal hearing.

15. Request an assessment of expenses within 30 days from the date of the order of the arbitrator.

16. An order for an assessment of expenses is issued within 60 to 85 days of the conclusion of the expense assessment hearing.

Mediation procedural rules: Section A, part 2

The procedural rules for the mediation and neutral evaluation processes are set out in rules 12 to 24. The rules contemplate that the parties begin with mediation and move on to arbitration (rule 21.3). To request mediation, the applicant must be an insured person or claimant or an insurance company. A claimant who is not the policy holder is still referred to as "the insured" under these rules. There must be a dispute about an insured's entitlement under the *Statutory Accident Benefits Schedule* about the amount to be paid where the insurance company has denied a claim, or about a failure by the insurer to reply to the claim within the time provided by the *Insurance Act*.

Abigail is a claimant and an insured person for the purposes of the *Insurance Act* because she has been injured and has claimed a benefit, even though she is not named in the policy and is not the policy owner. The principal dispute is about whether the payment of a benefit should continue. Abigail meets the prerequisites for mediation and must now file a completed application for mediation in form A. The form appears to be lengthy and complex, but it is designed to be user friendly to a non-lawyer. However, where the mediation is likely to involve complex evidentiary issues, Abigail would be wise to hire I.M. Just to represent her. Since the issues to be mediated are identified from form A and are likely to be carried forward into arbitration, I.M. Just should draft form A so that Abigail's case is put forth as persuasively as possible from the earliest possible opportunity.

Contents of the application for mediation

Form A must describe each issue in dispute. In this case the only issue is whether or not loss of income benefits should continue to be paid because Abigail is unable to return to work. I.M. Just must list all documents he intends to rely on at mediation that are in his possession or that he will produce. He need not, therefore, produce privileged documents or even identify them on the list if he is not going to refer to them at mediation. These documents might include medical assessments and reports from Abigail's family doctor, neurologist, or psychologist; reports on Abigail's ability to work; and a report from Abigail's employer describing her core functions at work and the skills she needs for her job.

Form A must also list other documents that Abigail does not have but that she wishes to rely on in settlement discussions and that can be produced from other persons, including the insurer. These might include reports of "return to work" counsellors employed by the insurer or medical reports from specialists retained by the insurer.

If the applicant was the insurer, the name and contact information for the insurer's representative must also be included.

Designated assessments

designated assessment centre
neutral health care provider or facility designated by FSCO to provide objective assessments of a claimant's injuries for use at mediation and in other dispute resolution procedures

Abigail may be asked by the mediator or by the insurer or may volunteer to attend a **designated assessment centre** to obtain an objective assessment of her medical condition.[3] These centres are health care facilities appointed under the authority of the *Statutory Accident Benefits Schedule* to carry out these independent assessments. If Abigail is asked to attend and does not do so, she may be barred from proceeding with mediation or any other procedure. This is an alternative to the more traditional approach where the insurance company asks the claimant to attend for an examination by a medical specialist chosen by the insurer to obtain a second opinion.

Power to remedy deficiencies in the application

The group has the power to stop proceedings and require that defects apparent in the mediation application be remedied or satisfactorily explained before proceedings continue. This may be done where the application:

- is incomplete;

- arrives after the time required for commencing proceedings;

- raises issues that are beyond the dispute resolution powers given to the group under the Act; or

- is frivolous, vexatious, or an abuse of process.

If the applicant cannot satisfy the group's concerns or remedy the deficiencies, the group may reject the mediation application. If the matter has been previously mediated, it cannot be mediated again.

Completed application

Abigail's application is set out in figure 25.1. You should read it carefully because it contains useful information about how the process works and about what needs to be included. The form appears to be lengthy. This is because we have included the pages that refer to accidents that occurred before 1996 so that you can see and compare the differences as the legislation changed since 1990. You may be involved with claims involving coverage for chronic disability and illness arising from collisions that occurred before 1996. Remember that when you file a form, only include the part for the time period in which the accident occurred.

Once Abigail delivers form A to the group, it sends a copy to the insurer together with a blank form B, response to the application for mediation. The group also appoints a mediator (rule 13). The parties have no choice of mediator, as they have with mediation in the Superior Court.

Response by the insurer

The insurer (or responding party if the insurer is the applicant) has 10 days to file form B. In it, the insurer must respond to each issue raised by Abigail. Here the only issue is the duration of the payment of the loss of income benefit. The insurer can raise other issues and add them to the mediation process. The insurer must include a copy of the statement of benefits denying further payments, or other explanatory document, if Abigail did not include a copy of the one she received. Like Abigail, the insurer must list documents it relies on and list ones it is requesting from other parties, including Abigail. The insurer must also identify its representative and include contact information for that person. Once it is completed, the insurer must deliver the response to the group and to Abigail (rule 14). The insurer's completed form B is set out in figure 25.2.

Power to control proceedings

Because a car accident can involve a number of injured claimants and a number of insurers, the group has the power to control potentially complicated proceedings where there are common issues of fact, common parties, or common legal issues. Provided that it is fair to do so, under rule 15 the group may:

- combine applications;

- have mediations follow one after the other, using the same mediator, where there are several applications; and

- conduct all mediation sessions as one session with all parties present, if the parties consent.

Rule 16 makes it clear that the mediator controls the process. He or she may (and probably will) conduct mediation with the parties in adjoining rooms or the same room. Alternatively, the mediator may choose to mediate by telephone conference where the issues are not complex.

Providing relevant documents and attending mediation

At least 10 days before mediation, the parties must engage in a form of discovery of documents by furnishing the mediator and other parties with copies of the documents on which they rely (rule 16).[4] Rule 17 indicates that all parties are expected to participate in mediation in good faith and to attend mediation as the mediator directs even if they have a named representative. The representative speaks for the party but does not stand in for him or her. The party must be there to agree to any settlement. If a party does not attend, the mediator may adjourn proceedings. If a party refuses to attend or is uncooperative, the mediator may report that mediation has failed.

Privileged information in the mediation process

Because mediation requires that parties make a frank attempt to settle, whatever their legal rights, all statements and offers made by them are made "without prejudice"; this means that the statements cannot be used to bind the person who made them in subsequent proceedings before an adjudicator (rule 18). The mediator also maintains confidentiality if asked to do so with respect to things said to him or her or with respect to documents he or she is shown. When mediation is concluded, the only document or information available is the mediator's report.

Time limits in mediation

One party cannot drag mediation out forever. Rule 19 requires it to be concluded within 60 days of the filing of an application for mediation. The parties may agree to extend time beyond the 60-day limit, but they must consult with the mediator and confirm the dates agreed on for further mediation sessions. Should the parties settle, rule 20 requires them to inform the mediator. A settlement has the usual legal consequences. If it involves persons under legal disability, it must be confirmed by the court. Once an issue is settled, neither party can relitigate it. The settlement bars further legal action.

Mediation succeeds when the parties settle one or more issue. It fails when the mediator is of the view that mediation cannot succeed, and he or she tells the parties this. It also fails when the time limits for concluding mediation have passed, including extensions of time, and the parties have not reached an agreement. If mediation fails, rule 21.2 requires the insurer to provide the mediator with its last offer. No party can resort to the courts, file for arbitration, or agree to private arbitration unless they have participated in the mandatory mediation process (rule 21.3).

Mediation report

Once the mediation has been completed, the mediator files a report, which contains the following:

- a description of the issues in dispute;

- an identification of issues that were resolved and the terms of settlement;

- the insurer's last offer as required under rule 21.2 — for example, an offer to continue benefits if Abigail tries an alternative treatment;

- a description of steps agreed to by the parties to help them settle outstanding issues — for example, Abigail might agree to a course of alternative treatment as a condition for continued benefit payments;

- a list of documents the parties failed to produce that the mediator thought were required; and

- the mediator's recommendation as to whether or not remaining issues should be referred to neutral evaluation before proceeding to arbitration (rule 22.1). A mediator will recommend neutral evaluation if he or she thinks a party can be persuaded to settle an issue, even if it has not settled at mediation.

The mediator's report is sent to the group, which distributes it to the parties, to the neutral evaluator appointed by the director of the group, and to an arbitrator appointed by the director. If a party believes anything in the mediator's report is inaccurate, he or she must notify the mediator and the other parties in writing within 10 days of receiving the report. The mediator may amend the report if he or she considers it appropriate, and the amendments are distributed to all those originally entitled to a copy of the report (rule 23).

Neutral evaluation

Rule 24 sets out the steps for neutral evaluation. Neutral evaluation functions in the same manner as a pretrial conference in the Superior Court. It creates an opportunity for parties to have an objective and frank appraisal of their chances at arbitration on the issues outstanding on completion of mediation. That appraisal also gives a further opportunity to settle.

A mediator or the parties may jointly ask for neutral evaluation. If so, the parties may jointly retain a private neutral evaluator,[5] or in their referral to arbitration (form C) they may jointly request neutral evaluation under the rules in part 3 of the code.[6] If the parties jointly ask for private neutral evaluation, the director must appoint the person they select once he or she has provided contact information and once he or she has confirmed that a neutral evaluation will be conducted at the parties' expense in accordance with the requirements of the *Insurance Act*. Otherwise, the director will appoint a neutral evaluator who will act through FSCO at no charge to the parties. Once the parties have agreed to neutral evaluation, they must complete it. They cannot resort to the courts or push ahead with arbitration until the evaluation process has been completed (rule 24).

Arbitration and neutral evaluation procedural rules: Section A, part 3

Let us suppose that Abigail is adamant on the question of medication and alternate treatment plans and insists that she is entitled to further payments of loss of income benefits. Her next step is to apply for arbitration with or without neutral evaluation. These procedures are governed by rules 25 to 49. An aggrieved claimant must file a completed application for arbitration in form C. A completed application for arbitration appears in figure 25.3. The rules do not seem to contemplate an insurer's launching an arbitration because it is the insurer's decision not to pay that is the subject of an arbitration when mediation fails.

The arbitration process here is not simply a gallop to an adversarial proceeding. There are a number of side excursions possible for neutral evaluation and further attempts at settlement before slugging it out at arbitration. Abigail will still have some opportunities to think about compromise and settlement, as will the insurance company.

Application for arbitration

When Abigail files form C, the application for arbitration, she must include in it:

- a description of each issue to be arbitrated, provided that the issue has been mediated, and mediation has failed;

- an explanation of why she failed to provide documents requested by the other side, as reported in the report of the mediator;

- a list of other key documents that she intends to rely on (this will probably be the same as the documents relied on at mediation);

- a list of other documents that she intends to obtain from others, including the insurer (if she received these documents at mediation, this may be a short list); and

- an indication of her preference for an oral hearing (the usual), a hearing based on written submissions, or a hearing conducted by way of telephone conference (rule 25.1).

Abigail must also include with the application for arbitration:

- a cheque in the amount of the required arbitration filing fee (currently $100) as established in part D of the code;

- a copy of the report of the mediator relating to issues to be arbitrated; and

- a copy of the report of the neutral evaluator or a confirmation that the parties received it if the parties jointly agreed to private neutral evaluation before filing for arbitration (rules 25.1 and 25.2).

The claimant may also request neutral evaluation at FSCO in the application for arbitration if there has been no private neutral evaluation, as may the insured in its response. If conducted through FSCO, the neutral evaluation follows the procedures in rule 44, which will be discussed later.

As was the case with mediation, the rules contemplate that an unrepresented claimant may make an application. If the arbitration application is incomplete or is otherwise procedurally or substantially defective, rule 25.4 gives control of the process to the group's registrar. If an arbitrator has been appointed, the arbitrator also may exercise the powers of the registrar to adjourn proceedings and hold the application for 20 days until the defects are remedied. If they are not remedied or if the applicant is abusing the process, the registrar or the arbitrator may reject the application.

Once the application has been delivered to FSCO and reviewed by the registrar, he or she will deliver a copy to other parties.

Insurer's response options to an application for arbitration

Once Imperialist Payless receives Abigail's application for arbitration, it has some options. Within 20 days of the receipt of the application, it must do one of the following:

1. *Proceed to arbitration under rule 27.* If the insurer wishes to proceed directly to arbitration without neutral evaluation because both parties have not agreed to it, the insurer files form E, the response by insurer, together with form F, the statement of service, to prove delivery. The insurer then follows directions in rule 27.

2. *Proceed to private neutral evaluation under rule 44 at claimant's request.* If there was no private neutral evaluation and Abigail requested this evaluation at the commission in the application for arbitration, the insurer must file form D, the agreement to neutral evaluation, if it agrees to neutral evaluation. This form is sent by fax, the parties then follow rule 44.

3. *Proceed to private neutral evaluation under rule 44 at own request.* If there was no private neutral evaluation and Abigail did not request it in her application but the insurer wishes to request it, the insurer must propose it to Abigail, obtain her written consent, and file the consent with form D. The parties then follow the procedure in rule 44.

Response by insurer

Where the parties do not agree to neutral evaluation by the commission, the insurer must respond with form E, response by insurer to an application for arbitration, and follow the procedure in rule 27. The insurer must include in form E:

- a response to each issue raised by Abigail in her application for arbitration;

- a description of any additional issues the insurer wants arbitrated, provided that they were submitted to mediation and were not resolved (these should appear in the insurer's form B, the response to the application for mediation);

- an explanation of why the insurer failed to provide documents requested by the applicant where those documents are identified in the mediator's report;

- a list of documents on which the insurer intends to rely (probably the documents at mediation, perhaps including some of Abigail's if they help the insurer's case);

- a list of documents the insurer intends to obtain from other sources; and

- an indication of whether the insurer prefers the usual oral hearing, a hearing based on written submissions, or a hearing conducted by telephone conference.

If the insurer's response is substantively or procedurally deficient and the deficiencies are not rectified, the registrar or an arbitrator may reject the response, and the matter will proceed as if it were uncontested. Figure 25.4 sets out a completed form E.

Reply by the insured

The insurer must then serve the response on Abigail and the group. On receiving the response, Abigail has 10 days to reply to any new issue that was included in the response, using form G, reply by the applicant for arbitration. Suppose that Imperialist Payless replied in its response to the issue about Abigail's refusal to change her treatment plan and then went on to state that Abigail had used this medication before in another connection without any danger to herself. In this situation, Abigail would need to reply because this is a point not previously raised by either party. Abigail's form G, reply by the applicant for arbitration, appears in figure 25.5. Form G is served on the insurer and any other party, and a copy of the reply is filed together with a statement of service in form F with the group. Figure 25.6 sets out form F.

You will recognize that forms C, E, and G resemble the statement of claim, statement of defence, and reply in civil proceedings in the Superior Court. The approach should flush out all issues the arbitrator has to deal with. As in the Superior Court rules, the reply is optional. It is not used to get in a last word on all issues relied on by the insurer but to answer a new issue that is raised in the response.

Let us suppose for the moment that Abigail and the insurance company have not agreed to either private neutral evaluation or evaluation at the commission, and they wish to fight it out at arbitration. Abigail will file an application for arbitration in form C and deliver it to the commission. The insurer will deliver form E to Abigail and file form E together with form F at the commission.

Control of arbitration

Once the parties have exchanged documentation, the director of the group appoints an arbitrator under rule 28. As with mediation under rule 30, the registrar or the arbitrator may combine arbitrations or hear them one after the other where there are common questions of fact, law, or policy, provided that there is no injustice, delay, or extra cost. Under rule 30.1, a party may raise objections to consolidation or other procedural decisions involving multiple issues or parties, and the arbitrator must consider the objection, hear from all parties, and make a decision that appears to be just. Under rule 31, the registrar or arbitrator may, where appropriate, separate the issues in an application for arbitration by having them heard separately. A party may object to this procedure under rule 31.1 by notifying the group in writing, and the arbitrator is required to hear argument by all parties and make whatever order is just.

Prehearing discussion

Under rule 33, an arbitrator may hold a prehearing. The function of a prehearing is similar to a pretrial conference or trial conference in case management: organizing the presentation of the case, eliminating unnecessary steps and issues, and generally speeding up the proceeding. The arbitrator's powers at a prehearing include:

- identifying and narrowing the issues in dispute;

- obtaining an agreed statement of facts;

- making orders with respect to any dispute about the production of documents (under rule 32, the arbitrator may require documents to be exchanged at least 10 days before the prehearing and require that they be filed; under rule 32.3, the arbitrator may order production of a disputed document and set timelines for delivery, provided that the timelines comply with rule 39);

- dealing with preliminary issues, including requests for interim expenses;

- identifying the witnesses to be called;

- determining the length of the hearing;

- setting hearing dates; and

- arranging the format for a document brief or joint book of documents.

Failure to comply with time requirements

Because arbitrations are conducted expeditiously, meeting time limits is important. Rule 34 sets out various penalties for parties that are engaging in delaying tactics. Under Rule 34, where a party fails to meet the time limits imposed by these rules, by an order, or where a time limit has been agreed to, an arbitrator has broad discretionary to

- make a punitive expenses (costs) award,
- refuse to permit a party to file a document,
- impose a new timetable for compliance,
- draw an adverse inference against a party that refuses to produce a document or otherwise meet a time limit, and
- make any other order that is just.

Settlement conference

In addition to prehearing discussions, any party may ask the registrar to schedule a settlement conference before arbitration under rule 35, provided that all other parties consent, and the proposed dates are acceptable to all. An arbitrator may also initiate a settlement conference if the parties agree. But the arbitrator who presides over the conference may not preside over the hearing unless the parties consent. This is because the arbitrator will likely hear various "without prejudice" statements and admissions and be privy to other privileged information that might compromise his or her impartiality.

Rule 36 makes it clear that statements made for the purpose of settlement and offers to settle made during a prehearing discussion or settlement conference are not admissible in any subsequent proceeding, including the arbitration, appeal from an arbitration order, application to vary an order, or revocation of an order. No mediator, adjudicator, arbitrator, or person appointed to facilitate settlement can be compelled to give evidence about anything heard or seen during the settlement proceeding.

Arbitration hearings

The arbitrator is empowered under rule 37 to determine the form of hearing: oral, written, electronic (telephone conference), or a combination. A written hearing or an electronic hearing will not occur where a party gives good reason — where, for example, witness credibility is in issue. However, the arbitrator may use written and electronic hearings in the face of objections if the matter is only procedural. The arbitrator must give reasonable notice to the parties of the date of hearing and their right to object to written and electronic hearings. Where a party who has been given timely notice fails to appear at the hearing, the arbitrator may proceed in that party's absence.

Timelines for written hearings

Rule 38 permits an arbitrator to request additional written materials or submissions to be filed within 30 days after the last day on which the claimant could file a reply. If a party does not file within the time provided, the arbitrator may proceed on the basis of the materials filed when the time for filing has expired. The arbitrator may then make his or her order on the later of:

- 60 days after the last day on which the insured person is entitled to file a reply, or

- 30 days after the last day on which the parties are required to file additional materials.

This rule permits the arbitrator to obtain additional material on a written hearing if he or she is of the opinion that the material filed to date is insufficient to make findings. Rule 38 also sets timelines so that the hearing can proceed expeditiously. In an oral hearing, where the parties are before the arbitrator, further information can be obtained more efficiently.

Evidence

TIMELINES

Rule 39 requires parties to serve copies of all documents they intend to rely on at least 30 days before the hearing, although an arbitrator has authority to extend the time for serving documents in an extraordinary case. This rule covers situations where documents were not supplied after a prehearing or with applications, responses, or replies. It permits each party to have ample time to review relevant documents relied on by the other before the hearing.

ADMISSIBILITY

Rule 39.3 gives the arbitrator broad powers to decide whether or not to admit oral or written evidence based on whether the evidence is material, relevant, or prejudicial. The arbitrator may decide to hear evidence that would not be admitted in a court. For example, hearsay evidence may be admitted where a court would not permit it to be given. However, there are some restrictions on the arbitrator. He or she may not admit evidence that is

- privileged, such as solicitor–client correspondence;

- barred by the *Insurance Act*, or

- not served first on the other party in accordance with rules 39.1 and 39.2 unless there are extraordinary reasons for doing so — for example, where the evidence has just been discovered.

SURVEILLANCE

Where an insured claims to be unable to work, the insurance company may use investigators to covertly observe the insured in the course of his or her daily activities. For example, if Abigail claims to have memory problems and headaches, one would expect her not to engage in activities that tax her memory. One would also expect to see her giving some sign of suffering from headache, such as repairing to a dark room from time to time. But if Abigail is observed by an investigator to play non-stop bridge or to skip about like a young lamb day after day, this may be evidence that she is lying about, or at least exaggerating, her disability.

If the insurer wishes to introduce surveillance evidence, including investigator's reports, videotapes, or photographs, rule 40 requires the insurer to provide the names and qualifications of the persons carrying out the surveillance and to provide copies of all videotapes, photographs, reports, or other documentary evidence at least 30 days before the hearing.

WITNESSES

Rule 41 requires each party to provide to the other a list of witnesses he or she intends to call and to provide a list of persons he or she requires to attend for cross-examination on any report filed by the other party at least 30 days before the hearing.

Further, every party must give at least 30 days notice before the hearing to any witness he or she intends to call. A witness who is not given proper notice may be excused from testifying if the witness's name was not revealed at the prehearing or the witness was not given at least 30 days' notice of the hearing date. This ensures that witnesses are given time to arrange to attend. A witness who is given proper notice and who does not attend or who may not attend may have his or her attendance enforced by the arbitrator's issuing a summons. A summons requires the witness to attend and to bring with him or her various named documents. A party may ask the arbitrator to issue a summons without explaining why. The summons must be served on the witness by the party who asks for it using the summons to witness in form N in accordance with rule 73.[7] You should also prepare an affidavit of service for summons to witness in form O, but do not file it unless the witness fails to attend the hearing. Generally, if you are calling your mother as a witness, you need not use a summons. But if the party is a stranger or adverse in interest, you should issue a summons. Then, if the party fails to attend, you have a right to an adjournment and to have the summons enforced in the same way as a Superior Court summons: by contempt proceedings. A summons to witness in form N is set out in figure 25.7, and an affidavit of service for summons to witness in form O is set out in figure 25.8.

EXPERT WITNESSES

An expert report, if submitted as a document to be relied on, must contain the full name of the expert and his or her qualifications. Filing the report, together with the expert's resume, can do this. If the party also wishes to call the expert to give oral evidence, the party must serve and file a document containing the name and qualifications of the expert. Again, the resume is sufficient. But the document must also go on to identify the subject matter of the testimony to be presented and the substance of the facts and opinion that the witness will give. This is particularly important if an expert is called without his or her having prepared a report in advance. This rule prevents the opposing party from being taken by surprise and gives the opposing party the opportunity to prepare a cross-examination of the expert to test the evidence. In the case of a report or oral evidence summaries, the timelines in rules 39 and 41 must be observed. If not, an arbitrator can exclude the evidence. Each party is limited to two experts unless the arbitrator permits more to be called.

Reopening a hearing

Under rule 43, an arbitrator may reopen a hearing after having heard the parties, provided that he or she has not made a decision. While parties are expected to marshal their information within the timelines provided by the rules, the relatively short time limits may result in situations where evidence on, for example, a continuing disability becomes available only after all the other evidence has been heard.

If the evidence becomes available after the decision is made, there are provisions for appealing or revoking a decision or varying it. These procedures are discussed later in this chapter.

Neutral evaluation at the commission

Rule 44 permits the parties to agree to neutral evaluation after the claimant has filed an application for arbitration if the applicant requests it and the insurer agrees, or the insurer requests it and the applicant agrees. In either case, the insurer can follow the rule 44 route and file form D, agreement to neutral evaluation at the commission. Figure 25.9 sets out form D. The filing of form D puts the arbitration on hold. The director of the group suspends the arbitration, appoints a neutral evaluator, and confirms the appointment with the parties.

Once the parties have agreed to neutral evaluation, the director appoints the neutral evaluator. Within 30 days of receiving the notice of appointment, the parties must collaborate on a joint statement for neutral evaluation at the commission in form H. In this form, which appears in figure 25.10, the parties describe, in neutral and objective terms, the legal and factual issues to be evaluated and confirm that the relevant documents are before the evaluator. The parties must also agree on two proposed half days for the evaluation process within the 60-day period following the appointment of the evaluator. If the form is not properly completed, the evaluator may require that necessary information be provided if the evaluation is to proceed.

Now that the evaluator knows what the issues are, he or she requires more information about the position of the parties. Ten days before the evaluation hearing is held, each party must exchange and file a case summary. There is no prescribed form, but the summary must include:

- a summary of the submissions of fact and law on the issues, and

- copies of key documents.

If the evaluator feels that he or she needs more information than the case summary provides, he or she has the right to ask for it (rules 44 and 45). If the evaluator does not receive the cooperation of either or both parties, the evaluator will terminate the proceeding. A party who withdraws, is required to notify the director. Either way, the director will immediately appoint an arbitrator (rule 46).

At the hearing, the neutral evaluator is supposed to give an oral opinion, although it may be possible for the evaluator to reserve on his or her opinion if more time is needed. In any event, the neutral evaluator should furnish a written report. There is no specific time limit for this: The rule requires only that it be done "promptly." The report identifies those issues that were evaluated and those that were settled. The purpose of neutral evaluation is to help parties assess their chances, and if they are not very good, to settle the matter. Any issues outstanding for arbitration are also identified, as is the insurer's last offer on those issues. The report does not contain the evaluator's opinion: That information, like a mediator's views, is confidential (rules 47 and 48). Two days after delivery of the report, the matter is referred by the director to arbitration, and an arbitrator is promptly appointed.

Appeal procedures: Section A, part 4

WHAT MAY BE APPEALED?

A party may appeal a preliminary, interim, or final order of an arbitrator only on a point of law. An appeal on the ground that an arbitrator made an error in finding certain facts is not permitted. If a party wishes to appeal an interim or preliminary order (often a procedural matter, as is the case with court motions), he or she must wait until the final order and raise matters in one appeal (rule 50). The aim here is to prevent the process from getting out of hand with further costs and delay.

PROCEDURE TO START AN APPEAL

An appeal lies to the director.[8] The director does not hear the appeal himself or herself. Instead, the director appoints someone to hear the appeal and to exercise all of the director's powers with respect to the appeal (rule 56.1). To start the appeal, the appellant completes a notice of appeal in form I and serves it on the respondent or his or her lawyer if one appeared at arbitration. Form I appears in figure 25.11. The appellant then files a copy of the notice of appeal and the statement of service in form F with the director and pays the prescribed fee.[9] An appeal must be filed within 30 days of the making of the arbitration order appealed from (rule 52). If it is incomplete or otherwise defective, the director must notify the parties and give an opportunity to remedy the defect. If the defect is remedied and the appeal is in order, it will be acknowledged by the director (rule 51).

Once the appeal has been served and the respondent has received the director's acknowledgment of the appeal, he or she has 20 days to serve the appellant and file a response to appeal in form J together with a statement of service in form F (rule 53). An example of form J is set out in figure 25.12. The notice of appeal and the response to appeal set out the parties' positions on the issues, but these documents do not tell the person hearing the appeal what the arguments are. Unless the issue on appeal is so straightforward that the director dispenses with it, the appellant is required to file written submissions at least 30 days before the appeal. There is no prescribed form or content for this, but you may model your submission on the appellant's statement of fact and law used in an appeal in the Superior Court. Set out each issue with a brief summary of the facts and the principle or rule of law on which you rely, citing cases where necessary. Remember that, with a password, you can download case decisions from the FSCO Web site.

The appellant serves his or her written submissions on the respondent no later than 30 days before the appeal, and the respondent serves his or her submissions within 20 days of receiving the appellant's written statement (rules 53 and 54).

In some cases, a respondent on an appeal from an arbitrator's decision may also wish to appeal the arbitrator's decision. This is done by filing a cross-appeal. A cross-appeal re-invents the wheel as far as procedure goes: A respondent who is also a cross-appellant acts as an appellant in filing his or her own notice of appeal and his or her own submissions on that issue. The appellant in the main appeal, if contesting the cross-appeal, files respondent's documents on the cross-appeal. Both the appeal and the cross-appeal should be heard together, and the appeal adjudicator may give directions on how the parties are to proceed (rule 55).

APPEAL RECORD

The record on the appeal is made up of the notice of appeal, the response to appeal, written submissions, transcripts of the arbitration hearing (if any), and arbitration exhibits. A hearing may be conducted on the written record or by way of an oral hearing at the discretion of the adjudicator. If the hearing is oral, the adjudicator delivers a notice of hearing to the parties.

PRELIMINARY CONFERENCE

Once again, the adjudicator reserves the right to hold a prehearing session — in this case, a preliminary conference in order to clarify issues, establish procedures, and promote settlement on an issue.

INTERVENTIONS

Rule 59 provides for persons who are not parties to an appeal to make submissions on any issue of law in the appeal. This may happen where certain parties to the arbitration do not choose to participate in an appeal, but because of the way the issues on appeal are framed, the adjudicator or the director is of the view that their rights will be affected, and so they should be invited to appeal. Another possibility is that a non-party is of the view that issues raised in the dispute might affect the non-party in other disputes and therefore asks to intervene. For example, in Abigail's case, the Canadian Patient Rights Group might wish to make submissions on the issue of whether or not a mentally competent person should be compelled to consent to possibly dangerous treatment in order to continue to receive insurance benefits. Note that the director (or adjudicator) can ask someone to intervene, or the person may ask to intervene.

An intervener must file an application for intervention in form K after serving every other party with the document. An application for intervention is set out in figure 25.13. In the application, the intervener must satisfy the director that he or she has a good reason for intervening. The intervener then sets out his or her submissions on the issue he or she is intervening on. Within 10 days of receiving the application for intervention, other parties may indicate that they support the intervention or object to it, or they may express no opinion.

The director or adjudicator has jurisdiction to reject an application for intervention if the document does not set out the reasons for intervention and submissions on the issue or issues. The intervener in this situation may remedy the deficiency and participate in the proceedings. There does not seem to be a power to reject an attempt to intervene if the intervener complies with the requirements of the rules. Once an intervention has been made, the intervener follows the rules for appeals, particularly rules 56 to 58.

Variation procedures: Section A, part 5

An order may address a situation correctly at the time the order is made, but the situation may change, and the order may result in a remedy that is inadequate, irrelevant, or wrong. For example, suppose Abigail had applied for a caregiver benefit because she was looking after her elderly mother. An order may grant the benefit, but what happens if the elderly mother dies after the order is made? Should Abigail continue to receive the benefit because an arbitrator or appeal coordinator ordered it?

Alternatively, suppose the arbitrator rules against Abigail on her right to refuse a change in treatment on the ground that there is no compelling evidence that the medication is dangerous. What happens if three weeks after the arbitrator makes an order, a medical research report is released indicating that the medication is just as dangerous as Abigail claims? In these cases, the rules permit orders to be varied by changing the terms of the order or revoked by cancelling the order. An application to revoke or vary is different from an appeal. An appeal is used where the adjudicator made an error in law. An application to vary or revoke is made where the circumstances at the time the order was made have changed in a material way.

Rule 61.1 permits any party to apply to the commission to vary or revoke a preliminary or final order. However, no application may be made in respect of a preliminary or interim order until the final order has been made. Usually interim or preliminary orders can be corrected at the time the final order is made. The grounds for applying to vary or revoke an order are as follows:

1. *There is a material change in circumstances.* This means that there has been a significant change in relation to the issue previously raised. A minor or superficial change is not enough. What constitutes a material change depends on the adjudicator's judgment, though cases may be cited to present similar situations where an application to vary or revoke was successful.

2. *Evidence not available before the order has become available.* You cannot hide and then "find" evidence. To apply on this basis, you must show that the evidence that has surfaced was not available before the order was made despite reasonable attempts to find it.

3. *There is an error in the order.* An example is a situation in which the amount of a benefit is incorrectly calculated.

VARIATION/REVOCATION PROCEDURE

To apply for variation or revocation of an order, a party must complete an application for variation/revocation in form L, serve it on all other parties, and file it with a statement of service in form F with the commission. Figure 25.14 sets out an application for variation/revocation. You must also pay the application fee set out in part D of the code. As usual, the application may be rejected if it is not complete, the fee is not paid, or it is in respect of an interim or preliminary order. A party is given the usual opportunity to correct the deficiencies or have the application dismissed.

Once an application is received by the director and found to be in order, the director acknowledges it, in writing, to all parties. Within 20 days of receipt of the acknowledgment, the respondent must serve the applicant and then file a response to application for variation/revocation in form M. Figure 25.15 sets out form M. The director usually appoints an adjudicator, who may be the person who made the original order. The hearing procedure, which is like an appeal, follows rules 54, 57, and 58.

Hearing procedures: Section A, part 6

Rules 64 to 82 set out general hearing procedures that apply to all arbitrations, appeals, interventions, and variations/revocations. They do not, generally, apply to mediations. Some of the procedural rules are obvious; others are less so. Some of the more important ones are described here. However, if you work in this area you should become familiar with all of the rules.

ORDERS

Rule 65 permits orders to be given orally with oral reasons, but they can be reduced to writing if a party requests it. A final order must be supported by written reasons although an interim order need not be so supported unless a party requests it. An order that is straightforward may be given orally. A request to "put it in writing" is likely to be made if a party intends to appeal the order. An adjudicator who makes a writing or calculation error may correct it at any time.

ENFORCEMENT OF ORDERS

Suppose Imperialist Payless is ordered to pay Abigail but refuses to do so. Rule 66 permits a party to file a copy of an order with the Superior Court, but the party must give the director notice that this has been done. This treatment is similar to the treatment given generally to the orders of administrative tribunals: Civil court enforcement provisions are made available to tribunals, which have no enforcement powers of their own.

MOTIONS

Rule 67 permits a party to make a motion in writing to the adjudicator, setting out the nature of the order being sought, the grounds for the order, and a list of documents relied on. You should also set out the time, date, and manner of hearing the motion. You can model your written request on a court motion form. You serve the other party with the request and file it. There does not seem to be a requirement that you file with the director a statement of service with the request, but you are advised to do so.

If the motion is for production of documents from a third party, you must serve the third party, other parties, and file the request with the director. A statement of service is clearly required here. There are some protections for third parties so that they are not harassed by proceedings that may be none of their concern (rules 67.4 and 67.7)

A responding party has 10 days to serve and file any respondent's material. A motion for a preliminary order or interim order may be made orally at any hearing or preliminary meeting.

ADJOURNMENTS

Adjournments look very attractive to a party who wishes to delay. In order to forestall this kind of abuse, rule 72 sets out certain procedural requirements that must be met before an adjournment is granted:

- a request to adjourn a prehearing or arbitration must be made to the registrar in writing;
- a request to adjourn an appeal or variation/revocation must be made to the director in writing;

- a request must outline the reasons for adjournment, indicate whether all parties consent, and provide alternative dates that are acceptable to all parties; and

- a request must be served on other parties and filed seven days in advance of the proceeding for which the request is made unless the registrar or director allows for a shorter period.

To ensure that the adjournment policy is not abused, the adjudicator must refer to practice note 9 for guidance on the appropriateness of the request.

TRANSCRIPTS

There is no formal record of what is said at hearings unless one or both parties decide they wish to have a transcript. If both decide on having a transcript, they can save expense by agreeing to share the cost. Because transcripts can be expensive, careful thought must be given as to whether transcripts are necessary. Transcripts are usually necessary if there are factual or credibility issues. Rule 74 sets out the rules for transcripts. Generally, parties must use a court reporter who swears to take down the evidence accurately. This kind of reporter is often specially trained. Court reporting services are listed in the Yellow Pages, should you wish to use a reporter. The parties are responsible for hiring and paying the reporter and for the costs of preparing the transcript. If they use a transcript, they must inform the adjudicator and provide a copy to the adjudicator and all other parties at their own expense.

COSTS

As in the court system, adjudicators have authority to award costs, which are called "expenses" in rule 75. Generally, costs are awarded to the successful party, although the adjudicator has broad discretion in awarding costs.[10] The criteria to be considered are set out in rule 75.2:

- a party's degree of success;

- the parties' conduct in facilitating or obstructing proceedings;

- the degree of complexity, novelty, or significance of issues in case; and

- at the request of a party, any written offer to settle, having regard to the outcome of the proceeding.

As noted above, an award of expenses can be affected by a written offer to settle. This is similar to the use of an offer to settle in the Superior Court. If one party makes an offer to the other side that would give the other side more than it received as a result of the adjudicator's order, the adjudicator may decide that the offeree unnecessarily prolonged proceedings by failing to take the offer. In that case, the adjudicator may award expenses to the party who made the offer. Similarly, if a party makes an order that is less generous than the adjudicator's award, that party may be made to pay the other side's expenses.

In determining an expense award, an adjudicator will consider an offer that was made in writing, served on the other party, sets out the full terms of the offer, contains the date when the offer was served, and shows the time in which it remains open for acceptance (usually to the date of hearing). An offer must also be made between the close of mediation and the opening of the hearing, but particular attention is paid to offers made at the conclusion of a prehearing discussion or at a preliminary conference, when there are focused attempts to encourage settlement. A response to an offer to settle will be considered as an expense award factor if it was made in writing and served on the other parties before the conclusion of the hearing.

Adjudicators should not know about offers to settle until after they have made an order so that their judgment is not affected by this knowledge. At the end of a hearing, the parties may inform the adjudicator that there were no offers made by either party so that the adjudicator will make an expense award without reference to offers. If a party seeks to have an offer considered as a factor in making a costs award, the parties must jointly advise the adjudicator at the conclusion of the hearing, and file any written offers made in accordance with rules 76 and 77 with the adjudicator.

EXPENSES OF REPRESENTATIVES

A party may be awarded expenses, including expenses for legal fees.[11] The amount is calculated using the hourly rates prescribed under the *Legal Aid Services Act, 1998* for lawyers appearing in the Superior Court, adjusted by application of the experience allowance. If the adjudicator believes a higher amount is justified, he or she may award expenses based on an hourly rate of $150. If a party uses a law clerk, paralegal, or other agent, the allowable fee is based on the rate for law clerks in the *Legal Aid Services Act, 1998*.

Under rule 79, the parties are expected to settle the expenses issues themselves following the principle that a successful party gets his or her expenses at or near the rates in rule 78. If the parties cannot agree on expenses, rule 79 provides a procedure for having the adjudicator decide the matter.

CHAPTER SUMMARY

Since 1990, persons injured in automobile accidents have not had an untrammelled right to sue in tort in the courts. While injured persons may still sue for pain and suffering if the injuries are catastrophic, they are otherwise expected to rely on no fault benefits prescribed by the *Insurance Act*. Since the no fault regimes were introduced in 1990, the disputes that have frequently arisen between insurance companies and claimants about payment of benefits are resolved by FSCO's Dispute Resolution Group. The group provides a number of services, including mediation, neutral evaluation, arbitration, appeals of orders, revocation, and variation of orders.

In this chapter, we provided an overview of the procedures set out in The Dispute Resolution Practice Code and the forms filed in support of the adjudication or mediation processes. A claimant first applies for mediation. When mediation is not successful, a claimant may refer a claim for neutral evaluation, and if it is not settled there, for arbitration. If a claimant or an insurer thinks the arbitrator has made an error of law, the party may appeal the order. After the appeal process has been exhausted, the only other remedy that can arise under these rules is an application to vary or revoke an order on the basis that the circumstances that existed at the time the order was made have changed in a material way. Finally, we reviewed certain general procedures governing hearings, including adjournments, formal offers to settle, and expenses awarded to successful parties.

KEY TERMS

tort reform

no fault

Financial Services Commission of Ontario (FSCO)

Dispute Resolution Group

Dispute Resolution Practice Code

arbitration

neutral evaluation

Statutory Accident Benefits Schedule

natural justice

procedural fairness

director of arbitrations

registrar

designated assessment centre

NOTES

1 Since June 1990, there have been restrictions and prohibitions on the right to sue in tort. At present, a plaintiff may sue in tort for general damages for pain and suffering and loss of the enjoyment of the quality of life if there has been a catastrophic injury.

2 J.M. Flaherty and Catherine Zingg, eds., *Financial Services Commission of Ontario (Motor Vehicle Insurance Law and Practice)* (Aurora, ON: Canada Law Book, 2001); R.A. Robinson and Harry P. Brown, eds., *No Fault Arbitration Manual, Ontario*, 3 vols. (Toronto: Carswell 2000); and Eric Grossman, ed., *Ontario Accident Benefits Case Summaries* (Toronto: CCH Canadian, 1999). Quicklaw also maintains case summary reports available for subscribers online.

3 Information about designated assessment centres is found at http:// www.fsco.gov.on.ca/ under "insurance." See also practice notes 1 and 12 in part C of the code.

4 See practice note 4, section C of the code.

5 See practice note 5, section C of the code.

6 See practice note 6, section C of the code.

7 See practice note 8, section C of the code.

8 The rules governing appeals usually refer to actions undertaken by "the director." Usually it is not the director who acts, but the director's nominee, whom we refer to here as "the adjudicator."

9 The prescribed fee is set out in section D of the code.

10 See the expense regulation schedule, part F of the code.

11 See also the expense regulation schedule, part F of the code.

REFERENCES

Automobile Insurance Rate Stability Act, 1996, SO 1996, c. 21.

Financial Services Commission of Ontario, *Dispute Resolution Practice Code* (Toronto: Queen's Printer, 2001).

Flaherty, J. M. and Catherine Zingg, eds., *Financial Services Commission of Ontario (Motor Vehicle Insurance Law and Practice)* (Aurora, ON: Canada Law Book, August 2001).

French Language Services Act, RSO 1990, c. F.32.

Grossman, Eric, ed., *Ontario Accident Benefits Case Summaries* (Toronto: CCH Canadian, 1999).

Insurance Act, RSO 1990, c. I.8, as amended.

Insurance Statute Law Amendment Act, 1993, SO 1993, c. 10.

Legal Aid Services Act, 1998, SO 1998, c. 26.

Robinson, R.A. and Harry P. Brown, eds., *No Fault Arbitration Manual, Ontario*, 3 vols. (Toronto: Carswell, 2000).

Rules of Civil Procedure, RRO 1990, reg. 194.

Statutory Accident Benefits Schedule — Accidents After December 31, 1993 and Before November 1, 1996, O. reg. 776/93.

Statutory Accident Benefits Schedule — Accidents Before January 1, 1994, RRO 1990, reg. 672.

Statutory Accident Benefits Schedule — Accidents On or After November 1, 1996, O. reg. 403/96.

Statutory Powers Procedure Act, RSO 1990, c. S.22.

Substitute Decisions Act 1992, SO 1992, c. 30.

REVIEW QUESTIONS

1. What disputes can be heard by FSCO?

2. Do all insurance disputes go to FSCO?

3. How does the dispute resolution process start?

4. What is involved in mediation?

5. What happens if mediation fails?

6. How does the arbitration process work?

7. Is there a right of appeal from an arbitrator's order?

8. When is an application for revocation or variation made?

9. How much time does a party have to apply for mediation or arbitration?

10. How much time do you have to file an appeal?

11. How long do you have to file a request for assessment of expenses?

12. How long do you have to file a request for revocation/variation?

1. Eaton Shredlu was badly injured in an automobile accident on September 1, 2000. He weighs about 180 pounds (81 kilograms). He is now a paraplegic and confined to a wheelchair. His spouse, Shirley Shredlu, weighs 90 pounds (about 41 kilograms). Eaton needs help with a variety of things and must be lifted from time to time. Shirley has tried to do this but has injured her back twice and refuses to continue to do so. The Shredlus have asked for the attendant care benefit so that they can hire an attendant to do the heavy lifting. The insurance company has refused, saying Shirley can manage and that the exercise will be good for her. The insurer denied benefits on November 13, 2000. The Shredlus live at 60 Oriole Birdway, North York, Ontario, M2R 1X5. Their phone number is 416-491-5123. Their insurer is Imperialist Payless Insurance Co., and the adjuster is Norbert Nopay. The Shredlus are friends with Abigail Boar, who recommended I.M. Just to represent them at FSCO. The Shredlus have retained I.M. Just, and Imperial Payless has retained their usual lawyer, Giacomo Brown. The Shredlus have several reports from their family doctor, Roger Ramalujam, dated October 1, 2000, January 12, 2000, and August 15, 2001. They also have an assessment report from Dr. Susan Quitewell, a specialist in rehabilitation medicine, dated October 5, 2001, stating that Eaton will be unable to walk for the rest of his life. There is also a needs assessment, dated November 21, 2001, from Maria Dunnow, RN, a staff person from the Roadwill Rehabilitation Hospital, which says that Shirley Shredlu is not physically capable of doing the required lifting of Eaton without injuring herself in the process. The insurance company asked for an independent assessment through a disability assessment centre, and the Shredlus attended the centre at Cloudybrook Hospital in North York, Ontario. The centre's report, written by Dr. Joan Shadewell on December 10, 2001, indicates that if bars are installed in the bathroom and in other places, Eaton can pull himself out of his wheelchair, make use of the bathroom, and pull himself into bed with minimal assistance from his spouse. The insurance company is refusing to reconsider the benefit claim on the basis of Dr. Shadewell's report. It is now January 15, 2002.

   a. Draft the application for mediation for Eaton in form A, and draft the insurance company's response in Form B.

   b. At mediation, the insurance company does not agree to provide the benefit requested. Draft the application for arbitration and the response to arbitration.

   c. Assume the Shredlus were not successful at arbitration and that three months after the arbitration order was made, Eaton began to lose upper body strength, is not strong enough to pull himself up on the bars mounted around the house, and is unable to lift himself out of his wheelchair. Draft an application for variation/revocation of an order.

FIGURE 25.1   APPLICATION FOR MEDIATION (FORM A)

Financial
Services
Commission
of Ontario

Dispute
Resolution
Group

Application for Mediation
Form A

Use this application form after a motor vehicle accident, when a dispute arises about whether the claimant qualifies for benefits under the *Statutory Accident Benefits Schedule ("SABS")* and how much those benefits should be. Mediation is an informal process in which a neutral third party (the mediator) helps the parties resolve the issues in dispute. The mediator works with the parties to find resolutions that are acceptable to everyone involved. There is no cost to the injured person for mediation. The benefits that can be mediated are described in this booklet.

Before filing an application for mediation, the parties or their representatives should contact each other to identify the issues in dispute, clarify the facts, exchange documents relevant to the dispute and discuss settlement. Parties are expected to take part personally in the mediation process and to be available during the 60-day mediation period.

After completing the application, return it to the Financial Services Commission of Ontario (the "Commission") at the address below.

Personal information requested on this form is collected under the authority of the *Insurance Act*, R.S.O. 1990, c.I.8 as amended. This information, including documents submitted with this application, will be used in the dispute resolution process for accident benefits. This information will be available to all parties to the proceeding. Any questions about this collection of information may be directed to the Office of the Registrar, Dispute Resolution Group, at the address below.

If you have any questions about this application, or want more information, contact:

Mediation Services
Dispute Resolution Group
Financial Services Commission of Ontario
5160 Yonge Street, 15th Floor, Box 85
North York ON M2N 6L9

In Toronto: (416) 250-6714, extension 7210

Toll Free: 1-800-517-2332, extension 7210

Fax: (416) 590-7077

Mediation Hotline: (416) 590-7210

Commission website: www.fsco.gov.on.ca

Instructions, page 1

Ce formulaire est également disponible en français.

1974 (03/01)

FIGURE 25.1 CONTINUED

Please print. Read the instructions carefully. To complete the application more easily, remove the section you are filling out and place it beside the relevant instructions.

For a complete set of the rules about mediation, refer to the Dispute Resolution Practice Code.

How to complete the Application

SECTION 1

This section must be completed no matter what date the motor vehicle accident occurred.

General Information

Please answer all questions. Note that if you prefer a language other than English or French, it is up to you to make arrangements and pay the cost for your own interpreter.

Claimant

For the purposes of this application, a claimant is any person making a claim for statutory accident benefits to an insurance company as a result of a motor vehicle accident. The claimant is not necessarily the motor vehicle insurance policyholder. Fill in the name and address of the claimant and provide telephone numbers so that we can contact the claimant without delay to discuss the dispute. A minor is anyone under the age of 18.

Claimant's Representative

If the claimant will be represented in mediation by someone else, fill in the name, title, firm name, address and telephone numbers so that we can contact the representative to discuss the dispute. Please include your file reference number, if any. Complete the question concerning the relationship of the representative to the claimant. **The claimant must provide full authorization to the representative to discuss all issues in dispute, to negotiate and to enter into agreements or a settlement of any and all issues in dispute.**

Insurance Company

Fill in the full name of the insurance company and the person you have been dealing with at the insurance company. Please provide the name of the policyholder, the policy number and the claim number.

Insurance Company's Representative

If you are filing on behalf of the claimant, please leave this blank. However, if you are the insurer, please provide the name of the insurance company's representative, the representative's title, firm name, address, telephone numbers and file reference number. **The insurance company's representative must be authorized to settle the dispute on behalf of the insurance company.**

Signature and Certification

The claimant **must** sign and date the bottom of Section 1. We will not accept an application unless it is signed by the claimant, the insurance company or an authorized representative. Please read the declaration before signing. After completing the application, make two copies. Keep one copy for yourself and send the original application plus a copy to Mediation Services at the Commission. The address is on the front page of this application. You should attach a copy of any information about your dispute. For example: the insurance company's written explanation of why they denied the benefit; doctor's reports; tax returns; and financial statements.

SECTIONS 2, 3, 4

This application form is designed to accommodate 3 different Statutory Accident Benefits Schedules.

You need to complete only ONE of these sections depending on the date of the motor vehicle accident. Discard unused sections.

Section 2 – Complete if the motor vehicle accident occurred on or after November 1, 1996.

Section 3 – Complete if the motor vehicle accident occurred on or between January 1, 1994 and October 31, 1996, inclusive.

Section 4 – Complete if the motor vehicle accident occurred on or between June 22, 1990 and December 31, 1993, inclusive.

SECTION 5 – Documents at the Mediation

The claimant must complete Section 5. List key documents in the claimant's possession to which reference will be made in the mediation. Also list key documents that the claimant wishes to obtain from other sources including the other party to the mediation, for the purpose of discussing settlement.

Instructions, page 2

1974 (03/01)

FIGURE 25.1 CONTINUED

Steps in the Mediation Process

Step 1

Return the following items to Mediation Services at the Commission. The full address is on the front of this form.

- Two copies of the completed *Application for Mediation*, signed and dated (keep one copy for yourself).
- A copy of the insurance company's written explanation of why they denied the benefit, if available.
- Any information about your dispute that is relevant (i.e., doctor's reports, tax receipts or financial statements). **Send copies only – keep originals of all your documents.**

Failure to comply with all these instructions will result in your application being returned to you.

Step 2

The Commission will review your application for completeness and will contact you if additional information is required before appointing a mediator. The Commission may reject the application for deficiencies or jurisdictional concerns. Once complete, your application will be forwarded to the other party along with a *Response to an Application for Mediation* form and a mediator will be appointed. The other party will provide the completed Response form to you and the Commission. A letter will be sent notifying you of the name of the mediator.

Step 3

When you receive this letter you should immediately contact the mediator to discuss the issues in dispute and to arrange for a mediation meeting if appropriate. You are requested to produce and exchange all relevant documents and reports *before* the mediation meeting.

Step 4

In cases where there is a mediation date set, you will participate in person or by teleconference as the mediator considers appropriate. Appointing a representative does not relieve any party of the obligation to participate in the mediation.

Step 5

At the end of the mediation period, the mediator will produce a report indicating the disputed issues discussed and the outcome of the mediation. The Commission will deliver a copy of the *Report of Mediator* to the parties.

For additional information concerning the mediation process please refer to the *Dispute Resolution Practice Code* and the Commission's website at *www.fsco.gov.on.ca*

Note: You may settle your dispute with the other party directly at any time during the mediation process. Please notify Mediation Services of any settlement.

Instructions, page 3

1974 (03/01)

FIGURE 25.1 CONTINUED

S A M P L E A P P L I C A T I O N

Description of Dispute

Check the box beside the benefits you are disputing. Please refer to *Available Benefits* in the Instructions, page 5, for a description of the types of statutory accident benefits available. Give the details of the dispute and state the amount that is in dispute, if possible. **Be as specific as possible when you are explaining your reasons for mediation.** List the details of each claim separately. Describe what was claimed, what was paid, what was denied and when.

If you need more space, attach extra sheets.

		For each benefit checked, briefly explain the details of the dispute. (Attach extra sheets if necessary.) ▼
[X] **Weekly Benefits**	Which weekly benefit are you disputing? [X] income replacement [ ] non-earner What are you disputing? [ ] initial entitlement to benefits [X] length of time benefits were paid [ ] amount of weekly benefits [ ] entitlement to benefits past 104 weeks [ ] benefits after age 65 [ ] other, specify ▼ If you received income benefits, state weekly amount and duration of payments. $ *300.00* From — *Jan. 8, 1999* To — *May 14, 1999* Is the insurance company claiming a repayment of benefits? [X] No [ ] Yes If Yes, amount ▼ $	*I remain unable to return to work as a result of my motor vehicle accident. I am unable to perform the physical requirements of my job. I am enclosing the doctor's report and the insurance company's notice terminating benefits.*
[X] **Medical Benefits**	Amount in dispute? $ *350.00* *($35/week for 10 weeks)* Does this claim involve catastrophic impairment? [X] No [ ] Yes	*My doctor recommended chiropractic treatments at the ABC Clinic. I had 10 sessions from Feb. 1, 1999 to April 1, 1999. The insurer has refused to pay the expense. Attached is the insurance company's assessment form.*
[X] **Interest**	Amount in dispute? Set out calculations.	

$ *2% per month from May 14th, 1999 to date on amount of $300 per week.*

My insurance company hasn't paid weekly benefits since May 14, 1999, and I claim interest on the money that they owe me.

FIGURE 25.1   CONTINUED

Available Benefits

The types of benefits available, the minimum and maximum available and the rules to qualify for benefits may be different depending on the date of the motor vehicle accident. Complete only the section which relates to the date of the accident.

The following benefits are available for motor vehicle accidents that occurred on or after November 1, 1996.

Income Replacement Benefits pay a claimant for lost income.

Non-Earner Benefits pay a claimant if he/she suffers a complete inability to carry on a normal life and does not qualify for income replacement or caregiver benefits.

Caregiver Benefits pay a claimant if he/she cannot continue as the main caregiver for a member of their household who is under 16 years of age, or who is over 16 years of age and who requires care because of a physical or mental incapacity.

Medical Benefits pay for reasonable and necessary medical expenses required because of the claimant's injuries. These are expenses that are not covered by any other medical coverage plan such as Ontario Health Insurance or supplementary insurance plans at the claimant's workplace.

Rehabilitation Benefits pay for reasonable and necessary rehabilitation expenses that are required because of the claimant's injuries and are not covered by any other insurance plan.

Attendant Care Benefits pay a claimant for the expense of an aide or attendant, or services provided by a long term care facility.

Case Manager Services Benefits pay for reasonable and necessary expenses related to coordination of goods and services if the claimant sustained a catastrophic impairment as a result of the accident.

Other Expenses (compensation for other pecuniary losses) pay for other reasonable expenses such as the cost of visiting a claimant during treatment or recovery. It also pays for home maintenance and housekeeping services, repairing or replacing items lost or damaged in the accident and lost educational expenses.

Death Benefits pay money to survivors of a person who dies as a result of the accident.

Funeral Expenses pay for funeral expenses of a person who dies as a result of the accident.

The following benefits are available for motor vehicle accidents that occurred on or between January 1, 1994 and October 31, 1996 inclusive.

Income Replacement Benefits pay a claimant for lost income.

Education Disability Benefits pay a claimant if he/she is unable to continue his/her education or to carry out normal daily activities. It also covers a claimant who completed their education less than one year before the accident, but is unable to get a job matching their education or training.

Caregiver Benefits pay a claimant if he/she cannot continue as the main caregiver for a member of their household who is under 16 years of age, or who is over 16 years of age and who requires care because of a physical or mental incapacity. It also covers a caregiver who cannot carry on his or her normal daily activities.

Loss of Earning Capacity Benefits replace the above weekly benefits after two years. It provides income to a claimant who has a long term reduction in their ability to earn income as a result of an accident.

Other Disability Benefits pay a claimant if he/she cannot carry out normal daily activities and does not qualify for a Weekly Income Replacement Benefit, Education Disability Benefit or Caregiver Benefit.

Supplementary Medical Benefits pay for reasonable medical expenses required because of the claimant's injuries. These are expenses that are not covered by any other medical coverage plan such as Ontario Health Insurance or supplementary insurance plans at the claimant's workplace.

Rehabilitation Benefits pay for reasonable rehabilitation expenses that are required because of the claimant's injuries and are not covered by any other insurance plan.

Attendant Care Benefits pay a claimant for the expense of an aide or attendant.

Other Expenses (compensation for other pecuniary losses) pay for other reasonable expenses such as the cost of visiting a claimant during treatment or recovery. It also pays for care for dependants, home maintenance and housekeeping services and repairing or replacing items lost or damaged in the accident.

Death Benefits pay money to survivors of a person who dies as a result of the accident.

Funeral Expenses pay for funeral expenses of a person who dies as a result of the accident.

The following benefits are available for accidents that occurred on or between June 22, 1990 and December 31, 1993 inclusive.

Weekly Benefits pay a claimant for lost income. It also covers a claimant who cannot carry out normal daily activities.

Caregiver Benefits pay a claimant if he/she cannot continue as the main caregiver for a member of their household who is under 16 years of age, or who is over 16 years of age and who requires care because of a physical or mental incapacity.

Supplementary Medical and Rehabilitation Benefits pay for reasonable medical and rehabilitation expenses required because of the claimant's injuries. These are expenses that are not covered by any other medical coverage plan such as Ontario Health Insurance or supplementary insurance plans at the claimant's workplace.

Care Benefits pay a claimant for the expense of an aide or attendant.

Death Benefits pay money to survivors of a person who dies as a result of the accident.

Funeral Expenses pay for funeral expenses of a person who dies as a result of the accident.

Instructions, page 5

1974 (03/01)

FIGURE 25.1 CONTINUED

Financial
Services
Commission
of Ontario

Ontario

Dispute
Resolution
Group

Application for Mediation
Form A

Commission file number

M-1234

Section 1   This section MUST be completed.

**General
Information**

1. What was the date of the motor vehicle accident?

Month	Day	Year
0 9	1 4	1 9 9 9

2. Who is making this application?

☐ Claimant   ☒ Claimant's representative   ☐ Insurance company   ☐ Insurance company's representative

3. Have you applied for mediation before?

☒ No   ☐ Yes

4. Language preferred

☒ English   ☐ French   ☐ Other, specify ▶

5. Have you contacted the other party and tried to settle the dispute before applying for mediation?

☐ No   ☒ Yes

Claimant

	Last name	First name	Middle name
☐ Mr. ☐ Mrs. ☒ Ms.	Boar	Abigail	Elfreida

Street address	City	Province	Postal Code
72 Sumach Street	Toronto	Ontario	M4R 1Z5

Home phone number	Work phone number	Fax number	Birthdate
(416) 928-0001	(416) 635-1234	(416) 928-0002	Month 02 Day 03 Year 1975

1. What is the best way to reach you?

☐ phone   ☐ mail   ☐ fax   ☒ through my representative

2. Where is the best place to reach you?

☐ home   ☐ work   ☒ other, specify ▶ *representative's office*

3. When is the best time to reach you? Specify days of the week and time.

on business days during business hours

4. Is the Claimant under a legal disability (a minor or mentally incapable)?

☒ No   ☐ Yes   If Yes, has a family member, or guardian, or court appointed guardian, been named?   ☐ No   ☐ Yes

**Claimant's
Representative**

	Last name	First name	File reference number
☒ Mr. ☐ Mrs. ☐ Ms.	Just	I.M.	—

Title	Firm name
Lawyer	Just + Coping, Barristers and Solicitors

Street address	City	Province	Postal Code
365 Bay Street	Toronto	Ontario	M3J 4A9

Work phone number	Fax number	Electronic mail address
(416) 762-1342	(416) 762-2300	imjust@isp.on.ca

Relationship to the insured person

☒ lawyer   ☐ para legal   ☐ parent with whom the child resides   ☐ spouse or family relation   ☐ executor/ administrator/ trustee   ☐ court appointed guardian   ☐ other, specify ▶

Section 1, page 1

1974 (03/01)

FIGURE 25.1 CONTINUED

Section 1 *continued*

Insurance Company	Company name *Imperialist Payless Insurance Co.*

	Claim representative name *Dietrich Seljani*	Claim number *1A201301-99*
	Policyholder name *Rattle Motors Ltd.*	Policy number *A123456*

Insurance Company's Representative

☐ Mr. ☐ Mrs. ☐ Ms.	Last name *Unknown*	First name	File reference number
Title		Firm name	
Street address		City	Province Postal Code
Work phone number ( )	Fax number ( )	Electronic mail address	

Mediation

1. Do you wish the mediation to be conducted in French?
   ☒ No   ☐ Yes

2. Will you require the services of an interpreter at the mediation?
   ☒ No   ☐ Yes   If Yes, what language? ▶

   Please note that it is up to the Claimant to arrange interpretation or translation during the mediation in languages other than English or French.

3. Do you wish a face-to-face meeting with the other party?
   ☐ No   ☒ Yes

   Please note that it is within the mediator's discretion to conduct the mediation by telephone conference.

Signature and Certification

I certify that all information in this Application and attachments is true and complete. I authorize the insurance company to release all medical reports and information relating to the issues in dispute to Mediation Services of the Commission. I realize that information filed with this Application may be given to the other party in this dispute.

Claimant name (please print) *Abigail Boar*	Claimant Signature X *Abigail Boar*
Representative name (please print) *I.M. Just*	Representative Signature X *[signature]*
	Date *April 4, 2000*

If your representative is NOT a lawyer, please certify that you have provided your representative with full authorization to discuss all issues in dispute, to negotiate and to enter into an agreement or settlement of any and all issues in dispute, on your behalf in connection with this Application.

I certify that my representative ▼

I.M. Just   **has full authorization as described above**

Claimant Signature *Abigail Boar*
Date *April 4, 2000*

Section 1, page 2

1974 (03/01)

FIGURE 25.1 CONTINUED

ISSUES IN DISPUTE

The types of benefits available, the minimum and maximum amounts available and the rules to qualify for benefits may be different depending on when your motor vehicle accident took place. Fill in only that section covering the date of your accident.

You need to complete only ONE of sections 2, 3 or 4. (Discard unused sections.)

Section 2 – Complete if your motor vehicle accident occurred on or after November 1, 1996.

Section 3 – Complete if your motor vehicle accident occurred on or between January 1, 1994 and October 31, 1996, inclusive.

Section 4 – Complete if your motor vehicle accident occurred on or between June 22, 1990 and December 31, 1993, inclusive.

Section 2	Complete this section ONLY for motor vehicle accidents that occurred on or after November 1, 1996.

Insurer Examination (Medical) (I.E.) and Designated Assessment Centre (D.A.C.) Information

1. Was the Claimant **asked by the insurance company** to attend an **Insurer Examination (Medical)** (I.E.) relating to any of the issues in dispute?

☐ No ☒ Yes If Yes, did the Claimant attend? ▶ ☐ No ☒ Yes If No, give reason(s). ▼

Is the Claimant willing to attend a rescheduled I.E. within the next 30 days?

☐ No ☒ Yes If Yes, state available dates. ▶ *any time on 10 days' notice*

Please note that in some cases, mediation cannot take place until the Claimant has made him/herself reasonably available for an I.E.

2. Was the Claimant **asked by the insurance company** to attend an **assessment at a D.A.C.** relating to any of the issues in dispute?

☒ No ☐ Yes If Yes, did the Claimant attend? ▶ ☐ No ☐ Yes If No, give reason(s). ▼

Is the Claimant willing to attend a rescheduled D.A.C. assessment within the next 30 days?

☐ No ☐ Yes If Yes, state available dates. ▶ *N/A*

Please note that in some cases, mediation cannot take place until the Claimant has made him/herself reasonably available for a D.A.C. assessment.

To what benefit claim was the D.A.C. assessment related?	Name(s), address(es) and code(s) of the D.A.C.(s) *(Attach extra sheets, if necessary.)*
☐ medical benefits	D.A.C. Code ⌶ ⌶ ⌶ ⌶
☐ rehabilitation benefits	
☐ attendant care benefits	
☐ determination of catastrophic impairment	
Do you dispute the outcome of the D.A.C.? ☐ No ☐ Yes ☐ Partially	D.A.C. Code ⌶ ⌶ ⌶ ⌶

3. Did the Claimant **ask to attend an assessment at a D.A.C.** relating to any of the benefits in dispute?

☒ No ☐ Yes If Yes, to what benefits was the assessment related?	Name(s), address(es) and code(s) of the D.A.C.(s) *(Attach extra sheets, if necessary.)*
☐ disability benefits (income replacement, non-earner or caregiver benefits)	D.A.C. Code ⌶ ⌶ ⌶ ⌶
☐ disability benefits past 104 weeks of accident (income replacement or caregiver)	
☐ determination of catastrophic impairment	
Do you dispute the outcome of the D.A.C.? ☐ No ☐ Yes ☐ Partially	D.A.C. Code ⌶ ⌶ ⌶ ⌶

Section 2, page 1

1974 (03/01)

FIGURE 25.1   CONTINUED

Section 2   *continued*

Description of Dispute

Please review the SAMPLE in the Instructions, page 4, before completing this part. Check all benefits that are in dispute. If there is more than one amount in dispute for a particular benefit, state those amounts in the explanation area. (Add extra sheets, if necessary.)

Does the Claimant have optional benefits?

[ ] No   [X] Yes

For each benefit checked, briefly explain the details of the dispute.
(Attach extra sheets if necessary.) ▼

[ ] **Weekly Benefits**

Which weekly benefit are you disputing?

[X] income replacement
[ ] non-earner

What are you disputing?

[ ] initial entitlement to benefits
[X] length of time benefits were paid
[ ] amount of weekly benefits
[ ] entitlement to benefits past 104 weeks
[ ] benefits after age 65
[ ] other, specify ▼

If the Claimant received income benefits, state weekly amount and duration of payments.

$ 600

From   To
09-15-99   03-15-2000

Is the insurance company claiming a repayment of benefits?

[X] No   [ ] Yes   If Yes, amount ▼

$

The insurer has terminated the income replacement benefit. I am still unable to perform the core functions of my job as an investment analyst because of headaches and memory loss. I enclose my neurologist's report and the insurer's statement of benefits terminating income replacement benefits.

[ ] **Caregiver Benefits**

Weekly amount in dispute?

$ _____

From   To

What are you disputing?

[ ] initial entitlement to benefits
[ ] length of time benefits were paid
[ ] amount of benefits
[ ] entitlement to benefits past 104 weeks
[ ] other, specify ▼

[ ] **Medical Benefits**

Amount in dispute?

$ _____

Does this claim involve catastrophic impairment?

[ ] No   [ ] Yes

[ ] **Rehabilitation Benefits**

Amount in dispute?

$ _____

[ ] **Attendant Care Benefits**

Amount in dispute?

$ _____

Section 2, page 2

1974 (03/01)

FIGURE 25.1 CONTINUED

Section 2 *continued*	For each benefit checked, briefly explain the details of the dispute. *(Attach extra sheets if necessary.)* ▼

☐ **Case Manager Services Benefits**

Amount in dispute?

$ _____

☐ **Other Expenses**

Amount in dispute?

$ _____

What are you disputing?

   ☐ lost educational expenses

   ☐ expenses of visitors

   ☐ housekeeping and home maintenance

   ☐ damage to clothing, glasses, etc.

   ☐ cost of examinations

☐ **Death Benefits**

Amount in dispute?

$ _____

☐ **Funeral Expenses**

Amount in dispute?

$ _____

☐ **Other Disputes**

Amount in dispute?

$ _____

☐ **Interest**

Amount in dispute? Set out calculations.

$ _____

After completing this Section, make sure that you have signed the Application at the end of Section 1, and that you have listed all of your documents in Section 5. Send two copies of Application Sections 1, 2 and 5 plus any extra sheets, to:

        Mediation Services
        Dispute Resolution Group
        Financial Services Commission of Ontario

at the address shown on the front of this form.

Section 2, page 3

1974 (03/01)

FIGURE 25.1   CONTINUED

Section 3	Complete this section ONLY for motor vehicle accidents that occurred on or between January 1, 1994 and October 31, 1996, inclusive.

Insurer Examination (Medical) (I.E.) and Designated Assessment Centre (D.A.C.) Information

1. Was the Claimant **asked by the insurance company to attend an Insurer Examination (Medical)** (I.E.) relating to any of the issues in dispute?

☐ No   ☐ Yes   If Yes, did the Claimant attend? ▶   ☐ No   ☐ Yes   If No, give reason(s). ▼

Is the Claimant willing to attend a rescheduled I.E. within the next 30 days?

☐ No   ☐ Yes   If Yes, state available dates. ▶

Please note that in some cases, mediation cannot take place until the Claimant has made him/herself reasonably available for an I.E.

2. Was the Claimant **asked by the insurance company to attend an assessment at a D.A.C.** relating to any of the issues in dispute?

☐ No   ☐ Yes   If Yes, did the Claimant attend? ▶   ☐ No   ☐ Yes   If No, give reason(s). ▼

Is the Claimant willing to attend a rescheduled D.A.C. assessment within the next 30 days?

☐ No   ☐ Yes   If Yes, state available dates. ▶

Please note that in some cases, mediation cannot take place until the Claimant has made him/herself reasonably available for a D.A.C. assessment.

To what benefit claim was the D.A.C. assessment related?

☐ supplementary medical benefits
☐ rehabilitation benefits
☐ attendant care benefits
☐ loss of earning capacity benefits

Name(s), address(es) and code(s) of the D.A.C.(s) *(Attach extra sheets, if necessary.)*

D.A.C. Code ☐☐☐☐

Do you dispute the outcome of the D.A.C.?

☐ No   ☐ Yes   ☐ Partially

D.A.C. Code ☐☐☐☐

3. Did the Claimant **ask to attend an assessment at a D.A.C.** relating to any of the benefits in dispute?

☐ No   ☐ Yes   If Yes, to what benefits was the assessment related?

☐ disability benefits (income replacement, education disability or caregivers benefits)
☐ loss of earning capacity benefits
☐ attendant care benefits

Name(s), address(es) and code(s) of the D.A.C.(s) *(Attach extra sheets, if necessary.)*

D.A.C. Code ☐☐☐☐

Do you dispute the outcome of the D.A.C.?

☐ No   ☐ Yes   ☐ Partially

D.A.C. Code ☐☐☐☐

Section 3, page 1

1974 (03/01)

FIGURE 25.1 CONTINUED

Section 3 *continued*

Description of Dispute

Please review the SAMPLE in the Instructions, page 4, before completing this part. Check all benefits that are in dispute. If there is more than one amount in dispute for a particular benefit, state those amounts in the explanation area.

For each benefit checked, briefly explain the details of the dispute.
(Attach extra sheets if necessary.) ▼

☐ **Weekly Benefits**

Which weekly benefit are you disputing?
☐ income replacement
☐ education disability
☐ caregiver
☐ other disability

What are you disputing?
☐ initial entitlement to benefits
☐ length of time benefits were paid
☐ amount of weekly benefits
☐ entitlement to benefits past 104 weeks
☐ benefits after age 65
☐ other, specify ▼

If the Claimant received income benefits, state weekly amount and duration of payments.

$ _____

From _____ To _____

Is the insurance company claiming a repayment of benefits?
☐ No   ☐ Yes   If Yes, amount ▼

$ _____

Does the Claimant have a Pre-determined income from Self-Employment Agreement?
☐ No   ☐ Yes

☐ **Loss of Earning Capacity Benefits**

Did the Claimant receive a Loss of Earning Capacity Benefits offer from the insurer?

☐ No   If No ▼
  ☐ Claiming Loss of Earning Capacity Benefits

☐ Yes   If Yes ▼
  What part(s) of the offer are you disputing?
  ☐ Pre-accident earning capacity
  ☐ Residual Earning capacity

☐ **Education Disability Benefits (Lump Sum Benefits)**

Amount in dispute?

$ _____

☐ **Medical Benefits**

Amount in dispute?

$ _____

☐ **Rehabilita-tion Benefits**

Amount in dispute?

$ _____

Section 3, page 2

1974 (03/01)

FIGURE 25.1   CONTINUED

Section 3   *continued*

For each benefit checked, briefly explain the details of the dispute.
(Attach extra sheets if necessary.) ▼

☐ **Attendant Care Benefits**

Amount in dispute?

$

☐ **Compensation for Other Pecuniary Losses**

Amount in dispute?

$

What are you disputing?

☐ expenses of visitors
☐ dependant care expenses
☐ housekeeping and home maintenance
☐ damage to clothing, glasses, etc.
☐ cost of examinations

☐ **Death Benefits**

Amount in dispute?

$

☐ **Funeral Expenses**

Amount in dispute?

$

☐ **Other Disputes**

Amount in dispute?

$

☐ **Interest**

Amount in dispute? Set out calculations.

$

After completing this Section, make sure that you have signed the Application at the end of Section 1, and that you have listed all of your documents in Section 5. Send two copies of Application Sections 1, 3 and 5 plus any extra sheets, to:

**Mediation Services
Dispute Resolution Group
Financial Services Commission of Ontario**

at the address shown on the front of this form.

Section 3, page 3

1974 (03/01)

FIGURE 25.1   CONTINUED

Section 4   Complete this section ONLY for motor vehicle accidents that occurred on or between June 22, 1990 and December 31, 1993.

Insurer Examination (Medical) (I.E.) Information

Was the Claimant **asked by the insurance company to attend an Insurer Examination (Medical)** (I.E.) relating to any of the issues in dispute?

☐ No   ☐ Yes   If Yes, did the Claimant attend? ▶   ☐ No   ☐ Yes   If No, give reason(s). ▼

Is the Claimant willing to attend a rescheduled I.E. within the next 30 days?

☐ No   ☐ Yes   If Yes, state available dates. ▶

Please note that in some cases, mediation cannot take place until the Claimant has made him/herself reasonably available for an I.E.

Description of Dispute

Please review the SAMPLE in the Instructions, page 4, before completing this part. Check all benefits that are in dispute. If there is more than one amount in dispute for a particular benefit, state those amounts in the explanation area. (Add extra sheets, if necessary.)

Do you have optional benefits?

☐ No   ☐ Yes

For each benefit checked, briefly explain the details of the dispute.
(Attach extra sheets if necessary.) ▼

☐ **Income Benefits**

Which income benefit are you disputing?

☐ employed benefits
☐ benefit if no income

What are you disputing?

☐ initial entitlement to benefits
☐ length of time benefits were paid
☐ amount of weekly benefits
☐ entitlement to benefits past 156 weeks
☐ other, specify ▼

If the Claimant received weekly income benefits, state amount per week and duration of payments.

$ _____
From _____   To _____

Is the insurance company claiming a repayment of benefits?

☐ No   ☐ Yes   If Yes, amount ▼
$ _____

☐ **Childcare Benefits**

What are you disputing?

☐ initial entitlement to benefits
☐ length of time benefits were paid
☐ amount of benefits
☐ other, specify ▼

If the Claimant received weekly Childcare Benefits, state amount per week and duration of payments.

$ _____
From _____   To _____

Section 4, page 1

1974 (03/01)

FIGURE 25.1   CONTINUED

Section 4 *continued*	For each benefit checked, briefly explain the details of the dispute. *(Attach extra sheets if necessary.)* ▼
☐ **Supple-mentary Medical/ Rehabilita-tion Benefits** — Amount in dispute? $	
☐ **Care Benefits** — Amount in dispute? $	
☐ **Death Benefits** — Amount in dispute? $	
☐ **Funeral Expenses** — Amount in dispute? $	
☐ **Other Disputes** — Amount in dispute? $	
☐ **Interest** — Amount in dispute? Set out calculations. $	

After completing this Section, make sure that you have signed the Application at the end of Section 1, and that you have listed all of your documents in Section 5. Send two copies of Application Sections 1, 4 and 5 plus any extra sheets, to:

Mediation Services
Dispute Resolution Group
Financial Services Commission of Ontario

at the address shown on the front of this form.

Section 4, page 2

1974 (03/01)

FIGURE 25.1 CONTINUED

Section 5   Document List   This section MUST be completed.

It is expected that both parties have exchanged key documents prior to filing this _Application for Mediation._   _(Attach extra sheets if necessary.)_

Documents   1. List key documents in your possession to which you will refer in the mediation.

Identify the type of document (letter, medical report, tax return), the name of the writer or issuing institution and the date of the document.

Medical report of Dr. Morris Furgazy, dated October 30, 1999

Medical report of Dr. Edwina Dhrool, dated March 1, 2000

Psychological assessment by Enid Lightweight, PhD, dated
     March 2, 2000

Journal article on medication risk by Dr. E.J. Clomp et al.,
     Lancet July 1998

Job description, human resources department, Megadoon
     Investments, February 1995

☐ Extra sheets attached

---

2. List key documents not currently in your possession, which you intend to get from other sources (such as employers, doctors, Revenue Canada) for use in the mediation. You should also include any documents requested from the other party (such as Insurer Examination (Medical) reports, surveillance evidence, a summary of benefits paid) which have not yet been provided.

Wherever possible, identify the type of document (letter, medical report, tax return), the name of the writer or issuing institution and the date of the document.

I have asked my employer to provide a return to
work assessment. Date not yet known.

I requested copies of all insurer medical reports and
all other documents on which Imperialist Pay less
Insurer Co. relies.

☐ Extra sheets attached

After completing this Section, make sure that you have signed the Application at the end of Section 1. Send two copies of Application Sections 1, 5, and ONE of Sections 2, 3, or 4, depending on the accident date, plus any extra sheets, to:

    Mediation Services
    Dispute Resolution Group
    Financial Services Commission of Ontario

at the address shown on the front of this form.

Section 5

1974 (03/01)

FIGURE 25.2   RESPONSE TO AN APPLICATION FOR MEDIATION (FORM B)

Financial Services Commission of Ontario	Dispute Resolution Group

Response to an Application for Mediation
Form B

Mediation file number

M – 1234

An *Application for Mediation* has been filed with the Dispute Resolution Group of the Financial Services Commission of Ontario. You are a party in this application. Use this form to respond to the reasons for the dispute.

Personal information requested on this form is collected under the authority of the *Insurance Act*, R.S.O. 1990, c.I.8, as amended. This information will be used in the dispute resolution process for statutory accident benefits. This information will be available to all parties to the mediation. Any questions about this collection of information may be directed to the Office of the Registrar, Dispute Resolution Group.

When you have completed this form, make three copies, keep a copy for yourself, send a copy to the other party in this dispute, and send the original to:

**Mediation Services
Dispute Resolution Group
Financial Services Commission of Ontario
5160 Yonge Street, 15th Floor, Box 85
North York ON M2N 6L9**

If you have any questions about this form, or want more information, contact the Commission in Toronto at:

(416) 590-7210

or toll free at 1-800-517-2332, ext. 7210.

Commission website: www.fsco.gov.on.ca

Claimant

For the purposes of this Response, a Claimant is any person making a claim for statutory accident benefits to an insurance company as the result of a motor vehicle accident. The Claimant is not necessarily the motor vehicle insurance policyholder.

☐ Mr.
☐ Mrs.
☒ Ms.

Last name	First name	Middle name
Boar	Abigail	Elfreida

Street address	City	Province	Postal Code
72 Sumach Street	Toronto	Ontario	M4R 1Z5

Home phone number	Work phone number	Fax number	Birthdate
(416) 928-0001	(416) 635-1234	(416) 928-0002	Month 0 2 Day 0 3 Year 1 9 7 5

1. What is the best way to reach you?

☐ phone   ☐ mail   ☐ fax   ☐ through my representative

2. Where is the best place to reach you?

☐ home   ☐ work   ☐ other, specify ▶

3. When is the best time to reach you? Specify days of the week and time.

4. Is the Claimant under a legal disability (a minor or mentally incapable)?

☐ No   ☐ Yes   If Yes, has a family member, or legal guardian, or court appointed guardian, been named?   ☐ No   ☐ Yes

---

Insurance Company

Company name	Claims representative
Imperialist Payless Insurance Co.	Dietrich Seljani

Insurer's claim number	Policyholder name	Policy number
1A 201301 - 99	Rattle Motors Ltd.	A123456

Respondent's Representative

☒ Mr.
☐ Mrs.
☐ Ms.

Last name	First name	File reference number
Brown	Giacomo	

Title	Firm name
Lawyer	Brown & Puce

Street address	City	Province	Postal Code
130 Adelaide St. W. – 1023	Toronto	Ontario	M3J 1P4

Work phone number	Fax number	Electronic mail address
(416) 597-1234	(416) 597-1851	jocko.b@isp.on.ca

Relationship to Respondent

☒ lawyer   ☐ paralegal   ☐ other, specify ▶

PAGE 1   *Ce formulaire est également disponible en français.*

1849 (03/01)

FIGURE 25.2 CONTINUED

Insurer Examination (Medical) (I.E.) and Designated Assessment Centre (D.A.C.) Information	1. Was the Claimant **asked by the insurance company to attend an Insurer Examination (Medical) (I.E.)** relating to any of the issues in dispute?

[ ] No   [X] Yes   If Yes, did the Claimant attend? ▶   [ ] No   [X] Yes   If No, give reason(s). ▼

Is the insurer willing to arrange a new appointment within the next 30 days?

[ ] No   [X] Yes   If Yes, state available dates. ▶   *at a time convenient to the claimant*

Please note that in some cases, mediation cannot take place until a Claimant has made him/herself reasonably available for an I.E.

To what benefits does the I.E. relate?

loss of income

2. Was the Claimant **asked by the insurance company to attend an assessment at a Designated Assessment Centre (D.A.C.)** relating to any of the issues in dispute?

[X] No   [ ] Yes   If Yes, did the Claimant attend? ▶   [ ] No   [ ] Yes   If No, give reason(s). ▼

Is the insurer willing to arrange a new appointment within the next 30 days?

[ ] No   [ ] Yes   If Yes, state available dates. ▶

Please note that in some cases, mediation cannot take place until a Claimant has made him/herself reasonably available for a D.A.C. assessment.

To what benefits does the D.A.C. relate?	Date(s), name(s), address(es) and code(s) of the D.A.C.(s) *(Attach extra sheets, if necessary.)*
	D.A.C. Code [| | |]
	D.A.C. Code [| | |]
Do you dispute the outcome of the D.A.C.? [ ] No [ ] Yes [ ] Partially	

3. Did the **claimant ask to attend an assessment at a D.A.C.** relating to any of the benefits in dispute?

[X] No [ ] Yes If Yes, to what benefits does the D.A.C. relate?	Date(s), name(s), address(es) and code(s) of the D.A.C.(s) *(Attach extra sheets, if necessary.)*
	D.A.C. Code [| | |]
	D.A.C. Code [| | |]

FIGURE 25.2 CONTINUED

Response
Respond to each issue raised in the *Application for Mediation* and identify any new issues that you wish to raise at mediation. *Attach extra sheets if necessary.*

The insurer's medical assessments and reports indicate that the claimant may return to work on a part-time basis if she takes prescribed medication. She has refused to take the necessary medication.

☐ Extra sheets attached

Document List – this section MUST be completed.

It is expected that both parties have exchanged key documents prior to filing this *Response to an Application for Mediation.*

Attach extra sheets if necessary.

List all available documents (medical reports, etc.) that the Respondent intends to refer to at mediation. Identify the type of document (letter, medical report, tax return) with the name of the writer or issuing institution and date of the document.

Medical report of Dr. Olive Ork, dated February 15, 2000
Psychological assessment by Dr. Alex Oliphant, dated February 20, 2000

☐ Extra sheets attached

List key documents not currently in your possession, which the Respondent intends to get from other sources (such as employers, doctors, Revenue Canada), which are required for discussing a settlement of the issues in dispute. The Respondent should also include any documents requested from the other party which have not yet been provided. *Wherever possible identify the type of document (letter, medical report, tax return), the name of the writer or issuing institution and the date of the document.*

We requested a copy of the claimant's return to work assessment referred to in her application.

☐ Extra sheets attached

Signature

Name *(please print)*	Title	Signature	Date
Dietrich Seljani	Claims representative	D S	April 10, 2000

COMMISSION USE ONLY

Insurance company / Lawyer code	Date received	Date registered	File number
Mediator	Caseworker	Assistant	Assistant

PAGE 3

1849 (03/01)

FIGURE 25.3   APPLICATION FOR ARBITRATION (FORM C)

Financial
Services
Commission
of Ontario

Dispute
Resolution
Group

Application for Arbitration
Form C

An insured person may use this form to apply for arbitration of disputes about entitlement to or the amount of benefits under the *Statutory Accident Benefits Schedule (SABS)*. You can apply for arbitration only if the issues in dispute have not been resolved through mediation. **You may also use this form to apply for Neutral Evaluation.**

After you complete the application, **keep one copy** for yourself and **return two copies** of the completed application form signed by you, along with relevant documents and the filing fee, to Arbitration Services at the Financial Services Commission of Ontario (the "Commission") at the address below.

Personal information requested on this form is collected under the authority of the *Insurance Act*, R.S.O. 1990, c.I.8, as amended. This information, including documents submitted with this application, will be used in the dispute resolution process for accident benefits. This information will be available to all parties to the proceeding. Any questions about this collection of information may be directed to the Office of the Registrar, Dispute Resolution Group, at the address below.

You must enclose an application fee of $100. Make your cheque or money order payable to the Minister of Finance. Cheques made out to the Commission cannot be accepted and will be returned. Failure to pay the application fee will result in the Commission returning your application to you.

If you have any questions about this application, or want more information, contact:

Arbitration Services
Dispute Resolution Group
Financial Services Commission of Ontario
5160 Yonge Street, 14th Floor, Box 85
North York ON M2N 6L9

In Toronto: (416) 250-6714, extension 7202

Toll Free: 1-800-517-2332, extension 7202

Fax: (416) 590-8462

Arbitration Hotline: (416) 590-7202

Commission website: www.fsco.gov.on.ca

Ce formulaire est également disponible en français.

1850 (03/01)

FIGURE 25.3 CONTINUED

Applying for Arbitration

For a complete set of the rules about Arbitration and Neutral Evaluation, refer to the Dispute Resolution Practice Code.

How to Complete the Form

PLEASE PRINT

SECTION 1

General Information

Answer all six questions.

Applicant

Fill in your name, address and phone numbers, and tell us the best place to reach you. Be sure to fill in the mediation file number. You can find the mediation file number on the front of the Mediator's Report.

Applicant's Representative

You may choose to have someone represent you. Although many people are represented by a lawyer during arbitration or Neutral Evaluation, a lawyer is not required. If you have a representative, fill in the name, address and phone number of your representative. If it is a firm, please give the name of the firm in the box provided. *If your representative is NOT a lawyer, please provide written confirmation that the representative is authorized to act for you during the arbitration and can settle the dispute on your behalf. A minor (a person under the age of 18) or a person who has been declared mentally incapable, must have a representative.*

Insurance Company

Fill out the name of the insurance company and a contact or representative if known. Please provide the name of the policyholder and the policy number.

Neutral Evaluation

Neutral Evaluation may be appropriate for your case if the issues in dispute are clearly defined. *Neutral Evaluation* is an assessment of the issues in dispute by an experienced evaluator who will provide a non-binding opinion concerning the probable outcome if your case proceeds to court or arbitration. If your dispute has been referred to *Neutral Evaluation* by the mediator, please check off the appropriate box on the application.

Otherwise, if you wish to obtain *Neutral Evaluation* through the Commission, you must contact your insurance company. Both sides must agree to *Neutral Evaluation* and both sides must confirm that **all necessary documents and reports required for a determination of the issues have been obtained and exchanged.**

Arbitration Hearing

Please provide details concerning the arrangements you will require for an arbitration hearing. In most cases, both sides of a dispute want a hearing in person. However, in simple disputes where no witnesses will be called and little evidence will be filed, it is possible to speed up the arbitration process by holding a written or electronic hearing (e.g. by phone). In a written hearing, the arbitrator will decide the case based on the written materials submitted. *If you need an interpreter or other special services (such as sign language or wheelchair access), please give details in this section.*

Arbitration hearings are held at the Commission offices in North York for Applicants who live in the Greater Metropolitan Toronto Area. If you live outside the Greater Metropolitan Toronto Area, arrangements will be made to conduct a hearing in a location near your home.

Signature and Certification

Sign and date the form and return it along with two copies, to Arbitration Services of the Dispute Resolution Group at the Financial Services Commission of Ontario. Be sure to enclose a cheque or money order for **$100** payable to the **Minister of Finance**. *NOTE: Your application may be rejected if these steps have not been completed as requested.*

SECTIONS 2, 3, 4

You need to complete only ONE of these sections depending on the date of your motor vehicle accident. Discard unused sections.

Section 2 – Complete if your motor vehicle accident occurred on or after November 1, 1996.

Section 3 – Complete if your motor vehicle accident occurred on or between January 1, 1994 and October 31, 1996, inclusive.

Section 4 – Complete if your motor vehicle accident occurred on or between June 22, 1990 and December 31, 1993, inclusive.

Issues in Dispute

Please check all of the benefits you want arbitrated under the appropriate section. Check the benefits that are still being disputed (as they appear on the Mediator's Report). *New issues cannot be added at this stage until they have been mediated.* Make sure you fill in the section that applies to the date of your accident.

SECTION 5 – Documents at the Hearing

You must complete Section 5. List key documents in your possession to which reference will be made in the arbitration. Also list key documents you intend to obtain from other sources, including those requested from the insurer, such as surveillance evidence.

Instructions, page 1

1850 (03/01)

FIGURE 25.3 CONTINUED

Steps in the Arbitration Process

Step 1

Return the following items to Arbitration Services at the Commission. The full address is on the front of this form.

- Two copies of the completed Application for Arbitration, signed and dated (also keep one copy for yourself).

- Copy of the Mediator's Report (if available).

- Copy of Report of Neutral Evaluator, if neutral evaluation has taken place.

- Any information about your dispute that is relevant (i.e., doctor's reports, tax receipts or financial statements). **Send copies only – keep originals of all your documents.**

- **The $100 filing fee, payable to the Minister of Finance.**

Failure to comply with all these instructions may result in your application being returned to you.

Step 2

The Commission will send a copy of your completed Application to the insurance company. If you and the insurer jointly agree to refer your dispute to Neutral Evaluation at the Commission, a date will be set for the evaluation. If your case does not settle after the Neutral Evaluation, your case will move directly to Step 6 below.

Step 3

If your case is not referred to Neutral Evaluation, the insurance company must file a *Response by Insurer to an Application for Arbitration* with the Commission within 20 days of their receipt of your *Application for Arbitration*. The Response will state the company's position on the dispute and may raise further issues which were not resolved in mediation. You will get a copy of the Insurer's *Response by Insurer to an Application for Arbitration*.

Step 4 (optional)

You will have an opportunity to reply to what the insurance company has said. If you wish to reply, you can use the *Reply by the Applicant for Arbitration* form that is available from the Commission. You will have 10 days from the day you receive the insurance company's Response to reply. Send the insurance company and the Commission a copy of your reply.

Step 5

The Commission will set a date for a pre-hearing discussion with an arbitrator, before you have a hearing. You are required to produce and exchange all relevant documents and reports *before* the pre-hearing discussion. At the pre-hearing discussion, you and the insurance company will discuss the issues with an arbitrator and make arrangements for the hearing.

Step 6

If you have not settled the dispute after Neutral Evaluation or a pre-hearing discussion, a hearing will be scheduled. After the hearing, the written order of the arbitrator will be sent to you and the insurance company.

Note: You may settle your dispute with the insurance company directly at any time during the arbitration process.

FIGURE 25.3 CONTINUED

Financial Services Commission of Ontario	Dispute Resolution Group	**Application for Arbitration** Form C	Arbitration file number *A-1234*

Section 1 — This section MUST be completed.

General Information

1. What was the date of the motor vehicle accident?

Month	Day	Year
0 9	1 4	1 9 9 9

2. Who is making this application?

☐ Applicant   ☒ Applicant's representative

3. Have you applied for arbitration before?

☒ No   ☐ Yes   If Yes, please provide arbitration numbers ▶

4. Language preferred

☒ English   ☐ French   ☐ Other, specify ▶

5. Have you contacted the other party and tried to settle the dispute since mediation?

☒ No   ☐ Yes

6. Provide mediation file number

M-78910C

Have you attached a copy of the mediator's report?

☐ No   ☒ Yes

Applicant

☐ Mr. ☐ Mrs. ☒ Ms.

Last name: *Boar*   First name: *Abigail*   Middle name: *Elfreida*

Street address: *72 Sumach Street*   City: *Toronto*   Province: *Ontario*   Postal Code: *M4R 1Z5*

Home phone number: *(416) 928-0001*   Work phone number: *(416) 635-1234*   Fax number: *(416) 928-0002*

Birthdate: Month *0 2* Day *3* Year *1 9 7 5*

1. What is the best way to reach you?

☐ phone   ☐ mail   ☐ fax   ☒ through my representative

2. Where is the best place to reach you?

☐ home   ☐ work   ☒ other, specify ▶ *representative's office*

3. When is the best time to reach you? Specify days of the week and time.

contact my representative

4. Is the Applicant under a legal disability (a minor or mentally incapable)?

☒ No   ☐ Yes   If Yes, has a family member, or guardian, or court appointed guardian, been named?   ☐ No   ☐ Yes

Applicant's Representative

☒ Mr. ☐ Mrs. ☐ Ms.

Last name: *Just*   First name: *I.M.*   File reference number: *—*

Title: *Lawyer*   Firm name: *Just & Coping, Barristers and Solicitors*

Street address: *365 Bay Street*   City: *Toronto*   Province: *Ontario*   Postal Code: *M3J 4A9*

Work phone number: *(416) 762-1342*   Fax number: *(416) 762-2300*   Electronic mail address: *imjust@isp.on.ca*

Relationship to the insured person

☒ lawyer   ☐ para legal   ☐ parent with whom the child resides   ☐ spouse or family relation   ☐ executor/ administrator/ trustee   ☐ court appointed guardian   ☐ other, specify ▶

Insurance Company

Company name: *Imperialist Payless Insurance Co.*

Claim representative name: *Dietrich Seljani*   Claim number: *1A 201301-99*

Policyholder name: *Rattle Motors Ltd.*   Policy number: *A123456*

Section 1, page 1

1850 (03/01)

FIGURE 25.3 CONTINUED

Section 1 *continued*

Neutral Evaluation	1. Are any issues relating to this accident still in mediation? ☐ No ☒ Yes If Yes, provide mediation file number(s) ▶ M- 2. Does the mediator's report refer issues in dispute for neutral evaluation? ☒ No ☐ Yes

Neutral Evaluation

1. Are any issues relating to this accident still in mediation?
☐ No   ☒ Yes   If Yes, provide mediation file number(s) ▶ M-

2. Does the mediator's report refer issues in dispute for neutral evaluation?
☒ No   ☐ Yes

3. Have you referred any issues in dispute to a private sector neutral evaluator appointed by the Director of Arbitrations?
☒ No   ☐ Yes

4. Did the neutral evaluator issue a written report?
☒ No   ☐ Yes   If Yes, attach a copy of the report

5. Do you want Neutral Evaluation through the Commission?
☒ No   ☐ Yes   If Yes, *do you certify that all documents or reports listed in the Report of Mediator have been exchanged and that no other documents are required for the purpose of evaluating the issues in dispute?*
☐ Yes **Signature ▼**

Arbitration Hearing

1. Do you wish to have an oral arbitration hearing?
☐ No   ☒ Yes

2. In simple disputes, it is possible to speed up the arbitration process by holding a written or electronic hearing. Do you wish to have a hearing based on written or electronic (by telephone) submissions only?
☒ No   ☐ Yes

3. Do you wish the arbitration hearing to be conducted in French?
☒ No   ☐ Yes

4. Will you require the services of an interpreter at the arbitration hearing?
☒ No   ☐ Yes   If Yes, what language? ▶

5. Do you require other special services such as wheelchair access or sign language interpreter?
☒ No   ☐ Yes   If Yes, please describe ▶

6. Do you require the hearing to be held outside the Greater Metropolitan Toronto Area?
☒ No   ☐ Yes   If Yes, where? ▶

Signature and Certification

I certify that all information in this Application and attachments is true and complete. I authorize the insurance company to release all medical reports and information relating to the issues in dispute to Arbitration Services at the Commission. I realize that copies of all information filed with this Application will be given to the other party in this dispute.

Applicant name (please print)
Abigail Boar

Applicant Signature
X *Abigail Boar*

Representative name (please print)
I.M. Just

Representative Signature
X

☒ Cheque or money order enclosed

Date
May 10, 2000

If your representative is NOT a lawyer, please certify that you have provided your representative with full authorization to discuss all issues in dispute, to negotiate and to enter into an agreement or settlement of any and all issues in dispute, on your behalf in connection with this Application.

I certify that my representative ▼

has full authorization as described above

Applicant Signature

Date

FIGURE 25.3 CONTINUED

ISSUES IN DISPUTE

The types of benefits available, the minimum and maximum amounts available and the rules to qualify for benefits may be different depending on when your motor vehicle accident took place. Fill in only that section covering the date of your accident.

You need to complete only ONE of sections 2, 3 or 4. (Discard unused sections.)

Section 2 – Complete if your motor vehicle accident occurred on or after November 1, 1996.

Section 3 – Complete if your motor vehicle accident occurred on or between January 1, 1994 and October 31, 1996, inclusive.

Section 4 – Complete if your motor vehicle accident occurred on or between June 22, 1990 and December 31, 1993, inclusive.

Section 2   **Complete this section ONLY for motor vehicle accidents that occurred on or after November 1, 1996.**

Insurer Examination (Medical) (I.E.) and Designated Assessment Centre (D.A.C.) Information

1. Since you filed for mediation, has the insurer **asked you to attend an Insurer Examination (Medical) (I.E.)** relating to any of the issues in dispute?

   [X] No   [ ] Yes   If Yes, did you attend? ▶   [ ] No   [ ] Yes   If No, briefly explain. ▼

   Please note that in some cases, arbitration cannot take place until an Applicant has made him/herself reasonably available for an I.E.

2. Since you filed for mediation, has the insurer **asked you to attend an assessment at a D.A.C.** relating to any of the issues in dispute?

   [X] No   [ ] Yes   If Yes, did you attend? ▶   [ ] No   [ ] Yes   If No, briefly explain. ▼

   Please note that in some cases, arbitration cannot take place until an Applicant has made him/herself reasonably available for a D.A.C. assessment.

If Yes, to what benefit claim was the D.A.C. assessment related?	Name(s), address(es) and code(s) of the D.A.C.(s) if known *(Attach extra sheets, if necessary.)*
[ ] medical benefits	D.A.C. Code [| | | |]
[ ] rehabilitation benefits	
[ ] attendant care benefits	
[ ] determination of catastrophic impairment	
Do you dispute the outcome of the D.A.C.? [ ] No [ ] Yes [ ] Partially	D.A.C. Code [| | | |]

3. Since you filed for mediation have you **asked to attend an assessment at a D.A.C.** relating to any of the benefits in dispute?

[X] No   [ ] Yes   If Yes, to what benefits was the assessment related?

[ ] disability benefits (income replacement, non-earner or caregiver benefits)

[ ] disability benefits past 104 weeks of accident (income replacement or caregiver)

[ ] determination of catastrophic impairment

Do you dispute the outcome of the D.A.C.? [ ] No [ ] Yes [ ] Partially

Name(s), address(es) and code(s) of the D.A.C.(s) if known *(Attach extra sheets, if necessary.)*

D.A.C. Code [\| \| \| \|]

D.A.C. Code [\| \| \| \|]

Section 2, page 1

1850 (03/01)

FIGURE 25.3   CONTINUED

Section 2   *continued*

Description of Dispute

Check the benefits that were not resolved in mediation and which you now want evaluated or arbitrated. You cannot add new issues at this stage until they have been mediated. (Add extra sheets, if necessary.)

Do you have optional benefits?

☐ No   ☒ Yes

For each benefit checked, briefly explain the details of the dispute. Refer to disputed issues in mediation report. *(Attach extra sheets if necessary.)* ▼

☒ **Weekly Benefits**

Which weekly benefit are you disputing?

☒ income replacement
☐ non-earner

What are you disputing?

☐ initial entitlement to benefits
☒ length of time benefits were paid
☐ amount of weekly benefits
☒ entitlement to benefits past 104 weeks
☐ benefits after age 65
☐ other, specify ▼

If you received income benefits, state weekly amount and duration of payments.

$ 600

From _____   To
09-15-99   Present

Is the insurance company claiming a repayment of benefits?

☒ No   ☐ Yes   If Yes, amount ▼

$

I have been, and am, unable to return to work because I am physically and mentally incapable of performing my core job functions. The insurer has suggested alternative treatment to allow me to return to work on a part-time basis. I have refused this treatment because of unacceptable life-threatening risks to my health from side effects of the proposed medication.

☐ **Caregiver Benefits**

Amount in dispute?

$

What are you disputing?

☐ initial entitlement to benefits
☐ length of time benefits were paid
☐ amount of benefits
☐ entitlement to benefits past 104 weeks
☐ other, specify ▼

☐ **Medical Benefits**

Amount in dispute?

$

Does this claim involve catastrophic impairment?

☐ No   ☐ Yes

☐ **Rehabilita-tion Benefits**

Amount in dispute?

$

☐ **Attendant Care Benefits**

Amount in dispute?

$

Section 2, page 2

1850 (03/01)

FIGURE 25.3   CONTINUED

Section 2 *continued*	For each benefit checked, briefly explain the details of the dispute. Refer to disputed issues in mediation report. *(Attach extra sheets if necessary.)* ▼

☐ **Case Manager Services Benefits**

Amount in dispute?

$ _____

☐ **Other Expenses**

Amount in dispute?

$ _____

What are you disputing?

☐ lost educational expenses
☐ expenses of visitors
☐ housekeeping and home maintenance
☐ damage to clothing, glasses, etc.
☐ cost of examinations

☐ **Death Benefits**

Amount in dispute?

$ _____

☐ **Funeral Expenses**

Amount in dispute?

$ _____

☐ **Other Disputes**

Amount in dispute?

$ _____

☐ **Interest**

Amount in dispute? Set out calculations.

$ _____

☒ **Expenses of the Hearing**

Disbursements and fees paid to counsel for representing me.

☐ **Special Award**

After completing this Section, make sure that you have signed the Application at the end of Section 1, and that you have listed all of your documents in Section 5. Send two copies of Application Sections 1, 2 and 5, plus any extra sheets, to:

    Arbitration Services
    Dispute Resolution Group
    Financial Services Commission of Ontario

at the address shown on the front of this form.

Section 2, page 3

1850 (03/01)

FIGURE 25.3 CONTINUED

Section 3 **Complete this section ONLY for motor vehicle accidents that occurred on or between January 1, 1994 and October 31, 1996, inclusive.**

Insurer Examination (Medical) (I.E.) and Designated Assessment Centre (D.A.C.) Information

1. Since you filed for mediation, has the insurer **asked you to attend an Insurer Examination (Medical)** (I.E.) relating to any of the issues in dispute?

☐ No ☐ Yes If Yes, did you attend? ▶ ☐ No ☐ Yes If No, briefly explain. ▼

Please note that in some cases, arbitration cannot take place until an Applicant has made him/herself reasonably available for an I.E.

2. Since you filed for mediation, has the insurer **asked you to attend an assessment at a D.A.C.** relating to any of the issues in dispute?

☐ No ☐ Yes If Yes, did you attend? ▶ ☐ No ☐ Yes If No, briefly explain. ▼

Please note that in some cases, arbitration cannot take place until an Applicant has made him/herself reasonably available for a D.A.C. assessment.

If Yes, to what benefit claim was the D.A.C. assessment related?	Name(s), address(es) and code(s) of the D.A.C.(s) if known *(Attach extra sheets, if necessary.)*
☐ supplementary medical benefits	D.A.C. Code
☐ rehabilitation benefits	
☐ attendant care benefits	
☐ loss of earning capacity benefits	
Do you dispute the outcome of the D.A.C.?	D.A.C. Code
☐ No ☐ Yes ☐ Partially	

3. Since you filed for mediation have you **asked to attend an assessment at a D.A.C.** relating to any of the benefits in dispute?

☐ No ☐ Yes If Yes, to what benefits was the assessment related?	Name(s), address(es) and code(s) of the D.A.C.(s) if known *(Attach extra sheets, if necessary.)*
☐ disability benefits (income replacement, education disability or caregiver benefits)	D.A.C. Code
☐ loss of earning capacity benefits	
☐ attendant care benefits	
	D.A.C. Code
Do you dispute the outcome of the D.A.C.?	
☐ No ☐ Yes ☐ Partially	

Section 3, page 1

1850 (03/01)

FIGURE 25.3   CONTINUED

Section 3   *continued*

Description of Dispute

Check the benefits that were not resolved in mediation and which you now want evaluated or arbitrated. You cannot add new issues at this stage until they have been mediated. (Add extra sheets, if necessary.)

For each benefit checked, briefly explain the details of the dispute. Refer to disputed issues in mediation report. *(Attach extra sheets if necessary.)* ▼

Weekly Benefits

Which weekly benefit are you disputing?

☐ income replacement
☐ education disability
☐ caregiver
☐ other disability

What are you disputing?

☐ initial entitlement to benefits
☐ length of time benefits were paid
☐ amount of weekly benefits
☐ entitlement to benefits past 104 weeks
☐ benefits after age 65
☐ other, specify ▼

If you received income benefits, state weekly amount and duration of payments.

$ _____
From _____ To _____

Is the insurance company claiming a repayment of benefits?

☐ No   ☐ Yes   If Yes, amount ▼
$

Do you have a Pre-determined income from Self-Employment Agreement?

☐ No   ☐ Yes

Loss of Earning Capacity Benefits

Did you receive a Loss of Earning Capacity Benefits offer from the insurer?

☐ No   If No ▼
  ☐ Claiming Loss of Earning Capacity Benefits

☐ Yes   If Yes ▼
  What part(s) of the offer are you disputing?
  ☐ Pre-accident earning capacity
  ☐ Residual Earning capacity

Education Disability Benefits (Lump Sum Benefits)

Amount in dispute?

$ _____

Medical Benefits

Amount in dispute?

$ _____

Rehabilitation Benefits

Amount in dispute?

$ _____

Section 3, page 2

1850 (03/01)

FIGURE 25.3   CONTINUED

Section 3 *continued*	For each benefit checked, briefly explain the details of the dispute. Refer to disputed issues in mediation report. *(Attach extra sheets if necessary.)* ▼

☐ **Attendant Care Benefits**

Amount in dispute?

$

☐ **Compensation for Other Pecuniary Losses**

Amount in dispute?

$

What are you disputing?

☐ expenses of visitors

☐ dependant care expenses

☐ housekeeping and home maintenance

☐ damage to clothing, glasses, etc.

☐ cost of examinations

☐ **Death Benefits**

Amount in dispute?

$

☐ **Funeral Expenses**

Amount in dispute?

$

☐ **Other Disputes**

Amount in dispute?

$

☐ **Interest**

Amount in dispute? Set out calculations.

$

☐ **Expenses of the Hearing**

☐ **Special Award**

After completing this Section, make sure that you have signed the Application at the end of Section 1, and that you have listed all of your documents in Section 5. Send two copies of Application Sections 1, 3 and 5, plus any extra sheets, to:

Arbitration Services
Dispute Resolution Group
Financial Services Commission of Ontario

at the address shown on the front of this form.

Section 3, page 3

1850 (03/01)

FIGURE 25.3 CONTINUED

Section 4   **Complete this section ONLY for motor vehicle accidents that occurred on or between June 22, 1990 and December 31, 1993.**

Insurer Examination (Medical) (I.E.) Information

Were you **asked by the insurance company** to attend an **Insurer Examination (Medical) (I.E.)** relating to any of the issues in dispute?

☐ No   ☐ Yes   If Yes, did you attend? ▶   ☐ No   ☐ Yes   If No, briefly explain. ▼

Please note that in some cases, arbitration cannot take place until an Applicant has made him/herself reasonably available for an I.E.

Description of Dispute

Check the benefits that were not resolved in mediation and which you now want evaluated or arbitrated. You cannot add new issues at this stage until they have been mediated. (Add extra sheets, if necessary.)

Do you have optional benefits?

☐ No   ☐ Yes

For each benefit checked, briefly explain the details of the dispute. Refer to disputed issues in mediation report. *(Attach extra sheets if necessary.)* ▼

☐ **Income Benefits**

Which income benefit are you disputing?

☐ employed benefits
☐ benefit if no income

What are you disputing?

☐ initial entitlement to benefits
☐ length of time benefits were paid
☐ amount of weekly benefits
☐ entitlement to benefits past 156 weeks
☐ other, specify ▼

If you received weekly income benefits, state amount per week and duration of payments.

$ _____
From _____ To _____

Is the insurance company claiming a repayment of benefits?

☐ No   ☐ Yes   If Yes, amount ▼

$ _____

☐ **Childcare Benefits**

What are you disputing?

☐ initial entitlement to benefits
☐ length of time benefits were paid
☐ amount of benefits
☐ other, specify ▼

If you received weekly Childcare Benefits, state amount per week and duration of payments.

$ _____
From _____ To _____

Section 4, page 1

1850 (03/01)

FIGURE 25.3   CONTINUED

Section 4	*continued*	For each benefit checked, briefly explain the details of the dispute. Refer to disputed issues in mediation report. *(Attach extra sheets if necessary.)* ▼
☐ Supple-mentary Medical/ Rehabilita-tion Benefits	Amount in dispute? $	
☐ Care Benefits	Amount in dispute? $	
☐ Death Benefits	Amount in dispute? $	
☐ Funeral Expenses	Amount in dispute? $	
☐ Other Disputes	Amount in dispute? $	
☐ Interest	Amount in dispute? Set out calculations. $	
☐ Expenses of the Hearing		
☐ Special Award		

After completing this Section, make sure that you have signed the Application at the end of Section 1, and that you have listed all of your documents in Section 5. Send two copies of Application Sections 1, 4 and 5, plus any extra sheets, to:

Arbitration Services
Dispute Resolution Group
Financial Services Commission of Ontario

at the address shown on the front of this form.

Section 4, page 2

1850 (03/01)

FIGURE 25.3   CONTINUED

Section 5   Document List   This section MUST be completed.

It is expected that the Applicant and the Insurer have exchanged key documents prior to the filing of an Application for Arbitration.

(Attach extra sheets if necessary.)

Documents   1. Please explain why any document, identified in the **Report of Mediator** as having been requested by the insurer, has not been provided to the insurer prior to submitting your **Application for Arbitration.**

N/A

☐ Extra sheets attached

2. List key documents in your possession to which you will refer in the arbitration.

Identify the type of document (letter, medical report, tax return), the name of the writer or issuing institution and the date of the document.

Medical report of Dr. Morris Furgazy, dated October 30, 1999

Medical report of Dr. Edwina Dhrool, dated March 1, 2000

Psychological assessment by Enid Lightweight, PhD, dated March 2, 2000

Journal article on medication risk by Dr. E.J. Clomp et al., Lancet July 1998

Job description, human resources department, Megadoon Investments, February 1995

☐ Extra sheets attached

3. List key documents not currently in your possession, which you intend to get from other sources (such as employers, doctors, Revenue Canada) for use in your arbitration. You should also include any documents requested from the insurer (such as Insurer Examination (Medical) reports, surveillance evidence, a summary of benefits paid) which have not yet been provided.

Wherever possible, identify the type of document (letter, medical report, tax return), the name of the writer or issuing institution and the date of the document.

N/A

☐ Extra sheets attached

After completing this Section, make sure that you have signed the Application at the end of Section 1. Send two copies of Application Sections 1, 5, and ONE of Sections 2, 3, or 4, depending on the accident date, plus any extra sheets, to:

   Arbitration Services
   Dispute Resolution Group
   Financial Services Commission of Ontario

at the address shown on the front of this form.

Section 5

1850 (03/01)

FIGURE 25.4   RESPONSE BY INSURER TO APPLICATION FOR ARBITRATION (FORM E)

Financial Services Commission of Ontario	Dispute Resolution Group

Response by Insurer to an Application for Arbitration
Form E

Arbitration file number

A-1234

An **Application for Arbitration** has been filed with the Dispute Resolution Group of the Financial Services Commission of Ontario (the "Commission"). A copy of the **Application for Arbitration** is attached. Your company is named as a party in this arbitration. Use this form to respond to the issues raised in the Application. You can add new issues which have been mediated but not settled. You must serve a copy of this **Response** on the Applicant and provide proof of service to the Commission. This must be done within **20 days** of receiving this document. This **Response** need not be completed if the Insurer agrees to the applicant's request for Neutral Evaluation, or the Applicant consents to an **Agreement to Neutral Evaluation at the Commission** within **20 days** of receiving this document.

If the Applicant has not requested Neutral Evaluation through the Commission but the Insurer wishes to request Neutral Evaluation, the Insurer must contact the Applicant and his/her representative (if any), to obtain the Applicant's written consent to Neutral Evaluation. This written consent and an **Agreement to Neutral Evaluation at the Commission (Form D)** must be filed within **20 days** of receipt by the Insurer of the **Application for Arbitration**.

The Insurer must complete and sign Section 1.

The Insurer must complete ONE of Sections 2, 3, or 4, depending on the accident date, plus any required extra sheets.

The Insurer must complete Section 5. List key documents in the insurer's possession to which reference will be made in the arbitration, such as surveillance evidence. Also list key documents the Insurer intends to obtain from other sources, including those requested from the Applicant, such as financial or employment records.

Personal information requested on this form is collected under the authority of the *Insurance Act*, R.S.O. 1990, c. I.8, as amended. This information, including documents submitted with this form, will be used in the dispute resolution process for accident benefits. This information will be available to all parties to the proceeding. Any questions about this collection of information may be directed to the Office of the Registrar, Dispute Resolution Group, Financial Services Commission of Ontario.

Section 1   This section MUST be completed.

Applicant

Date of the motor vehicle accident?

Month	Day	Year
0 9	1 4	1 9 9 9

☐ Mr.
☐ Mrs.
☒ Ms.

Last name	First name	Middle name
Boar	Abigail	Elfrieda

Insurance Company

Company name

Imperialist Payless Insurance Co.

☒ Mr.
☐ Mrs.
☐ Ms.

Contact person – Last name	First name
Seljani	Dietrich

Street address	City	Province	Postal Code
681 University Avenue – 2300	Toronto	Ontario	M5G 1S2

Phone number	Fax number	Electronic mail address
(416) 597-1341	(416) 597-1342	sdiet@payless.com

Insurer's claim number	Policyholder name	Policy number
1A 201301-99	Rattle Motors Ltd.	A123456

Legal Representative

☒ Mr.
☐ Mrs.
☐ Ms.

Last name	First name	File reference number
Brown	Giacomo	

Title	Firm name
Lawyer	Brown & Puce

Street address	City	Province	Postal Code
130 Adelaide St. W. – 1023	Toronto	Ontario	M3J 1P4

Work phone number	Fax number	Electronic mail address
(416) 597-1234	(416) 597-1851	jocko.b@isp.on.ca

Section 1, page 1   Ce formulaire est également disponible en français.

1851 (03/01)

FIGURE 25.4 CONTINUED

Section 1 *continued*

Neutral Evaluation	1. Are any issues relating to this accident still in mediation? [X] No [ ] Yes If Yes, provide mediation file number(s) ▶ M-	2. Does the mediator's report refer issues in dispute for neutral evaluation? [X] No [ ] Yes

3. Have you referred any issues in dispute to a private sector neutral evaluator appointed by the Director of Arbitrations?

[X] No [ ] Yes

4. Did the neutral evaluator issue a written report?

[ ] No [ ] Yes If Yes, attach a copy of the report

5. Do you want Neutral Evaluation through the Commission?

[X] No [ ] Yes If Yes, *do you certify that all documents or reports listed in the Report of Mediator have been exchanged and that no other documents are required for the purpose of evaluating the issues in dispute?*

[ ] Yes *Signature* ▼

Type of Hearing

1. Does the insurer wish to have an oral hearing?

[ ] No [X] Yes

2. In simple disputes, it is possible to speed up the arbitration process by holding a written or electronic hearing where the arbitrator will decide the case based on the written materials submitted. Does the insurer wish to have a hearing based on electronic (by telephone) or written submissions only?

[X] No [ ] Yes

3. Does the insurer require special service such as audio visual equipment?

[X] No [ ] Yes If Yes, please describe. ▶

4. Will the insurer be arranging for the services of a Court Reporter?

[X] No [ ] Yes

Signature and Certification

I certify that all information in this Response and attachments is true and complete. I realize that copies of all information filed with this Response will be given to the other party in this dispute.

Name	Title	Signature
Dietrich Seljani	Claims representative	D S

Date

May 22, 2000

FIGURE 25.4 CONTINUED

ISSUES IN DISPUTE

The types of benefits available, the minimum and maximum amounts available and the rules to qualify for benefits may be different depending on when your motor vehicle accident took place. Fill in only that section covering the date of your accident.

You need to complete only ONE of sections 2, 3 or 4. (Discard unused sections.)

Section 2 – Complete if your motor vehicle accident occurred on or after November 1, 1996.

Section 3 – Complete if your motor vehicle accident occurred on or between January 1, 1994 and October 31, 1996, inclusive.

Section 4 – Complete if your motor vehicle accident occurred on or between June 22, 1990 and December 31, 1993, inclusive.

Section 2   Complete this section ONLY for motor vehicle accidents that occurred on or after November 1, 1996.

Insurer Examination (Medical) (I.E.) and Designated Assessment Centre (D.A.C.) Information

1. Since the conclusion of mediation did the **insurance company ask the Applicant to attend an Insurer Examination (Medical)** (I.E.) relating to any of the issues in dispute?

   [X] No   [ ] Yes   If Yes, did the Applicant attend? ▶   [ ] No   [ ] Yes   If No, state reason(s). ▼

2. Since the conclusion of mediation did the **insurance company ask the Applicant to attend an assessment at a D.A.C.** relating to any of the issues in dispute?

   [X] No   [ ] Yes   If Yes, did the Applicant attend? ▶   [ ] No   [ ] Yes   If No, state reason(s). ▼

   If Yes, to what benefit claim was the D.A.C. assessment related?

   [ ] medical benefits

   [ ] rehabilitation benefits

   [ ] attendant care benefits

   [ ] determination of catastrophic impairment

   Does the insurer dispute the outcome of the D.A.C.?

   [ ] No   [ ] Yes   [ ] Partially

   Name(s), address(es) and code(s) of the D.A.C.(s) *(Attach extra sheets, if necessary.)*

   D.A.C. Code | | | |

   D.A.C. Code | | | |

3. Since the conclusion of mediation did the **Applicant ask to attend an assessment at a D.A.C.** relating to any of the benefits in dispute?

   [X] No   [ ] Yes   If Yes, to what benefits was the assessment related?

   [ ] disability benefits (income replacement, non-earner or caregiver benefits)

   [ ] disability benefits past 104 weeks of accident (income replacement or caregiver)

   [ ] determination of catastrophic impairment

   Does the insurer dispute the outcome of the D.A.C.?

   [ ] No   [ ] Yes   [ ] Partially

   Name(s), address(es) and code(s) of the D.A.C.(s) *(Attach extra sheets, if necessary.)*

   D.A.C. Code | | | |

   D.A.C. Code | | | |

Section 2, page 1

1851 (03/01)

FIGURE 25.4 CONTINUED

Section 2 *continued*

Description of Dispute

Check the benefits that were not resolved in mediation and which the insurer now wants to respond to or now wants evaluated or arbitrated. The insurer may add new issues which have been mediated but not settled. (Add extra sheets, if necessary.)

Does the Applicant have optional benefits?

[ ] No   [X] Yes

For each benefit checked, briefly explain the insurer's position on the issues in dispute. (Attach extra sheets if necessary.) ▼

[X] **Weekly Benefits**

Which weekly benefits are being disputed?

[X] income replacement
[ ] non-earner

What is being disputed?

[ ] initial entitlement to benefits
[X] length of time benefits were paid
[ ] amount of weekly benefits
[X] entitlement to benefits past 104 weeks
[ ] benefits after age 65
[ ] other, specify ▼

If the insurer paid weekly benefits, state weekly amount and duration of payments.

$ **600**

From **9-15-99**   To **Present**

Is the insurance company claiming a repayment of benefits?

[X] No   [ ] Yes If Yes amount ▼

$

The insurer's position is that the claimant could return to work on a part-time basis with a change in treatment plan involving a change in medication. The claimant has refused to change treatment. The insurer's view is that the treatment proposed is safe and that the claimant is unreasonably refusing treatment and exaggerating the effect of her injuries. The claimant has used this medication before without being harmed.

[ ] **Caregiver Benefits**

Amount in dispute?

$

What is being disputed?

[ ] initial entitlement to benefits
[ ] length of time benefits were paid
[ ] amount of benefits
[ ] entitlement to benefits past 104 weeks
[ ] other, specify ▼

[ ] **Medical Benefits**

Amount in dispute?

$

Does this claim involve catastrophic impairment?

[ ] No   [ ] Yes

[ ] **Rehabilitation Benefits**

Amount in dispute?

$

[ ] **Attendant Care Benefits**

Amount in dispute?

$

Section 2, page 2

1851 (03/01)

FIGURE 25.4 CONTINUED

Section 2 *continued*

For each benefit checked, briefly explain the insurer's position on the issues in dispute.
(Attach extra sheets if necessary.) ▼

☐ **Case
Manager
Services
Benefits**

Amount in dispute?

$ _____

☐ **Other
Expenses**

Amount in dispute?

$ _____

What is being disputed?

☐ lost educational expenses
☐ expenses of visitors
☐ housekeeping and home
maintenance
☐ damage to clothing, glasses, etc.
☐ cost of examinations

☐ **Death
Benefits**

Amount in dispute?

$ _____

☐ **Funeral
Expenses**

Amount in dispute?

$ _____

☐ **Other
Disputes**

Amount in dispute?

$ _____

☐ **Claim for
Repayment**

Amount in dispute?

$ _____

☐ **Interest**

Amount in dispute? Set out calculations.

$ _____

☐ **Expenses
of the
Hearing**

☐ **Abuse of
process,
Frivolous or
Vexatious
Proceedings**

☐ **Response to
Special
Award Claim**

Section 2, page 3

1851 (03/01)

FIGURE 25.4 CONTINUED

| Section 3 | **Complete this section ONLY for motor vehicle accidents that occurred on or between January 1, 1994 and October 31, 1996, inclusive.** |

Insurer Examination (Medical) (I.E.) and Designated Assessment Centre (D.A.C.) Information

1. Since the conclusion of mediation did the **insurance company ask the Applicant to attend an Insurer Examination (Medical)** (I.E.) relating to any of the issues in dispute?

☐ No   ☐ Yes   If Yes, did the Applicant attend? ▶   ☐ No   ☐ Yes   If No, state reason(s). ▼

2. Since the conclusion of mediation did the **insurance company ask the Applicant to attend an assessment at a D.A.C.** relating to any of the issues in dispute?

☐ No   ☐ Yes   If Yes, did the Applicant attend? ▶   ☐ No   ☐ Yes   If No, state reason(s). ▼

If Yes, to what benefit claim was the D.A.C. assessment related?

☐ medical benefits

☐ rehabilitation benefits

☐ attendant care benefits

☐ loss of earning capacity benefits

Does the insurer dispute the outcome of the D.A.C.?

☐ No   ☐ Yes   ☐ Partially

Name(s), address(es) and code(s) of the D.A.C.(s) *(Attach extra sheets, if necessary.)*

D.A.C. Code ☐ ☐ ☐ ☐

D.A.C. Code ☐ ☐ ☐ ☐

3. Since the conclusion of mediation did the **Applicant ask to attend an assessment at a D.A.C.** relating to any of the benefits in dispute?

☐ No   ☐ Yes   If Yes, to what benefits was the assessment related?

☐ disability benefits
(income replacement, education disability or caregivers benefits)

☐ loss of earning capacity benefits

Does the insurer dispute the outcome of the D.A.C.?

☐ No   ☐ Yes   ☐ Partially

Name(s), address(es) and code(s) of the D.A.C.(s) *(Attach extra sheets, if necessary.)*

D.A.C. Code ☐ ☐ ☐ ☐

D.A.C. Code ☐ ☐ ☐ ☐

Section 3, page 1

1851 (03/01)

FIGURE 25.4   CONTINUED

Section 3   *continued*

Description of Dispute   *Check the benefits that were not resolved in mediation and which the insurer now wants to respond to or now wants evaluated or arbitrated. The insurer may add new issues which have been mediated but not settled.*
(Add extra sheets, if necessary.)

For each benefit checked, briefly explain the insurer's position on the issues in dispute. *(Attach extra sheets if necessary.)* ▼

Weekly Benefits

Which weekly benefit is being disputed?
- [ ] income replacement
- [ ] education disability
- [ ] caregiver
- [ ] other disability

What is being disputed?
- [ ] initial entitlement to benefits
- [ ] length of time benefits were paid
- [ ] amount of weekly benefits
- [ ] entitlement to benefits past 104 weeks
- [ ] benefits after age 65
- [ ] other, specify ▼

If the insurer paid weekly benefits, state weekly amount and duration of payments.

$ _____

From   To

Is the insurance company claiming a repayment of benefits?
- [ ] No
- [ ] Yes   If Yes, amount ▼

$

Does the Applicant have a Pre-determined income from Self-Employment Agreement?
- [ ] No
- [ ] Yes

Loss of Earning Capacity Benefits

Did the insurer offer a Loss of Earning Capacity Benefit to the Applicant?
- [ ] No   If No ▼
  - [ ] Disputing Loss of Earning Capacity Benefits
- [ ] Yes   If Yes ▼
  - What part(s) of the offer are being disputed?
  - [ ] Pre-accident earning capacity
  - [ ] Residual Earning capacity

Education Disability Benefits (Lump Sum Benefits)

Amount in dispute?

$ _____

Medical Benefits

Amount in dispute?

$ _____

Rehabilitation Benefits

Amount in dispute?

$ _____

Section 3, page 2   1851 (03/01)

FIGURE 25.4 CONTINUED

Section 3 *continued*

For each benefit checked, briefly explain the insurer's position on the issues in dispute. *(Attach extra sheets if necessary.)* ▼

☐ **Attendant Care Benefits**

Amount in dispute?

$ _____

☐ **Compensation for Other Pecuniary Losses**

Amount in dispute?

$ _____

What is being disputed?

☐ expenses of visitors

☐ dependent's care expenses

☐ housekeeping and home maintenance

☐ damage to clothing, glasses, etc.

☐ cost of examinations

☐ **Death Benefits**

Amount in dispute?

$ _____

☐ **Funeral Expenses**

Amount in dispute?

$ _____

☐ **Other Disputes**

Amount in dispute?

$ _____

☐ **Claim for Repayment**

Amount in dispute?

$ _____

☐ **Interest**

Amount in dispute? Set out calculations.

$ _____

☐ **Expenses of the Hearing**

☐ **Abuse of process, Frivolous or Vexatious Proceedings**

☐ **Response to Special Award Claim**

Section 3, page 3

1851 (03/01)

FIGURE 25.4 CONTINUED

Section 4	Complete this section ONLY for motor vehicle accidents that occurred on or between June 22, 1990 and December 31, 1993.

Insurer Examination (Medical) (I.E.) Information

Since the conclusion of the mediation did the **insurance company ask the Applicant to attend an Insurer Examination (Medical)** (I.E.) relating to any of the issues in dispute?

☐ No   ☐ Yes   If Yes, did the Applicant attend? ▶   ☐ No   ☐ Yes   If No, state reason(s). ▼

Description of Dispute

Check the benefits that were not resolved in mediation and which the insurer now wants to respond to or now wants evaluated or arbitrated. The insurer may add new issues which have been mediated but not settled. (Add extra sheets, if necessary.)

Does the Applicant have optional benefits?

☐ No   ☐ Yes

For each benefit checked, briefly explain the insurer's position on the issues in dispute. *(Attach extra sheets if necessary.)* ▼

☐ **Income Benefits**

Which income benefit is being disputed?

☐ employed benefits

☐ benefit if no income

What is being disputed?

☐ initial entitlement to benefits

☐ length of time benefits were paid

☐ amount of weekly benefits

☐ entitlement to benefits past 156 weeks

☐ other, specify ▼

If the insurer paid weekly income benefits, state amount per week and duration of payments.

$ _____

From _____   To _____

Is the insurance company claiming a repayment of benefits?

☐ No   ☐ Yes   If Yes amount ▼

$

☐ **Childcare Benefits**

What is being disputed?

☐ initial entitlement to benefits

☐ length of time benefits were paid

☐ amount of benefits

☐ other, specify ▼

If the insurer paid weekly income Childcare Benefits to the Applicant, state amount per week and duration of payments.

$ _____

From _____   To _____

Section 4, page 1

1851 (03/01)

FIGURE 25.4 CONTINUED

Section 4   *continued*

For each benefit checked, briefly explain why you want arbitration. Refer to disputed issues in mediation report. *(Attach extra sheets if necessary.)* ▼

☐ Supple-
   mentary
   Medical/
   Rehabilita-
   tion
   Benefits

Amount in dispute?

$ _____

☐ Care
   Benefits

Amount in dispute?

$ _____

☐ Death
   Benefits

Amount in dispute?

$ _____

☐ Funeral
   Expenses

Amount in dispute?

$ _____

☐ Other
   Disputes

Amount in dispute?

$ _____

☐ Claim for
   Repayment

Amount in dispute?

$ _____

☐ Interest

Amount in dispute? Set out calculations.

$ _____

☐ Expenses
   of the
   Hearing

☐ Abuse of
   process,
   Frivolous or
   Vexatious
   Proceedings

☐ Response to
   Special
   Award Claim

Section 4, page 2

1851 (03/01)

FIGURE 25.4 CONTINUED

Section 5   Document List   This section MUST be completed.

It is expected that the Applicant and the Insurer have exchanged key documents prior to the filing of a Response by Insurer to an Application for Arbitration.   *(Attach extra sheets if necessary.)*

Documents   1. Please explain why any document, identified in the **Report of Mediator** as having been requested by the Applicant, has not been provided to the Applicant prior to submitting your **Response by Insurer to an Application for Arbitration.**

N/A

☐ Extra sheets attached

2. List key documents in the insurer's possession to which you will refer in the arbitration.
   Identify the type of document (letter, medical report, tax return), the name of the writer or issuing institution and the date of the document.

medical report of Dr. Olive Ork, dated February 15, 2000

Psychological assessment by Dr. Alex Oliphant, dated February 20, 2000

Return to work assessment provided by claimant's employer, Megadoon Investments, dated February 20, 2000

☐ Extra sheets attached

3. List key documents not currently in the insurer's possession, which you intend to get from other sources (such as employment records, Ontario Health Insurance records, Revenue Canada records) for use in the arbitration. The insurer should also include any documents requested from the Applicant (such as financial or employment records) which have not yet been provided. *Wherever possible, identify the type of document (letter, medical report, tax return), the name of the writer or issuing institution and the date of the document.*

N/A

☐ Extra sheets attached

After completing this Section, make sure that you have signed the Response at the end of Section 1.

Compile one copy of the Response, Sections 1, 5, and ONE of Sections 2, 3, or 4, depending on the accident date, plus any extra sheets.

Keep one set of these documents.

Send one set of these documents to the Applicant at the address noted in the Application for Arbitration.

Send one set of these documents to the Commission at:

Arbitration Services
Dispute Resolution Group
Financial Services Commission of Ontario
5160 Yonge Street, 14th Floor, Box 85
North York ON M2N 6L9

Enquiries:
In Toronto: (416) 250-6714, extension 7202
Toll Free: 1-800-517-2332, extension 7202
Fax: (416) 590-8462
Arbitration Hotline: (416) 590-7202

Section 5

1851 (03/01)

FIGURE 25.5   REPLY BY APPLICANT FOR ARBITRATION (FORM G)

Financial Services Commission of Ontario	Dispute Resolution Group	**Reply by the Applicant for Arbitration**	Arbitration file number
		Form G	A-1234

Use this form to reply to any **point** made by the insurance company in its *Response* to your *Application for Arbitration*. You **must** reply to any **new issues raised by the insurance company in their** *Response*. If no new issues are raised by the insurance company, this *Reply* is optional. You must serve a copy of the *Reply* on the Insurance Company **within 10 days of your receipt of the** *Response by the Insurer* to your *Application*. You must also file the *Reply* and a *Statement of Service* with the Commission.

Personal information requested on this form is collected under the authority of the *Insurance Act*, R.S.O. 1990, c. I.8, as amended. This information, including documents submitted with this form, will be used in the dispute resolution process for accident benefits. This information will be available to all parties to the proceeding. Any questions about this collection of information may be directed to the Office of the Registrar, Dispute Resolution Group, Financial Services Commission of Ontario.

Applicant

☐ Mr. ☐ Mrs. ☒ Ms.

Last name	First name	Middle name
Boar	Abigail	Elfrieda

Legal Representative

If your representative has changed since you applied for Arbitration, give details of your new representative.

☐ Mr. ☐ Mrs. ☐ Ms.

Last name	First name	File reference number
N/A		

Title

Firm name

Street address

City   Province   Postal Code

Work phone number   Fax number   Electronic mail address
(   )   (   )

Insurance Company

Company name

Imperialist Payless Insurance Co.

Reply

Please reply to the insurance company's position on the issues in dispute. *Attach extra sheets if necessary.*

The claimant denies she previously used the medication referred to by the insurer without danger to herself. She previously used the medication very briefly and discontinued its use when it caused her to become depressed.

☐ Additional sheets attached

Signature

I certify that all information in this Reply and attachments is true and complete. I realize that copies of all information filed with this Reply will be given to the other party in this dispute.

Name		Signature	Date
I.M. Just	☐ Applicant ☒ Representative		June 3, 2000

Ce formulaire est également disponible en français.

1975 (03/01)

FIGURE 25.6 STATEMENT OF SERVICE (FORM F)

Financial
Services
Commission
of Ontario

Dispute
Resolution
Group

Statement of Service
Form F

This is a three part form.
White - Financial Services
Commission of Ontario
Canary - Insurance Company
Pink - Insured Person

The purpose of this statement is to verify that a copy of a document was delivered to a party. A *Statement of Service* must be completed for every document served and given to the insured person and the insurance company, or their representatives. **Do not use this form where proof of service of a** *Summons to Witness* **and payment is required to be filed with the Commission.** In this case, you should use an *Affidavit of Service for Summons to Witness* which is available at the Commission.

Case Information	Insured Person *Abigail Boar*	Insurance Company *Imperialist Payless Insurance*	Commission file number *A-1234*

Who are you?

	Last name	First name	Middle name
☐ Mr. ☐ Mrs. ☒ Ms.	*Snorglepuss*	*Sandra*	

Occupation
Office administrator, Imperialist Payless Insurance Co.

Street address	City	Province	Postal Code
681 University Avenue	*Toronto*	*Ontario*	*M5G 1S2*

Who was served?

	Last name	First name	Middle name
☐ Mr. ☐ Mrs. ☒ Ms.	*Boar*	*Abigail*	*Elfrieda*

Street address	City	Province	Postal Code
72 Sumach Street	*Toronto*	*Ontario*	*M4R 1Z5*

What was served?

Arbitration Documents
- ☒ Response by Insurer to an Application for Arbitration
- ☐ Reply by the Applicant for Arbitration
- ☐ Other (please specify below)

Appeal Documents
- ☐ Notice of Appeal
- ☐ Response to Appeal
- ☐ Application for Variation/Revocation
- ☐ Response to Application for Variation/Revocation
- ☐ Application for Intervention
- ☐ Other (please specify ▼)

How was it served?
- ☐ Personal Delivery
- ☐ Courier (give name of company ▼)
- ☐ Fax
- ☒ Regular mail
- ☐ Registered mail
- ☐ Other (please specify ▼)

Name of Service Used
Canada Post

Address Served To	Street address	City	Province	Postal Code
	2933 Yonge Street	*Toronto*	*Ontario*	*M2S 3X5*

Date of Service	Time of Service
May 22, 2000	*10:05 a.m.*

A copy of the fax transmission record, or the courier or postal receipt may be required as evidence to support this Statement.

Your Signature	Signature of Person Who Served *Sandra Snorglepuss*	Date *May 22, 2000*

Ce formulaire est également disponible en français.

1855 (03/01)

FIGURE 25.7   SUMMONS TO WITNESS (FORM N)

Financial
Services
Commission
of Ontario

Dispute
Resolution
Group

Summons to Witness
Form N

This form is in quadruplicate.
Page 1 – Witness
Page 2 – Commission
Page 3 – Insurance company
Page 4 – Insured person.

*This summons must be served at least **5 business days** before the first day of the hearing set out below. An adjudicator may order a shorter period of time for service. If so, a copy of the order setting out the shorter time for service must be served with this summons.*

Insurance Act, R.S.O. 1990, Chapter I.8 as amended **(the "Act")**

SUMMONS TO A WITNESS BEFORE the Financial Services Commission of Ontario

Re: *(Parties)* Commission File No. A - *1234*

Abigail Boar and Imperialist Payless Insurance Co.

TO: *(name and address of witness)*
Hatfield A. McCoy
80 Bay Street
Toronto, Ontario   M52 4A7

For oral hearing

YOU ARE REQUIRED TO ATTEND TO GIVE EVIDENCE at the hearing of this proceeding

on, *Monday* , *June 18, 2000* , at *10 a.m.*, at *480 Dundas St. W., Toronto* ,
 *(day)* *(date)* *(time)* *(place)*

and to remain until your attendance is no longer required.

YOU ARE REQUIRED TO BRING WITH YOU and produce at the hearing the following documents and things:
(Set out the type and date of each document and give sufficient particulars to identify each document and thing. Attach extra sheets as required.)

all employment records of Abigail Boar, including anything related to return to work assessments

Additional sheets attached. ☐

IF YOU FAIL TO ATTEND or to remain in attendance as this summons requires, the Ontario Superior Court of Justice may order that a warrant for your arrest be issued, or that you be punished in the same way as for contempt of that court.

For electronic hearing

YOU ARE REQUIRED TO PARTICIPATE IN AN ELECTRONIC HEARING

on, _____ , _____ , at _____ ,
 *(day)* *(date)* *(time)*

in the following manner: *(Give sufficient particulars to enable witness to participate.)*

_____

_____

IF YOU FAIL TO PARTICIPATE IN THE HEARING in accordance with the summons, the Ontario Superior Court of Justice may order that a warrant for your arrest be issued, or that you be punished in the same way as for contempt of that court.

Signature

Financial Services Commission of Ontario Office of the Registrar	Date

Note: *You are entitled to be paid the same fees or allowances for attending at or otherwise participating in the hearing as are paid to a person summoned to attend before the Ontario Superior Court of Justice. Refer to the attached Practice Note 8 for further information concerning this summons.*

Ce formulaire est également disponible en français.

1856 (03/01)

FIGURE 25.8 AFFIDAVIT OF SERVICE FOR SUMMONS TO WITNESS (FORM O)

Financial
Services
Commission
of Ontario

Ontario

Dispute
Resolution
Group

Affidavit of Service
for Summons to Witness

Form O

This is a three part form.

White - Financial Services
Commission of Ontario
Yellow - Insurance Company
Pink - Insured Person

The purpose of this Affidavit is to verify that a copy of the document named was personally served on the named person.
An *Affidavit of Service for Summons to Witness* must be prepared for service of a Summons.

Case Information	Insured Person *Abigail Boar*	Insurance Company *Imperial Payless Insurance Co.*	Commission file number *A-1234*

Declaration

I, ___*Delbert Foogle*___ ,
(Full Name)

of the ___*City*___ of ___*Toronto*___
(City, Town, etc.)   (Name of City, Town, etc.)

in the _____ of _____
(County, Regional Municipality, etc.)   (Name of County, Regional Municipality)

SWEAR OR SOLEMNLY AFFIRM THAT:

(1) At *12:30* a.m.(p.m.)on *Tuesday* , the *10th* of *June* , 20 *00* ,
(Time)   (Day of Week)   (Date)   (Month)   (Year)

I personally served ___*Hatfield A. McCoy*___
(Name of person served)

with a copy of ___*a summons to a witness*___
(Name of document served)

at ___*80 Bay Street, Toronto, Ontario M52 4A7*___ .
(Location where document was served)

(2) I was able to identify the person by ___*examining his driver's licence*___ .
(State means of identification)

(3) For a *Summons to Witness*, I paid the appropriate attendance monies to the person served, named above.

Signatures

Sworn (or Solemnly Affirmed) before me at the ___*City*___ of ___*Toronto*___
(City, Town, etc.)   (Name of City, Town, etc.)

in the _____ of _____
(County, Regional Municipality, etc.)   (Name of County, Regional Municipality)

on this ___*10th*___ of ___*June*___ , 20 *00* .
(Date)   (Month)   (Year)

_____   ___*Delbert Foogle*___
Signature of Commissioner of Oaths   Signature of Person Serving

Ce formulaire est également disponible en français.

1858 (03/01)

FIGURE 25.9 AGREEMENT TO NEUTRAL EVALUATION AT THE COMMISSION (FORM D)

Financial Services Commission of Ontario

Dispute Resolution Group

FORM D

AGREEMENT TO NEUTRAL EVALUATION AT THE COMMISSION
(FAX-BACK FORM)

Personal information requested on this form is collected under the authority of the *Insurance Act*, R.S.O. 1990, c.I.8 as amended. This information, including documents submitted with this Form, will be used in the dispute resolution process for accident benefits. This information will be available to all parties to the proceeding. Any questions about this collection of information may be directed to the Office of the Registrar, Dispute Resolution Group, FSCO.

An *Application for Arbitration* has been filed with the Dispute Resolution Group of the Financial Services Commission of Ontario (the Commission). Your company is named as a party in this arbitration. Use this Form to consent to a request for neutral evaluation raised in the *Application*.

This form may also be used by the insurer to request neutral evaluation through the Commission, where the applicant has NOT requested neutral evaluation in the *Application*, provided the insurer obtains the Applicant's written consent to neutral evaluation and no private neutral evaluation has been conducted in respect of the issues in dispute.

GENERAL INFORMATION

COMMISSION FILE NO. FOR ARBITRATION

A-1234

Applicant / Insured Person

Date of Accident

Last Name	First Name	Month	Day	Year
Boar	Abigail	09	14	99

Street Address	City	Province	Postal Code
72 Sumach Street	Toronto	Ontario	M4R 1Z5

Home Phone Number	Work Phone Number	Fax Number
(416) 928-0001	(416) 635-1234	(416) 928-0002

Insurance Company

Name Imperialist Payless Insurance Co.

Contact Person Dietrich Seljani

Street Address 681 University Avenue

City	Province	Postal Code
Toronto	Ontario	M5G 1S2

Phone Number	Fax Number	Electronic Mail Address
416-597-1341	416-593-1342	sdiet@payless.com

Insurer Claim Number	Policyholder Name	Policy Number
IA 201301-99	Rattle Motors Ltd.	A123456

(Rev.Mar/01)

FORM D : Page 1

FIGURE 25.9   CONTINUED

1.   Within **20 days** of the receipt by the insurer of the *Application for Arbitration*, the insurer must
      respond in ONE of the following ways:

      (a)   Where the insured person has requested neutral evaluation in the *Application for
             Arbitration*, the insurer may consent to neutral evaluation by serving and filing this form on
             the applicant and the Office of the Registrar of the Dispute Resolution Group. The
             Commission requires service of this form upon the Commission by facsimile transmission.

      (b)   Where the insured person has NOT requested neutral evaluation in the *Application for
             Arbitration*, the insurer may request neutral evaluation by obtaining the written consent of
             the applicant and serving and filing the written consent and this form on the office of the
             Registrar. The Commission requires service of this form upon the Commission by facsimile
             transmission.

      (c)   Upon receipt of the materials referred to in (a) or (b) above, the Director of Arbitrations will
             promptly appoint a person to perform the neutral evaluation and confirm the appointment
             with the parties. Where the insurer does not wish to refer the issues in dispute to neutral
             evaluation, the insurer must file a *Response by Insurer to an Application for Arbitration*
             in **Form E,** pursuant to Rule 27 of the Dispute Resolution Practice Code.

2.   The applicant requested neutral evaluation through the Commission in the *Application for
      Arbitration*:

                          Yes   ☒   No   ☐

      (a)   If **YES**, the insurer hereby **CONSENTS** to a referral of the issues in dispute in this
             arbitration, to a person appointed by the Director of Arbitrations, for a neutral evaluation of
             the probable outcome of a proceeding in arbitration.

      (b)   If **NO**, the insurer hereby **REQUESTS** a referral of the issues in dispute in this arbitration to
             a person appointed by the Director of Arbitrations for a neutral evaluation. The insurer has
             attached a copy of the written consent of the applicant to a referral of the issues in dispute
             in the arbitration to neutral evaluation at the Commission.

                          Yes   ☐

3.   The insurer hereby certifies that all documents required for an evaluation of the issues in dispute in
      this arbitration have been exchanged by the parties or will be exchanged **within 30 days** of the
      date of this Form, and that no other documents or reports are required for the neutral evaluation.

4.   The person identified below will be available for a neutral evaluation **within 60 days** from the date of
      this Form. The insurer confirms that the following two half-day dates are available to both parties:

             _____*July 4, 2000*_____ a.m._X_ p.m.__

             _____*July 8, 2000*_____ a.m.__ p.m._X

(Rev.Mar/01)

                                                                                        FORM D : Page 2

FIGURE 25.9   CONTINUED

THE PERSON HANDLING THIS FILE, WITH BINDING AUTHORITY, ON BEHALF OF THE INSURANCE COMPANY:

Name of Company Representative:

Last Name	First Name	Title

Phone Number	Fax Number	Electronic Mail Address

ADR Coordinator's Signature		Date

Or the Insurance Company's legal representative

Name	Law Firm	File Reference Number
Giacomo Brown	Brown & Puce	

Street Address		
130 Adelaide St. W. — 1023		

City	Province	Postal Code
Toronto	Ontario	M 3J 1P4

Phone Number	Fax Number	Electronic Mail Address
416 - 597 - 1234	416 - 597 - 1851	jocko.b@isp.on.ca

(Rev.Mar/01)

FORM D : Page 3

Financial Services
Commission
of Ontario

Dispute
Resolution
Group

FORM H
JOINT STATEMENT FOR NEUTRAL EVALUATION AT THE
COMMISSION
(FAX-BACK FORM)

THIS FORM MUST BE COMPLETED BY BOTH PARTIES AND RETURNED TO THE DISPUTE
RESOLUTION GROUP, ARBITRATION UNIT, OF THE FINANCIAL SERVICES COMMISSION
OF ONTARIO (THE COMMISSION) **WITHIN 30 DAYS** OF THE DATE OF THE **NOTICE OF
APPOINTMENT OF A NEUTRAL EVALUATOR** RECEIVED FROM THE DIRECTOR.

TO: _Eredu Diswuk_____   Arbitration Fax: (416) 590-8462
(Name of the Commission Case Administrator)

RE: **NAME OF CASE** _Boar and Imperialist Payless Insurance Co._

  COMMISSION FILE No. - A – _!234_____

We hereby certify that all documents listed in the **Report of Mediator** and all other documents necessary
for an evaluation of the issues in dispute have been exchanged by the parties.

Listed below are the issues remaining in dispute that are to be submitted to the neutral evaluator.
(Add more pages if required)

1.   _whether the claimant should be obliged to follow a new treatment plan_

2.   _whether the claimant should now return to work on a part-time basis_

3.   _____

The parties agree they are available on the following dates (**within 60 days** of the date of the **Notice of
Appointment of a Neutral Evaluator**) for a half day evaluation:

  Date:

1.   _July 4, 2000_____   a.m. X   p.m.__

2.   _July 8, 2000_____   a.m.__   p.m. X

SIGNATURES:	
Applicant or Applicant's Representative	Insurer or Insurer's Representative
(signature)	_DS (signature)_
Date _June 29, 2000_	Date _June 30, 2000_

(Rev. Mar/01)

FIGURE 25.11   NOTICE OF APPEAL (FORM I)

Financial
Services
Commission
of Ontario

Dispute
Resolution
Group

Notice of Appeal
Form I

Use this form to appeal an Arbitration decision. **Appeals are only allowed on questions of law.**

You must file your completed *Notice of Appeal* with the Financial Services Commission of Ontario (the "Commission") at the address below, **within 30 days** of the date of the arbitration order you wish to appeal. The Director of Arbitrations may extend the time based on the reasons for the delay and the apparent strength of the appeal. The steps you must take are set out in this form.

Personal information requested on this form is collected under the authority of the *Insurance Act*, R.S.O. 1990, c.I.8, as amended. This information, including documents submitted with this application, will be used in the dispute resolution process for accident benefits. This information will be available to all parties to the proceeding. Any questions about this collection of information may be directed to the Office of the Registrar, Dispute Resolution Group, at the address below.

If you have any questions or want more information, contact:

Appeals Unit
Dispute Resolution Group
Financial Services Commission of Ontario
5160 Yonge Street, 15th Floor, Box 85
North York ON M2N 6L9

In Toronto: (416) 590-7222

Toll Free: 1-800-517-2332, extension 7222

Fax: (416) 590-7077

Commission website: www.fsco.gov.on.ca

Ce formulaire est également disponible en français.

1976 (03/01)

FIGURE 25.11 CONTINUED

Appealing an Arbitration Decision

For a complete set of the rules for appeals, see the *Dispute Resolution Practice Code*.

Step 1

Complete this *Notice of Appeal* form within **30 days** of the date of the Arbitration order. If the *Notice of Appeal* is incomplete, it may be rejected. After completing the form, you must serve a copy on the respondent (the other party). If the respondent was represented at the arbitration hearing by a lawyer, you should serve the *Notice of Appeal* on the lawyer. If not, serve the respondent.

Service may be done by personal delivery, courier, fax, regular mail, registered mail or any other method allowed by the *Dispute Resolution Practice Code*.

Then file the following with the Commission:
- Completed *Notice of Appeal*
- Original *Statement of Service* form stating when and how you served the respondent with the *Notice of Appeal*
- The fee

Step 2

Upon receiving a properly completed *Notice of Appeal*, *Statement of Service* and the application fee, the Commission will promptly acknowledge the appeal.

Step 3

To oppose your appeal, the respondent must file a *Response to Appeal* within **20 days** of receiving acknowledgement of the appeal from the Commission. You will get a copy of the *Response to Appeal* from the respondent.

Step 4

Unless the Director of Arbitrations or an adjudicator delegated by the Director (known as Director's Delegate) advises you differently, your written submissions must be served on the respondent and filed with the Commission within **30 days** of the date the *Response to Appeal* was due. If a transcript is ordered, this time limit is extended to **30 days** from receipt of the transcript.

Step 5

The Director or Director's Delegate may decide the appeal with or without a hearing.

How to Complete the Notice of Appeal

PLEASE PRINT

Arbitration Decision Details

This information can be found in the arbitration decision.

Appellant's Name and Address

Fill in completely. Provide any alternative addresses, phone numbers, fax numbers or electronic mail addresses that will make it easier for us to contact you.

Appellant's Representative

You may choose to have someone represent you. Although many people are represented by a lawyer in an appeal, a lawyer is not required. If you have a representative, fill in the name, address and phone number of your representative. If it is a firm, please give the name of the firm in the box provided. **If your representative is NOT a lawyer, please provide written confirmation that the representative is authorized to act for you during the appeal. A minor (a person under the age of 18) or a person who has been declared mentally incapable, must have a representative.**

Reasons for the Appeal

Appeals are only available on questions of law. If your appeal does not involve a question of law, it may be rejected.

Briefly state what part(s) of the Arbitration order you are appealing and the error(s) of law you claim the arbitrator made. Attach extra sheets if necessary. Your *Notice of Appeal* must be sufficiently detailed to allow the other party to respond. It is not necessary, however, for you to file your complete written submissions until later.

Action Sought

Briefly state the remedy or outcome you are seeking in your appeal.

Transcript

Indicate if the Arbitration hearing was recorded by a reporting service. If it was recorded, indicate if you have ordered a transcript of the hearing. If you do not intend to order a transcript, you must state why a transcript is not needed for the appeal.

Stay

The usual rule is that an appeal does not stop the Arbitration order from taking effect. If you are asking that the Arbitration order not go into effect, you must explain why the usual rule should not apply.

It is likely that the stay will be decided without further submissions, so your reasons should be as complete as possible.

Appeal from a Preliminary or Interim Order

The usual rule is that a party may not appeal a preliminary or interim order of an arbitrator until all of the issues in the arbitration dispute have been finally decided. If you are seeking to appeal a preliminary or interim order, you must explain why the usual rule should not apply.

It is likely that this issue will be decided without further submissions so your reasons should be as complete as possible.

Evidence

Appeals are usually decided based on the evidence presented at the arbitration hearing. The Director's Delegate will have access to the arbitration exhibits and, therefore, it is not necessary to refile them.

If you want to rely on any additional or new evidence – documents or witnesses – you must explain what the evidence is and why it should be allowed in the appeal.

This issue may be decided without further submissions so your explanation should be as detailed as possible.

Signature

Sign the form and return it to the Appeals Unit at the Commission.

Fee

If you are an insured person, be sure to enclose the filing fee of $250 by cheque or money order made out to the **MINISTER OF FINANCE. The application will be rejected if the filing fee is not enclosed.**

If you are an insurer, the Commission will invoice your company for the filing fee ($250) and the insurer assessment (**$500**).

Note: You may settle your dispute with the respondent directly at any time during the appeal process.

Page 2

1976 (03/01)

FIGURE 25.11 CONTINUED

Financial
Services
Commission
of Ontario

Ontario

Dispute
Resolution
Group

Notice of Appeal

Complete ALL sections.
Attach extra sheets if necessary.

Commission file number

P-1234A

Arbitration Decision Details	Applicant *Abigail Boar*		Insurer(s) *Imperialist Payless Insurance Co.*	
	Date of Arbitration decision *July 31, 2000*	Arbitrator *Anju Prsykll*		Arbitration file number *A 00-78910C*

Appellant

Company name OR Last name ☐ Mr. ☐ Mrs. ☒ Ms. *Boar*	First name *Abigail*	Middle name *Elfreida*	
Street address *72 Sumach Street*	City *Toronto*	Province *Ontario*	Postal Code *M4K 1Z5*
Home phone number *(416) 928-0001*	Work phone number *(416) 635-1234*	Fax number *(416) 928-0002*	Electronic mail address

Appellant's Representative

Last name ☒ Mr. ☐ Mrs. ☐ Ms. *Just*	First name *I.M.*	File reference number
Title *Lawyer*	Firm name *Just & Coping, Barristers and Solicitors*	
Street address *365 Bay Street*	City *Toronto*	Province *Ontario* Postal Code *M3J 4A9*

Work phone number *(416) 762-1342*	Fax number *(416) 762-2300*	Electronic mail address *imjust@isp-on.ca*

Relationship to the Appellant

☒ lawyer ☐ para legal ☐ parent with whom the child resides ☐ spouse or family relation ☐ executor/ administrator/ trustee ☐ court appointed guardian ☐ other, specify ▶

Reasons for the Appeal

Briefly explain the reasons for your appeal (questions of law only).

The arbitrator erred in law in holding that I had no right to refuse treatment or withhold my consent to treatment unless there was clear and cogent evidence of risk, when the standard for refusal of consent should have been "some evidence of serious risk."

☐ Extra sheets attached

Actions Sought from the Appeal

Briefly explain what outcome or result you are looking for in the Appeal.

1. That the insurer be ordered to pay all arrears and to continue to pay the loss of income benefit until I have recovered. 2. That I not be compelled to undergo a treatment that is unsafe.

☐ Extra sheets attached

Page 3

1976 (03/01)

FIGURE 25.11   CONTINUED

Transcripts	Was the Arbitration recorded?	Are you ordering a transcript of the hearing?

☒ No   ☐ Yes   ☐ No   ☐ Yes   If Yes, you must inform the other party and arrange for a transcript copy to be provided to him/her and the Director's Delegate. State when you expect to receive the transcript. ▼

_____

If No, briefly explain why a transcript is not needed for the Appeal. ▼

☐ Extra sheets attached

Stay of the Arbitration Order   Are you asking for a Stay of the Arbitration Order?

☒ No   ☐ Yes   If Yes, briefly explain why you are asking for a Stay. Your reasons should be as complete as possible. ▼

☐ Extra sheets attached

Appeal from a Preliminary or Interim Order   Are you asking for an Appeal of a Preliminary or Interim Order?

☒ No   ☐ Yes   If Yes, briefly explain why you should be permitted to appeal a preliminary or interim order. Your reasons should be as complete as possible. ▼

☐ Extra sheets attached

Evidence   List any evidence that you intend to rely on that was not part of the Arbitration hearing. Explain why this evidence is necessary. Your explanation should be as complete as possible.

☐ Extra sheets attached

Signature and Certification   *I certify that all information in this Notice of Appeal and attachments is true and complete. I realize that copies of all information filed with this Notice of Appeal will be given to the other party in this dispute.*

Name (please print)	Title	
I. M. Just	*Counsel for appellant*	☐ Appellant ☒ Representative

Signature	Date	
(signature)	*August 10, 2000*	☒ Cheque or money order enclosed

If your representative is NOT a lawyer, please certify that you have provided your representative with full authorization to discuss all issues in dispute, to negotiate and to enter into an agreement or settlement of any and all issues in dispute, on your behalf in connection with this Appeal.

I certify that my representative (name of representative ▼)

has full authorization as described above

Appellant Signature	Date	**Total number of extra sheets attached**

Page 4

1976 (03/01)

FIGURE 25.12 RESPONSE TO APPEAL (FORM J)

Financial
Services
Commission
of Ontario

Dispute
Resolution
Group

Response to Appeal
Form J

Use this form if you want to oppose a *Notice of Appeal* filed by another party to the arbitration hearing.

You must file this *Response to Appeal* with the Commission (address below) within **20 days** of receiving a letter from the Commission acknowledging the appeal. The Director of Arbitrations may extend the time limit based on the reasons for the delay and the apparent strength of the appeal. The steps you must take are set out in this form.

Personal information requested on this form is collected under the authority of the *Insurance Act*, R.S.O. 1990, c.I.8, as amended. This information, including documents submitted with this application, will be used in the dispute resolution process for accident benefits. This information will be available to all parties to the proceeding. Any questions about this collection of information may be directed to the Office of the Registrar, Dispute Resolution Group, at the address below.

If you have any questions about this application, or want more information, contact:

Appeals Unit
Dispute Resolution Group
Financial Services Commission of Ontario
5160 Yonge Street, 15th Floor, Box 85
North York ON M2N 6L9

In Toronto: (416) 590-7222

Toll Free: 1-800-517-2332, extension 7222

Fax: (416) 590-7077

Commission website: www.fsco.gov.on.ca

Page 1

Ce formulaire est également disponible en français.

1848 (03/01)

FIGURE 25.12 CONTINUED

For a complete set of rules for appeals, see the *Dispute Resolution Practice Code.*

Responding to an Appeal

Upon receiving a properly completed *Notice of Appeal*, the Commission will promptly acknowledge the appeal by sending letters to all parties to the arbitration hearing.

If you want to oppose the *Notice of Appeal*, you must respond within **20 days** of receiving a letter from the Commission acknowledging the appeal. The Director of Arbitrations can extend the time limit based on the reasons for the delay and the apparent strength of the appeal.

Step 1

Complete this *Response to Appeal* form. After completing the form, you must serve a copy on the appellant. If the *Notice of Appeal* shows that the appellant is represented, you must serve the representative. If not, serve the appellant.

Service may be done by personal delivery, courier, fax, regular mail, registered mail or any other method allowed by the *Dispute Resolution Practice Code.*

Then file the following with the Commission:
- Completed *Response to Appeal*
- Original *Statement of Service* form stating when and how you served the appellant with the *Response to Appeal*

Fee

If you are an insured person, there is no fee for filing a *Response to Appeal.*

If you are an insurer, the Commission will invoice your company the insurer assessment **($500)**.

Cross-appeals

If, in addition to responding to the *Notice of Appeal*, you also want to appeal any part of the arbitration order, you must file your own *Notice of Appeal*. The rules for appeals apply to "cross-appeals" including time limits and filing fee **($250)** and insurer assessment.

Step 2

When you receive the appellant's written submissions, your written submissions must then be served on the appellant and filed with the Commission within **20 days**.

Step 3

The Director or Adjudicator delegated or appointed by the Director of Arbitrations (known as the Director's Delegate) may decide the appeal with or without a hearing.

How to Complete the *Response to Appeal*

Please print.

Appellant

This information can be found in the *Notice of Appeal.*

Respondent's Name and Address

Fill in completely. Provide any alternative addresses, phone numbers or fax numbers that will make it easier for us to contact you.

Respondent's Representative

You may choose to have someone represent you. Although many people are represented by a lawyer in an appeal, a lawyer is not required. If you have a representative, fill in the name, address and phone number of your representative. If it is a firm, please state the name of the firm. **If your representative is NOT a lawyer, please provide written confirmation that the representative is authorized to act for you during the appeal. A minor (a person under the age of 18) or a person who has been declared mentally incapable, must have a representative.**

Response to Appeal

Briefly state your response to the reasons for appeal set out in the *Notice of Appeal*. Attach extra sheets if necessary. Although you should state your position, it is not necessary for you to file your complete written submissions until later.

Response to Preliminary Matters

Provide your response to the preliminary matters raised in the *Notice of Appeal* (transcript, stay, preliminary or interim order, new evidence). The Director of Arbitrations or Director's Delegate may decide the preliminary matters without further submissions, so your response should be set out in detail. Attach extra sheets if necessary.

Transcript

If the appellant does not intend to order a transcript, you may state whether you think a transcript is needed for the appeal.

Stay of the Arbitration Order

The usual rule is that an appeal does not stop the arbitration order from taking effect. If you are asking that the arbitration order not go into effect, you must explain why the usual rule should not apply.

It is likely that the stay will be decided without further submissions, so your reasons should be as complete as possible.

Appeal from a Preliminary or Interim Order

The usual rule is that a party may not appeal a preliminary or interim order of an arbitrator until all of the issues in dispute in the arbitration have been finally decided. If you object to the appeal of the preliminary or interim order, you must explain your objection.

It is likely that the issue of the right to appeal from a preliminary or interim order will be decided without further submissions, so your reasons should be as complete as possible.

Evidence

Appeals are usually decided based on the evidence presented at the arbitration hearing. The Director's Delegate will have access to the arbitration exhibits and therefore, it is not necessary to refile them.

If you want to rely on any additional or new evidence – documents or witnesses – you must explain what the evidence is and why it should be allowed in the appeal.

If you object to the introduction of new evidence, you should explain why you object.

This issue may be decided without further submissions, so your explanation should be as detailed as possible.

Signature

Sign the form and return it to the Appeals Unit at the Commission.

Note: You may settle your dispute with the appellant directly at any time during the arbitration process.

FIGURE 25.12 CONTINUED

Financial
Services
Commission
of Ontario

Dispute
Resolution
Group

Response to Appeal
Form J

Complete ALL sections.
Attach extra sheets if necessary.

Appeal file number

P-1234A

Appellant	Company name OR Last name ☐ Mr. ☐ Mrs. ☒ Ms. *Boar*	First name *Abigail*	Middle name *Elfreida*

Respondent's name and address	Company name OR Last name ☐ Mr. ☐ Mrs. ☐ Ms. *Imperialist Payless Insurance Co.*	First name	Middle name

Street address *681 University Avenue*	City *Toronto*	Province *Ontario*	Postal Code *M5G 1S2*

Phone number *(416) 597-1341*	Fax number *(416) 597-1342*	Electronic mail address *sdiet@payless.com*

Respondent's Representative	Last name ☒ Mr. ☐ Mrs. ☐ Ms. *Brown*	First name *Giacomo*	File reference number

Title *Lawyer*	Firm name *Brown & Puce*

Street address *130 Adelaide St. W. – 1023*	City *Toronto*	Province *Ontario*	Postal Code *M3J 1P4*

Work phone number *(416) 597-1234*	Fax number *(416) 597-1851*	Electronic mail address *jocko.6@isp.on.ca*

Relationship to the Respondent

☒ lawyer ☐ para legal ☐ parent with whom the child resides ☐ spouse or family relation ☐ executor/ administrator/ trustee ☐ court appointed guardian ☐ other, specify ▶

Response to Appeal

Briefly explain your response to the appellant's reasons for appeal. (Questions of law only.)

The arbitrator was correct in law in holding that the appellant was required to consent to the treatment suggested by the respondent as a condition of continuing to receive loss of income benefits.

☐ Extra sheets attached.

1848 (03/01)

FIGURE 25.12   CONTINUED

Response to Preliminary Matters

Set out your response to the preliminary matters raised in the **Notice of Appeal** (transcript, stay, appeal of a preliminary or interim order, new evidence). *See instruction sheet for details.* **Your response should be as complete as possible.**

☐ Extra sheets attached.

Signature and Certification

I certify that all information in this Response to Appeal and attachments is true and complete. I realize that copies of all information filed with this Response to Appeal will be given to the other party in this dispute.

Name (please print) *G. Brown*	Title *Counsel for respondent*	☐ Respondent ☒ Representative
Signature	Date *August 15, 2000*	

If your representative is NOT a lawyer, please certify that you have provided your representative with full authorization to discuss all issues in dispute, to negotiate and to enter into an agreement or settlement of any and all issues in dispute, on your behalf in connection with this Appeal.

I certify that my representative (name of representative ▼)

has full authorization as described above

Respondent Signature	Date	Total number of extra sheets attached

FIGURE 25.13   APPLICATION FOR INTERVENTION (FORM K)

Financial
Services
Commission
of Ontario

Dispute
Resolution
Group

Application for Intervention
Form K

Commission file number

C-1234

Complete ALL sections.
Attach extra sheets if necessary.

Use this *Application* to intervene in an appeal before the Commission. You must serve a copy of this *Application* and any supporting submissions on all parties to the appeal. You must also file the *Application* and a *Statement of Service* with the Commission.

Any party to the appeal may support or object to this *Application* by filing written submissions with the Commission within **10 days** of being served with the *Application*. The submissions must include the party's reasons why the applicant should, or should not, be permitted to participate. You must serve a copy of the written submission on the representative of the person making the *Application for Intervention*, or, if

not represented, on the person seeking to intervene. You must then file a *Statement of Service* with the Commission.

Personal information requested on this form is collected under the authority of the *Insurance Act*, R.S.O. 1990, c. I.8, as amended. This information, including documents submitted with this form, will be used in the dispute resolution process for accident benefits. This information will be available to all parties to the proceeding. Any questions about this collection of information may be directed to the Office of the Registrar, Dispute Resolution Group, Financial Services Commission.

Appeal Case	Appellant *Boar, Abigail*	Respondent *Imperialist Payless Insurance Co.*	Appeal file number A 00-*13579*
Applicant	Company name **OR** Last name ☐ Mr. ☐ Mrs. ☐ Ms. *Canadian Patient Rights Group*	First name	Middle name
	Street address *123 Edward Street*	City *Toronto*	Province *Ontario* Postal Code *M3J 1X4*
	Home phone number ( )	Work phone number *(416)423-5678*	Fax number *(416) 423-7891* Electronic mail address *patients @ isp. on. ca*
Applicant's Representative	Last name ☒ Mr. ☐ Mrs. ☐ Ms. *Drood*	First name *Edmund*	File reference number
	Title *Lawyer*	Firm name	
	Street address *100 – 10 Yonge Street*	City *Toronto*	Province *Ontario* Postal Code *M6W 3P4*
	Work phone number *(416) 897-1011*	Fax number *(416) 897-1012*	Electronic mail address *edrood @ isp. on. ca*

Relationship to the Applicant

☒ lawyer   ☐ para legal   ☐ parent with whom the child resides   ☐ spouse or family relation   ☐ executor/ administrator/ trustee   ☐ court appointed guardian   ☐ other, specify ▶

Page 1

1978 (03/01)

FIGURE 25.13 CONTINUED

Submissions   1. I seek to intervene in this appeal for the following reasons.

> This case raises the issue whether a mentally competent patient should be compelled, in order to receive an insurance benefit, to undergo treatment that he or she believes, on reasonable grounds, to be dangerous.
>
> The balancing of a patient's right in this case has a potential effect on a wide variety of consent to treatment cases

☐ Extra sheets attached

2. I wish to make submissions on the following issues of law. (Include a reference to any statutory provision to be relied on.)

> Whether consent is compellable to receive a statutory benefit
>
> <u>Bjork v. Crumm</u> (1984), 24 OR (3d) 416 (CA)
>
> <u>Debert v. Ping</u> (1994), 6 CPC 802 (PEI CA)

☐ Extra sheets attached

Documents   I am relying on the following documents for the Application

☐ Copies of documents are attached

Signature and Certification

I certify that all information in this Application for Intervention and attachments is true and complete. I realize that copies of all information filed with this Application for Intervention will be given to the other parties in this dispute.

Name (please print)

Edmund Drood

Title Counsel, Canadian Patient Rights Group

☐ Applicant
☒ Representative

Signature

Date August 19, 2000

If your representative is NOT a lawyer, please certify that you have provided your representative with full authorization to discuss all issues in dispute, to negotiate and to enter into an agreement or settlement of any and all issues in dispute, on your behalf in connection with this Application for Intervention.

I certify that my representative (name of representative ▼)

has full authorization as described above

Applicant Signature	Date	Total number of extra sheets attached

Page 2

1978 (03/01)

FIGURE 25.14   APPLICATION FOR VARIATION/REVOCATION (FORM L)

Financial
Services
Commission
of Ontario

Dispute
Resolution
Group

Application for
Variation/Revocation
Form L

Use this form to apply for a Variation or Revocation of an Arbitration or
an Appeal decision.

An *Application for Variation/Revocation*, instead of a *Notice of Appeal*, is
appropriate if the circumstances of the insured person have changed
significantly since the hearing, new evidence not available at the
arbitration hearing or the appeal, has become available, or there is
some clear error in the order (for example, the order does not
correspond to the reasons for the decision).

After completing your *Application for Variation/Revocation* form, you
must file one copy with the Financial Services Commission of Ontario
(the "Commission") at the address below. The steps you must take are
set out in this form.

Personal information requested on this form is collected under the
authority of the *Insurance Act*, R.S.O. 1990, c.I.8, as amended. This
information, including documents submitted with this application, will be
used in the dispute resolution process for accident benefits. This
information will be available to all parties to the proceeding. Any
questions about this collection of information may be directed to the
Office of the Registrar, Dispute Resolution Group, at the address below.

If you have any questions or want more information, contact:

Appeals Unit
Dispute Resolution Group
Financial Services Commission of Ontario
5160 Yonge Street, 15th Floor, Box 85
North York ON M2N 6L9

In Toronto: (416) 590-7222

Toll Free: 1-800-517-2332, extension 7222

Fax: (416) 590-7077

Commission website: www.fsco.gov.on.ca

Page 1

Ce formulaire est également disponible en français.

1977 (03/01)

FIGURE 25.14   CONTINUED

Applying for Variation or Revocation of an Arbitration order or an order of an Appeal Decision

For a complete set of the rules for variations/revocations, see the *Dispute Resolution Practice Code.*

Step 1

Complete this *Application for Variation/Revocation* form. If it is incomplete, it may be rejected. After completing the form, you must serve a copy on the respondent (the other party). If the respondent was represented by a lawyer, you should serve the *Application for Variation/Revocation* on the lawyer. If not, serve the respondent.

Service may be done by personal delivery, courier, fax, regular mail, registered mail or any other method allowed by the *Dispute Resolution Practice Code.*

Then file the following with the Commission:

- Completed *Application for Variation/Revocation*
- Original *Statement of Service* form stating when and how you served the respondent with the *Application for Variation/Revocation*
- The fee

Step 2

Upon receiving a properly completed *Application for Variation/Revocation, Statement of Service* and the application filing fee, the Commission will promptly acknowledge the Application.

Step 3

To oppose your Application, the respondent must file a *Response to Application for Variation/Revocation* within **20 days** of receiving acknowledgement of the *Application for Variation/Revocation* from the Commission. You will get a copy of the *Response to Variation/Revocation* from the respondent.

Step 4

Unless the Director of Arbitrations or an adjudicator delegated by the Director (known as Director's Delegate) advises you differently, your written submissions must be served on the respondent and filed with the Commission within **30 days** of the date the *Response to Variation/Revocation* was due. If a transcript is ordered, this time limit is extended to **30 days** from receipt of the transcript.

Step 5

The Director or Director's Delegate may decide the Variation/Revocation with or without a hearing.

How to Complete the Application for Variation/Revocation

PLEASE PRINT

Decision Details

This information can be found in the arbitration or appeal decision.

Applicant's Name and Address

Fill your name and address as the person or insurance company making this *Application for Variation or Revocation*. Provide any alternative addresses, phone numbers, fax numbers or electronic mail addresses that will make it easier for us to contact you.

Applicant's Representative

You may choose to have someone represent you. Although many people are represented by a lawyer in these proceedings, a lawyer is not required. If you have a representative, fill in the name, address and phone number of your representative. If it is a firm, please give the name of the firm in the box provided. **If your representative is NOT a lawyer, please provide written confirmation that the representative is authorized to act for you during the proceeding. A minor (a person under the age of 18) or a person who has been declared mentally incapable, must have a representative.**

Reasons for the Application

Briefly state what part(s) of the Arbitration or Appeal decision you want varied or revoked and the reasons for your request. Attach extra sheets if necessary. Your *Application for Variation/Revocation* must be sufficiently detailed to allow the other party to respond. It is not necessary, however, for you to file your complete written submissions until later.

Action Sought

Briefly state the remedy or outcome you are seeking in your *Application for Variation/Revocation.*

Transcript

Indicate if the hearing was recorded by a reporting service. If it was recorded, indicate if you have ordered a transcript of the hearing. If you do not intend to order a transcript, you must state why a transcript is not needed for the Application.

Evidence

If you want to rely on any additional or new evidence in your Application for Variation or Revocation, you must identify the new evidence and explain why it should be allowed. This should include whether the evidence could have been presented at the hearing and whether it would have led the adjudicator to a different decision.

The Director's Delegate will have access to the Arbitration exhibits and, therefore, it is not necessary to refile them.

This issue may be decided without further submissions so your explanation should be as detailed as possible.

Preliminary or Interim Order of an Adjudicator

The usual rule is that a party may not apply to vary or revoke a preliminary or interim order of an adjudicator. If you are seeking to vary of revoke an interim or preliminary order, you must explain why the usual rule should not apply.

It is likely that this issue will be decided without further submissions, so your reasons should be as complete as possible.

Signature

Sign the form and return it to the Appeals Unit at the Commission.

Fee

If you are an insured person, be sure to enclose the filing fee of $250 by cheque or money order made out to the **MINISTER OF FINANCE. The Application will be rejected if the filing fee is not enclosed.**

If you are an insurer, the Commission will invoice your company for the filing fee ($250) and the insurer assessment ($500).

Note: You may settle your dispute with the respondent directly at any time during the appeal process.

FIGURE 25.14   CONTINUED

Financial
Services
Commission
of Ontario

Dispute
Resolution
Group

Application for Variation/Revocation

Form L

Commission file number

A-1234

Complete ALL sections.   Attach extra sheets if necessary.

Decision Details	Applicant	Insurer(s)
	Boar, Abigail	Imperialist Payless Insurance Co.

	Date of Decision	Adjudicator		Arbitration or Appeal file number
	July 25, 2000	E. Bogswamp		A 00-13579

Applicant

Company name OR Last name		First name	Middle name
☐ Mr. ☐ Mrs. ☒ Ms. Boar		Abigail	Elfreida

Street address	City	Province	Postal Code
72 Sumach Street	Toronto	Ontario	M4R 1Z5

Home phone number	Work phone number	Fax number	Electronic mail address
(416) 928-0001	(416) 635-1234	(416) 928-0002	

Applicant's Representative

Last name	First name	File reference number
☒ Mr. ☐ Mrs. ☐ Ms. Just	I.M.	

Title	Firm name
Lawyer	Just & Coping, Barristers and Solicitors

Street address	City	Province	Postal Code
365 Bay Street	Toronto	Ontario	M3J 4A9

Work phone number	Fax number	Electronic mail address
(416) 762-1342	(416) 762-2300	imjust@isp.on.ca

Relationship to the Applicant

☒ lawyer   ☐ para legal   ☐ parent with whom the child resides   ☐ spouse or family relation   ☐ executor/ administrator/ trustee   ☐ court appointed guardian   ☐ other, specify ▶

Reasons for the Application for Variation/ Revocation

Briefly explain the reasons for your Application.

Further evidence has become available since the order on appeal was made. A report has just been released showing that the medication treatment required as a condition for continued payment of an insurance benefit has been found to be clearly dangerous and to pose unacceptably high risks to patients.

☐ Extra sheets attached

Actions Sought from the Variation/ Revocation

Briefly explain what outcome or result you are looking for in the Application.

The order on appeal should be revoked and an order substituted requiring the insurer to pay the loss of income benefit from and after the date on which payment ceased.

Page 3

☐ Extra sheets attached

1977 (03/01)

FIGURE 25.14 CONTINUED

Transcripts

Was the hearing recorded?

[X] No   [ ] Yes

Are you ordering a transcript of the hearing?

[ ] No   [ ] Yes

If Yes, you must inform the other party and arrange for a transcript copy to be provided to him/her and the Director's Delegate. State when you expect to receive the transcript. ▼

If No, briefly explain why a transcript is not needed for the Variation/Revocation. ▼

[ ] Extra sheets attached

Preliminary or Interim Order of an Adjudicator

Are you asking for a Variation/Revocation of a Preliminary or Interim Order of an Adjudicator?

[X] No   [ ] Yes

If Yes, briefly explain why you should be permitted to vary or revoke a preliminary or interim order. Your reasons should be as complete as possible. ▼

[ ] Extra sheets attached

Evidence

List any evidence that you intend to rely on that was not part of the hearing. Explain why this evidence is necessary. Your explanation should be as complete as possible.

"A New Look at the Repoxil Treatment for Severe Headache and Migraine," by Q. Qwak, in *The Medical Quarterly* 2000, vol. 6, issue 12. This article demonstrates that the medication and treatment plan proposed by the insurer is untenable and that the medication should not have been required as a condition for the payment of the loss of income benefit.

[ ] Extra sheets attached

Signature and Certification

I certify that all information in this Application for Variation/Revocation and attachments is true and complete. I realize that copies of all information filed with this Application for Variation/Revocation will be given to the other party in this dispute.

Name (please print)

I. M. Just

Title

Counsel for the claimant

[ ] Applicant
[X] Representative

Signature

Date

August 30, 2000

[X] Cheque or money order enclosed

If your representative is NOT a lawyer, please certify that you have provided your representative with full authorization to discuss all issues in dispute, to negotiate and to enter into an agreement or settlement of any and all issues in dispute, on your behalf in connection with this Application.

I certify that my representative (name of representative ▼)

has full authorization as described above

Applicant Signature	Date	Total number of extra sheets attached

Page 4

1977 (03/01)

FIGURE 25.15 RESPONSE TO APPLICATION FOR VARIATION/REVOCATION (FORM M)

Financial
Services
Commission
of Ontario

Dispute
Resolution
Group

Response to Application for Variation/Revocation
Form M

Use this form if you want to oppose an *Application for Variation/ Revocation* filed by the other party to the arbitration or appeal.

You must file this *Response to Application for Variation/Revocation* form with the Commission (address below) **within 20 days** of receiving confirmation of the *Application for Variation/Revocation* from the Commission. The Director of Arbitrations may extend the time limit based on the reasons for the delay and the apparent strength of the Response. The steps you must take are set out in this form.

Personal information requested on this form is collected under the authority of the *Insurance Act*, R.S.O. 1990, c.I.8, as amended. This information, including documents submitted with this application, will be used in the dispute resolution process for accident benefits. This information will be available to all parties to the proceeding. Any questions about this collection of information may be directed to the Office of the Registrar, Dispute Resolution Group, at the address below.

If you have any questions about this application, or want more information, contact:

Appeals Unit
Dispute Resolution Group
Financial Services Commission of Ontario
5160 Yonge Street, 15th Floor, Box 85
North York ON M2N 6L9

In Toronto: (416) 590-7222

Toll Free: 1-800-517-2332, extension 7222

Fax: (416) 590-7077

Commission website: www.fsco.gov.on.ca

Page 1

Ce formulaire est également disponible en français.

1852 (03/01)

FIGURE 25.15 CONTINUED

For a complete set of the rules for a variation/revocation see the Dispute Resolution Practice code.

Responding to an Application for Variation/Revocation

Upon receiving a properly completed *Application for Variation/Revocation*, the Commission will promptly acknowledge the application by sending letters to all parties to the original arbitration or appeal.

If you want to oppose the variation/revocation, you must respond within **20 days** of receiving confirmation of the application from the Commission. The Director of Arbitrations can extend the time limit based on the reasons for the delay and the apparent strength of the Response.

Step 1

Complete this *Response to Application for Variation/Revocation* form.

After completing the form, you must serve a copy on the applicant. If the *Application for Variation/Revocation* shows that the applicant is represented, you must also serve the representative.

Service may be done by personal delivery, courier, fax, regular mail, registered mail or any other method allowed by the *Dispute Resolution Practice Code.*

Then file the following with the Commission:

- Completed *Response to Application for Variation/Revocation.*

- Original *Statement of Service* form stating when and how you served the applicant with the *Response to Application for Variation/Revocation.*

Fee

If you are an insured person, there is no fee for filing a *Response to Application for Variation/Revocation.*

If you are an insurer, the Commission will invoice your company the insurer assessment (**$500**).

Step 2

When you receive the applicant's written submissions, your written submissions must then be served on the applicant and filed with the Commission within **20 days**.

Step 3

The Director of Arbitrations or adjudicator delegated or appointed by the Director (known as Director' Delegate), may decide the *Application for Variation/Revocation* with or without a hearing.

How to Complete the *Response to Application for Variation/Revocation*

Please print.

Applicant for Variation/Revocation

This information can be found in the *Application for Variation/Revocation.*

Respondent's Name and Address

Fill in completely. Provide any alternative addresses, phone numbers or fax numbers that will make it easier for us to contact you.

Respondent's Representative

You may choose to have someone represent you. Although many people are represented by a lawyer in these proceedings, a lawyer is not required. If you have a representative, fill in the name, address and phone number of your representative. If it is a firm, please state the name of the firm. **If your representative is NOT a lawyer, please provide written confirmation that the representative is authorized to act for you during the proceeding. A minor (a person under the age of 18) or a person who has been declared mentally incapable, must have a representative.**

Response to Application for Variation/Revocation

Briefly state your response to the reasons for variation/revocation set out in the *Application for Variation/Revocation.* Attach extra sheets if necessary. Although you should state your position, it is not necessary for you to file your complete written submissions until later.

Response to Preliminary Matters

Provide your response to the preliminary matters raised in the *Application for Variation/Revocation* (transcript, preliminary or interim order, new evidence). The Director or Director's Delegate may decide the preliminary matters without further submissions, so your response should be set out in detail. Attach extra sheets if necessary.

Transcript

If the applicant does not intend to order a transcript, you may state whether you think a transcript is needed for the Response.

Preliminary or Interim Order

The usual rule is that a party may not vary or revoke a preliminary or interim order of an adjudicator. If you object to the Variation/Revocation of a preliminary or interim order, you must explain your objection.

Evidence

The Director or Director's Delegate will have access to the arbitration exhibits and therefore, it is not necessary to refile them.

If you want to rely on any additional or new evidence – documents or witnesses – you must explain what the evidence is and why it should be allowed.

If you object to the introduction of new evidence, you should explain why you object.

This issue may be decided without further submissions so your explanation should be as detailed as possible.

Signature

Sign the form and return it to the Appeals Unit of the Commission.

Note: You may settle your dispute with the applicant directly at any time during the arbitration process.

FIGURE 25.15 CONTINUED

Financial
Services
Commission
of Ontario

Dispute
Resolution
Group

Response to Application for Variation/Revocation

Form M

Complete ALL sections.
Attach extra sheets if necessary.

		Variation/Revocation file number
		P- *1234*

Applicant for Variation/Revocation

Company name **OR** Last name
☐ Mr. ☐ Mrs. ☒ Ms.
Boar

First name
Abigail

Middle name
Elfreida

Respondent's name and address

Last name
☐ Mr. ☐ Mrs. ☐ Ms.
Imperialist Payless Insurance Co.

First name

Middle name

Street address
681 University Avenue - 2300

City
Toronto

Province
Ontario

Postal Code
M5G 1S2

Respondent's Representative

Last name
☒ Mr. ☐ Mrs. ☐ Ms.
Brown

First name
Giacomo

File reference number

Title
Lawyer

Firm name
Brown & Puce

Street address
130 Adelaide St. W. - 1023

City
Toronto

Province
Ontario

Postal Code
M3J 1P4

Work phone number
(416) 597-1234

Fax number
(416) 597-1851

Electronic mail address
jocko.b @ isp. on. ca

Relationship to the insured person

☒ lawyer ☐ para legal ☐ parent with whom the child resides ☐ spouse or family relation ☐ executor/ administrator/ trustee ☐ court appointed guardian ☐ other, specify ▶

Response to Application for Variation/Revocation

Briefly explain your response to the Applicant's reasons for variation/revocation.

The evidence cited by the applicant does not amount to a material change in circumstances. The new evidence advanced by the applicant does not support the contention that the medication is dangerous to persons such as the applicant.

FIGURE 25.15 CONTINUED

Response to Preliminary Matters

Set out your response to the preliminary matters raised in the **Application for Variation/Revocation** (transcript, preliminary or interim order, new evidence). *See instruction sheet for details.* **Your response should be as complete as possible.**

☐ Extra sheets attached.

Signature and Certification

I certify that all information in this Response to Application for Variation/Revocation and attachments is true and complete. I realize that copies of all information filed with this Response to Application for Variation/Revocation will be given to the other party in this dispute.

Name (please print)	Title	
Giacomo Brown	*Counsel for respondent*	☐ Respondent ☒ Representative

Signature	Date	
[signature]	*September 10, 2000*	

If your representative is NOT a lawyer, please certify that you have provided your representative with full authorization to discuss all issues in dispute, to negotiate and to enter into an agreement or settlement of any and all issues in dispute, on your behalf in connection with this Appeal.

I certify that my representative (name of representative ▼)

has full authorization as described above

Respondent Signature	Date	Total number of extra sheets attached

Glossary of terms

absentee   person whose rights or interests are being determined in a proceeding and whose whereabouts are unknown

action   one of the two procedures by which a civil matter is commenced in the Superior Court; the other such procedure is an application

affidavit   written statement setting out the evidence of the person who swears or affirms its contents are true

alternative dispute resolution   term used to describe various ways of settling disputes without going to court, including arbitration, mediation, and conciliation

appeal as of right   appeal that a party has a legal right to bring and for which leave to appeal is not required

appellant   party that commences an appeal

appellate court   any court that hears an appeal

application   one of the two procedures by which a civil matter is commenced in the Superior Court; the other such procedure is an action

arbitration   court-like procedure where a neutral third party, chosen by the parties, hears each side of the dispute and renders a binding decision

assessment of costs   tally made by an assessment officer of a specific amount of costs payable after a court has determined which party is entitled to costs

assignee   person to whom rights, usually contract benefits, are granted by an assignor

assignor   person who grants contract rights to an assignee

attendance money   formerly called conduct money, composed of the *per diem* witness fee and an amount for transportation and lodging in accordance with tariff A

backsheet   part of every court document, containing the name and address of the lawyer who prepared the document, the short title of proceedings, the court and court file number, and a large space reserved for court officials to make entries on

balance of convenience   judicial determination of greatest convenience for all parties arrived at by judge after weighing all the relevant factors and merits of parties' arguments

bill of costs   list of allowable fees and disbursements that is used by an assessment officer to assess a litigant's costs after the litigant is successful in obtaining judgment; differs from an account because it does not include all fees charged to a client

boilerplate   standard wording that is part of every copy of a particular type of document

call-over courts   temporary courts set up in Toronto to bring all cases commenced before July 2001 into the case management system or otherwise to ready them for trial or settlement

carriage   responsibility for a file or a case

case conference   conference managed by the case management judge or master, who controls timetables and settles all procedural matters

case management judge or master   court official assigned to each case managed case to ensure court control over the case on its way to trial

cause of action   legal right to sue to obtain a legal remedy

children's lawyer   official of the Ontario Ministry of the Attorney General whose office oversees the rights of some minors involved in civil litigation and custody disputes

chose in action   intangible personal property whose value lies in what it represents

class proceeding fund   public fund of the Law Foundation of Ontario, administered by the Law Society of Upper Canada, to provide funding for the costs of class actions which otherwise might be beyond the financial reach of the parties

co-defendant   one defendant in multi-defendant proceeding

common law   law that is made by judges following precedents set by higher courts; often called "case law"

compendium   summary of material to be referred to at a hearing, designed for easy access by judge

contingency fee   fee payable to a lawyer only if he or she wins the case for a client

contracting state   country that is a signatory to a contract or convention

counterclaim   claim made by the defendant in the main action against the plaintiff or against the plaintiff and other persons

court of first instance   court that made a decision that is under appeal

cross-examination   series of questions asked of a witness by a lawyer for a party adverse in interest to the party that called the witness

crossclaim   claim brought by one defendant whom the plaintiff is suing against another defendant whom the plaintiff is suing

crossclaiming defendant   defendant in the main action who commences a crossclaim against one or more of the other defendants in that action

damages   compensation awarded by a court for harm done

defendant on the crossclaim   defendant in the main action against whom a crossclaim is brought

deponent   person who makes an affidavit

designated assessment centre   neutral health care provider or facility designated by FSCO to provide objective assessments of a claimant's injuries for use at mediation and in other dispute resolution procedures

director of arbitrations   person who oversees the arbitration, appeals, and adjudication system and who is given power under the rules to control the process

disbursements   amounts lawyers pay on behalf of clients to third parties that lawyers can recover from clients

discovery   process that occurs after close of pleadings in which parties obtain more information about each other's cases before trial

Dispute Resolution Group   branch of FSCO that oversees the settlement and adjudication of no fault benefit disputes between claimants and insurance companies

Dispute Resolution Practice Code   user's guide to dispute settlement procedures that are available to settle no fault benefit claims

draw an adverse inference   make a factual determination that is contrary to the interests of a party

endorsement   judge's handwritten order or judgment from which a successful party is expected to prepare a formal draft of the order or judgment

estate administrator   person appointed by a court to administer an estate where there is no will or where the appointment of an executor is ineffective

estoppel   term indicating that a witness is bound by his or her original position and evidence and cannot later take a contrary position

et al.   Latin phrase meaning "and others"

examination-in-chief   series of questions asked of a witness by the lawyer for the party who called the witness

executor   person appointed by a will maker to administer an estate under the provisions of the will; a female executor is sometimes called an executrix

exemplary damages   damages over and above the plaintiff's actual loss, paid to compensate the plaintiff for hurt feelings or mental stress caused by the defendant's particularly outrageous behaviour

factum   document that sets out the facts, statutes, and cases that a party relies on to obtain a favourable decision

fees   payment to lawyers for services rendered

fiduciary relationship   one-sided relationship where one party relies on the other party's honesty and advice given in the reliant party's best interests

final order   order that resolves all the outstanding issues between the parties

Financial Services Commission of Ontario (FSCO)   provincial body established in 1998 to supervise and regulate the financial services industry, including pension trusts, credit unions, cooperatives, mortgage brokers, provincial loan and trust companies, and insurance companies

fixing costs   making an order that a specific party pay a specific amount of costs

garnishee   order directed to a third party who owes money to a defendant as a means of enforcing a judgment

general damages   monetary damages for pain and suffering that cannot be determined on the basis of a formula

general heading   heading on all court documents identifying the court, the parties, the status of the parties, and the name of the document

impecunious   insolvent

interlocutory order   order that decides some of the matters at issue

issuing   official commencement of court proceedings whereby documents that are originating processes are signed by the registrar, dated, sealed with a court seal, and given a file number

judgment *in personam*   judgment that is binding only on the parties to the proceeding

judgment *in rem*   judgment that is binding on everyone, whether a party to the proceeding in which the judgment is pronounced or not

judgment-proof   unable to pay any amount of a judgment

jurat   part of an affidavit that appears at the bottom on the left side of the page and begins with the words "Sworn (or affirmed) before me"

law of equity   type of law developed several hundred years ago in England wherein judges, rather than following precedents, look at the issues in a case and apply certain principles to ensure a fair outcome

leading a witness   asking a witness a question that suggests the answer

leave of the court   permission of the court to take a procedural step

limitation period   specified time within which court proceedings must be commenced

litigation guardian   competent adult who directs and takes responsibility for the litigation of a legally disabled party, such as a minor, an absentee, or a mentally disabled person

main action   primary case brought by the plaintiff against the defendant

mandatory mediation   process in which disputants are required to allow a neutral third party to facilitate their communication and assist them in negotiating a settlement

master   minor judicial official with limited jurisdiction to hear and decide specific legal issues identified by the rules or a statute

mediation   process whereby a neutral third party facilitates communication between disputants and assists them in negotiating a solution

motion   proceeding within the main proceeding to settle an issue, usually one that has arisen at the pretrial stage

narrow questions questions in which the interviewer tries to elicit specific information

natural justice basic elements of a fair hearing, including one impartial judge, the right to be told the case against one, and the right to answer it

neutral evaluation optional procedure that may follow a failed mediation in which a neutral third party gives an assessment of the likely outcome of arbitration

no fault term that usually refers to a system where motor vehicle insurance claims are paid out by the claimant's own insurer regardless who is at fault and without the claimant's suing for damages

non-pecuniary non-monetary

notice of action document informing defendants that they have been sued

official examiner individual who is licensed to operate a business to conduct out-of-court examinations, such as cross-examinations on affidavits and discoveries

open-ended questions questions that allow the persons interviewed to choose what they want to talk about to the interviewer

order generic term used in the *Rules of Civil Procedure* to describe commands issued by courts on motions and at trials

originating process first document in a lawsuit that tells parties that they are being sued

partial indemnity usual order for costs, based on a cost grid that establishes hourly rates for tariff items listed in the grid; provides less than full recovery for the client

pecuniary of monetary value

perfecting an appeal taking all the necessary procedural steps to ensure that an appeal is ready to be heard

practice direction instructions set out by a chief justice to inform lawyers about special procedures that must be followed in particular courts as a result of administrative needs

pro bono abbreviation of a Latin term *pro bono publico*, meaning "for the public good," used where a lawyer takes on a case without charging a fee as part of a duty to see that justice is done

procedural fairness the idea that procedural rules are fair and fairly applied

punitive damages damages in the nature of a fine paid to the plaintiff when the defendant's behaviour has been particularly outrageous

ratio decidendi the legal reason for the judge's decision in a case

reference judicial proceeding used when it is necessary to delve into an issue in detail before a decision can be reached

refresh the retainer make a further deposit against future fees as a case progresses

registrar official who oversees the administration of some of the alternative dispute resolution processes offered by or through the Dispute Resolution Group

request to admit document in which one party requires the other to admit the truth of a fact or the authenticity of a document

res judicata Latin phrase meaning that a matter decided by a court is final and incapable of being relitigated in a subsequent proceeding

respondent party that answers or defends against an appeal

retainer contract between a lawyer and client describing the services to be provided by the lawyer and the terms of payment by the client; also refers to a cash deposit to be used by a lawyer to pay future fees and disbursements as they are incurred

return date the date on which the motion will be heard by the court

return of a motion day on which a motion is "returned" to court for a hearing; the hearing date is also referred to as "the return date"

service process by which documents are brought to the attention of a party in accordance with the rules or a court order

setting an action down for trial procedure that a party must follow in order to have its case placed on the trial list

sheriff official appointed by the provincial government to assist in various court-related functions, such as the enforcement of orders and judgments

sittings a time period during which a specific court may hear cases

solicitor of record lawyer recognized by the court as the legal representative of a party in a proceeding

special damages monetary damages that are specific, ascertainable, and measured on an objective basis; sometimes referred to as out-of-pocket expenses

Statutory Accident Benefits Schedule schedule attached to every automobile insurance policy issued in Ontario, setting out the mandatory no fault benefits, including amounts payable or a formula for determining them

stay proceedings stop proceedings for a given or indefinite period, pending the fulfillment of a condition, without dismissing the proceedings

substantial indemnity costs scale, usually used as a punitive costs award, that results in near indemnity for the winner on a dollar-for-dollar basis

substitute decisions cases cases involving the *Substitute Decisions Act*, under which a person may be named to handle the property and day-to-day affairs of a person who is not mentally competent to manage his or her own affairs

summary proceedings proceedings designed to be conducted quickly and with reduced formality

summons to a witness order of a court telling the person named on the summons to attend a trial and give evidence

testimony oral evidence given by a witness

third party claim claim brought by a defendant in the main action against a person who is not already a party to the main action

title of proceedings part of the general heading that identifies the parties and their status in a lawsuit

tort reform campaign to change provincial legislation to limit access by motor vehicle accident claimants to civil courts in order to claim damages

transcript written record of proceedings transcribed word for word

trial list list kept by the registrar in each courthouse of cases that are ready for trial

trial record bound set of documents prepared by the party setting the action down for trial and containing the pleadings of all parties, any relevant orders, all notices, and certificates

trier of fact judge or jury whose job is to determine the facts of the case from the evidence

true copy copy of an original document that is like the original in every particular, including copies of alterations, signatures, and court file numbers

truing up making a handmade copy of a document at the court counter

undefended action an action in which no statement of defence is delivered

unincorporated association association of persons formed to carry out a specific purpose and not formally incorporated

***viva voce* evidence** oral evidence

without prejudice term used, usually in correspondence, to indicate that an offer or admission cannot be used against its maker, admitted in evidence, or disclosed to the court

wood-shedded prepared for later cross-examination by opposing lawyer

writ of seizure and sale order from a court to a sheriff to enforce the court's order by seizing and selling the defendant's property and holding the proceeds to satisfy the judgment debt to the plaintiff; also known as a writ of execution

Index

Italicized page numbers indicate sample forms and precedents.

birth certificate, request for *38*
boilerplate 137, 594
book of authorities 394
brief of authorities 331
Business Corporations Act (Ontario) 481
business records 326

call-over courts
    defined 407, 594
    form *428*
    procedure 408
Canada Business Corporations Act 481
Canada Evidence Act 326
carriage 367, 594
case conference
    defined 406, 594
    effective use of 419
    how and when to convene 418
    judge or master, requirement for 419
    notice to attend *439, 440*
    rationale for 417
    request for 438
        Ottawa *445*
case management judge or master 411, 594
case management system
    applicable areas 406
    call-over court 408, *428*
    case conference 417-19, *438*
        notice to attend by telephone *440*
        notice to attend in person *439*
    case timetable 410-15, *431, 433*
    checklist *446*
    commencement of proceedings 408
    commercial list 483
    defined 23, 405
    motions 415-17, *435*
    Ottawa case conference request form *445*
    Ottawa differences 422
    purpose 406
    settlement conference 419-21
    Toronto practice direction re trial scheduling *441*
    transition rules 407
    trial management conference 421, *442*
case timetable
    case management timetable 411
    compliance with rules 412
    customization 412
    deadlines 410
    defendants and timetables 411
    forms 414, *431, 433*
    time requirements 412

cause of action
    defined 7, 594
    determination of 7, 35
certificate of assessment of costs *359*
certificate of non-compliance *458*
certificate of retainer *52*
certificate of service by sheriff *175*
children's lawyer 86, 594
chose in action 82, 594
city directories 41
civil law suit, *see* civil litigation
civil litigation
    process overview 4, *6*
    simplified procedure 467-77
claims, joiner of 78
class proceeding fund 102, 594
class proceedings
    application of rule 12 103
    overview 100
Class Proceedings Act, 1992 100, 102, 103, 467
    notice of proceeding under *104*
client accounts
    components of 368-70
    docketing 53
    draft account *372*
    information, gathering of 367
    file organization 54
client management
    communicating with client 62
    obtaining information from client 61
co-defendant 238, 594
commencement of proceedings 9
    by way of action 119
    by way of application 124
    simplified procedure 467
commercial list
    adjournments and settlements 483
    case management 483
    case settlement 483
    court documents 482
    dates for applications, motions, and trials 482
    materials for court use 484
    rationale 482
common law 67, 594
Companies' Creditors Arrangement Act 481
compendium of evidence and exhibits 394, 484, 594
confirmation form for all judges/masters civil motions/
  applications 202
conflicts of interest 48
consolidation of proceedings 83
Construction Lien Act 467